Benson and Hedges

Cricket Year

Benson and Hedges

Cricket Year

Nineteenth Edition
September 1999 to September 2000

Edited by **Jonathan Agnew**

with additional contributions by
Qamar Ahmed
Mark Baldwin
Tony Cozier
Neil Manthorp
Jim Maxwell
Robin Martin-Jenkins
Bryan Waddle

BLOOMSBURY

First published in 2000 by
Bloomsbury Publishing Plc
38 Soho Square
London W1V 5DF

www.bloomsbury.com

A copy of the CIP entry for this book is available from the
British Library

ISBN 0 7475 4987 7

10 9 8 7 6 5 4 3 2 1

Edited by Jonathan Agnew
with additional contributions by
Qamar Ahmed
Mark Baldwin
Mike Berry
Tim Boon
Tony Cozier
Haydn Gill
Neil Manthorp
Robin Martin-Jenkins
Jim Maxwell
Telford Vice
Bryan Waddle
Steve Whiting
and special thanks to Gul Hameed Bhatti,
Ramaswamy Mohan and Vijay Lokapally, and to Pradeep
Mandhani, who supplied Indian photographs

Statistics by Wendy Wimbush
Pictures researched and supplied by
David Munden at Sportsline Photographic
www.sportsline.org.uk

Typeset by Book Creation Services, London

Printed and bound in Great Britain
by Butler and Tanner Ltd, Frome

The symbol * indicates not out
and + indicates wicketkeeper.

Contents

Sponsor's Message

We were promised a Carnival of Cricket this summer, and although the English weather did its utmost to spoil Channel 4's promises, cricket delivered. A triumphant England turned yet another corner by sending the West Indies home after 31 years of domination by winning the series against them for the first time since 1969.

With the new two-division County Championship creating continuous competition and the arrival of central contracts, England needed a winning summer to aid this new structure. New coach Duncan Fletcher has added other dimensions; with aggressive captaincy from Nasser Hussain their partnership combines many attributes England have missed in past years.

For the first time, seven Test matches and a Triangular Tournament were included in a hectic domestic schedule. England beat the Zimbabweans before the West Indies arrived, and when the Triangular Tournament started in July the Test series stood at 1–1 after England's thrilling victory at Lord's. The Triangular Tournament developed into a two-horse race, and England discovered a possible answer to their opening partnership problem – Marcus Trescothick – as they swept aside the Zimbabweans at Lord's to win their first silverware since the Sharjah Cup.

The Test series resumed and the English dominated with bat and ball. For years Marshall, Holding *et al* tormented England; this time Gough, Caddick, Cork and White exploited the West Indies' batting with pace, movement and aggression. Of the five Tests played, two finished in three days and one in two days (the first time since 1946). England won the final Test at the Oval to take the series 3–1 in front of a full house on the fifth day and the whole country smiled.

On the domestic front, the Benson and Hedges Cup woke up early this summer. The zonal rounds started in April with the weather playing a major innings in a number of matches (19 were abandoned). As the Cup gathered momentum, Gloucestershire, the new self-styled one-day wonders, were on the hunt again. On 10 June they won the final, which will be remembered for two outstanding individual performances – the opening spell of Australian one-day specialist, Ian Harvey, and an exhilarating century from Glamorgan skipper, Matthew Maynard, who was supported by some 11,000 Welsh vocal chords and took the Gold Award.

In this, the nineteenth edition of *Benson and Hedges Cricket Year*, we look at all world cricket. Dominating the headlines for the wrong reasons were the betting and match-fixing scandals. On a brighter note, Bangladesh became the tenth Test-playing country. Asia has provided some of the world's greatest cricketers and nowhere is the sport so popular. One innovation to the international stage saw the Australians launch indoor cricket when Melbourne's Colonial Stadium hosted the World Super Cup against South Africa.

Last year Jonathan Agnew took over the captaincy of the *Benson and Hedges Cricket Year*. He delivered every first-class match played throughout the world in a concise and charming manner. Once again we thank him, the other notable contributors, as well as the publishers, Bloomsbury, for their part in making this yearbook even more colourful and more global in its recognition of world cricket.

Barry Jenner
Managing Director, UK
Gallaher Ltd

OCTOBER 1999

Aravinda de Silva (right) helps Sri Lanka humble Australia at Kandy for the first time on home soil, and go on to win the series one–nil.

NOVEMBER 1999

England face precision bowling by Allan Donald (below) and collapse to 2 for 4, losing the first Test against South Africa at Johannesburg. Malcolm Marshall, the great West Indian fast bowler, dies aged 41.

DECEMBER 1999

Matthew Sinclair (below left) scores a double century on his debut for New Zealand against the West Indies, who lose the series two–nil.

JANUARY 2000

History is made at Centurion Park when first, Hansie Cronje and then Nasser Hussain forfeit an innings of the final Test. Express bowler Brett Lee (left) makes a significant contribution to Australia's three-nil thrashing of India.

MARCH 2000

South Africa defeat India in Bombay and take the series two-nil. Sachin Tendulkar's second term as India's captain comes to an end (below).

FEBRUARY 2000

South Africa defeat England in the final of the Standard Bank One-Day Series in Johannesburg (below). England's women lose all nine One-Day Internationals against Australia and New Zealand.

APRIL 2000
Indian police announce that they have taped telephone conversations between Hansie Cronje (above) and a bookmaker that suggest Cronje is involved in match-fixing.

MAY 2000
A Pakistan report into match-fixing finds two players guilty and recommends that Wasim Akram should never captain his country again. Brian Lara (below) allegedly changes his mind and agrees to tour England.

JUNE 2000
After losing the first Test, England beat the West Indies in a historic match at Lord's to level the series (left). Cronje gives evidence to the King Commission in Cape Town and admits he was paid by a bookmaker to declare and forfeit an innings at Centurion Park.

JULY 2000

England beat Zimbabwe in the final at Lord's to take the trophy of the first NatWest triangular series (right).

AUGUST 2000

Alec Stewart (below) scores a century in his hundredth Test at Old Trafford. England then defeat the West Indies within two days at Headingley: the shortest Test match for 56 years.

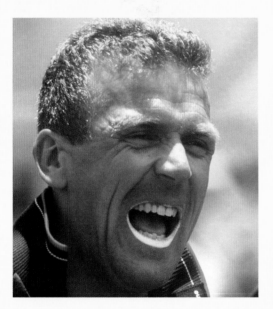

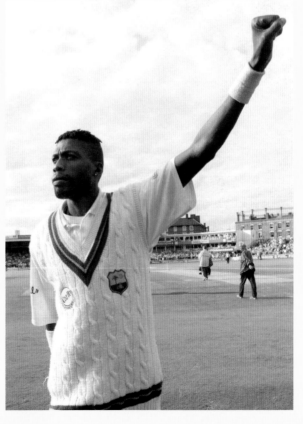

SEPTEMBER

England win at the Oval to beat the West Indies in a series for the first time in 31 years. Curtly Ambrose (right) retires from Test cricket. Gloucestershire win the National League and become the first team to win all three One-Day competitions.

INTRODUCTION

By Jonathan Agnew

Previous page: Nasser Hussain, Michael Vaughan and Alec Stewart are all smiles after winning the fifth Test in South Africa.

Above: Captain Nasser Hussain (left) and Darren Gough congratulate Graeme Hick on taking another wicket.

It had been fifteen long and, generally, fruitless summers since the Oval last saw anything like it: thousands of happy, singing England cricket followers swarming across the outfield to salute their heroes. In 1985, it was David Gower who stood, smiling, on the pavilion balcony unaware, as he held the Ashes urn aloft, that Ian Botham was about to tip a pint of beer over his head! This year, the celebrations ran to several bottles of champagne and it was Nasser Hussain – booed, of course, by the same crowd only the previous summer – who took the praise as England beat the once-mighty West Indies for the first time in 31 years.

Once, not so long ago, that seemed an impossible prospect. I remember running from the field at the Oval quite terrified as – piece by piece – my batting equipment was stolen from me by hundreds of marauding West Indian supporters. I had just seen Richard Ellison, my batting partner, dismissed by Joel Garner to complete the first 'blackwash' and if anyone had told me, as I battled back into the dressing room, that the West Indies would decline quite so quickly, I certainly would not have believed them.

That rapid fall from power is a huge concern for the Caribbean and, indeed, world cricket but I will not allow it to detract in any way from England's efforts this year. The first signs were evident in South Africa where Hussain and the new coach,

Duncan Fletcher got to know and respect each other. The players responded to a quiet, disciplined and, above all, calm approach and although the early selection of central contracts (more of that in a moment) threw up the occasional surprise, both captain and coach have been unswerving in following the course they have decided to pursue. The transformation of Hussain – once an 'angry young man' – to a responsible, level-headed leader has been dramatic and genuine: he fully deserves every ounce of praise that has been heaped upon him.

Marcus Trescothick emerged as an opening bat of real quality. To think that, at the start of the summer, the selectors were shoving a reluctant Mark Ramprakash up the order to partner Mike Atherton! This only shows how far from their plans the robust Somerset left-hander was only a couple of months before he replaced the injured Nick Knight in England's one-day team. His promise in the NatWest Series, which England also won, shone through in the Test series and with Michael Vaughan also making good progress, England appears to have an excellent opening pair for the future.

Super Challenge 2000, the first indoor cricket tournament at the Colonial Stadium in Melbourne, was won by Australia.

So to the thorny issue of central contracts: this was the hot topic on the county circuit this summer. There can be little doubt that, in the case of England's bowlers, the introduction of what amounted to enforced rest between Tests paid dividends. Darren Gough who, during the winter, was facing the real prospect of a premature end to his career, has never looked so fit as when he was charging in at top speed against the West Indies. Andy Caddick, too, benefited although he is a bowler who needs early overs under his belt and to rest him between the two Zimbabwe Tests was a mistake. I have little doubt that central contracts helped England to win Test matches this summer. However, the damaging effect on county cricket is profound and the authorities must be aware that, very soon, domestic cricket simply will not be worth watching, and the standard will drop still further. The early signs are already there: neither the Benson and Hedges or NatWest Trophy finals were sold out thanks to a combination of high prices and an excess of international one-day cricket. Remove the attraction of watching England's top players appearing for the counties, and there is little to entice supporters to county grounds.

This is a major concern and the only sensible answer is to raise, once again, the limit of overseas players from one to two. This was the level set in the 1980s since when county cricket has never been so strong, or nearly so interesting to watch.

I have written at length about Hansie Cronje's fall from grace later in this book but, nevertheless, it is impossible not to mention the most unsavoury episode in the game's history here as well. I was one of many people who hailed his declaration at Centurion Park as a turning point for cricket: a moment when, for once, the interests of the spectator came before anything else. How cruelly fooled we all were – and who knows how long greed and callous deception has been influencing matches all over the world. Cronje – and anyone else involved with match-fixing – deserves nothing more in return than the same measure of disdain he has shown to the game that made him one of the most respected sportsmen in the world. There is no room in any sport for men like Hansie Cronje, whose arrogance and avarice has irrevocably damaged the image and integrity of cricket.

Left: England captain Nasser Hussain and new England coach Duncan Fletcher established mutual respect during the year.

Above: PPP Healthcare County Champions Surrey celebrate their 2000 season win.

THE GAME IN 2000

(above) Who says county cricket is soft? Phil Tufnell and Mike Roseberry settle in to watch Mark Ramprakash score a century for Middlesex against Sussex at Southgate.

(right) Farewell to one of the finest: Curtly Ambrose bowed out of Test cricket at the Oval in September.

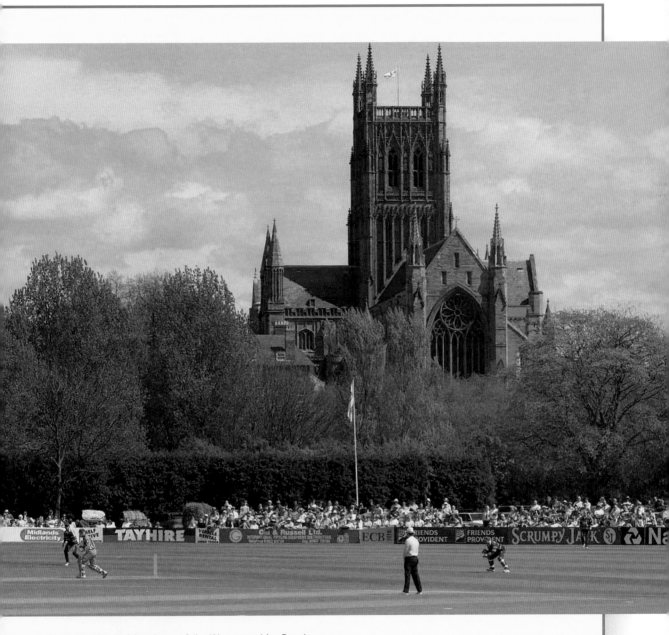

Not even the garish colours of the Worcestershire Royals
and Yorkshire Phoenix can detract from the beauty of a
sunny afternoon at New Road.

First, the traditionalists had to come to terms with indoor cricket: now this! The first one-day international to be played indoors, between Australia and South Africa at the Colonial Stadium in Melbourne.

(top left) Brought together in unhappy circumstances: Shane Warne and Brian Lara both played in the memorial match for the great fast bowler, Malcolm Marshall, who died in November 1999, aged 41.

(above) The 2000 season will not be remembered for weeks of unbroken sunshine. A lone spectator waits for play to resume at the Oval in the NatWest Trophy match between Surrey and Sussex.

(top right) The Gloucestershire team celebrate beating Glamorgan in the final of the Benson and Hedges Cup.

(above) As if the modern umpire does not have enough on his mind! Cyril Mitchley battles to save his cap at Potchefstroom where England beat North West in a floodlit match during their winter tour of South Africa.

(right) Despite scoring a half-century, Chris Schofield discovered that the Test arena can be a bruising experience when he played in the second Test against Zimbabwe.

(opposite) A triumphant Courtney Walsh having just taken his 435th Test wicket in front of a home crowd in Jamaica to beat Kapil Dev's world record.

(above) Somewhere amidst the jubilation is
Sri Lankan Muttiah Muralitharan, who has just
trapped Pakistan's Yousuf Youhana lbw at Peshawar.

(right) Ramnaresh Sarwen, the young West Indian
batsman, heads for cover again as rain blights the
Old Trafford Test.

(opposite) Zimbabwe's Heath Streak realises that
England are well on their way to clinching the
final of the NatWest series at Lord's.

(above) Floodlit international cricket finally arrived in England this summer. Bristol staged the first match, between West Indies and Zimbabwe.

(left) Penny for his thoughts. Hansie Cronje after South Africa's controversial defeat by England at Centurion Park. His generous declaration was later exposed as a sham and thanks to the grubby dealings of Cronje – and others – with bookmakers, the simple pleasure of watching cricket can never be the same again.

(opposite) England captain Nasser Hussain keeps his eye on pigeons in the outfield during England's successful run in the NatWest Triangular Series.

ENGLAND

Zimbabwe in England
The West Indies in England
NatWest Trophy Triangular Series
PPP Healthcare County Championship
First-Class Averages
Norwich Union National League
Benson and Hedges Cup
NatWest Trophy
Oxford and Cambridge Universities
Minor Counties

ATHERTON & STEWART by Jonathan Agnew

In 124 years of Test cricket, only five Englishmen have appeared in one hundred Tests or more. Given that statistic, it was remarkable that Mike Atherton and Alec Stewart should both choose Old Trafford to join Graham Gooch, David Gower, Colin Cowdrey, Geoff Boycott and Ian Botham on that celebrated list. Stewart, of course, will remember the game with enormous pride: his century in England's first innings was as commanding and attractive as any he has ever scored. Bursting with patriotic pride, he refrained, later, from dedicating his achievement to the Queen Mother – who was celebrating her 100th birthday on the same day – but only just!

Unfortunately, Atherton could not match Stewart. Walking out to bat to a standing ovation on his home ground, he was soon trudging ruefully back to the pavilion having scored just a single in the first innings and 28 in the rain-affected second. You felt, though, that this did not disappoint Atherton nearly to the extent that failure on the big day would have upset Stewart. Of course Atherton wanted to make a big score: he always does. But landmark occasions have never had an impact on the quietly spoken and thoughtful Cambridge graduate who had looked positively embarrassed by all the fuss made of him during the ECB presentation ceremony before the match began.

Stewart, on the other hand, is 'in your face'. Known in and around the England set-up as 'the Gaffer', his role within the England team has changed almost constantly, giving rise to passionate arguments within cricketing circles. With England lacking a genuine all-rounder, Stewart's wicketkeeping has been a godsend to the various captains, managers and coaches of the past ten years. No one settled on a consistent role for him and Stewart has batted in just about every position in the top six for England, sometimes while keeping wicket and sometimes not. Given this, his immeasurable contribution to English cricket is all the more remarkable, being virtually ever-present throughout the 1990s, during which he was the highest run-scorer throughout the world in international cricket.

Apart from his century at Old Trafford, Stewart's fondest memory would have to be the Barbados Test of 1994 when he became the first Englishman ever to score a century in both innings of a Test match against the West Indies. England won the game as well – the first victory by any visiting team to Kensington for 60 years – and thousands of sunburned, chanting English supporters were there to see it. Given his love of all things football – and especially Chelsea – it is in those situations that Stewart is in his element. If it were left to him, the Barmy Army would have free admission to every England match.

Atherton enjoys football – he is a Manchester United supporter – but he is rather more restrained about it all. He is the type of football fan that follows his team through the pages of *The Daily Telegraph*, while the Gaffer is probably a *Sun* man. Horse racing is another of Atherton's passions, and he will often be found frowning over his laptop at the latest form guide he has just downloaded from the Internet.

He is an intelligent man, which is why his extraordinary brush with the authorities over the 'dirt in the pocket affair' in 1994 surprised so many people. It was his first full summer as England captain, and it seemed astonishing that he came so close to throwing it all away through a moment's lack of thought. He was extremely lucky to survive – arguments about precisely what he was doing still simmer on in the press box, which remains deeply divided over the issue – but he went on to lead England 52 times, and no one has done that before.

His was an undistinguished team so it was Atherton's batting that made the greatest impression during that time. He has been England's most resolute and determined player of the past decade, and so crucial is Atherton's wicket that his early dismissal often spells disaster. The opposition has known this only too well, giving rise to some memorable duels between the slightly built opener and the fastest bowlers in the world. In November 1995, he defied the South African attack for nearly ten and three quarter hours to save a Test match that, on the fourth day, appeared to be a lost cause. His heated battle with Allan Donald, in particular, was Test cricket at its very best. The pair clashed again three years later at Trent Bridge when, with England chasing 247 to level the series, Donald appeared to have Atherton caught at the wicket. Atherton stood his ground with all the innocence of a choirboy, and proceeded to lead England to victory.

Stewart and Atherton have enormous respect for one another which has been created not necessarily by close friendship, but by rivalry. The 1993 tour of India was a disaster and it was clear that Graham Gooch's term as England's captain was coming to an end. A successor had to be found and the media was full of speculation about which of the two young men would succeed him. The pressure came to an ugly head in Bombay, during the final Test of that unhappy trip, when both batsmen ended up in the same crease and refused to budge when the stumps were broken at the other end. Neither batsman looked at the other as the umpires deliberated over which should be given out. Technically, it should have been Atherton, but he was going nowhere. Eventually, and in stony silence, it was Stewart who was dispatched. The incident will never be forgotten by those who witnessed it, but to his credit – and it says everything about the man – Stewart became a loyal and unstinting vice-captain during Atherton's long reign as captain. Finally, the opportunity came for him to lead his country, and his team beat the South Africans in 1998.

Atherton commiserates with Stewart: once again an Ambrose delivery had hit Stewart during the first West Indies Test in 1998.

Stewart remains extremely fit and could carry on for years. Atherton, though, is increasingly troubled by a long-standing back complaint. During the 1999 World Cup he joined the BBC commentary team, proving that once his playing days are over, he will be a most welcome and incisive addition. ∎

ZIMBABWE IN ENGLAND
By Jonathan Agnew

Hampshire v. Zimbabwe
27, 28, 29 and 30 April 2000 at Southampton
Hampshire 131 (53.5 overs)(DA Kenway 48) and 234
for 4 dec. (*RA Smith 60, WS Kendall 56)
Zimbabwe 364 for 7 dec. (106 overs)
(*ADR Campbell 150, MW Goodwin 70)
Match drawn

A second-day wash-out meant that this match never really developed as a contest, but there was much for the Zimbabweans to take out of the remaining cricket. Troubles at home, and a desperately disappointing tour of the West Indies, brought Andy Flower's side to England with much on their minds. But at least at Southampton, especially when the sun came out on the final two days, they could enjoy the simple pleasures of playing the game and trying to find form for the short Test series ahead.

Hampshire were bowled out unceremoniously on the opening day, Pommie Mbangwa taking 4 for 19 from his 16 accurate overs and Neil Johnson weighing in with 4 for 28. Zimbabwe, 19 for 1 on the first evening, proceeded to 281 for 6 when the match resumed on the third day with Alistair Campbell reaching three figures and Murray Goodwin hitting a cultured 70 from 118 balls.

Charlie van der Gucht, a young left-arm spinner on his first-class debut, bowled promisingly to take 3 for 53 from 20 overs, but on the final morning Campbell strode on to 150 not out while diminutive schoolboy wicketkeeper-batsman Tatendu Taibu, still just 17, scored 36 before the Zimbabweans declared at 364 for 7. Hampshire, in their second innings, ensured the draw and settled for batting practice themselves with Robin Smith (60) and Will Kendall (56 not out) doing their best to provide further entertainment.

Kent v. Zimbabwe
3, 4, 5 May 2000 at Canterbury
Zimbabwe 159 (78.4 overs)(ML Nkala 24,
*HH Streak 23) and 165 (NC Johnson 70, ML Nkala 40)
Kent 487 for 8 dec. (138 overs)(R Dravid 182,
JB Hockley 74)
Kent won by an innings and 163 runs

Kent picked up £11,000 from sponsors Vodafone for this beating of the troubled Zimbabweans at Canterbury. David Masters, a young seamer whose

Above: Pom Mbangwa tries to avoid a bouncer from Andy Caddick during the first Test, but the ball deflects from his helmet into the stumps and removes a bail.

father Kevin played a handful of matches for Kent in the early 1980s, picked up match figures of 9 for 81 on his first-class debut as Zimbabwe were tumbled out for 159 and 165. Min Patel matched Masters' 4 for 44 in the tourists' limp first innings and Masters then took 5 for 37 as only Neil Johnson (70) and Mluleki Nkala (40) made any lasting impression with the bat for Zimbabwe. In between, Rahul Dravid demonstrated his class with 182 as Kent, further boosted by 74 from James Hockley and half-centuries from Alan Wells and Paul Nixon, powered to 487 for 8 declared.

Sussex v. Zimbabwe
7 May 2000 at Hastings (50 over match)
Sussex 264 for 4 (RR Montgomerie 129 not out,
PA Cottey 85)
Zimbabwe 267 for 2 (NC Johnson 107 not out,
MW Goodwin 63)
Zimbabwe won by 8 wickets

The Zimbabweans, no doubt in a happier frame of mind after sorting out a tour pay dispute with Peter Chingoka and David Ellman-Brown, respectively the chairman and chief executive of the Zimbabwe

Cricket Union, trounced Sussex by eight wickets at Hastings. Richard Montgomerie's unbeaten 129 was the basis of Sussex's 50-over total of 264 for 4, Tony Cottey also weighing in with 85, but Zimbabwe romped home with three overs to spare. Grant Flower managed to find some semblance of form with 53, and Murray Goodwin hit 63, but chief honours went to Neil Johnson who underlined his prowess as a limited-overs batsman with 14 fours and a six in his 107 not out.

Essex v. Zimbabwe
9 May 2000 at Chelmsford (50 over match)
Essex 172 (47.2 overs)(DR Law 41, GR Napier 35)
Zimbabwe 175 for 3 (34.4 overs)(MW Goodwin 50, NC Johnson 41, *+A Flower 41)
Zimbabwe won by 7 wickets

The Zimbabweans at last began to string some results together, following up their win against Sussex with a trouncing of Essex at Chelmsford in another 50-over match. Essex, though, batted extremely poorly as they slipped to 20 for 4 and then 48 for 5 before Danny Law and Graham Napier hauled them up to the relative riches of 172. Bryan Strang took 4 for 22 but the Essex bowlers could not follow his example, some inaccurate fare allowing Murray Goodwin, Neil Johnson and Andy Flower to enjoy themselves as Zimbabwe reached their target with more than 15 overs remaining.

Essex v. Zimbabwe
11, 12, 13 and 14 May 2000 at Chelmsford
Zimbabwe 315 (105.3 overs)(NC Johnson 83, GJ Whittall 54) and 75 for 0 dec.
(TR Gripper 32, GW Flower28)
Essex 249 (99.3 overs)(N Hussain 33, SG Law 33)
Match drawn

A first-day wash-out consigned this match to an unsatisfactory draw, England captain Nasser Hussain using the occasion for some much-needed batting practice for himself ahead of the opening Test at Lord's, and ultimately asking his Essex team-mates to keep the Zimbabweans in the field for as long as possible on the fourth day in a bid to deny them extra time in the middle. Zimbabwe reached 143 for 4 on a rain-affected second day, finally being bowled out for 315 with Neil Johnson top-scoring with 83. Ricky Anderson took 5 for 69 and Hussain

Alec Stewart pulls Streak on the way to his century on the third day of the first Test.

then joint top-scored with 33 as Essex crawled to 249. In the small amount of time left on the final afternoon Grant Flower and Trevor Gripper, the out-of-touch openers, added 75 against Essex's two off-spinners – a form of bowling they would not encounter in the Test!

First Test
18, 19, 20 and 21 May 2000 at Lord's

There has never been an earlier start to a Test match in England, and with characteristically damp and miserable weather hanging over the country, it was inevitable that the game would be dominated by the seam bowlers. Since Zimbabwe, with the admirable exception of Heath Streak, were hopelessly outgunned in that department, their comprehensive thrashing was only to be expected. This was overlooked in some quarters which, before we knew it, had proclaimed England to be a ruthless team that now had Australia in its sights. Naturally, Nasser Hussain and Duncan Fletcher were quick to play down anything that went beyond the obvious satisfaction of having easily completed a straightforward job.

Much of the attention before the match was focused on the business of central contracts. Twelve of England's leading players were now employed by

Nick Knight is poised to gobble up the catch to dismiss Streak for a duck at Lord's – another wicket for Ed Giddins.

the England and Wales Cricket Board rather than by their counties. The selectors faced the almost impossible task of effectively choosing, in February, a team to play in May and two of their original choices – Dean Headley and Michael Vaughan – were already ruled out by injury. Further to this was the intriguing and, I felt, misguided decision to promote Mark Ramprakash to open the batting. Having spent the meaningful phase of his career in the middle order, this was asking an awful lot. Although he scored 93 for Middlesex against Northamptonshire in his new, unaccustomed position on a bleak day at Lord's, that was barely adequate preparation for what was to come later in the summer in the form of Curtly Ambrose and Courtney Walsh.

Another controversial selection was that of Chris Schofield, the young Lancashire leg-spinner, who had appeared in fewer than 20 first-class matches. In many ways, it was an admirable and bold step to take in that it was clear that England do not possess a finger-spinner who is good enough to win Test matches and, therefore, this was a positive route to pursue. Schofield was awarded a central contract on this basis yet, after only 18 overs (which were delivered in the second Test against Zimbabwe), he was dropped. No matter what new schemes are

introduced, England's short-term and short-sighted selection policy still manages to triumph regardless.

Zimbabwe had problems of their own, particularly off the field. Pre-election violence was becoming widespread in their troubled country and this was particularly directed at the white farming community, with which a number of their players were connected. Barely a day passed without more stories of barbarity and even murder, so the Zimbabweans deserved a great deal of credit for playing the match at all, let alone for not using the situation to excuse their abject performance.

There was, then, already a great deal in the melting pot as England gathered at Lord's, where their recent record had been appalling. Ed Giddins and Nick Knight substituted for Headley and Vaughan respectively – Knight being the third specialist opener in the team apart from Ramprakash – and moments after Hussain won the toss, Zimbabwe were effectively out of the match. Very rarely can anybody come back from 48 for 5, and with Andy Caddick and Giddins running rampant, Zimbabwe quickly found themselves on the rack. Caddick did the early damage, nipping out the first three batsmen with only eight runs on the board, and then handed over to Giddins whose pre-match publicity had been split between his extraordinary back-packing journey up the Amazon, which had accounted for the first half of his previous winter, and the time he then spent – at his own expense –

FIRST TEST – ENGLAND v. ZIMBABWE

18, 19, 20 and 21 May 2000 at Lord's

ZIMBABWE

	First innings		Second innings	
G Flower	b Caddick	4	lbw b Gough	2
TR Gripper	c Stewart, b Caddick	1	c Knight, b Gough●	5
MW Goodwin	c Knight, b Gough	18	lbw b Caddick	11
ADR Campbell	c Stewart, b Caddick	0	lbw b Gough	4
*A Flower (capt)	c Atherton, b Giddins	24	(6)lbw b Gough	2
C Johnson	c Gough, b Giddins	14	(7) c Hick, b Caddick	9
GJ Whittall	b Giddins	15	(8) c Hick, b Caddick	23
HH Streak	c Atherton, b Giddins	4	(9) c Knight, b Giddins	0
BC Strang	c Ramprakash, b Giddins	0	(10) not out	37
BA Murphy	c Stewart, b Gough	0	(5)lbw b Giddins	14
M Mbangwa	not out	1	b Caddick	8
	lb2	2	lb1, nb7	8
		83		**123**

	First Innings				Second Innings			
	O	M	R	W	O	M	R	W
Gough	12.3	1	36	2	15	3	57	4
Caddick	8	3	28	3	16.2	5	38	4
Flintoff	3	2	2	-				
Giddins	7	2	15	5	7	3	27	2

● TV replay decision

Fall of Wickets
1-5, 2-8, 3-8, 4-46, 5-48, 6-67, 7-77, 8-79, 9-82
1-2, 2-7, 3-18, 4-33, 5-36, 6-49, 7-74, 8-74, 9-82

ENGLAND

	First innings	
MA Atherton	lbw b Streak	55
MR Ramprakash	lbw b Streak	15
N Hussain (capt)	c Murphy, b Streak	10
GA Hick	lbw b Streak	101
*AJ Stewart	not out	124
NV Knight	c Johnson, b Whittall	44
A Flintoff	c Streak, b Whittall	1
CP Schofield	c Johnson, b Whittall	0
AR Caddick	c †A Flower, b Streak	13
D Gough	c Campbell, b Murphy	5
ESH Giddins	c Strang, b Streak	7
	b5, lb29, w1, nb5	40
		415

	First Innings			
	O	M	R	W
Streak	35.5	12	87	6
Strang	27	4	86	-
Mbangwa	21	5	69	-
Johnson	20	5	55	-
Whittall	7	0	27	3
Murphy	25	6	57	1

Fall of Wickets
1-29, 2-49, 3-113, 4-262, 5-376, 6-378, 7-378, 8-398, 9-407

Umpires: P Willey & DL Orchard
Toss: England
Test Debut: CP Schofield
Man of the Match: ESH Giddins

England won by an innings & 209 runs

getting fit at Lilleshall. Swinging the ball both ways, and enjoying a fair slice of good fortune, Giddins ran through the middle order to finish with 5 for 15: the cheapest five-wicket haul for England for more than 70 years. Zimbabwe's total of 83 was the lowest against England by anybody for 22 years.

Ramprakash might consider himself to have been unlucky to be dispatched leg before, half forward to Streak for 15 while Hussain's carved catch to backward point was just careless. England were 49 for 2, but Mike Atherton and Graeme Hick dug in, putting on 64 before Streak claimed his third victim: Atherton leg before for 55. By the close of the second day, Hick had progressed to 64 and England's lead was already a healthy 92.

Interest on the third day was divided: would Hick reach his first century against the country of his birth, and how would Alec Stewart concentrate on batting while his beloved Chelsea appeared in the FA Cup Final? Hick provided the first answer, albeit after 22 tortuous minutes on 99. It might have been that his nerves were shot, because he succumbed to the very next ball for 101, having proved little.

Stewart, too, reached three figures to complete what should have been a positive afternoon (Chelsea won), but England completely lost their way as Stewart, in particular, seemed unsure as to how they were supposed to be playing the game. The result was that the last six wickets fell quite needlessly for 39 runs and although the lead had already assumed match-winning proportions – 332 – England's lack of experience in driving home the advantage was again exposed as Streak took 6 for 67, the best figures by a Zimbabwean in Test cricket.

However, any Zimbabwean smiles were immediately wiped away by a superb opening burst from Darren Gough. Bowling as fast as any Englishman in recent years, he reduced Zimbabwe to an utterly hopeless 36 for 5 and the match was effectively over. All that remained was for Giddins to take his match haul to seven wickets, which was enough to seal, narrowly, the Man of the Match award. England's victory by an innings and 209 runs – which required only 205 overs of play – was their most emphatic since 1974.

Yorkshire v. Zimbabwe

24, 25, 26 and 27 May 2000 at Headingley, Leeds
Zimbabwe 235 (98.1 overs)(GJ Whittall 89, *A Flower 47) and 68 (30.3 overs)(GJ Whittall 15, *A Flower 15)
Yorkshire 124 (58.4 overs)(MJ Wood 32, †SM Guy 29) and 147 (54 overs)(MJ Lumb 66, GM Fellows 22)
Zimbabwe won by 32 runs

Murray Goodwin prepares to sweep Chris Schofield as Alec Stewart watches from behind the stumps.

Zimbabwe's cricketers bounced back from their highly disappointing defeat in the first Test at Lord's with a morale-boosting victory by 32 runs in a tense, low-scoring struggle on a difficult Headingley pitch. Grant Flower's horrid form continued when the opener was out to the first ball of the match but Guy Whittall, a stand-in opener, responded with a gutsy 89 and, chiefly in alliance with skipper Andy Flower (47), lifted Zimbabwe to 235 all out. In reply, Yorkshire were skittled for 124, Pommie Mbangwa taking a career-best 6 for 14 – the best bowling by an overseas player against Yorkshire since the even more exotically named Xenophon Balaskas took 8 for 99 for South Africa at Sheffield in 1935. Yorkshire were not finished, however, with Gavin Hamilton (5 for 22) and Matthew Hoggard (3 for 18) undermining the tourists to such an extent that they were bowled out in their second innings for just 68. A target of 180, though, proved just out of Yorkshire's reach on such a pitch, Mbangwa (4 for 39) this time being well supported by Bryan Strang (4 for 41). Considerable consolation for Yorkshire, nevertheless, came in the shape of a brave, unbeaten 66 on his first-class debut by Michael Lumb, the 20-year-old son of the county's former opener Richard Lumb.

SECOND TEST
1, 2 (no play), 3, 4 and 5 June 2000 at Trent Bridge

Poor Trent Bridge! Having spent a small fortune on developing one of the most friendly grounds in the country, the reward has so far consisted of one low-key England game in last year's World Cup (against Zimbabwe) and now as unattractive a Test match as one can imagine. Played in foul weather and on the back of such a one-sided encounter at Lord's, it was a great credit to Nottinghamshire that they managed to entice anybody into the ground at all.

Those hardy souls who did brave the elements were rewarded by a heartening Zimbabwean fightback despite the most terrible bad luck. First, on the opening day of the match, the father of Jason Oates – a Zimbabwean first-class cricketer – was murdered on his farm in Zimbabwe. Guy Whittall's aunt (the mother of Andy Whittall, who was commentating for Channel 4) died suddenly, and this tragedy was followed by the death of Gary Brent's mother from a heart attack. It is possible for such an unbelievably sad sequence of events to bond a beleaguered team together, and this is what happened at Trent Bridge.

England were understandably buoyed after their comprehensive victory at Lord's and, for the first time since 1998, named the same eleven. Zimbabwe made only two changes – it could have been many more after their disastrous effort – leaving out Trevor Gripper and Bryan Strang. In the continued absence of Henry Olonga, Mluleki Nkala – only 19 years old – was drafted in to strengthen the attack.

Zimbabwe took one look at the conditions – and the forecast – and put England in to bat. On the face of it, England's total of 374 does not look at all bad, but take out the contributions of Atherton (136) and Schofield (57) and you are not left with a great deal. Ramprakash also passed 50 as he and Atherton put on 121 for the first wicket to raise hopes of a confidence-boosting second century in this, his 40th Test match. Sadly, this was not to be as he edged a lifter from Johnson into the gully. Hussain, unbelievably, drove a second catch into the off side and when Hick, Stewart and Knight all departed cheaply, England had subsided from 182 for 1 to 221 for 5.

The stage was set, therefore, for Andy Flintoff to repay the faith the selectors have shown in him with a meaningful contribution. However, after an hour of prodding about, he missed a pull stroke and fell leg before for 16 to leave Schofield to play the most refreshing and entertaining knock of the innings. He faced only 119 balls, played an up-and-under as well as a reverse sweep or two and was finally the last man out as he tried to protect Giddins from the bowling.

Zimbabwe lost a couple of wickets before the close of the third day (the second having been completely washed out) but any thoughts of another collapse were laid to rest by Murray Goodwin, who scored an unbeaten 148. His partnership of 127 with Neil Johnson for the third wicket was the highest for Zimbabwe against England and, with a day to go, Zimbabwe were only 89 behind.

What followed was extraordinary as England were dismissed for only 147 having at one stage been 110 for 7 – only 199 ahead. They could not even claim to have been taken by surprise by Zimbabwe's overnight declaration because, sportingly – and quite unnecessarily – Andy Flower informed Hussain of his decision an hour before the start of play. Yet, before they knew it, England were 44 for 4 and Zimbabwe realised they had a real chance of levelling the series.

As is so often the case, Atherton's wicket was crucial and he stood firm, despite a stomach upset – as chaos reigned at the other end. Atherton was the ninth man out, for 34, by which time England had clawed their

Right: How to play short-pitched fast bowling – Mike Atherton gets right up on his toes to ease the ball away into the leg side.

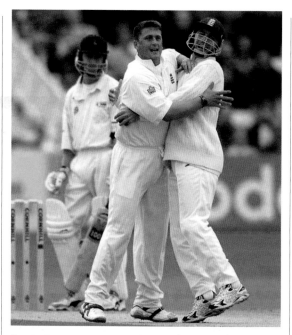

Darren Gough is congratulated by catcher Mark Ramprakash after dismissing Grant Flower for nought.

SECOND TEST – ENGLAND v. ZIMBABWE
1, 2 (no play), 3, 4 and 5 June 2000 at Trent Bridge

TEST MATCH AVERAGES
England v. Zimbabwe

ENGLAND

	First innings		Second innings	
MA Atherton	c G Flower, b Mbangwa	136	(7) c A Flower, b Whittall	34
MR Ramprakash	c G Flower, b Johnson	56	c A Flower, b Nkala	4
N Hussain (capt)	c Streak, b Nkala	21	lbw b Nkala	0
GA Hick	c Murphy, b Nkala	5	c A Flower, b Johnson	30
*AJ Stewart	lbw b Whittall	9	c A Flower, b Johnson	15
NV Knight	lbw b Whittall	1	(1) b Streak	6
A Flintoff	lbw b Mbangwa	16	(6) c A Flower, b Streak	16
CP Schofield	b Murphy	57	c Campbell, b Murphy	10
AR Caddick	c G Flower, b Nkala	13	c A Flower, b Whittall	12
D Gough	c Campbell, b Streak	9	c Murphy, b Whittall	3
ESH Giddins	not out	3	not out	0
	b9, lb13, w16, nb10	48	b5, lb8, w1, nb3	17
		374		**147**

	First Innings				Second Innings			
	O	M	R	W	O	M	R	W
Streak	32	7	82	1	17	8	13	2
Nkala	31	7	82	3	11	5	22	2
Johnson	22	7	63	1	12	2	41	2
Mbangwa	18	6	40	2	15	8	25	–
Murphy	12.2	1	36	1	12	6	19	1
Whittall	19	7	47	2	8	3	14	3
Flower GW	1	0	2	–				

Fall of Wickets
1-121, 2-182, 3-188, 4-209, 5-221, 6-264, 7-303, 8-335, 9-358
1-6, 2-6, 3-12, 4-44, 5-73, 6-95, 7-110, 8-139, 9-140

Atherton had been unable to field and could not bat until the fall of the 5th wicket

ZIMBABWE

	First innings		Second innings	
GW Flower	c Ramprakash, b Gough	0	c Hick, b Caddick	12
GJ Whittall	lbw b Giddins	28	not out	12
MW Goodwin	not out	148	not out	1
NC Johnson	c Stewart, b Gough	51		
*A Flower (capt)	b Gough	42		
BA Murphy	not out	0		
SV Carlisle				
ADR Campbell				
HH Streak				
ML Nkala				
M Mbangwa				
	b5, lb5, nb6	16		
	(for 4 wickets dec.)	**285**	(for 1 wicket)	**25**

	First Innings				Second Innings			
	O	M	R	W	O	M	R	W
Gough	20	2	66	3	2	0	15	–
Caddick	18.3	4	57	–	2	1	9	1
Giddins	16	5	46	1				
Schofield	18	2	73	–				
Flintoff	10	3	33	–				
Ramprakash	1	1	0	1				

Fall of Wickets
1-1, 2-33, 3-162, 4-284 1-17

Umpires: MJ Kitchen & DL Orchard
Toss: Zimbabwe
Test Debut: ML Nkala
Man of the Match: MW Goodwin
Players of the Series: MA Atherton (Eng) & HH Streak (Zim)

Match drawn

ENGLAND

Batting	M	Inns	NO	HS	Runs	Av	100	50
MA Atherton	2	3	0	136	225	75.00	1	1
AJ Stewart	2	3	1	124*	148	74.00	1	–
GA Hick	2	3	0	101	136	45.33	1	–
MR Ramprakash	2	3	0	56	75	25.00	–	1
CP Schofield	2	3	0	57	67	22.33	–	1
NV Knight	2	3	0	44	51	17.00	–	–
AR Caddick	2	3	0	13	38	12.66	–	–
A Flintoff	2	3	0	16	33	11.00	–	–
N Hussain	2	3	0	21	31	10.33	–	–
ESH Giddins	2	3	2	7	10	10.00	–	–
D Gough	2	3	0	9	17	5.66	–	–

Bowling	Overs	Mds	Runs	Wkts	Av	Best	10/m	5/inns
ESH Giddins	30	10	88	8	11.00	5–15	–	1
AR Caddick	44.5	13	132	8	16.50	4–38	–	–
D Gough	49.3	6	174	9	19.33	4–57	–	–

Also bowled: A Flintoff 13–5–35–0; MR Ramprakash 1–0–1–0; CP Schofield 18–2–73–0

Fielding Figures
4–AJ Stewart; 3 – GA Hick, NV Knight.2 – MA Atherton, MR Ramprakash; 1 – D Gough

ZIMBABWE

Batting	M	Inns	NO	HS	Runs	Av	100	50
MW Goodwin	2	4	2	148*	178	89.00	1	–
GJ Whittall	2	4	1	28	78	26.00	–	–
NC Johnson	2	3	0	51	74	24.66	–	1
+A Flower	2	3	0	42	68	22.66	–	–
BA Murphy	2	3	1	14	14	7.00	–	–
GW Flower	2	4	0	12	18	4.50	–	–

Also batted: ADR Campbell (2 Tests) 0, 4; TR Gripper (1 Test) 1, 5; M Mbangwa (2 Tests) 1*, 8;
BC Strang (1 Test) 0, 37*; HH Streak (2 Tests) 4, 0
SV Carlisle and M Nkala played in one Test but did not bat

Bowling	Overs	Mds	Runs	Wkts	Av	Best	10/m	5/inns
GJ Whittall	34	10	88	8	11.00	3–14	–	–
HH Streak	84.5	27	182	9	20.22	6–87	–	1
M Nkala	42	12	104	5	20.80	3–82	–	–

Also bowled: G Flower 1–0–2–0; NC Johnson 54–14–159–3; M Mbangwa 54–19–134–2;
BA Murphy 49.2–13–112–3; BC Strang 27–4–86–0

Fielding Figures
6 – A Flower; 4 – GW Flower; 3 – ADR Campbell, BA Murphy; 2 – NC Johnson, HH Streak;
1 – BC Strang

Chris Schofield falls over as he hits a four off Neil Johnson during his ungainly but effective innings of 57 at Trent Bridge. It was to be Scofield's last appearance of the season for England.

way to safety despite the efforts of Whittall, who nabbed his 50th Test wicket as he took 3 for 14.

England's celebrations at winning the series – the first under the leadership of Hussain – were muted that evening. It had been a thoroughly lacklustre performance and one that called into question the concept of allowing too much rest for the contracted players between Tests. Caddick, for instance, was a shadow of the bowler who terrorised Zimbabwe at Lord's because he was rusty, and for no other reason. These are early days for the new system, and England's management learned a lesson at Trent Bridge. It almost cost them the match.

Zimbabwe v. West Indies
10, 11 and 12 June at Arundel Castle
West Indies 407 (114.5 overs)(BC Lara 176, SL Campbell 146) and 200 for 5 dec. (60 overs) (S Chanderpaul 103 not out)
Zimbabwe 275 for 8 (83.5 overs)(MW Goodwin 126) and 108 for 1 (36 overs)(TR Gripper 66 not out)
Match drawn

Two touring teams met in a first-class match on English soil for the first time since 1912 – the year of the experimental Triangular Test series between England, Australia and South Africa – and the three days at Arundel provided some fine entertainment for good crowds. Most spectacular of all was the return to form, on the opening day, of Brian Lara.

The former West Indies captain, previously struggling for runs since his return to cricket

following a self-imposed four-month lay-off, hit a superb 176 from 163 balls to announce his readiness for the First Cornhill Test against England. Coming in at 55 for 2, Lara dominated a fine stand with opener Sherwin Campbell, who himself went on to reach an unbeaten 141 out of 364 for 6 by the close, and 146 in all. Quickly into his stride – his first fifty occupying just 43 balls – Lara struck five sixes and 25 fours to the delight of all those fortunate enough to be present. Bryan Strang, the left-arm seamer, somehow escaped much of the carnage to finish with 5 for 68 in a West Indian first-innings total of 407.

In reply, Murray Goodwin again underlined his class with the bat by hitting 126 as Zimbabwe totalled 275 for 8 declared. Nixon McLean was the best of the Caribbean bowlers with 4 for 64 and, after reaching 12 for no wickets by the close, the West Indians reached 200 for 5 declared on the final day with Shivnarine Chanderpaul including 19 boundaries in his 103 not out. Left with an impossible target, the Zimbabweans were happy to see out the draw on 108-1 with Trevor Gripper unbeaten on 66.

Lara said: 'My break from the game was very good for me, and spending time with my family, my daughter and my friends was very important to me. I would not take any of it back. Now, coming back to cricket, the enthusiasm is there again.'

Gloucestershire v. Zimbabwe
16, 17, 18 and 19 June at Gloucester
Zimbabwe 568 (142.2 overs)(MW Goodwin 194) and 258 for 2 dec. (57 overs)(*+A Flower 116 not out)
Gloucestershire 167 (69.2 overs)(MGN Windows 47) and 135 (57.5 overs)(+RC Russell 28)
Zimbabwe won by 524 runs

Rain stops play: the perpetual enemy of English cricket featured quite heavily in this season's fixtures.

At Archdeacon Meadow in Gloucester the Zimbabweans inflicted the heaviest defeat in their history on Gloucestershire, winning by 524 runs after using the better part of the four days available as batting practice. First, the tourists ran up 568 in their first innings with Murray Goodwin leading the way with 194 and Trevor Gripper, Alistair Campbell and Bryan Strang all hitting half-centuries. Ironically, in the midst of all this run-scoring, Jon Lewis picked up a career-best 8 for 95! Gloucestershire, with a weakened team, subsided to 167 all out in reply, with Matt Windows the only lengthy resister with 47 and Heath Streak proving too potent for many of the rest with 5 for 72. Imran Mohammad, the son of Sadiq and nephew of the three other Test-playing Pakistani brothers Hanif, Mushtaq and Wazir, bagged a fifth-ball duck in his first first-class innings for the county. Zimbabwe chose not to enforce the follow-on, allowing the Flower brothers to gorge themselves on runs before a declaration at 258 for 2. By the close of the third day Gloucestershire were 98 for 4, Streak having taken two more wickets with the new ball, and Pommie Mbangwa then took 4 for 7 in 35 balls on the final morning to finish with 5 for 23 as the county were dismissed for 135. Jack Russell, typically, fought hard with 28 off 100 balls, but the size of Gloucestershire's defeat eclipsed the previous record – the 470-run loss to Sussex at Hove in 1913.

British Universities v. Zimbabwe
21, 22 and 23 June 2000
British Universities 261 for 8 dec. (113.3 overs)
(JJ Porter 93, MJ Banes 51)
Zimbabwe 441 for 6 dec. (124 overs)
(CB Wishart 116, DP Viljoen 72, HH Streak 71)
Match drawn

Joe Porter, a crisp-driving left-hander from Oxford Brookes, finished the opening day on 90 not out as the British Universities reached 247 for 7 against the Zimbabweans at Fenner's. But the following morning he mishit a pull and was out for 93. After the Universities had declared their first innings on 261 for 8 the Zimbabweans reacted to a loss of some play on the second day by batting all through the final day to total 441 for 6 declared and make the contest meaningless. Craig Wishart top-scored with 116.

Somerset v. Zimbabwe
25 June 2000 at Taunton (50-over match)
Zimbabwe 248 for 4 (NC Johnson 101)
Somerset 227 (⁺M Burns 68, PCL Holloway 55)
Zimbabwe won by 21 runs

Neil Johnson showed yet again what an accomplished one-day batsman he is by hitting the Somerset bowlers for 101 at Taunton. Alistair Campbell, keeping wicket in this game, also contributed an unbeaten 45 and the Zimbabweans' 50-over total of 248 for 4 proved just too much for the home county. Piran Holloway made 55 and

The 'new-look' Trent Bridge, as seen from the pavilion. Next year, Nottinghamshire's investment in the ground will be rewarded by a Test match against Australia.

Michael Burns threatened to win the match with a 68-ball 68, but Heath Streak (3 for 27) and Gary Brent (4 for 36) then ensured a 21-run victory for the tourists.

Durham v. Zimbabwe
27 June 2000 at Chester-le-Street (50-over match)
Durham 168 (JJB Lewis 37, NC Phillips26)
Zimbabwe 169 for 2 (40.2 overs)(NC Johnson 81)
Zimbabwe won by 8 wickets

An unbroken stand of 90 between Neil Johnson (81 not out) and Stuart Carlisle (35 not out) swept the Zimbabweans to an easy eight-wicket victory against Durham at Chester-le-Street. Jon Lewis (37) was the only home batsman to flourish for long as Bryan Strang took 3 for 37 and Dirk Viljoen 2 for 20 from ten overs of cleverly varied slow left-arm spin. Durham's eventual total of 168 was wholly inadequate, and the tourists passed it with almost ten overs to spare.

Nottinghamshire v. Zimbabwe
29 June 2000 at Nottingham (50-over match)
Nottinghamshire 207 (GE Welton 94)
Zimbabwe 211 for 5 (41.3 overs)(GJ Whittall 44)
Zimbabwe won by 5 wickets

The Zimbabweans, cranking up their preparations for the triangular NatWest series, demolished Nottinghamshire by five wickets at Trent Bridge after restricting the county to 207. Paul Strang's comeback from injury continued with the leg-spinner taking 3 for 31 against his old team-mates, although Guy Welton's 94 was another innings of high promise from the 22-year-old opener. Guy Whittall (44) gave the tourists a rapid start, Alistair Campbell added an unbeaten 39, and Neil Johnson applied the finishing touches with a half-hour 40 not out after coming in at number seven.

Northamptonshire v. Zimbabwe
1 July 2000 at Northampton (50-over match)
Northamptonshire 264 for 3 (MB Loye 112, AS Rollins 75)
Zimbabwe 244 (42.1 overs)(GW Flower 84)
Zimbabwe won by 5 wickets D/L Method

An opening stand of 218 by Mal Loye and Adrian Rollins, plus a little help from Duckworth/Lewis, proved too much for the Zimbabweans at Northampton. Loye hit 112 and Rollins 75 as Northants ran up a challenging 45-over total of 264 for 3. Because the game had been reduced by rain, though, the Zimbabweans found themselves needing 287 from 45 overs in reply and, despite 84 from Grant Flower and 58 from Stuart Carlisle, they could score only 244 from 42.1 overs. Michael Strong was the best home bowler with 5 for 39.

THE WEST INDIES IN ENGLAND
By Jonathan Agnew

Worcestershire v. West Indies
2, 3 and 4 June 2000 at Worcester
West Indies 164 and 301 for 9 dec.
(S Chanderpaul 161*)
Worcestershire 232 (VS Solanki 51)
Match drawn

Most of the interest in the West Indies' opening tour match at Worcester was centred on Brian Lara's comeback to cricket following his self-imposed five-month exile. What an anticlimax! In the first innings Lara contributed just a fourth-ball one to West Indies' 164 and then, after Worcestershire had replied with 232, the great left-hander was out for a second-ball single. Shivnarine Chanderpaul, however, hit a superb unbeaten 161 (the next-best score was Ramnaresh Sarwan's 30) as the West Indies made sure of the draw at 301 for 9 declared.

Looks good – but Adams is about to be caught at point just two runs short of a deserved century.

Glamorgan v. West Indies
6, 7 and 8 June 2000 at Cardiff
West Indies 176 (WW Hinds 105*,
RDB Croft 5 for 26) and 97
Glamorgan 140 and 113 (NAM McLean 5 for 30)
West Indies won by 20 runs

The West Indians boosted their morale with a hard-fought 20-run win against Glamorgan on a painfully slow and dusty pitch at Cardiff. Brian Lara's early-tour struggle for runs continued with 0 and 11: he was stumped in the first innings overbalancing as he played forward to Robert Croft, and the England off-spinner had him rather harshly adjudged leg before in the second innings. At least Lara showed he had not lost his sense of calm, though. When a swarm of bees buzzed the ground on the second afternoon when he was batting, he simply lay on the ground until the danger had passed! Wavell Hinds' brilliant 105 not out was the feature of the opening day, although Croft forced his way back into Test contention by taking 5 for 26 from 34 overs as the West Indians totalled just 176. Glamorgan, 44 for 2 at the close, ground on to 140 on the second day – leg-spinner Nahendra Nagamootoo announcing himself to English audiences with figures of 19–11–12 for 4. Only Ridley Jacobs (43) came to terms with the deteriorating conditions in the West Indians' second innings 97. Steve James and Matthew Elliott then added 49 for the first wicket as Glamorgan seemed to be on their way to a famous victory, but the West Indians were not giving up and, slowly but surely, they regained control. Runs almost dried up, Keith Newell taking 91 balls over his 12, and Nixon McLean (5 for 30) provided the cutting edge which eventually brought victory for the tourists. 'I thought this game gave us good mental preparation for the rest of the tour,' said West Indies skipper Jimmy Adams.

FIRST TEST
15, 16 and 17 June 2000 at Edgbaston

Edgbaston has been a batsman's nightmare in recent years. Ever since, in fact, Curtly Ambrose's first delivery of the corresponding match four years ago took off from short of a length and sailed over Mike Atherton's head for four byes. The pitch, on that occasion, resembled a cabbage patch but England this time around appeared to be so confident that they pre-selected their final eleven two days in advance. At the time, it seemed unnecessary and potentially foolish. So it proved.

West Indies captain, Jimmy Adams, congratulates Courtney Walsh on taking another wicket as England subsided in their second innings.

The day before the Test began – England having already committed themselves to playing a spinner and, therefore, apparently determined to bat first – Edgbaston was one vast lake. The rain had hammered down and it was inconceivable that some moisture would not freshen the pitch. Jimmy Adams called correctly and put England in to bat. Nasser Hussain later claimed that he would have inserted the West Indies, but that would have contradicted the selection he and his colleagues had made two days before.

Graeme Hick walked out to bat at 44 for 2 and returned at 45 for 3. It was a stroke horribly reminiscent of 1991, when he first appeared against the West Indies, and Campbell gratefully snaffled the inadequate grope to second slip that gave Walsh his third wicket of the morning. When Hussain and Stewart – who was the brilliant Ambrose's only victim of the innings – both followed, England were on the brink of total calamity on 82 for 5.

It is not often that England's lower order scores more runs than the top but, for once, some gritty resistance paid dividends and only the hapless Giddins – who had an awful match – failed to make double figures. The stand between Caddick and Gough was especially encouraging: 39 for the ninth wicket before Gough was run out by Jacob's throw to the non-striker's end.

Brian Lara drives Robert Croft through the covers on the way to his half century in the first Test at Edgbaston.

It was crucial that England's seam bowlers discovered the same assistance as had Walsh (5 for 36) and Ambrose. Gayle fell immediately to Gough and Hinds was not far behind, but Campbell and Lara took the West Indies to 123 for 2 before Campbell was scuppered by a ball that kept a little low. Lara reached his 50 in two and a quarter hours and seemed absolutely determined to make a big score on his old stamping ground. The admirable Gough, however, had other ideas and ran one across the left-hander which Lara obligingly edged to Stewart. That was 136 for 4 and England might have hoped to concede a lead of only 50 or so, but Adams produced an innings of great patience and not a great deal less skill. He batted, in all, for nearly seven hours and it was the partnership of 94 with Chanderpaul, who scored 73, that pushed the West Indies into their winning position. Franklyn Rose played some extravagant blows, making 48 from only 54 balls but, as Adams carved the stroke that should have brought his century, Flintoff grabbed a superb catch at point to dismiss him for 98.

England were soon batting again, 218 behind and within no time were effectively out of the match at 24 for 4. Although nothing should be taken away from Walsh, who took the first three, their demise was feeble in the extreme. Ramprakash became Walsh's 450th test wicket when he fell leg before for no runs. Hussain edged to Jacobs for no runs and Hick completed a pair in the same manner although slow motion replays suggested that he might have been unlucky on this occasion.

Knight stood firm, as he had in the first innings but, quickly, the only point of interest became whether or not the West Indies could wrap up proceedings within three days. This they achieved when Giddins successfully bagged his pair by missing a straight delivery from Adams whose innings of concentration and resolve had proved to be the difference between the two teams.

Any hope that England might have entertained of beating the West Indies for the first time in more than thirty years seemed nothing more than a pipe dream, although Courtney Walsh and Curtly Ambrose apart, the visitors' bowling attack lacked the depth, hostility and experience of their recent predecessors.

West Indies v. New Zealand 'A'
21, 22, 23 and 24 June 2000 at Chelmsford
West Indies 232 (WW Hinds 61, MG Croy 4ct/1st) and 381 for 7 dec. (AFG Griffith 130, WW Hinds 74, CH Gayle 65, RR Sarwan 53)

FIRST TEST ENGLAND V. WEST INDIES
15, 16 and 17 June 2000 at Edgbaston

ENGLAND

	First innings		Second innings	
MA Atherton	c Jacobs, b Walsh	20	b King	19
MR Ramprakash	c Hinds, b Walsh	18	lbw b Walsh	0
N Hussain (capt)	c Jacobs, b Rose	15	c Jacobs, b Walsh	8
GA Hick	c Campbell, b Walsh	0	c Jacons, b Walsh	0
+AJ Stewart	b Ambrose	6	b Rose	8
NV Knight	c Lara, b King	26	c Hinds, b Adams	34
A Flintoff	c Lara, b Walsh	16	b King	12
RDB Croft	c Jacobs, b Walsh	18	c Hinds, b King	1
AR Caddick	not out	21	c Hinds, b Rose	4
D Gough	run out (Jacobs)	23	not out	23
ESH Giddins	c Jacobs, b King	0	b Adams	0
	lb6, w1, nb9	16	lb7, w1, nb8	16
		179		**125**

	First innings				Second innings			
	O	M	R	W	O	M	R	W
Ambrose	20.5	10	32	1	14	8	16	–
Walsh	21	9	36	5	19	10	22	3
King	14.1	2	60	2	9	4	28	3
Rose	13	3	45	1	10	1	43	2
Gayle					3	0	4	–
Adams	3	1	5	2				

Fall of Wickets
1–26, 2–44, 3–45, 4–57, 5–82, 6–112, 7–112, 8–134, 9–173
1–0, 2–14, 3–14, 4–24, 5–60, 6–78, 7–83, 8–94, 9–117

WEST INDIES

	First Innings	
SL Campbell	b Gough	59
CH Gayle	lbw b Gough	0
WW Hinds	c Hussain, b Caddick	12
BC Lara	c Stewart, b Gough	50
S Chanderpaul	c Stewart, b Flintoff	73
JC Adams (capt)	c Flintoff, b Gough	98
+RD Jacobs	c Stewart, b Caddick	5
CEL Ambrose	lbw b Croft	22
FA Rose	lbw b Gough	48
RD King	st Stewart, b Croft $	1
CA Walsh	not out	3
	b6, lb14, nb6	26
		397

	First innings			
	O	M	R	W
Gough	36.5	7	109	5
Caddick	30	6	94	2
Giddins	18	4	73	–
Croft	29	9	53	2
Flintoff	23	10	48	1

$ TV decision

Fall of Wickets
1–5, 2–24, 3–123, 4–136, 5–231, 6–237, 7–292, 8–354, 9–385

Umpires: DR Shepherd & S Venkataraghavan
Toss: West Indies
Test Debuts: nil

West Indies won by an innings and 93 runs

New Zealand 'A' 193 and 206 for 6 (MH Richardson 74)
Match drawn

New Zealand 'A', for some reason denied a chance to meet England 'A' on English soil despite having hosted them Down Under six months previously, grabbed the offer of a four-day match against the West Indians at Chelmsford. The game provided the Kiwis with a focal point to their otherwise haphazard tour schedule and they fought hard to emerge with a creditable draw. The West Indians, despite Wavell Hinds' classy 61, slid from 181 for 3 to 232 all out on day one, but the New Zealand youngsters could only manage 193 in reply. In their second innings the West Indian batsmen fared better, Adrian Griffith reaching 130 and Hinds, again, Chris Gayle and Ramnaresh Sarwan all going past fifty. An overnight declaration on 381 for 7 set New Zealand 'A' an impossible target, but they did not fold and opener Mark Richardson led the way to 206 for 6 with a gritty 74.

Hampshire v. West Indies
25 June 2000 at Southampton (50-over match)
Hampshire 189 (AD Mascarenhas 52, *RA Smith 30)
West Indies 190 for 6 dec. (CH Gayle 47, WW Hinds 36)
West Indies won by 4 wickets

The West Indians made hard work of beating Hampshire by four wickets at Southampton, despite a fine spell of 1 for 27 in ten overs from Shane Warne. Earlier Curtly Ambrose, with figures of 9.1–6–11–2, and Courtney Walsh (3 for 36) had done much to restrict Hampshire to 189, with only Dimitri Mascarenhas getting on top of the West Indian bowlers with 52. Chris Gayle then made 47, Wavell Hinds 36 and Jimmy Adams 32, but the West Indians still needed five to win when the final over began. Ridley Jacobs, however, settled things with a pulled four.

Second Test
29, 30 June and 1 July 2000 at Lord's

The series exploded into life as a result of one of the most extraordinary and gripping Tests in the history of the game. It was absolutely unique in that part of all four innings took place on the second day which, apart from yielding 21 wickets, also produced another first: England's opening batsmen were cheered from the field after accepting an offer for bad light! Lord's had truly neither seen nor heard anything quite like it before in its previous ninety-nine Tests.

Nasser Hussain was forced to watch the remarkable events unfold from the England balcony. He suffered a broken thumb while fielding for Essex and Alec Stewart was temporarily restored to the captaincy. Stewart's first task was to insert the West Indians on a pitch that, without being particularly threatening, offered something throughout the match to unsettle two inconsistent batting line-ups.

There were few signs of what was to come as the West Indies accepted Stewart's challenge and rattled up 50 without loss in the first hour of play. It required the absurd run-out of Adrian Griffith – who attempted a suicidal second run to Caddick's arm at long leg in the first over after lunch – for England to secure a breakthrough. Even then, their joy was only temporary as Campbell and Hinds took the score along to 162. Dominic Cork, restored to the ranks after a spell in the wilderness, tempted Campbell to pull straight down Hoggard's throat for 82 and the wickets began to tumble. After Lara flung his bat at a wide one to fall to Gough once again, Hinds appeared most unfortunate to be given out caught at short leg, apparently off the glove but more likely off the forearm, for a very good 59. From 185 for 4, the West Indies slid to 267 for 9 at the close as Gough and Cork harried their way through the middle and lower order.

A grey second morning greeted Courtney Walsh, the number 11, who promptly missed the first delivery of the day from Caddick and the players trooped from the field once again. The capacity crowd – most of which had not yet settled in their seats – can have had no idea of what lay ahead.

In no time, England were 9 for 3. The hapless Ramprakash was the first to go, caught by Lara at slip off Ambrose, and Lara did the same for Walsh when Atherton was lured into following one that held its own. Vaughan was bowled by a ball that clipped his pad for 4 and, although Hick promised an authoritative innings by punishing the erratic Rose, he was bowled by Ambrose for 25. Stewart made 28 and White 27 to go out on 35 for the sixth wicket but from 50 for 5, England were bundled out for 134, giving the West Indies a potentially match-winning lead of 133.

The West Indies team of fifteen years ago would certainly have steamrollered on at this stage, pushing the match well out of reach of an England team that was used to accepting that kind of treatment from them. But times have changed and this West Indies team has little confidence in its batting and none whatsoever in its change bowling. England, too, are nothing like the resigned force that used to roll over

Wavell Hinds evades a short ball from Dominic Cork on the second day of the second Test.

Curtly Ambrose produced a beauty to rattle Michael Vaughan's stumps in the first innings.

in these situations. Unbelievably, the West Indies were dismissed in less than 27 overs for a truly feeble 54. The spectators cheered England, just as a Wimbledon crowd would urge on Tim Henman to win a singles final. It was not the impartial, sporting reception that the England players resent and that we have grown accustomed to at Lord's, but this was a special day indeed.

It was when the West Indies were 24 for 5 that the realisation dawned that they really could be skittled. Gough and Caddick had shared the wickets, including Lara, who was caught by Cork in the gully. Soon it was 41 for 9, still short of the humbling 45 that England were shot out for at Port-of-Spain. A couple of blows from King saved that ignominy, but when Cork trapped him leg before for 7 to finish with 3 for 13, England needed 188 to win and level the series.

When, early on the third morning, Ramprakash played Walsh into his stumps and England were 3 for 1, the pessimists who have seen English collapses all over the world would not have offered them a price. However, there is more determination in these ranks and this was exemplified, typically, by Atherton and, encouragingly, by Vaughan. Between them, they carried the score to 93, almost halfway to victory, before Walsh returned to find the edge of Vaughan's bat. The young Yorkshireman had scored 41 in 160 minutes and looked every inch a Test batsman. Hick edged Walsh to slip for 15 and Atherton was trapped in front for 45, but it was Stewart's wicket, which left England foundering on 140 for 5, that really gave the West Indies hope.

England seemed on course for a dramatic nosedive as, first, White for no runs and then Knight for 2 were dispatched. It was now 149 for 7 – still 39 from victory – and Walsh, in particular, was rampant. However, Cork has always promised much with the bat and he relishes a situation in which he can wind up the opposition. This he did with great effect by scampering singles and clubbing the occasional four. Caddick was lost for 7, but Gough battled away for 42 minutes, scoring only 4 himself, as Cork finally hit the winning boundary through the covers and gestured aggressively to a section of the crowd.

As the England batsmen dashed for the pavilion armed with souvenir stumps, Walsh led his colleagues, slowly and deliberately, to the West Indian supporters at the Nursery End. With a wave and a smile, he was saying goodbye. Ambrose joined him. Neither of these great fast bowlers will ever play at Lord's again, and while they would love to have bowed out with a victory, they had both played their parts in one of the most memorable Tests there has even been.

West Indies v. New Zealand 'A'
4 July 2000 at Bristol (Floodlit)
Match abandoned without a ball bowled

Curtly Ambrose appeals to the gods as Mike Atherton looks on, following his run of good luck during the first over.

SECOND TEST – ENGLAND v. WEST INDIES
29, 30 June and 1 July 2000 at Lord's

WEST INDIES

	First innings		Second innings	
SL Campbell	c Hoggard, b Cork	82	c Gough, b Caddick	4
AFG Griffith	run out $ (Caddick/Stewart)	27	c Stewart, b Gough	1
WW Hinds	c Stewart, b Cork	59	c Ramprakash, b Caddick	0
BC Lara	c Stewart, b Gough	6	c Cork, b Caddick	5
S Chanderpaul	b Gough	22	c Ramprakashm b Gough	9
JC Adams (capt)	lbw b Gough	1	lbw b Cork	3
+RD Jacobs	c Stewart, b Cork	10	c Atherton, b Caddick	12
CEL Ambrose	c Ramprakash, b Cork	5	c Ramprakash, b Caddick	0
FA Rose	lbw b Gough	29	c & b Cork	1
RD King	not out	12	lbw b Cork	7
CA Walsh	lbw b Caddick	1	not out	3
	b1, lb8, w2, nb2	13	lb8, w1	9
		267		54

	First innings				Second innings			
	O	M	R	W	O	M	R	W
Gough	21	6	72	4	8	3	17	2
Caddick	20.3	3	58	1	13	8	16	5
Hoggard	13	3	49	-				
Cork	24	8	39	4	5.4	2	13	3
White	8	1	30	-				
Vaughan	3	1	10	-				

$ TV decision

Fall of Wickets
1–80, 2–162, 3–175, 4–185, 5–186, 6–207, 7–216, 8–253, 9–258
1–6, 2–6, 3–10, 4–24, 5–24, 6–39, 7–39, 8–39, 9–41

ENGLAND

	First innings		Second innings	
MA Atherton	c Lara, b Walsh	1	lbw b Walsh	45
MR Ramprakash	c Lara, b Ambrose	0	b Walsh	2
MP Vaughan	b Ambrose	4	c Jacobs, b Walsh	41
GA Hick	b Ambrose	25	c Lara, b Walsh	15
+AJ Stewart (capt)	c Jacobs, b Walsh	28	lbw b Walsh	18
NV Knight	c Campbell, b King	6	c Jacobs, b Rose	2
C White	run out $ (Adams)	27	c Jacobs, b Walsh	0
DG Cork	c Jacobs, b Walsh	4	not out	33
AR Caddick	c Campbell, b Walsh	6	lbw b Ambrose	7
D Gough	c Lara, b Ambrose	13	not out	4
MJ Hoggard	not out	12		
	lb5, nb3	8	b3, lb8, w1, nb12	24
		134	(for 8 wickets)	191

	First innings				Second innings			
	O	M	R	W	O	M	R	W
Ambrose	14.2	6	30	4	22	11	22	1
Walsh	17	6	43	4	23.5	5	74	6
Rose	7	2	32	-	16	3	67	1
King	10	3	24	1	8	2	17	-

$ TV decision

Fall of Wickets
1–1, 2–1, 3–9, 4–37, 5–50, 6–85, 7–100, 8–100, 9–118
1–3, 2–95, 3–119, 4–120, 5–140, 6–140, 7–149, 8–160

Umpires: JH Hampshire & S Venkataraghavan
Toss: England
Test Debut: MJ Hoggard

England won by two wickets

NATWEST TROPHY TRIANGULAR SERIES
By Jonathan Agnew

Contrary to what some believed, this was not the first triangular one-day tournament to be staged in England. Because the three participants – England, the West Indies and Zimbabwe – were all involved in Test series here, it did at least give the feel of being more like an Australian 'World Series', upon which this competition was based.

Changes were promised and indeed delivered, but whether the introduction of meaningless blasts of pop music at every opportunity proved to be popular is more than simply a moot point. If the reaction to the listeners to Test Match Special was anything to go by, it was a sure way of driving people away from the game, rather than attracting them to it. The lunchtime 'entertainment' was just about as banal as anything that has been offered anywhere in the world and, much more seriously, the future of floodlit international cricket in this country is now highly questionable because the quality of the lights – particularly at Edgbaston – simply was not good enough.

Nine round-robin matches would eliminate one team and since there was nothing to choose between all three, the early games promised a great deal. Unfortunately, there were hardly any close finishes to get excited about. The fact is that this is what spectators wish to experience – not thumping music – and the string of low scores in the tournament (only seven innings out of a possible 19 reached 200) again points the finger of suspicion at the white ball. Once more, I urge the authorities to rethink this policy for the good of the one-day game in this country.

In Hussain's continued absence, Stewart led England, and Marcus Trescothick, the fresh-faced opener from Somerset, was called in to the squad. The 24-year-old was the success of the tournament, despite the script being torn up in England's very first match, which Zimbabwe won by five wickets. Trescothick scored 79 in his first innings for England from only 102 balls, but apart from Hick, who made an even fifty, the rest of the batting fell away to set Zimbabwe 208 to win. Thanks to Alistair Campbell's 80 and 61 from Andy Flower, the visitors eased home with ten balls to spare. When the third game between England and the West Indies was washed out, and Zimbabwe beat the West Indies in the fourth, the table looked remarkable: Zimbabwe had a clean six points, England and the West Indies one apiece courtesy of the Lord's downpour.

England fought back at Old Trafford where Andy Flintoff, smarting from some savage and personal criticism in the press, blasted 42 from 45 deliveries to beat Zimbabwe's paltry total of 114 with 30 overs to spare. Flintoff's excess weight had been a talking point all week but he bit back in the best possible way even if he did miss a golden opportunity to answer his critics face to face by boycotting the post-match press conference. England's thumping victory was followed by an even more emphatic win over the West Indies – who still had to win a game. Stewart and Trescothick knocked off the 170-run target with 15 overs to spare at Chester-le-Street. Trescothick made 87 and Stewart 74, which he bettered under lights at Edgbaston three days later. Zimbabwe were again derailed following another victory over the hapless West Indies, but this was not entirely their fault. The lights at Birmingham were totally inadequate and the team batting second had little chance of winning in the gloom. Stewart's 101 led the way and White's three wickets sealed Zimbabwe's fate, but at least Stewart had the good

Brian Lara hits a six at Bristol during the first floodlit international to be staged in England.

Andy Flower runs Mark Ealham down to third man as Zimbabwe beat England at the Oval.

grace, and the sense, to join the all-round condemnation of the floodlights.

The West Indies were already out of contention for the final when they met England for the last time at Trent Bridge and their total of 195 did not seem to be enough. However, although Stewart made another unbeaten century, the visitors secured a win in the best finish of the competition. Stewart was stranded at the non-striker's end in the final over as first Gough and then Mullally were defeated by the alleged off-spin of Chris Gayle. The match did not matter one jot, but it did provide the West Indies – who had been without Walsh and Ambrose throughout – with a consolation victory.

So to Lord's for the final between England and Zimbabwe, which proved to be another tame game. Zimbabwe were determined to make up for their disastrous showing in the first Test of the summer but were undone by Gough, whose 3 for 20 pegged them back to only 169 for 7. The match needed some early England wickets to add some excitement – and when Trescothick and Flintoff went for 0 and 1, an upset was at least a possibility. But Stewart rose again to score 97 – his last four innings now reading 74 not out, 101, 100 not out, 97 to steer England to the first NatWest Trophy with six wickets and five overs to spare.

Match One – West Indies v. Zimbabwe
6 July 2000 at Bristol (floodlit)
West Indies 232 for 7 (50 overs)(BC Lara 60, WW Hinds 51)
Zimbabwe 233 for 4 (45 overs)(NC Johnson (95*))
Zimbabwe (2 pts) won by six wickets
Man of the Match: NC Johnson

Match Two – England v. Zimbabwe
8 July 2000 at Kennington Oval
England 207 (50 overs)(ME Trescothick 79, GA Hick 50, GJ Whittall 4ct)
Zimbabwe 210 for 5 (48.2 overs)(ADR Campbell 80, A Flower 61)
Zimbabwe (2 pts) won by five wickets
Man of the Match: ADR Campbell

Match Three – England v. West Indies
9 July 2000 at Lord's
England 158 for 8 (43.5 overs)
West Indies did not bat
Match abandoned – 1 pt each

Match Four – West Indies v. Zimbabwe
11 July 2000 at Canterbury
Zimbabwe 256 for 4 (50 overs)(GJ Whittall 83,
ADR Campbell 77*, NC Johnson 51)
West Indies 186 for 8 (50 overs)(NAM McLean 50*)
Zimbabwe (2 pts) won by 70 runs
Man of the Match: GJ Whittall

Match Five – England v. Zimbabwe
13 July 2000 at Old Trafford (floodlit)
Zimbabwe 114 (38.4 overs)
England 115 for 2 (20.3 overs)
England (2 pts) won by eight wickets
Man of the Match: A Flintoff

Match Six – England v. West Indies
15 July 2000 at Chester-le-Street
West Indies 169 for 8 (50 overs)(BC Lara 54)
England 171 for 0 (35.2 overs)(ME Trescothick 87*,
AJ Stewart 74*)
England (2 pts) won by ten wickets
Man of the Match: ME Trescothick

Match Seven – West Indies v. Zimbabwe
16 July 2000 at Chester-le-Street
West Indies 287 for 5 (50 overs) (SL Campbell 105,
BC Lara 87
Zimbabwe 290 for 4 (49.1 overs)(MW Goodwin 112*,
GW Flower 96*)
Zimbabwe (2 pts) won by six wickets
Man of the Match: MW Goodwin

Match Eight – England v. Zimbabwe
18 July 2000 at Edgbaston (floodlit)
England 262 for 8 (50 overs)(AJ Stewart 101)
Zimbabwe 210 for 9 (50 overs)(ADR Campbell 60,
NC Johnson 52)
England (2 pts) won by 52 runs
Man of the Match: AJ Stewart

Match Nine – England v. West Indies
20 July 2000 at Trent Bridge
West Indies 195 for 9 (50 overs)
England 192 (49.5 overs)(AJ Stewart 100*)
West Indies (2 pts) won by 3 runs
Man of the Match: CH Gayle

Alistair Campbell is run out by Alec Stewart at Old Trafford.

Stuart Carlisle tried to rally the lower order in the final, but Zimbabwe's total of 169 for 7 was never likely to trouble England.

FINAL – ENGLAND v. ZIMBABWE
22 July 2000 at Lord's

ZIMBABWE

Batting			Bowling	O	M	R	W
NC Johnson	b Caddick	21	Caddick	10	2	23	1
GJ Whittall	c Hick, b Gough		Gough	10	2	20	3
MW Goodwin	b Gough	3	Mullally	10	1	32	1
ADR Campbell	c White, b Mullally	1	White	10	2	46	2
+A Flower (capt)	c Stewart, b White	48	Ealham	10	0	41	–
GW Flower	not out	53					
SV Carlisle	c Caddick, b White	14					
HH Streak	lbw b Gough	18	**Fall of Wickets**				
BC Strang	not out	0	1–4, 2–12, 3–21, 4–31, 5–120				
DP Viljoen			6–143, 7–169				
M Nkala							
	b1, lb6, w2, nb2	11					
	50 overs (for 7 wickets)	**169**					

ENGLAND

Batting			Bowling	O	M	R	W
ME Trescothick	c Campbell, b Streak	1	Streak	10	3	30	3
+AJ Stewart	c A Flower, b Streak	97	Nkala	5	0	30	–
A Flintoff	b Streak	0	Strang	10	3	26	–
GA Hick	c & b Viljoen	41	Johnson	6	0	22	–
GP Thorpe	not out	10	Viljoen	10	0	35	1
N Hussain (capt)	not out	9	Whittall	4	0	20	–
C White			Campbell	0.2	0	2	–
MA Ealham							
AR Caddick			**Fall of Wickets**				
D Gough			1–9, 2–9, 3–143, 4–149				
AD Mullally							
	lb5, w5, nb2	12					
	45.2 overs (for 4 wickets)	**170**					

Umpires: DR Shepherd & P Willey
Toss: England
Man of the Match: AJ Stewart
Player of the Series: AJ Stewart

England won by six wickets

A happy man: Nasser Hussain shows off the first-ever NatWest triangular series trophy.

THIRD TEST
29, 30 June and 1 July 2000 at Old Trafford

After the excitement and celebrations of Lord's, it was a great shame that five weeks passed between the second and third Tests in order to accommodate the NatWest one-day series. To be fair to the authorities (for once!) they were not to know in advance, when the fixtures were planned, exactly what this wonderful Test series held in store. However, the ECB has acknowledged its mistake and, next summer, the triangular limited-overs tournament will split the Test series' involving Pakistan and Australia rather than interrupt either of them.

That said, it did not take long for the excitement and anticipation to resurrect itself at Old Trafford – and this despite a deluge before the game and several rain breaks during it. Inadequate covers did little to help the situation – Old Trafford really must address this problem – and too much time was lost to the elements to force a result on the final day, which found the West Indies firmly in the driving seat.

Ramnaresh Sarwan is struck a painful blow by Darrren Gough at Old Trafford. It was later revealed that the youngster had cracked a rib.

Mark Trescothick and Graeme Thorpe celebrate following Lara's dismissal to a brilliant catch by Thorpe, restored in England's slip cordon.

The miserable weather did not dampen the various celebrations at the ground to mark this, the hundredth Test match played by both Mike Atherton and Alec Stewart. Before the start, they were each presented with a glass trinket or two, and also with a unique ECB cap (they are no longer traditional England caps, I am afraid) which bears the figure 100 beneath the three lions and coronet. Neither player appeared to wear his cap during the match!

Jimmy Adams won the toss and, despite the damp conditions, elected to bat. The belief was that the pitch would take spin later on, but while the West Indies resisted the temptation to play Ramnarine, the leg-spinner, England recalled Robert Croft who, arguably, was playing for his international future. History will record that the Welshman did not make the most of his opportunity. He was one of four changes as the experiment of opening with Ramprakash was, not surprisingly, abandoned.

As at Lord's, England's seamers, led by Gough and Caddick, bowled superbly. Both openers were dismissed with 12 on the board and when Gough again dismissed Lara, beautifully taken by Thorpe at slip, the West Indies were 49 for 4. Adams, no doubt fearing what his critics might say about his decision to bat, played with customary patience while he and young Ramnaresh Sarwan put on 69 for the fifth wicket. Sarwan received a horrible blow in the ribs that clearly discomforted him and he finally became the first of three late victims for Cork who, with Caddick, restricted the West Indies to a hardly imposing 157 all out.

Atherton, on his home ground, emerged to a rousing cheer, but was soon returning to the pavilion courtesy of Walsh for 1. Hussain's miserable summer continued when he edged to Adams and when Thorpe was deceived first ball by as good a slow delivery as there can ever have been, England were 17 for 3.

'The Gaffer' would never let such a moment pass, however, and bristling with fierce patriotic pride on the Queen Mother's hundredth birthday, Stewart stroked a superb century from only 136 balls. Rarely has he played better for his country, and while he narrowly stopped short of dedicating his innings to the royal birthday girl, his timing, nonetheless, was impeccable. Thanks to Stewart – and Trescothick, whose first innings in Test cricket realised 66 – England swept past the West Indies and on to a lead of 146.

Any hopes of a West Indian collapse à la Lord's were laid to rest by their openers, Campbell and Griffith, who fought back to put on 96 for the first wicket. White split them and Gough then nipped out Hinds for 25 with the West Indies still a single run in arrears. This brought in Lara, who had been troubled during much of the one-day series with a hamstring injury and had hardly raised his bat in anger. It says everything about the man that what followed was batting of pure brilliance – he even managed to put Stewart in the shade. It was clear that Lara meant business when he decided against eating lunch and, instead, headed for the nets. After the interval, when England took the second new ball, he simply went up another gear. It seemed the only way that England could get him out would be to run him out, and so it proved. A sensational piece of fielding from Hussain, who threw down the non-striker's stumps with a direct throw from mid-wicket, did the trick – Lara's hunger for the strike proving to be his downfall as he set off for an impossible single despite Adams' vain attempt to send him back.

Helped by 42 from Jacobs and his own 53, Adams declared on the final morning with a lead of 292. The forecast suggested that the weather would have

THIRD TEST – ENGLAND v. WEST INDIES
29, 30 June and 1 July 2000 at Lord's

WEST INDIES

	First innings			Second innings	
SL Campbell	c Thorpe, b Gough	2		c Cork, b White	55
AFG Griffith	lbw b Caddick	2		lbw b Croft	54
WW Hinds	c Stewart, b Cork	26		c Stewart, b Gough	25
BC Lara	c Thorpe, b Gough	13		run out (Hussain)	112
JC Adams (capt)	c Thorpe, b White	24		lbw b Cork	53
RR Sarwan	lbw b Cork	36		lbw b Caddick	19
†RD Jacobs	b Caddick	5		not out	42
FA Rose	lbw b Croft	16		lbw b White	10
CEL Ambrose	c Hussain, b Caddick	3		not out	36
RD King	not out	3			
CA Walsh	lbw b Cork	7			
	b1, lb12, nb7	20		b14, lb4, w2, nb12	32
		157		(for 7 wickets dec.)	
438					

	First innings				Second innings			
	O	M	R	W	O	M	R	W
Gough	21	3	58	2	27	5	96	1
Caddick	24	10	45	3	23	4	64	1
Cork	17.1	8	23	4	28	9	64	1
White	9	1	18	1	27	5	67	2
Croft					47	8	124	1
Trescothick					1	0	2	–
Vaughan					1		3	–

Fall of Wickets
1–3, 2–12, 3–49, 4–49, 5–118, 6–126, 7–130, 8–135, 9–148
1–96, 2–145, 3–164, 4–302, 5–335, 6–373, 7–384

ENGLAND

	First innings			Second innings	
MA Atherton	c Campbell, b Walsh	1		c Jacobs, b Walsh	28
ME Trescothick	b Walsh	66		not out	38
N Hussain (capt)	c Adams, b Walsh	10		not out	6
GP Thorpe	lbw b Walsh	0			
†AJ Stewart	c Jacobs, b Ambrose	105			
MP Vaughan	c Lara, b Ambrose	29			
C White	b King	6			
DG Cork	c Jacobs, b Ambrose	16			
RDB Croft	not out	27			
AR Caddick	lbw b Ambrose	3			
D Gough	c Ambrose, b King	12			
	b10, lb6, nb12	28		b4, lb1, nb3	8
		303		(for 18 wicket)	80

	First innings				Second innings			
	O	M	R	W	O	M	R	W
Ambrose	27	7	70	4	12	2	31	–
Walsh	27	14	50	4	14	6	19	1
Rose	20	3	83	–				
King	12.2	3	52	2	2.4	0	15	–
Adams	11	4	32	–	5	1	10	–

Fall of Wickets
1–1, 2–17, 3–17, 4–196, 5–198, 6–210, 7–251, 8–275, 9–283, 1–61

Umpires: P Willey & DB Cowie
Toss: West Indies
Test Debut: ME Trescothick

Match drawn

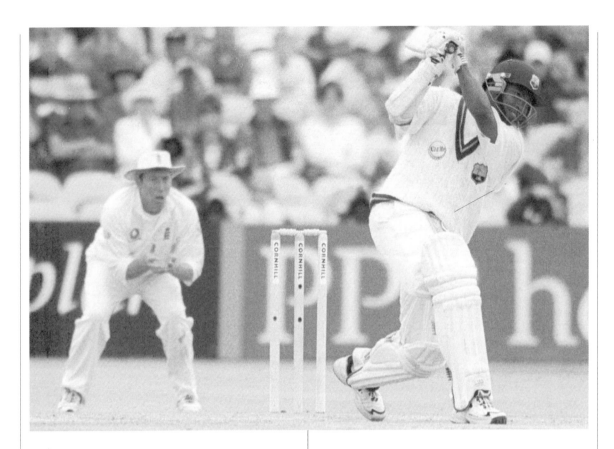

Brian Lara was back to his very best at Old Trafford: there are few finer sights in the modern game.

the final say, and so it proved, but not before Walsh continued his domination of Atherton, dismissing him for the fifth time in the series. Trescothick's unbeaten 38, meanwhile, meant that his Test average, after one game, stood at a more than healthy 104.

At the end of another entertaining match, English attention began to focus on the forthcoming tours to Pakistan and Sri Lanka: how, in those arid conditions, and against Saqlain and Muralitharan, will England possibly compete? Here, on a pitch that took decent spin and with an array of left-handers to bowl at, England's premier spinner, Croft, took 1 for 124 from 47 unthreatening overs. It might be a very long winter indeed.

Yorkshire v. West Indies
24 and 25 July at Leeds
Yorkshire 126 (63 overs)(VJ Craven 53) and 94 (36.5 overs)(*D Byas 30)
West Indies 209 (87.1 overs)(MV Nagamootoo 40, +W Phillip 38) and 12 for 0 (5.2 overs)(CH Gayle 7)
West Indies won by 10 wickets

A poor, seamer-friendly pitch left an understrength Yorkshire side with little hope against a West Indies team welcoming back Courtney Walsh following his injury lay-off. And so it proved, Yorkshire being tumbled out for 126 on the opening day with Walsh taking 5 for 19 from 16 overs and looking virtually unplayable in his new-ball spell. Only a gutsy fifth-wicket stand of 70 between Vic Craven (53) and David Byas (41 not out) prevented a total rout. That came in the second innings, with Yorkshire dismissed for just 94 with Nixon McLean (5 for 49) the chief executioner this time. The West Indians, in between, totalled 209 with Mahendra Nagamootoo top-scoring with 40 and Ramnaresh Sarwan rallying them initially from 38 for 4 with a delightful 32. Lesroy Weekes, a burly 29-year-old former Leeward Islands fast bowler now plying his trade in the Huddersfield League, took 6 for 56 and troubled the best batsmen to show what an asset he will be to Yorkshire when he becomes England-qualified by residence in January. Yorkshire's second-innings

Mike Atherton and Alec Stewart proudly wearing their 100th Test caps, presented to them at Old Trafford on the Queen Mother's hundredth birthday.

demise left the West Indians needing just 12 runs to complete victory inside two days in this scheduled four-day fixture.

Derbyshire v. West Indies
9, 10 and 11 August at Derby
West Indies 390 for 9 dec. (106 overs)(CH Gayle 128, WW Hinds 104) and 221 for 8 dec. (52 overs) (CH Gayle 57, *SL Campbell 52)
Derbyshire 242 for 5 dec. (79.4 overs)(*RJ Bailey 112) and 145 (54.2 overs)(*RJ Bailey 65 not out, SD Stubbings 23)
West Indies won by 224 runs

The West Indians defeated a weakened Derbyshire by 224 runs at Derby in a match featuring brilliant first-innings hundreds by Jamaican left-handers Wavell Hinds and Chris Gayle – and memorable batting too by Derbyshire's stand-in captain Rob Bailey. Hinds (104) and Gayle (128) added 202 for the third wicket with a stream of fine strokes against a below-strength Derbyshire attack that was further diluted when Trevor Smith broke down with ankle trouble. But Lian Wharton, wheeling away with his slow left-arm spinners, was eventually rewarded by a burst of 5 for 6 in 47 balls as the West Indians, for whom Ramnaresh Sarwan also stroked 52, slipped from 282 for 2 to 390 for 9.

Wharton ended up with 5 for 96, and also took 4 for 83 before the West Indians declared their second innings on 221 for 8. But that declaration was, in itself, rather a small-minded response to Bailey's imaginative decision to close Derbyshire's own first-innings response on 242 for 5 in an effort to open up the match as a contest. But Derbyshire, set a daunting 370 in 62 overs on the final afternoon, collapsed to 145 all out with Reon King and Corey Collymore picking up three wickets apiece. Bailey, however, could hold his head high. He finished the match 65 not out, hitting a six and ten fours, in addition to his first-innings unbeaten 112. In becoming the first Derbyshire batsman to score a hundred against the West Indians since 1906 (or, in 15 matches) he gained some measure of revenge, too, for being given out controversially to a disputed leg-side catch against the West Indies in Barbados in 1990 in what turned out to be his fourth and final Test appearance for England.

Scotland v. West Indies
13 August 2000 at Uddingston, Glasgow
West Indies 204 for 7 (43 overs)(JC Adams 48, CH Gayle 45)
Scotland 183 for 7 (43 overs)(DR Lockhart 48)
West Indies won by 21 runs

Alec Stewart is superbly caught by Sherwin Campbell in the slips off Walsh in what was to become the shortest Test match in fifty-four years.

Brian Lara pads up and is out lbw, offering no stroke, for the second time in the match.

FOURTH TEST
17 and 18 August 2000 at Headingley

We thought we had seen more than our fair share of excitement at Lord's, but following the stalemate in the third Test at Old Trafford, this fluctuating series burst into life once again in the most spectacular fashion.

Headingley has become renowned over the years for producing pitches that favour seam bowlers. Nasser Hussain, frowning, said before the game that the strip looked 'ugly', which is an unusual description of 22 yards of rolled soil, but we knew what he meant. There were cracks on the first morning and, in several bare patches devoid of grass, the tell-tale signs of uneven bounce. But while there was some strong criticism for the way in which the pitch eventually played, there can be no excuses for the astonishing demise of the West Indians. In being dismissed for only 61 in their second innings, Jimmy Adams' men became the first team for fifty-six years to lose a Test match within two days – since pitches were covered, in other words. It was the first time England had won inside that time span since defeating the South Africans at the Oval in 1912.

Although there were some raised West Indian eyebrows in the Test Match Special commentary box, Adams had little choice but to bat when he called correctly. The pitch was not going to improve: he had to make first use of it at its best. At 50 for 1, the West Indies had made a decent start but the introduction of Craig White at the Football Stand End changed all that. Bowling at a sharp pace and

FOURTH TEST – ENGLAND v. WEST INDIES
17 and 18 August 2000 at Headingley

WEST INDIES

	First innings		Second innings	
SL Campbell	c Trescothick, b Gough	8	c Hick, b Gough	12
AFG Griffith	c Stewart, b Gough	22	b Gough	0
WW Hinds	c Stewart, b White	16	lbw b Gough	0
BC Lara	lbw b White	4	lbw b Gough	2
JC Adams (capt)	b White	2	b Cork	19
RR Sarwan	not out	59	not out	17
RD Jacobs	c Caddick, b Cork	35	lbw b Caddick	1
NAM McLean	c Stewart, b White	7	b Caddick	0
CEL Ambrose	b Cork	1	b Caddick	0
RD King	lbw b Gough	6	b Caddick	0
CA Walsh	c Caddick, b White	1	b Caddick	3
	lb2, nb9	11	lb3, nb4	7
		172		**61**

	First Innings				Second Innings			
	O	M	R	W	O	M	R	W
Gough	17	2	59	3	10	3	30	4
Caddick	10	3	35	0	11.2	5	14	5
White	14.4	4	57	5				
Cork	7	0	19	2	5	0	14	1

Fall of Wickets
1-11, 2-50, 3-54, 4-56, 5-60, 6-128, 7-143, 8-148, 9-168
1-3, 2-3, 3-11, 4-21, 5-49, 6-52, 7-52, 8-52, 9-53

ENGLAND

	First innings	
MA Atherton	c Lara, b Ambrose	6
ME Trescothick	c Lara, b Ambrose	1
N Hussain (capt)	lbw b Walsh	22
GP Thorpe	lbw b Walsh	46
+AJ Stewart	c Campbell, b Walsh	5
MP Vaughan	c Jacobs, b Ambrose	76
AR Caddick	c Jacobs, b Ambrose	6
GA Hick	st Jacobs, b Adams	59
C White	c Jacobs, b McLean	0
DG Cork	not out	11
D Gough	c Griffith, b Walsh	2
	b4, lb13, w3, nb18	38
		272

	First Innings			
	O	M	R	W
Ambrose	18	3	42	4
Walsh	24.5	9	51	4
King	11	2	48	0
McLean	22	5	93	1
Adams	6	1	21	1

Fall of Wickets
1-7, 2-10, 3-80, 4-93, 5-96, 6-124, 7-222, 8-223, 9-269

Umpires: G Sharp & DB Cowie
Toss: West Indies
Test Debut: nil

England won by an innings and 39 runs

Wavell Hinds drops the easiest of catches offered by Dominic Cork during the fourth Test.

from round the wicket at the array of left-handers, he quickly reduced the West Indies to 60 for 5. Lara shouldered arms and fell leg before for 4 – unbelievably, he was to repeat that form of dismissal in the second innings – Adams edged into his stumps, and the situation could have been even worse had umpire Doug Cowie not given Sarwan the benefit of the doubt when he appeared to have gloved Gough to Stewart.

The youngster remained to play the only innings of authority in the brief afternoon session that saw the visitors bundled out within 49 overs. He and Jacobs added 68 for the sixth wicket before Cork returned to remove Jacobs, and the rest of the lower order succumbed meekly. White finished with 5 for 57 – his first five-wicket haul for England and although his line to the left-handers was mighty impressive, there was a worrying lack of discipline within the visitors' ranks.

Even so, when England were quickly 10 for 2, and Ambrose was celebrating his 400th wicket (Atherton, neatly caught by Lara at first slip), 172 seemed a half-decent total after all. Hussain emerged in the middle of his worst trot as a Test player and was hit, nastily, on the bottom hand. As was feared, though, the West Indian support bowling, which had let the team down throughout the summer, could not maintain the pressure. Hussain and Thorpe added a priceless 70 and although Walsh returned to nip them out leg before and have Stewart taken at slip before the close of the first day, England were only 67 runs adrift.

Fifteen wickets had already fallen, but the Headingley faithful had no idea what lay in store when they gathered and filled the Western Terrace by 11 o'clock the following morning. How they cheered when one of their own – the fast-improving Michael Vaughan – teamed up with Graeme Hick to take England into the lead. Hick, following the nightwatchman, Caddick, found himself at number eight, but seldom has an English pair run so positively between the wickets. A regulation single to third man was turned into a scrambled two and the West Indian fielding began to buckle. There were overthrows and misfields as Hick – so shy and introverted when in England colours – took control. Even his nemesis, Ambrose, failed to dislodge him and, having passed 50, Hick's cameo was ended when he was stumped by Jacobs off a despairing

Adams. Fancy! A West Indian team calling on an occasional spinner at the world's most seamer-friendly Test venue before lunch on the second day!

Vaughan edged Ambrose to Jacobs for 76, but the mental state of the West Indies was best illustrated by the appalling miss by Hinds at square leg. It was as regulation a dolly – from Cork's top-edged pull – as you could wish to see, requiring no more than a couple of steps backwards. Somehow, the fielder managed not to get a hand to the ball and, amid howls of laughter from all parts of the ground, the realisation began to dawn that the West Indies were there for the taking.

Their second innings could not have begun any worse. Griffith drove casually at Gough and was spectacularly bowled. Hinds was trapped by the perfect in-swinging yorker next ball, and had the brilliant hat-trick delivery been bowled at anyone else but Lara, Gough would have entered the record books for the second time in his Test career. The Western Terrace was already baying, but when Gough trapped Lara leg before, offering no stroke for the second time in the match, it produced the most deafening ovation of the summer. The wheels were off and, at 21 for 4, a West Indian defeat seemed certain, but even now, optimists still believed that the game would go into a third day.

Andy Caddick swept those hopes away after tea with the most devastating over bowled by an Englishman since Chris Old in 1978. His four wickets – off the first, third, fourth and final legitimate delivery – settled the issue in the most extraordinary way. Fittingly, it was Caddick who blew Walsh away to finish with the most economical five-wicket haul since Botham's 5 for 11 against Australia – and beating Ed Giddins' effort against Zimbabwe earlier this summer.

As the startled crowd celebrated with England's jubilant players, the recriminations began in the West Indian camp. Their batting had been thoroughly spineless and their spirit appeared to be broken. From Edgbaston to this in two months: England's dream of winning a series for the first time in 13 attempts was soon to become a reality.

Ever the showman! Dominic Cork celebrates the dismissal of a disappointed Wavell Hinds.

Somerset v. West Indies
23, 24, 25 and 26 August at Taunton
Somerset 488 (135.5 overs)(KA Parsons 193 not out, M Burns 55) and 240 for 6 dec. (69 overs)(M Burns 78, ARK Pierson 48)
West Indies 290 (90.2 overs)(MV Nagamootoo 100, +W Phillip 67) and 169 (55 overs)(AFG Griffith 77)
Somerset won by 269 runs

Somerset won themselves £11,000 from sponsors Vodafone for defeating an uninspired West Indian team by the crushing margin of 269 runs at Taunton. The win was built on a career-best 193 not out from Keith Parsons, which helped Somerset to post a challenging first-innings total of 488. But the West Indian batting, in reply, was criminally poor and only a maiden first-class hundred by Mahendra Nagamootoo, and a career-best 67 not out by reserve wicketkeeper Wayne Phillip, hauled the tourists from 118 for 6 to 290 all out. Joe Tucker, a 20-year-old fast bowler, marked his first-class debut by having Brian Lara caught at long leg for 18 from his second delivery – a great moment for Tucker, even though it was not the best ball he has ever bowled. Somerset opted not to follow on, building on their lead instead largely through the efforts of Michael Burns (78 not out) and his 98-run stand with Ian Blackwell. Given seven overs to bat before the close of the third day, the West Indians slipped to 5 for 1; then, on the final day, they disintegrated to 169 all out with only opener Adrian Griffith (77) showing the necessary application.

Dominic Cork congratulates Craig White on taking five wickets for the second time in consecutive Tests.

FIFTH TEST
31 August, 1, 2, 3 and 4 September 2000 at the Oval

Thirty-one years of history and, in England's case, misery was swept away on a tide of emotion as a last-day crowd of 19,000 people celebrated a famous victory. The ECB's policy of allowing children into the ground for free was a triumph – as many as 5,000 fans were turned away – and even the vacated sponsors' boxes were opened up to accommodate the unexpected invasion. It was an extraordinary final day, during which Courtney Walsh and Curtly Ambrose were applauded to the crease and even given a guard of honour by England's fielders. Whether or not that would have happened if the West Indies were on the verge of victory themselves is a moot point, but the gesture illustrated what a sporting series this had been, with barely an angry word exchanged between any of the players involved.

The West Indies had to win the match, and England merely to draw it, making Jimmy Adams' decision to put England in to bat a curious one. At a

No doubt about that! Nixon McClean is clean bowled by Craig White.

Farewell to two cricketing giants: Curtly Ambrose and Courtney Walsh, reflective in defeat, say goodbye to the Oval.

stroke he handed England the advantage, and on a pitch that has – for some seasons now – become too dusty and dry during the course of every match. It was a gamble; an opportunity for a final hurrah for Walsh and Ambrose but by the time Atherton and Trescothick were parted after an opening stand of 159, England were already in firm control. The balance shifted a little when Hussain's desperate run of poor form continued – he was caught at the wicket by the second ball of the leg-spinner, Nagamootoo – Atherton had his bails trimmed by McLean for 83 and Stewart slipped in the crease to fall leg before to McLean, also for a duck. As the middle order risked being swept away, Thorpe and Hick added 40 for the sixth wicket on a rain-affected second day, but England lost their last five wickets for 60 in a collapse that typified the inconsistent

batting of both teams throughout the series.

Campbell and Griffith resumed on the third morning, but were quickly parted when Campbell was bowled off the inside edge by Cork for 20. That was 32 for 1; 22 balls later, the West Indies were 51 for 6 and out of the match. The killer blow was struck by White. Operating from round the wicket, as usual, he bowled Lara, first ball, behind his legs and hit an exposed leg stump. The crowd roared on as Hinds fell leg before to Cork for 2, Sarwan was brilliantly caught in the gully for 5 by the diving Trescothick and, finally, Adams was taken at slip by Hick.

Brief resistance came in the form of Jacobs, Nagamootoo and McLean but the first-ball swipe of Ambrose spoke volumes about the team's hopelessness and, particularly, of his personal frustrations. Judging by that shot, it would be a

FIFTH TEST – ENGLAND v. WEST INDIES
31 August, 1, 2, 3 and 4 September 2000 at The Oval

ENGLAND

	First innings		Second Innings	
MA Atherton	b McLean	83	c Jacobs, b Walsh	108
ME Trescothick	c Campbell, b Nagamootoo	78	c Lara, b Ambrose	7
N Hussain (capt)	c Jacobs, b Nagamootoo	0	lbw b Mclean	0
GP Thorpe	lbw b Walsh	40	c Griffith, b Walsh	10
+AJ Stewart	lbw b McLean	0	c Campbell, b Nagamootoo	25
MP Vaughan	lbw b Ambrose	10	lbw b Walsh	9
GA Hick	lbw b Ambrose	17	c Campbell, b Walsh	0
C White	not out	11	run out (Griffith) $	18
DG Cork	lbw b McLean	0	lbw b McLean	26
AR Caddick	c Hinds, b Walsh	4	c Jacobs, b McLean	
D Gough	b Walsh	8	not out	1
	b4, lb15, w1, nb10	30	b1, lb7, nb5	13
		281		**217**

	First innings				Second Innings			
	O	M	R	W	O	M	R	W
Ambrose	31	8	31	2	22	8	36	1
Walsh	35.4	16	68	3	38	17	73	4
McLean	29	6	80	3	22	5	60	3
Nagamootoo	24	7	63	2	1	7	29	1
Adams	4	0	13	–	7	3	11	–

$ TV decision

Fall of Wickets
1-159, 2-159, 3-184, 4-184, 5-214, 6-254, 7-254, 8-255, 9-264
1-21, 2-29, 3-56, 4-121, 5-139, 6-139, 7-163, 8-207, 9-207

WEST INDIES

	First Innings		Second Innings	
SL Campbell	b Cork	20	c Hick, b Gough	28
AFG Griffith	c Hick, b White	6	c Stewart, b Caddick	20
WW Hinds	lbw b Cork	2 (4)	lbw b Caddick	7
BC Lara	b White	0 (3)	lbw b Gough	47
JC Adams (capt)	c Hick, b Cork	5	c White, b Caddick	15
RR Sarwan	c Trescothick, b White	5	run out (Thorpe) $	27
+RD Jacobs	not out	26	c Hick, b Caddick	1
MV Nagamootoo	c Trescothick, b Gough	18	lbw b Gough	13
CEL Ambrose	lbw b Caddick	0 (10)	c Atherton, b Cork	28
NAM McLean	b White	29 (9)	not out	23
CA Walsh	b White	5	lbw b Cork	0
	lb3, nb6	9	lb3, w1, nb2	6
		125		**215**

	First innings				Second Innings			
	O	M	R	W	O	M	R	W
Gough	13	3	25	1	20	3	64	3
Caddick	18	7	42	1	21	7	54	4
White	11.5	1	32	5	11	2	32	–
Cork	8	3	23	3	15	1	50	2
Vaughan					3	1	12	–

$ TV decision

Fall of Wickets
1-32, 2-32, 3-32, 4-34, 5-39, 6-51, 7-74, 8-75, 9-119
1-50, 2-50, 3-58, 4-94, 5-140, 6-142, 7-150, 8-167, 9-215

Umpires: DR Shepherd & DJ Harper
Toss: West Indies
Test Debuts: MV Nagamootoo
Players of the Series: D Gough (England) & CA Walsh (West Indies)

England won by 158 runs

TEST MATCH AVERAGES
West Indies v. England

ENGLAND

Batting	M	Inns	NO	HS	Runs	AV	100	50
ME Trescothick	3	5	1	78	190	47.50	–	2
MA Atherton	5	9	0	108	311	34.55	1	1
MP Vaughan	4	6	0	76	169	28.16	–	1
+AJ Stewart	5	8	0	105	195	24.37	1	–
GP Thorpe	3	4	0	46	96	24.00	–	–
DG Cork	4	6	2	33*	90	22.50	–	–
D Gough	5	8	3	23*	86	17.20	–	–
NV Knight	2	4	0	34	68	17.00	–	–
GA Hick	4	7	0	59	116	16.57	–	1
C White	4	6	1	27	62	12.40	–	–
N Hussain	4	7	1	22	61	10.16	–	–
AR Caddick	5	8	1	21*	51	7.28	–	–
MR Ramprakash	2	4	0	18	20	5.00	–	–

Also batted: RDB Croft (2 Tests) 18, 1, 27*; A Flintoff (1 Test) 16, 12; ESH Giddins (1 Test) 0, 0; MJ Hoggard (1 Test) 12*

Bowling	Overs	Mds	Runs	Wkts	Av	Best	10m	5/inn
DG Cork	109.5	31	245	20	12.25	4-23	–	–
C White	81.3	14	236	13	18.15	5-32	–	2
AR Caddick	170.5	53	422	22	19.18	5-14	–	2
D Gough	173.5	32	530	25	21.20	5-109	–	1

Also bowled: RDB Croft 76-17-177-3; A Flintoff 23-10-48-1; ESH Giddins 18-4-73-0; MJ Hoggard 13-3-49-0; ME Trescothick 1-0-2-0; MP Vaughan 8-3-25-0

Fielding
14 – AJ Stewart (13ct,1st); 5 – GA Hick; 4 – MR Ramprakash; 3 – DG Cork, GP Thorpe, ME Trescothick; 2 – MA Atherton, AR Caddick, N Hussain; 1 – A Flintoff, D Gough, MJ Hoggard, C White

WEST INDIES

Batting	M	Inns	NO	HS	Runs	Av	100	50
RR Sarwan	3	6	2	59*	163	40.75	–	1
SL Campbell	5	9	0	82	270	30.00	–	3
BC Lara	5	9	0	112	239	26.55	1	1
JC Adams	5	9	0	98	220	24.44	–	2
FA Rose	3	5	0	48	104	20.80	–	–
NAM McLean	2	4	1	29	59	19.66	–	–
+RD Jacobs	5	9	2	42*	137	19.57	–	–
AFG Griffith	4	8	0	54	132	16.50	–	1
WW Hinds	5	9	0	59	147	16.33	–	1
CEL Ambrose	5	9	1	36*	95	11.87	–	–
RD King	4	6	2	12*	29	7.25	–	–
CA Walsh	5	8	2	7	23	3.83	–	–

Also batted: S Chanderpaul (2 Tests) 73, 22, 9; CH Gayle (1 Test) 0; MV Nagamootoo (1 Test) 18, 13

Bowling	Overs	Mds	Runs	Wkts	Av	Best	10m	5/inn
CA Walsh	220.2	92	436	34	12.82	6-74	1	2
CEL Ambrose	181.1	63	317	17	18.64	4-30	–	–
RD King	67.1	16	244	8	30.50	3-28	–	–
NAM McLean	73	16	233	7	33.28	3-60	–	–

Also bowled: JC Adams 36-10-92-3; CH Gayle 3-0-4-0; MV Nagamootoo 43-14-92-3; FA Rose 66-12-270-4

Fielding
21 – RD Jacobs (20ct,1st); 10 – BC Lara; 8 – SL Campbell; 5 – WW Hinds; 2 – AFG Griffith; 1 – JC Adams, CEL Ambrose

mistake to persuade Curtly out of retirement: he appeared to have had enough.

England's first innings was 156 and, at 56 for 3 and Hussain out for his second duck of the match, the West Indies were at least competing. But if ever the stage were set for an Atherton special, then this was it. He drove Walsh to despair – five times in one over Atherton groped at thin air, and a number of very close leg-before appeals were rejected by umpire Shepherd. As wickets fell regularly at the other end, Atherton stood firm and came within a whisker of carrying his bat throughout a Test innings for the second time. With the last man, Darren Gough, standing at the other end and the game undoubtedly England's, it was a desperate shame that Atherton touched a catch to Jacobs off the persevering Walsh to complete a marathon innings that lasted for 7 hours and 25 minutes. It is also worth noting that his 108 was his 15th Test century, but his first in London.

As the England last-wicket pair left the stage, Ambrose and Walsh linked arms to walk from a cricket field together for the very last time. It was a moving scene – something that makes sport so special – as the entire ground cheered in appreciation for all that the great fast bowlers have achieved over the years. For all the smiles, though, the West Indians knew they faced defeat.

There was the usual talk about a run-chase for the 374 to win, but this so very rarely works out. Only two teams have ever recorded more than 400 to win a Test in the final innings, and the West Indies had never achieved this particular target before. Shots were played, but wickets fell, too. Lara avoided a king pair and batted beautifully with young Sarwan, who made a promising 27, but the pressure was always on and Lara's 47 came in 36 overs.

Cork wrapped up the match by taking the last three wickets, and when he bamboozled Walsh with a slower ball, his captain, Hussain, fell to his knees for a moment: the job was done.

There were mixed feelings as the crowd sprinted across the sunlit ground for the presentations. In the Test Match Special box, the proud figure of Viv Richards looked on in dismay at quite how quickly the legacy founded by himself and Clive Lloyd before him had disintegrated. Beside him Graeme Fowler – England's bruised and battered opening batsman in 1984 – smiled proudly. It was the moment English cricket has been praying for and now that success has finally been achieved, it is the responsibility of all concerned with the future of the game to ensure that it is not a missed opportunity.

A year ago, on the very same spot, Nasser Hussain was booed by England's frustrated supporters. Now, twelve months on, it is time to celebrate the long-awaited return of the Wisden Trophy. Many of the current England team were not born the last time it was in English hands.

PPP HEALTHCARE COUNTY CHAMPIONSHIP
By Mark Baldwin
(who spent the summer monitoring the mood, as well as the many changes and developments on the county circuit)

It happens in all walks of life. Someone goes on about how good something is so often that after a while, well, you think they must be right. After all, if they are so certain, who are you to disagree?

Politicians, of course, are always trying to play this trick. For instance, we apparently need rather urgently to join a splendid new currency called the Euro, otherwise all our businesses will go bang and every financial institution will come crashing down around our ears. Come to think of it, how was it exactly that we ended up with the dreaded Dome?

Even small children get up to it. They've simply got to have the latest PlayStation, Pokemon game or Teenage Mutant Turtle 'because everyone says it's the best thing ever! Dad, pleeease!'

In cricket, we have now just had the first two-division county championship since the whole shooting match was set up back in 1864. And a lot of people already seem to be going on about how good it is – including quite a number who have hardly seen a championship ball bowled.

So, is it here to stay? Or is it just the latest craze?

To my mind, it is most important to keep an eye on what championship cricket is really trying to achieve. Keeping an eye on the ball, and not being distracted by passing fancies, is after all a crucial aspect of any long innings.

Many voices, and some of them influential ones, have been raised this summer in praise of how much more competitive championship cricket has suddenly become, and of the way the two divisions maintained interest right up to the final day of the season. Fine: on one level they are right.

The only relevant question, as far I can see, is however a very different one. Has the switch to two divisions begun to raise standards? No one has yet claimed that, to my knowledge, and after spending the whole summer covering county cricket for *The Times* I can certainly say that I am not aware that the standard of play on view is much different.

Considering how much cricket the players play, how much travelling they do, and how they are constantly jiggled about month after month by one of the craziest and most unstructured fixture lists that can ever have been inflicted on a sport, the standard seems to me to be much as it has always been: generally sound, occasionally fierce, sometimes poor and often sloppy.

Shane Warne and Glenn McGrath have gone on record since the end of their respective first seasons in county cricket to admit that the overall standard is better than they had expected. And they're Australians, don't forget, and so would gladly rubbish the Poms if they thought anything else!

What Warne and McGrath instantly recognised, however, as being the root cause of perceived low standards in English cricket, was that the vast majority of county pitches are simply not good enough. Warne joined Jack Birkenshaw, the estimable Leicestershire coach, and many other independent observers, in calling for visiting captains only to be given the choice of whether to bat or bowl first.

That may well be a worthwhile initiative, and less costly than having to employ every groundsman centrally, although the England and Wales Cricket Board have begun to acknowledge at last the grave damage to the game being done by the 'result' pitch cheats. This is seen in their setting up for last summer a new policing force of 'pitch liaison officers' under the command of Mike Denness. The former England captain was quickly dubbed the 'Pitchfinder General', and his panels duly penalised three counties – Derbyshire, Yorkshire and Hampshire.

Yet their worthy efforts were undermined by too many inconsistencies in the system, and too many other sub-standard pitches escaped to undermine yet more techniques and the self-confidence of young players.

So, let's get it clear about two divisions in championship cricket. If it's artificial excitement you're after, or an end-of-season frisson, then let the two divisions of the National League provide that fix for you. With the overdue increase of floodlit cricket, and, it is to be hoped, with more of that played at the right time of year – in late July to early September when it actually gets dark – the National League is a highly marketable product that is further enhanced by two divisions.

But, if the ECB are serious about actually raising the standard of our first-class game (and we must assume they are!), if they really want to improve (dramatically) the quality of championship pitches, and if they want to help advance the England team by expanding the central contracts system, then let's get back to a one-division championship. Graded prize money all the way down the table would also provide just as much incentive to get into the top nine – without the harmful effects of relegation.

Central contracts, the success of which was the true reason for England's uplifting Test victories this past summer, and not a two-tier championship, are naturally destructive to the concept of two divisions for the simple reason that they take the best players out of the competition.

England beat the West Indies mainly because Darren Gough and Andy Caddick stayed fit and firing for the whole summer – the first pair of England opening bowlers to do this since Trueman and Statham in 1960. Yet Gough and Caddick only made three championship appearances apiece for Yorkshire and Somerset. That caused unrest enough in those two counties, but what would have happened if either Yorkshire or Somerset had been relegated?

The incentive to produce young stars is diluted if the counties realise that they will then soon be taken away for huge chunks of the season by England and, in the medium to long term, only the very richest counties will have the resources to miss their top players and still stay in the top division. For an example of this you only have to look at how Derbyshire's fortunes plummeted once Dominic Cork won back his regular place in the Test team.

Expect the transfer system to mushroom now, too, with bigger-city clubs inevitably picking off young talent from elsewhere to offset the losses of their England players. And watch the salaries of good journeymen pros go up as counties realise that shelling out for them, or a big-name overseas player, is the most cost-effective way of getting short-term results.

But let's get back to standards. That's what we should be concentrating on – remember? How intelligent was it then, this past season, to have half our best young batsmen being denied a rare and valuable chance to mix in championship cricket with the great Glenn McGrath, while the other half were denied a crack at Shane Warne!

Selection of England teams is hard enough, too, without muddying the waters with two divisions. For instance, David Graveney and his panel were this past summer denied a valuable look at Marcus Trescothick, say, batting against McGrath or Donald, or the likes of Jason Brown or Paul Franks bowling against Dravid, Lehmann or even Flintoff, Crawley and Habib.

To sum up, think hard about the hidden costs of two divisions. Read the small print, and don't believe everything the politicians of cricket try to sell you. In the meantime, digest the following words from John Bracewell, the Gloucestershire coach. As a New Zealander, he's got no axes to grind, and – being Bracewell – he will just tell it to you straight.

'The condition of the pitches is a massively worrying trend across the country, but if you are going to have divisional cricket you are going to have that problem,' said Bracewell, instantly exposing the humbug that lies behind the current official 'policy' of raising standards by virtue of the split (and literally divisive) championship. 'Also, if you are going to produce England cricketers out of four-day cricket, then you are not going to do it on some of the pitches we play on.'

The answer to the need for better standards is, I believe, to revert immediately to a true championship, giving every professional English cricketer the chance, every year, of winning the most coveted prize. Take away the fear of relegation, and the inevitable accompanying short-termism, and demand in return far better pitches for our first-class cricket.

Moreover, do what New Zealand are now doing as they begin to develop deeper resources of international-class young talent – expand the 'A' team programme to include a home schedule as well as just an annual, 'one-off', overseas tour, and use that as a natural bridge between the county system and the unforgiving Test arena. And, on top of all that, redraw the domestic fixture list so that it is coherent to players and public alike. To prove that all this is plausible, we've even drawn up our very own 'possible' fixture list for the year 2001 – turn to page 200 and see!

English cricket is still producing good young players, and thankfully Trescothick and Michael Vaughan came along this year to show it is not necessarily just a two-division championship system that will create it.

Yet, as proved in Trescothick's case, when it was only because of injuries to Nasser Hussain and Nick Knight that he was given his international chance at all, those good young players need opportunity above all else. Give them the right stage, give them the right pitches, and give them a logical, gimmick-free structure through which to progress.

Meanwhile Hampshire, the seventh best championship team in the country, cannot challenge for the title next year – whereas Glamorgan, who scraped in 12th, can!

I could go on...but just one final point: what kind of current crazy system is it that allows Essex, runners-up in the championship second division but in essence 11th in the pecking order, to receive £35,000 in prize money while Somerset – who finished fifth in the so-called first division 'elite' – were awarded just £4,000!

DERBYSHIRE CCC

Home Ground:
Derby
Address:
County Ground, Nottingham Road,
Derby DE21 6DA
Tel: 01332 383211
Fax: 01332 290521
Email: derby@ecb.co.uk
Directions:
By road: From the south, exit M1 at junction 25,
follow A52 into Derby. The ground is off Pentagon
Island. From the north, exit M1 at junction 28, join
A38 into Derby and then follow directional signs.
Capacity: 4,000
Other grounds used: Chesterfield
Year formed: 1870

Chief Executive: John Smedley
Cricket Manager: Colin Wells
Other posts: Commercial Manager: Keith
Stevenson; County Development Officers: John
Brown, Colin Davies; Head Groundsman: Barry
Marsh
Captain: Dominic Cork
County colours: Blue, brown and gold

HONOURS

COUNTY CHAMPIONSHIP
1936
SUNDAY LEAGUE
1990
BENSON & HEDGES CUP
1993
GILLETTE CUP/NATWEST TROPHY
1981

CGU National Cricket League
nickname:
DERBYSHIRE SCORPIONS

Website:
www.dccc.org.uk

ROUND ONE: 26–29 APRIL 2000

Rain once again grabbed the initial headlines as the first split championship in history tried to get under way. For the first time since 1966, the whole championship programme was washed out on the opening day. Perhaps Nature was having her say, too, on the whole new concept! In the end, all six matches (three from each division) ended in watery draws.

Division One
26, 27, 28 and 29 April
at Derby
Derbyshire 359 (140.3 overs)(RJ Bailey 118, MJ di Venuto 70, KM Krikken 51) and 2 for 0 dec.
Leicestershire 309 (94.5 overs)(PAJ DeFreitas 79, DI Stevens 78)
Match drawn – no play was possible on the first day
Derbyshire 10 pts, Leicestershire 9 pts

at Canterbury
Lancashire 186 (56.5 overs)(A Flintoff 77, MA Ealham 4 for 53)
Kent 29 for 1 (9 overs)
Match drawn – no play was possible on the first and fourth days
Kent 7 pts, Lancashire 4 pts

at Taunton
Surrey 185 (45 overs)(AJ Hollioake 59, PS Jones 5 for 41)
Somerset 302 for 8 (95.2 overs)(ME Trescothick 85, M Burns 81)
Match drawn – no play was possible on the first day
Somerset 10 pts, Surrey 6 pts

Rob Bailey scored 118 on his championship debut for Derbyshire, Michael di Venuto hit 70 from 89 balls, and Karl Krikken made 51, as a total of 359 brought them three batting points at Derby. Under new regulations, five batting points are available for scoring up to 400 inside 130 overs, with bowling points reduced to a maximum of three. Leicestershire slipped to 100 for 5 in reply but then, in the only time left available by more bad weather, rallied to 309 thanks to a hard-hitting 78 from Darren Stevens, which included 12 fours, and an equally robust 79 from Phillip de Freitas.

The second day at Taunton was notable for some superb fast bowling from Somerset pair Andy Caddick (3 for 71) and, perhaps more surprisingly, Steffan Jones. Surrey, struggling at 38 for 4 and briefly roused by Adam Hollioake (59) and Alistair Brown (47), were dismissed for 185 as the strong

and pacy Jones ended up with figures of 5 for 41. Only five overs were possible right at the start of the third day, Somerset slipping from 4 for 0 to 15 for 2 as Martin Bicknell took wickets with both his second and sixth deliveries, but on an academic final day the home side made sure of three batting points by recovering to 302 for 8. Ian Salisbury bowled his leg-spinners gamely in unappealing conditions, but Marcus Trescothick (85) and Michael Burns (81) held sway for much of the day.

Mark Ealham's splendid early-season form continued amid the rainstorms at Canterbury, the chunky Kent all-rounder including Saurav Ganguly (lbw first ball for nought on his championship debut, offering no stroke) among his victims in a return of 4 for 63. Lancashire were bowled out for 186 but Andy Flintoff impressed with a much tighter technique allied to the raw power which brought him thirteen fours in his 82-ball 77. There was no play at all on the fourth day, despite sunshine, following a violent overnight downpour.

Division Two
26, 27, 28 and 29 April
at Bristol
Sussex 110 for 5 (39 overs)
Gloucestershire did not bat
Match drawn – no play was possible on the first, second and fourth days
Gloucestershire 5 pts, Sussex 4 pts

at Trent Bridge
Northamptonshire 153 (54.4 overs)(DJ Millns 5 for 58, CMW Read 5 ct)
Nottinghamshire 79 for 9 (26 overs)(DE Malcolm 5 for 45, DM Cousins 4 for 31)
Match drawn – no play was possible on the first, second and fourth days
Nottinghamshire 7 pts, Northamptonshire 7 pts

at Worcester
Worcestershire 206 for 7 (53.1 overs)(GA Hick 76)
Glamorgan did not bat
Match drawn – no play was possible on the first, second and fourth days
Worcestershire 5 pts, Glamorgan 6 pts

The three division two matches were similarly decimated by the weather, with Sussex having time after an eventual start on the third day to reach only 110 for 5 before the rain came again, for the final rites. At least Mike Smith's 3 for 13 from ten overs earned Gloucestershire a bowling point.

Rob Bailey marked his championship debut for Derbyshire with a century against Leicestershire.

APRIL DIARY by Robin Martin-Jenkins

The usual story: beautiful blue skies during early March turn to monsoons and freezing Arctic winds just as the first ball of the season is about to be bowled. This year there is more interest in the competition for Sussex because it means we play against Shane Warne and I'm pleased to report that I faced him and survived! I was rather nervous and decided to test out a theory I had heard that if ever you felt intimidated by someone, just think of that person in a pair of oversized Y-fronts! I'd like to point out that I'm a happily married man and these thought processes are purely for professional reasons!

The cricketers at Hove were surprised to hear the accusations being thrown at Hansie Cronje, but were absolutely stunned to see that he had admitted to receiving money from bookmakers in return for certain inside information. After the recent debacle over a similar situation involving Shane Warne and Mark Waugh, it takes a very foolish person to even dream of talking with bookmakers, let alone accepting money from them.

It was mentioned in 1997, when Sussex were going through a torrid time and heading quite distinctly for the wooden spoon, that perhaps we were throwing games on purpose and receiving large bonuses into the bargain from bookies. I can assure everyone that that was not the case. We didn't need to try and throw games in those days!

Anyone who was at Bristol and Leicester, or even anyone watching Ceefax or reading the reports in the papers, will have gathered that Sussex managed to produce two of their less capable performances with the bat in the championship. Both games should have been won and we should now be sitting proudly at the top of division one with eight points securely in the bag. It is clear, however, that the inconsistencies that have plagued our team in the past few years remain. No longer are they the virus that eats its way through the season, but a few germs are still there. It was the bubonic plague. It's now just an irritating cold. It may be true that, just as there is no foreseeable cure for the common cold, ironing out batting flaws in English batsmen is no easy task. It must be possible, however, to be able to build up the immunity, thus restricting batting collapses to maybe only twice a season. If that is the case, then we've already used up our quota of batting disasters: against Surrey we were bowled out for less than 100, having been 30 without loss; against Hampshire we were 29 for 5 at one stage. Now if you include the collapses of the past week it adds up to a pretty impressive portfolio for the season so far.

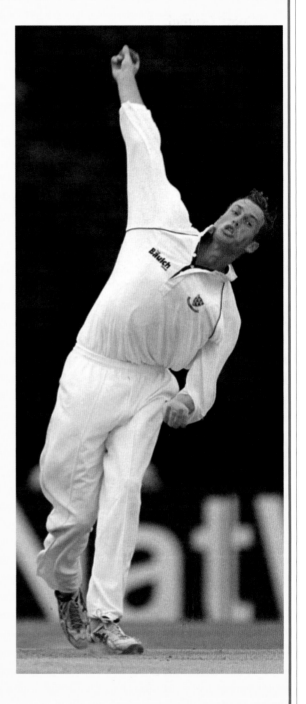

DURHAM CCC

Home Ground:
Chester-le-Street
Address:
County Ground, Riverside,
Chester-le-Street,
Co. Durham DH3 3QR
Tel: 0191 387 1717
Fax: 0191 387 1616
Email: marketing@durham-ccc.org.uk
Directions:
By rail: Chester-le-Street (approx. 5 minutes by taxi or a
10-minute walk).
By road: Easily accessible from junction 63 of the A1(M).
Nearby car parking is available on match days.
Disabled access:
Viewing points for spectators in wheelchairs; Members'
Lounge has induction loop system for members who are
hard of hearing; guide dogs allowed into ground.
Capacity: 10,000
Other grounds used:
Darlington CC (Feethams); Hartlepool CC;
Stockton CC 01642 672835.
Year formed: 1882

Chairman: DW Midgley
Director of Cricket: Geoff Cook
First Team Coach: Norman Gifford MBE
Captain: Nick Speak
Vice-captain: Jonathan Lewis
County colours:
Yellow, blue, burgundy

HONOURS

NONE YET

CGU National Cricket League
nickname:
DURHAM DYNAMOS

Website:
www.durham-ccc.org.uk

At Trent Bridge both sides grabbed maximum bowling points on an extraordinary third day. After the match had finally begun Northants were dismissed for 153, with David Millns taking 5 for 58 for his new county. Then, however, it was the turn of Devon Malcolm (5 for 45) and new signing from Essex, Darren Cousins (4 for 31), to take advantage of perfect seam-bowling conditions and reduce Notts to a sorry 79 for 9. A result might have been possible on the final day, after the clatter of those 19 wickets on day three, but the weather then intervened once again.

Only 53.1 overs were possible in the match at New Road, again on the scheduled third day. In that time Worcestershire managed to claim one batting point, clambering to 206 for 7 mainly as a result of Graeme Hick's 76 off 80 balls.

ROUND TWO: 2–6 MAY 2000

Division One
2, 3 and 4 May
at Chester-le-Street
Durham 234 (75.4 overs)(N Peng 98, PD Collingwood 66, BC Hollioake 4 for 41) and 186 (SM Katich 65, MP Bicknell 5 for 85)
Surrey 104 (55.5 overs) and 85
Durham won by 231 runs
Durham 16 pts, Surrey 3 pts

3, 4 and 5 May
at Southampton
Hampshire 232 (91.5 overs)(DA Kenway 93*, AR Caddick 5 for 62) and 126 (GW White 78* (carried bat), AR Caddick 7 for 64)
Somerset 319 (111.1 overs)(J Cox 153, PD Bowler 56, RJ Turner 56) and 40 for 1
Somerset won by nine wickets
Somerset 18 pts, Hampshire 4 pts

at Headingley
Derbyshire 239 (75 overs)(MJ di Venuto 70) and 190 (RJ Bailey 54*)
Yorkshire 508 for 5 dec. (152.3 overs)(MP Vaughan 155 ret hurt, MJ Wood 100*, DS Lehmann 95, PJ Aldred 4 for 97)
Yorkshire won by an innings and 79 runs
Yorkshire 20 pts, Derbyshire 2 pts

3, 4, 5 and 6 May
at Old Trafford
Leicestershire 265 (104.5 overs)(VJ Wells 56, PJ Martin

7 for 67) and 198 (CP Schofield 4 for 82)
Lancashire 488 (143.1 overs)(NH Fairbrother 138, A Flintoff 119, CP Schofield 66, J Ormond 4 for 122)
Lancashire won by an innings and 25 runs
Lancashire 20 pts, Leicestershire 4 pts

Champions Surrey were stunned at Chester-le-Street by a Durham side inspired by Nicky Peng, a 17-year-old who had decided to abandon his studies at the Royal Grammar School, Newcastle, to pursue a full-time cricket career. Peng, not 18 until September, captured the nation's attention by scoring 98 on his first-class debut – and left Surrey captain Adam Hollioake to exclaim: 'He is an incredible talent, the finest young player I have ever seen.'

Peng, who comes from a moneyed background and has been driven to matches in the past in his father's Bentley, was last man out as he tried to cap his fairytale debut by reaching three figures. But he had batted beautifully to guide Durham to 234 all out, displaying all the promise shown when he hit a double hundred for England Under-17s in 1999. Paul Collingwood scored 66, with Ben Hollioake (4 for 41) and Martin Bicknell (3 for 52) Surrey's best bowlers. Peng's joy became Durham's joy, too, on the second day when Surrey collapsed from their overnight 48 for 2 to 104 all out – Simon Brown and Neil Killeen both picking up three wickets. It was the lowest total made against Durham since Yorkshire were tumbled out for 108 in the north-east county's debut season in 1992.

Peng then made 23 from number six to help Simon Katich steady the Durham second innings after it slipped to 14 for 4, and Katich went on to 65 as he and Martin Speight (36) rallied Durham to 186. Surrey, initially reaching 41 without loss as they set off towards a distant target, then folded in astonishing fashion to 85 all out, Brown and Killeen again doing most of the damage. Fittingly, it was Peng who led triumphant Durham off at the end of the match. Surrey had beaten Durham in all 17 of their previous meetings, in all competitions, and this was their first defeat in the championship since Leicestershire beat them in the final match of the 1998 season.

An interesting opening day at Southampton included a third-ball duck on his championship debut for Shane Warne, an eye-catching 93 not out by 21-year-old Derek Kenway, and some high-class bowling on a good pitch by Andy Caddick (5 for 62). The result was a Hampshire first-innings total of 232 and, although they were 14 for 2 at the close, Somerset took charge of the game on the second day with Jamie Cox hitting a superb 153 and both Peter Bowler and Rob Turner completing half-centuries in support. Warne managed just 1 for 83 from 33 overs as Somerset reached 319. The third day belonged completely, and compellingly, to Caddick – the England fast bowler picking up 7 for 64 with a performance of rhythmical and sustained hostility as Hampshire plunged to 126 all out. Warne made another duck, his first 'pair' in more than 150 first-class matches, and only Giles White offered lengthy resistance. White, in fact, became the first Hampshire opener since Paul Terry in 1994 to carry his bat and was 78 not out at the end. Somerset soon knocked off the few runs they required for a thumping victory, and the only clouds on their horizon were injuries picked up during the match by Matthew Bulbeck and Steffan Jones.

Yorkshire thrashed Derbyshire at Headingley by an innings and 79 runs, with only an injury to Michael Vaughan tarnishing their display. Vaughan also had the disappointment of knowing he would miss England's short Test series against Zimbabwe after having a finger broken by a ball from Matt Cassar. Vaughan, though, had scored 155 at the time which, with Matthew Wood's 100 not out and Darren Lehmann's 95, enabled Yorkshire to pile up 508 for 5 declared in reply to Derbyshire's first-day 239. Then, when Derbyshire batted again, only Rob Bailey with an unbeaten 54 held up Darren Gough and Craig White and the rest of Yorkshire's eager attack.

A similar pattern emerged across the Pennines at Old Trafford where Leicestershire found themselves overwhelmed by Lancashire and beaten by an innings and 25 runs. Bowled out for 265, with Peter Martin picking up a magnificent 7 for 67, Leicestershire then found it impossible to contain Andy Flintoff and Neil Fairbrother. Flintoff struck 18 boundaries in a controlled 119 and Fairbrother batted more than five hours for 138 – the 41st first-class hundred of his career. Just to round things off, the chirpy Chris Schofield then hit 66 to push Lancashire up to 488. Glen Chapple took three early wickets in the Leicestershire second innings, which was finished off by a spell of 3 for 27 in 10.1 overs from Schofield on the fourth morning.

Division Two
3, 4, 5 and 6 May
at Chelmsford
Essex 2274 (79.2 overs)(SG Law 120, AP Grayson 58, DS Lucas 4 for 61) and 263 (SG Law 55)
Nottinghamshire 340 (119.1 overs)(P Johnson 100, DJ Bicknell 59, PJ Franks 53, CM Tolley 51, RC Irani 4 for

57) and 150 for 6
Match drawn
Essex 9 pts, Nottinghamshire 10 pts

at Lord's
Middlesex 427 for 8 dec. (126.3 overs)(JL Langer 120, MR Ramprakash 93, OA Shah 76, DM Cousins 5 for 123) and 243 for 3 dec. (AJ Strauss 111*)
Northamptonshire 280 (113.2 overs)(AS Rollins 100, AL Penberthy 59, ARC Fraser 4 for 49) and 237 for 3 (AS Rollins 96, ML Hayden 93)
Match drawn
Middlesex 12 pts, Northamptonshire 8 pts

at Edgbaston
Warwickshire 551 for 6 dec. (150 overs)(NV Knight 233, TL Penney 85, MJ Powell 73)
Glamorgan 400 (130 overs)(SP James 166, MTG Elliott 117, AF Giles 5 for 89) and (following on) 194 for 6 (AD Shaw 56*, MP Maynard 52)
Match drawn
Warwickshire 12 pts, Glamorgan 10 pts

Three hard-fought draws made up the action from the second division, although Nottinghamshire and Warwickshire came within sniffing distance of victory at Chelmsford and Edgbaston respectively.

A sparkling 120 at little more than a run a ball by Stuart Law, his 22nd first-class hundred for Essex, lit up a shortened first day at Chelmsford, although 21-year-old left-arm seamer David Lucas took 4 for 3 in 13 balls as Essex slipped to 216 for 6. On the second morning last man Ricky Anderson hit a jaunty 31 to push Essex up to 274, but by the close Notts were almost on level terms as Paul Johnson struck 100 from 153 balls, with fifteen fours, and Darren Bicknell offered a solid 59. Nottinghamshire, in fact, pushed on from their overnight 340 thanks to Chris Tolley (51) and Paul Franks (53) and, despite Law's 55, Essex were in some trouble at 184 for 7 going into the final day. A last-wicket stand of 62 between Ashley Cowan and the underrated Anderson, however, frustrated Notts and Essex's eventual 263 meant a win target of 198 from 51 overs. When John Morris was going well it looked possible, but then the former England batsman wafted at Mark Ilott and was caught behind for 44 and Nottinghamshire could only finish on 150 for 6.

A monumental 233 by Nick Knight, which included 27 fours and spanned almost nine hours, put Warwickshire into a commanding position at 551 for 6 declared against Glamorgan. Knight, clearly

ESSEX CCC

Home Ground:
The County Ground, Chelmsford
Address:
County Cricket Ground, New Writtle Street,
Chelmsford, Essex CM2 0PD
Tel: 01245 252420
Fax: 01245 491607
Prospects of play: 01245 287921
Email: administration.essex@ecb.co.uk
Directions:
By rail: Chelmsford Station (8 minutes' walk away).
By road: M25 then A12 to Chelmsford.
Exit Chelmsford and follow AA signs
to 'Essex Cricket Club'.
Capacity: 6,000
Other grounds used: Castle Park, Colchester; Valentine's
Park, Ilford; Southchurch Park, Southend-on-Sea.
Year formed: 1876

Chairman: DL Acfield
Chief Executive: DE East
Cricket Development Manager: AW Lilley
Other posts: 2nd XI Coach/Captain: John Childs;
Manager/Coach Cricket School: Norman Bambridge;
Head Groundsman: SG Kerrison
Captain: Nasser Hussain
Vice-captain: Ronnie Irani
County colours: Blue, gold and red

HONOURS

COUNTY CHAMPIONSHIP
1979, 1983, 1984, 1986,
1991, 1992
SUNDAY LEAGUE
1981, 1984, 1985
REFUGE ASSURANCE CUP
1989
BENSON & HEDGES CUP
1979, 1998
GILLETTE CUP/NATWEST TROPHY
1985, 1997

CGU National Cricket League nickname:
ESSEX EAGLES

Website:
www.essexcricket.org.uk

intent on winning back his England Test place, was joined principally by Trevor Penney (85), but Glamorgan fought back with the bat to score 400 themselves on a fine pitch. Steve James top-scored with 166 and Matthew Elliott (117) also featured in an opening stand of 203. Ashley Giles, however, pegged away to take 5 for 89 from 42 overs and Glamorgan were forced to follow on. At 95 for 5 it looked as if Warwickshire would win, but Matthew Maynard (52) and Adrian Shaw (56 not out) stood firm in an 81-run stand for the sixth wicket.

Runs were also in abundance at Lord's with Justin Langer (120) and Mark Ramprakash (93) kicking things off with an opening partnership of 196 in 45 overs for Middlesex. The home side finally declared at 427 for 8, Owais Shah making 76, and it took a determined 100 from Adrian Rollins, supported by 59 from Tony Penberthy, to keep Angus Fraser and Phil Tufnell at bay. With a good first-innings lead, Middlesex then reached 243 for 3 declared with Andrew Strauss scoring a maiden first-class hundred. Rollins and Matthew Hayden, however, dampened any Middlesex hopes of victory with a first-wicket stand of 152. Hayden hit a typically robust 93 and Rollins was eventually dismissed for 96 as Northants reached 237 for 3, having spent 10 hours and 40 minutes at the crease during the match.

ROUND THREE: 11–15 MAY 2000

Division One
11, 12 and 13 May
at Chester-le-Street
Lancashire 263 (80 overs)(SC Ganguly 73, CP Schofield 50, SJ Harmison 4 for 74) and 134 (SJE Brown 7 for 51)
Durham 164 (68.4 overs)(G Chapple 6 for 42) and 92 (MP Smethurst 7 for 50)
Lancashire won by 141 runs
Lancashire 17 pts, Durham 3 pts

at Leicester
Somerset 262 (101.5 overs)(ME Trescothick 105, ID Blackwell 58) and 246 (A Kumble 5 for 61)
Leicestershire 387 (139.5 overs)(Aftab Habib 172*, JM Dakin 135, GD Rose 5 for 74, JO Grove 5 for 90) and 124 for 4
Leicestershire won by six wickets
Leicestershire 19, Somerset 4 pts

at the Oval
Surrey 417 (142.5 overs)(MP Bicknell 73, AD Brown 60, AJ Hollioake 51, IDK Salisbury 50) and 17 for 0 dec.

Kent 115 for 2 dec. (45 overs) and 255 for 8 (MA Ealham 83, R Dravid 71, PA Nixon 50*)
Match drawn – no play was possible on the first day
Surrey 8 pts, Kent 6 pts

12, 13 and 14 May
at Headingley
Hampshire 101 (52.3 overs)(D Gough 4 for 23) and 198 (W S Kendall 78*)
Yorkshire 399 (120.3 overs)(GM Hamilton 125, DS Lehmann 85)
Yorkshire won by an innings and 100 runs
Yorkshire 19 pts, Hampshire 3 pts

After an inauspicious winter in South Africa, Yorkshire's Gavin Hamilton grabbed some early headlines by scoring a century against Hampshire.

MAY DIARY by Robin Martin-Jenkins

Who says that English cricket isn't innovative? We started our championship match against Worcestershire at 12 noon, having had an hour's extra kip due to the day/night game the previous evening. There were gasps of horror going around the Sussex dressing room when we looked at the fixture list and realised that we would have to finish one game and start another in the space of 12 hours. The bowlers among us were particularly dreading the prospect of possibly bowling second in the evening, finishing at 11:00 p.m., and then us losing the toss and having to bowl again at 11:00 a.m.! Luckily the kind-hearted souls at the ECB agreed that we could start the four-day game an hour later. The time would be made up by adding half an hour to the last session of each of the first two days. This sort of flexibility will have to be seen more often if our fixture list continues to be so jam-packed.

We were fortunate enough, this month, to be able to play Zimbabwe at the lovely new ground at Hastings, Horntye Park. Many tears were shed when first-class cricket came to an end 11 years ago when the old ground at Hastings was sold and turned into a supermarket. The new ground is magnificent. A large, lush oval is surrounded by banks of grass and a pavilion, complete with indoor school, and it puts a lot of county headquarters to shame (not least Hove!). Zimbabwe appear a competent outfit with some extremely talented batsmen. Neil Johnson and Murray Goodwin looked the best players, although Andy Flower didn't get to bat, so easily did they chase our large total. Their bowling, however, looked weak, even as a county attack.

England made them look like a very ordinary side. Usually Lord's inspires opposition sides to produce their best performances but it seemed the atmosphere intimidated Zimbabwe. It reminded me of my pair against Middlesex at Lord's this time last year. Having to walk back through the long room past some very disapproving looks from elderly MCC members was daunting. To my surprise an elderly voice piped up, just loud enough for everyone in the room to hear; 'take up journalism' was his advice. My head bowed even lower at this stage and I could still hear the rumbles of laughter as I climbed the many stairs back to the dressing room. I didn't have the nerve to tell him that I already did that as well!

Yorkshire, Lancashire and Leicestershire maintained their status as early-season pace-setters with emphatic victories at Headingley, Chester-le-Street and Leicester respectively. In the other first division game, champions Surrey were involved in a rain-ravaged draw against Kent at the Oval.

Despite the loss of Andy Caddick, rested due to a blistered foot ahead of England's first Test against Zimbabwe, Somerset were potentially awkward opponents for Leicestershire at Grace Road. And that looked especially true when the home side slumped to 34 for 4 in reply to Somerset's first-innings 262, in which Marcus Trescothick had scored 105 and had been rewarded for his fine anchor role by a stand of 100 for the eighth wicket with Ian Blackwell (58). But then Aftab Habib, who went on to remain 172 not out, put on a magnificent 275 for the fifth wicket with Jon Dakin. With his innings of 135, powerful all-rounder Dakin underlined his emergence as one of the most-improved county cricketers of the season. Graham Rose and Jamie Grove claimed an equal share of Leicestershire's ten wickets, but a total of 387 gave the Midlanders a handy lead. Anil Kumble then got to work on Somerset's second innings, taking 5 for 61 as only Trescothick (43) and Peter Bowler (48) resisted for any length of time. Phil deFreitas demonstrated his worth with 3 for 48 from 27 overs, but it still took some imagination from acting captain Ben Smith to finish off Somerset when time seemed to be running short on the final afternoon. Darren Maddy, called up to purvey his occasional medium pace, grabbed two wickets in four overs as the visitors were dismissed in the 114th over of their innings for 246. Smith and Maddy then teamed up with the bat, scoring an unbeaten 45 and 39 respectively, as Leicestershire swept to their modest target for the loss of only four wickets.

Yorkshire matched Leicestershire's 19-point haul by crushing Hampshire, who were tumbled out for 101 on the first day. Robin Smith top-scored with 15 as Darren Gough, bowling with real venom, took 4 for 23 and was well supported by Craig White (3 for 12). Yorkshire then replied with 399, Gavin Hamilton hitting 125 from number eight and helping Darren Lehmann (85) add 111 for the seventh wicket. That stand, which began at 160 for 6, spelt the end for Hampshire and Shane Warne, the Australian leg-spinner, found life difficult against the two Yorkshire left-handers. Warne, leg before to off-spinner James Middlebrook for nought in the first-innings, then sliced Hamilton to gully in Hampshire's second-innings slide to 198 all out. His unhappy pair meant that Warne's first four knocks in the championship had brought three third-ball ducks followed by a second-ball one. Quite a way to make an impact on English cricket! Will Kendall remained defiant on 78 not out, even adding 45 for the last wicket with Peter Hartley, but Yorkshire's win by an innings and 100 runs was not long in being confirmed. Mike Denness, head of the ECB's new pitches liaison force, did visit Headingley to study the quality of the pitch, but his subsequent all-clear became merely further condemnation of Hampshire's batting inadequacies.

Mike Smethurst and Glen Chapple were the quick bowlers behind Lancashire's 141-run victory at Durham. Chapple's 6 for 42 was the main reason Durham were bowled out for 164 in reply to Lancashire's first-innings 263; he also took three wickets in four balls during a destructive spell of 5 for 19 at one stage, Mel Betts denying Chapple a hat-trick. Saurav Ganguly, who twice hit Paul Collingwood for on-driven sixes during his 73, added 78 in 17 overs for the seventh wicket with Chris Schofield (50), while Peter Martin's 25-ball 40 further boosted Lancashire on the opening day. In their second innings, however, they stuttered to 134 all out with only Neil Fairbrother (41) being able to withstand a career-best onslaught of 7 for 51 from left-arm paceman Simon Brown. Smethurst, though, the highly promising 23-year-old from Oldham, responded by taking a career-best 7 for 50 himself to send Durham tumbling to 92 all out.

The first day at the Oval was washed out, and the match between Surrey and Kent finished in a draw in spite of the efforts by both captains to forge a meaningful contest. Initially, Surrey were content on achieving maximum batting points, an objective they realised thanks to half-centuries from Alistair Brown and Adam Hollioake and then an eighth-wicket partnership of 113 between Martin Bicknell and Ian Salisbury. Bicknell ended up as top-scorer with 73 while Salisbury also reached 50. Graham Thorpe, still struggling for any sort of form following his voluntary winter off, added just 11 to the three ducks and only one half-century that had come from his seven previous innings of the season. Then came the understandable collusion between the two sides, Kent declaring their first innings on 115 for 2 and Surrey following suit on 17 for nought, having agreed not to force the follow-on. The result was a Kent target of 320 in 93 overs, although at 45 for 4 the visitors did not seem to have a hope. Rahul Dravid (71) and Mark Ealham (83) nevertheless rallied Kent, Ealham striking two sixes and eight

fours. Dravid, though, skied to cover and, in the end, Paul Nixon (50 not out) and David Masters needed to hold out for seven overs as Kent won themselves their four extra draw points at 255 for 8.

Division Two
11, 12, 13 and 14 May
at Cardiff
Glamorgan 250 (102.4 overs)(AD Shaw 88*, SL Watkin 51, J Lewis 6 for 73) and 300 for 4 dec. (MP Maynard 119*, SP James 109)
Gloucestershire 242 (101.5 overs)(IJ Harvey 79, KJ Barnett 76) and 174 for 9 (RDB Croft 4 for 65)
Match drawn
Glamorgan 9 pts, Gloucestershire 8 pts

at Northampton
Northamptonshire 585 (144.3 overs)(DJG Sales 276, ML Hayden 101, AL Penberthy 62, RD Stemp 4 for 127)
Nottinghamshire 333 (120 overs)(JE Morris 88, DJ Millns 50*) and (following on) 128 (DM Cousins 4 for 41)
Northamptonshire won by an innings and 124 runs
Northamptonshire 20 pts, Nottinghamshire 4 pts

at Hove
Sussex 224 (68.2 overs)(CJ Adams 70, A Richardson 4 for 69) and 277 (RR Montgomerie 51)
Warwickshire 548 for 7 dec. (160 overs)(DR Brown 203, AFG Griffith 128*, DL Hemp 90)
Warwickshire won by an innings and 47 runs
Warwickshire 20 pts, Sussex 3 pts

at Worcester
Middlesex 161 (46 overs)(SR Lampitt 4 for 44, A Sheriyar 4 for 55) and 181 (JL Langer 73)
Worcestershire 182 (65 overs)(EJ Wilson 104* (carried his bat), ARC Fraser 4 for 29, TF Bloomfield 4 for 57) and 161 for 3 (GA Hick 115*)
Worcestershire won by seven wickets
Worcestershire 15 pts, Middlesex 3 pts

Warwickshire and Worcestershire recorded good wins against Sussex and Middlesex, respectively, to strengthen their positions at the top end of the second division, with Northamptonshire also keeping in touch with an important victory at home to Nottinghamshire. Glamorgan, however, were denied a win of their own by Gloucestershire's last pair at Cardiff.

A superb 276 by David Sales – just back from an England training camp in Manchester – was the highlight of Northants' success at Wantage Road. The richly talented 22-year-old accelerated from 31

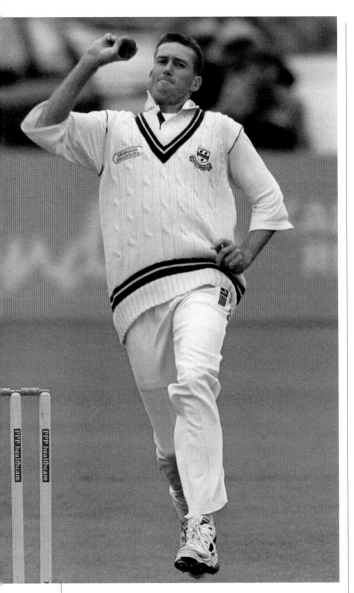

Warwickshire's Glenn McGrath was quickly into his stride taking 9 wickets in the match against Sussex at Hove.

to 102 in just 58 balls and then, having subjugated the Nottinghamshire attack, simply eased his way on to a score that threatened to eclipse his 303 not out against Essex in 1999. After facing 375 balls, however, Sales was run out and the Northants innings finally closed on 585. Matthew Hayden, batting at number seven because of a back strain, hit 101 to help Sales add 197 for the sixth wicket, and earlier Tony Penberthy had scored 62. Notts fought hard to reach 333 in reply, John Morris hitting 88,

but then collapsed to 128 after being asked to follow on. Northants picked up maximum points for their innings and a 124-run triumph.

Another double hundred, Dougie Brown's career-best 203, was at the heart of Warwickshire's innings and 47-run win over Sussex at Hove. The lack of variety in the seam-obsessed Sussex attack was fully exposed as Brown and Ashley Giles (128 not out – also a career-best) built a county-record seventh-wicket stand of 289 to push Warwickshire up to a mammoth 548 for 7 declared. Sussex, on the opening day, had been dismissed for 224 and, second time around, they could only muster 277.

Centuries from Elliott Wilson and Graeme Hick underpinned Worcestershire's seven-wicket win at New Road, with batting never easy in seam-friendly conditions. Middlesex made 161 on the first day, Andrew Strauss hooking Glenn McGrath for six in his 47, but Alamgir Sheriyar and Stuart Lampitt both picked up four wickets. Wilson, a tall and well-organised young opener, then played a near lone hand – carrying his bat for 104 not out in a Worcestershire reply of 182. David Hughes, a member of the ECB pitch panel, carried out a thorough examination of the pitch before deeming it satisfactory, but only Justin Langer (73) and Strauss again (37) overcame the conditions as Middlesex reached just 181 in their second innings. Worcestershire's target could, nevertheless, have proved tricky had not Hick pummelled them for 115 not out off 106 balls. The Worcestershire captain celebrated his latest Test recall with his 109th first-class hundred, moving him past Zaheer Abbas of Pakistan into 15th place on the all-time list of century-makers. Hick finished the game in some style, smiting Paul Weekes' off-spin for four, four, six off successive deliveries.

The match at Cardiff ended, by contrast, in desperate defence and high tension, Gloucestershire's ten-wicket pair of James Averis and Tom Cotterell surviving two overs with nine fielders around the bat as Robert Croft and Dean Cosker tried to clinch victory for Glamorgan. Spinners Croft (4 for 65 from 41 overs) and Cosker (2 for 40 from 38 overs) had earlier looked to have fatally wounded Gloucestershire at 90 for 7, but after tea Jack Russell (46) led a rearguard action which also involved Averis (25 not out from 127 balls), Jon Lewis (20) and then Cotterell. In all, Gloucestershire batted for 107 overs to reach 174 for 9 and the sanctuary of the draw, and perhaps Glamorgan captain Matthew Maynard was left to rue his decision not to declare his side's second innings earlier than at 300 for 4. Maynard himself

GLAMORGAN CCC

Home Ground:
Cardiff
Address:
Sophia Gardens, Cardiff CF1 9XR
Tel: 0292 040 9380
Fax: 0292 040 9390
Indoor school: 0292 041 9308
Email: glam@ecb.co.uk
Directions:
By rail: Cardiff Central Train Station.
By road: From north, A470 and follow signs to Cardiff until
junction with Cardiff by-pass then A48 Port Talbot and City
Centre. Cathedral Road is situated off A48 for Sophia
Gardens. From east, M4 Junction 29 then A48.
Capacity: 4,000
Other grounds used: Pontypridd, Mid Glamorgan; St Helens,
Swansea; Rhos-on-Sea, Colwyn Bay; Pen-y-Pound Ground,
Abergavenny.
Year formed: 1888

Chief Executive: Mike Fatkin
Coach: Jeff Hammond
Other posts: Grounds Supervisor: Len Smith; Manager
Indoor School: Peter Ingram; Marketing Executive:
Matthew Telling
Captain: Matthew Maynard
County colours: Navy blue and yellow/gold

HONOURS

COUNTY CHAMPIONSHIP
1948, 1969, 1997
SUNDAY LEAGUE
1993

CGU National Cricket League nickname:
GLAMORGAN DRAGONS

Website:
www.glamorgancricket.com

was 119 not out when he settled on leaving Gloucestershire a target of 308, Steve James having earlier scored 109. The match, though, had been evenly poised at the halfway stage, Gloucestershire replying with 242 to Glamorgan's first-innings 250. Lewis picked up 6 for 73 in the opening exchanges, but Glamorgan were boosted by a last-wicket stand of 84 between Adrian Shaw (88 not out) and Steve Watkin, whose joyous 51 was a career-best. Ian Harvey (79) and Kim Barnett (76) led the Gloucestershire reply, but the visitors then lost their last five wickets for eight runs in only six overs.

ROUND FOUR: 17–21 MAY 2000

Division One
17, 18, 19 and 20 May
at Derby
Derbyshire 303 (100.1 overs) and 209 for 1
(SD Stubbings 84*, MJ di Venuto 81*)
Yorkshire 349 (128.1 overs)(DS Lehmann 133,
VJ Craven 58, ME Cassar 6 for 76)
Match drawn
Derbyshire 10 pts, Yorkshire 10 pts

at Leicester
Hampshire 229 (95.4 overs)(AN Aymes 74*) and 123
for 8 (PAJ DeFreitas 4 for 41)
Leicestershire 289 (129 overs)(ND Burns 67*, Aftab
Habib 66, SK Warne 5 for 86, AN Aymes 3ct/2st)
Match drawn
Leicestershire 9 pts, Hampshire 8 pts

More bad weather ravaged this round of games, with both first division fixtures – at Derby and Leicester – suffering from lengthy interruptions and ending in draws.

Leicestershire came closest to forcing a victory, reducing Hampshire to 123 for 8 in their second innings – a lead of just 63 – when time ran out. There were 12 overs left, in fact, when Shaun Udal was eighth out, and when the lead was only 57, but Shane Warne put his previous bad form with the bat behind him to hold on tenaciously. In Hampshire's first innings, indeed, Warne had survived a huge leg before appeal to his first ball from Phil deFreitas, which if upheld would have presented the Australian with a fifth successive championship duck! Hampshire totalled 229, with Adrian Aymes returning from his knee injury to hit 74 not out in his first championship innings of the season. In reply,

Leicestershire struggled to score at the rate which, on the final afternoon, would surely have resulted in them pressing home their advantage – with Warne, for instance, taking 5 for 86 from 43 of the 129 overs it took the Midlanders to reach 289 all out. Aftab Habib made 66, Neil Burns a spirited unbeaten 67 and Jon Dakin a useful 36. DeFreitas then got to work with the ball, picking up 4 for 41 as only Robin Smith (31) put up much resistance – until Warne arrived at the crease. The rain took 115.3 overs from the first three days.

Both Derbyshire and Yorkshire claimed ten points from their draw at Derby, with the weather allowing time for only 21 wickets in all to fall. Derbyshire's first-innings 303 was a solid, no-frills affair notable chiefly for a debut wicket for Gary Ramsden, a 17-year-old seamer plucked out of Huddersfield New College on the morning of the match to answer Yorkshire's chronic injury problems. Another Yorkshire youngster, opener Victor Craven, then scored 58 as he added 112 with David Byas (49) for the first wicket, before Darren Lehmann took over. The big Aussie left-hander, such a favourite with the Yorkshire public, was eventually last man out for 133. James Middlebrook, the off-spinner, also chipped in with 45 and helped Lehmann put on 114 for the eighth wicket as Yorkshire totalled 349. Matthew Cassar, showing previously unrealised pace, took a career-best 6 for 76 and then sat back in his dressing room chair to watch Steve Stubbings and Michael di Venuto enjoy themselves as Derbyshire batted out time on 209 for 1 in their second innings. Tim Munton, the Derbyshire seamer, could not bowl in the match after an accident in practice in the indoor school prior to the second day required 40 stitches to a wound over his left eye.

Division Two
17, 18, 19 and 20 May
at Trent Bridge
Nottinghamshire 215 (70.2 overs)(GE Welton 74,
J Lewis 5 for 55) and 207 for 8 (IJ Harvey 4 for 63)
Gloucestershire 290 (117.2 overs)(MW Alleyne 126,
PJ Franks 4 for 43)
Match drawn
Nottinghamshire 8 pts, Gloucestershire 9 pts

at Edgbaston
Warwickshire 400 for 8 dec. (128.3 overs)(DP Ostler
144, NMK Smith 68*, DR Law 5 for 78)
Essex 298 for 4 (89 overs)(RC Irani 91*, SG Law 83)
Match drawn – no play was possible on the second day
Warwickshire 10 pts, Essex 8 pts

18, 19, 20 and 21 May
at Hove
Sussex 258 (63.5 overs)(GD McGrath 5 for 54) and 148 (GD McGrath 4 for 30)
Worcestershire 311 for 8 dec. (93.5 overs)(VS Solanki 98) and 96 for 3
Worcestershire won by seven wickets
Worcestershire 18 pts, Sussex 4 pts

The only positive result in this round of matches came at Hove, where the game between Sussex and Worcestershire had begun a day later than the others and as a consequence escaped some of the bad weather. Worcestershire, however, almost ran out of time as they dismissed Sussex for a second time late on the final day and then reached their victory target of 96 in 26 overs with 11 balls to spare. Vikram Solanki added a magical 33 to his first-innings 98 as he and Elliott Wilson (47) made sure of the win. Worcestershire's main hero, though, was Glenn McGrath who took 5 for 54 and 4 for 30 as Sussex were dismissed for 258 and 148. Stuart Lampitt supported the great Australian paceman well, picking up six wickets in all himself, and Worcestershire's seven-wicket win took them into second place in the second division table, just four points behind Warwickshire.

No play was possible on the second day of Warwickshire's home match against struggling Essex, and a draw was always likely on a good batting strip. Dominic Ostler made his first championship hundred since 1995, going on to reach 144 as Warwickshire ran up 400 for 8 declared. In reply Essex scored 298 for 4 before more rain denied them extra batting bonus points, Ronnie Irani finishing 91 not out and Stuart Law's 83 giving him his 45th score above 50 in 113 innings for Essex.

Nottinghamshire, after a few frights, secured a draw at home to Gloucestershire at Trent Bridge, finishing on 207 for 8 in their second innings in a match in which the highlight was undoubtedly Jon Lewis' first hat-trick of his career. The 24-year-old Gloucestershire seamer, who ended with 5 for 55 as Notts were dismissed for 215 in their first innings, had Jason Gallian and Usman Afzaal leg before seeing John Morris caught off a leading edge by Tom Cotterell at mid-on. Guy Welton hit 74 as Notts recovered from 40 for 5, and Gloucestershire were themselves 47 for 5 at the end of the first day before Mark Alleyne, with a brilliant 126, guided his side to 290 with dogged support from both Jack Russell and Lewis. The

pitch was inspected by David Hughes, of the ECB panel, but deemed satisfactory.

ROUND FIVE: 23–27 MAY 2000

More poor weather, sweeping across the country in waves for several days, wrecked this round of championship games. No positive result was gained in either division, leaving little movement in the two tables.

Division One
23, 24, 25 and 26 May
at Southampton
Lancashire 215 (63.5 overs)(AD Mascarenhas 4 for 52)
Hampshire 175 for 4 (69 overs)
Match drawn – no play was possible on the first and fourth days
Hampshire 7 pts, Lancashire 6 pts

at Canterbury
Surrey 348 for 8 (118 overs)(IJ Ward 158*)
Kent did not bat
Match drawn – no play was possible on the third day
Kent 6 pts, Surrey 7 pts

24, 25, 26 and 27 May
at Chester-le-Street
Leicestershire 336 (129.3 overs)(JM Dakin 89, PAJ de Freitas 81*, DL Maddy 50)
Durham 302 for 8 dec. (117.2 overs)(SM Katich 137*, ID Hunter 63)
Match drawn
Durham 10 pts, Leicestershire 9 pts

at Taunton
Somerset 240 (70.5 overs)(PD Bowler 57)
Derbyshire 101 for 0 (26 overs)
Match drawn – no play was possible on the third and fourth days
Somerset 5 pts, Derbyshire 7 pts

The wisdom of staging back-to-back championship fixtures in May between two such old rivals was again questioned at Canterbury, where Kent and Surrey could not even complete one innings over the four days. The scheduled third day was washed out completely, 106 overs were lost during the first two days, and only 15 overs were possible on the fourth day. Ian Ward, the Surrey opener, remained unbeaten at the end of all of this – but, on 158 not out and with Surrey 348 for 8, he could not hit the two runs

GLOUCESTERSHIRE CCC

Home Ground:
Bristol
Address:
The Sun Alliance Ground, Nevil Road,
Bristol BS7 9EJ
Tel: 0117 910 8000
Directions:
By road: M5, M4, M32 into Bristol: exit at second
exit (Fishponds/Horfield), then third exit – Muller
Road. Almost at end of Muller Road (bus station on right),
turn left at Ralph Road. Go to the top, turn left and then
right almost immediately into Kennington Avenue. Follow
the signs for County Cricket.
Capacity: 8,000
Other grounds used: College Ground, Cheltenham;
Kings School, Gloucester
Year formed: 1870

Chairman: John Higson
Director of Cricket: Andy Stovold
Other posts: Chief Executive: CL Sexstone; Youth
Development Officer: Richard Holdsworth
Captain: Mark Alleyne
Coaching contact: Andy Stovold, Director of Coaching
0117 910 8004
County colours: Blue, brown, gold, green and red,
sky blue

HONOURS

BENSON & HEDGES CUP
1977, 1999, 2000
GILLETTE CUP/NATWEST TROPHY
1973, 1999, 2000

CGU National Cricket League nickname:
GLOUCESTERSHIRE GLADIATORS

Website:
www.glosccc.co.uk

HAMPSHIRE CCC

Home Ground:
Southampton
Address:
The Hampshire Rose Bowl, Botley Road,
West End, Southampton SO32 3XA
Tel: 02380 333788
Fax: 02380 330121
Indoor school: 02380 334393
Email: enquiries.hants@ecb.co.uk
Directions:
By rail: Southampton Parkway – 4 miles.
By road: From M27, exit junction 7 and take the
A334 then the B3035 (Botley Road, West End).
Capacity: 7,800
Year formed: 1863

Chief Executive: Tony Baker
Director of Cricket & Coaching: Tim Tremlett
Coach: Jimmy Cook
Other posts: Head Groundsman: Nigel Gray
Cricket Development Officer: Mark Garaway
Youth Development Officer: Alan Rowe
Women's Cricket Development Officer: Clare Slaney
Captain: Robin Smith
Vice-captain: Shaun Udal
County colours: Navy blue, old gold

HONOURS

COUNTY CHAMPIONSHIP
1961, 1973
SUNDAY LEAGUE
1975, 1978, 1986
BENSON & HEDGES CUP 1988,
1992
GILLETTE CUP/NATWEST TROPHY
1991

CGU National Cricket League
nickname:
HAMPSHIRE HAWKS

Website:
www.hampshire.cricket.org

off the last three balls bowled in increasingly heavy rain before play was abandoned with Surrey still just short of another batting bonus point. Alex Tudor at least livened up the final overs of a frustrating match by hitting 33 not out off 32 balls.

Almost two completed innings were achieved at Chester-le-Street but that too was scant consolation for the frustrated Durham and Leicestershire teams. After Darren Maddy's 50, Leicestershire were indebted to Jon Dakin (89), Phil deFreitas (81 not out) and Carl Crowe who, in stands for the last two wickets, more than doubled their side's score. Dakin and deFreitas put on 85 in 30 overs at the end of an opening day that was sternly fought and always interesting; then, on the second morning, deFreitas and last man Crowe stretched their tenth-wicket stand to 84 as Leicestershire's total was pushed up to 336. DeFreitas followed up his batting contribution by taking 3 for 33 as Durham were reduced to 82 for 5 by the end of the second day, but on a truncated third day Simon Katich went on to reach 102 not out in company with 20-year-old seamer Ian Hunter. The Darlington-born former Durham Academy player was 59 not out by the close in his maiden championship innings, and in the little play possible on the fourth day he went on to 63 before leaving Katich (127 not out) to steer Durham to a third batting point.

A first day wash-out at Southampton was followed by a Lancashire struggle to 215 all out early on the third day, Chris Schofield making a perky unbeaten 39. In reply, Hampshire reached 175 for 4 by the close, Robin Smith hitting 61 and Giles White 45 not out, but no play at all on the fourth day condemned this match to a watery grave.

An even sadder story unfolded at Taunton, with no play possible on both the scheduled third and fourth days. In the 40 overs bowled on the opening day Somerset stumbled to 117 for 4 despite first use of a good pitch. That became 240 all out on the second day, Peter Bowler top-scoring with 57 and Keith Parsons chipping in with 47. But there was only time for Derbyshire to reach 101 for no wicket in reply, from 26 overs, before terminal rain arrived.

Division Two
23, 24, 25 and 26 May
at Chelmsford
Essex 255 (79 overs) (RSG Anderson 67*) and 22 for 0
Sussex 374 for 7 dec. (117.2 overs)(PA Cottey 154, MTE Peirce 86, UBA Rashid 61*)
Match drawn
Essex 8 pts, Sussex 11 pts

at Cardiff
Warwickshire 280 for 5 (92 overs)(NV Knight 80, MJ Powell 73, DR Brown 54*, SP Jones 4 for 47)
Glamorgan did not bat
Match drawn – no play was possible on the first and fourth days
Warwickshire 6 pts, Glamorgan 5 pts

at Bristol
Gloucestershire 199 (62.1 overs)(IJ Harvey 70, A Sheriyar 4 for 51)
Worcestershire 310 for 6 (81 overs)(VS Solanki 161*, DA Leatherdale 65)
Match drawn – no play was possible on the first and fourth days
Gloucestershire 6 pts, Worcestershire 10 pts

at Northampton
Middlesex 217 (69.4 overs)(MR Ramprakash 54, RJ Logan 5 for 61) and 24 for 0
Northamptonshire 319 (115 overs)(ML Hayden 69, D Ripley 55, PCR Tufnell 6 for 92, TF Bloomfield 4 for 46)
Match drawn – no play was possible on the third day
Northamptonshire 10 pts, Middlesex 8 pts

Phil Tufnell has long been portrayed as the Artful Dodger of English cricket, and at Northampton the 34-year-old proved he can still pick a batsman's pocket or two with his slow left-arm wiles. A mesmeric 30-over spell on day two, broken only by tea, was the highlight of an ultimately rain-ruined match between Northamptonshire and Middlesex, and Tufnell finally finished with figures of 6 for 92 – his best in the championship for four years – as Northants reached 319 all out. On the opening day Richard Logan, the young Northants seamer, had picked up a career-best 5 for 61 as Middlesex were dismissed for 217 despite Mark Ramprakash's 54 and considerable bravery from opener Andrew Strauss. Cut over the eyebrow as he top-edged a hook at Devon Malcolm in the game's third over – blood dripped into the crease from the wound after the ball squeezed between the peak and grille of his helmet – Strauss returned with seven stitches at the fall of the sixth wicket to battle on to 18. Matthew Hayden scored 69 and David Ripley a lower-order 55, but Northants' handy first-innings lead counted for nothing once the third day was washed out and rain allowed little play on the Saturday.

After a first day on which only 18 overs were possible, Essex were boosted from 140 for 8 to 255 all out at Chelmsford by a magnificent 67 not out from Ricky Anderson, their number ten. Playing strokes that hinted at a future as an all-rounder, the 23-year-old seamer made his runs from just 87 balls and dominated a stand of 86 for the ninth wicket with Barry Hyam (34). Shown how good a surface it was for batting, Sussex replied with an eventual 374 for 7 declared – despite early on sliding to 24 for 3. Tony Cottey, who came in at the fall of that third wicket, hit 154 from 264 balls, with one six and 18 fours, and added 198 in 59 overs with opener Toby Pierce. Umer Rashid ended up 61 not out, but on a rain-wrecked final day there was time for Essex to reach just 22 without loss in their second innings.

Another big century-maker in this round of games was Worcestershire's Vikram Solanki. Unfortunately, his unbeaten 161 at Bristol was prevented from being a match-winning knock by the bad weather. Both the first and fourth days were complete wash-outs, but in-between Gloucestershire were tumbled out for 199 – despite Ian Harvey (70, with a six and 11 fours) and Jeremy Snape (43) adding 98 for the seventh wicket. Solanki then hit two sixes and 25 fours in his classy innings, supported by David Leatherdale's 65, to take Worcestershire to 310 for 6 before the rain came again.

Even less play was possible at soggy Cardiff, with only 92 overs being bowled on days two and three. In between the blank first and fourth days Warwickshire reached 280 for 5 with Nick Knight scoring 80, Michael Powell 73 and Dougie Brown an unbeaten 54. Glamorgan's attack looked blunt, apart from one rapid spell by 21-year-old Simon Jones – son of former Glamorgan and England left-arm quickie Jeff – which brought him 4 for 1 in 12 balls.

ROUND SIX: 31 MAY–5 JUNE 2000

Division One
31 May, 1, 2 and 3 June
at Tunbridge Wells
Kent 177 (110.2 overs)(J Wood 5 for 36) and 237 for 9 dec. (MA Ealham 72*)
Durham 81 (64.2 overs)(DD Masters 6 for 27) and 143 (MM Patel 4 for 38)
Kent won by 190 runs
Kent 15 pts, Durham 3 pts

at Old Trafford
Derbyshire 170 (80.5 overs)(PJ Martin 5 for 44) and 24 for 2
Lancashire 213 (70.5 overs)
Match drawn – no play was possible on the third and

fourth days
Lancashire 8 pts, Derbyshire 7 pts

at Headingley
Leicestershire 296 (101.5 overs)(PAJ deFreitas 70, DL Maddy 63)
Yorkshire 146 for 4 (64.4 overs)
Match drawn – no play was possible on the fourth day
Yorkshire 8 pts, Leicester 7 pts

1, 2, 3 and 4 June
at the Oval
Surrey 333 (110.1 overs)(AJ Tudor 64*, MP Bicknell 59, GP Thorpe 58, SRG Francis 4 for 95) and 142 (SK Warne 5 for 31, AD Mullally 4 for 31)
Hampshire 210 (92 overs)(GW White 96, MP Bicknell 4 for 52) and 263 (AD Mascarenhas 59, SK Warne 50, AJ Tudor 5 for 57)
Surrey won by 2 runs
Surrey 18 pts, Hampshire 4 pts

Champions Surrey finally shrugged off their sluggish start to the campaign with one of the most exciting and dramatic victories seen in English first-class cricket. Losers Hampshire played their, part, too in events at the Oval, which culminated in a two-run win for Surrey.

A last-wicket stand of 55 between Alex Tudor and Saqlain Mushtaq boosted Surrey's first-innings total to 333 and was a strange precursor of what was to come on the final afternoon. Graham Thorpe and Martin Bicknell both hit half-centuries, too, before Bicknell (4 for 52), Tudor (3 for 52) and Saqlain (3 for 65) got to work with the ball to dismiss Hampshire for 210 in reply. Giles White, the opener, played well for 96, but only Adrian Aymes (44) made any other significant contribution. Surrey's dominance, however, was suddenly threatened as Shane Warne began to spin his web around their batsmen. The Australian leg-spinner took 5 for 31 as, in tandem with fellow big-money winter signing Alan Mullally (4 for 31), he skittled Surrey for 142. A magnificent third day ended with Hampshire reaching 58 for 2 by the close but, on a tense final morning, their quest for 266 took some serious blows as they declined to 87 for 6. Now, though, Warne took over with the bat – making 50 and inspiring some determined Hampshire resistance. All looked lost, however, when Dimitri Mascarenhas was joined by last man Simon Francis with 93 runs still required. Despite batting with a runner, Mascarenhas played some quality strokes and Francis, despite coming in one place lower than Mullally, showed that

KENT CCC

Home Ground:
Canterbury
Address:
St Lawrence Ground,
Old Dover Road,
Canterbury,
Kent CT1 3NZ
Tel: 01227 456886
Fax: 01227 762168
Indoor school: 01227 473605
Email: kent@ecb.co.uk
Directions:
By rail: Canterbury East/West.
By road: AA roadsigns
Capacity: 10,000
Other grounds used: The Mote, Maidstone;
The Nevill, Tunbridge Wells
Year formed: 1870

Chief Executive: Paul Millman
First Team Coach: John Wright
Other posts: Head Groundsman: Mike Grantham;
Second Team Coach: Chris Stone; Marketing Manager: Adele
Aylwin
Captain: Matthew Fleming
County colours: Blue and white

HONOURS

COUNTY CHAMPIONSHIP
1906, 1909, 1910, 1913, 1970,
1977, 1978
SUNDAY LEAGUE
1972, 1973, 1976, 1995
BENSON & HEDGES CUP
1973, 1976, 1978
GILLETTE CUP/NATWEST TROPHY
1967, 1974

**CGU National Cricket League
nickname:**
KENT SPITFIRES

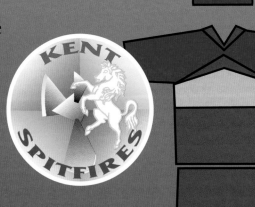

Website:
www.kentcountycricket.co.uk

he too could play a bit. Inch by inch, they crept closer to the target until, amid unbearable tension, Mascarenhas top-edged a pull at Tudor and was caught and bowled for 59. Francis was left 30 not out, and the joyous Tudor celebrated with a soccer-style charge and slide towards the Vauxhall End stands – with all his teammates charging after him and submerging him under a pile of bodies. No wonder Surrey were ecstatic – they had not only won a magnificent match, but had also signalled their intent to defend their crown tenaciously.

Kent's determined attempt to kick-start their season resulted in a 190-run win over Durham at Tunbridge Wells. Torrential rain in the lead-up to the match left the council-owned pitch soft and slow, but Kent adapted to the conditions far more readily than their opponents, who seemed miffed that the pitch – though far from dangerous – was imperfect. In the long years of uncovered pitches, of course, first-class cricketers were often asked similar questions of technique and temperament by the suddenly changing conditions: they had to learn to adapt, or die. Here, tellingly, was a kind of throwback to those days – and a majority of players proved either unable, or unwilling, to work out ways of dealing with a different sort of examination. Matthew Fleming, the Kent captain, was more than willing to adapt, however. On the opening day, fighting hard against the constant seam movement, he laboured 57 overs for an invaluable 37 not out as Kent reached 171 for 8. Then, on day three, after a clearly disillusioned Durham had been shot out for just 81 with David Masters taking a career-best 6 for 27, Fleming was more characteristically forthright as Kent recovered from 76 for 7 to 237 for 9 declared. Fleming biffed 40, as did Min Patel, and both batsmen lent fine support to Mark Ealham, who battled away for four hours to compile an unbeaten 72. Fleming capped his performance by taking 3 for 14 as Durham, also undermined by Patel's 4 for 38 from 30 overs, fell away to 143 all out.

Rain ruined the matches at Old Trafford and Headingley, which both ended in draws. No play was possible on either of the last two days at Old Trafford, where Lancashire replied to Derbyshire's first-innings 170 by being bowled out for 213 themselves. A lack of application lay behind Derbyshire's demise, Peter Martin bagging 5 for 44, but Martin was unluckily hit on the thumb by a ball from Dominic Cork near the end of Lancashire's first innings; a fractured dislocation meant he would be out of action for two months.

Phil Tufnell gave the selectors a timely – but fruitless – nudge by bowling 30 overs on the trot and claiming six Northampton wickets at Wantage Road.

At Headingley leaders Leicestershire totalled 296 on day one, Darren Maddy striking ten fours in his 63 and Phil deFreitas maintaining his fine early-season form with the bat by hitting 70 from number nine. In fact, deFreitas put on 61 with Jimmy Ormond for the ninth wicket. Chris Elstub, a 19-year-old pace bowler from the Yorkshire Academy, picked up a maiden first-class wicket in Darren Stevens, but rain on the second and third days allowed Yorkshire to reach only 146 for 4 in reply. The final day was a complete wash-out.

Division Two
31 May, 1, 2 and 3 June
at Ilford
Northamptonshire 114 (47 overs)(RSG Anderson 6 for 34) and 327 (ML Hayden 73, MB Loye 62, RSG Anderson 5 for 77)
Essex 216 (82.5 overs)(RC Irani 53, DM Cousins 4 for 44, DE Malcolm 4 for 53) and 228 for 5 (DDJ Robinson 93*, RC Irani 55)
Essex won by five wickets
Essex 16 pts, Northamptonshire 3 pts

at Lord's
Gloucestershire 259 (85.4 overs)(CG Taylor 104, JN Snape 52, RL Johnson 5 for 83) and 242 (KJ Barnett 82, MGN Windows 54, RL Johnson 4 for 66)
Middlesex 204 for 9 dec. (79.2 overs)(AM Smith 5 for 52) and 212 (MW Alleyne 6 for 49)
Gloucestershire won by 85 runs
Gloucestershire 17 pts, Middlesex 4 pts

at Hove
Glamorgan 185 (78 overs)(A Dale 75, JD Lewry 4 for 40) and 284 (RSC Martin-Jenkins 5 for 94)
Sussex 463 for 9 dec. (MG Bevan 107, CJ Adams 90, RR Montgomerie 71, MTE Peirce 60, UBA Rashid 51*, SL Watkin 4 for 102) and 7 for 0
Sussex won by ten wickets
Sussex 20 pts, Glamorgan 2 pts

An incredible opening partnership of 406, unbeaten, by Darren Bicknell and Guy Welton was the biggest talking point of this round of second division matches – but the record-breaking stand, against Warwickshire at Edgbaston, could not in the end help Nottinghamshire force the victory the pair's batting heroics deserved.

Seventy minutes were lost to rain on the final day, with Warwickshire managing to hang on for the draw at 305 for 8 in their second innings thanks to Dominic Ostler's 93, resistance from both Trevor

Penney and David Hemp, and a 54-run eighth-wicket stand in 18 overs between Dougie Brown (51 not out) and Keith Piper. For Notts, this was cruel after the way they had bundled out the home side for just 110 on the opening day and then, through Bicknell and Welton, batted Warwickshire out of the game. Notts were 194 for 0 at the end of the second day and, when play resumed the following morning, Bicknell and Welton motored on to 180 and 200 not out respectively before the declaration at 406 for 0. It was a maiden first-class hundred for Welton, a former Grimsby Town footballer and MCC Young Cricketer. Both openers hit 23 boundaries and, unsurprisingly, it was a county first-wicket record stand. It was, in fact, the 13th-highest partnership in championship history, and a county record for any wicket – beating the 398 put on by Arthur Shrewsbury and William Gunn against Sussex at Trent Bridge in 1890. Also, it was the biggest opening stand at Edgbaston, and the biggest against Warwickshire – overhauling the 352 put together by Jack Hobbs and Tom Hayward at the Oval in 1909.

There was another little piece of history made at Lord's, where 23-year-old Chris Taylor became not only the first Gloucestershire player to score a hundred in his first championship match, but also the first batsman of any county to hit a maiden championship ton at Lord's. It was quite a moment for the diminutive Taylor, and for the cricketers of Western League club Optimists – with whom the youngster first learned to play the game. Taylor's innings was all the more notable for the fact that he came in with Gloucestershire 29 for 4, but Jeremy Snape stayed with him to make 52 and a total of 259, despite Richard Johnson's 5 for 83, was soon confirmed as enough to earn them a handy first-innings lead. Mike Smith took 5 for 52 and Middlesex captain Justin Langer declared at 204 for 9 in order to get a shot at the Gloucestershire openers before the end of the second day. From their overnight 20 for 0, however, Gloucestershire reached 242 with Kim Barnett (82) and Matt Windows (54) taking particular advantage of some Middlesex sloppiness in the field. Needing 298, Middlesex were always struggling once Langer went for 49 and, from 154 for 3, they slipped ignominiously to 212 all out and defeat by 85 runs. Mark Alleyne, the jubilant Gloucestershire captain, picked up a career-best 6 for 49 with his medium-pacers.

At Ilford there was joy, at last, for Essex, who forced their first championship win of the season with a five-wicket success against Northants. Ricky Anderson, the fast-improving paceman, took a career-best 6 for 34 – including a spell of 5 for 2 in 14 balls – as the visitors were shot out for 114 on the first day. Essex, looking like gaining a big lead at 162 for 3, slipped themselves to 216 by losing their last six wickets for 12 runs against a fired-up Devon Malcolm and Darren Cousins, who was bowling against his former county. Northants then tried to keep the tide of the match turning towards them, reaching 327 in their second innings, thanks largely to a stand of 118 in 31 overs between Matthew Hayden (73) and Mal Loye (62). But Anderson snatched 5 for 77 and Essex, riding out a new-ball burst of 3 for 9 in seven overs from Malcolm, rallied to 170 for 4 by the third evening. Darren Robinson, who added 121 for the fourth wicket with Ronnie Irani (55), then converted his overnight unbeaten 70 into 93 not out as Essex cruised past their 226 target.

Sussex showed Glamorgan little mercy at Hove, dismissing their visitors for 185 on the opening day and then running up 463 for 9 declared in an attempt to grind Glamorgan into submission. Chris Adams, smarting from being handed a £500 ECB fine for pushing Danny Law of Essex in a Benson and Hedges Cup match in April, included three sixes and nine fours in his 90 and dominated a stand of 131 in 34 overs with Michael Bevan. The Australian left-hander went on to score 107 – and all this after Richard Montgomerie (71) and Toby Pierce (60) had put on 106 for the first wicket. An unbeaten 51 from Umer Rashid added to Glamorgan's misery, but at least the Welsh county put up a fight as they ground out 284 in their second innings. Robin Martin-Jenkins, with 5 for 94, was chiefly responsible for chipping away at the Glamorgan resistance and, in the end, Sussex needed just seven runs to complete a satisfying ten-wicket win.

ROUND SEVEN: 6–10 JUNE 2000

Division One
6, 7 and 8 June
at Liverpool
Hampshire 95 (44 overs)(MP Smethurst 4 for 15) and 139 (A Flintoff 4 for 18)
Lancashire 269 (92.4 overs)(NH Fairbrother 77*, A Flintoff 73, SK Warne 4 for 61)
Lancashire won by an innings and 35 runs
Lancashire 17 pts, Hampshire 3 pts

6, 7, 8 and 9 June
at Bath
Kent 261 (81.5 overs)(R Dravid 90, AR Caddick 6 for 57) and 223 (MJ Walker 61, AR Caddick 4 for 40)
Somerset 295 (118.5 overs)(KA Parsons 62, J Cox 52, PCL Holloway 50, KD Masters 5 for 55) and 193 for 8)
Somerset won by two wickets
Somerset 17 pts, Kent 5 pts

7, 8 and 9 June
at Derby
Surrey 138 (51.5 overs)(TA Munton 7 for 34) and 218 (AD Brown 75)
Derbyshire 191 (50.1 overs)(MP Dowman 69, AJ Tudor 5 for 64, MP Bicknell 4 for 75) and 167 for 3 (MJ di Venuto 92*)
Derbyshire won by seven wickets
Derbyshire 7 pts, Surrey 3 pts
Derbyshire had 8 pts deducted from their original total of 15 pts after an enquiry deemed their pitch to have been unsuitable for a first-class match.

at Chester-le-Street
Durham 189 (73.5 overs)(JJB Lewis 52, MJ Hoggard 5 for 57) and 201 (D Gough for 63)
Yorkshire 294 (98.3 overs)(MP Vaughan 94, DS Lehmann 79, ID Hunter 4 for 73) and 97 for 4
Yorkshire won by six wickets
Yorkshire 17 pts, Durham 3 pts

The first big pitch controversy of the season accompanied Derbyshire's initially striking seven-wicket triumph over champions Surrey at the Racecourse Ground. After Mike Denness, the England and Wales Cricket Board's chief pitches liaison officer, had docked Derbyshire eight points, all hell broke loose.

Derbyshire immediately announced an intention to appeal against the penalty, amid allegations that the ECB had deliberately picked on a small club in a bid to warn off others tempted to flout their tougher pitch directives. Surrey's attitude towards the conditions, during an ill-tempered match, also attracted private criticism – while Derbyshire also pleaded mitigating circumstances and argued that they had the support of both umpires, Barry Dudleston and Vanburn Holder. 'To say that we are deeply upset is putting it mildly,' said John Smedley, Derbyshire's chief executive. Denness' three-man panel penalised Derbyshire for what they saw as a pitch with too much moisture in it at the start. The club retorted that groundsman Barry Marsh had begun preparing the pitch 12 days before the match,

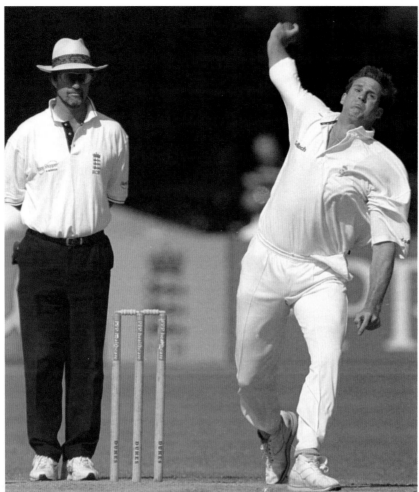

Tim Munton managed to ignore the distractions of the fashion-conscious umpire Willey to take 7 Surrey wickets as Derbyshire beat the holders by 7 wickets.

during the ensuing game. Surrey, having decided to bat first, were bundled out for 138 in 51.5 overs. Tim Munton, exploiting the warm muggy atmosphere and the moisture beneath the surface, took 7 for 34 from his 19.5 overs and only Ian Ward (41) held out for long. In reply, Derbyshire also struggled against Alex Tudor (5 for 64) and Martin Bicknell (4 for 75), and 19 wickets in all fell on the opening day. Mathew Dowman's 69 did earn Derbyshire a first innings lead of 53, and later on the second day Surrey had been bowled out again for 218. This time Alistair Brown (75) and Alec Stewart (42) resisted well, but Dominic Cork and Matt Cassar shared six wickets. Faced with a win target of 166, Derbyshire lost early wickets but were rallied by a stand for the fourth wicket between Michael di Venuto and Rob Bailey. The pair had taken Derbyshire to 119 for 3 by the close of the second day, and they turned down the chance to claim the extra half-hour because of low sunshine shining into their eyes. The next morning, however, the match ended in a flurry of boundaries as di Venuto (92 not out) and Bailey (40 not out) sped to the finishing line. The match was won and lost; all that remained was rancour, a pitch penalty and an appeal that was to be rejected.

but had been hampered by persistent bad weather – and by the fact that the ECB itself had requisitioned Derbyshire's waterhog equipment to help Trent Bridge (at nearby Nottingham) stage the Second Test between England and Zimbabwe. This equipment was only returned after a violent thunderstorm had soaked the ground on the Tuesday before the game. Moreover, umpires Dudleston and Holder argued against the imposition of the penalty, agreeing to represent Derbyshire as witnesses and saying that the pitch was as dry as it was possible to be at the start of the match. County officials also pointed to the fact that Adam Hollioake, the Surrey captain, had chosen to bat first after winning the toss and had also chosen to include a second spinner. Derbyshire members were particularly offended that Hollioake – and some of the Surrey players – then moaned about the pitch

By contrast, a magnificent game of pure and unsullied four-day cricket was unfolding at Bath,

LANCASHIRE CCC

Home Ground:
Old Trafford
Address:
Old Trafford, Manchester M16 0PX
Tel: 0161 282 4000 (switchboard)
      0161 282 4040 (ticket/membership office)
Fax: 0161 873 8353 (ticket office)
Indoor cricket centre: 0161 282 4039
Email: sales.lancs@ecb.co.uk (ticket office)
Directions:
By rail: Manchester Piccadilly or Victoria then
Metro link to Old Trafford (station alongside
ground).
By road: M63, Stretford slip road (junction 7) on to
A56; follow signs.
Capacity: 21,500
Other grounds used: Blackpool (Stanley Park);
Liverpool (Aigburth); Southport (Trafalgar Road);
Lytham (Church Road).
Year formed: 1864

Chairman: Jack Simmons MBE
Chief Executive: Jim Cumbes
Other posts: Cricket Secretary: David Edmundson; Head
Groundsman: Peter Marron; Sales & Marketing Manager:
Geoff Durbin
Captain: John Crawley
Vice-captain: Warren Hegg
County colours: Red, blue, green

HONOURS

COUNTY CHAMPIONSHIP
1881, 1897, 1927, 1928, 1930, 1934
JOINT CHAMPIONS
1878, 1882, 1889, 1950
NATIONAL LEAGUE
1999
BENSON & HEDGES CUP
1984, 1990, 1995, 1996
GILLETTE CUP/NATWEST TROPHY
1970, 1971, 1972, 1975, 1990,
1996, 1998

**CGU National Cricket League
nickname:**
LANCASHIRE LIGHTNING

Website:
www.lccc.co.uk

with Somerset destined to win by dint of holding their nerve as the match ebbed and flowed deep into its final session. Kent batted first, and the opening day featured a terrific duel between Rahul Dravid, the elegant Indian, and Andy Caddick. The angular Caddick, obtaining lift and movement where lesser bowlers could not, took 6 for 57 but could not ensnare Dravid. That Kent reached 261 was almost entirely due to Dravid's 90, and perhaps even the home supporters sighed with regret when the Indian vice-captain touched a legside delivery from Graham Rose when within sight of a deserved first championship century. A solid Somerset reply saw them gain a small lead at 295 all out, David Masters continuing his promising start to his first-class career with 5 for 55. In their second innings Matthew Walker (61) and Mark Ealham (43) fought hard, but Caddick again caused huge problems with 4 for 40 from 25 overs, and a total of 223 left the outcome of the match in the balance. By the close of play on day three Somerset were 50 for 3, and an engrossing game seemed to be sliding the visitors' way when the home side declined first to 97 for 6 and then 142 for 8. Enter Caddick, however, to off-drive his second ball for four and then hit the previously miserly Min Patel for six over mid-wicket. With Ian Blackwell also playing positively for 27 not out, Caddick went on to 21 and the pair steered Somerset home at the last.

Lancashire's thrashing of Hampshire at Liverpool, by an innings and 35 runs, confirmed their own title challenge as well as condemning the visitors to bottom spot in the championship's first division. Lancashire won the toss, bowled first in helpful conditions and their seamers, led by Mike Smethurst (4 for 15), skittled Hampshire for 95. In reply, Neil Fairbrother grafted for more than five hours to make 77 not out while Andy Flintoff's 73 also helped to keep Shane Warne and Alan Mullally at bay. By the close of the second day Hampshire were in deep trouble at 45 for 3, and that became 139 all out on the third morning when Flintoff added 4 for 18 to his first innings 3 for 12.

Yorkshire overcame Durham at Chester-le-Street to maintain their early-season form, with Darren Gough's second innings 6 for 63 denying Durham any escape route after they had conceded a deficit of 105 on the first innings. Durham could only score 201 to add to their first innings 189, in which Jonathan Lewis hit 52 and Matthew Hoggard took 5 for 67. Nick Speak, suffering unhappy form in his first season as captain, made 11 – his highest

score of the season but giving him a tally of just 30 runs from eight innings. Michael Vaughan confirmed his successful recovery from his broken finger, after a five-week absence, with a composed 94 and Darren Lehmann hit 79 as Yorkshire totalled 294. Martin Speight's 44 was then the only real Durham resistance as Gough stamped his authority on proceedings, leaving Richard Blakey (34 not out) to ease Yorkshire home by six wickets.

Division Two
2, 3, 4 and 5 June
at Edgbaston
Warwickshire 110 (44.5 overs) and 305 for 8 (DP Ostler 93, DR Brown 51*)
Nottinghamshire 406 for 0 dec. (GE Welton 200*, DJ Bicknell 180*)
Match drawn
Warwickshire 4 pts, Nottinghamshire 12 pts

6, 7 and 8 June
at Bristol
Essex 263 (102.2 overs)(PJ Prichard 96, BJ Hyam 53, RC Irani 52) and 199 (AP Grayson 52, J Lewis 6 for 47)
Gloucestershire 268 (94.3 overs)(MG Windows 107, JN Snape 54) and 85 (DR Law 4 for 15)
Essex won by 109 runs
Essex 17 pts, Gloucestershire 5 pts

7, 8, 9 and 10 June
at Trent Bridge
Worcestershire 402 (112.5 overs)(GA Hick 122, DA Leatherdale 117, DJ Millns 4 for 92) and 292 for 7 dec. (VS Solanki 80, EJ Wilson 54, AJ Harris 4 for 85)
Nottinghamshire 313 (96.1 overs)(U Afzaal 151*, GD McGrath 8 for 86) and 275 (PJ Franks 60, GE Welton 60, SR Lampitt 4 for 42)
Worcestershire won by 106 runs
Worcestershire 20 pts, Nottinghamshire 6 pts

at Horsham
Middlesex 370 (122.4 overs)(DC Nash 76*, JL Langer 64, OA Shah 60, RSC Martin-Jenkins 4 for 66) and 337 for 6 dec. (MA Roseberry 87, OA Shah 55)
Sussex 300 for 9 dec. (90 overs)(MG Bevan 72, UBA Rashid 51*, RL Johnson 6 for 71)
Match drawn – no play was possible on the third day
Sussex 10 pts, Middlesex 11 pts

Not even a record Nottinghamshire last wicket stand could prevent Worcestershire from recording a 106-run win at Trent Bridge and moving to the top of the second division table.

Usman Afzaal and Andrew Harris were the record-equallers. In fact, their 152-run stand in Notts' first innings 313 putting them alongside Ted Alletson and William Riley's mark at Hove in 1911. For a moment, actually, most spectators at the ground thought the modern-day pair had created a new record when Harris pushed Glenn McGrath away off the back foot for a single. But, in playing the stroke, last man Harris had dislodged a bail with his boot and was out for 39. Afzaal remained unbeaten for a fine 151, and he was particularly impressive against the hostile McGrath, but even his heroics could not prevent Worcestershire from – eventually – earning the sizeable first innings advantage that had always looked likely following a first day 122 from Graeme Hick (the 111th first-class ton of his career) and 117 from David Leatherdale. Vikram Solanki then made 80 as Worcestershire reached 292 for 7 declared second time around – and Notts' fate was sealed when they were dismissed on the final day for 275 despite 60s from Guy Welton and Paul Franks.

Slow handclapping disfigured events on the final day at Horsham, where Middlesex opted not to open the game out against Sussex following the frustrations of a third-day washout. The home crowd could not understand why the visitors, despite being 270 ahead by mid-afternoon, did not want to give themselves the chance of victory, but – in the two-division climate – four points for the draw (and denying the opponent chance of victory) represents a prize often worth having. Spectators? What do they matter when promotion or relegation is at stake? For the record, Middlesex made a first innings 370, Robin Martin-Jenkins was capped during the second day's tea interval, and Sussex replied with 300 for 9 declared in which Michael Bevan thrashed a 67-ball 72, with 15 fours, and Richard Johnson took an impressive 6 for 66 by extracting more lift and bounce from an excellent pitch than anyone else. In their second innings Middlesex reached 337 for 6 declared on that tedious final day.

Essex's season, meanwhile, took an upturn as Gloucestershire disfigured the supposedly more cut-throat championship by resting four key players from their fixture at Bristol. Jack Russell, Kim Barnett, Mike Smith and Ian Harvey were all pulled out of the game in order to keep them fresh for the Benson and Hedges Cup final – which was to be played at Lord's immediately after this match. Although one could understand the thinking, what did it say for Gloucestershire's commitment to

championship cricket? Essex totalled a first innings 263, with Paul Prichard making 96 before a direct hit from Tim Hancock ran him out, and both Ronnie Irani and Barry Hyam making gritty half-centuries. Nasser Hussain, the England captain, was desperate for runs but reached just three in seven balls before being leg before to Mike Cawdron. Gloucestershire seemed to be in control when Matt Windows was making 107, but although Jeremy Snape weighed in with 54 their total of 268 merely left the game in the balance. Hussain then bagged a duck as Essex, largely through Paul Grayson's 52 and Irani's 42, reached 199 in their second innings. Jon Lewis continued his good season with 6-47, but then the Essex seamers went to work and Gloucestershire, tumbled out for 85 in less than 32 overs, lost by 109 runs.

ROUND EIGHT: 14–18 JUNE 2000

Division One
14, 15 and 16 June
at Basingstoke
Hampshire 340 (128.1 overs)(SJE Brown 4 for 62)
Durham 83 (49.4 overs)(SK Warne 4 for 34) and (following on) 93 (SK Warne 4 for 22)
Hampshire won by an innings and 184 runs
Hampshire 18 pts, Durham 3 pts

at the Oval
Surrey 548 (154.3 overs)(GP Thorpe 115, JN Batty 100*, MA Butcher 82, N Shahid 77, PS Jones 4 for 103)
Somerset 145 (63.2 overs)(Saqlain Mushtaq 6 for 47, IDK Salisbury 4 for 31) and (following on) 190 (IDK Salisbury 8 for 60)
Surrey won by an innings and 213 runs
Surrey 20 pts, Somerset 2 pts

at Headingley
Kent 129 (75.2 overs)(RJ Sidebottom 5 for 27) and 82 (A Sidebottom 6 for 16)
Yorkshire 149 (68 overs) and 63 for 4
Yorkshire won by six wickets
Yorkshire 15 pts, Kent 6 pts

14, 15, 16 and 17 June
at Leicester
Leicestershire 310 (90.3 overs)(A Habib 164, KJ Dean 4 for 47 including the hat trick, ME Cassar 4 for 62) and 47 for 0
Derbyshire 133 (56.5 overs)(J Ormond 6 for 50) and (following on) 223 (VJ Wells 4 for 58)

JUNE DIARY by Robin Martin-Jenkins

Another week has passed in the blinking of an eye. It is June already and at last we have a championship win under our belts. A great all-round team performance against Glamorgan should have given us a huge confidence boost for the next few weeks. There wasn't time to reflect on the win as we had to drive down the M4 for our national league game against Somerset at Bath the following day. If you asked every professional cricketer in the country if he thought we played too much cricket in this country, 90 per cent would say yes. Yet nothing is ever done about it.

However, I've obviously managed to impress someone enough for Sussex to award me my county cap! I was given it in the tea interval of the match against Middlesex at Horsham. It was a good touch as I've lived near, and played at, Horsham since I was ten. I have fond memories of practising every Wednesday evening at the ground as a boy. I remember receiving my Sussex under-11 cap on the same ground (along with Justin Bates, the Sussex off-spinner). Little did I know that 13 years later I'd receive the senior version standing in almost exactly the same place.

I missed our brilliant demolition of Worcestershire due to a niggling side strain but the boys clearly enjoyed their two-day victory. With the sun forecast to remain it will give everyone a chance to top up their tans. We are often very envious of the spectators, who can shed their shirts while watching cricket on hot days. One such gentleman, who sunbathes on the roof of one of the houses behind the main scoreboard at Hove, is cause for much amusement, for not only is he one of the most tanned people you will ever see, but he seems to wear a pair of tan-coloured Speedos. From a distance, this makes him look like something from Brighton nudist beach!

It was a strange feeling watching the day/night game against Kent as the month drew to a close. It was the first game I had watched since the start of my injury and I was itching to be out on the park with the chaps. It was so frustrating not being able to take part in the game and I knew that no matter how much I willed them on, it wasn't going to have any effect on the result of the game. It looks as though we are going to have to put together a run of wins in the national league if we are not going to get relegated. With nine games remaining we will have to win six if we are to be sure of safety. The nature of one-day cricket is such that it is quite possible to get on a roll and win a number of games in a row. Last year we managed it, but we seemed to play our games at more regular intervals. This year it has been very stop-start. We won our first game against Leicestershire but then didn't have another national league game for the next two weeks. It can be difficult to get into that winning rhythm, but the games come thick and fast from now on so we've definitely got a chance.

Leicestershire won by ten wickets – no play was possible on the first day
Leicestershire 18 pts, Derbyshire 3 pts

Ian Salisbury outshone even his more celebrated spin twin Saqlain Mushtaq as Surrey crushed Somerset by an innings and 213 runs at the Oval to crank up their attempt to defend the championship title. But Yorkshire stayed top with victory against Kent on a controversial pitch at Headingley. Leicestershire also maintained their challenge by beating Derbyshire, while there was a welcome win for struggling Hampshire. Shane Warne took eight wickets in the match as Durham were spun out for 83 and 93 at Basingstoke.

Salisbury's career-best 8 for 60, in addition to his first-innings 4 for 31, underlined his status as England's leading leg-spinner, despite the awarding of a central contract to young Lancastrian pretender Chris Schofield. At 30, Salisbury might even be coming into his prime at a time when he seems to have little future as a Test bowler. A record of just 19 wickets in 12 Tests between 1992 and 1998, at 70 runs apiece, is a harsh reflection of Salisbury's true ability – and it is interesting to hear Saqlain's assertion that, if Salisbury were Pakistani, he would be a fully fledged Test performer. Saqlain, in fact, undermined Somerset's first innings by taking 6 for 47 but, perhaps struggling with a knee complaint, he could only pick up 1 for 75 second time around as Salisbury totally bamboozled the visiting batsmen with his well-varied leg-breaks and vicious googlies. Somerset were bowled out for 145 and 190, even after reaching 73 for no wicket in their first innings, and all this came after Surrey had amassed 548 themselves with Graham Thorpe (115), Jon Batty (100 not out from 173 balls), Nadeem Shahid (77) and Mark Butcher (82) all enjoying themselves.

A treacherous Headingley pitch was marked below average by the umpires, but ECB pitch liaison officer AC Smith arrived only on the third day and said he had not seen enough of the play to take action. In fact, 11 wickets fell on that third and final day as Kent, in their second innings, slid from an overnight 36 for 3 to 82 all out with Ryan Sidebottom, the left-arm fast bowler, adding 6 for 16 to his first innings 5 for 27 to achieve ten wickets or more for the first time in a first-class match. Then, Yorkshire lost four wickets in knocking off the 63 runs they required but, farcically, Smith still had not seen enough. The bottom line is that pitches like this one are not going to improve the standard of English cricket – which, apparently, is the aim of the

LEICESTERSHIRE CCC

Home Ground:
Grace Road, Leicester
Address:
County Ground,
Grace Road,
Leicester LE2 8AD
Tel: 0116 283 2128
Fax: 0116 244 0363
Directions:
By road: Follow signs from city centre, or from southern ring road from M1 or A6.
Capacity: 5,500
Other grounds used: None
Year formed: 1879

Manager: Jack Birkenshaw
General Manager/Secretary: James Whitaker
Other posts: County coaches: Russell Cobb, John Smith, Phil Whiticase, Lloyd Tennant; Administrative Secretary: Kevin Hill
Captain: Vince Wells
Vice-captain: Ben Smith
County colours: Dark green and scarlet

HONOURS

COUNTY CHAMPIONSHIP
1975, 1996, 1998
SUNDAY LEAGUE
1974, 1977
BENSON & HEDGES CUP
1972, 1975, 1985

CGU National Cricket League nickname:
LEICESTERSHIRE FOXES

Website:
www.leicestershireccc.com

He might have been born in Yorkshire, but Gary Keedy bowled Lancashire to victory in the Roses Match.

administrators as they tinker endlessly with the structure of the domestic game – and should therefore be condemned. End of story. Derbyshire, still aggrieved at being docked eight points for their poor pitch at Derby, and despite clearly extenuating circumstances, would have looked on at Yorkshire's escape in despair. For the record, Kent were 26 for 5 on a weather-affected first day before the skill of Indian Test batsman Rahul Dravid, who battled for more than four hours to score 45 not out, enabled them to reach 127 for 7 from 71 overs by the close. That, though, became 129 all out on the second morning and Darren Lehmann, with 28, was the top-scorer as Yorkshire struggled against disciplined Kent seam bowling to total 149 in reply. Sixteen wickets fell on that second day and the pitch, criss-crossed with cracks even at the start, was becoming yet more uneven. What a lottery, and what a 'brave new world' this new two-division championship will be if pitches like this remain unpunished.

The pitch at May's Bounty, however, was not to blame for Durham's abject surrender to Hampshire – it was more the genius of Shane Warne, and the inadequate techniques of the visiting batsmen. This match could be the last first-class game at Basingstoke, although a campaign is on to reinstate this fixture from 2002 onwards. A good crowd turned up despite chilly conditions on the opening day, and they saw Hampshire reach 255 for 4 by the close. That total became 340 all out the following morning – and although eight batsmen scored 27 or more, Derek Kenway was the top-scorer with 47. When Durham replied, they were soon in trouble, Alan Mullally and Dimitri Mascarenhas taking three wickets each and Warne wrapping up the innings for just 83 with 4 for 34. Durham were 12 for 1, following on, by the end of the second day and Hampshire, though pleased with the imminent victory, were still left to rue that an expected bumper Saturday crowd would have no cricket to watch. That duly happened, with Warne (4 for 22) and fellow spinner Shaun Udal (3 for 35) skittling Durham again for 93 to clinch victory by an innings and 164 runs.

Tremendous batting by Aftab Habib and hostile bowling by James Ormond spearheaded Leicestershire's ten-wicket win over Derbyshire at Leicester – a result that put them into second place behind Yorkshire. Habib's 164, out of a Leicestershire first-innings total of 310, was described by Jack Birkenshaw, the county's cricket manager, as 'the best innings he has ever played', while Ormond's 6 for 50 destroyed the Derbyshire reply. Bowled out for 133, Derbyshire were asked to follow on and, by the close of the second day, were already down and out at 116 for 5. Anil Kumble did much to undermine the Derbyshire second innings and only Matt Cassar and Steve Titchard resisted for long. Vince Wells ended with 4 for 58 and Trevor Ward then breezed Leicestershire past their small victory target.

Division Two
14, 15, 16 and 17 June
at Lord's
Nottinghamshire 265 (102.2 overs)(JE Morris 67, PCR Tufnell 4 for 56) and 293 for 6 dec. (U Afzaal 127)
Middlesex 166 (53.4 overs)(JL Langer 96, PJ Franks 7 for 56) and 223 (JL Langer 104, AJ Harris 5 for 34)
Nottinghamshire won by 169 runs
Nottinghamshire 17 pts, Middlesex 3 pts

at Northampton
Warwickshire 568 for 9 dec. (DP Ostler 145, MJ Powell 145, G Welch 55, A L Penberthy 5 for 54)
Northamptonshire 266 (83.5 overs)(MB Loye 93, AF Giles 4 for 45) and (following on) 249 (AS Rollins 76, GP Swann 72, AF Giles 8 for 90)
Warwickshire won by an innings and 53 runs
Warwickshire 20 pts, Northamptonshire 4 pts

15 and 16 June
at Worcester
Worcestershire 230 (65.4 overs)(RC Driver 64, DA Leatherdale 56) and 110 (JD Lewry 5 for 29)
Sussex 277 (78.2 overs)(PA Cottey 76, CJ Adams 55) and 64 for 2
Sussex won by eight wickets
Sussex 17 pts, Worcestershire 4 pts

15, 16, 17 and 18 June
at Cardiff
Essex 410 for 7 dec. (203 overs)(RC Irani 168*, PJ Prichard 59, TJ Mason 52*) and 102 (SL Watkin 6 for 26)
Glamorgan 263 for 8 dec. (MP Maynard 98, AD Shaw 80*) and 177 for 5 (MTG Elliott 52)
Match drawn
Glamorgan 8 pts, Essex 8 pts

The left-arm spin of Ashley Giles propelled Warwickshire to an innings-and-53-run thrashing of Northamptonshire at Wantage Road. Giles took 4 for 45 in Northants' first-innings 266, and then a career-best 8 for 90 from 44 overs as the home side could muster only 249 second time around. Neil Smith lent faithful support, but Giles used his height and effective quicker ball to extract extra bounce from a surface that was otherwise blameless. Warwickshire began the match by batting for the best part of two days, running up 568 for 9 declared after 145 from both Michael Powell and Dominic Ostler. Tony Penberthy's 5 for 54 contained, remarkably amid the carnage, a spell of 5 for 5 in 35 balls! Powell and Ostler put on 306 and Warwickshire's total was their highest ever against Northants and their third score above 500 this season. Mal Loye was the only batsman to shape up in the Northants first innings and, on the final day, Adrian Rollins could add only five more to his overnight 71 not out. Graeme Swann merely delayed the inevitable by hitting sixes off successive balls from Giles, following a straight six off Smith, in his 72.

Warwickshire's great rivals, Worcestershire, meanwhile, slipped to a humbling eight-wicket defeat against Sussex on their home ground at New Road. Despite a career-best 64 from Ryan Driver, and 56 from David Leatherdale, Worcestershire managed only 230 in overcast conditions on day one. Chris Adams then seized the initiative for Sussex, including a six and 11 fours in his run-a-ball 55 as the visitors replied with 144 for 3 in just 38 overs before the close. Tony Cottey's 76 then earned Sussex a 47-run first-innings lead, and that looked riches indeed when Jason Lewry and Billy Taylor skittled Worcestershire for a second-innings 110. Elliott Wilson top-scored with just 36 and Lewry's 5 for 29 left Sussex with a comparatively simple task. Victory was achieved, in a rush of strokes, before the second day was done.

Middlesex captain Justin Langer could not conceal his disgust at another terrible batting performance by his side as Nottinghamshire grabbed a thumping 169-run victory at Lord's. Langer, the Australian left-hander, scored 96 in Middlesex's first-innings slump to 166 and then, in the second innings, made 104 out of 223 with two sixes and 13 fours before being eighth out. On the opening day, as Nottinghamshire reached 218 for 6 in the 82 overs possible, Phil Tufnell had claimed his 900th first-class wicket (Guy Welton) and the former England slow left-armer went on to take 4 for 56 from 36 overs as the visitors totalled 265. The Notts victory, however, was set up first by Paul Franks – who finished with 7 for 56 in the Middlesex first innings – and then Usman Afzaal, whose patient five-and-a-half-hour 127, allied to Chris Read's 56 not out, enabled

MIDDLESEX CCC

Home Ground:
Lord's Cricket Ground
Address:
Lord's Cricket Ground,
St John's Wood, London NW8 8QN
Tel: 020 7289 1300
Fax: 020 7289 5831
Email: enquiries.middx@ecb.co.uk
Directions:
By underground: St John's Wood on Jubilee Line
(five minutes' walk).
By bus: 13, 82, 113 stop along east side of
ground; 139 at south-west corner; 274 at top
of Regent's Park
Capacity: 28,000
Other grounds used: Southgate; Richmond
Year formed: 1864

Chairman: Phil Edmonds
Secretary: Vinny Codrington
Captain: Justin Langer
County colours: Navy

HONOURS

COUNTY CHAMPIONSHIP
1903, 1920, 1921, 1947,
1949 (JOINT), 1976, 1977 (JOINT),
1980, 1982, 1985, 1990, 1993
SUNDAY LEAGUE
1992
BENSON & HEDGES CUP
1983, 1986
GILLETTE CUP/NATWEST TROPHY
1977, 1980, 1984, 1988

CGU National Cricket League nickname:
MIDDLESEX CRUSADERS

crusaders

Website:
www.middlesexccc.co.uk

Notts to declare their second innings on 293 for 6. Andy Harris (5 for 34) and Richard Stemp cleaned up around Langer.

Glamorgan almost won a memorable victory at Cardiff, which Welsh fans would have seen as natural justice after what they perceived to be Essex go-slow tactics on the first couple of days. Ronnie Irani, the Essex captain, batted for nine hours and 20 minutes and faced 479 balls in making a career-best unbeaten 168 and, with Tim Mason taking 220 balls over his 52 not out, Essex declared only on 410 for 7 after 203 overs. In the 45 minutes available before the close of the second day, Glamorgan made 47 for 1 and, despite sliding to 72 for 6 the next morning, rallied through Matthew Maynard and Adrian Shaw to throw down the gauntlet by declaring at 263 for 8. Maynard's brilliant 98 contained a six and 11 fours and he and Shaw, who remained 80 not out, added 135. Then, on a slow and low pitch, Steve Watkin turned in one of the bowling performances of the season to take 6 for 26 in 14.2 overs to send Essex tumbling to 102 all out. Suddenly, on the final day, the match was alive again with Glamorgan needing 250 from a minimum of 68 overs. To the frustration of the home supporters, and to most neutrals, the sluggish pitch had the final say. Matthew Elliott hit 52, and Maynard 44, but once they were gone it would have been impossible for Glamorgan to have sustained a run chase in the conditions and, after 66 overs, the draw was agreed at 177 for 5. Essex won few friends in this match, which underlined another negative by-product of the split into two divisions.

ROUND NINE: 28 JUNE–2 JULY 2000

Division One
28, 29 and 30 June
at Feethams, Darlington
Derbyshire 151 (49 overs)(MM Betts 7 for 30) and 249 (SP Titchard 87*, MP Dowman 61, TA Munton 52, SJE Brown 6 for 40)
Durham 479 for 9 dec. (SM Katich 114, PD Collingwood 111, NJ Speak 78, MM Betts 55)
Durham won by an innings and 79 runs
Durham 20 pts, Derbyshire 2 pts

Mal Loye made a defiant 93, but could not prevent Northants losing to Warwickshire in Round Eight.

at Maidstone
Somerset 475 (154.4 overs)(PD Bowler 108,
ME Trescothick 90, ID Blackwell 69)
Kent 261 (106.4 overs)(R Dravid 88, RWT Key 51) and
(following on) 338 for 3 (DP Fulton 115, R Dravid 95,
AP Wells 60*, RWT Key 54)
Match drawn
Kent 8 pts, Somerset 11 pts

29, 30 June, 1 and 2 July
at Southampton
Surrey 331 (99.2 overs)(AD Brown 71, MP Bicknell 56*,
AD Mullally 6 for 75) and 228 for 6 dec. (MA Butcher
116*, SK Warne 5 for 90)
Hampshire 167 (63.3 overs)(Saqlain Mushtaq 6 for 51)
and 272 (GW White 73, AN Aymes 50)
Surrey won by 120 runs
Surrey 18 pts, Hampshire 3 pts

at Old Trafford
Yorkshire 164 (59.2 overs)(RJ Blakey 56) and 151
Lancashire 269 (85.4 overs)(WK Hegg 58) and 47 for 1
Lancashire won by nine wickets
Lancashire 17 pts, Yorkshire 3 pts

Bobby Simpson, the Lancashire coach, claimed his
side were on the march towards a first outright
championship title for 66 years after seeing off
Yorkshire by nine wickets at Old Trafford and
earning themselves a third successive Roses Match
victory for the first time since 1893. Moreover, the
17 points Lancashire won took them to within two
of leaders Yorkshire at the top of the first-division
table. Only Richard Blakey (56) put up much of a
fight on the opening day as Glen Chapple, with 4
for 27, helped to bowl out Yorkshire for just 164.
Saurav Ganguly and Graham Lloyd led the reply as
Lancashire got almost beyond their opponents'
score by the close, and on the second morning
Warren Hegg's 58 was chiefly responsible for a first-
innings lead of 105. Once the Lancashire spinners
got to work the game was up for Yorkshire, who,
despite reaching 65 for 1, then fell away to 130 for 7
by the end of the day and 151 all out early on the
third morning. Slow left-armer Gary Keedy,
ironically born in Yorkshire and on his native
county's staff until six years earlier, was the main
destroyer with 4 for 47.

Surrey, however, served notice of their intent to
defend their county title strongly, overturning
Hampshire by 120 runs at Southampton to move
into third place. Saqlain Mushtaq and Ian Salisbury,
the most potent spin partnership in the county

game, spearheaded the Surrey effort after the
champions had given themselves a solid platform
with a first-innings total of 331 on the opening day.
Alistair Brown hit 71, Martin Bicknell a valuable 56
not out but Graham Thorpe played his part, too, by
dealing impressively with the threat of Shane Warne
during his 74-ball 44. Alan Mullally was
Hampshire's most successful bowler with 6 for 75,
but Saqlain then responded with 6 for 51 as the
home side were tumbled out for just 167 in reply.
Surrey declined to enforce the follow-on, preferring
to put up their feet in the dressing room while
opener Mark Butcher reached 116 not out and led a
second-innings surge to 228 for 6 declared. Warne
took 5 for 90, but it was Saqlain and Salisbury who
held the upper hand as they steadily worked their
way through the Hampshire batting. Nine wickets
were down by the close of the third day and, 14
balls into the final morning, it was all over with
Hampshire dismissed for 272 and both Surrey
spinners finishing with 4 for 84.

Durham's chances of staying in the top division
were improved by a thumping innings and 79-run
victory against Derbyshire, themselves one of the
favourites for the drop. Melvyn Betts kicked them
off towards the win by taking a magnificent 7 for 30
on day one as Derbyshire were shot out for 151.
Betts bowled with sustained hostility and now has
three of Durham's four best bowling performances
since their elevation into first-class cricket in 1992.
Tim Munton tried all he knew to limit Durham's
reply, taking 2 for 30 in an 18-over new-ball spell in
the day's final session, but Durham converted their
overnight 88 for 2 into a mammoth 479 for 9 on the
second day. Simon Katich, the Australian left-
hander, hit 114 and Paul Collingwood an excellent
111 as the pair put on 157 for the third wicket and,
after Nick Speak had scored 78, Betts had fun with
the bat, too, as he swung his way to 55. Simon
Brown then took 6 for 40 as Derbyshire were
bowled out again for 249, with Betts adding 3 for 58
to his first-innings effort. Only an eighth-wicket
stand of 81 between Steve Titchard (87 not out) and
Munton (52) held up Durham for long.

Kent's battle for a draw against Somerset at
Maidstone probably hinged on one moment deep
into the third day. Following on after being bowled
out for a disappointing 261 in reply to Somerset's
first-innings 475, opener David Fulton was dropped
on four when he offered a simple catch to Michael
Burns at square leg off Steffan Jones. By the close,
Kent were 124 without loss and Fulton, up till then
enduring a wretched season, had moved to 65 not

out. On the final day Fulton went on to reach 115 and with Rob Key making 54, Rahul Dravid 95 and Alan Wells an unbeaten 60, Kent were able to cruise to 338 for 3 on a still-true pitch. A 90-minute rain delay on that last day did not help Somerset's cause either, and the visitors left the Mote a frustrated team. Peter Bowler's 108, Marcus Trescothick's 90 and a belligerent 69 from Ian Blackwell had enabled them to dominate the first two days and then only Key (51) and Dravid, his 88 full of wonderful wristy strokes, had held them up in Kent's reply.

Division Two
28, 29, 30 June and 1 July
at Chelmsford
Middlesex 222 (78 overs)(KP Dutch 55, PM Such 5 for 51) and 293 (KP Dutch 91, RL Johnson 69, PM Such 7 for 167)
Essex 136 (84 overs)(SD Peters 54*) and 142 (KP Dutch 6 for 62)
Middlesex won by 237 runs
Middlesex 16 pts, Essex 3 pts

at Swansea
Glamorgan 218 (87.5 overs)(MTG Elliott 62) and 311 (MJ Powell 70, A Dale 66, MTG Elliott 57)
Worcestershire 196 (70.5 overs)(DA Leatherdale 59*, SD Thomas 5 for 72) and 252 (DA Leatherdale 50)
Glamorgan won by 81 runs
Glamorgan 16 pts, Worcestershire 3 pts

at Edgbaston
Gloucestershire 350 (116.5 overs)(KJ Barnett 106, RC Russell 70) and 232 for 7 (DR Hewson 58, MGN Windows 56)
Warwickshire 233 (83.3 overs)(MJ Powell 96, NMK Smith 58*, BW Gannon 5 for 58) and 108 for 2 (MA Wagh 52*)
Match drawn
Warwickshire 8 pts, Gloucestershire 11 pts

Glamorgan, the bottom club before this game, turned the form-book upside down by beating Division Two leaders Worcestershire by 81 runs at Swansea. Matthew Elliott made 62 on the opening day, and his battle with fellow Aussie Glenn McGrath was a real treat for spectators, but Glamorgan collapsed from 126 for 1 to 218 all out. Worcestershire's first-innings reply, however, fell short at 196 with Darren Thomas taking 5 for 72. By the halfway stage of the match, Glamorgan had forced themselves ahead on points, reaching 156 for 3 by the close of day two and going on to total 311

with Michael Powell's 70 and Adrian Dale's 66 building a solid structure on the foundations again laid by Elliott (57). Chasing the highest score of the match to win, Worcestershire were never in the hunt despite a second half-century for David Leatherdale, who added 50 to his first-innings 59. A seventh-wicket partnership of 70 between Stuart Lampitt and Richard Illingworth held up the Welsh county, but slow left-armer Dean Cosker finished with 4 for 82.

Middlesex were another team to begin to try to brush off an uncertain first half of the season with victory, Justin Langer's side overpowering Essex by 237 runs at Chelmsford in a game that was a real triumph for Keith Dutch, the off-spinning all-rounder rarely used in championship cricket. A first-innings 55 bolstered Middlesex, who otherwise fell away to 222 following an opening stand of 84 between Langer and Andrew Strauss. Then, after Angus Fraser and Phil Tufnell had combined to dismiss Essex for 136, Dutch hit a career-best 91 as Middlesex reached 293 in their second innings. Richard Johnson's hard-hitting 69 supported Dutch in a stand of 108 for the ninth wicket, and the pair at last put a dent in the figures of Peter Such who finished with 7 for 167 in addition to his first-innings 5 for 51. Dutch's final trick, though, was to complete his double of career-bests by taking 6 for 62 as Essex were swept away second time around for 142.

The new leaders of Division Two, however, following this round of games, were Warwickshire – who perhaps needed the assistance of bad weather on the final day to finish with a draw against Gloucestershire at Edgbaston. The visitors, after totalling 350 in their first innings thanks to Kim Barnett's 106 and fellow veteran Jack Russell's 70, won a lead of 117 despite a five-hour 96 from Michael Powell, who showed fine judgement throughout yet another promising display with the bat. Neil Smith, the captain, also ended up 58 not out, but Ben Gannon's 5 for 58 put Gloucestershire in command, and they built on their good lead by reaching 232 for 7 declared in their second innings with half-centuries from Dominic Hewson and Matt Windows. The start of the final day, however, was delayed by 90 minutes and after a mini-session of 33 balls another two-hour hold-up for rain left Gloucestershire with little chance of forcing victory. The last session of the game was fairly meaningless, with Warwickshire making sure of their four draw-points on 108 for 2.

Alastair Brown scored a superb 295 not out against Leicestershire at Oakham School as the holders returned to the top of the table.

Round Ten: 7–10 July 2000

Division One
7, 8 and 9 July
at Oakham School
Surrey 505 (148.5 overs)(AD Brown 295*, Saqlain Mushtaq 66)
Leicestershire 143 (57.2 overs) and (following on) 184 (DI Stevens 68, Saqlain Mushtaq 5 for 35, JN Batty 4ct/1st)
Surrey won by 178 runs
Surrey 20 pts, Leicestershire 3 pts

7, 8, 9 and 10 July
at Derby
Derbyshire 307 (106.4 overs)(SD Stubbings 64, TM Smith 53*, DG Cork 52) and 80 for 4
Lancashire 172 (61 overs)(DG Cork 6 for 41)

Match drawn – no play was possible on the fourth day
Derbyshire 10 pts, Lancashire 7 pts

at Headingley
Durham
314 (125.5 overs)(JJB Lewis 66, NJ Speak 61*, SM Katich 55, RJ Sidebottom 5 for 66)
Yorkshire 129 (60.4 overs) and 386 for 4 dec. (DS Lehmann 136, MP Vaughan 118)
Match drawn
Yorkshire 7 pts, Durham 10 pts

at Taunton
Hampshire 142 (41.1 overs) and 319 for 5 (WS Kendall 161, DA Kenway 54)
Somerset 368 (110.3 overs)(PCL Holloway 113, M Burns 56)
Match drawn – no play was possible on the fourth day
Somerset 11 pts, Hampshire 7 pts

Surrey moved to the top of the division table by annihilating Leicestershire by an innings and 178 runs at Oakham School, a venue that drew much praise for the quality of the pitch and the surroundings.

Alistair Brown certainly enjoyed the setting, compiling a brilliant, epic 295 not out in Surrey's first-innings total of 505. It beat his previous career-best, 265, and Brown was joined in a last-wicket partnership of 141 by Saqlain Mushtaq, who batted with some style to reach 66 and thoroughly demoralise the Leicestershire team. Indeed, Surrey's great depth of batting was underlined as Brown and the tail rallied their side from 190 for 7. Jimmy Ormond produced a fine new-ball spell, but after that it was Brown who dominated proceedings, moving remorselessly to 200 from 257 balls and ending the first day on 211 not out. That opening day was watched by a good crowd, including 80-year-old guest of honour George Dawkes, a former Leicestershire wicketkeeper and the only known survivor of the previous championship match played on the ground, back in 1938. The previous best score made in Rutland, Percy Chapman's 252 for Uppingham School in 1918, was soon eclipsed on the second day as Brown faced in all 392 balls, in 517 minutes, and hit a six and 32 fours. By tea Leicestershire, in reply, were a pathetic 51 for 7 – and although they made it to 143 the follow-on was as inevitable as the final result. Only Darren Stevens (68) made any real impression in Leicestershire's second-innings 184, and Saqlain (5 for 35) quickly finished things off by claiming the last three wickets in ten balls.

NORTHAMPTONSHIRE CCC

Home Ground:
Northampton
Address:
The County Ground, Wantage Road,
Northampton NN1 4TJ
Tel: 01604 514455
Fax: 01604 514488
Email: post@nccc.co.uk (general enquiries) or
commercial@nccc.co.uk (commercial enquiries)
Directions:
By rail: Castle Station, three miles.
By road: M1 to J15, A508 and follow RAC signs.
RAC signs from all other areas. Parking on ground when
space permits otherwise ample local street parking.
By coach: regular service from Greyfriars coach station.
Capacity: 4,250
Other grounds used: Campbell Park, Milton Keynes.
Year formed: 1878

Chairman: Lynn Wilson
Chief Executive: Stephen Coverdale
Director of Excellence: David Capel
Director of Cricket: Bob Carter
Captain: Matthew Hayden
Vice-captain: David Ripley
Coaching contact: Ian Lucas 01604 632917
County colours: Claret and gold

HONOURS

BENSON & HEDGES CUP
1980
GILLETTE CUP/NATWEST TROPHY
1976, 1992

**CGU National Cricket League
nickname:**
STEELBACKS

Website:
www.nccc.co.uk

Superb batting on the final two days at
Headingley by Michael Vaughan and Darren
Lehmann enabled second-placed Yorkshire to
emerge with a draw after following on against
Durham. The home side had folded to 129 all out in
reply to Durham's 314, a total launched by the
county's highest first-wicket stand of the season, 60,
between Michael Gough and Jon Lewis. Lewis,
Simon Katich and Nick Speak all hit half-centuries,
but Yorkshire then fought back on a third day cut
short by 45 overs by rain. Vaughan, 94 not out
overnight in a total of 149 for 1, looked an England
opener in the making as he reached 118, while
Lehmann, the Australian left-hander, clubbed 136
with 18 fours despite, on 40, calling for a runner
because of a back strain!

Fourth-day wash-outs ruined potentially good
finishes in the other two first-division games, at
Derby and Taunton.

Hampshire, largely through Will Kendall's 161 –
the county's first championship hundred of the
season – had fought back strongly against Somerset
after losing an important toss and being bowled out
for a first-innings 142 in bowler-friendly conditions.
Somerset had replied with 386 with Piran Holloway,
missed badly at 55 by John Stephenson, going on to
hit his first championship ton for almost 12 months.
But Hampshire rallied on the second evening
through Kendall and Robin Smith and, although
only 44 overs were possible on day three, the visitors
continued to flourish. The weather, though, wrecked
any Hampshire hopes of Shane Warne bowling out
Somerset on the final afternoon.

Derbyshire were particularly miffed at their last-day
wash-out at the Racecourse Ground, especially as the
third day had provided just an hour's action. All that,
too, after Dominic Cork had starred with both bat
and ball to leave Lancashire right up against it.
First, Cork struck a sparky 52 from 86 balls as, with
Steve Stubbings and Trevor Smith also hitting half-
centuries, Derbyshire totalled 307. Then, beginning
with the prized wicket of Mike Atherton for a duck,
Cork tore into the Lancashire batting and, with 6 for
41, left them well adrift on first innings at 172 all out.

Division Two
7, 8, 9 July
Glamorgan 234 (73.2 overs)(AG Wharf 101*) and 255
(SP James 62, A Dale 53)
Northamptonshire 167 (62.4 overs) and 178
(DJG Sales 61)
Glamorgan won by 144 runs
Glamorgan 16 pts, Northamptonshire 3 pts

at John Walker's Ground, Southgate
Middlesex 303 (108.2 overs)(MR Ramprakash 101,
AJ Strauss 90, MJ Rawnsley 5 for 125)
Worcestershire 141 (83.1 overs) and 95 for 5
Match drawn
Middlesex 10 pts, Worcestershire 7 pts

at Trent Bridge
Essex 505 for 9 dec. (146 overs)(SG Law 165,
AP Grayson 144, DR Law 68*, AJ Harris 5 for 139)
Nottinghamshire 180 for 5 (59.3 overs)(U Afzaal 65*,
DJ Bicknell 64)
Match drawn – no play was possible on the fourth day
Nottinghamshire 6 pts, Essex 10 pts

at Edgbaston
Warwickshire 252 (84 overs)(AF Giles 98, NMK Smith
87, JD Lewry 6 for 66) and 165 for 2 (MJ Powell 70*,
DP Ostler 66*)
Sussex 158 (71.5 overs)(AF Giles 6 for 58)
Match drawn – no play was possible on the fourth day

A 144-run defeat at home to Glamorgan condemned
Northamptonshire to remain rock bottom of the
championship. It was their third successive beating
and, if the loss to Oxford University was added,
their fourth first-class defeat on the trot. Alex Wharf
was their first tormentor in this match, hitting his
maiden championship century and finishing 101 not
out in Glamorgan's 234. Wharf struck 16
boundaries and rallied his team from 77 for 6. In
reply, however, Northants were soon 78 for 6
themselves and, by the close of an eventful opening
day, 85 for 7. There was a partial recovery to 167, but
half-centuries from Steve James and Adrian Dale
kept Glamorgan on top and, in their second-innings
178, only David Sales (61) delayed the Welsh county
for long. Steve Watkin took 3 for 31 before limping
off with a hamstring strain just one wicket short of
his 800 in first-class cricket.

Middlesex were cruelly denied a certain victory at
Southgate when rain arrived six overs after lunch on
the final day with Worcestershire 95 for 5 in their
second innings and Phil Tufnell, with seven wickets
already to his name in the match, tying their
batsmen up in knots. But at least the match saw
Mark Ramprakash, back in his rightful place at
number four after England's ridiculous attempt to
turn him into a Test batsman, return to form with a
chanceless 101 – his first hundred of the summer.
Andrew Strauss, the opener, also impressed with 90
as Middlesex made 303. Worcestershire were then
reduced to 111 for 8 by the close of the second day.

However, although Tufnell wrapped up their innings for 141 with 4 for 48, less than 21 overs of play were possible on the third day as un-July-like weather shrouded the country.

Warwickshire were another county to feel aggrieved by the unseasonable rain, being well on the way to disposing of Sussex at Edgbaston before the loss of 72 overs on the third day and a total wash-out on the fourth. Ashley Giles and Neil Smith dominated what play there was, hitting 98 and 87 respectively to haul Warwickshire up from 39 for 6 to 252 all out and then combining with the ball to shoot out Sussex for 158 in reply. Giles' 6 for 58 was then followed by some positive batting from Michael Powell and the in-form Dominic Ostler, before the bad weather set in.

A similar weather pattern wrecked the match at Trent Bridge, in which Essex ran up a mammoth 505 for 9 declared and Nottinghamshire replied with 180 for 5 before 69 overs were lost on day three and the fourth day was washed out. Stuart Law, who thumped eight first-class hundreds in 1999, rediscovered much of his misplaced form by hitting 165 – only his second championship century of the season – and Paul Grayson anchored the innings with a solid 144. Danny Law's 68 was the most aggressive innings of the game, including three sixes and seven fours, but Darren Bicknell and Usman Afzaal also batted well for the home side before the rain came.

ROUND ELEVEN: 12–15 JULY 2000

Division One
12, 13 and 14 July
at Leicester
Leicestershire 222 (94.4 overs)(BF Smith 111*, J Wood 5 for 60) and 259 (DL Maddy 77, Aftab Habib 52, SJE Brown 5 for 70)
Durham 171 (71.1 overs) and 93 (J Ormond 5 for 34)
Leicestershire won by 217 runs
Leicestershire 16 pts, Durham 3 pts

12, 13, 14 and 15 July
at Derby
Derbyshire 181 (81.5 overs)(SD Stubbings 72, DG Cork 58) and 269 (SP Titchard 74, MM Patel 6 for 77)
Kent 280 (116 overs)(RWT Key 83, R Dravid 55, TA Munton 6 for 54) and 171 for 2 (DP Fulton 66*)
Kent won by eight wickets
Kent 17 pts, Derbyshire 3 pts

at Taunton
Lancashire 239 (65.5 overs)(MA Atherton 113, KA Parsons 5 for 13) and 417 for 9 (JP Crawley 120, SC Ganguly 99, MA Atherton 58)
Somerset 565 (177 overs)(J Cox 171, M Burns 108, PD Bowler 95, RJ Turner 75)
Match drawn
Somerset 11 pts, Lancashire 7 pts

at Kennington Oval
Surrey 226 (81.5 overs)(RJ Sidebottom 5 for 40) and 345 for 8 dec. (AD Brown 140*, N Shahid 80)
Yorkshire 242 (86.4 overs)(MP Vaughan 80, DS Lehmann 55, Saqlain Mushtaq 6 for 63) and 126 (Saqlain Mushtaq 5 for 41)
Surrey won by 203 runs
Surrey 16 pts, Yorkshire 4 pts

Matthew Elliott enjoyed his first taste of county cricket with Glamorgan. He averaged 54 in the championship, with four centuries, and 47 in the National League.

NOTTINGHAMSHIRE CCC

Home Ground:
Trent Bridge
Address:
Trent Bridge,
Nottingham NG2 6AG
Tel: 0115 982 3000
Fax: 0115 945 5730
Ticket line: 0870 168 88 88
Email: administration.notts@ecb.co.uk
Alternative website: www.nottsccc.co.uk
Directions:
By road: Follow signs from Ring Road, towards
city centre.
Capacity: 14,500 (16,000 during Test Matches/ODIs)
Other grounds used: Worksop
Year formed: 1841

Chief Executive: David Collier
Cricket Manager: Clive Rice
Other posts: Head Groundsman: Steve Birks Sales;
Marketing Manager: Lisa Pursehouse
Captain: Jason Gallian
County colours: Green and gold

HONOURS

COUNTY CHAMPIONSHIP
1907, 1929, 1981, 1987
SUNDAY LEAGUE
1991
BENSON & HEDGES CUP
1989
GILLETTE CUP/NAT WEST TROPHY
1987

CGU National Cricket League
nickname:
NOTTS OUTLAWS

Website:
www.trentbridge.co.uk

NOTTS
OUTLAWS

SOMERSET CCC

Home Ground:
Taunton
Address:
The Clerical Medical County Ground,
Taunton,
Somerset TA1 1JT
Tel: 01823 272 946
Fax: 01823 332 395
Centre of Cricketing Excellence: 01823 352266
Email: somerset@ecb.co.uk
Directions:
By road: M5 junction 25. Follow A358 to town centre.
Signposted from there.
Other grounds used: None
Year formed: 1875

Chief Executive: Peter Anderson
First XI Coach: Kevin Shine
Captain: Jamie Cox
Other posts: Head Groundsman: Phil Frost; Second
XI Coach: Julian Wyatt
County colours: Black, white and maroon

HONOURS

SUNDAY LEAGUE
1979
BENSON & HEDGES CUP
1981, 1982
GILLETTE CUP/NATWEST TROPHY
1979, 1983

CGU National Cricket League nickname:
SOMERSET SABRES

unofficial **Website:**
www.somersetcountycricket.co.uk

JULY DIARY   by Robin Martin-Jenkins

The pitch at Hove has come under scrutiny after we recently played New Zealand 'A' and only four wickets were taken by seamers in the whole game. To get anything out of it as a seam bowler, you really have to work your socks off, or have a bit of luck (or preferably both). I'd far rather see wickets like ours than some of the atrocious surfaces we sometimes have to play on around the country, but there should be a balance and I feel that it has tipped too much in favour of the batsmen in recent years. It was no coincidence that the crowd got smaller each day and we mustn't forget that cricket is an arm of the entertainment business and as such should be as entertaining as possible. Despite the increasing demand for one-day cricket, there are many spectators who prefer to watch first-class cricket. However, they like to see an even contest between bat and ball where boundaries are hit and stumps are shattered. Time to re-lay a few strips I would suggest.

I was lucky enough to have a substantial and extremely enjoyable partnership with Michael Bevan in the recent championship match at Arundel. He seems completely unfazed by anyone and anything on the pitch and his composed demeanour can't help but rub off on you when you are batting with him. At one stage, when he had scored about 80, Mark Ilott was bowling a tight spell and was landing the ball more or less in the right spot every ball. At our between-over conference we discussed how we were going to score off him. Bev remarked; 'He's putting the ball in the same spot all the time, so if he's still bowling when I'm on 94 I'll run down the wicket and hit him over mid-off for six to get my hundred'. I laughed and looked down at him expecting to see him smiling at his joke. He was looking at me with not even a glint of humour in his eye. I realised that he wasn't joking at all; he really would do it. To have that confidence in your ability is a prerequisite of top international cricketers. As it happened Ilott came off after the next over and Bev had to make do with making the required runs off some other poor soul. Ilott probably never knew how lucky he was!

Surrey moved 16 points clear at the top of the championship tree with a resounding 203-run win against near rivals Yorkshire at the Oval. The visitors actually won themselves a first-innings lead, after dismissing Surrey for 226 through the efforts of Ryan Sidebottom (5 for 40) and Matthew Hoggard (4 for 70), but from 158 for 2 they were desperately disappointed to fall away to 242 all out following a stand of 94 between Michael Vaughan (80) and Darren Lehmann (55). The left-handed Lehmann was at first brutally dismissive of Ian Salisbury's leg-breaks but the bowler got him eventually and, at the other end, Saqlain Mushtaq employed his sorcery to great effect with 6 for 63. Martin Bicknell, meanwhile, took the only wicket that didn't fall to spin to complete 800 first-class scalps. Surrey, after this fightback in the field, were soon in control with Nadeem Shahid playing well for 80 and Alistair Brown living up to his nickname 'Lord' with a majestic 140 not out. Brown drove James Middlebrook contemptuously for six to reach a 106-ball hundred and when the declaration came at 345 for 8 the scene was set for Saqlain and Salisbury. Bicknell, as is his wont, nipped in with both openers before Saqlain (5 for 41) and Salisbury (3 for 36) sent Yorkshire sliding to 126 all out.

Kent hauled themselves off the bottom of Division One by beating Derbyshire by eight wickets at Derby. Martin Saggers took a championship-best 4 for 62 as Derbyshire were dismissed for a pitiful 181 on day one, and despite the best efforts of Tim Munton (6 for 54) Kent built a 99-run first-innings lead thanks to solid contributions from Robert Key (83), Rahul Dravid (55) and Matthew Fleming (47). The home side battled better second time around, Steve Titchard leading the way with 74, but Min Patel patiently chipped away at the Derbyshire batting and a burst of three wickets in four balls helped him to 6 for 77. Derbyshire's 269 all out left Kent with a seemingly awkward target, especially with Dravid nursing a dislocated finger. But David Fulton hit an unbeaten 66 and, with Matthew Walker scoring 41 not out, they eased themselves comfortably over the finishing line.

Leicestershire saw off Durham by 217 runs at Grace Road to keep up their championship challenge, but even home officials admitted afterwards that they were fortunate to escape pitch censure after problems with preparation produced a surface with erratic bounce and which the umpires reportedly marked 'below average'. Ben Smith's unbeaten 111 rallied Leicestershire from 37 for 4 to 222 all out on the first day, and then Anil Kumble and James Ormond combined to dismiss Durham for 171. In front of a watching Phil Sharpe, one of the ECB's pitch police, Leicestershire now reached 259 with Darren Maddy (77) and Aftab Habib (52) responding to a slide to 25 for 3 with a stand of 100 for the fourth wicket. By the end of the third day, however, the match was all over, with Durham bowled out for 93 and with only Simon Katich and John Wood reaching double figures.

At Taunton, by contrast, bat was mostly on top of ball, and Somerset, despite bowling out Lancashire on the opening day for 239 – after the visitors had been 216 for 4 with Mike Atherton hitting 113 – and then reaching a massive 565 themselves, could not force victory. In the Lancashire first innings, a combination of sloppy batting and inspired medium pace from Keith Parsons (a career-best 5 for 13 from 7.5 overs) had caused their collapse. But, second time around, John Crawley hit 120 and Saurav Ganguly 99 from 119 balls as Lancashire batted out time on 417 for 9. Atherton, who during his first-innings hundred had once hooked Steffan Jones into the car park, added 58 to put behind him a run of poor championship form that had brought him just 47 runs in five previous innings. The Somerset total was built around two big partnerships: first 199 in 64 overs between Jamie Cox, who hit a six and 19 fours in his 171, and Peter Bowler (95), and then a 166-run seventh-wicket alliance between Michael Burns (108) and Rob Turner (75).

Division Two
12, 13 and 14 July
at Cheltenham
Northamptonshire 543 (154.3 overs)(JW Cook 137, DJG Sales 76, ML Hayden 75, AS Rollins 63)
Gloucestershire 116 (59.1 overs) and (following on) 328 (RC Russell 110*, DR Hewson 57, IJ Harvey 52, GP Swann 6 for 118)
Northamptonshire won by an innings and 99 runs
Northamptonshire 20 pts, Gloucestershire 2 pts

at John Walker's Ground, Southgate
Middlesex 164 (57.1 overs)(MR Ramprakash 83) and 374 (AJ Strauss 73, JL Langer 61, A Dale 5 for 25)
Glamorgan 232 (77.2 overs)(A Dale 81) and 307 for 8 (MTG Elliott 127)
Glamorgan won by two wickets
Glamorgan 16 pts, Middlesex 3 pts
Middlesex had eight points deducted from their season's total because the pitch was deemed unfit for first-class cricket. Seventeen wickets fell on the first day.

at Arundel Castle
Sussex 265 (86.4 overs)(RSC Martin-Jenkins 86, PA Cottey 83) and 321 for 8 dec. (MG Bevan 151*, CJ Adams 53)
Essex 277 (107 overs)(DDJ Robinson 61, RJ Kirtley 6 for 85) and 254 for 7 (PJ Prichard 66, DDJ Robinson 65)
Match drawn
Sussex 9 pts, Essex 9 pts

at Worcester
Worcestershire 284 (122.4 overs)(EJ Wilson 102, PR Pollard 53, WPC Weston 52) and 431 (SJ Rhodes 103, PR Pollard 74, GD McGrath 55, Kabir Ali 50*, RD Stemp 5 for 123)
Nottinghamshire 358 (104.2 overs)(U Afzaal 86, CMW Read 50) and 24 for 0
Match drawn
Worcestershire 9 pts, Nottinghamshire 11 pts

Glamorgan won an astonishing match at Southgate, pipping Middlesex by two wickets late on the final day after being set more than 300 on a pitch condemned two days earlier by Mike Denness, the ECB's chief pitch officer. Alan Fordham, the Board's cricket operations manager, had been summoned by Denness to Southgate after 17 wickets tumbled on the opening day – ten of them leg before. The result was an eight-point penalty, despite Middlesex's pleas of mitigating circumstances, and the fact that they had rung Lord's on the day before the match to warn them that the pitch would be starting damp following a decision to play through rain during a previous game. By the close of that eventful first day Glamorgan were 144 for 7 in reply to Middlesex's 164, a total almost entirely due to a brilliant innings of great skill against the moving ball by Mark Ramprakash (83). Adrian Dale, 42 not out overnight, went on to 81 as Glamorgan earned themselves a useful lead, but by now the pitch had dried out and its true character was revealed. Middlesex, announcing that they were to appeal against the penalty, and livid at being punished for what they saw as being honest, responded by totalling 374. Andrew Strauss and Justin Langer hit fine half-centuries, and Glamorgan were further frustrated by a ninth-wicket stand of 74 between Richard Johnson and Angus Fraser. Dale's 5 for 25, meanwhile, was his best bowling return for seven years, but it took a magnificent 127 from Australian opener Matthew Elliott, scored off 214 balls, to propel Glamorgan towards their distant victory target. In the end, what a game, and – a week later – a happy ending all round as Middlesex's appeal was successful.

Northamptonshire did to Gloucestershire at Cheltenham what the home county had inflicted on many visitors themselves down the years – batting first to post a massive total, and then spinning their opponents to defeat on an increasingly turning pitch. Jeff Cook, a tall left-hander born and bred in Sydney but who settled in England seven years ago, marked only his second championship appearance by hitting 137 and, with David Sales, Matthew Hayden and Adrian Rollins all weighing in with significant contributions, Northants ran up an intimidating 543. Darren Cousins then struck several early blows with the new ball, and Gloucestershire never recovered. All out for 116, with only young Chris Taylor resisting, they were soon following on. Jack Russell, cussed to the last, remained 110 not out off 321 balls. But Gloucestershire, despite reaching 328 second time around, still lost by an innings and 99 runs.

Worcestershire fought back defiantly to earn a draw with Nottinghamshire at New Road, Steve Rhodes leading the resistance with a second-innings 103 and Kabir Ali (50 not out) and Glenn McGrath, his 55 a maiden first-class fifty, setting the seal on it with a last-wicket stand of 103. Paul Pollard passed 50 twice against his old county, and Elliott Wilson compiled a first-innings 102, but Notts held the upper hand after bowling out the home side for 284 early on the second day and then totalling 358 with Usman Afzaal continuing his fine mid-season form with 86. Worcestershire, however, then hit back with 431 to prevent Notts from leaping to the top of the congested and hard-fought second-division table.

There was a draw, too, between Sussex and Essex at Arundel but not until after an engrossing, tight, four-day struggle that provided further evidence that it is the county out-grounds (such as Oakham, Horsham, Bath and Maidstone), and not the established headquarters (such as Headingley, Worcester, Bristol and Derby) that are increasingly staging proper four-day cricket. A fifth-wicket stand of 150 in 38 overs between Tony Cottey (83) and Robin Martin-Jenkins (86) was the feature of the opening day, and honours were even when James Kirtley, with a season's-best 6 for 85, helped to peg Essex back to 277 in reply and a lead of just 12 runs. The next day, however, belonged to Michael Bevan as the Australian cruised to 105 not out by the close and an unbeaten 151 overall. Essex, set 310, were briefly in the hunt before a clatter of wickets persuaded them to see out time on 254 for 7.

ROUND TWELVE: 19–22 JULY 2000

Division One
19, 20 and 21 July
at Guildford
Leicestershire 318 (108.1 overs)(BF Smith 102, MP Bicknell 7 for 72) and 87 (MP Bicknell 9 for 47)
Surrey 288 (81 overs)(IJ Ward 107, J Ormond 6 for 87) and 119 for 0 (IJ Ward 61*)
Surrey won by ten wickets
Surrey 17 pts, Leicestershire 6 pts

at Scarborough
Somerset 182 (61 overs) and 212 (PS Jones 56*, MJ Hoggard 5 for 50)
Yorkshire 400 (130.1 overs)(D Byas 84, DS Lehmann 77)
Yorkshire won by an innings and 6 runs
Yorkshire 20 pts, Somerset 3 pts

19, 20, 21 and 22 July 2000
at Portsmouth
Hampshire
320 (93.3 overs)(JS Laney 81, SK Warne 69) and 136 (GW White 80*, MM Patel 5 for 46)
Kent 252 (100.2 overs)(R Dravid 137) and 205 for 4 (R Dravid 73*, RWT Key 60)
Kent won by six wickets
Kent 17 pts, Hampshire 6 pts

at Old Trafford
Durham 370 (111.5 overs)(SM Katich 129, PD Collingwood 60) and 206 (G Keedy 6 for 56)
Lancashire 445 (140.1 overs)(JP Crawley 117, GD Lloyd 86, SC Ganguly 65, MA Atherton 64) and 132 for 4 (MA Atherton 64*)
Lancashire won by six wickets
Lancashire 20 pts, Durham 6 pts

Martin Bicknell was the undoubted star of this round of games, producing one of the great performances of the season as Surrey kept up their lead of division one by beating Leicestershire at Guildford. Lancashire, however, who also have a game in hand, gained three more points than Surrey from their victory over Durham and so cut Surrey's lead to 13 points.

Bicknell's heroics brought him match figures of 16 for 119 – including a remarkable second-innings haul of 9 for 47 – and Leicestershire's own championship challenge probably died with their sudden, astonishing second-innings batting collapse on the second evening. Until then, Leicestershire had even looked slightly on top after earning

SURREY CCC

Home Ground:
The Fosters' Oval
Address:
The Fosters' Oval, Kennington,
London SE11 5SS
Tel: 0207 582 6660
Fax: 0207 735 7769
Email: membership enquiries to
jblakesley@surreyccc.co.uk
Directions:
By rail: Vauxhall, SouthWest lines, five
minutes' walk away.
By underground: Northern Line, Oval Tube 100 yds
away; Victoria Line, Vauxhall is five minutes away.
By road: Situated on A202 near junction of A24 and A3
south of Vauxhall Bridge.
By bus: 36 and 185 from Victoria
Capacity: 16,500
Other grounds used: Guildford Cricket Club,
Woodbridge Road, Guildford.
Year formed: 1845

Chairman: Michael Soper
Chief Executive: Paul Sheldon
Captain: Adam Hollioake
Vice-captain: Mark Butcher
County colours: Brown and silver

HONOURS

COUNTY CHAMPIONSHIP
1890, 1891, 1892, 1894, 1895,
1899, 1914, 1952–1958, 1971,
1999, 2000
SUNDAY LEAGUE
1996
BENSON & HEDGES CUP
1974, 1997
GILLETTE CUP/NATWEST TROPHY
1982

CGU National Cricket League
nickname:
SURREY LIONS

Website:
www.surreyccc.co.uk

themselves a useful 30-run first-innings lead. Ben Smith's determined 102, with 15 fours, had boosted them to 318 despite Bicknell's superb 7 for 72, and then Jimmy Ormond – mixing pace with ever-improving off-spin – replied by taking 6 for 87 as Surrey were dismissed for 288 with only Ian Ward (107 in five and a quarter hours) and Nadeem Shahid (47) suggesting permanence. In 13.2 overs before the close, however, Leicestershire crashed to 33 for 6 as Bicknell, glorying in his home ground's hard and fast pitch, took 5 for 24 from seven destructive overs with the new ball. The next morning saw Bicknell grab four more wickets from another 35 balls, and Leicestershire's 87 all out left Surrey needing only 118 for victory. The in-form Ward (61 not out) made sure, in company with opening partner Mark Butcher (47 not out). Bicknell's 16 for 119 match analysis was the best in England since Jim Laker's famous haul of 19 for 90 for England against the Australians in the 1956 Old Trafford Test, and the best for Surrey since Laker's spin twin Tony Lock took 16 for 83 against Kent at Blackheath earlier in that same 1956 summer. The 31-year-old, so unfortunate not to have won more than two Test caps, had also achieved the best match figures by a fast-medium bowler since Cliff Gladwin's 16 for 84 for Derbyshire against Worcestershire at Stourbridge in 1952.

Lancashire had their spinners, Gary Keedy and Gary Yates, to thank for a maximum 20-point six-wicket victory over Durham at Old Trafford. The match, in fact, did not turn Lancashire's way until the third evening when Durham slipped to 123 for 6 in their second innings, with Keedy and Yates sharing the wickets to fall. The next morning, despite John Wood's 44, Durham were bowled out for 206 with Keedy finishing with 6 for 56 and off-spinner Yates 4 for 91. That left Lancashire requiring just 132 for victory and Mike Atherton, adding 64 not out to his first-innings 64, saw them home. John Crawley's 117 was the other main feature of Lancashire's performance, although Graham Lloyd (86) and Saurav Ganguly (65) also made significant contributions as the home side replied with 445 to Durham's first-innings 370, in which Simon Katich hit a fine 129 from 213 balls and added 146 for the third wicket with Paul Collingwood (60).

Perhaps the best cricket of this week, and possibly of the season, came at Portsmouth, where Kent's Rahul Dravid responded to the threat of Hampshire's Shane Warne with matchwinning innings of 137 and 73 not out. The Indian vice-captain was simply majestic, repelling all Warne's best efforts to dismiss him – although the Australian maestro had his fair share of moral victories as their duel raged on. Warne had actually dominated the opening day with the bat, striking two sixes and 11 fours in a 62-ball 69 that gave the crowd 77 minutes of marvellous entertainment. Hampshire totalled 320, with Jason Laney top-scoring with 81, and Warne than took the first two Kent wickets to fall as the visitors struggled to 31 for 2 by the close. But that rich first day's entertainment was just the warm-up act for the Dravid v. Warne battle that ran almost throughout the second day. Warne took 4 for 81 from 37 overs, but he did not get Dravid. Kent's 252 was almost entirely down to the Indian's skill, and his soft hands in defence and wristy elegance in attack, allied to Warne's varied armoury, made for pure theatre. This was county cricket fit to grace any great arena, and the spectators who turned up at the United Services Ground were utterly captivated by the contest and joyous that the money they had paid to see it represented one of the bargain buys of the sporting year. Unfortunately for those of a Hampshire persuasion, the third day brought only disappointment as the home team subsided to 136 all out. Only opener Giles White, carrying his bat for the second time this season and ending unbeaten on 80, had any answers to Kent's spinner – slow left-armer Min Patel, who added 5 for 46 to his four first-innings wickets. Kent, however, still had to score 205 for victory. Surely, Warne could yet emerge as the true matchwinner. Dravid, though, was not to be denied that honour. After David Fulton had made a valuable 42, Dravid marched in to play a decisive innings of 73 not out. He was well supported, too, by an obdurate Robert Key (60) and the mighty Warne's 31.4 overs left him nursing figures of 0 for 69. Indeed, Shaun Udal's off-breaks proved the bigger threat and brought him 4 for 42, but it was not enough to prevent Kent – and Dravid – from celebrating an important six-wicket win.

Somerset, badly missing both Andy Caddick and Marcus Trescothick, were swept aside by Yorkshire at Scarborough. Bowled out for 182 and 212, they showed frailty against the short ball and eventually lost by an innings and six runs despite a late assault by number 11 Steffan Jones that brought him a second-innings 56 not out, off just 50 balls. Matthew Hoggard took 5 for 50 on the third, and final, day and Yorkshire's win earned them a maximum 20 points and revived their championship challenge. The home side's 400 was built on a gritty, unpretty, fourth-wicket stand between Darren Lehmann (77) and skipper David Byas (84), although Chris Silverwood livened up the crowd by smiting three sixes and five fours in his 45-ball 48.

Division Two
19, 20 and 21 July
at Chelmsford
Worcestershire 240 (109.4 overs)(PR Pollard 77, DA Leatherdale 62) and 176 (VS Solanki 53, PM Such 5 for 39, BJ Hyam 4ct/1st)
Essex 131 (53.3 overs)(GD McGrath 5 for 40) and 287 for 6 (80.5 overs)(SG Law 133*, AP Grayson 69)
Essex won by four wickets
Essex 5 pts, Worcestershire 4 pts

19, 20, 21 and 22 July
at Cardiff
Northamptonshire 229 (87.2 overs)(JW Cook 53, SD Thomas 5 for 43) and 277 (102.3 overs)(AL Penberthy 57, ML Hayden 51, DJG Sales 51, RDB Croft 5 for 108)
Glamorgan 198 (85.2 overs)(MTG Elliott 76) and 310 for 5 (MTG Elliott 117, MJ Powell 53)
Glamorgan won by five wickets
Glamorgan 15 pts, Northamptonshire 4 pts

at Cheltenham
Warwickshire 260 (102.5 overs)(MA Wagh 59, DL Hemp 58, IJ Harvey 5 for 29) and 316 (KJ Piper 69, DP Ostler 54)
Gloucestershire 254 (89.2 overs)(MGN Windows 79) and 237 for 5 (DR Hewson 67, MGN Windows 62*
Match drawn
Gloucestershire 9 pts, Warwickshire 9 pts

at Hove
Sussex 472 (122 overs)(MG Bevan 166, RR Montgomerie 133, CJ Adams 55) and 278 for 3 dec. (MG Bevan 174, RR Montgomerie 95)
Nottinghamshire 344 (119 overs)(JE Morris 76, RJ Kirtley 6 for 90) and 379 for 8 (JER Gallian 120, JE Morris 115, U Afzaal 54)
Match drawn
Sussex 12 pts, Nottinghamshire 10 pts

Nineteen wickets fell on day two of Essex's match against Worcestershire at Chelmsford, prompting a visit by one of the ECB's pitch inspectors Raman Subba Row. But what he saw instead, on a remarkable third day, was Essex complete a stirring fightback by successfully chasing a seemingly distant target of 286 to win by four wickets. Stuart Law, their Australian batsman, was the architect of victory, finishing 131 not out and relishing the all-Aussie

battle against Glenn McGrath, whose 5 for 40 had wrecked the Essex first innings on the previous day. Paul Grayson lent faithful support and Law's mastery was such that the runs were knocked off before the end of the 81st over. A five-and-a-quarter-hour 77 by Paul Pollard had dominated the opening day, with David Leatherdale also reaching 62 as Worcestershire closed on 232 for 7. Andrew McGarry, an 18-year-old pace bowler, impressed by taking 3 for 29 from 16 overs on debut, but Essex then slumped to 131 in reply to Worcestershire's 240. By the end of the day, however, the visitors themselves had slid to 124 for 7, despite Vikram Solanki's fluent 53 off 57 balls, and on the third morning not even a quick-fire 43 by tail-ender Kabir Ali could haul Worcestershire into a winning overall lead. Peter Such was the other Essex hero, picking up 5 for 39 as Worcestershire were dismissed for 176.

Fine batting by another Australian, Matthew Elliott, helped to bring Glamorgan victory by five wickets against Northamptonshire at Cardiff. Elliott, the tall left-handed opener, added a brilliant 117 to his first-innings 76 as Glamorgan made the highest score of the match in the fourth innings. It was a notable result, too, in that Steve Watkin, their chief strike bowler, limped out of the game soon after taking his 800th first-class wicket early on the opening day. Darren Thomas stepped into the breach for Glamorgan, taking 5 for 43 as Northants were bowled out for 229 midway through the final session. Jeff Cook made 53 and Graeme Swann a typically adventurous 48 off just 51 deliveries, and Northants hit back with the ball to have Glamorgan 39 for 2 by the close. Despite Elliott's resistance, the Welsh county could muster only 198 on day two, seamer Michael Strong (4 for 50) and off-spinner Jason Brown (4 for 56) doing much of the damage. Matthew Hayden, David Sales and Tony Penberthy then scored half-centuries, but Robert Croft kept wheeling away to take 5 for 108 from 46 overs. Northants, all out for 277, had failed to bat Glamorgan out of the game and Michael Powell (53) then gave Elliott the necessary support as a victory target of 309 was achieved with relative comfort.

Yet another Australian, Michael Bevan, stamped his authority on proceedings at Hove – although, in the end, Nottinghamshire came close to a memorable win against Sussex on a batting paradise of a pitch. Bevan hit 166 and 174 and Notts, despite being flayed in the field, hit back to reach 379 for 8 in a brave chase of a 407 win target. John Morris was the pick of the visiting batsmen, adding 115 (his 50th first-class hundred) to his first-innings 76.

SUSSEX CCC

Home Ground:
Hove
Address:
County Ground, Eaton Road, Hove,
East Sussex BN3 3AN
Tel: 01273 827100
Fax: 01273 771549
Membership: 01273 827133
Scoreline (home games only): 01273 827145
Email: Fran@sccc.demon.co.uk
Directions:
By rail: Hove station is a ten-minute walk.
By road: Follow AA signs. Street parking at no cost.
Capacity: 5,500
Other grounds used: Eastbourne, Horsham, Arundel
Year formed: 1839

Chief Executive: David Gilbert
Cricket Manager: Peter Moores
Cricket Development Manager: Ian Waring
Other posts: Director of Excellence: Chris Waller;
Second XI Coach: Keith Greenfield; Pro Cricket
Administrator: Chris Pickett; Cricket Development Officer:
Steve Peyman; Marketing Manager: Neil Lenham
Captain: Chris Adams
Vice-captain: Michael Bevan
County colours: Dark blue, light blue and gold

HONOURS

SUNDAY LEAGUE
1982
GILLETTE CUP/NATWEST TROPHY
1963, 1964, 1978, 1986

CGU National Cricket League nickname:
SUSSEX SHARKS

Website:
www.sccc.demon.co.uk

Jason Gallian, the Notts captain, also hit form on the final day with 120 – putting on 222 in 52 overs with Morris and going a long way to making up for his decision, on the first morning, to put Sussex into bat. Usman Afzaal's 54 then threatened to sweep Notts to their target, but too many batsmen got themselves out trying for the big shot, rather than pushing the ones and twos, and Sussex took enough wickets to slow the Notts advance and earn themselves 12 points for the draw. Richard Montgomerie was the other Sussex batsman to enjoy himself, hitting 133 and 95 and sharing in stands of 292 and 265 with Bevan. Before Montgomerie top-edged a risky sweep in the second innings, indeed, he and Bevan looked like becoming only the second pair of batsmen in county history (and the fourth worldwide) to each hit two hundreds in the same match. Well though Montgomerie played, however, and especially so considering that 14 previous championship knocks had brought him just 276 runs, the match belonged to Bevan. The left-hander, acknowledged as the world's best one-day batsman, unleashed his whole repertoire of strokes on the hapless Notts bowlers. In the first innings he hit 20 boundaries from 213 balls and then, as he rushed to his third successive championship score above 150, Bevan struck 22 fours and two sixes from only 177 deliveries. His third fifty, in fact, took just 30 balls – a fitting celebration, in its way, of becoming the 13th Sussex batsman to score two hundreds in a match.

Another draw was fought out at Cheltenham, where Gloucestershire's batsmen (notably Dominic Hewson with 67 and Matt Windows with an unbeaten 62) held off the twin threat of Allan Donald's pace and Ashley Giles' left-arm spin on a tense final day. Technically, Gloucestershire were chasing 323 after the first three innings of the match had fitted neatly into the first three days. But, with Donald trying to whip up a storm and Giles toiling through 45 overs unchanged to take 4 for 74, survival was always the likeliest best option. Windows, in fact, had a fine match: his first-innings 79 was mainly responsible for Gloucestershire getting to within six runs of Warwickshire's opening-day total of 260, of which Mark Wagh made 59 and David Hemp 58. Ian Harvey was the other Gloucestershire hero, taking 5 for 29 from 23 overs in the Warwickshire first innings and then picking up 4 for 71 when they batted again to reach 316. Wicketkeeper Keith Piper, promoted to number three, responded by hitting 69 – his highest score for three seasons.

ROUND THIRTEEN: 28–31 JULY 2000

Division One
28, 29, 30 and 31 July
at Chester-le-Street
Durham 292 (105 overs)(JJB Lewis 115) and 73 for 3
Somerset 280 (126 overs)(PD Bowler 107, GD Rose 82*, J Wood 5 for 88)
Match drawn – no play was possible on the fourth day
Durham 9 pts, Somerset 9 pts

at Canterbury
Derbyshire 279 (115.5 overs)(MP Dowman 77, SP Titchard 52) and 293 for 0 (SP Titchard 141*, SD Stubbings 135*)
Kent 251 for 9 dec. (116.1 overs)(PA Nixon 80*, MM Patel 60, KJ Dean 8 for 52)
Match drawn
Kent 9 pts, Derbyshire 9 pts

at Headingley
Lancashire 267 (92 overs)(WK Hegg 75) and 127 for 2
Yorkshire 376 (124.5 overs)(DS Lehmann 83, D Byas 81)
Match drawn – no play was possible on the fourth day
Yorkshire 11 pts, Lancashire 9 pts

The 235th Roses Match was one of two first division matches ruined by a fourth-day total wash-out – the other game affected was at Chester-le-Street – and so much of the interest in this round of matches came in the Division Two promotion dogfight, with important victories being gained by Sussex, Northamptonshire and Worcestershire.

At Headingley, there was consternation about the standard of the pitch ahead of the Fourth Cornhill Test, due to start on 17 August, but despite being mysteriously damp at the outset of the Yorkshire-Lancashire clash, it did dry out enough on subsequent days for both sides to reach good first-innings totals. How ironic, then, that a prolonged downpour should wash away any possibility of a positive result. On the opening day Lancashire struggled to 128 for 6 before Warren Hegg hit 75 in his usual combative manner to haul the total up to 267. There was a distinguished scalp for Chris Elstub, a 19-year-old pace bowler, when he had Mike Atherton leg before with his third ball on his Roses debut. On weather-affected second and third days, Yorkshire reached 376 all out in reply, Darren Lehmann (83) and David Byas (81) adding 100 after the home side had slipped initially to 108 for 4.

The fourth day was sunlit and beautiful at Canterbury, in contrast, yet that did not prevent a slow handclap ringing around the St Lawrence Ground by mid-afternoon as Derbyshire and Kent brought to a sorry end a match in which neither side seemed willing to take even the slightest risk. One of the negative aspects of two divisions became painfully clear as Derbyshire, understrength because of injuries and the England management decree that Dominic Cork should miss the match, refused to set Kent a target. Not that Kent were blameless in the stalemate: they had batted turgidly after an early collapse before declaring at 251 for 9 in reply to Derbyshire's hardly cavalier first-innings 279 from 115.5 overs. Mathew Dowman (77) put on 68 for the seventh wicket with Simon Lacey, who took 159 balls to score 48, while Kent wicketkeeper Paul Nixon battled for five and a half hours to make 80 not out and was joined by Min Patel (60) in a stand of 131 in 59 overs for the eighth wicket. The outstanding bowling in the match came from left-arm paceman Kevin Dean who, on the second evening, took 4 for 17 from ten overs to undermine the Kent top order and, overall, picked up 8 for 52. On the pointless final day, by the way, all 11 Kent players had a bowl, and Derbyshire openers Steve Stubbings (135 not out) and Steve Titchard (141 not out) created a county record: they took the total to 293 for no wicket declared, which was the first time Derbyshire had not lost a wicket in a full day's play.

There was attritional batting at Chester-le-Street, too, with Somerset replying with 280 to Durham's 292. Durham had stretched their lead to 85 by the close of the third day, for the loss of three second-innings wickets, only for rain to wash away the final day. Durham's first innings was based on 115 from Jon Lewis, who batted with great application either side of a thunderstorm that, between lunch and tea, took 31 overs out of the opening day. Somerset, struggling on 144 for 6 from 70 overs by the close of the second day, were revived thanks to a six-and-a-half hour 107 from Peter Bowler and fine support from Graham Rose, who curbed most of his naturally aggressive instincts to end on 82 not out. John Wood was the most successful home bowler with 5 for 88.

Division Two
28, 29 and 30 July
at Edgbaston
Northamptonshire 318 (99.3 overs)(ML Hayden 122, GP Swann 58, AF Giles 6 for 118) and 176 (ML Hayden 72, NMK Smith 5 for 66, AF Giles 5 for 78)
Warwickshire 236 (81.1 overs)(DP Ostler 88 , JF Brown 5 for 88) and 205 (NMK Smith 67, JF Brown 6 for 90)

Steve Stubbings batted throughout the final day with Steve Titchard: the first time Derbyshire had never lost a wicket in a completed day. Mind you, all eleven of Kent's fielders had a bowl in the stalemate!

Northamptonshire won by 54 runs
Northamptonshire 18 pts, Warwickshire 4 pts

at Worcester
Worcestershire 98 (50.2 overs) and 225 (DA Leatherdale 56, SJ Rhodes 52*, IJ Harvey 6 for 100)
Gloucestershire 87 (31.5 overs)(GD McGrath 7 for 29) and 184 (SJ Rhodes 5 catches)
Worcestershire won by 52 runs
Worcestershire 15 pts, Gloucestershire 3 pts

at Southgate
Middlesex 227 (57.5 overs)(MR Ramprakash 110*, RJ Kirtley 5 for 50) and 283 (MR Ramprakash 112,

RL Johnson 52)
Sussex 243 (101.1 overs) and 270 for 3 (MG Bevan 173*)
Sussex won by seven wickets
Sussex 16 pts, Middlesex 4 pts

Sussex went to the top of the second division table with a stirring seven-wicket win over Middlesex at Southgate. Despite the brilliant batting of Mark Ramprakash, who scored two hundreds in the match, Middlesex could total only 227 and 283 and, on a good pitch, a coruscating unbeaten 173 by Michael Bevan on the final day proved to be the match-winning effort. James Kirtley also had a fine match for Sussex, taking 5 for 50 and then 4 for 65 in the second innings to continue his push for further international honours. Sadly, the Ramprakash whose 110 not out and 112 in this game made him the first Middlesex batsman to score two centuries in a match four times has seldom, if ever, been seen at England level. Even more sadly, the misguided experiment in trying to convert him into a Test opener has been exposed for the folly it was by his magnificent form since returning both to the county circuit and to his favoured number four berth. At Southgate during the past fortnight, moreover, Ramprakash has scored 446 runs from five innings. Yet, for all Ramprakash's class, supported finally in the Middlesex second innings by Richard Johnson (52) in an eighth-wicket stand of 104, this game belonged to Bevan. On the third evening, with Sussex 118 for 3, he was poised at 57 not out to play the matchwinning innings. The next day, however, he simply destroyed the Middlesex attack with a breathtaking assault that also brought him the honour of becoming the first player to reach 1,000 first-class runs for the season. Phil Tufnell and Keith Dutch, the Middlesex spinners, had exercised a tight hold on Sussex during their first innings, but now they were powerless as Bevan took just 191 balls to score his unbeaten 173. It was his fourth score of more than 150 in five innings and, with nightwatchman Kirtley hanging on determinedly at the other end – and no doubt thoroughly enjoying his close-up view of the entertainment on offer – Sussex were swept home on a tidal wave of Australian stroke-play.

In a match dominated by spin, Northamptonshire beat Warwickshire by 54 runs at Edgbaston to continue the transformation of their championship season. Jason Brown and Graeme Swann, their youthful off-spinners, were again the source of inspiration as Warwickshire were bowled out for 204 in the final innings. The home side, in fact,

fought hard after initially collapsing to 48 for 6. Nick Knight (43) and skipper Neil Smith (67) made Brown and Swann work hard to finish the job. But Brown, fast-emerging as an England 'A' tour and possibly even senior winter tour candidate, ended with 6 for 90 – giving him match figures of 11 for 178. In Warwickshire's first innings of 236 he had taken 5 for 88 and Swann 4 for 74, with only Dominic Ostler (88) thriving. Brown has now taken five or more wickets in an innings six times in only 21 first-class appearances. Northants, however, were greatly indebted to their captain, Matthew Hayden, and without his first-innings century and second-innings 72 the spinners would have had nothing to bowl at. Swann, with a six and eight fours in a belligerent 58, helped Hayden take Northants to 318 on the opening day and a bit – Hayden's superb 122 occupying just 178 balls and featuring no fewer than four sixes and 14 fours. Thanks to Hayden, again, Northants managed to scrape together 176 in the second innings and set Warwickshire a tough target. Defeat for the home side was particularly rough on Ashley Giles, who took 6 for 118 and 5 for 78 with his slow left-arm. Off-spinner Smith, too, enjoyed the conditions with 5 for 66 as Warwickshire fought back on the third day.

Worcestershire gained their first win in any form of cricket since 24 June when they beat Gloucestershire by 52 runs at New Road. Glenn McGrath spearheaded their victory, blowing away Gloucestershire's batting to take 7 for 29 in their first-innings capitulation to 87 all out, and then following up with three more scalps as the visitors were dismissed for 184 on the third afternoon. The pitch came under scrutiny from Phil Sharpe, the former England batsman now acting on the ECB's inspectorate, but he decided it was not poor enough to warrant a penalty – even though, for the first time in 100 years at Worcester, both teams' first innings did not reach 100. Worcestershire, indeed, were bowled out for 98 on the opening day, Mike Smith leading the Gloucestershire seam battery with 4 for 16, but the visitors were 57 for 5 themselves by the close, with McGrath producing an irresistible new-ball burst of 11–7–16–4. The Australian continued with his destruction on the second morning and Worcestershire, with an unexpected 11-run lead, managed to reach 225 second time around mainly thanks to a sixth-wicket stand of 63 between David Leatherdale (56) and the ever-committed Steve Rhodes (52 not out). Ian Harvey picked up 6 for 100 for Gloucestershire, but the visitors never looked capable of attaining their victory target.

WARWICKSHIRE CCC

Home Ground:
Edgbaston
Address:
County Ground,
Edgbaston,
Birmingham, B5 7QU
Tel: 0121 446 4422
Fax: 0121 446 4949
Ticket Hotline: 0121 446 5506
Indoor cricket centre: 0121 446 3633
Email: info@thebears.co.uk
Alternative website: www.warwickccc.org.uk
Directions:
By rail: New Street station, Birmingham
By road: M6 to A38M, to city centre, then follow signs to
County Ground.
Capacity: 20,000
Other grounds used: None
Year formed: 1882

Chairman: MJK Smith OBE
Chief Executive: Dennis Amiss MBE
Director of Coaching: Bob Woolmer
Other posts: 2nd XI Coach: Steve Perryman; Marketing
Manager: Peter Thompson; Indoor cricket centre coach:
RN Abberley
Captain: Neil MK Smith

HONOURS

COUNTY CHAMPIONSHIP
1911, 1951, 1972, 1994, 1995
SUNDAY LEAGUE
1980, 1994, 1997
BENSON & HEDGES CUP
1994
GILLETTE CUP/NATWEST TROPHY
1989, 1993, 1995

CGU National Cricket League
nickname:
THE BEARS

The Bears

Website:
www.thebears.co.uk

WORCESTERSHIRE CCC

Home Ground:
Worcester
Address:
New Road, Worcester WR2 4QQ
Tel: 01905 748474
Fax: 01905 748005
Ticket office: 01905 422694
Cricket Development Admin Officer (Allan Scrafton): 01905 429147
Directions:
By rail: Worcester Foregate Street Station (city centre), half a mile from ground. Worcester Shrub Hill Station, one mile from ground.
By road: From the north, M5 junction 6 then follow signposted route to Worcester and city centre, then take A44 for New Road.
By bus: Midland Red West Nos 23–6.
Disabled access: designated viewing area for disabled visitors; free admission for carers; disabled toilet facilities.
Capacity: 4,500
Other grounds used: Kidderminster CC, Chester Road North, Kidderminster
Year formed: 1865

Secretary: The Reverend Michael Vockins OBE
Senior Coach: Bill Athey
Coach: Damian D'Oliveira
Other posts: Head Groundsman: Roy McLaren
Captain: Graeme Hick
Vice-captain: Steve Rhodes
County colours: Green, black and white

Website:
www.wccc.co.uk

HONOURS

COUNTY CHAMPIONSHIP
1964, 1965, 1974, 1988, 1989
SUNDAY LEAGUE
1971, 1987, 1988, 1991
BENSON & HEDGES CUP
1991
GILLETTE CUP/NATWEST TROPHY
1994

CGU National Cricket League nickname:
WORCESTERSHIRE ROYALS

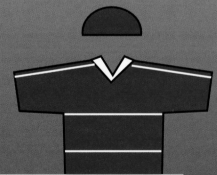

ROUND FOURTEEN: 2–7 AUGUST 2000

Division One
2, 3, 4 and 5 August
at Derby
Derbyshire 310 (115.3 overs)(MP Dowman 110,
SJ Lacey 55*, AD Mullally 9 for 93) and 293 (LD Sutton
79, MJ di Venuto 78*, AD Mullally 5 for 95)
Hampshire 394 (131.2 overs)(DA Kenway 136,
AD Mascarenhas 100, RA Smith 50)
Match drawn
Derbyshire 10 pts, Hampshire 11 pts

at Canterbury
Leicestershire 375 (133.5 overs)(Aftab Habib 78,
VJ Wells 72, A Kumble 56)
Kent 201 (88.2 overs) and (following on) 187 for 7
(A Kumble 6 for 44)
Match drawn
Kent 8 pts, Leicestershire 11 pts

at Taunton
Somerset 359 (128 overs)(GD Rose 124, PD Trego 62)
and 368 for 3 (PD Bowler 139*, KA Parsons 108*)
Yorkshire 327 (98.4 overs)(A McGrath 74, ID Fisher
68*, DS Lehmann 56)
Match drawn
Somerset 11 pts, Yorkshire 10 pts

at the Oval
Surrey 310 (110.5 overs)(AJ Holliaoake 80, AD Brown
54, MP Smethurst 6 for 63) and 227 for 4 dec.
(MA Butcher 95, N Shahid 62)
Lancashire 120 (39.1 overs)(AJ Tudor 7 for 48) and
145 (IDK Salisbury 5 for 46)
Surrey won by 272 runs
Surrey 18 pts, Lancashire 3 pts

Alex Tudor produced the most eye-catching
individual performance in another irresistible Surrey
team display as the county champions brushed off
challengers Lancashire at the Oval to signal their
intention of defending their title in style. Adam
Holliaoake, the Surrey skipper, even had the
confidence to pass up the chance to make
Lancashire follow on after Tudor (7 for 48) had
destroyed their first innings. Instead, in order to give
Tudor a rest, his own batsmen the opportunity of
rubbing Lancastrian noses in the south London soil,
and his two spinners their best chance of inflicting
maximum last-day damage, he batted again. Surrey,
who had totalled 310 in their first innings with
Holliaoake himself hitting a fine 80 and Alistair

Brown 54, this time reached 227 for 4 with Mark
Butcher stroking 95 off 134 balls before the
declaration came. Lancashire, tumbled out for 120
by Tudor's pace and movement early on the third
day, could muster only 145 at the second attempt.
And, as Holliaoake had expected, it was spinners Ian
Salisbury (5 for 46) and Saqlain Mushtaq (3 for 45)
who wrapped up the crushing 272-run victory. This
was Surrey's sixth successive win and, in a sequence
that took them ahead of the field, no fewer than
nine different players had contributed to a tally of
six centuries and ten five-wicket hauls.

Kent's struggle to hold on to first-division status,
despite chronic injury problems to their leading fast
bowlers, went on at Canterbury as Robert Key and
Matthew Walker led the resistance that finally
denied Leicestershire the innings win that could
have rekindled their championship hopes. The time
lost on the second day, when just 20 overs were
bowled, did not help Leicestershire either, although
they chose to bat on to 375 all out on the third
morning when Anil Kumble (56) enjoyed himself
with the bat rather than having a ball in his hand.
Kent, who then slid to 184 for 8 by the close, faced
a tense final day after being bowled out for 201 and
being asked to follow on. Kumble caused constant
problems, taking 6 for 44, but Key fought his way to
53 and Walker added an unbeaten 24 to his first-
innings 48 not out to see Kent to safety and four
vital draw points.

Derbyshire also resisted strongly on the last day of
their match against fellow strugglers Hampshire at
Derby, Luke Sutton (79) and Michael di Venuto (78
not out) doing most to secure a draw. Di Venuto,
who came in at number seven because of an earlier
injury, then found more support from number ten
Kasir Shah (33). They put on 79 for the ninth wicket
and Derbyshire, who had begun the final day still 18
runs adrift at 66 for 4 in their second innings, battled
to 293 for 9 despite Alan Mullally's 5 for 95 and
Shane Warne's 2 for 63 from 36 overs. Mullally, in
fact, took 14 wickets in the match: his first-innings 9
for 93 was a quite magnificent effort and, not
surprisingly, a career-best as Derbyshire totalled 310.
Mathew Dowman, dropped five times, hit 110 and
also had another major slice of luck when a ball from
Dimitri Mascarenhas was squeezed on to his off-
stump and dislodged a bail – which then fell back
into its groove! Dowman shared a stand of 91 with
Sutton (36) for the fifth wicket and Simon Lacey
later finished 55 not out. Hampshire stuttered early
on against Kevin Dean, but Robin Smith steadied his
side with 50 and then, on the third day, Mascarenhas

joined Derek Kenway in a sixth-wicket partnership that finally realised 187 and threatened to win Hampshire the game. Kenway scored 136 and Mascarenhas a highly promising maiden hundred.

Only 37.3 overs were possible on the opening day of the match between Somerset and Yorkshire at Taunton, due to rain, and on a lovely, true pitch neither side was able to provide the cutting edge with the ball to make up for that lost time. Somerset's first-innings 359 was a triumph for the veteran all-rounder Graham Rose, who reached the tenth century of his 15-year career and featured in a fine eighth-wicket stand of 132 with 19-year-old Pete Trego. Rose's 124 came from 227 balls and included 14 fours, while the richly talented Trego struck ten boundaries in his 103-ball 62. Darren Lehmann, passing his 1,000 runs for the season, hit 56 from 79 balls in reply, putting on 91 with Anthony McGrath (74), and Yorkshire were further boosted to 327 by a 92-run stand for the seventh wicket between wicketkeeper Simon Guy (42) and spinning all-rounder Ian Fisher, whose hard-hitting unbeaten 68 off 83 balls included a six and 12 fours, and was a career-best. David Byas, the Yorkshire captain, tore a cartilage in his knee twisting away from a McGrath drive while at the non-striker's end. In the prevailing climate of two divisions, however, no deal was done to open up the game for the spectators and, on a glorious final day, Somerset merely cruised pointlessly to 368 for 3 with Peter Bowler cashing in with an unbeaten 139 and Keith Parsons helping him add an unbroken 227 by reaching 108 not out, a maiden first-class century more than slightly devalued by the situation.

Division Two
2, 3, 4 and 5 August
at Bristol
Glamorgan 122 (40.3 overs)(SD Thomas 52, MJ Cawdron 5 for 45) and 210 (MJ Powell 61)
Gloucestershire 308 (95.1 overs)(MGN Windows 82, MCJ Ball 53, MP Maynard 4ct/1st) and 27 for 0
Gloucestershire won by ten wickets – no play was possible on the second day
Gloucestershire 18 pts, Glamorgan 3 pts

at Lord's
Middlesex 287 (108 overs)(MR Ramprakash 84, BL Hutton 55) and 174 for 9 dec.
Essex 200 (97.2 overs)(RC Irani 76, PCR Tufnell 6 for 48) and 130 for 7)
Match drawn
Middlesex 9 pts, Essex 8 pts

3, 4, 5 and 6 August
at Trent Bridge
Nottinghamshire 368 (113 overs)(U Afzaal 82, CMW Read 52, DR Brown 5 for 87) and 232 for 8 dec. (PR Reiffel 60*)
Warwickshire 324 (108.3 overs)(DL Hemp 70, PR Reiffel 5 for 62) and 132 for 4
Match drawn
Nottinghamshire 11 pts, Warwickshire 10 pts

4, 5, 6 and 7 August
at Northampton
Northamptonshire 519 (170 overs)(ML Hayden 147, AL Penberthy 83, AS Rollins 63, RJ Warren 60, D Ripley 56, MB Loye 52, SR Lampitt 5 for 63)
Worcestershire 249 (109 overs)(DA Leatherdale 132*, JF Brown 5 for 100) and (following on) 198 (SR Lampitt 56*, GP Swann 5 for 55)
Northamptonshire won by an innings and 72 runs
Northamptonshire 19 pts, Worcestershire 2 pts

Off-spinners Jason Brown and Graeme Swann were at it again at Wantage Road as Northamptonshire completed their charge right through the second division ranks by beating Worcestershire by an innings and 72 runs. The victory, clinched just before lunch on the fourth day, put them top of a table in which the nine teams were separated by just 33 points. Northants began by amassing a mammoth 519, with Matthew Hayden, the captain, maintaining his fine run of form – and going past 1,000 runs for the season – by hitting 147 from 218 balls, with two sixes and 19 fours. Five other players topped fifty, with Tony Penberthy (83) and David Ripley (56) adding 108 for the seventh wicket, and by the close of the second day Worcestershire were already up against it at 97 for 4. Despite a wonderful unbeaten 132 by David Leatherdale, it became 249 all out the next day, with Brown picking up 5 for 100, and soon Worcestershire were 102 for 6 by the close after being instructed to follow on. Swann, who took four of those first six wickets to fall, ended with 5 for 55 as he and Brown (4 for 88) wrapped things up. Stuart Lampitt's unbeaten 56 was mere token defiance.

Glamorgan's promotion ambitions took a severe jolt at Bristol where, despite the loss of the entire second day to rain, Gloucestershire eased to a comfortable ten-wicket victory. It was quite an achievement, too, by the home side who were without a first-choice attack in the injured or unavailable quartet of Mike Smith, Ben Gannon, Ian

The ageless Somerset all-rounder, Graham Rose, reached his tenth first-class century against Yorkshire at Taunton.

Harvey and Jon Lewis. Into the breach stepped Michael Cawdron, who took a first-innings 5 for 45, and debutant Alistair Bressington, who picked up a second-innings 4 for 36. Tim Hancock's occasional seamers also did a good job for the home side as Glamorgan, bowled out for 122 on the opening day, reached just 210 second time around despite Michael Powell's 61 and number nine Darren Thomas adding an unbeaten 48 to a defiant first-innings 52. Gloucestershire, who

totalled 308 in their first innings as a result of a 94-run sixth-wicket stand between Matt Windows (82) and Jeremy Snape (40), plus some aggressive batting at opposite ends of the order from Mark Alleyne (38) and Martyn Ball (53 off 48 balls, with ten fours), were left needing just 25 for an 18-point victory haul.

Essex held on for a draw at Lord's after a grim struggle with Middlesex, for whom left-arm spinner Phil Tufnell was the game's outstanding bowler. Mark Ramprakash's classical 84 from 115 balls, plus a composed 55 from Ben Hutton, took Middlesex to 287 on the first two rain-affected days. Then, on the third morning, Tufnell got to work with a mesmeric spell that brought him season's-best figures of 6 for 48 from 353.2 overs. Angus Fraser supported him in equally miserly fashion, snatching 3 for 45 from 24 overs, and only Ronnie Irani's 76 dragged Essex to 200 all out. Middlesex, perhaps, delayed their declaration on the final day – Ramprakash again playing well for 49 in a total of 174 for 9 – and a combination of Tufnell and Simon Cook, the left-arm paceman, threatened to win the game. In the end, though, Essex hung on at 130 for 7 with Tufnell finishing with 3 for 45 from 31 overs and Cook 4 for 13.

Determined batting by the Nottinghamshire lower order, led by Paul Reiffel (60) and Chris Read (45) enabled the home side to frustrate Warwickshire at Trent Bridge. Notts, 85 for 5 in their second innings at the close of play on day three – an overall lead of 129 – rallied to 232 for 8 declared. That left Warwickshire a target of 277 from just 49 overs and, predictably, they settled for a draw at 132 for 4. A hailstorm cost the game 55 overs on the opening day, but Usman Afzaal's 82 and a perky 52 from Read enabled Notts to reach 368. In reply, Warwickshire totalled 324, David Hemp top-scoring with 70 and Reiffel taking his first five-wicket haul for his new county.

ROUND FIFTEEN: 8–12 AUGUST 2000

Division One
8, 9, 10 and 11 August
at Southampton
Leicestershire 266 (83.3 overs)(A Habib 61, JM Dakin 60, IJ Sutcliffe 53) and 240 (D Williamson 43)
Hampshire 228 (81 overs)(+AN Aymes 71) and 217 (AC Morris 60, GW White 50)
Leicestershire won by 61 runs
Leicestershire 17 pts, Hampshire 4 pts

YORKSHIRE CCC

Home Ground:
Headingley
Address:
Headingley Cricket Ground,
Leeds LS6 3BU
Tel: 0113 278 7394
Fax: 0113 278 4099
Email: cricket@yorkshireccc.org.uk
Other grounds used: Scarborough
Year formed: 1863

Chairman: Keith H Moss
Chief Executive: Chris Hassell
Secretary: David Ryder
Director of Coaching: Martyn Moxon
Coach: Arnie Sidebottom
Captain: David Byas
County colours: Oxford blue, Cambridge blue and gold

HONOURS

COUNTY CHAMPIONSHIP
1893, 1896, 1898, 1900, 1901,
1902, 1905, 1908, 1912, 1919,
1922, 1923, 1924, 1925, 1931,
1963, 1966, 1967, 1968
BENSON & HEDGES CUP
1987
SUNDAY LEAGUE
1983
GILLETTE CUP/NATWEST TROPHY
1965, 1969

CGU National Cricket League nickname:
YORKSHIRE PHOENIX

Website:
www.yorkshireccc.org.uk

Allan Mullally enjoyed his reunion with old Leicestershire teammates at Southampton where he took 9 wickets in the match.

9, 10, 11 and 12 August
at Chester-le-Street
Kent 170 (56.4 overs)(SJE Brown 5 for 59) and 354 for 7 dec. (ET Smith 175)
Durham 223 (84.5 overs)(NJ Speak 89*, MJ Saggers 7 for 79) and 157 for 3 (JJB Lewis 59*)
Match drawn
Durham 8 pts, Kent 7 pts

Hampshire's woes continued with a 61-run loss to Leicestershire at Southampton – despite the visitors being without both their first-choice pace attack and Anil Kumble, the Indian leg-spinner. Jack Birkenshaw, the Leicestershire coach, was upset initially at the way Hampshire had produced a pitch with a marked greenish hue, designed clearly for Alan Mullally who, in the absence of Warne, Kumble, deFreitas, Lewis and Ormond, was the

one bowler of established international class on either side. Birkenshaw's view, especially after Hampshire had won the toss and predictably inserted his side, was that the pitch preparation on view gave further ammunition to those who believe that visiting captains should always have the choice of batting or bowling first. In the event, and despite Mullally's 5 for 84 against his old county, Leicestershire were bowled out for 266 only in the opening minutes of the second day, and then won themselves a small but useful first-innings lead when Hampshire were dismissed for 228. Iain Sutcliffe, Aftab Habib and Jon Dakin all got past fifty in Leicestershire's first innings, but Adrian Aymes' 71 was the only Hampshire score of substance. Mullally, displaying great stamina and desire, slogged through 37 impressive overs to take 4 for 59 in Leicestershire's second-innings 240, but the visitors had set Hampshire a tough last-innings target and, by the close of the third day, they were already wobbling at 54 for 2. Carl Crowe (4 for 55) and Vince Wells, adding 4 for 54 to his first-innings 3 for 39, then bowled well enough to allow Hampshire no way back.

A fine innings of 175 by Ed Smith, who had previously endured an unhappy season, earned Kent an important draw at Chester-le-Street – Durham remaining 14 points behind Kent in the relegation zone's third-from-bottom spot. Only 32 overs were possible on the opening day, because of rain, but Kent were struggling at 88 for 7 early on day two before Martin McCague (45 from 44 balls) joined Matthew Fleming (35) in a stand worth 59 for the eighth wicket. Despite McCague's aggression, however, Kent were dismissed for 170, with Simon Brown picking up 5 for 59, and Durham had a useful lead by the close. In fact, the home side had slumped themselves to 130 for 8 before Nick Speak put a poor season behind him with an unbeaten 89. Neil Killeen joined him in a fighting 93-run partnership for the ninth wicket and Durham's eventual 223 all out put them in control. Martin Saggers, however, playing against his old county and returning his first five-wicket haul for Kent, finished with 7 for 79 to boost the morale in the visiting camp. Rahul Dravid got things going with a fluent 47, but it was 23-year-old former Cambridge University skipper Smith who really blossomed, ending the third day on 139 not out and then moving on to 175 before Kent eventually declared at 354 for 7. Jon Lewis scored an unbeaten 59 as Durham reached 157 for 3 in the time left.

Division Two
9, 10 and 11 August
at Trent Bridge
Middlesex 412 (109.4 overs)(JL Langer 108,
EC Joyce 51) and 27 for 0
Nottinghamshire 245 (79.5 overs)(CM Tolley 60) and
(following on) 192 (PJ Franks 50, ARC Fraser 6 for 64)
Middlesex won by ten wickets
Middlesex 20 pts, Nottinghamshire 4 pts

at Northampton
Sussex 232 (102.3 overs)(WG Khan 74) and 211
(PA Cottey 112, JF Brown 7 for 78)
Northamptonshire 460 (154.5 overs)(RJ Warren 151,
AL Penberthy 96, UBA Rashid 5 for 103)

Ronnie Irani was amongst the wickets at Kidderminster as
Essex beat Worcestershire by 10 wickets.

Northamptonshire won by an innings and 17 runs
Northamptonshire 19 pts, Sussex 3 pts

at Kidderminster
Worcestershire 302 (92 overs)(PR Pollard 123*,
VS Solanki 55, DA Leatherdale 52) and 282 (GA Hick
75, PR Pollard 69, VS Solanki 56, AP Cowan 5 for 54,
RC Irani 5 for 79)
Essex 462 (116.2 overs)(SG Law 189, PJ Prichard 74,
SD Peters 67) and 125 for 0 (PJ Prichard 62*,
AP Grayson 50*)
Essex won by ten wickets
Essex 20 pts, Worcestershire 6 pts

Northamptonshire seriously dented Sussex's own
promotion hopes, while strengthening their own, by
crushing the visitors to Wantage Road by an innings
and 17 runs. Jason Brown, the fast-emerging off-
spinner, was again the most successful of the
Northants bowlers as he took 4 for 53 from 32.3
overs in Sussex's first-innings 232 before wrapping
up the home victory by bagging 7 for 78 in the
second innings. Sussex, bowled out for 211 second
time around, batted poorly and were kept afloat
only by Wasim Khan's dedicated 74 on the first day
and Tony Cottey's combative second innings 112,
which just took the game into a final day. Darren
Cousins, enjoying a wonderful comeback season
after his switch from Essex and a catalogue of
injuries, produced fine figures of 4 for 36 on day
one, and the Northants cause was further helped by
sensible, disciplined and determined innings of 151
and 96 by Russell Warren and Tony Penberthy
respectively. Their superb fifth-wicket partnership
enabled Northants to total 460 and put Sussex
under the kind of pressure that, in turn, allowed
Brown to weave his spell. During his second-innings
haul, Brown took his 100th first-class wicket (in only
his 23rd match) and when he dismissed Cottey to
secure victory he had taken his season's tally to 50
(from just seven appearances).
  Essex, meanwhile, moved above Worcestershire
into second place by beating them by ten wickets at
Kidderminster in another significant contest. The
home side, initially, looked to have recovered well
from 17 for 3 when they totalled 302 on the opening
day. Vikram Solanki and David Leatherdale scored
half-centuries, while Paul Pollard completed his first
championship hundred since 1995 and went on to
remain unbeaten on 123. But then Essex, and Stuart
Law in particular, made the most of Glenn
McGrath's enforced absence by running up a huge
462. Law, irrepressible, hit 189 while Paul Prichard

AUGUST DIARY by Robin Martin-Jenkins

It is frightening to think how quickly this season seems to have passed and how little cricket we have left. The first team have 26 days of competitive cricket remaining and the second team have just 13. It goes without saying that every day is vitally important but the next three weeks are probably the most important days of the summer. With our maestro, Michael Bevan, overseas everyone else is going to have to put in that extra 10 per cent for us to win games. In fact, the way it's been going recently, with Bev scoring 150 every time he bats, it will mean everyone in the team will have to score an extra 15 runs each to compensate!

The worlds of sport and technology fuse ever closer. The other day I received a call from a university friend who has been working with a new Internet company to set up a website that is exclusively about cricket. In an attempt to break into a new market their website is more than just an information site about professional cricket: 'www.playcricket.com' is designed to help anyone who wants to play cricket whatever his or her standard. By creating a database of every club in the country, they are hoping that people will use the site to get information about their nearest club so that they can join in. Mailing lists/newsgroups will be set up so that players can find out if they are playing in the next match, for example, or if they are required to come to training.

It is a great idea, which quite rightly has the backing of the ECB; club cricket in this country has to improve if English cricket as a whole is to progress. One of the problems in the past has been a lack of communication between cricket clubs and local populations. Aspiring young cricketers have been blocked because their parents have been unaware of how to access their nearest club. So if this new website improves interaction between clubs and accessibility to them, then all well and good.

A shocking fortnight has seen us lose twice to Northants and now our chances of being promoted to the first division of the championship next year are getting slimmer by the day. I wonder how it will affect a team, in terms of sponsorship and player transfers, if they remain in the second division for more than a couple of years.

As I write, I am sitting with my feet up in our hotel in Colwyn Bay having had probably the worst day of cricket of my life. The day started quite well. Opening the curtains we were relieved to see that the sun was out and there wasn't a cloud in the sky. Little were we to know that we were set to suffer a horrendous day being panned around the park by Steve James and Matthew Elliot. At 500 for 2 in walked Matthew Maynard to carry on where his colleagues had left off. Anyone who has watched him play will know that he's not the sort of chap you want to see walk to the wicket when the score has just reached 500.

(74) and Stephen Peters (67) both played innings that were important to their own seasons as well as to their team's. Ronnie Irani (5 for 79) and the impressive Ashley Cowan, following up his first-innings 4 for 69 with 5 for 54, then bowled out Worcestershire for 282 – leaving a relatively simple victory target, which Prichard (62 not out) and Paul Grayson (50 not out) soon reached. Remarkably, Worcestershire's second innings had included two century stands, 136 between Graeme Hick (75) and Solanki (56) and then the 100 put on by Pollard (69) and Leatherdale, but precious little else.

At Trent Bridge there was satisfaction at last for Middlesex, who beat Nottinghamshire by ten wickets to haul themselves off the bottom of the second division table. A surfeit of loose bowling on the opening day allowed Middlesex to rattle up 377 for 8, with Justin Langer cashing in with 108, and an eventual total of 412 was too intimidating for Notts, who slid to 245 all out in reply. Angus Fraser, Richard Johnson and Phil Tufnell each took three wickets and, when Notts followed on, it was Fraser and Johnson who did virtually all the damage. Fraser, defying a sore knee and an aching Achilles tendon, earned himself 6 for 64 while Johnson ended with 3 for 76. A ninth-wicket stand of 68 between Paul Franks (50) and David Lucas rallied Notts from 82 for 7 to 192 all out, but all it really achieved was delaying the end and forcing Middlesex to bat again.

ROUND SIXTEEN: 16–20 AUGUST 2000

Division One
16 and 17 August
at the Oval
Derbyshire 118 (53.3 overs)(GP Butcher 5 for 18, including four wickets in five balls) and 97 (Saqlain Mushtaq 7 for 11)
Surrey 260 (79.3 overs)(MA Butcher 78, IJ Ward 57, KJ Dean 6 for 51)
Surrey won by an innings and 45 runs
Surrey 17 pts, Derbyshire 3 pts

16, 17, 18 and 19 August
at Leicester
Leicestershire 351 (110.3 overs)(DL Maddy 66, Aftab Habib 59, ND Burns 58)
Yorkshire 340 (111.1 overs)(DS Lehmann 115, GM Hamilton 66)
Match drawn – no play was possible on the third day
Leicestershire 11 pts, Yorkshire 10 pts

Following an impressive 1999, this was an important season for Sussex's James Kirtley. He responded with 63 Championship wickets, and 26 victims in the National League.

at Taunton
Durham 378 (127.1 overs)(NJ Speak 78, PD Collingwood 74)
Somerset 362 for 8 (111.4 overs)(GD Rose 102, M Burns 89)
Match drawn
Somerset 11 pts, Durham 10 pts

17, 18 and 19 August
at Old Trafford
Lancashire 236 (87.3 overs) and 198 (CP Schofield 70*)
Kent 155 (55 overs)(PJ Martin 5 for 42) and 125
Lancashire won by 154 runs
Lancashire 16 pts, Kent 3 pts

Surrey called up Gary Butcher for his first championship appearance of the season, against Derbyshire at the Oval, and the 25-year-old all-rounder could hardly have made a bigger or more immediate impact after being preferred to Ben Hollioake. On the opening day Butcher became the first championship bowler for 28 years to take four wickets in four balls as Derbyshire were skittled for 118. Bursting from the shadows of his Test-playing father Alan and brother Mark, the younger Butcher took his wickets from the last ball of his seventh over and the first three deliveries of his eighth. Brother Mark, in fact, had a hand in his achievement – catching hold of a rebound off third slip Martin Bicknell to give Gary the first scalp of his four-wicket blitz. Butcher had taken 1 for 12 from an initial six-over spell when he was recalled. It proved to be one of the most inspired bowling changes made by skipper Adam Hollioake all season! In order, Butcher's victims were Paul Aldred, Tim Munton, Kevin Dean and Lian Wharton – not the full glorious flower of English batsmanship but still a worthy bag! Bicknell, by the way, might have made the first three wickets a real collector's item hat-trick – after spilling Aldred, and seeing Mark Butcher at second slip scoop up the ball, he managed to hang on to nicks from Munton and Dean. Wharton was then leg before. Only 31 bowlers have managed four in four throughout the history of first-class cricket worldwide, and the last of the 15 to do it in county championship competition was Pat Pocock, also of Surrey, against Sussex at Eastbourne in 1972. Butcher finished with 5 for 18, and the rest of the day belonged to his brother Mark, who hit 78 in an opening stand of 137 with Ian Ward (57). By the close Surrey were completely in command at 161 for 2 and, despite Dean's 6 for 51, that pegged back their first innings to 260 all out, the champions were soon celebrating the innings and 45-run win which avenged their early-season defeat at Derby and also kept them moving remorselessly towards another title. Saqlain Mushtaq, with a brilliant 7 for 11 from 9.3 overs, simply decimated the Derbyshire batting in their second innings and, with Ian Salisbury supporting well with 3 for 25, the visitors were tumbled out for 97.

Lancashire clung on to hopes of championship success by beating Kent by 154 runs at Old Trafford to keep up their dogged chase. Neil Fairbrother's 48 was the best score in a workmanlike first innings of 236 – Saurav Ganguly making a duck and returning to total silence through the members' enclosure once dubbed the 'pit of hate' by a local journalist.

ENGLAND UNDER-19S by Tim Boon

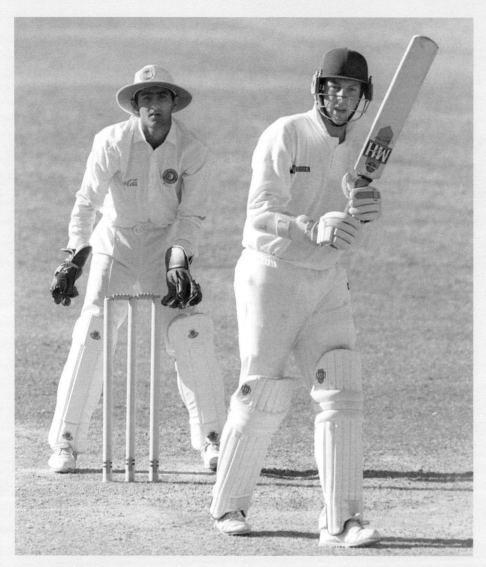

The under-19s of today are the Test players of
the future. Marcus Trescothick batted for England
v. South Africa under-19s at Taunton in 1995.

It was a marvellous opportunity for the England Under-19 team to travel to Sri Lanka and play in the Junior World Cup 2000 in order to experience a different climate and culture. Our aim, obviously, was to retain the World Cup after the huge 1998 success in South Africa, but this was a completely different side with very different characters and preparation going to Sri Lanka.

We profiled the players who worked on individual programmes in conjunction with their county coaches, as well as visiting Impact, 'team building' specialists from the Lake District. We were fortunate to be able to practise and acclimatise in the intense heat of Malaysia before going on to Sri Lanka – which was noticeably cooler by comparison. Given that preparation, I was disappointed to come home after the Super League stage but, on reflection, a semi-final place would have been a fine achievement.

England's players were immature compared to the Asians, who had at least one member on the fringe of the Test squad. We lacked runs, and scored too many twenties and thirties – the only exception being Gary Pratt who averaged more than 50. Our bowling was plagued by inconsistency but improved as the tour progressed. The fielding department was athletic and, in fact, proved to be our best area of skill. However, even this can still improve under pressure.

I can assure you that the technical department within the England and Wales Cricket Board is moving at breakneck speed as we restructure the coaching scheme and the development of excellence under the guidance of Technical Director Hugh Morris. It is hoped the first National Academy will be up and running by November 2001, together with the University Centres of Excellence and County Academies to form a more progressive structure.

In the National Academy, the coaches will be of a minimum Level three/four standard and implement individually based programmes. A broad range of topics will be covered in the Academy, with best practice from around the world employed. These topics will be drip-fed into the lower age groups, creating a more inclined measurable structure all the way through to Test cricket. Communication will depend on maturity, learning styles and individual needs. Skill acquisition will be drill-based initially to promote self-learning and give solid foundations from which to build, moving on to match practice under pressure.

Batsmen need to be technically and tactically adept and have the mindset to keep the tempo of runs flowing without selling their wicket cheaply, while the bowlers must be balanced, applying their trade with control from a sound injury-free base. Fielders must become specialists: athletes who thrive under pressure.

If we are to become the most successful and respected cricket nation in the world, we will require young people with a tremendous desire to succeed, an insatiable appetite for knowledge and the persistence to complete the task in hand! The philosophy that drives much of the development discussed above is encapsulated by a quote from John Whitmore: 'When we truly accept or take responsibility for our thoughts and our actions, our commitment to them rises and so does our performance.' ■

Mark Ramprakash drives Ashley Giles past the jumping Graeme Welch during his undefeated century against Warwickshire.

But Peter Martin, fighting his way back to full fitness, won Lancashire a useful lead by picking up 5 for 42 as Kent, slumping first to 14 for 4, could only reach 155. Now, though, it was the home side's turn to struggle, and at 43 for 6 the match was in the balance. Fairbrother, however, responded again with 43 and a last-wicket stand of 54 between the irrepressible Chris Schofield (70 not out) and Martin gave Lancashire the advantage. Kent needed a big innings from Rahul Dravid, but the Indian could not this time answer the call and – with spinners Schofield and Gary Keedy sharing seven wickets – Lancashire dismissed their visitors for just 125.

Yorkshire, like Lancashire desperate for a win to keep up the pressure on Surrey, could only draw with Leicestershire at Grace Road in a match that lost the whole of its third day to rain. Yorkshire, however, were fielding a severely weakened side and

might have been grateful for the four extra points available for a draw after Leicestershire had reached 351 in their first innings. Darren Maddy, Aftab Habib, Neil Burns and Darren Stevens all made runs against a team missing seven first-choice players and also including just four capped players. Yorkshire, in reply, slipped to 123 for 5 despite a determined effort from opener Simon Widdup, but then acting captain Darren Lehmann joined Gavin Hamilton in an excellent partnership. Hamilton was out for 66 soon after the match resumed on the final day, but Lehmann – who had come in at number seven because of a stiff back – surged on to 115 as Yorkshire used the time left to search for more batting bonus points.

Rain on days two and three, allowing just 47.1 overs in that period, also wrecked the prospect of a result at Taunton. Durham totalled 378 before the first downpour, with Nick Speak (78) and Paul Collingwood (74) enjoying one of the best batting surfaces in the country, and on the final day Somerset merely concentrated on securing maximum batting points as they reached 362 for 8. Graham Rose (102) scored his second championship century in successive innings and figured in a stand worth 170 for the sixth wicket with Michael Burns (89).

Division Two
16, 17 and 18 August
at Eastbourne
Northamptonshire 110 (45.2 overs)(RJ Kirtley 6 for 41) and 270 (JW Cook 116)
Sussex 153 (56.3 overs)(CJ Adams 84) and 65 (JP Taylor 6 for 27)
Northamptonshire won by 162 runs
Northamptonshire 15 pts, Sussex 3 pts

at Colchester
Gloucestershire 324 (121.2 overs)(JN Snape 54*) and 197 (KJ Barnett 57, AP Cowan 5 for 66)
Essex 174 (67.3 overs)(AP Grayson 56) and 243 (SG Law 58)
Gloucestershire won by 104 runs
Gloucestershire 18 pts, Essex 3 pts

at Cardiff
Glamorgan 288 (96.5 overs)(SP James 77, MP Maynard 77) and 99 for 6
Nottinghamshire 343 (124 overs)(Usman Afzaal 103, GE Welton 74)
Match drawn – no play was possible on the third day
Glamorgan 9 pts, Nottinghamshire 10 pts

17, 18, 19 and 20 August
at Edgbaston
Middlesex 380 for 8 dec. (111 overs)(MR Ramprakash 120*, JL Langer 109, MA Roseberry 62) and 126 for 1 dec. (JL Langer 69*)
Warwickshire 211 for 4 dec. (DL Hemp 78*) and 191 for 5 (MJ Powell 55)
Match drawn – no play was possible on the second day
Warwickshire 7 pts, Middlesex 7 pts

Northamptonshire's dramatic late-season surge towards the second division title continued apace in a remarkable match at Eastbourne. Preparing a well-grassed strip, possibly in order to nullify the Northants spinners, might be seen to have backfired on Sussex after they were shot out for 65 in their second innings. Paul Taylor, adding 6 for 27 to his first-innings 4 for 42, cut a swathe through the home batting with his left-arm seam and swing, while Darren Cousins also had a ball, taking 4 for 16 on the second evening, and 4 for 25 overall, as Sussex collapsed spectacularly to 25 for 7. Chris Adams, following up his first-innings

84 with 24 not out, watched in horror from the other end and all that Sussex could take from the debacle was that Mike Denness, the ECB's chief pitch inspector, marked the surface only 'below average' and therefore did not deduct any points. Nineteen wickets, however, fell on the opening day with James Kirtley taking 6-41 as Northants were dismissed for 110 but then Sussex struggling to 151-9 in reply with only Adams flourishing in the conditions. Poor batting, though, was more than partly responsible for the carnage and, on the second day, Jeff Cook certainly showed that run-scoring was not an impossible occupation. The Australian-raised left-hander hit 116, displaying superb stroke selection, and David Ripley's unbeaten 39 also helped to take Northants to 270 and a lead decisive enough soon to earn them victory by 162 runs.

Sloppy batting by Essex was also at the core of their 104-run defeat against Gloucestershire at Colchester – a win that took the visitors off the bottom of the table. Gloucestershire looked to have underachieved when a succession of batsmen got in, but then got out, as they reached 278 for 9 by the close of the opening day. However, Jeremy Snape (54 not out) was then joined by last man Ben Gannon in a final-wicket stand of 58 – Gannon scoring a career-best 28 – and the frustration of seeing their opponents move on to 324 clearly got the better of Essex. One by one, apart from Paul Grayson (56), they came and went before, finally, Essex were bowled out for 174. Mark Alleyne, the Gloucestershire captain, opted not to enforce the follow-on – preferring to try to bat Essex out of the game on a pitch that all expected to deteriorate. But, after Gloucestershire had rather unsteadily reached 197 in their second innings, the pitch seemed to be playing as well as at any stage in the match as Essex reached 123 for 1 towards the close of the third day. Stuart Law and Grayson were producing the first real quality batting of the match, and suddenly a shock win looked possible for Essex. Then, however, the illusion was broken as Grayson was leg before playing no stroke and Law (58) edged a flamboyant drive to first slip. Essex, 141 for 4 at the close, declined to 243 the next day despite Ronnie Irani's defiant 33 not out.

Bad weather brought draws at both Cardiff and Edgbaston, with no play being possible at all on the third day of Glamorgan's match against Nottinghamshire and the second day of the meeting between Warwickshire and Middlesex. Notts were particularly peeved at Cardiff, having replied with 343 to Glamorgan's 288 with Usman Afzaal compiling a determined 103 to build on an earlier fine comeback in the field. Linked with fellow slow left-armer Richard Stemp, Afzaal then helped to put Glamorgan under severe pressure on the final day before time ran out with the home side struggling for survival at 99 for 6. Justin Langer (109) and Mark Ramprakash (120 not out) were both in imperious form at Edgbaston but the loss of a day ultimately meant that deals had to be done by the respective captains if a result was to be achieved. Both teams, though, were wary of giving anything away and – eventually – Warwickshire finished on 191 for 5, David Hemp adding 44 to his first-innings 78, after being set a target of 296 in 80 overs.

ROUND SEVENTEEN: 21–25 AUGUST 2000

Division One
22, 23, 24 and 25 August
at Derby
Derbyshire 167 (50.3 overs)(RJ Bailey 54) and 476 for 7 dec. (DG Cork 200*, MP Dowman 140)
Durham 144 (47.5 overs)(KJ Dean 6 for 52) and 267 (SM Katich 70, PD Collingwood 66)
Derbyshire won by 232 runs
Derbyshire 15 pts, Durham 3 pts

at Canterbury
Kent 323 (120.5 overs)(PA Nixon 134*, AD Mullally 5 for 90) and 146 (SK Warne 6 for 34)
Hampshire 156 (51.1 overs)(LR Prittipaul 52, MJ Saggers 5 for 47) and 298 (WS Kendall 72, MJ McCague 5 for 52)
Kent won by 15 runs
Kent 18 pts, Hampshire 3 pts

at Leicester
Leicestershire 372 (109 overs)(PAJ deFreitas 97, Aftab Habib 93, JM Dakin 50) and 408 for 6 (PAJ deFreitas 123*, Aftab Habib 73, IJ Sutcliffe 52)
Lancashire 574 for 5 dec. (177 overs)(JP Crawley 139, NH Fairbrother 100*, SC Ganguly 87, WK Hegg 65*, A Flintoff 55)
Match drawn
Leicestershire 9 pts, Lancashire 12 pts

Kent all but assured themselves of retaining first division status with an exciting, nerve-tingling 15-run victory against a gallant, but now doomed, Hampshire at Canterbury. In one of the best finishes to one of the best matches of the season, Martin McCague produced the decisive contribution just

when it seemed as if Hampshire were going to reach their stiff fourth-innings target of 314 and give themselves a lifeline in the fight against relegation. A remarkable match began with Shane Warne flying in from Melbourne on the morning of the game, jumping from his car from Heathrow and going straight into the field. Ever the showman, of course, he took a wicket with his fifth ball and went on to take 3 for 88 from 28 overs on an opening day that initially went Hampshire's way but finally belonged to Paul Nixon, the combative Kent wicketkeeper. Nixon attacked Warne, and nullified the threat of five-wicket Alan Mullally, in a magnificent innings. What is more, he inspired last man David Masters to tough it out alongside him, and by the close of play they had taken Kent from 198 for 9 to 268 for 9. The following morning saw Nixon convert his unbeaten 92 into a superb 134 not out, while Masters' resolute 21 played a huge part in an unexpected but vital last-wicket stand of 125. In reply, a no-doubt-demoralised Hampshire slid to 156 all out, with Martin Saggers continuing his fine form with 5 for 47 and Masters adding a gleeful 4 for 31 to his great batting effort. Only Lawrence Prittipaul (52) and Warne (45) put up worthy resistance but Alan Wells, the acting Kent captain, opted not to enforce the follow-on. Perhaps it was a negative move, and revealed Kentish fears of facing Warne on a final-day pitch, but it failed to pay off, with Hampshire now fighting back with the ball to reduce the home side to 83 for 5 by the close of the second day. David Fulton, holding the innings together with 40 not out overnight, could add just eight more runs when play resumed and only McCague's hard-hit 24 hauled Kent's total up to 146. Warne, bowling quite brilliantly and sensing a way back into the match, took 6 for 34 from his 20.2 overs. Will Kendall (72) now added 108 for the second wicket with Giles White and, when Jason Laney also got among the runs, Hampshire moved menacingly to 251-6 by the close. An almost unbearably tense final morning began with McCague snatching two important wickets with the old ball. But, against the second new-ball spells of Saggers and Masters, the ninth-wicket pair of Adrian Aymes and Shaun Udal began to flourish and soon their partnership was worth 38. Wells now threw the ball again to McCague, even though the big Irish-Australian was struggling for fitness and had suffered an unhappy season following ankle surgery in the winter. The result was joy for Kent, and for McCague, as he threw himself into the fray to trap Udal leg before with an off-cutter and then, two balls later, clean bowling hapless last man Mullally for a duck.

In another bottom-of-the-table clash, at Derby, a stunning unbeaten 200 from Dominic Cork spearheaded a 232-run victory over Durham. Cork and Mathew Dowman transformed a match that had previously been dominated by the ball by putting on a massive 258 for the seventh wicket in Derbyshire's second innings – which was not surprisingly a new county record, beating the 241 posted by George Pope and Bert Rhodes against Hampshire at Portsmouth in 1948. Cork's superb innings, a career-best, included three sixes and 32 fours and took him 264 balls. His final fifty came off just 30 balls and, when Dowman (140) was out, Cork and Tim Munton added a further 97 in nine overs. The result of all this mayhem was that Derbyshire, who had been struggling on 121 for 6, were eventually able to declare at 476 for 7 and set Durham to score 500 in just over five sessions. Cork, typically, then unstrapped his pads to remove Jon Lewis with the very first ball of the Durham second innings, and not even a fine stand between Simon Katich (70) and Paul Collingwood (66) could hold up Derbyshire for long. The visitors were finally bowled out soon after the start of the final day, with Munton picking up 3 for 44 and Kevin Dean adding 3 for 49 to his first-innings 6 for 52. That first Dean haul had helped Derbyshire bounce back on an astonishing opening day when Durham, having dismissed the home side for 167, were themselves sent packing for 144. Rob Bailey's 54 and Cork's 53-ball 45 were the only clues amid all the poor-quality batting on day one of the rich stroke-play to come. And, despite the clatter of 20 wickets on that first day, ECB pitch inspector Alan Smith had quickly absolved the pitch of any blame.

Phil deFreitas and Aftab Habib were Leicestershire's batting stars at Grace Road as the home side held out for a high-scoring draw that greatly harmed Lancashire's chances of winning an elusive championship title. DeFreitas made 97 and Habib 93 as Leicestershire, with Jon Dakin also hitting 50, reached 372 in their first innings. But, on a shirtfront of a surface, Lancashire then set out to earn themselves a potentially match-winning lead and, by totalling 574 for 5, they succeeded. John Crawley led the way with 139, Saurav Ganguly hit 87 and Neil Fairbrother ended 100 not out. By the close of the third day Leicestershire were 75 for 1, but Lancashire hopes that spinner Chris Schofield and Gary Keedy could win the game for them were misplaced. Keedy was tidy but rarely threatening while Schofield, who

managed just 3 for 149 from his 43 overs, was particularly disappointing in a situation set up for the leg-spinner. Habib's 73 and Iain Sutcliffe's solid 52 made sure there were no early alarms, and deFreitas then enjoyed himself by reaching 123 not out as the bowling grew ever friendlier.

Division Two
21, 22 and 23 August
at Worcester
Worcestershire 338 (113.2 overs)(VS Solanki 160, DJ Pipe 54) and 36 for 1
Warwickshire 142 (54.2 overs)(MJ Powell 75, CG Liptrot 6 for 44) and (following on) 231 (A Singh 79, TL Penney 51, SR Lampitt 7 for 45)
Worcestershire won by nine wickets
Worcestershire 18 pts, Warwickshire 3 pts

21, 22, 23 and 24 August
at Bristol
Middlesex 207 (73.1 overs)(JL Langer 77, RCJ Williams 4ct/1st) and 124
Gloucestershire 188 (101.3 overs)(PCR Tufnell 5 for 23) and 147 for 3 (MGN Windows 70*)
Gloucestershire won by seven wickets
Gloucestershire 15 pts, Middlesex 4 pts

at Colwyn Bay
Glamorgan 718 for 3 dec. (162 overs)(SP James 309*, MTG Elliott 177, MP Maynard 67, MJ Powell 64)
Sussex 342 (108.5 overs)(CJ Adams 156, UBA Rashid 110, AG Wharf 5 for 68) and (following on) 316 (RSC Martin-Jenkins 77, CJ Adams 68, UBA Rashid 54, A Dale 5 for 46)
Glamorgan won by an innings and 60 runs
Glamorgan 20 pts, Sussex 3 pts

Glamorgan, Gloucestershire and Worcestershire all stepped up their promotion pushes with important victories in this round of games. As for the three beaten counties, Sussex seemed to be slipping inexorably out of contention – after leading the division not so long before – while both Middlesex and Warwickshire looked to be quite incapable of mounting a consistent challenge.

Two long-standing batting records fell at Colwyn Bay as Steve James and Matthew Elliott gave the Sussex attack a fearful roasting in the North Wales sunshine. James and Elliott put on no fewer than 374 for Glamorgan's first wicket, eclipsing the 330 of Alan Jones and Roy Fredericks against Northants at Swansea in 1972. By the close of a memorable opening day, Glamorgan were 457 for 1 with Elliott the only casualty after smashing seven sixes and 15 fours in his 177. James, on 193 overnight, strode on to a mammoth 309 not out the following day as Glamorgan showed no mercy to their shell-shocked opponents. Michael Powell, Matthew Maynard and Adrian Dale also made runs but it was James' day as he went past Emrys Davies' previous Glamorgan

Alex Tudor took four wickets in an ill-tempered match at Scarborough that took Surrey one step closer to retaining the title.

best of 287 not out in 1939. A difficult return catch to James Kirtley, on 285, was James' only chance – and Glamorgan's final total of 718 for 3 declared could not have been more intimidating. Chris Adams' decision to bowl, on winning the toss, won't go down as one of the season's better decisions – although it was perhaps a small consolation to hear Maynard confess that he, too, would have been seduced into bowling first by a pitch that initially looked a little damp (but that soon dried out!). Adams, to his credit, did his best to rally his downcast side after Alex Wharf had made two early strikes with the new ball and Steve Watkin had grabbed two more important wickets just before the close of the second day. From their overnight 112 for 5, Sussex were boosted by a stand of 232 for the sixth wicket by Adams (156) and Umer Rashid (110), but then Wharf (5 for 68) and Watkin (4 for 76) hit back to bowl out the visitors for 342. Following on, Sussex slipped at first to 50 for 4 before Adams once more dug in. Robin Martin-Jenkins helped his captain take Sussex to 168 for 4 by the close, but on the last day Adams could not add to his overnight 68 and a subsequent partnership of 84 between Martin-Jenkins (77) and Rashid (54) merely delayed the inevitable. Dale (5 for 46) polished off the fragile Sussex tail and Glamorgan took a maximum 20 points from their innings-and-60-run victory.

Gloucestershire warmed up for the NatWest Trophy final by moving off the bottom of the congested second division table and into fourth place as a result of outfighting Middlesex in a low-scoring and attritional contest at Bristol. A rain-affected opening day made it 17 weather-hit days out of 25 on the ground this season, but Middlesex were still able to reach 151 for 5 from 53.5 overs thanks to Justin Langer's unbeaten 76. The Australian left-hander added just a single to his score on the resumption the following day, Jon Lewis finishing with 4 for 72 as Middlesex were dismissed for 207. Only 213 runs came from the six and a half hours of play on day two, in fact, Gloucestershire struggling to 157 for 7 in reply by the close with Phil Tufnell, the slow left-arm spinner, taking 3 for 16 from no fewer than 28 overs. Reggie Williams, deputising for the rested Jack Russell, made 43, but when Gloucestershire were bowled out for 188 with Tufnell returning figures of 5 for 23 from 36.3 overs (21 of them maidens), it looked as though Middlesex had the upper hand. Soon, however, the visitors were 45 for 5, and although the promising Ed Joyce remained 49 not out, Middlesex were all out for 124 with Lewis again the leading home bowler with 4 for 36. At first, Gloucestershire concentrated only on preserving wickets, and at the end of the third day they had reached just 44 for 1 from 31 overs. But, the next morning, the stroke-play of Matt Windows blossomed and, in an unbroken stand of 72 with Chris Taylor, he saw Gloucestershire home by seven wickets.

The West Midlands derby at Worcester was a triumph for Vikram Solanki, whose brilliant 160 proved to be the match-winning innings. Worcestershire were denied the services of the travelling Glenn McGrath because the ECB decreed the game had to be moved forward 24 hours because of Warwickshire's involvement in the NatWest Trophy final, and although they were unhappy at the ruling they overcame a terrible start to claim a convincing nine-wicket win. Jamie Pipe hit a rousing 54 on his championship debut to join Solanki in a fourth-wicket stand of 100 in 20 overs – the perfect riposte to the plunge to 8 for 3 against a new ball. Rain and bad light cut 40 overs from the day, but Solanki had still reached 113 not out by the close and, with Steve Rhodes contributing a dour 46, Worcestershire went on to total 338. By that evening Warwickshire were in desperate trouble at 140 for 8 in reply, with only opener Michael Powell (75) putting up lengthy resistance and Chris Liptrot (5 for 43) thoroughly enjoying himself in McGrath's absence. Liptrot took his figures to 6 for 44 the next morning, and Warwickshire's 142 all out condemned them to following on. This time it was Stuart Lampitt's medium-pace cut and in-swing that did the damage: he finished with 7 for 45 as Warwickshire could total just 231. Anurag Singh scored a fluent 79 and Trevor Penney a cussed 51, but Worcestershire were left with a straightforward task as they knocked off the 36 runs needed.

ROUND EIGHTEEN: 30 AUGUST – 4 SEPTEMBER 2000

Division One
30, 31 August, 1 and 2 September
at Scarborough
Surrey 356 (110.3 overs)(IJ Ward 59, IDK Salisbury 57*) and 89 for 3 dec.
Yorkshire 158 (41.1 overs)(DS Lehmann 66) and 68 for 0
Match drawn – Yorkshire had 8 pts deducted from their season's total for producing an unsatisfactory pitch for this fixture
Yorkshire 7 pts, Surrey 11 pts

31 August, 1, 2 and 3 September
at Chester-le-Street
Durham 320 for 9 dec. (92.3 overs)(JJB Lewis 70, SM Katich 60, MP Speight 55, JA Daley 50) and 39 for 1 dec.
Hampshire 69 for 0 dec. (20 overs) and 292 for 4 (WS Kendall 119*, JS Laney 52)
Hampshire won by six wickets
Hampshire 15 pts, Durham 3 pts

1, 2, 3 and 4 September
at Taunton
Somerset 411 for 7 dec. (ID Blackwell 109, J Cox 58) and 90 for 2
Leicestershire 470 (122.2 overs)(DL Maddy 102, VJ Wells 98, Aftab Habib 72, BF Smith 69, ND Burns 57)
Match drawn
Somerset 8 pts, Leicestershire 7 pts

A controversial, bad-tempered and at times farcical match at Scarborough ended with Yorkshire's championship ambitions in ruins because of a pitch penalty and Surrey taking away the 11 points that, almost, clinched them the county title. The bad feeling between the two teams started even before the match began, with Surrey's players being openly critical of the pitch produced for such a crucial game. Well-grassed, it looked greener than the rest of the square, and Yorkshire captain David Byas had no hesitation in asking Surrey to bat when he won the toss. The tactic backfired, however, as the Yorkshire bowlers failed to make the most of the conditions; by the close Surrey, despite slipping at one stage to 197 for 7, had rallied to 330 for 8 thanks to a stand of 78 between Ian Salisbury and Jon Batty, and then further resistance by Salisbury and Alex Tudor. The next morning saw Surrey claim a further batting point, reaching 356 all out with Salisbury unbeaten on 57. Umpires John Harris and Barry Dudleston, however, had already seen enough and they expressed their concerns about the pitch to Mike Denness, also in attendance at North Marine Road in his capacity as head of the ECB's pitch liaison team. In turn, Denness asked Alan Fordham, the ECB's cricket operations manager, to form an adjudicating panel and he called in Chris Wood, the Board's pitches consultant. The verdict, confirmed late in the evening on the second day, was an eight-point penalty for 'undue seam movement and unevenness of bounce on the first day, with no extenuating circumstances'. By then, moreover, Yorkshire had folded to 158 all out in their first innings, Tudor taking wickets with the first two deliveries and finishing with 4 for 75 despite feeling the force of a furious counter-attack by Darren Lehmann (66). Ben Hollioake, who also struck quickly with the new ball, as Yorkshire were reduced initially to 4 for 3, took 3 for 67 and Saqlain Mushtaq needed only seven balls to wrap up the innings – at a personal cost of no runs. Surrey opted not to enforce the follow on but, as the third day dawned, an already infamous contest turned into pure farce. Inadequate pitch covering (or was it a deliberate act of vandalism?) resulted after torrential overnight rain in a serious leak which left a waterlogged patch of turf right on the bowlers' take-off point at the Pavilion End. No more than a yard square, it nevertheless took an age to clear up – while, all the time, the sun beat down and spectators grew ever more agitated. Finally, four hours late, the match resumed. Eleven overs later, however, the heavens opened during the tea interval and further play was impossible. Surrey, having moved to 89 for 3, then declared overnight but more bad weather meant there was time only for Yorkshire to reach 68 without loss before, mercifully, the whole affair was over. On a strained third day, to boot, the Yorkshire players made a point of moving to another part of the pavilion to take lunch – rather than share facilities, as is the Scarborough tradition, with their opponents. It was an act of petulance quite out of keeping with a professional sports team – but, then again, events surrounding the match itself should have no part in championship cricket. Yorkshire, afterwards, announced that they would not be appealing against the pitch penalty, but at the end of the season would be tackling the ECB about what they see as serious inconsistencies in the actions of the pitch liaison committee. Having been fortunate to get away with some dodgy pitches at Headingley earlier in the summer, however, Yorkshire should not try to claim any moral high ground.

An old-fashioned bout of bartering between acting Durham captain Jon Lewis and his Hampshire counterpart Robin Smith produced a positive result out of a rain-afflicted match at Chester-le-Street. Unfortunately for Lewis, his offer of 291 in 91 overs on the final day proved too soft a target, with Hampshire's in-form Will Kendall hitting a match-winning 119 not out. Kendall faced just 147 balls, stroking 16 fours, with Jason Laney, Smith himself and young Lawrence Prittipaul all making valuable contributions to an eventual six-wicket victory. The win, achieved in the end with 13.5 overs to spare, just about kept alive Hampshire's mathematical chances of avoiding relegation. In Durham's stop-start first innings of

320 for 9 declared, which spilled well into the third day because of the weather interruptions, Lewis (70) and Simon Katich (60) added 125 while Jimmy Daley (50) and Martin Speight (55) put on a further 112 for the fifth wicket. Then came the two declarations that made up the deal, but not before Adrian Aymes, the Hampshire wicket-keeper, had claimed only the fourth first-class wicket of his career during an over of 'cafeteria' bowling.

Poor weather also affected the game between Somerset and Leicestershire at Taunton, but there no deal was done between Jamie Cox and Vince Wells in an attempt to make up for lost time. An excellent pitch, and the unwillingness of either

Ian Harvey enjoyed another superb all-round year for Gloucestershire: wickets, runs and 3 more one-day titles in the championship.

captain to risk defeat, resulted in a high-scoring draw. Ian Blackwell made a powerful maiden first-class century in Somerset's first innings 411 for 7 declared, and Darren Maddy replied with his first championship hundred for 14 months. Wells, however, was out two runs short of his ton as Leicestershire reached 470 on a final day when both sides merely went through the motions.

Division Two
30, 31 August, 1 and 2 September
at Southend-on-Sea
Essex 292 (103.2 overs)(RC Irani 95, SG Law 70, JS Foster 52) and 350 for 8 (RC Irani 83*, SG Law 82, AP Cowan 67)
Glamorgan 507 for 9 dec. (162.5 overs)(MJ Powell 128, MP Maynard 102, IJ Thomas 82)
Match drawn
Essex 8 pts, Glamorgan 12 pts

at Northampton
Northamptonshire 469 (179 overs)(AL Penberthy 116, AJ Swann 61*, RJ Warren 61, DJG Sales 55)
Gloucestershire 186 (80 overs) and (following on) 209
Northamptonshire won by an innings and 74 runs
Northamptonshire 18 pts, Gloucestershire 1 pt

at Trent Bridge
Nottinghamshire 351 (112.4 overs)(DJ Bicknell 144, PR Reiffel 74, JD Lewry 6 for 89) and 238 for 4 dec. (JER Gallian 110*)
Sussex 287 (85.1 overs)(RR Montgomerie 129, AJ Harris 6 for 110) and 4 for 0
Match drawn
Nottinghamshire 11 pts, Sussex 9 pts

at Edgbaston
Worcestershire 263 (89 overs)(VS Solanki 71) and 181 for 1 (WPC Weston 58*, VS Solanki 57*, EJ Wilson 51)
Warwickshire 407 for 8 dec. (129.4 overs)(MA Wagh 130, DP Ostler 88, MJ Powell 69, GD McGrath 6 for 90)
Match drawn
Warwickshire 12 pts, Worcestershire 8 pts

Northamptonshire's great surge towards the second division title continued apace at Wantage Road, where Gloucestershire became the latest victims. More fine bowling by Darren Cousins and Jason Brown earned Northants victory by an innings and 74 runs, with only Jack Russell (40 and 41) putting up prolonged resistance in both the Gloucestershire innings. On a bone-dry pitch Northants ran up an intimidating 469 with fine half-centuries from

Russell Warren and David Sales, a worthy 116 from Tony Penberthy (including three sixes and 12 fours) and 61 not out by Alec Swann on his first championship appearance of the season. By the close of the second day Brown already had two wickets to his name and Gloucestershire were 65 for 3. Brown, going past 50 wickets for the summer, made it 4 for 68 the next day and, with Cousins coming in with 4 for 41, Gloucestershire were soon bowled out for 186. Following on, the visitors did only a little better, this time reaching 209 with Cousins and Brown picking up another three wickets apiece.

The other three matches in the second division all ended in draws, despite some memorable individual performances.

At Southend, the Glamorgan fourth wicket pair of Michael Powell (128) and Matthew Maynard (102) put on 227 – Powell being awarded his county cap at tea on the second day. Ian Thomas, a 21-year-old making his first-class debut, then hit a brisk 82 as Glamorgan reached 507 for 9 declared

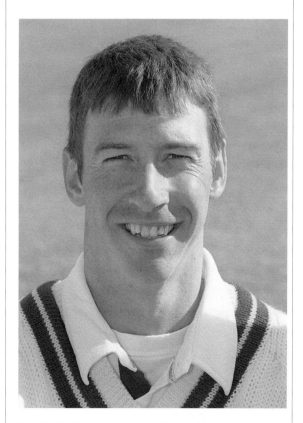

Tony Penberthy's century against Gloucestershire maintained Northamptonshire's progress toward the second-division title.

in reply to the Essex first innings of 292. Ronnie Irani and Stuart Law, who had scored 95 and 70 respectively to rescue their side from 13 for 3 on the first morning, were in the runs a second time as Essex successfully batted out for a draw on 350 for 8. Law made 82, nightwatchman Ashley Cowan enjoyed himself immensely with 67 and Irani remained 83 not out. Catching the eye in this match, too, was 20-year-old wicket-keeper Jamie Foster, who marked an impressive debut with composed innings of 52 and 34.

Rain for much of the final day prevented any chance of a result at Trent Bridge, where Darren Bicknell, Richard Montgomerie and Jason Gallian all scored hundreds. Bicknell's 144, and an eighth wicket stand of 143 with Paul Reiffel (74) helped Nottinghamshire post 351 in their first innings. Andy Harris (6 for 110) then all but matched Jason Lewry's 6 for 89 as Sussex were dismissed for 287 in reply. Montgomerie's 129 meant that, in three championship innings against Notts this summer, he had scored 357 runs. Gallian, dropped on 10, then strode on to 110 not out, but the rain arrived soon after Notts had declared their second innings on 238 for 4.

The second and third days at Edgbaston were badly hit by the weather, so it was no surprise when time ran out for both Warwickshire and Worcestershire too. Vikram Solanki's 71, and Allan Donald's 4 for 69, were the highlights of the opening day as Worcestershire were bowled out for 263, but it was well into the fourth and final day before Warwickshire could reach a declaration at 407 for 8. Mark Wagh scored an excellent 130, from 256 balls, and Dominic Ostler passed 1,000 runs for the first time since 1994 during his forthright 88, but Glenn McGrath (6 for 90 from 42.4 overs) made sure the Warwickshire batsmen had to work hard for a good many of their runs and, in the end, Worcestershire batted out time comfortably to reach 181-1.

ROUND NINETEEN: 5–10 SEPTEMBER 2000

Division One
6, 7, 8 and 9 September
at Southampton
Hampshire 522 (134.3 overs)(LR Prittipaul 152, WS Kendall 143, AD Mascarenhas 62)
Derbyshire 352 (113.2 overs)(RJ Bailey 90, LD Sutton 77, MJ di Venuto 52) and (following on) 167 (RJ Bailey 53, SD Udal 5 for 58)
Hampshire won by an innings and 3 runs
Hampshire 20 pts, Derbyshire 6 pts

Anthony McGrath continues to make progress at Yorkshire as the Tykes promise to become a dominant force in the future.

at the Oval
Surrey 453 for 4 dec. (128.5 overs)(MA Butcher 191,
IJ Ward 144)
Durham 241 (82.3 overs)(SM Katich 77, IDK Salisbury
7 for 105) and (following on) 144
Surrey won by an innings and 68 runs
Surrey 20 pts, Durham 2 pts

7, 8, 9 and 10 September
at Canterbury
Yorkshire 401 (115 overs)(A McGrath 133, DS Lehmann
116, MP Vaughan 69) and 145 (MA Ealham 5 for 35)
Kent 317 (123.1 overs)(R Dravid 72) and 197
(MJ McCague 72)
Yorkshire won by 32 runs
Yorkshire 20 pts, Kent 6 pts

8, 9 and 10 September
at Old Trafford
Somerset 132 (49.4 overs)(J Cox 53) and 222
(PD Bowler 75)
Lancashire 463 for 9 dec. (127.2 overs)(WK Hegg 128,
GD Lloyd 126, MA Atherton 57)
Lancashire won by an innings and 109 runs
Lancashire 20 pts, Somerset 3 pts

Surrey virtually made sure of their second successive
championship title by overwhelming Durham by an
innings and 68 runs at the Oval – and then allowed
themselves quite a celebration anyway in front of
their home fans. Although, with Lancashire beating
Somerset at Old Trafford, a couple more points
were technically still required, Surrey knew that they
themselves could deny their nearest rivals the title by
merely declaring their first innings at any time
during the scheduled meeting of the two top
counties in the season's final week.

And so the Surrey players accepted the applause
and the plaudits, with captain Adam Hollioake
saying he believed the 2000 team were a stronger
unit than 12 months previously – despite a slow
start that had seen them beaten twice and win-less
until their fifth match. Durham, one of those sides
to topple the champions in the early part of the
campaign, were totally outclassed this time, with
Surrey openers Mark Butcher and Ian Ward both
hitting big hundreds in a first wicket stand of 359,
and then leg-spinner Ian Salisbury bamboozling the
visiting batsmen with match figures of 11 for 154 to
celebrate his winter tour recall by England. Surrey
were 243 for 0 after an opening day trimmed to 76
overs by rain, Butcher and Ward reaching their
centuries from consecutive balls in the penultimate

over before the close. The next morning saw
Butcher reach 191 and Ward 144 – and at one stage
the venerable county record opening stand of 428,
established against Oxford University in 1926 by
Jack Hobbs and Andy Sandham, looked under
threat. Durham, despite 77 from Simon Katich, had
slipped to 165 for 6 by the game's halfway stage,
and Salisbury ended with 7 for 105 as the visitors
were bundled out for 241. Following on, they were
soon 43 for 5, and from that position there could be
no escape. Salisbury's 4 for 49 and Alex Tudor's 3
for 41 made sure the end was not long delayed,
with Durham being bowled out a second time for
just 144.

Yorkshire, forced to face disappointment on both
championship and National League fronts, cheered
themselves up a touch by beating Kent by 32 runs in
an intriguing match at Canterbury. Yorkshire
seemed unbeatable when they ran up 401 in their
first innings, despite a slide from 327 for 2 following
a very fine stand of 195 between Darren Lehmann
(116) and Anthony McGrath (133). That, itself,
followed a partnership worth 123 from McGrath
and Michael Vaughan (69). Rahul Dravid led the
Kent reply, scoring 72 as his parents watched from
the Kent committee room as guests of the club and
adding 117 with Ed Smith (46). But Matthew
Hoggard's four wickets helped to restrict Kent to
317, and Yorkshire still seemed on top. Back,
however, came Kent with Mark Ealham (5 for 35)
and Martin Saggers (4 for 45) combining to great
effect to dismiss the visitors for just 145 in their
second innings. With 230 to win, could Kent turn
the tables? At 33 for 6, and then 59 for 7, it didn't
look likely – but that was before Matthew Fleming
was joined by Martin McCague in an eighth wicket
stand that produced 102 runs. McCague thumped a
career-best 72, from just 80 deliveries, but his
downfall to a missed heave to leg was soon followed
by Fleming (42) driving straight to extra cover. Kent
could now find no further heroics, and were soon all
out for 197.

Hampshire, finding some championship form
after it was too late, destroyed Derbyshire by an
innings and three runs at Southampton with the 20-
year-old Lawrence Prittipaul, an England-qualified
cousin of the West Indies batsman Shivnarine
Chanderpaul, marking only his fourth first-class
knock with a magnificent 152. Exactly 100 of his
runs came from boundaries as Prittipaul helped Will
Kendall (143 with fourteen fours) add 248 in 59
overs. Dimitri Mascarenhas contributed a late-order
62 to a massive first innings total of 522 – but at 346

SEPTEMBER DIARY by Robin Martin-Jenkins

A frustrating season for my Sussex teammates and myself was compensated for by the superb performances of the England team. While it seems as though we have taken a step backwards in the development of our team at Hove, English cricket as a whole has taken a huge leap forward. We will find out if this is indeed a giant leap for mankind, or just a small step for man, when we return from Asia. Will the introduction of central contracts for the core of the England team, which appears to be the most significant factor contributing to the improvement thus far, enable our batsmen to develop their techniques to be able to cope with Saqlain, Murali and co? Judging by the ease with which the best spinners in England took wickets in the county championship this year, it doesn't bode well.

The county season was as busy as ever, although with the introduction of two divisions in the championship it meant we played 16 games instead of 17. Significantly, this gave each team an extra week that could be used for practice or, if late in the season, the recharging of batteries. The glamour that the names Warne and McGrath (among others) brought to the daily treadmill of games under leaden skies was the tonic that many county supporters needed. Two divisions definitely helped to produce meaningful contests right to the end and so in that respect the idea has proved a success.

Who was the best player we came up against? A popular question at this time of year. On the bowling front there is only one name that springs to mind: Big G. McGrath. In the one-day games he bowled so tight anyone might think he had Scottish blood in him. He went at a little over two runs per over throughout the season, and the pace and bounce he generates from his rhythmical action makes him almost impossible to confront. When facing him in the four-day game, as throat ball followed throat ball, which followed the yorker and then the one that nips away off the seam, I didn't know where my next run was coming from.

The two batsmen who impressed us most are both under the age of 25 and have both been picked for the 'A' tour, which augurs well. Vikram Solanki scored a dazzling 98 at Hove in the championship, an innings brimming with the most brilliant natural talent. He is still a bit uncontrolled at times, but anyone who scores 1,000 runs at Worcester two seasons in a row must be worth a look. Likewise David Sales looks to have it all: a good temperament, sound defence and breathtaking strokes. He destroyed our bowling attack in a Sunday league game at Eastbourne. These guys will surely feature in Test cricket before too long.

Gloucestershire and Surrey are obviously the teams of the year and Marcus Trescothick took his chance superbly to be named PCA player of the year. So although Sussex picked up the wooden spoon in both leagues, and Hansie Cronje and pals did their best to sully its name, cricket marches on as gloriously as ever. If I were a football manager I'd know how to sum it all up: cricket was the winner.

for 4 in reply, Derbyshire seemed to have few worries. Then, with a suddenness that only Shane Warne could induce, Derbyshire collapsed unbelievably to 352 all out and by the close of that third day, following on, they were 32 for 2 and struggling. Shaun Udal, who took both those two early second innings wickets, took 5 for 58 overall with his off-breaks and Derbyshire's only resistance, as they crumbled to 167 all out, was Rob Bailey who added 53 to his first innings 90. Warne's match haul of six wickets, meanwhile, was an inadequate reflection of the impact he made on the game.

Lancashire headed for their third successive runners-up championship finish as they trounced Somerset by an innings and 109 runs at Old Trafford. Glen Chapple grabbed 4 for 34 as the visitors were dismissed for just 132 on the first morning – and then Lancashire set about running up a match-winning total with grim determination

(and at least one eye on events at the Oval). After a patient 57 from Mike Atherton came a punchy 152-run stand between Graham Lloyd (126) and Warren Hegg (128) and, following Lancashire's declaration on 463 for 9, Somerset were soon in trouble again at 65 for 4. That soon became 101 for 6 on the third morning and, although Peter Bowler clung on with 75, Somerset reached only 222. Hegg's fine match was complete when he broke George Duckworth's pre-War county wicket-keeping record of 635 catches.

Division Two
5, 6, 7 and 8 September
at Lord's
Warwickshire 416 (117.3 overs)(DL Hemp 129, MJ Powell 92, DP Ostler 52) and 109 for 1 (MA Wagh 74*)
Middlesex 350 for 5 dec. (111.4 overs)(MR Ramprakash 88*, AJ Strauss 75, JL Langer 70)

Match drawn – no play was possible on the fourth day
Middlesex 11 pts, Warwickshire 10 pts

6, 7 and 8 September
at Trent Bridge
Nottinghamshire 371 (93 overs)(JER Gallian 150,
PR Reiffel 50, SL Watkin 5 for 99) and 66 for 3
Glamorgan 187 (47.3 overs)(RDB Croft 56, AJ Harris
5 for 69) and (following on) 246 (MA Wallace 59*,
PJ Franks 6 for 59)
Nottinghamshire won by seven wickets
Nottinghamshire 19 pts, Glamorgan 3 pts

Division Two
at Northampton
Essex 233 (68.4 overs)(SG Law 59) and 225 for 4
(SG Law 119*, SD Peters 50*)
Northamptonshire 410 (120.3 overs)(ML Hayden 164,
DJG Sales 61, D Ripley 54)
Match drawn
Northamptonshire 12 pts, Essex 8 pts

7 and 8 September
at Hove
Sussex 138 (52 overs)(IJ Harvey 6 for 19) and 71
Gloucestershire 227 (72.3 overs)(IJ Harvey 60)
Gloucestershire won by an innings and 18 runs
Gloucestershire 16 pts, Sussex 3 pts

Gloucestershire, their one-day triumphs complete,
now turned the full focus of their attention on
gaining promotion to the championship first division,
and an innings and 18-run humbling of Sussex at
Hove – inside two days – certainly underlined their
intentions. Michael Bevan was badly missed, but the
Sussex batting was still nothing less than pathetic as
Ian Harvey in particular scythed through their team.
Harvey's swing and seam brought him 6 for 19 on
the first day as Sussex mustered just 138, and then
the Australian all-rounder hit 60 as Gloucestershire
replied with 227. That, too, was rather an
underachievement from 159 for 2, but the visitors'
slide was nothing compared to the Sussex second
innings. Just 25 overs were needed to send them
crashing to a dire 71 all out – from 40 for 0! Harvey
this time took 4 for 13, and the shocked Sussex
members were rightly angry with what they had
witnessed.

At Trent Bridge a second successive championship
hundred by Jason Gallian, who then motored on to
150, his highest score for the county, set up
Nottinghamshire's seven-wicket victory over a
Glamorgan side still harbouring designs of

promotion. Gallian struck a six and twenty-two fours
but Paul Reiffel's 50 from 67 balls was another
important innings as Notts reached 371 and then put
pressure on their opponents by bowling them out for
187. Andy Harris (5 for 69) was the chief destroyer
of the Glamorgan first innings but, after they had
been asked to follow on, Paul Franks made sure of
victory by taking 6 for 59. A last wicket stand of 51
between Mark Wallace 59 not out) and Steve Watkin
(28) irritated Notts, and then Watkin added 3 for 31
to his first innings 5 for 99 to make Notts' task of
scoring just 63 for victory as uncomfortable as
possible. Chris Hewison, meanwhile, a 20-year-old
former Durham Academy batsman, had a Notts
debut to remember on the opening day. Called up as
a last-minute replacement for the injured John
Morris, Hewison was summoned from the county's
second eleven match at the Boots Ground in
Nottingham, where he had already batted and had
been out for a second-ball duck. In his second
innings (and second match) of the day, however,
Hewison reached a more assured 24!

Northamptonshire were made to endure a scare
over the state of their pitch for the match at home to
Essex before they could celebrate promotion to
division one. Phil Sharpe, one of the ECB pitch
liaison panel, called up his colleague Alan Smith for
a second opinion about a surface that started out
dry and bare. Jason Brown, the fast-emerging off-
spinner, took 4 for 34 on the opening day as Essex
were bowled out for 233. But, after 24 hours of
uncertainty, because any penalty would have left
Northants still short of the points required to
become the first team certain to be promoted,
Matthew Hayden smashed a mocking 164 from 260
balls and the pitch inspectors reported they were
happy. David Sales' 61 and David Ripley's 54
pushed Northants on to 410 and Bob Carter, the
county's director of cricket, said: 'It has been a quite
stressful day or so. We obviously wanted to start
celebrating our promotion before now, but the
champagne had to be put on ice for 24 hours. We
will be having a few drinks now, but we still want to
win this game and go on to clinch the second
division championship'. Frustratingly, however, bad
weather took all but 18 overs from the third day's
play and, on the final afternoon, Essex withstood a
four-wicket burst from their former fast bowler
Darren Cousins to bat it out for a draw at 225 for 4.
Stuart Law, maintaining his superb end-of-season
form, added an unbeaten 119 to his first innings 59.

The match between Middlesex and Warwickshire
was heading for a probable draw even before rain

washed out the entire final day. But, at that stage, Warwickshire were 175 runs ahead at 109 for 1 in their second innings, Middlesex having challenged them to make a game of it by declaring their own first innings on 350 for 5 – 66 runs behind. David Hemp made a fine 129 in Warwickshire's first innings 416, and Michael Powell another accomplished knock of 92. Mark Wagh, finding excellent late-season form, was 74 not out in the visitors' second innings. In between, the Lord's spectators were treated to an aggressive 70 from Justin Langer, the Australian left-hander hitting Allan Donald out of the attack as he raced to fifty from just 25 balls, another promising innings of 75 from Andrew Strauss and an effortless 88 not out by Mark Ramprakash who, in 12 innings since being dropped by England, has scored 796 runs.

ROUND TWENTY: 13–16 SEPTEMBER 2000

Division One
13, 14, 15 and 16 September
at Derby
Somerset 311 for 9 (94.3 overs)(PD Bowler 117*)
Derbyshire did not bat
Match drawn – no play was possible on the second, third and fourth days
Derbyshire 7 pts, Somerset 7 pts

at Southampton
Yorkshire 205 (60.1 overs)(SK Warne 5 for 92) and 265 DS Lehmann 92, GM Hamilton 61)
Hampshire 213 (66.5 overs)(WS Kendall 73, SK Warne 65, JD Middlebrook 6 for 82) and 185 (DA Kenway 58)
Yorkshire won by 72 runs – no play was possible on the third day
Yorkshire 16 pts, Hampshire 4 pts

at Old Trafford
Lancashire 324 (87.5 overs)(WK Hegg 93*, SC Ganguly 54) and 304 for 9 dec. (NH Fairbrother 90, MP Smethurst 66, SC Ganguly 65, MA Butcher 5 for 86)
Surrey 359 (106.1 overs)(MP Bicknell 79*, GP Butcher 66, Saqlain Mushtaq 54)
Match drawn – no play possible on the third day
Lancashire 10 pts, Surrey 11 pts

at Leicester
Kent 228 for 8 (92 overs)(R Dravid 77, WF Stelling 5 for 49)
Leicestershire did not bat
Match drawn – no play was possible on the second,

third and fourth days
Leicestershire 6 pts, Kent 5 pts

Nadeem Shahid did some awful impressions of Bob Willis, Adam Hollioake tried out some leg-breaks, and Alex Tudor took over the wicketkeeping gloves. In short, champions Surrey decided to have some fun on the last day of their rain-affected draw with nearest challengers Lancashire at Old Trafford. Amazingly, they still managed to have Lancashire wobbling on 161 for 7 in their second innings – but then opted not to go for the jugular and decided to party instead. Lancashire eventually ended on 304 for 9, Neil Fairbrother reaching 90 and Mike Smethurst posting a maiden fifty, the draw confirming their runners-up finish. Mark Butcher perhaps enjoyed himself on that final day, taking the new ball and, in all, picking up a career-best 5 for 86 with his medium pace. Surrey had gone into the game needing just one point to secure the championship title. It was, in truth, a formality and the first bowling bonus point soon arrived as Lancashire were bowled out for 324, Warren Hegg ending 93 not out and Saqlain Mushtaq taking 4 for 81. Surrey's players celebrated that evening by going to watch Manchester United play at the other Old Trafford just up the road – appropriate, in a way, given their own domination of cricket's championship. On the second day, despite the hangovers, Surrey reached 297 for 9 in reply – skipper Hollioake blasting 49 from 39 balls and Gary Butcher hitting 66. But, by the close, last pair Martin Bicknell and Saqlain had added a further 54 and – after the washed-out third day which ruined the match as a contest – they went on to take their tenth-wicket stand to 116. Bicknell ended 79 not out, with Saqlain finally dismissed for 54. Keith Medlycott, the Surrey cricket manager, said: 'Over the last few years some sides have not wanted to play against us, and if that means there is an aura about this Surrey team then so be it'.

The 565th and final first-class match at Hampshire's Northlands Road ground, meanwhile, could not have had a more memorable finish – except that it was visitors Yorkshire and not the home side that won the game from the very last ball. Hampshire, set 258 to win in a minimum of 54 overs, had fallen away to 185 for 9 (despite Derek Kenway's 58) when the final over began. Alex Morris blocked the first five balls from slow left-arm spinner Ian Fisher – with every single Yorkshire fielder crouched around the bat – but then edged the last ball of that last over to Gavin Hamilton at

It had been a disappointing season for Stephen Peters until his highest score of the year earned Essex promotion for 2001.

second slip. There was a further sting in the tail, too, for Hampshire as they bade farewell from the ground which had been their county headquarters since 1885 – a pitch penalty of eight points was confirmed the next day. Umpires John Holder and Trevor Jesty had reported a surface too dry and uneven at the start following the fall of 16 wicket on the opening day – and that prompted ECB chief pitch liaison officer Mike Denness to convene an adjudicating panel which also comprised Raman Subba Row and Chris Wood. Their conclusion was that the pitch had offered excessive spin on the first day – although Darren Lehmann counter-attacked his Aussie compatriot Shane Warne so effectively during the match, scoring 46 and 92, that Yorkshire were able to post totals of 205 and 265. Hampshire, 78 for 6 on that hectic first day before Will Kendall (73) and Warne (65) added 95 for the seventh wicket, replied with 213 in their first innings but could not make the highest total of the match in conditions dominated by spin. James Middlebrook, the Yorkshire off-spinner, earned himself match figures of 10 for 170 and, during his first innings haul of 6 for 82, he took four wickets in the space of

five balls that spanned two separate overs. The poor quality of the pitch also, of course, enabled a full game to be fitted in despite the loss of the third day to bad weather.

The other two games in division one were totally wrecked by rain, with each of the last three days being washed away at both Derby and Leicester. Peter Bowler hit 117 not out, his fifth hundred of the season and third against his former county, as Somerset reached 311 for 9 at Derby, while at Leicester there was a four-and-a-half hour 77 from Rahul Dravid – the determined Indian seeming to make it his personal business to make sure Kent scored at least 200 to secure the one bonus point they required, at the start, to retain their first division status. Billy Stelling took 5 for 49 for Leicestershire as Kent ground their way to 228 for 8.

Division Two
13, 14, 15 and 16 September
at Chelmsford
Warwickshire 400 for 8 dec. (125.2 overs) (MA Wagh 137, MJ Powell 106) and 8 for 0 dec.
Essex 208 for 5 dec. (77 overs)(DDJ Robinson 92, RC Irani 72*) and 202 for 4 (SD Peters 77*, RC Irani 64*)
Essex won by six wickets – no play was possible on the third day
Essex 15 pts, Warwickshire 6 pts

at Cardiff
Glamorgan 325 (103.1 overs)(MJ Powell 114, A Dale 57, RDB Croft 50) and 93 for 0
Middlesex 387 (98.5 overs)(JL Langer 213*, MR Ramprakash 51)
Match drawn
Middlesex 11 pts, Glamorgan 10 pts

at Bristol
Nottinghamshire 216 (96.1 overs) and 103 for 3 dec.
Gloucestershire 73 for 1 dec. (21.4 overs) and 248 for 7 (RC Russell 53)
Gloucestershire won by three wickets – no play was possible on the third day
Gloucestershire 15 pts, Nottinghamshire 1 pt

at Worcester
Northamptonshire 260 (73.2 overs)(TMB Bailey 96*) and 125 (GD McGrath 8 for 41)
Worcestershire 124 for 7 dec. (37.1 overs) and 119 for 6
Match drawn – no play was possible on the second and third days
Worcestershire 7 pts, Northamptonshire 8 pts

WOMEN'S CRICKET by Jonathan Agnew

By Christmas 2000 (and after publication of this book) we should know where English women's cricket is going. Or has gone. With scant regard for the stirring of the plum pudding somebody has managed to arrange the final of the Cricinfo World Cup 2000 on 23 December on the other side of the globe in New Zealand – with the reserve day on Christmas Eve!

The only way England can celebrate Christmas at home is to arrange to be knocked out in the eight-team round robin stage. And that is not in the plans of team manager Paul Farbrace, the former Kent and Middlesex wicketkeeper, whose own two-year contract as boss of the England girls comes to an end at the same time... unless.

Unless, that is, England win the World Cup, which is not beyond them, and the England and Wales Cricket Board ask Farbrace to carry on the work which has seen the girls progressing on an upward curve ever since he took over. It has to be said there was room for improvement when he started. The England team that won the World Cup at home in 1993 had stood still. The Aussies and the Kiwis, both smarting at England's triumph, had done something about it.

Both countries had been miffed that they hadn't won the World Cup in 1993. Almost as hard to bear was the fact that England had won it. Australia were doubly miffed as England had toppled them from the lofty perch they had occupied by winning both the previous World Cups – in New Zealand in 1982 and at home in

Australia in 1988. So they won it in India in 1997 and beat England four–nil earlier this year. That four–nil drubbing had an effect on the England team that is still being felt as the World Cup approaches.

After a particularly horrendous 220-run defeat in Newcastle, New South Wales, skipper Karen Smithies, already nominated by Farbrace to lead England into the World Cup and even beyond, resigned. Smithies had played a record 69 one-day internationals for England and had been skipper since leading them to the World-Cup triumph seven years earlier in 1993. It was well into the small hours of the morning after the Newcastle game before Smithies finally called it a day. It was an abdication on a regal scale and the rumours rumble to this day.

Brighton teacher Clare Connor was installed as captain, but the ship still foundered. England travelled straight across the Tasman from Australia to be beaten five–nil by New Zealand and the dominance of the southern hemisphere looked as well established as ever. Even a three–two defeat of South Africa in England this summer could not paper over the cracks – even if it did give rise to a game plan for the World Cup.

That plan will be hatched in Christchurch on two days in December, Saturday the 2nd and Monday the 4th. On those days England meet South Africa and India and Farbrace knows they have to beat at least one of them. 'I expect Australia to win the round robin stage,' he said. 'Without being unpatriotic you would be silly to bet

against them. The top team will meet the fourth team in the semi-finals, so we don't want to be that fourth team.'

Farbrace has identified South Africa as the team to go for. India looked a good side when they toured England in 1999 and the fanaticism for cricket in the sub-continent has seized on the women's game every bit as fiercely as it has always dominated the men. But in South Africa it is different. That colonial passion for winning, and especially 'licking the Limeys', may be present in their players – but certainly not the authorities.

This summer's series against England was meant to be played in South Africa, but they couldn't raise the rands to stage it. Cricket supremo Dr Ali Bacher is by all accounts not very interested and apparently one major South African cricket sponsor has even had written into their contract a clause forbidding any of their money to be used for the women's game.

'It is almost certain New Zealand will get through with us, South Africa or India filling two of the other three places,' says Farbrace. 'We want to finish either second or third in the round robin stages so that we can avoid the No.1 team. We all know that in one-day cricket anything can happen on the day – if we get to the final we can win it – even against Australia.' ■

Karen Smithies, the England captain, who resigned during the New Zealand tour following a string of poor results.

There was no denying the frantic excitement on a final day that finally resulted in Essex and Glamorgan emerging from a six-county dogfight to join Northants in the second division promotion places, but the vagaries of the British weather made it all a bit of a lottery too as Gloucestershire, Warwickshire, Nottinghamshire and Worcestershire failed to manoeuvre themselves instead into the top three. All good knock-about stuff, but was it raising the standard?

Warwickshire, for example, were palpably winning their struggle against Essex at Chelmsford before a

Despite Neil Fairbrother's 90, Lancashire were unable to defeat champions Surrey.

third-day wash-out forced the visiting captain to offer Essex a tempting fourth innings target in his own desperation for promotion. Essex were therefore able to declare their own first innings on 208 for 5, in reply to Warwickshire's initially intimidating 400 for 8 declared, and a brief Warwickshire second innings of 8 for 0 declared, from three balls, left Essex wanting 201 from 56 overs to make sure of promotion themselves. For a while, the gamble seemed to be paying off for Warwickshire as Essex slumped to 64 for 4. But enter Stephen Peters, the 21-year-old former Young England batsman who had suffered two long summers of frustrating under-achievement. Now, with daring strokeplay, he reached 77 not out in a

match-winning stand of 64 with Ronnie Irani, his captain. Irani, who with Darren Robinson (92) had rallied Essex's wobbly first innings with 72 not out, now added an unbeaten 64 as victory came with a whopping 17.2 overs to spare. Soon, Irani was leading the Essex celebrations and no one could deny him his joy after a season of great personal performance. But were not Essex just that little bit lucky, too?

Gloucestershire also benefited from Nott's need to gamble the risk of defeat in the pursuit of victory – again, after rain had spoilt the original tightly fought contest. Two declarations early on the fourth day left Gloucestershire needing 248 for victory from 59 overs – and they eventually got home with Jack Russell digging deep into his reserves of cussedness with 53 and young Chris Taylor again playing a bright innings with 38 not out. But Gloucestershire, in the end, were denied adding championship promotion to their one-day trophy treble simply because the rain-abbreviated match had not allowed the time to attempt to gain the number of batting bonus points required to accompany a 12-point victory reward. What a lottery, indeed.

Spare a thought, moreover, for Glenn McGrath and Worcestershire, who had also been condemned by the England management to battling for first division status without their captain and leading batsman Graeme Hick. No play on both the scheduled second and third days at Worcester left the home side needing a miracle on the final day against opponents Northants, who had no interest in doing any sort of deals similar to the ones forced upon Warwickshire's Neil Smith and Nottinghamshire's Jason Gallian. The second division champions would have to be bowled out after Worcestershire had begun the day by thumping 74 quick runs in an effort to get as close to Northants' hardly intimidating first innings 260 as they could. Again, of course, time lost meant they had no opportunity to gain any batting points themselves. McGrath, responding like the great champion he is, then took 8 for 41 in a quite superb piece of sustained pace bowling as Northants were tumbled for 125. Yet even that superb, genuinely classy cricket effort left Worcestershire with time only to chase an improbable 262 off a minimum of 43 overs. They could reach just 119 for 6 and once again the weather, and not cricket ability, had directly affected a promotion issue. It did not help Worcestershire to recall that they had also reduced Northants to 96 for 7 on the opening day before Toby Bailey, with a gutsy 96 not out, shared in three

half-century stands with Tony Penberthy, Paul Taylor and then last man Darren Cousins.

All this left Glamorgan knowing that a draw in another weather-hit game would squeeze them into the top division and provide Matthew Maynard with a fine end to his five-year stint as captain. The Welsh county, who had begun the match thinking that they required an 18-point victory to guarantee their elevation, were grateful indeed on the final morning that Middlesex did not consider declaring their own first innings on the overnight 101 for 4 because they required batting bonus points themselves – plus the four points for the draw – to move off bottom place and condemn Sussex instead to the wooden spoon. If Middlesex had needed to win they would surely have declared, in an effort to force a result, and that would have thus denied Glamorgan the chance to collect the three bowling points which – ultimately – took them just past Gloucestershire and into the final promotion position. Yet at least Glamorgan had batted positively themselves on the opening day, reaching the 300 they knew was their first minimum requirement thanks largely to an aggressive 114 by Michael Powell. Adrian Dale and Robert Croft also got stuck in with half-centuries, while Richard Johnson and Phil Tufnell shared eight of the Glamorgan wickets in a final total of 325. Heavy rain, however, allowed just 15.2 and 12.4 overs on the second and third days respectively, which led to that fateful last day. Justin Langer, supported by David Nash and Johnson, batted beautifully to reach an unbeaten 213 off 250 balls after Mark Ramprakash had gone early for 51. But Glamorgan didn't care – all they needed to do was to keep taking wickets and, after Middlesex had been at last dismissed for 387 in the 99th over, they only had to bat out the remaining hour's play. Then, more through the happy result of circumstance, and not through any great standard of play that they had achieved in this vital last round of matches, Glamorgan were able to celebrate as if they had actually won a trophy rather than, in essence, finishing up 12th in the championship pecking order.

The concept of two-division championship cricket has enjoyed much early support – especially from those whose main aim is to 'beef up' the image of county cricket. Image is one thing, of course, but content is – or should be – the main issue here. It may be heresy to say it, but I don't believe I am alone in seeing a two-divisional championship as cricket's equivalent of the Emperor's New Clothes. It all looks fine and dandy if you want it to, but if you peer closer then I'm afraid there really isn't very much of substance.

FIRST-CLASS AVERAGES

BATTING

	M	Inns	NO	HS	Runs	Av	100	50
MG Bevan	12	18	3	174	1124	74.93	5	1
MH Richardson	6	11	2	212*	642	71.33	1	4
S Chanderpaul	5	9	3	161*	418	69.66	2	1
PR Reiffel	7	8	4	74	275	68.75	–	3
DS Lehmann	16	23	1	136	1477	67.13	4	9
MW Goodwin	8	12	2	194	651	65.10	3	1
PD Bowler	18	26	5	157*	1305	62.14	5	4
JL Langer	16	27	3	213*	1472	61.33	5	7
ML Hayden	15	22	0	164	1270	57.72	4	6
R Dravid	16	25	3	182	1221	55.50	2	8
SG Law	16	27	2	189	1385	55.40	5	6
RC Irani	17	29	7	168*	1196	54.36	1	9
AD Brown	16	23	5	295*	935	51.94	2	4
MTG Elliott	13	21	0	177	1076	51.23	4	4
DP Ostler	16	24	2	145	1096	49.81	2	7
MR Ramprakash	17	28	4	120*	1183	49.29	4	7
RJ Bailey	13	19	4	118	728	48.53	2	5
Aftab Habib	17	23	1	172*	1038	47.18	2	8
NH Fairbrother	15	23	5	138	823	45.72	2	3
KJ Barnett	11	16	2	118*	640	45.71	2	3
MA Wagh	9	16	3	137	592	45.53	2	3
JP Crawley	15	22	1	156	951	45.28	5	–
PAJ deFreitas	14	18	3	123*	677	45.13	1	4
Usman Afzaal	16	26	3	151*	1018	44.26	3	4
VS Solanki	16	28	2	161*	1138	43.76	2	8
MJ Powell (Wa)	17	26	2	145	1046	43.58	2	8
SM Katich	16	28	3	137*	1089	43.56	3	5
ME Trescothick	12	19	2	105	738	43.41	1	5
MP Vaughan	13	21	1	155rh	866	43.30	2	4
MA Butcher	16	25	4	191	891	42.42	2	3
DG Cork	14	17	4	200*	542	41.69	1	2
JM Dakin	9	12	1	135	458	41.63	1	3
AL Penberthy	15	21	2	116	785	41.31	1	5
WS Kendall	18	31	3	161	1156	41.28	3	5
SP James	17	28	2	309*	1070	41.15	3	2
M Burns	15	20	1	160	775	40.78	2	5
TL Penney	13	18	4	100*	569	40.64	1	2
IJ Ward	16	25	3	158*	894	40.63	3	3
AF Giles	13	14	3	128*	444	40.36	1	1
CJ Adams	16	26	3	156	913	39.69	1	7
NV Knight	10	15	0	233	593	39.53	1	1
J Cox	17	26	1	171	983	39.32	3	3
GD Rose	15	18	5	124	510	39.23	2	1
DA Leatherdale	17	30	5	132*	975	39.00	2	7
DR Brown	16	22	6	203	622	38.87	1	2
MA Atherton	18	29	1	136	1068	38.14	3	6
DL Hemp	17	24	2	129	834	37.90	1	5
KA Parsons	15	22	2	193*	745	37.25	2	1
MGN Windows	19	31	3	166	1042	37.21	2	6
WW Hinds	11	19	1	150	669	37.16	3	3
ADR Campbell	8	10	2	150*	292	36.50	1	1
N Shahid	9	12	0	80	434	36.16	–	3
DJG Sales	13	20	0	276	713	35.65	1	5
AD Shaw	12	18	5	88*	462	35.53	–	3
WK Hegg	17	23	5	128	639	35.50	1	4
JN Snape	15	20	3	69	598	35.17	–	4
GA Hick	14	24	2	122	773	35.13	3	3
DDJ Robinson	12	19	3	93*	561	35.06	–	4
A Flintoff	13	19	1	119	631	35.05	1	4
A Dale	17	27	3	81	837	34.87	–	5
RJ Warren	9	13	1	151	417	34.75	1	2
JER Gallian	16	26	3	150	796	34.60	3	–
DJ Bicknell	16	28	8	180*	858	34.32	2	2
RWJ Howitt	6	10	2	118*	274	34.25	1	1
MP Maynard	15	22	1	119*	716	34.09	2	5
RSG Anderson	9	8	3	67*	170	34.00	–	1
OJ Hughes	6	10	3	119	237	33.85	1	1
A Flower	7	10	1	116*	300	33.33	1	–
NC Johnson	7	8	0	83	266	33.25	–	3
AJ Strauss	17	28	2	111*	862	33.15	1	3
MJ di Venuto	16	25	3	92*	725	32.95	–	6
BF Smith	17	23	2	111*	686	32.66	2	2
MA Roseberry	11	20	3	139rh	549	32.29	1	2

FIRST-CLASS AVERAGES

BATTING

	M	Inns	NO	HS	Runs	Av	100	50
AJ Stewart	10	15	1	124*	451	32.21	2	–
PA Cottey	16	23	0	154	740	32.17	2	2
MJ di Venuto	16	25	3	92*	725	32.95	–	6
BF Smith	17	23	2	111*	686	32.66	2	2
MA Roseberry	11	20	3	139rh	549	32.29	1	2
AJ Stewart	10	15	1	124*	451	32.21	2	–
PA Cottey	16	23	0	154	740	32.17	2	2
PA Nixon	18	25	7	134*	578	32.11	1	3
RR Montgomerie	17	30	2	133	899	32.10	2	4
GE Welton	13	23	2	200*	674	32.09	1	3
MP Dowman	17	29	3	140	833	32.03	2	4
SC Ganguly	14	21	0	99	671	31.95	–	6
SD Stubbings	18	32	4	135*	889	31.75	1	4
D Ripley	13	18	3	56	475	31.66	–	1
SL Campbell	12	20	0	146	629	31.45	1	4
JW Cook	11	17	1	137	502	31.37	2	1
MP Bicknell	15	18	2	79*	500	31.25	–	4
SP Titchard	11	19	2	141*	530	31.17	1	3
SB Styris	5	9	1	72	247	30.87	–	1
UBA Rashid	15	22	3	110	585	30.78	1	4
GJ Whittall	7	11	1	89	304	30.40	–	2
IJ Harvey	10	14	1	79	395	30.38	1	2
RG Smalley	6	10	1	83	272	30.22	–	1
RR Sarwan	9	16	2	59*	423	30.21	–	3
CH Gayle	8	14	1	128	392	30.15	1	2
AR Danson	6	9	2	117*	211	30.14	1	–
MJ Powell (Gm)	18	28	0	128	843	30.10	2	4
JE Morris	13	20	0	115	601	30.05	1	3
AJ Holliaoke	16	23	0	80	689	29.95	–	3
JJ Porter	6	10	0	93	297	29.70	–	4
RC Russell	16	23	3	110*	593	29.65	1	2
MB Loye	12	18	1	93	504	29.64	–	3
MV Fleming	14	18	2	47	471	29.43	–	–
NJ Speak	14	24	5	89*	552	29.05	–	4
GD Lloyd	16	22	1	126	608	28.95	1	2
VJ Wells	15	19	0	98	549	28.89	–	4
A McGrath	10	14	1	133	375	28.84	1	1
BC Lara	10	18	0	176	519	28.83	2	1
GM Hamilton	13	16	2	125	402	28.71	1	2
TR Gripper	6	11	2	66*	258	28.66	–	2
GW White	18	32	4	96	797	28.46	–	5
PR Pollard	14	24	1	123*	652	28.34	1	5
A J Tudor	14	16	6	64*	283	28.30	–	1
CM Tolley	6	9	1	60	223	27.87	–	2
DJ Millns	8	11	4	50*	195	27.85	–	1
EC Joyce	6	8	1	51	195	27.85	–	1
AP Grayson	17	31	2	144	807	27.82	1	5
ID Blackwell	18	23	2	109	582	27.71	1	2
PJ Prichard	17	31	3	96	775	27.67	–	5
MHW Papps	5	10	2	63	220	27.50	–	1
SD Peters	16	28	6	77*	602	27.36	–	4
MV Nagamootoo	9	16	2	100	381	27.21	1	–
LD Sutton	10	16	1	79	407	27.13	–	2
EJ Wilson	17	31	2	104*	779	26.86	2	4
SJ Rhodes	18	28	6	103	591	26.86	1	1
AS Rollins	16	24	0	100	636	26.50	1	4
CP Schofield	17	22	2	70*	528	26.40	–	4
DA Kenway	15	27	1	136	685	26.34	1	3
PJ Franks	13	18	1	60	447	26.29	–	2
DS Lucas	10	12	5	46*	184	26.28	–	–
DL Maddy	17	25	1	102	630	26.25	1	4
ND Burns	16	21	4	67*	445	26.17	–	3
CG Taylor	12	22	3	104	492	25.89	1	–
SD Thomas	17	20	7	52	336	25.84	–	1
NMK Smith	17	20	2	87	464	25.77	–	4
MJ Walker	15	25	4	61	536	25.52	–	1
PD Collingwood	16	27	0	111	681	25.22	1	4
VJ Craven	8	11	1	58	251	25.10	–	2
GP Swann	16	24	0	72	597	24.87	–	3
D Byas	17	26	2	84	596	24.83	–	2
JJB Lewis	16	28	2	115	645	24.80	1	4
JI Englefield	6	11	1	90	248	24.80	–	1
OA Shah	12	20	0	76	489	24.45	–	3

FIRST-CLASS AVERAGES

BATTING

	M	Inns	NO	HS	Runs	Av	100	50
AFG Griffith	11	21	1	130	486	24.30	1	2IDK
Salisbury	16	19	6	57*	313	24.07	–	2
CMW Read	16	23	3	56*	479	23.95	–	3
J Scuderi	9	13	2	51	261	23.72	–	1
RD Jacobs	8	14	2	78	283	23.41	–	1
GP Thorpe	11	16	0	115	376	23.50	1	1
AN Aymes	13	22	5	74*	398	23.41	–	3
RC Driver	11	20	4	64	372	23.25	–	1
ET Smith	11	18	0	175	415	23.05	1	–
RSC Martin–Jenkins	15	23	1	86	499	22.68	–	2
ID Fisher	6	10	2	68*	181	22.62	–	1
GP Sulzberger	6	11	0	60	248	22.54	–	1
MA Ealham	11	14	1	83	293	22.53	–	2
DR Hewson	11	21	1	67	448	22.40	–	3
JP Pyemont	11	15	1	124	313	22.35	1	–
DP Fulton	14	24	1	115	512	22.26	1	1
MJ Chilton	10	14	1	46	286	22.00	–	–
AG Wharf	10	15	2	101*	285	21.92	2	–
RDB Croft	14	17	4	56	282	21.69	–	2
SK Warne	15	22	2	69	431	21.55	–	3
A Richardson	13	9	7	17*	43	21.50	–	–
GM Fellows	14	20	4	46	341	21.31	–	–
A Pratt	7	10	1	38	191	21.22	–	–
ARK Pierson	6	9	3	48	126	21.00	–	–
RWT Key	17	29	1	83	584	20.85	–	5
MP Speight	11	18	1	55	354	20.82	–	1
DI Stevens	15	22	0	78	457	20.77	–	2
P Johnson	12	19	2	100	353	20.76	1	–
RL Johnson	15	23	3	69	413	20.65	–	2
AD Mascarenhas	16	24	1	100	473	20.56	1	2
RA Smith	17	29	0	61	595	20.51	–	3
RJ Turner	18	26	2	75	492	20.50	–	2
JS Laney	14	25	1	81	489	20.37	–	2
PN Weekes	8	13	1	39	244	20.33	–	–_
MCJ Ball	9	14	2	53	244	20.33	–	1
DC Nash	17	24	2	76*	446	20.27	–	1
IJ Sutcliffe	12	17	1	53	319	19.93	–	2
PCL Holloway	13	20	1	113	377	19.84	1	1
MN Lathwell	9	14	1	54*	257	19.76	–	1
JN Batty	13	16	2	100*	276	19.71	1	–
SM Guy	6	9	2	42	136	19.42	–	–
MTE Peirce	14	24	1	86	446	19.39	–	2
THC Hancock	15	22	1	85	407	19.38	–	1
W Phillip	6	11	3	67*	155	19.37	–	1
SD Udal	12	21	3	85	346	19.22	–	1
PD Trego	7	8	1	62	134	19.14	–	1
ME Cassar	14	20	2	77*	341	18.94	–	1
RMS Weston	6	10	1	39	170	18.88	–	–
SJ Lacey	11	17	4	55*	242	18.61	–	1
JC Adams	10	17	0	98	311	18.29	–	2
MJ Wood	11	17	3	100*	256	18.28	1	–
Saqlain Mushtaq	12	14	2	66	217	18.08	–	2
DR Law	15	23	3	68*	360	18.00	–	2
MM Patel	14	16	1	60	269	17.93	–	1
MP Smethurst	16	19	10	66	161	17.88	–	1
SL Watkin	13	13	6	51	125	17.85	–	1
K Newell	13	21	1	64	356	17.80	–	1
Kabir Ali	10	15	3	50*	213	17.75	–	1
SW Weenik	6	9	2	72*	124	17.71	–	1
MG Croy	5	8	3	28	88	17.60	–	–
AP Cowan	14	20	6	67	245	17.50	–	1
AP Wells	12	19	2	60*	297	17.47	–	2
SR Lampitt	18	27	8	56*	331	17.42	–	1
MJ McCague	7	11	0	72	191	17.36	–	1
KJ Piper	16	18	3	69	260	17.33	–	1
CEW Silverwood	9	11	1	48	173	17.30	–	–
PJ Hartley	9	11	5	23*	103	17.16	–	–
CD Crowe	8	8	2	30	103	17.16	–	–
MW Alleyne	16	24	0	126	410	17.08	1	–
KM Krikken	10	13	0	51	221	17.00	–	1
PJ Martin	9	11	3	40	134	16.75	–	–
NJ Wilton	8	11	2	46	150	16.66	–	–

FIRST-CLASS AVERAGES

BATTING

	M	Inns	NO	HS	Runs	Av	100	50
G Welch	7	8	1	55	116	16.57	–	1
G Welch	7	8	1	55	116	16.57	–	1
N Peng	8	14	0	98	231	16.50	–	1
GW Flower	7	13	2	76*	180	16.36	–	1
RJ Cunliffe	9	14	0	74	229	16.35	–	1
FA Rose	8	11	1	48	162	16.20	–	–
WL Law	8	11	1	85	161	16.10	–	1
WPC Weston	10	19	2	58*	269	15.82	–	2
MJ Cawdron	6	8	0	32	125	15.62	–	–
RJ Blakey	12	18	1	56	264	15.52	–	1
S Widdup	9	14	1	44	201	15.46	–	–
RK Illingworth	10	12	2	44*	154	15.40	–	–
AJ Harris	11	14	4	39	153	15.30	–	–
JAH Marshall	5	9	0	69	133	14.77	–	1
MA Gough	7	12	0	33	176	14.66	–	–
CEL Ambrose	6	10	2	36*	117	14.62	–	–
JA Daley	10	17	0	50	247	14.52	–	1
SJ Cook	7	10	0	43	145	14.50	–	–
BL Hutton	10	15	2	55	188	14.46	–	1
ARC Fraser	15	22	6	30	227	14.18	–	–
AC Morris	8	12	1	60	154	14.00	–	1
TM Smith	10	13	2	53*	152	13.81	–	1
MM Betts	11	18	4	55	192	13.71	–	1
AM Smith	9	10	6	54	54	13.50	–	–
JD Middlebrook	11	15	0	45	201	13.40	–	–
MC Ilott	10	13	4	25	119	13.22	–	–
DM Cousins	16	23	7	29*	210	13.12	–	–
D Gough	10	13	3	23*	131	13.10	–	–
TA Munton	16	22	7	52	191	12.73	–	1
C White	7	9	1	27	100	12.50	–	–
WJ House	6	10	1	35	112	12.44	–	–
BW Gannon	8	10	4	28	74	12.33	–	–
TR Ward	7	10	1	39	110	12.22	–	–
G Chapple	16	19	1	41	218	12.11	–	–
J Wood	10	15	0	44	181	12.06	–	–
G Keedy	13	15	3	34	144	12.00	–	–
J Ormond	12	15	7	30*	95	11.87	–	–
CA Sayers	6	8	2	46	71	11.83	–	–
TJ Mason	10	14	2	52*	140	11.66	–	1
P Aldred	11	14	1	38	149	11.46	–	–
A Kumble	12	16	0	56	181	11.31	–	1
JO Grove	10	10	5	17	56	11.20	–	–
IN Flanagan	4	8	0	23	89	11.12	–	–
N Hussain	10	16	1	33	166	11.06	–	–
BC Hollioake	10	14	1	29	142	10.92	–	–
SJW Lewis	6	10	1	26	98	10.88	–	–
AR Caddick	10	15	2	21*	141	10.84	–	–
BJ Hyam	15	24	0	53	256	10.66	–	1
SRG Francis	9	13	7	30*	64	10.66	–	–
JP Taylor	7	10	1	27	96	10.66	–	–
N Killeen	10	15	1	38*	144	10.28	–	–
PS Jones	15	16	4	56*	122	10.16	–	1
M Mbangwa	8	8	5	9*	30	10.00	–	–

Qualification: 8 innings, averages 10.00

BOWLING

	Overs	Mds	Runs	Wkts	Av	Best	10/m	5/m
CA Walsh	242.2	106	457	40	11.42	6–74	1	3
RJ Sidebottom	134.2	46	300	24	12.50	6–16	1	4
GD McGrath	415.4	132	1057	80	13.21	8–41	3	6
M Mbangwa	211.5	86	428	30	14.26	6–14	1	2
Saqlain Mushtaq	451.2	127	1016	66	15.39	7–11	2	6
AR Caddick	329.4	98	848	55	15.41	7–64	2	5
PJ Martin	236.2	83	464	30	15.46	7–67	–	3
GP Sulzberger	189.3	61	458	28	16.35	5–55	–	1
IJ Harvey	254.2	79	658	40	16.45	6–19	1	3
AD Mullally	343.5	105	832	49	16.97	9–93	1	5
OT Parkin	108	30	291	17	17.11	4–14	–	–
C White	157.3	32	430	25	17.20	5–32	–	2
MP Bicknell	413.2	115	1052	60	17.53	9–47	1	3
KJ Dean	246	57	785	44	17.84	8–52	–	4

FIRST-CLASS AVERAGES

FIRST-CLASS AVERAGES

BOWLING

	Overs	Mds	Runs	Wkts	Av	Best	10/m	5/m
GJ Whittall	106	31	290	16	18.12	3–14	–	–
MM Betts	354	91	832	44	18.90	7–30	1	1
IDK Salisbury	380.3	101	984	52	18.92	8–60	2	3
D Gough	324.1	61	949	50	18.98	6–63	–	2
A Flintoff	135.2	47	290	15	19.33	4–18	–	–
DM Cousins	510.4	143	1318	67	19.67	5–123	–	1
MJ Saggers	425.2	99	1148	57	20.14	7–79	–	2
J F Brown	517.5	142	1258	61	20.62	7–78	2	4
AM Smith	250.4	70	623	30	20.76	5–52	–	1
J Lewis	562.3	169	1506	72	20.91	8–95	–	4
SR Lampitt	412.5	108	1173	56	20.94	7–45	–	2
MP Smethurst	380.1	90	1176	56	21.00	7–37	–	3
DG Cork	356.4	94	886	42	21.09	6–41	–	1
MJ Cawdron	199.5	64	534	25	21.36	6–25	1	2
KP Dutch	142.4	45	365	17	21.47	6–62	–	1
SJE Brown	442.2	110	1208	56	21.57	7–51	–	4
GM Hamilton	313.4	80	866	40	21.65	5–22	–	1
SL Watkin	389.4	108	1067	48	22.22	6–26	–	2
AL Penberthy	131	30	358	16	22.37	5–54	–	1
CEL Ambrose	207.1	65	403	18	22.38	4–30	–	–
MR Strong	84.2	15	269	12	22.41	4–46	–	–
JP Taylor	212.3	50	540	24	22.30	6–27	1	1
AJ Tudor	304.3	71	1071	47	22.78	7–48	–	3
NAM McLean	271.3	68	803	35	22.94	5–30	–	2
PCR Tufnell	738.3	255	1500	65	23.07	6–48	–	3
AF Giles	526.4	163	1200	52	23.07	8–90	2	5
SK Warne	639.4	183	1620	70	23.14	6–34	–	5
ARC Fraser	475.3	150	1112	48	23.16	6–64	–	1
DR Tuffey	116	23	373	16	23.31	5–74	–	1
ME Cassar	212.2	54	702	30	23.40	6–76	–	1
J Scuderi	120	28	333	14	23.78	4–58	–	–
JN Snape	113.3	44	239	10	23.90	3–70	–	–
G Chapple	431.5	101	1175	49	23.97	6–42	–	1
RC Irani	407.3	120	1008	42	24.00	5–79	–	1
DD Masters	435.2	104	1161	48	24.18	6–27	–	3
CD Collymore	126.4	44	369	15	24.60	3–18	–	–
RD King	195.1	45	618	25	24.72	3–28	–	–
RJ Kirtley	521.4	138	1559	63	24.74	6–41	–	4
JD Middlebrook	281.1	68	771	31	24.87	6–82	1	1
AP Cowan	398.5	98	1175	47	25.00	5–54	–	2
BC Strang	187.3	59	452	18	25.11	5–68	–	1
MM Patel	570.3	202	1157	46	25.15	6–77	–	2
A Kumble	498.3	139	1133	45	25.17	6–44	1	2
BW Gannon	201.5	38	732	29	25.24	5–58	–	1
J Ormond	380.3	75	1116	44	25.36	6–50	–	3
AG Wharf	256.3	51	940	37	25.40	5–68	–	1
PM Hutchison	129.3	35	420	16	26.25	3–62	–	–
MJ Hoggard	501.4	135	1323	50	26.46	5–50	–	2
AA Donald	205.3	61	530	20	26.50	4–50	–	–
DA Leatherdale	154	34	508	19	26.73	3–17	–	–
MV Fleming	278.1	72	753	28	26.89	4–77	–	–
SB Styris	115.4	27	325	12	27.08	3–45	–	–
G Keedy	478	142	1005	37	27.16	6–56	1	1
SD Udal	350.3	104	818	30	27.26	5–58	–	1
MW Alleyne	254.5	72	684	25	27.36	6–49	–	1
M Burns	132.2	33	387	14	27.64	3–11	–	–
J Wood	319.4	66	918	33	27.81	5–36	–	3
MC Ilott	283.2	85	724	26	27.84	3–37	–	–
PR Reiffel	233.3	60	586	21	27.90	5–62	–	1
ESH Giddins	285.5	92	813	29	28.03	5–15	–	1
A Dale	240.4	54	645	23	28.04	5–25	–	2
VJ Wells	222.3	48	648	23	28.17	4–54	–	–
CP Schofield	374	80	1102	39	28.25	5–48	–	1
AD Mascarenhas	313.5	88	796	28	28.42	4–52	–	–
DE Malcolm	184.1	46	541	19	28.47	5–45	–	1
RL Johnson	473	129	1429	50	28.58	6–71	–	2
RD Stemp	398.2	140	946	33	28.66	5–123	–	1
SD Thomas	488	93	1612	56	28.78	5–43	–	2
MA Ealham	271.5	67	703	24	29.29	5–35	–	1
PM Such	422.4	101	1055	36	29.30	7–167	1	3
CEW Silverwood	292.3	80	762	26	29.30	4–60	–	–
DJ Millns	226.1	42	880	30	29.33	5–58	–	1
MJ McCague	129.4	21	412	14	29.42	5–52	–	1
JD Lewry	524.4	137	1569	53	29.60	6–66	–	3
PJ Franks	394.1	81	1252	42	29.80	7–56	–	2
CD Crowe	185.3	50	453	15	30.20	4–55	–	–

BOWLING

	Overs	Mds	Runs	Wkts	Av	Best	10/m	5/m
RSG Anderson	234.4	56	729	24	30.37	6–34	1	3
SJ Cook	137	41	335	11	30.45	4–13	–	–
AJ Harris	384.3	62	1358	44	30.86	6–110	–	4
FA Rose	153	33	527	17	31.00	4–63	–	–
TA Munton	439.3	122	1093	35	31.22	7–34	–	2
AC Morris	183.1	43	562	18	31.22	3–48	–	–
NMK Smith	310.4	70	875	28	31.25	5–66	–	1
GD Rose	332.3	79	908	29	31.31	5–74	–	1
SJ Harmison	304.1	69	822	26	31.61	4–74	–	–
N Killeen	288.3	84	697	22	31.68	3–14	–	–
PS Jones	403.4	88	1294	40	32.35	5–41	–	1
DA Cosker	429.5	141	944	29	32.55	4–82	–	–
DS Lucas	271.5	57	888	27	32.88	4–61	–	–
GP Swann	467.3	92	1366	41	33.31	6–118	–	2
PAJ deFreitas	459.2	122	1105	33	33.48	4–41	–	–
PD Trego	165.1	34	603	18	33.50	4–84	–	–
MA Robinson	228	77	537	16	33.56	3–88	–	–
DR Law	291.4	50	1042	30	34.73	5–78	–	1
JO Grove	193.1	27	733	21	34.90	5–90	–	1
RDB Croft	586.1	153	1432	40	35.80	5–26	–	2
TF Bloomfield	222.3	35	834	23	36.26	4–46	–	–
RSC Martin-Jenkins	360.1	75	1202	33	36.42	5–94	–	1
P Aldred	203.3	44	624	17	36.70	4–97	–	–
ID Fisher	211.1	48	588	16	36.75	3–40	–	–
BC Hollioake	117.5	25	407	11	37.00	4–41	–	–
RK Illingworth	221.5	72	483	13	37.15	3–34	–	–
A Sheriyar	278.2	59	1048	28	37.42	4–51	–	–
BP Martin	133	35	378	10	37.80	3–43	–	–
MV Nagamootoo	328.4	93	801	21	38.14	4–12	–	–
DR Brown	268.2	49	917	24	38.20	5–87	–	1
NC Johnson	158.5	44	500	13	38.46	4–28	–	–
A Richardson	368.2	96	1040	27	38.51	4–69	–	–
LJ Wharton	164	42	464	12	38.66	5–96	–	1
SJ Lacey	241.5	68	626	16	39.12	4–84	–	–
PD Collingwood	214.2	61	474	12	39.50	2–21	–	–
SRG Francis	170.2	37	602	15	40.13	4–95	–	–
KA Parsons	150.4	41	443	11	40.27	5–13	–	1
Kabir Ali	219	41	811	20	40.55	4–114	–	–
TC Hicks	147	29	570	14	40.71	5–54	–	1
RJ Logan	133.1	33	453	11	41.18	5–61	–	1
IBA Rashid	343.5	84	994	23	43.21	5–103	–	1
JP Stephenson	172.1	33	566	13	43.53	4–68	–	–
MCJ Ball	243.1	58	658	15	43.86	3–31	–	–
ID Blackwell	411.3	123	1010	23	43.91	4–18	–	–
AP Grayson	178	39	443	10	44.30	3–55	–	–
JM Dakin	211.4	50	453	15	30.20	4–55	–	–
PJ Hartley	204.2	33	697	15	46.46	3–91	–	–
TJ Mason	239.3	55	710	14	50.71	3–38	–	–

The following bowlers took 10 wickets in fewer than 8 innings:–

	Overs	Mds	Runs	Wkts	Av	Best	10/m	5/m
HH Streak	156.1	50	346	18	19.22	6–87	–	2
LJ Hamilton	94	22	287	14	20.50	5–55	–	1
CR Pimlott	93	32	303	12	25.25	3–42	–	–
SP Jones	104	12	374	10	37.40	4–47	–	–

LEADING FIELDERS

55 – SJ Rhodes (54ct,1st), BJ Hyam (49ct,6ct); 54 – RC Russell (50ct,4st); 49 – PA Nixon (47ct,2st); 45 – WK Hegg (39ct,6st); 43 – RJ Blakey (41ct,2st); 42 – D Ripley (38ct,4st); 40 – CMW Read; 39 – RJ Turner; 38 – AN Aymes (32ct,6st); 37 – ND Burns (36ct,1st); 36 – JN Batty (29ct,7st), DC Nash (32ct,4st); 33 – AD Shaw (29ct,4st); 31 – KJ Piper (28ct,3st); 29 – DP Fulton, MP Speight; 27 – AJ Hollioake; 25 – RD Jacobs (23ct,2st), JL Langer, AJ Stewart (24ct,1st); 23 – JER Gallian, SM Guy (21ct,2st), W Phillip (22ct,1st), VS Solanki; 22 – D Byas 21 – ML Hayden, SM Katich, LD Sutton (20ct,1st); 20 – KM Krikken (18ct,2st), GD Lloyd; 19 – PD Collingwood, MTG Elliott, SG Law, MP Maynard (17ct,2st), RR Montgomerie, DP Ostler, AS Rollins, NJ Wilton; 17 – MG Croy (14ct,3st), A Flower (16ct,1st), WS Kendall, KA Parsons; 16 – AD Brown, NH Fairbrother, GA Hick, DL Maddy; 15 – CJ Adams, MA Atherton, R Dravid, BC Lara, AD Patterson, MR Ramprakash; 14 – MW Alleyne, DA Kenway (13ct,1st), SK Warne, GW White; 13 – MCJ Ball, MA Butcher, SL Campbell, RL Johnson, SR Lampitt, MM Patel, N Shahid 12 – MJ di Venuto, A Flintoff, JS Laney, SD Peters, MJ Walker, RCJ Williams (11ct,1st); 11 – DR Brown, ADR Campbell, MP Dowman, WW Hinds, JAH Marshall, MJ Powell (Gm), IJ Sutcliffe, ME Trescothick; 10 – MJ Birks (8ct,2st), MJ Chilton, DG Cork, RJ Cunliffe, GW Flower, SC Ganguly, AP Grayson, IJ Harvey, P Johnson, AL Penberthy, MJ Powell (Wa), PJ Prichard, RG Smalley (6ct,4st), BF Smith, MA Wallace

FEATURES OF 2000 FIRST-CLASS SEASON

+ 2nd innings

FIRST PLAYER TO 1,000 FIRST-CLASS RUNS

MG Bevan (**Sussex**) on 31 July 2000 v. **Middlesex** at Southgate

MOST FIRST-CLASS WICKETS

80   GD McGrath (**Worcestershire**)

TOTALS 500

718–3 dec.	**Glamorgan** v. **Sussex**	at Colwyn Bay
585	**Northamptonshire** v. **Nottinghamshire**	
		at Northampton
574–5	**Lancashire** v. **Leicestershire**	at Leicester
568–9 dec.	**Warwickshire** v. **Northamptonshire**	at Northampton
568	**Zimbabwe** v. **Gloucestershire**	at Bristol
565	**Somerset** v. **Lancashire**	at Taunton
551–6 dec.	**Warwickshire** v. **Glamorgan**	at Edgbaston
548–7 dec.	**Warwickshire** v. **Sussex**	at Hove
548	**Surrey** v. **Somerset**	at the Oval
543	**Northamptonshire** v. **Gloucestershire**	
		at Cheltenham College
541–6 dec.	**Gloucestershire** v. **Oxford Universities**	at Bristol
522	**Hampshire** v. **Derbyshire**	at Southampton
519	**Northamptonshire** v. **Worcestershire**	at Northampton
508–5 dec.	**Yorkshire** v. **Derbyshire**	at Headingley
507–9 dec.	**Glamorgan** v. **Essex**	at Southend
505–9 dec.	**Essex** v. **Nottinghamshire**	at Trent Bridge
505	**Surrey** v. **Leicestershire**	at Oakham School

TOTALS UNDER 100

+54	**West Indies** v. **England**	at Lord's
+61	**West Indies** v. **England**	at Headingley
+65	**Sussex** v. **Northamptonshire**	at Eastbourne
+68	**Zimbabwe** v. **Yorkshire**	at Headingley
+71	**Sussex** v. **Gloucestershire**	at Hove
+74	**Oxford Universities** v. **Somerset**	at Taunton
81	**Durham** v. **Kent**	at Tunbridge Wells
+82	**Kent** v. **Yorkshire**	at Headingley
83	**Zimbabwe** v. **England**	at Lord's
83	**Durham** v. **Hampshire**	at Basingstoke
84	**Cambridge University** v. **Derbyshire**	at Cambridge
+85	**Surrey** v. **Durham**	at Chester-le-Street
+85	**Gloucestershire** v. **Essex**	at Bristol
+87	**Leicestershire** v. **Surrey**	at Guildford
87	**Gloucestershire** v. **Worcestershire**	at Worcester
+92	**Durham** v. **Lancashire**	at Chester-le-Street
+93	**Durham** v. **Hampshire**	at Basingstoke
+93	**Durham** v. **Leicestershire**	at Leicester
+94	**Yorkshire** v. **West Indies**	at Headingley
95	**Hampshire** v. **Lancashire**	at Liverpool
97	**West Indies** v. **Glamorgan**	at Cardiff
+97	**Derbyshire** v. **Surrey**	at the Oval
98	**Worcestershire** v. **Gloucestershire**	at Worcester

FEATURES OF 2000 FIRST-CLASS SEASON

INDIVIDUAL SCORES OF 200

309*	SP James	**Glamorgan** v. **Sussex**	at Colwyn Bay
295*	AD Brown	**Surrey** v. **Leicestershire**	at Oakham School
276	DJG Sales	**Northamptonshire** v. **Nottinghamshire**	
			at Northampton
233	NV Knight	**Warwickshire** v. **Glamorgan**	at Edgbaston
213*	JL Langer	**Middlesex** v. **Glamorgan**	at Cardiff
212*	MH Richardson	**New Zealand 'A'** v. **Sussex**	at Hove
203	DR Brown	**Warwickshire** v. **Sussex**	at Hove
+200*	DG Cork	**Derbyshire** v. **Durham**	at Derby

TWO HUNDREDS IN THE SAME MATCH

166	174	MG Bevan	**Sussex** v. **Nottinghamshire**	at Hove
110*	112	MR Ramprakash	**Middlesex** v. **Sussex**	at Southgate

HUNDRED & 0 IN THE SAME MATCH

105*	0	WW Hinds	**West Indies** v. **Glamorgan**	
				at Cardiff
100	0	SP James	**Glamorgan** v. **Warwickshire**	
				at Edgbaston
0	109	SP James	**Glamorgan** v. **Gloucestershire**	
				at Cardiff
108	0	AJ Swann	**Northamptonshire** v. **Oxford**	
			Universities	at Oxford
107	0	MGN Windows	**Gloucestershire** v. **Essex**	at Bristol
0	151*	MG Bevan	**Sussex** v. **Essex**	at Arundel
0	103	SJ Rhodes	**Worcestershire** v. **Nottinghamshire**	
				at Worcester

PLAYERS WHO CARRIED THE BAT

78* (+126)	GW White	**Hampshire** v. **Somerset**	Southampton
104* (182)	EJ Wilson	**Worcestershire** v. **Middlesex**	Worcester
80 (+136)	GW White	**Hampshire** v. **Kent**	Portsmouth

FEATURES OF 2000 FIRST-CLASS SEASON

TEN WICKETS IN A MATCH

16–169	MP Bicknell	Surrey v. Leicestershire	at Guildford
14–188	AD Mullally	Hampshire v. Derbyshire	at Derby
12–91	IDK Salisbury	Surrey v. Somerset	at the Oval
12–116	GD McGrath	Worcestershire v. Northamptonshire	
			at Worcester
12–126	AR Caddick	Somerset v. Hampshire	at Southampton
12–135	AF Giles	Warwickshire v. Northamptonshire	
			at Northampton
12–218	PM Such	Essex v. Middlesex	at Chelmsford
11–43	RJ Sidebottom	Yorkshire v. Kent	at Headingley
11–104	Saqlain Mushtaq	Surrey v. Yorkshire	at the Oval
11–111	RSG Anderson	Essex v. Northamptonshire	at Ilford
11–131	JF Brown	Northamptonshire v. Sussex	Northampton
11–154	IDK Salisbury	Surrey v. Durham	Oval
11–178	JF Brown	Northamptonshire v. Warwickshire	
			at Edgbaston
11–196	AF Giles	Warwickshire v. Northamptonshire	
			at Edgbaston
10–32	IJ Harvey	Gloucestershire v. Sussex	at Hove
10–53	M Mbangwa	Zimbabwe v. Yorkshire	at Headingley
10–69	GD McGrath	Worcestershire v. Gloucestershire	
			at Worcester
10–69	JP Taylor	Northamptonshire v. Sussex	at Eastbourne
10–74	MJ Cawdron	FC Counties v. New Zealand 'A'	
			at Milton Keynes
10–88	MM Betts	Durham v. Derbyshire	at Darlington
10–97	AR Caddick	Somerset v. Kent	at Bath
10–105	A Kumble	Leicestershire v. Kent	at Canterbury
10–117	CA Walsh	West Indies v. England	at Lord's
10–135	Saqlain Mushtaq	Surrey v. Hampshire	at Southampton
10–143	GD McGrath	Worcestershire v. Nottinghamshire	
			at Trent Bridge
10–155	G Keedy	Lancashire v. Durham	at Old Trafford

FEATURES OF 2000 FIRST-CLASS SEASON

HAT TRICK

J Lewis	Gloucestershire v. Nottinghamshire	at Trent Bridge
KJ Dean	Derbyshire v. Leicestershire	at Leicester
JID Kerr	+Somerset v. West Indies	at Taunton

FOUR WICKETS IN SUCCESSIVE BALLS

GP Butcher	Surrey Derbyshire	at the Oval

FOUR WICKETS IN AN OVER

A R Caddick	West Indies v. England	at Headingley

FIVE DISMISSALS IN AN INNINGS

+6	6	SJ Rhodes	Worcestershire v. Nottinghamshire	
				at Trent Bridge
5	4/1	RC Russell	Gloucestershire v. Oxford Universities	
				at Bristol
5	5	MP Speight	Durham v. Lancashire	at Chester-le-Street
5	5	ND Burns	Leicestershire v. Somerset	at Leicester
5	3/2	AN Aymes	Hampshire v. Leicestershire	at Leicester
5	4/1	DC Nash	Middlesex v. Northamptonshire	
				at Northampton
5	5	RJ Blakey	Yorkshire v. Kent	at Headingley
5	5	SJ Rhodes	Worcestershire v. Sussex	at Worcester
5	4/1	MG Croy	New Zealand A v. West Indies	
				at Chelmsford
5	5	A Flower	Zimbabwe v. England	at Trent Bridge
+5	4/1	JN Batty	Surrey v. Leicestershire	
				at Oakham School
+5	4/1	BHJ Hyam	Essex v. Worcestershire	at Chelmsford
+5	5	SJ Rhodes	Worcestershire v. Gloucestershire	
				at Worcester
5	4/1	MP Maynard	Glamorgan v. Gloucestershire	at Bristol
5	5	AN Aymes	Hampshire v. Leicestershire	
				at Southampton
4	1	RCJ Williams	Gloucestershire v. Middlesex	at Bristol
5	5	SM Guy	Yorkshire v. Surrey	at Scarborough
5	5	ND Burns	Leicestershire v. Kent	at Leicester

EIGHT DISMISSALS IN A MATCH

9	9	SJ Rhodes	Worcestershire v. Gloucestershire	
				at Worcester
9	8/1	AN Aymes	Hampshire v. Leicestershire	
				at Southampton
8	8	SJ Rhodes	Worcestershire v. Nottinghamshire	
				at Trent Bridge

FEATURES OF 2000 FIRST-CLASS SEASON

SEVEN WICKETS IN AN INNINGS

+9-47	MP Bicknell	**Surrey** v. **Leicestershire**	at Guildford
9-93	AD Mullally	**Hampshire** v. **Derbyshire**	at Derby
+8-41	GD McGrath	**Worcestershire** v. **Northamptonshire**	
			at Worcester
8-52	KJ Dean	**Derbyshire** v. **Kent**	at Canterbury
+8-60	IDK Salisbury	**Surrey** v. **Somerset**	at the Oval
8-86	GD McGrath	**Worcestershire** v. **Nottinghamshire**	
			at Trent Bridge
+8-90	AF Giles	**Warwickshire** v. **Northamptonshire**	
			at Northampton
8-95	J Lewis	**Gloucestershire** v. **Zimbabwe**	
			at Bristol
+7-11	Saqlain Mushtaq	**Surrey** v. **Derbyshire**	at the Oval
7-29	GD McGrath	**Worcestershire** v. **Gloucestershire**	
			at Worcester
7-30	MM Betts	**Durham** v. **Derbyshire**	at Darlington
7-34	TA Munton	**Derbyshire** v. **Surrey**	at Derby
+7-45	SR Lampitt	**Worcestershire** v. **Warwickshire**	
			at Worcester
7-48	AJ Tudor	**Surrey** v. **Lancashire**	at the Oval
+7-50	MP Smethurst	**Lancashire** v. **Durham**	
			at Chester-le-Street
7-56	PJ Franks	**Nottinghamshire** v. **Middlesex**	at Lord's
+7-64	AR Caddick	**Somerset** v. **Hampshire**	at Southampton
7-67	PJ Martin	**Lancashire** v. **Leicestershire**	
			at Old Trafford
7-72	MP Bicknell	**Surrey** v. **Leicestershire**	at Guildford
+7-78	JF Brown	**Northamptonshire** v. **Sussex**	
			at Northampton
7-79	MJ Saggers	**Kent** v. **Durham**	at Chester-le-Street
+7-167	PM Such	**Essex** v. **Middlesex**	at Chelmsford
7-105	IDK Salisbury	**Surrey** v. **Durham**	at the Oval

FEATURES OF 2000 FIRST-CLASS SEASON

HIGHEST TOTAL

718-3 dec.   **Glamorgan** v. **Sussex**   at Colwyn Bay

LOWEST TOTAL

+54   **West Indies** v. **England**   at Lord's

HIGHEST INDIVIDUAL SCORE

309*   SP James **Glamorgan** v. **Sussex**   at Colwyn Bay

BEST INNINGS BOWLING

+9-47   MP Bicknell **Surrey** v. **Leicestershire**   at Guildford

BEST MATCH BOWLING

16-169   MP Bicknell **Surrey** v. **Leicestershire**   at Guildford

FOUR WICKETS IN SUCCESSIVE BALLS

GP Butcher   **Surrey** v. **Derbyshire**   at the Oval

FOUR WICKETS IN AN OVER

AR Caddick   **England** v. **West Indies**   at Headingley

MOST DISMISSALS IN AN INNINGS

6ct   SJ Rhodes   +**Worcestershire** v. **Nottinghamshire**
                                                      at Trent Bridge

MOST DISMISSALS IN A MATCH

9 ct   SJ Rhodes   **Worcestershire** v. **Gloucestershire**
                                                      at Worcester
8ct/1st AN Aymes   **Hampshire** v. **Leicestershire**
                                                      at Southampton

MOST FIELD CATCHES

29   DP Fulton (**Kent**)

NORWICH UNION NATIONAL LEAGUE
By Mark Baldwin

30 April 2000: Division One
at Bristol
Gloucestershire 145 (43.5 overs)(KJ Barnett 50)
Sussex 135 (43.4 overs)(MG Bevan 52*,
JMM Averis 4 for 21)
Gloucestershire (4 pts) won by 10 runs

at Canterbury
Kent v. Lancashire
No play – 2 pts each

at Worcester
Yorkshire 151 for 8 (45 overs)(GD McGrath 4 for 9)
Worcestershire 132 (43.2 overs)
Yorkshire (4 pts) won by 19 runs

Gavin Hamilton and Yorkshire picked up a solid opening-day win, beating Worcestershire by 19 runs.

Holders Lancashire suffered the frustration of having their first match, against Kent at Canterbury, abandoned without a ball being bowled. Elsewhere in the first division, however, there were wins for Gloucestershire and Yorkshire.

Gloucestershire successfully defended a total of just 145, built around Kim Barnett's 55, on a Bristol pitch that had been juiced up by the almost constant rainfall of previous weeks. In reply, Sussex initially looked to be in complete control – especially with Michael Bevan in such magnificent early-season form. But, with James Averis taking 4 for 21 and Ian Harvey 2 for 15, Sussex collapsed, losing their last six wickets for just ten runs in 43 balls. Bevan was left stranded, on 52 not out, and Gloucestershire had won by ten runs.

At Worcester it was Yorkshire who defended a smallish total, leaving Glenn McGrath on the losing side despite the awesome bowling that brought him figures of 9–6–9–4. McGrath's new-ball spell was six straight maidens but his fellow Australian, Darren Lehmann, hit back with 46 and Yorkshire eventually totalled 151 for 8 from their 45 overs. Worcestershire never looked comfortable in the conditions, seamers Craig White and Gavin Hamilton both picking up three wickets, and they were bowled out in the 44th over for 132.

30 April 2000: Division Two
at Cardiff
Surrey 185 for 9 (45 overs)(GP Thorpe 61)
Glamorgan 175 (44.1 overs)(AJ Hollioake 4 for 39)
Surrey (4 pts) won by 10 runs

at Chelmsford
Essex 143 (22.4 overs)(N Hussain 60,
ARC Fraser 4 for 18)
Middlesex 83 for 9 (23 overs)
Essex (4 pts) won by 60 runs

at Trent Bridge
Durham 208 for 6 (45 overs)(JA Daley 53)
Nottinghamshire 209 for 6 (JER Gallian 74,
JE Morris 50)
Nottinghamshire (4 pts) won by four wickets

Middlesex, enduring a miserable start to the season, were an astonishing 16 for 7 by the middle of the eighth over at Chelmsford as they replied to a challenging Essex total of 143 in a match reduced by the weather to 23 overs per side. Nasser Hussain hit 60 from 52 balls for Essex, and Danny Law a powerful 37, before Mark Ilott and Ronnie Irani created mayhem in the visitors' batting ranks. Middlesex eventually scraped together 83 for 9 and were beaten by 60 runs.

Surrey beat Glamorgan by ten runs at Cardiff, with left-handers Graham Thorpe (61) and Mark Butcher (47) scoring the bulk of their 185 for 9. The Welsh county were always struggling in reply, despite Matthew Maynard's 46 – Adam Holby oake took 4 for 39 and Martin Bicknell 3 for 28, but the bowling of young all-rounder Ben Holioake also caught the eye as his nine overs cost just 19 runs.

The most exciting finish of the day, however, came at Trent Bridge where Nottinghamshire needed two runs to win off the final ball of the match against Durham. Steve Harmison bowled a wide, Paul Franks scrambled through for a bye – and Notts were home with one ball still remaining! Durham's 208 for 6 was built around 53 from Jimmy Daley and 49 from Nick Speak, the skipper, while Jason Gallian also played a captain's innings of 74 for Notts and John Morris, with 50 from 45 balls, passed 5,000 one-day league runs.

1 May 2000: Division One
at Canterbury
Northamptonshire 76 (40.4 overs)(BJ Phillips 4 for 25)
Kent 77 for 3 (18.5 overs)
Kent (4 pts) won by seven wickets

at Leicester
Leicestershire 164 for 8 (45 overs)
(MA Robinson 4 for 23)
Sussex 164 for 9 (45 overs)(MG Bevan 59, CC Lewis 4 for 34)
Match tied – 2 pts each

at Taunton
Somerset 181 (43.5 overs)(KA Parsons 66, IJ Harvey 5 for 33)
Gloucestershire 173 (44.2 overs)(PS Jones 4 for 32)
Somerset (4 pts) won by 8 runs

Kent were missing almost their entire first-string pace attack at Canterbury, with Dean Headley, Martin McCague and Julian Thompson all injured. Nevertheless, they dismissed Northamptonshire for just 76, the visitors struggling woefully through 40.4 overs as Ben Phillips (4 for 25) and David Masters (2 for 10 from his nine overs) wrought havoc. In reply, and despite the loss of two early wickets, an assured unbeaten 31 from Rahul Dravid and a promising 26 from 21-year-old James Hockley swept Kent to a comfortable seven-wicket victory.

There was much excitement at Leicester, with Sussex last pair Mark Robinson and James Kirtley scampering a bye from Chris Lewis' last ball to clinch a thrilling tie. Lewis ended the match with 4 for 34 but could not prevent Sussex taking nine runs off that vital final over to reach 164 for 9. Richard Montgomerie had earlier launched the innings with a solid 42, while Michael Bevan's 59 from 83 balls took his run-tally from three limited-overs innings to 274. In Leicestershire's total of 164 for 8 Aftab Habib hit a 59-ball unbeaten 39 while Robinson's medium-pace deliveries earned him 4 for 23 from his allotted nine overs.

Somerset came out on top in another exciting finish in the West Country derby at Taunton, Gloucestershire's Mike Smith being run out by a direct hit from Piran Holloway as he tried to pinch a run from the second ball of the final over. Gloucestershire, all out for 173 despite 44 not out from skipper Mark Alleyne and 38 from Matt Windows, were beaten by eight runs. Steffan Jones was the most successful Somerset bowler with 4 for 32. Earlier Smith's waspish left-arm seam and swing had brought him 2 for 11 from nine overs and only a fighting boundary-less 66 from Keith Parsons hauled Somerset up to 181 as Ian Harvey, the leading wicket-taker with 33 in the 1999 National League, grabbed his best figures in the competition with 5 for 33.

1 May 2000: Division Two
at Derby
Middlesex 185 for 6 (45 overs)
Derbyshire 114 (36.5 overs)(PN Weekes 4 for 26)
Middlesex (4 pts) won by 71 runs

at Southampton
Warwickshire 215 for 8 (45 overs)(TL Penney 51)
Hampshire 118 (35.5 overs)
Warwickshire (4 pts) won by 97 runs

A freak injury to Allan Donald overshadowed Warwickshire's trouncing of Hampshire by 97 runs at Southampton. Donald's magnificent spell of 6–2–9–3 had reduced the home side to the hopeless position of 58 for 6 in reply to Warwickshire's 215 for 8, but then the South African fast bowler tried to catch a big hit from Shane Warne and fell heavily into the advertisement hoardings beyond long on. Donald had to leave the field for X-rays, which later confirmed a double rib fracture. Hampshire were bowled out for 118, a poor effort on a good pitch. Warwickshire's innings, by contrast, had been launched by an opening stand of 70 between Nick

Knight (46) and Graeme Welch (39) and boosted by a partnership of 84 in the last 12 overs between Trevor Penney (51) and Mohammad Sheikh (36).

A combination of Angus Fraser's miserly seam (5–3–7–2) and Paul Weekes' effective off-spin (4 for 26) proved too potent for Derbyshire, who slid to 114 all out at Derby and a 71-run defeat against Middlesex, for whom Mark Ramprakash (38) and Owais Shah (37) top-scored in a total of 185 for 6.

6 May 2000: Division Two
at Chester-le-Street
Surrey 230 for 7 (45 overs)
Durham 164 (41.3 overs)(AJ Hollioake 5 for 29)
Surrey (4 pts) won by 66 runs

The Hollioake brothers were in good form at Chester-le-Street as Surrey saw off Durham by the comfortable margin of 66 runs. Ben Hollioake struck 42 off 50 balls, after Alec Stewart had hit 41, as Surrey totalled 230 for 7 from 45 overs. Durham, who did not help their cause by bowling no fewer than 26 wides, then crumbled to 164 all out in reply with Adam Hollioake cashing in with 5 for 29.

7 May 2000: Division One
at Old Trafford
Lancashire 177 for 7 (45 overs)(SC Ganguly 61)
Leicestershire 177 for 9 (45 overs)(BF Smith 90)
Match tied – 2pts each

at Northampton
Gloucestershire 150 for 9 (35 overs)
Northamptonshire 112 (29.5 overs)(JMM Averis 5 for 20)
Gloucestershire (4 pts) won by 49 runs (DL Method: Northamptonshire target 162 from 35 overs)

at Headingley
Worcestershire 173 for 8 (45 overs)(PR Pollard 55)
Yorkshire 164 for 9 (45 overs)
Worcestershire (4 pts) won by 9 runs

Remarkably, Leicestershire were involved in their second tie of the season (in their second match!), with Ben Smith their batting hero at Old Trafford. Smith's 90 from 118 balls kept Leicestershire on course to challenge Lancashire's total of 177 for 7, in which Saurav Ganguly had scored a lovely 61 from 78 balls and Mike Atherton a more workmanlike 46. Two runs were required from the final delivery of the day, from Peter Martin, and Leicestershire's Jon Dakin and non-striker Anil Kumble managed to sprint a bye.

James Averis was in excellent early season form for Gloucestershire. Here he is taking 5 for 20 to demolish Northants.

James Averis picked up 5 for 20 at Northampton as Gloucestershire bowled out Northants to win by 49 runs. The home side had actually needed 162, under the Duckworth/Lewis regulations, after Gloucestershire had totalled 150 for 9 from their allotted 35 overs. But only Jeff Cook, with 33 from 40 balls, made an impression on the well-oiled Gloucestershire one-day attack.

Yorkshire were narrowly beaten at Headingley despite a promising 28 off 33 balls from 19-year-old Victor Craven, a left-hander from Harrogate. Darren Lehmann also made 39, but Yorkshire finished on

164 for 9, falling just short in reply to 173 for 8 by Worcestershire, for whom Paul Pollard hit 55 and Reuben Spring 49.

7 May 2000: Division Two
at Chelmsford
Nottinghamshire 190 for 7 (42 overs)
Essex 187 for 9 (42 overs)(N Hussain 55)
Nottinghamshire (4 pts) won by 3 runs

at Lord's
Hampshire 147 (44.5 overs)(RA Smith 71)
Middlesex 148 for 6 (43.2 overs)
Middlesex (4 pts) won by four wickets

at Edgbaston
Glamorgan 125 (39.2 overs)
Warwickshire 127 for 1 (26.5 overs)(NV Knight 68*)
Warwickshire (4 pts) won by nine wickets

Essex threw away a clear advantage at Chelmsford and ended up losing by three runs to Nottinghamshire. In a match reduced to 42 overs per side, Notts made 190 for 7 with Paul Johnson top-scoring with 37 and Paul Grayson taking 3 for 23. Essex, in reply, were cruising at 121 for 2, Nasser Hussain having scored 55 and Stuart Law 39. But then a rash of dreadful shots produced a sickly procession with only Ronnie Irani (42 not out) standing firm at the crease. Finally, eight runs were needed from the last over ... and it proved too much as they managed just five.

Shane Warne took 3 for 33 from his nine-over allocation at Lord's, but it was not enough to prevent Middlesex snatching a four-wicket win after a tense contest. Robin Smith played the innings of the day, his 71 guiding Hampshire to 147, but Owais Shah then hit 39 as Middlesex got home with ten balls to spare.

Brilliant fielding by Trevor Penney illuminated proceedings at Edgbaston, where Warwickshire trounced Glamorgan by nine wickets. Penney pulled off a superb catch to get rid of Glamorgan's Australian opener Matthew Elliott for 21, and then ran out Matthew Maynard with a direct hit on the one stump he could see. Later, Penney also ran out Adrian Shaw with another direct hit as Glamorgan slid to 125 all out. Nick Knight then hit an unbeaten 68 as Warwickshire romped home to victory.

17 May 2000: Division One
at Hove (floodlit)
Worcestershire 206 for 7 (45 overs)(KR Spring 71,
RJ Kirtley 4 for 41)
Sussex 103 for 4 (23.1 overs)
Worcestershire (4 pts) won by 4 runs (DL Method: at 23.1 overs, when rain stopped play, Sussex should have reached 108)

Worcestershire won a hollow victory at Hove, by four runs on the Duckworth/Lewis calculations, when rain allowed Sussex to reach only 103 for 4 in reply to the visitors' 206 for 7. A poor crowd saw Reuben Spring (71) and Paul Pollard (49) put on 99 for the Worcestershire first wicket and, later, Glenn McGrath open up with a spell of 6–3–7–2 with the new ball. As the weather closed in, McGrath returned to take another vital wicket and finish with 3 for 19 from eight overs, but Sussex still had Michael Bevan unbeaten on 49 when play was stopped and could claim that they were still in a good position to have won a full-length match.

21 May 2000: Division One
at Leicester
Kent 141 for 9 (45 overs)
Leicestershire 142 for 7 (39 overs)(TR Ward 53, K Adams 4 for 19)
Leicestershire (4 pts) won by three wickets

at Taunton
Northamptonshire 240 (44.4 overs)(GP Swann 57)
Somerset 243 for 6 (42.1 overs)(ME Trescothick 68, KA Parsons 54*)
Somerset (4 pts) won by four wickets

at Headingley
Yorkshire 160 for 3 (39 overs)
Gloucestershire 129 (30.2 overs)
Yorkshire (4 pts) won by 35 runs (DL Method: Gloucestershire target 165 from 33 overs)

More runs from the emerging Marcus Trescothick and a fine unbeaten stand of 85 in ten overs by Keith Parsons and Ian Blackwell earned Somerset a four-wicket victory over Northamptonshire in front of a contented crowd at Taunton. Graeme Swann's 57 followed a typically robust 47 from Matthew Hayden in a Northants total of 240, but Trescothick then hammered 68, with a six and eight fours, to set Somerset off in rapid pursuit. Much still needed to be done, however, when Parsons was joined by Blackwell but with unbeaten knocks of 54 and 45 respectively the seventh-wicket pair made light of the challenge.

At Leicester the individual honours went to Kristian Adams, a 23-year-old left-arm seamer from

Cleethorpes who took three wickets in his first 11 balls on his debut for Kent and finished up with 4 for 19. But his heroics were not enough to prevent Leicestershire overhauling Kent's 141 for 9. Trevor Ward, in his first match against the county he left after 14 seasons during the winter, led a recovery from 23 for 4 with a gritty 53, and the hard-won victory was sealed by an unbroken stand of 42 for the eighth wicket by Chris Lewis and Jon Dakin.

Yorkshire, though, moved to the top of the Division One table (as one of five teams on eight points) by beating Gloucestershire by 31 runs in a weather-restricted match at Headingley. David Byas made 48 and Richard Blakey an unbeaten 43 as Yorkshire totalled 160 for 3 from their allotted 33 overs. The Yorkshire off-spinner James Middlebrook then took 3 for 16 from five overs as Gloucestershire slid to 129 all out in reply.

21 May 2000: Division Two
at Chester-le-Street
Durham 91 for 3 (28 overs)
Glamorgan 70 for 2 (18 overs)
Glamorgan (4 pts) won by 15 runs (DL Method: Glamorgan target 105 from 28 overs)

at Trent Bridge
Derbyshire 186 (44.3 overs)(SD Stubbings 59)
Nottinghamshire 189 for 6 (41.2 overs)(JE Morris 54, DJ Bicknell 51)
Nottinghamshire (4 pts) won by four wickets

at The Oval
Surrey v. Middlesex
No play possible – 2 pts each

at Edgbaston
Hampshire 154 (44.4 overs)(JS Laney 69)
Warwickshire 158 for 5 (39.3 overs)
Warwickshire (4 pts) won by five wickets

Nottinghamshire overcame local rivals Derbyshire by four wickets at Trent Bridge to go to the top of the Division Two table. Steve Stubbings, run out for 59, top-scored in Derbyshire's total of 186 – three wickets going down on 70 – and Notts proceeded to a comfortable victory thanks to half-centuries from John Morris (54) and Darren Bicknell (51), while skipper Jason Gallian also made a significant contribution with 37.

Warwickshire, who stayed level on points with Notts, looked shaky at 71 for 5 in reply to Hampshire's 154 at Edgbaston, in which Jason

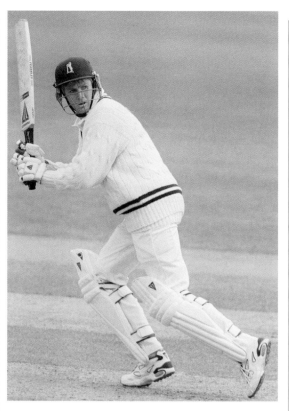

Trevor Penney's unbeaten 36 helped Warwickshire recover from an uncertain start to beat Hampshire at Edgbaston.

Laney hit 69 and John Stephenson an unbeaten 33. But then Dougie Brown (45 not out) and Trevor Penney (36 not out) added 87 in 20 overs.

Rain interrupted proceedings at Chester-le-Street, with Durham 91 for 3 from 28 overs and Simon Katich holding the fort on 47 not out. Glamorgan, replying with 70 for 2 from 18 overs thanks largely to Matthew Elliott's unbeaten 26, won by 15 runs on the Duckworth/Lewis formula.

The London derby between Surrey and Middlesex at The Oval was washed out.

28 May 2000: Division One
at Tunbridge Wells
Kent v. Sussex
No play possible – 2 pts each

at Worcester
Worcestershire 207 for 4 (34 overs)(PR Pollard 89)
Northamptonshire 133 for 9 (27 overs)
Worcestershire (4 pts) won by 47 runs (DL Method: Northamptonshire target 181 from 27 overs)

A fine innings of 89 by Paul Pollard and yet more controlled hostility from Glenn McGrath spearheaded Worcestershire's win against bottom side Northamptonshire at New Road. Richard Logan suffered more than most with 47 runs taken off his four overs as Worcestershire totalled 207 for 4 from 34 overs – the duration of the match having been cut due to bad weather. More rain brought down Northants' target to 181 from 27 overs, but McGrath responded with a spell of 6–2–15–2 and young Kabir Ali showed more signs of benefiting from the great Australian's presence by taking 3 for 19 from his own six-over allocation.

At Tunbridge Wells, where Kent were due to meet neighbours Sussex, the first match of festival week fell victim to prolonged rain – with parts of the Nevill Ground's outfield so waterlogged that groundsman John Bravey said he had never seen the playing arena in such a state.

28 May 2000: Division Two
at Chester-le-Street
Nottinghamshire 199 for 6 (45 overs)(JE Morris 73)
Durham 190 for 8 (43 overs)(PJ Franks 6 for 27)
Nottinghamshire (4 pts) won by 3 runs (DL Method: Durham target 194 from 43 overs)

Paul Franks was the undoubted hero of Nottinghamshire's thrilling three-run victory over Durham at Chester-le-Street. After John Morris (73 from 82 balls) had inspired Notts to 199 for 6, a brief rain shower meant Durham's target became 194 in 43 overs. Simon Katich hit 45 but Franks was a constant thorn in Durham's side, eventually finishing with the outstanding figures of 6 for 27 as the home side fell just short of what was needed with 190 for 8.

29 May 2000: Division Two
at Cardiff
Derbyshire 185 for 7 (45 overs)
Glamorgan 186 for 4 (43 overs)(MTG Elliott 88)
Glamorgan (4 pts) won by six wickets

at The Oval
Surrey v. Essex
No play possible – 2 pts each

A stand of 92 in 22 overs between Matthew Elliott (88) and Matthew Maynard (40) eased Glamorgan home by six wickets, and with two overs to spare, against Derbyshire at Cardiff. The Derbyshire total of 185 for 7, from their 45 overs, was merely a

workmanlike affair, and the flair of the two Matthews soon left the outcome of the match in little doubt. At The Oval, bad weather caused the abandonment of the Surrey/Essex match.

30 May 2000: Division Two
at The Oval (floodlit)
Hampshire 94 (30.2 overs)(AJ Tudor 4 for 26)
Surrey 95 for 3 (21.1 overs)
Surrey (4 pts) won by seven wickets

Surrey finally managed to avoid the bad weather as they tried to stage a floodlit match at The Oval – but then the game was over almost before the lights had been turned on! Alex Tudor (4 for 26) and Martin Bicknell (3 for 18) decimated the Hampshire top order and, from 42 for 6, only a stand of 32 between Robin Smith and Shane Warne prevented total humiliation for the visitors. Warne, with just 57 runs from 12 innings in all competitions to his name before this knock, displayed all his competitive spirit to hit 34 in trying conditions but a Hampshire total of just 94 was never going to be enough. Ian Ward's 44 from 51 balls ensured a quick finish ...and most of the evening was unused!

31 May 2000: Division Two
at Edgbaston (floodlit)
Warwickshire 222 for 7 (45 overs)(DP Ostler 55, G Welch 55)
Nottinghamshire 184 for 8 (45 overs)
Warwickshire (4 pts) won by 38 runs

A 5,000-strong crowd turned up for the first of three floodlit games being staged at Edgbaston this season by Warwickshire, who have declared their desire to install permanent lights at their headquarters. Graeme Welch and Dominic Ostler both scored 55, with David Hemp's stirring 53-ball 45 also helping to push Warwickshire's total up to 222 for 7. Guy Welton (42) and Jason Gallian (30) took the Nottinghamshire reply up to a promising 102 for 2 but from there the visitors fell away to 184 for 8 – leaving the home side victors by the comfortable margin of 38 runs.

4 June 2000: Division One
at Tunbridge Wells
Gloucestershire 192 for 5 (45 overs)(KJ Barnett 62, IJ Harvey 58*)
Kent 186 (44.4 overs)(DP Fulton 69)
Gloucestershire (4 pts) won by 6 runs

at Northampton
Lancashire 187 for 6 (45 overs)(NH Fairbrother 66*)
Northamptonshire 191 for 3 (43.2 overs)(MB Loye 61, DJG Sales 51*)
Northamptonshire (4 pts) won by seven wickets

at Bath
Somerset 197 (44.1 overs)(ME Trescothick 72)
Sussex 181 for 8 (45 overs)(MG Bevan 69)
Somerset (4 pts) won by 16 runs

at Headingley
Yorkshire 189 for 3 (45 overs)(GM Fellows 65, RJ Blakey 62)
Leicestershire 193 for 7 (43.2 overs)(BF Smith 88*)
Leicestershire (4 pts) won by three wickets

Holders Lancashire continued to endure a disappointing start to their title defence with a hefty seven-wicket defeat at Northampton. Only Neil Fairbrother, with an unbeaten 66, came to grips with the Northamptonshire bowlers as Lancashire totalled 187 for 6 from their 45 overs. Mal Loye (61), Jeff Cook (45) and David Sales, with an unbeaten 51, then eased Northants to their victory target with 10 balls to spare.

Gloucestershire warmed up for the Benson and Hedges Cup final with a fine performance in the field, and a six-run win, against Kent at Tunbridge Wells. They needed to be at their best to defend a total of 192 for 5, in which Kim Barnett had made 62 and Ian Harvey a typically robust 58 not out, especially after David Fulton launched the Kent reply with 69, curiously the first one-day half-century of his career. Fulton added 71 for the third wicket with Alan Wells (41) but, from 130 for 2, Kent's batsmen were squeezed and squeezed by Gloucestershire's out-cricket and, eventually, they subsided to 186 all out with just two balls remaining.

Somerset put in a similarly suffocating display in the field at Bath, defeating Sussex in the end by 16 runs and even withstanding an assault by Michael Bevan, the world's best one-day batsman. Bevan had already taken 3 for 17 in a Somerset total of 197 that would undoubtedly have been more but for the unlucky run out of Marcus Trescothick (72) from a deflected drive. Then, the Australian left-hander hit 69 to take Sussex within striking distance, but Somerset held firm in front of an appreciative festival crowd – with Graham Rose the pick of the home attack with figures of 9–4–18–2.

Ben Smith, dropped by James Middlebrook when on 55, led Leicestershire to a strange-looking three-

David Hemp's 45 in 53 balls bolstered Warwickshire's match-winning total of 222 against Nottinghamshire at Edgbaston.

wicket victory against Yorkshire at Headingley with an unbeaten 88. Earlier Yorkshire had seemed in little trouble against the Leicestershire attack, despite Chris Lewis' 2 for 19 from nine overs, and innings of 65 from Gary Fellows and 62 from Richard Blakey had taken them to 189 for 3. Michael Vaughan, returning from injury, faced four balls right at the end of the 45-over allocation.

4 June 2000: Division Two
at Ilford
Durham 182 for 7 (45 overs)(SM Katich 61, JJB Lewis 60)
Essex 175 (44.5 overs)(SG Law 63, ID Hunter 4 for 29)
Durham (4 pts) won by seven runs

at Lord's
Middlesex 185 for 9 (45 overs)
Glamorgan 185 for 9 (44 overs)(SP James 54*)
Match tied – 2 pts each

Glamorgan, given the perfect Benson and Hedges Cup final rehearsal for 10 June, failed to score a single off the last ball to beat Middlesex at Lord's. Mike Roseberry went past 3,000 one-day league runs in his 41, and Paul Weekes contributed 43, but Middlesex's 185 for 9 always looked in range for Glamorgan – even after a mid-innings slide. Steve James, coming in at number six, regained the initiative with a sensibly aggressive 54 not out, but

Middlesex fought hard to defend their total and – in a thrilling climax – Weekes ran in and dived rugby-style from point to hit the stumps with his underarm throw as Alex Wharf attempted to pinch what would have been the winning single from the last ball. Glamorgan at least had the consolation of two points from the tie, but the Welsh county were also left to reflect on their slow over-rate earlier that had resulted in them being docked an over when they batted. How handy those extra six balls would have been several hours later!

Somehow, at Ilford, Essex contrived to lose a match to Durham after being in total command at 137 for 4. Replying to Durham's 182 for 7, a total built around Simon Katich (61) and Jonathan Lewis (60), Essex were launched towards their target by Stuart Law's 63. But Ian Hunter weighed in with 4 for 29 and no one was capable of supporting Paul Grayson, who was left stranded on 32 not out when Essex were finally bowled out for 175 with just one ball outstanding.

11 June 2000: Division One
at Old Trafford
Lancashire 216 for 7 (45 overs)(VS Solanki 59*)
Worcestershire 204 (43.4 overs)(NH Fairbrother 75, A Flintoff 64)
Worcestershire (4 pts) won by 12 runs

at Taunton
Kent 179 for 9 (45 overs)(MV Fleming 63)
Somerset 180 for 1 (35.1 overs)(ME Trescothick 92*, J Cox 62)
Somerset (4 pts) won by nine wickets

at Horsham
Sussex 219 (45 overs)(CJ Adams 52)
Leicestershire 208 (44.4 overs)(VJ Wells 81)
Sussex (4 pts) won by 11 runs

The burgeoning talent of Marcus Trescothick was on show at Taunton as Somerset blitzed Kent by nine wickets to maintain their position at the top of the Division One table. Trescothick's unbeaten 92, plus 62 from skipper Jamie Cox, swept the home side past Kent's painfully inadequate 179 for 9 – a total that approached respectability only thanks to 63 off 75 balls from Matthew Fleming. Andy Caddick's 9–2–15–2 was also impressive before Trescothick and Cox added 145 in 29 overs.

Leicestershire suffered their first defeat of the season, failing to get past Sussex's 219 at Horsham despite an opening stand of 76 in just 12 overs

between Vince Wells and Trevor Ward. Although Wells went on to hit 81, no one else could settle in support and Leicestershire were eventually bowled out for 208 with only two balls remaining unbowled. Earlier Chris Adams' 52 had spearheaded a solid Sussex batting effort, but what crazy scheduling for this match: less than 20 miles down the road at Arundel the West Indians were still playing their first-class fixture against the Zimbabweans! Which match were Sussex-based cricket fans supposed to support on a summery Sunday? Both?

No Sussex supporter could have been as disgruntled as the followers of Lancashire, though, as Worcestershire edged out the home side at Old Trafford. Lancashire have come to expect one-day success almost by right – but this season it was just not happening. Paul Pollard and Elliott Wilson had put on 81 for the first wicket, and Vikram Solanki's 59 not out from 65 balls had pushed them on to a 45-over score of 216 for 7, but Worcestershire looked like finishing second when Andy Flintoff and Neil Fairbrother were adding 68 for the third wicket. Flintoff, however, was out for a 47-ball 64, which included a six and 11 fours, and although Fairbrother went on to reach 75 it was not enough. Warren Hegg, too, struck a late 33, but Lancashire kept on losing wickets and Glenn McGrath returned to telling effect as he took 3 for 11 from 8.4 overs. In the end, to the frustration of the Old Trafford regulars, last man Mike Smethurst was run out when 13 more runs were still needed from nine balls.

11 June 2000: Division Two
at Derby
Derbyshire 197 for 9 (45 overs)(ME Cassar 56)
Surrey 198 for 7 (42 overs)(IJ Ward 53)
Surrey (4 pts) won by three wickets

at Trent Bridge
Hampshire 135 (44 overs)(AJ Harris 5 for 35)
Nottinghamshire 136 for 2 (36.4 overs)
Nottinghamshire (4 pts) won by eight wickets

Nottinghamshire stayed top of Division Two, casting aside some of their disappointment at the news that Shoaib Akhtar would not be fit to join them this season by overpowering Hampshire at Trent Bridge. Andy Harris snatched 5 for 35 as Hampshire were tumbled out for 135, and old campaigners Darren Bicknell and John Morris ensured there would be no slip-ups in reply. Bicknell ended up with 58 not out, while Morris struck 38 in his side's eight-wicket romp.

Surrey's upward progress also continued with a seven-wicket win at Derby. The home side, in fact, were 135 for 2 with 17 overs remaining before tailing off to 197 for 9 – Saqlain picking up 3 for 36. Graham Thorpe had to battle through a testing spell from Dominic Cork (3 for 31) before steering Surrey home with an unbeaten 45 from 74 balls.

13 June 2000: Division Two
at Cardiff (floodlit)
Glamorgan 220 (44.2 overs)(MTG Elliott 94)
Essex 200 (42.4 overs)(DDJ Robinson 51)
Glamorgan (4 pts) won by 20 runs

Glamorgan bounced back from their Benson and Hedges Cup Final defeat by beating Essex by 20 runs under the floodlights at Cardiff. The sounds of Tom Jones ushered batsmen to and from the wicket as Glamorgan totalled 220 with Matthew Elliott (94) and Matthew Maynard (50) adding 98 in 18 overs. Ashley Cowan took four wickets for Essex, but then came three wickets apiece for Darren Thomas, Keith Newell and Dean Cosker as the visitors were successfully reined in for 200.

14 June 2000: Division One
at Worcester (floodlit)
Worcestershire 141 (44.4 overs)(IJ Harvey 4 for 23)
Gloucestershire 120 (29.5 overs)(GD McGrath 4 for 12)
Worcestershire (4 pts) won by 21 runs

Inspirational bowling from Glenn McGrath was instrumental in keeping Worcestershire top of the Division One table with a 21-run win over Gloucestershire. In a low-scoring affair at New Road there was fine bowling, too, from McGrath's fellow Australian Ian Harvey, who took 4 for 23 and was well supported by both Mike Smith and James Averis. Paul Pollard's 41 was the highest score of the match and Worcestershire's 141 was too much for Gloucestershire. Stuart Lampitt and Kabir Ali also revelled in the seam-friendly conditions, picking up three wickets apiece, but it was McGrath who was the indubitable star of the show with figures of 9–3–12–4 as the Benson and Hedges Cup winners were bowled out for a mere 120.

18 June 2000: Division One
at Northampton
Northamptonshire 251 for 8 (45 overs)(DJG Sales 72, MB Loye 54, ME Trescothick 4 for 50)
Somerset 229 (44.1 overs)(PD Bowler 69)
Northamptonshire (4 pts) won by 22 runs

Glenn McGrath was one of the 'signings of the season'. He routed Gloucestershire with figures of 4 for 12 from 9 overs.

at Headingley
Yorkshire 163 for 9 (45 overs)(D Byas 52)
Kent 139 (42.4 overs)
Yorkshire (4 pts) won by 24 runs
A 4,000-strong crowd was at Headingley to see Craig White stun Kent with a hat-trick that clinched Yorkshire a 24-run win. Kent, replying to Yorkshire's 163 for 9, slumped to 97 for 6 despite Rahul Dravid's 49 but then rallied through a seventh-wicket partnership of 41 between Paul Nixon and skipper

Matthew Fleming. But Fleming, having just hit White for four to reach 29, was then caught at cover before the England all-rounder followed up by trapping Min Patel and David Masters leg before with his next two deliveries. Nixon was left on 30 not out when the end came one run later.

David Sales hit a powerful 72 off just 55 balls at Northampton as Somerset were beaten by 22 runs. Mal Loye (54) was the other main contributor to the challenging Northants total of 251 for 8, and despite Peter Bowler's 69 the visitors could reach only 229 in reply.

18 June 2000: Division Two
at Basingstoke
Hampshire 222 for 5 (45 overs)(JP Stephenson 83*)
Durham 204 (44 overs)(JJB Lewis 55*)
Hampshire (4 pts) won by 18 runs

at Lord's
Derbyshire 186 for 8 (45 overs)(DG Cork 64)
Middlesex 171 (43.5 overs)(JL Langer 56)
Derbyshire (4 pts) won by 15 runs

Pitiful batting by Durham condemned them to defeat by 18 runs against Hampshire at Basingstoke. An opening stand of 95 in 20 overs between Paul Collingwood (51) and Muazam Ali (36) had set them up for a comparative stroll past Hampshire's 222 for 5, an innings based on opener John Stephenson's sometimes tortuous unbeaten 83 and a far freer 43 off 56 balls by Robin Smith. But then, for no accountable reason, Durham slumped to 126 for 7 before Jon Lewis, with 55 not out, did his best to haul them back into contention. In the end, however, Alan Mullally took 4 for 40 as Durham were bowled out for 204 with one over remaining.

At Lord's there was a first National League win of the season for Derbyshire, who beat Middlesex by 15 runs. Dominic Cork, batting at number three, top-scored with a responsible 64, and Simon Lacey, coming in at number eight, contributed an invaluable 40 as Derbyshire reached 186 for 8. Justin Langer hit 56 in reply, but Middlesex were dismissed for 171 with seven balls left.

23 June 2000: Division One
at Hove (floodlit)
Kent 215 for 7 (45 overs)(AP Wells 90,
RJ Kirtley 4 for 32)
Sussex 212 for 4 (45 overs)(CJ Adams 82,
RR Montgomerie 65)
Kent (4 pts) won by 3 runs

at Old Trafford (floodlit)
Northamptonshire 178 (41 overs)
Lancashire 118 for 3 (25.5 overs)
Lancashire (4 pts) won by 24 runs (DL method: Lancashire should have reached 95 from 25.5 overs when rain stopped play)

Kent won a remarkable floodlit game at Hove, in which Sussex failed to score five runs from the final over with seven wickets remaining. Even more remarkably, that final over was bowled by Matthew Walker, the Kent batsman not previously known for his ability with the ball. Chasing Kent's 215 for 7, in which Alan Wells made 90 against his old county, Sussex seemed to be cruising as Chris Adams hit 82 and Richard Montgomerie 65 while Michael Bevan was going nicely on 41. But Adams was yorked by Matthew Fleming during the penultimate over and Kent's captain, gambling by calling up Walker to bowl his skiddy seamers, saw Will House fail to score from the first four balls of the final over. A single at last put Bevan on strike, but the world's best one-day batsman chipped the final ball of the contest to David Fulton at deep mid-wicket and Kent had won by three runs! Walker, mobbed by his teammates, strode off with figures of 1–0–1–1.

On a wet and windy night at Old Trafford a hardy crowd of around 5,000 braved the cold to see Lancashire overcome Northamptonshire by 24 runs on Duckworth/Lewis calculations. Rain eventually forced the issue, but before then one of the floodlights shut down and there was an irritating delay while it was mended. Earlier, gusting winds had meant the lights could not be switched on until the 29th over of the Northants innings. Matthew Hayden's 48 was the main contribution to the visitors' 178, and Saurav Ganguly then added to his 3 for 22 by reaching 47 not out as Lancashire, chasing an initial target of 182 from 42 overs, got themselves ahead of the asking rate at 118 for 3 off 25.5 overs. Mike Atherton batted beautifully for 43.

23 June 2000: Division Two
at Edgbaston (floodlit)
Warwickshire 162 for 7 (45 overs)(NV Knight 82)
Surrey 166 for 3 (41.1 overs)(AJ Stewart 72*)
Surrey (4 pts) won by seven wickets

A stand of 75 in 18 overs between Alec Stewart (72 not out) and Alistair Brown (45) swept Surrey to a seven-wicket win against previously unbeaten Warwickshire at Edgbaston. The home side had earlier struggled to 162 for 7 with Saqlain Mushtaq,

Martin Bicknell and Ben Hollioake all impressing with their accuracy and control.

24 June 2000: Division One
at Bristol
Gloucestershire 211 (44.5 overs)(IJ Harvey 52, MP Vaughan 4 for 27)
Yorkshire 160 (42 overs)
Gloucestershire (4 pts) won by 51 runs

at Taunton
Worcestershire 222 for 8 (45 overs)(GA Hick 101)
Somerset 218 for 8 (45 overs)(PD Bowler 67, M Burns 56)
Worcestershire (4 pts) won by 4 runs

Brilliant wicketkeeping by the irrepressible Jack Russell provided two of the highlights of Gloucestershire's 51-run win against Yorkshire at Bristol. On a slow pitch the home side totalled 211 with Ian Harvey hitting 52 but Michael Vaughan's off-spin bringing him 4 for 27 and Craig White snapping up 3 for 30. Early in the Yorkshire reply, Russell brought off a quicksilver stumping to send back Vaughan and then a high-class catch as Richard Blakey tried to cut. Both times, Russell was standing up to the wicket to the whippy new-ball bowling of Mike Smith. David Byas (38) was thereafter the only visiting batsman to threaten as Smith finished with 3 for 20 and James Averis 3 for 26.

Worcestershire kept themselves on top of the Division One table by beating Somerset, who stayed second, by just four runs in an exciting finish at Taunton. Graeme Hick hit 101 in Worcestershire's 222 for 8, his 143rd hundred in all forms of senior cricket, while Steve Rhodes contributed a useful unbeaten 36 in the closing overs. Peter Bowler and Michael Burns both hit half-centuries in reply, but Worcestershire kept taking wickets at crucial times and, in the end, it all came down to whether Paul Jarvis could hit the last ball of the match, from Richard Illingworth, for six. He couldn't.

24 June 2000: Division Two
at Cardiff
Glamorgan 236 for 7 (45 overs)(MP Maynard 67)
Hampshire 185 for 9 (45 overs)(SD Udal 51*)
Glamorgan (4 pts) won by 51 runs

at Trent Bridge
Essex 177 for 9 (45 overs)(RC Irani 52, DS Lucas 4 for 38)
Nottinghamshire 179 for 6 (42.3 overs)
Nottinghamshire (4 pts) won by four wickets

The match between Nottinghamshire and Essex at Trent Bridge provided the news of the day – but it wasn't good news at all for England as Nasser Hussain suffered a bad fracture of his left thumb joint. The England captain was trying to stop a booming cover drive by Chris Read as Notts were closing in on a four-wicket victory, and the result was that Hussain would be ruled out of the second Test against the West Indies, and much of the triangular one-day series that followed. David Lucas, the emerging left-arm fast bowler, took 4 for 38 as Essex totalled 177 for 9, but Notts fell away to 128 for 6 in reply, despite 41 from Jason Gallian and 40 from Guy Welton, before Read and Paul Franks rallied them to victory with an unbroken seventh-wicket stand of 51.

Shane Warne took a severe hammering at Cardiff, conceding 58 runs from his eight overs, as Glamorgan romped to a 51-run win over Hampshire. Matthew Maynard top-scored with 67, while Keith Newell and Michael Powell weighed in with 43 each. When Hampshire replied, Robert Croft provided the tightest spin-bowling of the day with 2 for 22 from his nine overs and Hampshire slumped to 91 for 7 before Shaun Udal's unbeaten 51 at least salvaged some pride.

Gloucestershire's Mike Smith: 'I still have sleepless nights about giving him only one Test', admitted the chairman of selectors, David Graveney.

25 June 2000: Division One
at Leicester
Leicestershire 218 for 5 (45 overs)(DL Maddy 87*,
VJ Wells 59)
Gloucestershire 180 (43.3 overs)
Leicestershire (4 pts) won by 38 runs

at Headingley
Northamptonshire 189 for 7 (45 overs)(DJG Sales 71*)
Yorkshire 129 (39 overs)(GP Swann 4 for 14)
Northamptonshire (4 pts) won by 60 runs

A superb 87 not out from only 76 balls spearheaded
Leicestershire's 38-run victory against
Gloucestershire at Leicester. Vince Wells also hit 59
as the home side reached 218 for 5, and then Anil
Kumble's unique style of leg-spin proved too much
for the Gloucestershire batsmen. Kim Barnett (45)
and Jack Russell (49) did add 66 for the third
wicket, but Kumble began the slide to 180 all out by
bowling Barnett. The Indian finished with 3 for 28
from his nine-over stint.

David Sales played the dominant innings at
Headingley, his unbeaten 71 taking
Northamptonshire to 189 for 7 despite Matthew
Hoggard's 3 for 43. Yorkshire's batting faded badly
in reply, with only Anthony McGrath (32) shaping
up for long. The end came quickly, Graeme Swann's
off-breaks claiming 4 for 14 from just five overs as
Northants wrapped up victory by 60 runs.

25 June 2000: Division Two
at Chester-le-Street
Middlesex 233 (44.2 overs)(AJ Strauss 90)
Durham 180 (40.1 overs)(NJ Speak 53*,
AW Laraman 6 for 51)
Middlesex (4 pts) won by 53 runs

at Edgbaston
Essex 163 for 7 (45 overs)
Warwickshire 139 (40.2 overs)
Essex (4 pts) won by 24 runs

Splendid batting by Andrew Strauss and Mark
Ramprakash was at the forefront of Middlesex's 53-
run beating of Durham at Chester-le-Street. Strauss
scored 90 from 110 balls, and Ramprakash 46 from
67 deliveries, as Middlesex were propelled towards a
challenging 233. Angus Fraser then put Durham
seriously behind the clock with a new-ball spell of
6–2–7–1 before Aaron Laraman, a 21-year-old fast
bowler from Enfield, enjoyed himself hugely by
working through the rest of the Durham order to

Jack Russell played a key role in Gloucestershire's one-day
success, both batting and behind the wicket.

finish with 6 for 51. Only Nick Speak (53 not out)
put up any sort of resistance as Durham were
eventually dismissed for 180.

Warwickshire members were vocal in their
disappointment, and frustration, as the home side's
batting let them down against Essex at Edgbaston.
An Essex total of 163 for 7, boosted only by a stand
of 53 in ten overs between Paul Grayson (41 not
out) and Stephen Peters (39), should have been well
within the capabilities of the Warwickshire players –
especially when Nick Knight, the opener, gave them
a fine start with 42. But then Grayson's left-arm spin
brought him 3 for 21 from nine overs on a sluggish
surface and, suddenly under pressure, Warwickshire
collapsed pitifully to 139 all out. The last seven
wickets fell for just 39 runs, and the home
supporters were not happy.

Stuart Law: an unbeaten century against Middlesex in yet another high-scoring season for Essex.

final eight overs when Lucas was recalled into the attack, but only Rob Bailey (30) could master his rapid in-swinging yorkers.

27 June 2000: Division One
at Old Trafford (floodlit)
Yorkshire 225 for 5 (45 overs)
(DS Lehmann 62, GM Fellows 57)
Lancashire 138 (34.4 overs)
(JP Crawley 71*)
Yorkshire (4 pts) won by 69 runs (DL Method after light failure: Lancashire target 208 from 40.2 overs)

An Old Trafford crowd of 11,850 had to endure a floodlight failure at 9:20 p.m. that took 15 minutes to fix, the sight of Roses rivals Yorkshire batting beautifully to reach 225 for 5 from their 45 overs, and finally a poor effort from their own heroes as Lancashire slid to 138 all out in reply. Darren Lehmann hit 62, Gary Fellows 57, and 77 runs were taken from the last ten overs by Yorkshire. But, for Lancashire, only John Crawley (71 not out) resisted. Chris Silverwood set the tone of the innings by removing Mark Chilton's off-stump with the second ball, a delivery that measured 88mph on the speed gun, and then producing one that touched 90mph to dismiss Sourav Ganguly for just five. In the end, because of a Duckworth/Lewis adjustment necessary due to a delay caused by the failure of floodlights, Yorkshire won by 69 runs.

26 June 2000: Division Two
at Derby (floodlit)
Nottinghamshire 212 for 8 (45 overs)(DJ Bicknell 90, DG Cork 4 for 40)
Derbyshire 182 (42.3 overs)(DG Cork 51, DS Lucas 4 for 27)
Nottinghamshire (4 pts) won by 30 runs

David Lucas settled Derbyshire's first floodlit match with a superb four-wicket burst in the closing stages. Lucas' victims were all bowled, Nottinghamshire running out 30-run winners in front of an animated 2,500 crowd who thoroughly enjoyed both the entertainment and the balmy evening weather at the Racecourse Ground. Darren Bicknell made a good 90 for Notts, but Dominic Cork took 4 for 40 to restrict them to 212 for 8 and then promoted himself to number three to score 51 and help Michael Di Venuto (46) add 92 for Derbyshire's second wicket. But Richard Stemp bowled Cork during a steady spell of left-arm spin, and Lucas then got to work. Derbyshire needed 51 from the

27 June 2000: Division Two
at Southampton
Surrey 116 (38 overs)
Hampshire 73 (32.4 overs)
Surrey (4 pts) won by 43 runs

Surrey moved to the top of Division Two with a determined 43-run win over Hampshire in a low-scoring, but strangely compelling, contest at Southampton. All the Hampshire bowlers performed well on a pitch offering some bounce as Surrey were dismissed for just 116, and with seven overs unused. Ben Hollioake's 37 was a fine, correct innings that made one yearn for much more of the same from this highly talented young cricketer – and he even had the temerity to drive Shane Warne over long on for six. But Surrey's attack, led by Martin Bicknell (3 for 14) and Saqlain Mushtaq (3 for 12) fought back superbly – using the conditions perfectly to bowl out Hampshire for only 73. Well beaten, the home side remained rock bottom of the league.

2 July 2000: Division One
at Maidstone
Somerset 295 for 7 (45 overs)(ME Trescothick 71, J Cox 51)
Kent 241 (40.2 overs)(MJ Walker 63, AP Wells 59)
Somerset (4 pts) won by 54 runs

at Northampton
Sussex 260 for 3 (33 overs)(CJ Adams 100, MG Bevan 54*)
Northamptonshire 217 (30.5 overs)
Sussex (4 pts) won by 43 runs

at Worcester
Worcestershire 108 for 8 (38 overs)
Leicestershire did not bat
Match abandoned – 2 pts each

A high-class and powerful 71 from Marcus Trescothick, which took him just 50 balls and included a six and 11 fours, gave Somerset such a flying start against Kent at Maidstone that they always looked to have too much in the bank for the home side. Jamie Cox (51), Keith Parsons (49 not out) and Ian Blackwell, with a no-nonsense 39, all made good contributions too as Somerset totalled a formidable 295 for 7. And, despite Matthew Walker's 63 off 68 balls, and 59 from Alan Wells, Kent were never up with the asking rate. Trescothick even had the cheek to take 3 for 45 and, with Blackwell (3 for 30) also impressing with the ball, Somerset's margin of victory was eventually 54 runs.

Chris Adams was hurtful enough, hitting a fine hundred, but Michael Bevan's 27-ball unbeaten 54 was a murderous exhibition of one-day batting as Sussex totalled 260 for 3 from just 33 overs at Northampton and unsurprisingly went on to win by 43 runs in a match shortened by rain. Umer Rashid (3 for 38) was one of the few bowlers to taste success as Northants made a brave stab at matching Sussex's display by reaching 217 from 30.5 overs themselves.

Worcestershire, meanwhile, were highly fortunate to escape with two points in their match against Leicestershire at New Road. After collapsing to 41 for 6, and then struggling to 108 for 8 after 38 overs, on a blameless pitch, rain arrived to wash away any further thoughts of play.

2 July 2000: Division Two
at Darlington
Durham 182 for 6 (37 overs)(SM Katich 67*, MP Speight 55)
Derbyshire 87 (24 overs)
Durham (4 pts) won by 95 runs

at Chelmsford
Middlesex 213 for 9 (45 overs)(MA Roseberry 72)
Essex 214 for 3 (37 overs)(SG Law 104*)
Essex (4 pts) won by seven wickets

at Swansea
Glamorgan 167 for 4 (38 overs)(MTG Elliott 84*, SP James 53)
Warwickshire 201 for 7 (38 overs)
Match tied – 2 pts each (DL Method: Warwickshire target 202 from 38 overs)

Chris Taylor rescued Gloucestershire's innings with a dogged 37 not out at Cheltenham that helped condemn Worcestershire to defeat.

One of the finest one-day batsmen in the world – Michael Bevan – adds more runs for his adopted Sussex.

The Duckworth/Lewis formula produced an exciting tussle at Swansea, with Warwickshire clinching a tie against Glamorgan by reaching 201 for 7 in reply to the Welsh county's 167 for 4 from 38 overs. Matthew Elliott (84 not out) and Steve James (53) put on 101 for the second wicket, but the hitting of Michael Powell, Ashley Giles and Neil Smith saw the two sides sharing the four points.

An unbeaten 104 from 96 balls by Stuart Law, his highest score in all cricket since the start of May, swept Essex to victory by seven wickets against Middlesex at Chelmsford. Earlier Mike Roseberry had scored 72 as Middlesex totalled 213 for 9, with Paul Grayson taking 3 for 31 from nine overs of slow left-arm spin.

Mark Davies, a product of Durham's academy, took 3 for 15 to help the north-eastern county destroy Derbyshire at Darlington. Simon Katich (67 not out) and Martin Speight (55) led Durham to 182 for 6, from 37 overs, and then Derbyshire were blown away for just 87 as Davies and Nicky Phillips (3 for 4) got among the wickets.

16 July 2000: Division One

at Cheltenham
Worcestershire 145 for 9 (45 overs)
Gloucestershire 149 for 7 (44.5 overs)
Gloucestershire (4 pts) won by three wickets

at Leicester
Leicestershire 187 (44.4 overs)(Aftab Habib 70)
Northamptonshire 192 for 6 (43.3 overs)
(ML Hayden 96*)
Northamptonshire (4 pts) won by four wickets

at Taunton
Somerset 198 (44 overs)
Lancashire 202 for 3 (38 overs)(MA Atherton 105, SC Ganguly 82)
Lancashire (4 pts) won by seven wickets

at Arundel
Sussex 272 for 6 (45 overs)(MG Bevan 89*, CJ Adams 54)
Yorkshire 202 (42 overs)(DS Lehmann 89)
Sussex (4 pts) won by 70 runs

Leaders Worcestershire were beaten by Gloucestershire at Cheltenham, despite Glenn McGrath's 9–4–15–3 and despite the home side collapsing to 76 for 7 in reply to the visitors' 145 for 9. Chris Taylor (37 not out) and Martyn Ball (30 not out) answered their team's emergency with an eighth-wicket stand of 73. Earlier Mike Smith had produced figures of 9–5–9–1 with the new ball and only Vikram Solanki, with 45, looked like flourishing in the conditions.

An unbeaten 96 from Mathew Hayden, with three sixes and eight fours, spearheaded Northamptonshire's drive to a four-wicket win at Leicester. David Sales also hit 40, and earlier Aftab Habib's 109-ball 70 had contained no fewer than 42 singles as Leicestershire struggled to 187 all out.

Magnificent batting by Mike Atherton and Saurav Ganguly, who put on 192 for the first wicket (a county one-day league record against Somerset) swept Lancashire to victory by seven wickets at Taunton. Only Jamie Cox (45) looked fluent as Somerset totalled 198, but both Atherton (105) and Ganguly (82 from 93 balls) made batting look easy.

Michael Bevan, who was cast aside as Yorkshire's overseas player in 1998 after two seasons with them, enjoyed sweet revenge at Arundel as his brilliant 81-ball 89 not out helped Sussex trounce Yorkshire by 70 runs. Ironically, Darren Lehmann, the fellow Australian who was preferred to Bevan, also hit 89 (off 90 balls).

16 July 2000: Division Two
at Derby
Warwickshire 150 for 8 (45 overs)(KJ Dean 4 for 30)
Derbyshire 105 (40.5 overs)
Warwickshire (4 pts) won by 45 runs

at Southgate
Middlesex 173 (43.4 overs)(N Killeen 4 for 18)
Durham 172 for 9 (45 overs)(SM Katich 70*)
Middlesex (4 pts) won by 1 run

at the Oval
Surrey 268 for 5 (45 overs)(AJ Hollioake 111,
IJ Ward 90*)
Glamorgan 201 (41.2 overs)(BC Hollioake 4 for 42)
Surrey (4 pts) won by 67 runs

Surrey went top of Division Two when they
overpowered Glamorgan by 67 runs at the Oval.
Adam Hollioake, the captain, hit his maiden one-day
century as Surrey reached 268 for 5 from their 45
overs. Ian Ward provided the anchor role by batting
through the innings for 90 not out, but it was
Hollioake who produced the acceleration during a
partnership of 181 in 30 overs for the fourth wicket.
His 111 took 98 balls, with his second 50 spanning
just 38 deliveries. Adam then picked up a wicket
and two catches in the Glamorgan reply of 201 and,
to complete the Hollioakes' day, younger brother
Ben finished with 4 for 42.
Middlesex won a thriller at Southgate, beating
Durham by just one run despite a fighting 70 not
out by the visitors' Australian left-hander Simon
Katich. Durham had slipped to 135 for 9 in reply to
Middlesex's 173, but Neil Killeen, who had earlier
taken 4 for 18, joined Katich and the last-wicket pair
began to inch their team towards victory. Crucially,
however, in a nervy final over from Simon Cook,
which had begun with Durham needing 11 to win,
Katich lost the strike off the penultimate ball and –
with three still required – Killeen managed only a
leg-bye.
Derbyshire's wretched form continued at Derby
where, despite restricting Warwickshire to 150 for 8
with Kevin Dean taking 4 for 30, the home side
could reach only 105 all out in reply. Both Dougie
Brown and Neil Smith picked up three cheap
wickets, and Warwickshire's 45-run win kept them
in contention for promotion.

23 July 2000: Division One
at Cheltenham
Kent 199 for 6 (45 overs)

Gloucestershire 200 for 5 (40.1 overs)(RC Russell 55*)
Gloucestershire (4 pts) won by five wickets

at Leicester
Lancashire 162 for 9 (45 overs)(SC Ganguly 58)
Leicestershire 165 for 3 (36.5 overs)(Aftab Habib 63,
BF Smith 54*)
Leicestershire (4 pts) won by seven wickets

at Scarborough
Yorkshire 141 (43 overs)(PS Jones 4 for 33)
Somerset 246 for 8 (40.3 overs)(ID Blackwell 50*)
Somerset (4 pts) won by two wickets

Somerset and Gloucestershire maintained their West
Country challenge for the National League title,
cutting Worcestershire's lead to just two points by
beating Yorkshire and Kent respectively.
At Cheltenham, a highly successful festival was
rounded off in style as Gloucestershire romped home
by five wickets thanks to a hugely popular unbroken
sixth-wicket stand of 91 between Jack Russell and
Mark Alleyne. Gloucestershire were stuttering at 109
for 5, in reply to Kent's 199 for 6, when the
wicketkeeper and the skipper came together. Russell
ended 55 not out, and Alleyne 35 not out, as victory
eventually arrived with almost five overs to spare.
Earlier, local boy Dominic Hewson (45) and Ian
Harvey (41) had added 72 in 13 overs for the second
wicket, while Mark Ealham top-scored with 49 not
out from 52 balls in the Kent innings. The total
attendance at the Cheltenham Festival approached
40,000 – generating record receipts.
Ian Blackwell, well supported by Graham Rose,
was the Somerset hero at Scarborough. The visitors,
despite restricting Yorkshire to 141 all out, were
struggling at 107 for 8 until Blackwell met the
growing crisis by producing some power-hitting that
Lance Klusener would be proud of. Blackwell's
unbeaten 50 occupied just 41 balls, and included
two sixes and two fours. With Rose staying calm on
13 not out, Somerset cruised home in the end with
27 balls unused. Somerset's fine effort with the ball,
spearheaded by Steffan Jones (4 for 33) and Paul
Jarvis (3 for 23 against his former and native
county), also featured two wickets for Marcus
Trescothick, who demonstrated his commitment to
the Somerset cause by insisting on cutting short his
England celebrations following the NatWest Series
success at Lord's, rising at 6:00a.m. and driving
250 miles to play in the game. For Yorkshire there
was a milestone for David Byas, the captain, who
when he had made 14 became only the second

Yorkshire player after Geoff Boycott to complete 5,000 one-day league runs.

Leicestershire won the other Division One match, beating Lancashire by seven wickets after restricting the visitors to 162 for 9 from their 45 overs. Saurav Ganguly (58) was the only batsman to trouble the home attack, for whom Anil Kumble (3 for 29) was again outstanding. Aftab Habib (63) and Ben Smith (54 not out) made short work of the victory target.

23 July 2000: Division Two
at Chelmsford
Essex 203 for 8 (45 overs)
Derbyshire 197 (44.5 overs)
Essex (4 pts) won by 6 runs

at Portsmouth
Hampshire 190 for 9 (45 overs)
Middlesex 192 for 6 (44.2 overs)(MA Roseberry 54)
Middlesex (4 pts) won by four wickets

at Guildford
Surrey 273 for 3 (45 overs)(GP Thorpe 126*, IJ Ward 51)
Nottinghamshire 146 (35.2 overs)
Surrey (4 pts) won by 127 runs

at Edgbaston
Durham 198 for 6 (45 overs)(SM Katich 64, PD Collingwood 53)
Warwickshire 148 (40.1 overs)
Durham (4 pts) won by 50 runs

Surrey beat their nearest challengers Nottinghamshire by a crushing 127 runs at Guildford to stretch their lead at the top of the Division Two. A magnificent 126 not out by Graham Thorpe, from 127 balls and with 14 fours, was instrumental in helping Surrey post an imposing 273 for 3. Ian Ward hit 51 and David Lucas' nine overs cost 68. In reply, Jason Gallian (42) and Darren Bicknell, playing on his hometown ground for the first time in Notts colours, put on 57 for the first wicket. But, after that, it was downhill all the way as Notts were bowled out for 146.

At the other end of the table Derbyshire plunged to their eighth league defeat in nine games despite a late assault from tail-ender Kasir Shah, whose 20 from nine balls, including a six and three fours, took them to within six runs of Essex's 203 for 8 at Chelmsford. Nasser Hussain (47) top-scored for Essex, while Tim Munton's steadiness was rewarded with 3 for 24 off his nine overs.

Hampshire, too, suffered another defeat – this time failing to defend a total of 190 for 9 against Middlesex at Portsmouth. Robin Smith hit 42 but Hampshire fell away after reaching 121 for 2 with 14 overs remaining, and Mike Roseberry (54) and Mark Ramprakash (46) helped the visitors to claim a four-wicket victory.

At Edgbaston there was a morale-boosting win for Durham, for whom Simon Katich made 64 and Paul Collingwood 53 in a total of 198 for 6. That proved too much for Warwickshire, who struggled to 148 all out with Neil Killeen picking up 3 for 24.

30 July 2000: Division Two
at Southampton
Essex 158 for 9 (45 overs)(SD Peters 51, SK Warne 4 for 32)
Hampshire 162 for 4 (42.2 overs)(WS Kendall 46*)
Hampshire (4 pts) won by six wickets

Fine bowling from Shane Warne (4 for 32) and a forthright 46 not out from Will Kendall helped Hampshire to a comfortable six-wicket win against

Ben Smith eased Leicestershire to a comfortable victory over Lancashire.

Essex at Southampton. Stephen Peters (51) and Nasser Hussain (34) batted well during the Essex innings but no one else made an impression and a 45-over total of 158 for 9 was simply not enough.

1 August 2000: Division Two
at Trent Bridge (floodlit)
Warwickshire 244 for 6 (45 overs)(DP Ostler 79*, NV Knight 50, A Singh 43, RD Stemp 4 for 36)
Nottinghamshire 149 (43.5 overs)(DKJ Bicknell 61)
Warwickshire (4 pts) won by 85 runs

Warwickshire overwhelmed Nottinghamshire by 95 runs at Trent Bridge, despite the steady bowling that brought Richard Stemp, the left-arm spinner, figures of 4 for 36 from his nine-over allocation. Openers Nick Knight (50) and Anurag Singh (43) put on 91 at a run-a-ball and Warwickshire were further propelled towards their eventual 244 for 6 by an unbeaten 79 from 93 balls by the in-form Dominic Ostler. Darren Bicknell made 61 for Notts, but they never mounted a challenge and were finally bowled out for 147.

2 August 2000: Division One
at Northampton (floodlit)
Worcestershire 179 for 9 (45 overs)(SJ Rhodes 43, DA Leatherdale 40)
Northamptonshire 183 for 3 (36.4 overs)(MB Loye 75, DJG Sales 58*)
Northamptonshire (4 pts) won by seven wickets

A full house at Northampton were uneasy before the start of this match, especially because their own skipper Matthew Hayden was unfit. Glenn McGrath, Worcestershire's great Australian, was playing on the eve of his departure for the inaugural indoor one-day international series in Melbourne. They need not have worried, with Worcestershire being undermined initially at 83-6, recovering only to 179 for 9 thanks to Steve Rhodes and Stuart Lampitt, and McGrath then taking just 1 for 35 despite having previously plundered 22 wickets at a mere 6.36 runs apiece in this competition. Mal Loye (75) and David Sales (58 not out) swept Northants home by seven wickets with more than eight overs remaining.

6 August 2000: Division One
at Canterbury
Kent 214 (44.2 overs)(MJ McCague 56, JB Hockley 44)
Leicestershire 139 (38.4 overs)
Kent (4 pts) won by 75 runs

at Taunton
Yorkshire 249 for 3 (45 overs)(A McGrath 85*, GM Hamilton 43*)
Somerset 217 (43.3 overs)(RJ Turner 44, PD Bowler 40)
Yorkshire (4 pts) won by 32 runs

Somerset, bowling and fielding poorly, missed the chance of going to the top of the Division One table when they were beaten by 32 runs by Yorkshire at Taunton. Anthony McGrath, however, made an impressive 85 not out, from 77 balls, and with Gavin Hamilton (43 not out) was joined in an unbroken partnership of 124 in 18 overs. Yorkshire's total of 249 for 3 proved too much for the home side. Despite being 91 for 1 in the 21st over, Somerset fell away to 217 all out.

The re-emergence of Kent's forgotten former England fast bowler Martin McCague was the talking point at Canterbury. McCague, now 31, was playing in just his second league game of the season and – despite Kent's long list of injured quicker bowlers – he had also only figured in two championship fixtures. Now, though, McCague was back as he hammered 56 off 25 balls and followed up this superb display of power-hitting by taking two wickets as Kent thumped Leicestershire by 75 runs. McCague thrashed three sixes and eight fours, completing his fifty from just 20 deliveries – four less than Graham Rose's ten-year-old league record – and transforming the game. James Hockley also contributed a well-compiled 44 and Kent's 214 was more than enough. Martin Saggers, impressing more with every game, took 3 for 26 and Matthew Fleming, the skipper, bowled brilliantly to finish with 3 for 7 from his seven overs. Leicestershire, thus strangled, were dismissed for a disappointing 139 and the only cloud for rejuvenated Kent was the X-ray that revealed a crack in Mark Ealham's right index finger.

6 August 2000: Division Two
at Derby
Hampshire 233 for 3 (45 overs)(WS Kendall 73*, RA Smith 61*, DA Kenway 53)
Derbyshire 197 (42.4 overs)(MJ di Venuto 47, ME Cassar 44, JP Stephenson 4 for 40, DA Kenway 2ct, 3st)
Hampshire (4 pts) won by 36 runs

at Cardiff
Durham 202 for 5 (45 overs)(SM Katich 70, PD Collingwood 66)
Glamorgan 205 for 7 (44.5 overs)(A Dale 76*, MJ Powell 48)
Glamorgan (4 pts) won by three wickets

at Lord's
Middlesex 167 for 8 (45 overs)(MR Ramprakash 53)
Surrey 170 for 5 (39.1 overs)(N Shahid 50*,
AJ Hollioake 47)
Surrey (4 pts) won by five wickets

Surrey strode on towards the Division Two title by
dismissing their nearest challengers, Middlesex, by
five wickets at Lord's. Mark Ramprakash made 53,
but the home side could score only 167 for 8 from
their 45 overs and Surrey made short work of that
target with Adam Hollioake hitting 47 and Nadeem
Shahid finishing 50 not out.

Glamorgan kept up their promotion push, beating
Durham by three wickets from the penultimate ball
at Cardiff. Adrian Dale was the hero, ending on 73
not out, but Michael Powell also played his part in
the win with a well-played 48. Earlier, Durham's 202
for 5 was built on a third wicket stand of 92 in 17
overs between Simon Katich (70 from 93 balls) and
Paul Collingwood (66 off 76 deliveries).

Hampshire, meanwhile, drew eight points clear of
rock-bottom club Derbyshire by beating them by a
36-run margin at Derby. Will Kendall was the star of
their batting show, walloping an unbeaten 73 from
just 42 balls to send Hampshire rocketing to 233 for
3 from their 45 overs. Robin Smith, with 61 not out,
watched in admiration from the non-striker's end
as Kendall flew to his fifty from 30 balls and, overall,
struck three sixes and eight fours. An opening stand
of 87 between Matt Cassar and Michael Di Venuto
gave Derbyshire hope, but once they were split
John Stephenson (4 for 40) spearheaded a steady
whittling away of the rest of the order. In the end
Derbyshire were bowled out for a total of 197 in the
43rd over.

7 August 2000: Division One
at Hove (floodlit)
Sussex 213 for 6 (45 overs)(WJ House 80*,
B Zuiderent 68)
Lancashire 192 (39.2 overs)(NH Fairbrother 41,
A Flintoff 41, RJ Kirtley 4 for 45)
*Sussex (4 pts) won by 26 runs (DL Method: Lancashire
target 219 from 41 overs)*

Bungee jumping was part of the off-field menu at
Hove, and Sussex batsman Tony Cottey even had a
go himself after being run out cheaply early in this
encounter! Later, however, several Lancashire
batsmen complained that the adrenalin-rush
jumping – going on behind the sightscreen at one
end – was affecting their concentration. Lancashire,

though, had been out of sorts in this competition all
summer, and a 26-run loss here kept them glued to
the bottom of the Division One table. Sussex's 213
for 6, from 41 permitted overs, was reached thanks
to a superb partnership of 141 in 24 overs between
Bas Zuiderent, the 23-year-old Dutchman, and Will
House, who joined the club from Kent during the
winter. Zuiderent's fluent 68 was a plea in itself for
further first-team chances, while House displayed all
his limited-overs flair by hitting 80 not out from just
81 balls. Andy Flintoff and Neil Fairbrother reacted
to the loss of two early wickets by adding 85, but
Lancashire's challenge fizzled out once they had
both been dismissed for 41.

9 August 2000: Division One
at Leeds
Lancashire 68 (45 overs)(A Flintoff 28)
Yorkshire 72 for 1 (13.5 overs)(*DS Lehmann 54 not out)
Yorkshire won by nine wickets

at Bristol
Somerset 223 (45 overs)(ME Trescothick 53,
KA Parsons 47)
Gloucestershire did not bat
Match abandoned – 2pts each

Yorkshire kept up their title challenge in highly
dramatic style at Headingley, demolishing Roses
rivals Lancashire by nine wickets after bowling them
out for a shocking 68. Darren Lehmann then
thrashed 54 not out and the match was over before
the floodlights had a chance to shine! Yorkshire,
however, were too busy celebrating a marvellous
bowling and fielding performance to worry about the
lack of evening entertainment on show for a large
crowd. Only Lancashire's Andy Flintoff, with 28, had
shown any ability to get after the Yorkshire attack –
and he too fell to a rash stroke as Craig White added
4 for 14 to Matthew Hoggard's earlier 3 for 15.

It was Gloucestershire and Somerset, nevertheless,
who moved into a three-way share of the lead with
Worcestershire after the clash of the West Country
rivals at Bristol was abandoned at the halfway stage
because of heavy drizzle. Marcus Trescothick led the
way with eight powerful boundaries in his 53 as
Somerset, further boosted by Keith Parsons'
ebullient 47, totalled 223 from their 45 overs before
the weather closed in to give both teams two points.

9 August: Division Two
at Croydon
Surrey 211 for 9 (45 overs)(GP Thorpe 62)

Warwickshire 108 (TL Penny 35)
Surrey won by 103 runs

A special match at Whitgift School in Croydon, staged as part of the school's 400th anniversary celebrations, ended with a popular home win as Surrey marked their first appearance at the venue with a 103-run beating of Warwickshire. Graham Thorpe's 62 from 57 balls was easily the most impressive batting display of the day, and Warwickshire fell away to a disappointing 108 in reply to Surrey's 211 for 9. It was Surrey's tenth successive win in the league and stretched their lead at the top of the Division Two table.

11 August 2000: Division One
at Manchester
Gloucestershire 137 for 9 (45 overs)(+RC Russell 40)
Lancashire 138 for 0 (32.1 overs)
(SC Ganguly 101 not out)
Lancashire won by ten wickets

Lancashire won this meeting with Gloucestershire, two days before the sides were due to meet in the NatWest Trophy semi-finals, thanks to a superb bowling display from Ian Austin (9–2–14–4) and then a dismissive unbeaten 101 at the crease from Saurav Ganguly. Jack Russell's 40 was the only innings of note in Gloucestershire's total of 137 for 9, and Ganguly's onslaught soon brought victory by ten wickets.

13 August 2000: Division One
at Northampton
Leicestershire 220 for 7 (45 overs)(TR Ward 61)
Northamptonshire 123 for 2 (27.1 overs)
(ML Hayden 69*, DJG Sales 43*)
Northamptonshire (4 pts) won by eight wickets
(DL Method: Northamptonshire target 122 from 28 overs)

at Worcester
Sussex 15 for 1 (3.1 overs)
Worcestershire did not bat
Match abandoned – 2 pts each

Powerful batting by Matthew Hayden and David Sales, plus a little bit of help from Messrs Duckworth and Lewis, swept Northamptonshire to an eight-wicket win over Leicestershire at Northampton. The Leicestershire total of 220 for 7, based on Trevor Ward's 61 off 75 balls, was a decent effort – but Hayden and Sales were well on their way to making it look inadequate when rain

arrived to drive the players off. When the match was able to continue Northants needed just 19 more runs from three remaining overs to meet the Duckworth/Lewis requirements. Hayden scored 18 of them from his own bat to finish 69 not out, while Sales ended unbeaten on 43.

Just 3.1 overs of play were possible at Worcester, in which Sussex scored 15 for 1, but the subsequent abandonment – and the two points awarded to both teams – was enough to send Worcestershire back to the top of Division One.

13 August 2000: Division Two
at Derby
Essex 204 for 8 (45 overs)(GR Napier 78)
Derbyshire 14 for 1 (4 overs)
Match abandoned – 2 pts each

at Trent Bridge
Middlesex 241 for 3 (37 overs)(MR Ramprakash 61*, D Alleyne 58, EC Joyce 40*)
Nottinghamshire did not bat
Match abandoned – 2 pts each

A fine 78 off 83 balls by the 20-year-old all-rounder Graham Napier was ultimately to no avail as rain prevented a positive result at Derby. The match was, in fact, just six overs from being 'live', with Derbyshire on 14 for 1 in reply to Essex's 204 for 8, when bad weather swept in from the south-west ending play.

A similar story, unsurprisingly, occurred at nearby Trent Bridge where Nottinghamshire might have been grateful for the rain after seeing Middlesex total a formidable 241 for 3 from the 37 overs that intermittent drizzle allowed. But then the weather closed in completely before Notts could set off on a chase for what, under Duckworth/Lewis regulations, would have been 257 from their 37 overs. David Alleyne, the wicketkeeper, set Middlesex in motion with a well-made 58 before Mark Ramprakash, with a brilliant 61 not out from just 49 balls, was joined in a highly entertaining unbroken stand of 86 by Ed Joyce (40 not out). The two points awarded to Notts took them into second place in Division Two.

14 August 2000: Division Two
at Chester-le-Street
Durham 202 for 7 (45 overs)(PD Collingwood 73*)
Warwickshire 203 for 3 (42.3 overs)(NV Knight 75, AF Giles 45)
Warwickshire (4 pts) won by seven wickets

at Southampton
Glamorgan 263 for 5 (45 overs)(MTG Elliott 68,
K Newell 64, SP James 50*)
Hampshire 258 for 9 (45 overs)(WS Kendall 85*,
DA Kenway 47, SD Thomas 4 for 42)
Glamorgan (4 pts) won by 5 runs

Warwickshire overtook Notts and settled into
second place in the table after cruising past Durham
by seven wickets at Chester-le-Street. Durham's 45-
over total of 202 for 7 owed much to Paul
Collingwood, whose unbeaten 73 came from 99
balls, while Ashley Giles maintained his fine form in
all competitions by taking 3 for 40. Giles then hit 45
with the bat, coming in at number three, and he and
Nick Knight (75) swung the game firmly
Warwickshire's way. Dominic Ostler finished things
off with an unbeaten 38.

Glamorgan, meanwhile, had to survive a
remarkable blitz by Hampshire's final-wicket pair
Will Kendall and Chris Tremlett in the last three
overs of the match before they could celebrate the
five-run win at Southampton that kept them on
course for a promotion spot. Glamorgan's
challenging 263 for 5, built on an opening stand of
126 in 21 overs between Keith Newell (64 from 61
balls) and Matthew Elliott (68) and then a 51-ball
fifty not out from Steve James, looked far too much
for Hampshire – especially when they slumped to
205 for 9 in the 42nd over. But, from the last three
overs, Kendall (85 not out) and Tremlett, with an
astonishing 30 not out, plundered no fewer than 51
runs to leave Hampshire tantalisingly short on 258
for 9 of what would have been one of the great one-
day victories. Darren Thomas took Glamorgan, while
Robert Croft (2 for 36 from his nine overs) showed
all his experience to record tidy figures in a game
where the overall run-rate was almost six an over.

15 August 2000: Division One
at Old Trafford (floodlit)
Lancashire 136 for 7 (21 overs)(SC Ganguly 52)
Kent 141 for 3 (18.5 overs)(R Dravid 60*)
Kent (4 pts) won by seven wickets

Kent won a floodlit match reduced to 21 overs per
side with some thrilling batting from Rahul Dravid
and Martin McCague, and it was a victory that
boosted their hopes of avoiding relegation from
Division One. Lancashire, however, looked doomed
after failing to defend a total of 136 for 7 and much
was made of the fact that none of his teammates
appeared on the balcony to applaud when Sourav

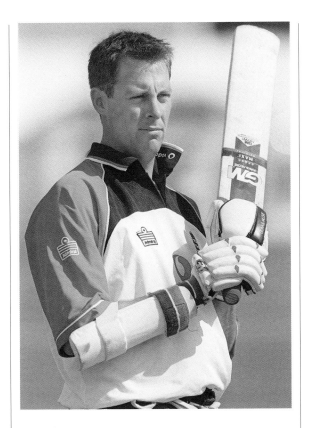

Marcus Trescothick who, with Mark Lathwell, put together an
opening stand of 68 from 11 overs against Warwickshire.

Ganguly, having been involved in the run-outs of both
Andy Flintoff and Neil Fairbrother, completed his
half-century. Ganguly was soon out for 52 but his
Indian Test colleague Dravid certainly had the full
backing of his Kent colleagues as he set about leading
the victory hunt. The chase was nip and tuck until
McCague, promoted up the order after some lusty
hitting in previous matches, set about the Lancashire
attack as if they were schoolboy bowlers. While
Dravid moved elegantly to 60 not out, the beefy
McCague thumped three big sixes in a violent 16-ball
31 not out to sweep Kent home with 13 balls to spare.

16 August 2000: Division One
at Edgbaston (floodlit)
Middlesex 201 for 9 (45 overs)(JL Langer 93)
Warwickshire 186 (44 overs)(BL Hutton 4 for 32)
Middlesex (4 pts) won by 15 runs

Inspired medium-pace bowling from Ben Hutton
helped to bring Middlesex victory by 15 runs in a
floodlit contest against Warwickshire. Middlesex's

201 for 9 was based on a fine 93 from Justin Langer – ended only when he was run out by a direct hit from Dominic Ostler. Mark Ramprakash and Ed Joyce also made useful contributions, but Dougie Brown (3 for 35) restricted the Middlesex middle order and Warwickshire set off confidently in pursuit of their target. No home batsman, however, could play a major innings and Middlesex – and Hutton – kept chipping away until Warwickshire ran out of time, and wickets.

20 August 2000: Division One
at Leicester
Leicestershire 53 (20.3 overs)(MJ Hoggard 5 for 28, CEW Silverwood 4 for 11)
Yorkshire 54 for 2 (14.5 overs)
Yorkshire (4 pts) won by eight wickets

at Eastbourne
Sussex 196 (45 overs)(RR Montgomerie 89)
Northamptonshire 199 for 4 (39 overs)(DJG Sales 84*)
Northamptonshire (4 pts) won by six wickets

at Worcester
Somerset 227 for 9 (45 overs)(J Cox 57, M Burns 51)
Worcestershire 174 (40.3 overs)(DA Leatherdale 43, ID Blackwell 4 for 36)
Somerset (4 pts) won by 53 runs

Somerset moved to the top of Division One with a comfortable victory over rivals Worcestershire at New Road, reaching 227 for 9 through half-centuries from Jamie Cox (57) and Michael Burns (51 off 58 balls) after Marcus Trescothick and Mark Lathwell had provided a first-wicket stand of 68 in 11 overs. Ian Blackwell picked up 4 for 36 as only David Leatherdale (43) made any lasting impression.

The most explosive performance of the day, however, came at Grace Road where Yorkshire blew away Leicestershire by bowling them out for just 53 and then romping to an eight-wicket victory. Darren Gough, allowed a rare outing with his county, went wicketless in six overs as Matthew Hoggard (5 for 28) and Chris Silverwood (4 for 11) did all the damage. No Leicestershire player reached double figures and the whole match lasted just two hours and 32 minutes – making it a minute quicker than Yorkshire's similar National League destruction of Lancashire 11 days earlier.

Northamptonshire joined Yorkshire in second place by overwhelming Sussex by six wickets at Eastbourne. Richard Montgomerie (89) provided the anchor role but nobody could stay with him for long as Tony Penberthy took 4 for 32 and Sussex totalled 196. Mal Loye kicked off the reply with 54 but it was David Sales' 82-ball unbeaten 84 that really powered the visitors towards the finishing line.

20 August 2000: Division Two
at Colchester
Essex 184 for 8 (45 overs)(AD Mullally 4 for 30)
Hampshire 188 for 4 (36.3 overs)(RA Smith 62, DA Kenway 56)
Hampshire (4 pts) won by six wickets

at Colwyn Bay
Glamorgan 104 for 4 (26 overs)
Nottinghamshire 131 for 2 (21.3 overs)(DJ Bicknell 59*)
Nottinghamshire (4 pts) won by eight wickets
(DL Method: Nottinghamshire target 131 from 26 overs)

at The Oval
Derbyshire 175 for 9 (45 overs)(RJ Bailey 43)
Surrey 176 for 4 (44 overs)(AJ Hollioake 48*, JD Ratcliffe 42*)
Surrey (4 pts) won by six wickets

Top versus bottom at the Oval was a surprisingly tight affair until an unbroken fifth-wicket stand of 93 between Adam Hollioake and Jason Ratcliffe won the game for Surrey. Earlier, Rob Bailey had scored 43 in Derbyshire's 175 for 9, with leg-spinner Ian Salisbury taking 3 for 32 from his nine overs.

Nottinghamshire went four points clear in second place after beating Glamorgan by eight wickets in a rain-affected contest at Colwyn Bay. Paul Reiffel's superb spell of 7–3–8–3 was chiefly responsible for keeping Glamorgan to 104 for 4 from 26 overs, and then Darren Bicknell (59 not out) and Paul Johnson (49 not out) made short work of a win target revised under Duckworth/Lewis regulations.

An opening stand of 120 between skipper Robin Smith (62) and Derek Kenway (56) led to Hampshire comfortably overhauling Essex's total of 184 for 8 at Colchester. Alan Mullally (4 for 30) was the pick of the bowlers on show and Essex were underachieving even before Danny Law and young Justin Bishop plundered 34 from the final four overs of their innings.

23 August 2000: Division Two
at Colchester (floodlit)
Essex 206 for 8 (45 overs)(SG Law 92, N Hussain 57, IDK Salisbury 4 for 32, AJ Hollioake 4 for 38)
Surrey 183 (43.3 overs)
Essex (4 pts) won by 23 runs

A crowd of more than 6,000 enjoyed Essex's first venture into floodlit cricket, especially as the home side toppled the previously unbeaten leaders of the division, Surrey, on a balmy evening and under impressive temporary floodlights at Castle Park in Colchester. The Essex 45-over total of 206 for 8 was, in fact, an underachievement following a superb first-wicket stand of 161 between Stuart Law and Nasser Hussain. Law, the prolific Australian, completed his first fifty from just 45 balls, once pulling Alex Tudor venomously for six, and out-of-touch England captain Hussain drove the same bowler for three successive fours during the early part of an innings that did much to boost his confidence with the bat ahead of the final Test against the West Indies at The Oval. Hussain made 57 (giving him 256 National League runs at an average of 44 this season) and Law 92, but Essex then collapsed alarmingly against a high-class spell of leg-spin by Ian Salisbury. Surrey, in reply, never got into a position of strength, but they still required an achievable 63 from the last ten overs with six wickets in hand. Essex, however, bowled and fielded like demons – Danny Law bringing off one stupendous outfield catch – and, dismissed for 183, Surrey were left to nurse their first defeat of the season in the competition on a night when they could have clinched the Division Two championship.

27 August 2000: Division One
at Canterbury
Kent 228 for 8 (45 overs)(R Dravid 104, JB Hockley 64)
Worcestershire 184 (41 overs)(WPC Weston 47, DJ Pipe 45, SJ Rhodes 40)
Kent (4 pts) won by 44 runs

Kent moved out of the relegation zone with a 44-run victory at Canterbury that also badly knocked Worcestershire's chances of winning the National League title. Yet, so closely fought was the division, only six points now separated fourth-from-bottom Kent and leaders Somerset! A magnificent 104, from 96 balls, by Rahul Dravid was the highlight of the Kent innings of 228 for 8 – although a 79-ball 64 by 21-year-old James Hockley also had the home crowd on their feet. Dravid and Hockley added 99 and Kent posted a demanding total despite figures of 9–3–17–3 from the incomparable Glenn McGrath. Worcestershire, however, were then given a racing start by Philip Weston (47) and Jamie Pipe (45), who added 81 for the first wicket from just 11 overs. Pipe, in particular, was striking the ball with great power but Martin McCague dragged Kent back into the game by having Pipe caught at mid on after a

highly entertaining 24-ball knock and quickly adding the important wicket of Vikram Solanki for a duck. Matthew Fleming, the Kent captain, also dismissed Graeme Hick for nought and, with McCague taking 3 for 29 in a fine spell, Worcestershire suddenly found themselves losing seven wickets for 29 runs. Steve Rhodes (40) tried to rescue the situation but Darren Scott, the off-spinner, picked up 3 for 21 in the closing stages as Worcestershire were dismissed for 184 with four overs remaining.

27 August 2000: Division Two
at Derby
Derbyshire 211 for 8 (45 overs)(RJ Bailey 64, ME Cassar 44)
Glamorgan 212 for 9 (44.5 overs)(SP James 56, MJ Powell 53)
Glamorgan (4 pts) won by one wicket

at Chester-le-Street
Durham 188 for 8 (43 overs)(SM Katich 63, PD Collingwood 50)
Essex 167 for 9 (32.1 overs)(WI Jefferson 51, N Killeen 4 for 32)
Essex (4 pts) won by one wicket (DL Method: Essex should have 167 runs from 33 overs when rain stopped play)

Glamorgan's attempt to win promotion from Division Two was boosted by a thrilling one-wicket win against Derbyshire at Derby – with the clinching run coming from the penultimate ball of a hard-fought game. Matt Cassar's aggressive 44, from just 35 balls, gave Derbyshire early impetus but only Rob Bailey (64) flourished thereafter and a total of 211 for 8 left the contest wide open. For a while, with Steve James scoring 56 and Michael Powell 53, it seemed as though Glamorgan would get to their target reasonably comfortably, but Derbyshire kept chipping away and when the ninth Welsh wicket fell at 202 the home side were perhaps favourites. Glamorgan's last pair, Dean Cosker and Owen Parkin, required ten more runs from the remaining 14 deliveries – but, keeping their heads despite deteriorating light, they inched their way towards and then over the finishing line.

Essex also won a narrow victory against Durham at Chester-le-Street, Danny Law's dramatic six and four from successive balls by Neil Killeen clinching a similar one-wicket margin. Up until then Killeen's bowling had looked to be taking Durham to a rare win, and he finished with 4 for 32, but the home side were left kicking themselves in particular for failing to make the most earlier of a 71-run stand between Simon Katich (63) and Paul Collingwood (50) that, at one stage, had left them 140 for 2. An eventual total of 188 for 8, from 43 overs, was disappointing – and a rain squall left Essex with a recalculated target under the Duckworth/Lewis formula. Will Jefferson, aged 20, impressed with a 64-ball fifty, but off-spinner Nicky Phillips also bowled well to take 3 for 34 and, in the end, Essex badly needed Law's timely unbeaten 27.

28 August 2000: Division One
at Bristol (floodlit)
Gloucestershire 269 for 9 (45 overs)(JN Snape 71, IJ Harvey 66, MGN Windows 61)
Leicestershire 222 (45 overs)(DL Maddy 86, BF Smith 77, IJ Harvey 4 for 26)
Gloucestershire (4 pts) won by 47 runs

at Northampton
Northamptonshire 109 (37.3 overs)
(MJ Hoggard 5 for 30)
Yorkshire 111 for 4 (30.3 overs)
Yorkshire (4 pts) won by six wickets

at Hove (floodlit)
Somerset 212 for 8 (45 overs)(J Cox 49)
Sussex 213 for 4 (45 overs)(MG Bevan 85*, CJ Adams 68)
Sussex (4 pts) won by six wickets

Yorkshire shattered Northants' title aspirations by shooting them out for just 109 on their home ground and then easing to a six-wicket win. A good-sized crowd of almost 4,000 had assembled at Wantage Road to cheer on Northants, but instead the spectators were forced to marvel at some irresistible fast bowling by Matthew Hoggard and Darren Gough that rapidly had Matthew Hayden's side reeling at 22 for 5. Both bowlers swung the new ball at pace, but Hoggard also found dangerous movement off the seam and his final figures of 5 for 30 took him past Howard Cooper's Yorkshire record of 29 wickets in a one-day league season. Gough ended with 3 for 19 and, when Yorkshire replied, Darren Lehmann (37) and Anthony McGrath (36 not out) ensured there were no slip-ups.

Ian Harvey's all-round skills shone out brightly once again as, under the Bristol lights, Gloucestershire maintained their late charge for the title by running up a season's-league-best total of 269 for 9 and then restricting Leicestershire to 222 in reply. Harvey's first contribution was a hurricane 66 from just 35 balls, and Gloucestershire's forward momentum was kept up by Jeremy Snape (71 from

85 balls) and Matt Windows (61), who added 130 in 23 overs for the fourth wicket. Leicestershire had a bad start, slipping to 28 for 3, but Darren Maddy (86) and Ben Smith (77) then produced a fighting partnership of 138. Harvey, however, defied a bruised hip (suffered during the indoor international series against South Africa in Melbourne) to finish with 4 for 26, while skipper Mark Alleyne also came up with a couple of important wickets.

Somerset, meanwhile, were in the process of wasting their opportunity to stay out in front in the Division One table by batting poorly at Hove and eventually going down by six wickets in an exciting finish under the Sussex lights. Jamie Cox reached 49 but no Somerset batsman really got to grips with the home attack, and a 45-over total of 212 for 8 always looked shy of a par score. Somerset did have the considerable bonus of having Andrew Caddick in their side, for the first time since June, but not even the England paceman could stop Chris Adams and, especially, the great Michael Bevan. Adams was finally dismissed for 68, but Bevan characteristically saw it out to the end as Somerset fought tigerishly to defend their score – the Australian finishing 85 not out as victory arrived from the last ball of the game.

28 August 2000: Division Two
at Old Deer Park, Richmond
Middlesex 148 for 3 (21 overs)(MR Ramprakash 53*)
Nottinghamshire 125 for 7 (21 overs)(JER Gallian 43)
Middlesex (4 pts) won by 23 runs

Middlesex's imaginative venture into Old Deer Park, Richmond, was rewarded with a 23-run win against Nottinghamshire in a game reduced to 21 overs per side. Mark Ramprakash, dashing to 53 not out from only 31 balls with two sixes and four fours, found a willing ally in Ed Joyce as 75 were added in double-quick time for the fourth wicket to boost Middlesex's total to a fine 148 for 3. And it proved too hot for Notts to handle, the visitors managing to reach just 125 for 7 in reply.

29 August 2000: Division Two
at Chester-le-Street (floodlit)
Durham 161 for 8 (45 overs)(JJB Lewis 40*)
Hampshire 165 for 3 (39.1 overs)(RA Smith 88*)
Hampshire (4 pts) won by seven wickets

A powerful unbeaten 88 from Robin Smith, which followed another masterclass of leg-spin bowling from Shane Warne, enabled Hampshire to cruise past a troubled Durham side at Chester-le-Street.

Victory was achieved by seven wickets, and with almost six overs to spare, after Warne's spell of 9–2–19–2 had helped to restrict Durham to 161 for 8 from their 45-over allocation. Jon Lewis, leading Durham following the announcement earlier in the day that Nick Speak had been stripped of the captaincy after less than a season in charge, did his best with 40 not out – but Hampshire were simply too strong in every department.

30 August 2000: Division One
at Taunton (floodlit)
Leicestershire 267 for 6 (45 overs)(JM Dakin 68*, BF Smith 48, Aftab Habib 45, VJ Wells 40)
Somerset 205 (38.3 overs)(M Burns 97, KA Parsons 69, DL Maddy 4 for 16)
Leicestershire (4 pts) won by 62 runs

Leicestershire won a high-scoring affair under the floodlights at Taunton, their 267 for 6 proving to be out of Somerset's reach despite a superb stand of 134 between Michael Burns (97 from 115 balls) and Keith Parsons (69). A procession followed Parsons' dismissal, caught at deep square leg, with Darren Maddy picking up 4 for 16 in four overs of medium-pace bowling.

3 September 2000: Division One
at Northampton
Northamptonshire 195 for 9 (45 overs)
Kent 190 (45 overs)(R Dravid 68, KJ Innes 4 for 36)
Northamptonshire (4 pts) won by 5 runs

at Worcester
Worcestershire 188 for 8 (45 overs)(RC Driver 52, SJ Rhodes 48*)
Lancashire 191 for 8 (45 overs)
Lancashire (4 pts) won by two wickets

at Scarborough
Yorkshire 192 for 8 (45 overs)(DS Lehmann 80, GM Hamilton 57*)
Sussex 143 (35.3 overs)(GM Hamilton 5 for 34)
Yorkshire (4 pts) won by 49 runs

Yorkshire stayed on top of the Division One table with victory by 49 runs over Sussex at Scarborough – a happier end to a sour festival week for the home side. Darren Lehmann (80) and Gavin Hamilton (57 not out) richly entertained the 5,500 crowd as Yorkshire totalled 192 for 8 from their 45 overs. In reply, Sussex were going well while Chris Adams (47) and Michael Bevan (67 off 69 balls) were

adding 113 for the third wicket – but when Hamilton bowled Bevan it proved to be the start of a dramatic collapse as the visitors lost no fewer than eight wickets for just 28 runs in the space of seven overs. Hamilton (5 for 34) deserves credit, of course, but this was still shabby batting by Sussex as they were dismissed for 143.

Worcestershire, meanwhile, the National League leaders a fortnight before, were suddenly left staring relegation in the face after losing out in a thrilling last-ball finish against Lancashire at Worcester. The visitors looked as if they were struggling to match Worcestershire's 188 for 8, in which Ryan Driver made 52 and Steve Rhodes a determined 48 not out, but then Chris Schofield hit out for 34 and an asking rate of more than seven runs an over was being matched. Lancashire, finally, won a fine victory when Ian Austin – needing two – drove the last ball of the match from Richard Illingworth for four runs.

Rahul Dravid did his best to lead Kent to victory at Northampton, in company with tailenders Martin McCague and Darren Scott, but in the end the task of scoring ten runs from the final two overs was too much and a brave Kent effort fell five runs short of Northants' 195 for 9. A one-day best of 4 for 36 from Kevin Innes pinned down the Kent middle order, but Dravid (68) was boosted by McCague's violent 29 off 23 balls and then given faithful support by Scott (27) in a partnership of 47 for the ninth wicket. Paul Taylor and Darren Cousins, however, both bowled exemplary final overs to deny Dravid and Scott.

3 September 2000: Division Two
at Southend-on-Sea
Essex 289 for 5 (45 overs)(SD Peters 73*, WI Jefferson 65, GR Napier 52)
Glamorgan 285 (45 overs)(SP James 88*, K Newell 78, MP Maynard 61, AP Cowan 4 for 44)
Essex (4 pts) won by 4 runs

at Trent Bridge
Nottinghamshire 288 for 4 (45 overs)(DJ Bicknell 115, JER Gallian 84)
Surrey 225 for 3 (45 overs)(N Shahid 109*, IJ Ward 46)
Nottinghamshire (4 pts) won by 63 runs

at Edgbaston
Warwickshire 233 for 8 (45 overs)(MJ Powell 41)
Derbyshire 189 (43 overs)(MJ di Venuto 84, SD Stubbings 41, CE Dagnall 4 for 34)
Warwickshire (4 pts) won by 44 runs

Tim Hancock, with 44, helped to maintain Gloucestershire's extraordinary dominance over Lancashire.

Glamorgan's promotion hopes took a sizable knock at Southend, where Essex fast bowler Ashley Cowan produced a sensational final over to shock the Welshmen. Chasing Essex's mammoth 289 for 5, which featured fine efforts from youngsters Will Jefferson (65), Stephen Peters (73 not out) and Graham Napier (52), Glamorgan seemed to be cruising to an impressive victory at 254 for 2. Keith Newell's 78, and 61 from Matthew Maynard, had helped to put Glamorgan into a commanding position while Steve James was still there on 88. However, with just six runs required from the final over, and with four wickets in hand, Darren Thomas was run out

from the first ball. Panic set in, with Cowan clean bowling Dean Cosker, Mark Wallace and Owen Parkin with his third, fifth and sixth deliveries. The home crowd were shell-shocked too, wandering home in a daze after seeing 574 runs, four wickets in the final over ... and an Essex win by four runs.

Allan Donald marked an emotional last match for Warwickshire at Edgbaston by taking the final Derbyshire wicket to fall in a 44-run win. Charles Dagnall (4 for 34) did most of the damage, though, as Derbyshire were dismissed for 189 – despite Michael Di Venuto's 84 – in reply to a Warwickshire total of 233 for 8.

Surrey, already promoted, rested eight first-team regulars at Trent Bridge – and went down by 63 runs to Nottinghamshire. Darren Bicknell, hitting 115 against his former county, had earlier featured in a 196-run opening stand with Jason Gallian (84) as Notts reached 288 for 4. In reply, Nadeem Shahid's unbeaten 109 amounted to little more than batting practice as Surrey never looked like getting near the Notts total.

4 September 2000: Division One
at Bristol
Lancashire 157 (45 overs)(GD Lloyd 46)
Gloucestershire 160 for 5 (38.3 overs)(THC Hancock 44)
Gloucestershire (4 pts) won by five wickets

Gloucestershire's extraordinary one-day season just kept on getting better as they defeated Lancashire for the third time in a big match at Bristol to move into second place in the Division One table. A crushing five-wicket win against the dethroned former limited-overs kings of county cricket put Gloucestershire just two points behind leaders Yorkshire ... with a game in hand. As so often before, left-arm paceman Mike Smith set the tone for another fine Gloucestershire performance in the field, taking 2 for 13 from a nine-over new-ball spell and not even a 56-run stand between Graham Lloyd and Neil Fairbrother could haul Lancashire up beyond a distinctly average 157. Tim Hancock's solid 44, and a breezy 34 in 30 balls from Ian Harvey, ensured no slip-ups with the bat by Gloucestershire on a pitch that in truth was never ideal for strokeplay.

5 September 2000: Division One
at Canterbury (floodlit)
Kent 217 (44.4 overs)(MV Fleming 79)
Yorkshire 153 (40.2 overs)(GM Hamilton 44)
Kent (4 pts) won by 64 runs

at Hove (floodlit)
Sussex 148 for 8 (31 overs – rain stopped play)
(MG Bevan 82*)
Gloucestershire 174 for 4 (29.1 overs)(THC Hancock 50,
IJ Harvey 44)
Gloucestershire (4 pts) won by six wickets (DL Method:
Gloucestershire target 171 from 31 overs)

Kent's first venture into floodlit cricket was a real
success at Canterbury, with almost 7,000 spectators
turning up to see Matthew Fleming inspire his side
to a vital 64-run win over Yorkshire with a top-class
all-round performance. Yorkshire's title hopes may
have been dashed, but Kent were too busy
celebrating a win that could keep them in Division
One to offer any sympathy. Opening the Kent
innings, after winning an important toss, Fleming
immediately went for his strokes. The skipper made
79 in the end, out of 136, and his assault enabled
Kent to reach 217 even with a mid-innings stutter.
Then, after Mark Ealham had split a dangerous
71-run stand between Michael Vaughan and Gavin
Hamilton, on came Fleming to take 3 for 19 from
his nine-over bowling stint to help wrap up victory.
Martin Saggers, too, bowled well for Kent under the
lights – snatching the prized early wicket of Darren
Lehmann and finishing with 3 for 22.

Despite Martin McCague's best efforts, Kent were beaten by
5 runs at Northampton.

Meanwhile, down on the South Coast at Hove,
Gloucestershire were doing Kent a big favour by
beating their fellow relegation candidates Sussex –
as well as clasping one hand themselves on the
National League title.

In a match reduced to 31 overs per side because of
afternoon rain, Gloucestershire restricted Sussex to
148 for 8 despite a brilliant unbeaten 82 from 87 balls
by Michael Bevan. Then, pacing their reply superbly
in pursuit of a revised target of 171, Gloucestershire
accelerated to a six-wicket win that would – when
Somerset failed to beat Lancashire 24 hours later –
clinch them their first-ever domestic league trophy,
and an unprecedented clean sweep of the three one-
day competitions. Tim Hancock hit 50, but yet again
Ian Harvey underlined his all-round expertise by
adding a brutal 30-ball 44 to his earlier 3 for 25.

6 September 2000: Division One
at Old Trafford (floodlit)
Lancashire 236 for 4 (45 overs)(SC Ganguly 102,
NH Fairbrother 62)
Somerset 226 for 8 (45 overs)(J Cox 110,
MN Lathwell 53)
Lancashire (4 pts) won by 10 runs

Somerset's last hope of pipping Gloucestershire for
the National League title disappeared in a tight
finish under the lights at Old Trafford. A
courageous 110 by their captain, Jamie Cox, took
Somerset agonisingly close to Lancashire's
challenging total of 236 for 4, in which Sourav
Ganguly had hit 102 and Neil Fairbrother a dazzling
62. Mark Lathwell's 53 helped to give Somerset a
fine start, and while Cox remained the West
Countrymen had a chance. But then, sent back by
Keith Parsons, Cox was run out by Glen Chapple's
super stop and direct hit from short fine leg. After
that, the task of scoring 20 runs from the last two
overs was beyond Somerset, who finished on 226 for
8 to leave Lancashire the ten-run victors.

8 September 2000: Division One
at Leicester (floodlit)
Leicestershire 152 (44.2 overs)
Worcestershire 145 (45 overs)
Leicestershire (4 pts) won by 7 runs

9 September 2000: Division Two
at Lord's
Warwickshire 172 (42.5 overs)(A Singh 74)
Middlesex 135 (41 overs)(BL Hutton 49)
Warwickshire (4 pts) won by 37 runs

10 September 2000: Division Two
at Southampton
Derbyshire 195 for 9 (45 overs)(LD Sutton 53,
JP Pyemont 50, SK Warne 4 for 23)
Hampshire 191 for 9 (45 overs)(DA Kenway 90,
ME Cassar 4 for 29)
Derbyshire (4 pts) won by 4 runs

at Trent Bridge
Nottinghamshire 229 for 9 (45 overs)(P Johnson 62,
U Afzaal 51)
Glamorgan 226 for 9 (45 overs)(MP Maynard 88*)
Nottinghamshire (4 pts) won by 3 runs

at The Oval
Durham 251 for 5 (45 overs)(JA Daley 105,
PD Collingwood 86)
Surrey 192 (40.3 overs)(AD Brown 51, IJ Ward 41,
NC Phillips 4 for 30)
Durham (4 pts) won by 59 runs

Nottinghamshire were promoted to Division One
amid joyous scenes at Trent Bridge, where Jason
Gallian's side held on in an exciting finish to beat
promotion rivals Glamorgan by just three runs.
A Notts total of 229 for 9 was built on a stand of
107 for the fourth wicket by Paul Johnson (62) and
Usman Afzaal (51), but it looked as if it might not
be enough as Matthew Maynard, the Glamorgan
captain, steered his side ever closer to their target.
A six swung high over straight mid-wicket off the
suffering Andy Harris helped Maynard keep
Glamorgan in touch with an asking rate of 71 from
the last 10 overs. But, even though Maynard ended
88 not out, wickets kept tumbling at the other end
and, finally, Maynard could not manage to hit Harris
for six from the last ball of the match.

Surrey were presented with their Division Two
championship trophy at the Oval, but by then they
had gone down by 59 runs to Durham in what was
rather an anti-climactic afternoon. With only four
first-team regulars in the side, Surrey could not
prevent Durham from piling up 251 for 5 – Jimmy
Daley hitting a six and 10 fours in his 109 as he put
on 177 for the third wicket with Paul Collingwood
(86). Alistair Brown briefly threatened some
fireworks with a 36-ball 51, dominating an opening
partnership of 87 with Ian Ward (41), but Durham
off-spinner Nicky Phillips picked up 4 for 30 as
Surrey's reply slipped away to 192 all out.

Shane Warne took three wickets in four balls at
Southampton, finishing with 4 for 23 against
Derbyshire and taking his wicket-tally for the season

to 101 in all competitions. But Derbyshire, boosted
by a sixth wicket stand of 99 between Luke Sutton
(53 not out) and James Pyemont (50), still managed
to reach 195 for 9 – and that proved just too much
for Hampshire, who batted badly to end up 191 for
9 in reply. Derek Kenway escaped much of the
blame, with 90, while Matt Cassar's underrated fast-
medium brought him figures of 4 for 29.

17 September 2000: Division One
at Bristol
Northamptonshire 129 (42.5 overs)(IJ Harvey 5 for 19)
Gloucestershire 101 (33.4 overs)(IJ Harvey 43)
*Northamptonshire (4 pts) won by 27 runs (DL Method:
Gloucestershire target 119 from 43 overs)*

at Old Trafford
Sussex 195 for 9 (45 overs)(MG Bevan 52, PA Cottey 45*,
RR Montgomerie 44, G Keedy 4 for 30)
Lancashire 154 for 4 (30 overs)(MA Atherton 51)
*Lancashire (4 pts) won by six wickets (DL Method:
Lancashire target 153 runs from 33 overs)*

at Leicester
Leicestershire 220 for 8 (45 overs)(IJ Sutcliffe 53)
Somerset 143 (39.1 overs)
Leicestershire (4 pts) won by 77 runs

at Worcester
Worcestershire 98 (36.3 overs)
Kent 101 for 2 (26.5 overs)
Kent (4 pts) won by eight wickets

Kent won the relegation battle at Worcester to save
their own Division One skins but condemn the home
county to Division Two National League cricket next
season. It all made for a sad finale for Glenn
McGrath as Worcestershire crumbled to 98 all out
in the face of some accurate and committed bowling
from Kent's five-man seam battery. Then, in his last
game of a faithful 19-season Kent career, 39-year old
Steve Marsh went in first against McGrath and took
everything the Australian could hurl at him as he
scored a vital 38. James Hockley, one of Kent's next
generation, also batted well to reach 36 not out as
Kent swept to victory by eight wickets.
Worcestershire, the leaders little more than a month
before, had lost seven of their last nine league games
– and the other two were abandoned! Just a final
word, though, about McGrath. His final analysis of
9–4–9–0 might not have been all he wanted, in the
final column that is, but his 30 league wickets at an
average of just 8.13 also came with a remarkable

economy rate of 2.16, which not surprisingly was a one-day league record. In all competitions for Worcestershire, McGrath took 114 wickets.

League champions Gloucestershire, meanwhile, paraded their trophy in front of a large home crowd at Bristol – and did not seem to mind losing to Northants, who thus finished third. On a poor-quality pitch, Ian Harvey took 5 for 19 to take his season's league tally to 34 and later hit 43 on the day it was announced that the Australian all-rounder had been offered a new two-year contract. But, with Tony Penberthy taking 5 for 29, Gloucestershire were bowled out for just 101 in reply to Northants' total of 129.

Mike Atherton scored 51 as Lancashire, with the aid of Duckworth and Lewis, ended their disappointing league season by beating the also-relegated Sussex by six wickets at Old Trafford. Earlier Michael Bevan had hit 52 and Tony Cottey an unbeaten 45 in a Sussex total of 195 for 9 that was mainly notable for perennial number eleven Mark Robinson's 15 not out. In 14 seasons of playing one-day league cricket it was his first score in double figures!

At Leicester the home side began their match against Somerset knowing that they needed to win to make sure of Division One status for 2001. And, after Iain Sutcliffe's 53 had provided the base for a good score of 220 for 8, Leicestershire then dismissed the visitors for 143 with Billy Stelling picking up 3 for 35.

17 September 2000: Division Two
at Derby
Durham 229 for 7 (45 overs)(JA Daley 54, PD Collingwood 52)
Derbyshire 228 for 8 (45 overs)(ME Cassar 126, N Killeen 6 for 31)
Durham (4 pts) won by 1 run

at Chelmsford
Essex 152 (41.2 overs)(AP Grayson 64)
Warwickshire 153 for 4 (35.1 overs)(NMK Smith 75*)
Warwickshire (4 pts) won by six wickets

at Cardiff
Glamorgan 191 for 9 (42 overs)(MJ Powell 86, AW Laraman 6 for 42)
Middlesex 193 for 4 (42 overs)(JL Langer 76*, AJ Strauss 40)
Middlesex (4 pts) won by six wickets

at Southampton
Nottinghamshire 234 for 8 (45 overs)(U Afzaal 95*, P Johnson 43)

Hampshire 231 for 8 (45 overs)(WS Kendall 63, LR Prittipaul 61)
Nottinghamshire (4 pts) won by 3 runs

The last round of matches in Division Two were academic in terms of promotion, but that did not prevent a thrilling finish to the game between Glamorgan and Middlesex at Cardiff. Ed Joyce, requiring three from the final ball, hit it for four to take Middlesex past Glamorgan's 191 for 9 in a contest reduced to 42 overs per side. Justin Langer's unbeaten 76 was also a big factor in the six-wicket victory, after Aaron Laraman had earlier returned figures of 6 for 42 in a Glamorgan innings boosted by a superb 86 from number six by Michael Powell. Middlesex ended up needing 16 from the last two overs, and then six from the last three balls. Glamorgan fought hard, but the promising 21-year-old Joyce was equal to the occasion.

There were close and exciting games at Derby and Southampton, too, with Derbyshire pipping Durham by just one run and Nottinghamshire holding off Hampshire by only three runs in a high-scoring final match at Northlands Road. Hampshire, due to move during the winter to their new county headquarters on the outskirts of Southampton, fell agonisingly short of Nottinghamshire's total of 234 for 8, in which Usman Afzaal (95 not out) and Paul Johnson (43) had put on 94. Shane Warne, pushed up to number three, contributed a hard-hit 29 in what he hopes will not be his last match for Hampshire, but the home side's reply only really got going when Will Kendall (63) and Lawrence Prittipaul (61) added a highly attractive 127 for the fifth wicket.

Matt Cassar, with 126, could not have done more to take Derbyshire past Durham's 229 for 7 at the Racecourse Ground – a visiting total that featured half-centuries from Jimmy Daley and Paul Collingwood. But Cassar could find no significant partner and, in a breathtaking final over, Derbyshire ended up on 228 for 8. Neil Killeen performed heroics with the ball for Durham, finishing with a memorable 6 for 31.

In the remaining game Neil Smith, in possibly his last innings as Warwickshire captain, hit an unbeaten 75 at Chelmsford to take his side to a comfortable six-wicket win against Essex, for whom Paul Grayson had top-scored with 64 in an otherwise disappointing total of 152.

DIVISION ONE FINAL RESULTS

	Won	Tied	Lost	NR	Pts
Gloucestershire	**9**	**–**	**6**	**1**	**38**
Yorkshire	9	–	7	–	36
Northamptonshire	9	–	7	–	36
Leicestershire	7	2	6	1	34
Kent	7	–	7	2	32
Somerset	7	–	8	1	30
Worcestershire	6	–	8	2	28
Lancashire	6	1	8	1	28
Sussex	5	1	8	2	26

Worcestershire, Lancashire & Sussex will be relegated to Division Two for the 2001 season

DIVISION TWO FINAL RESULTS

	Won	Tied	Lost	NR	Pts
Surrey	**11**	**–**	**3**	**2**	**48**
Nottinghamshire	11	–	4	1	46
Warwickshire	10	1	5	–	42
Middlesex	8	1	5	2	38
Essex	7	–	7	2	32
Glamorgan	7	2	7	–	32
Durham	5	–	11	–	20
Hampshire	5	–	11	–	20
Derbyshire	2	–	13	1	10

Surrey, Nottinghamshire & Warwickshire will be promoted to Division One for the 2001 season

FEATURES OF NATIONAL LEAGUE 2000

HIGHEST TOTAL

295-7	45	**Somerset** v. **Kent** at Maidstone	2 July

HIGHEST TOTAL BATTING SECOND

285	45	**Glamorgan** v. **Essex** at Southend	3 September

LOWEST TOTAL

53	20.3	**Leicestershire** v. **Yorkshire** at Leicester	20 August

HIGHEST INDIVIDUAL SCORE

126*	GP Thorpe	**Surrey** v. **Nottinghamshire** at Guildford	23 July

14 centuries were scored in the competition

SIX WICKETS IN AN INNINGS

6–27	PJ Franks	**Nottinghamshire** v. **Durham** at Chester-le-Street	28 May
6–31	N Killeen	**Durham** v. **Derbyshire** at Derby	17 September
6–42	AW Laraman	**Middlesex** v. **Glamorgan** at Cardiff	17 September
6–51	AW Laraman	**Middlesex** v. **Durham** at Chester-le-Street	25 June

There were 67 instances of four wickets in an innings

TIED MATCHES

Leicestershire tied with **Sussex** at Leicester	1 May
Lancashire tied with **Leicestershire** at Old Trafford	7 May
Middlesex tied with **Glamorgan** at Lord's	4 June
Glamorgan tied with **Warwickshire** at Swansea	2 July

WINNING BY TEN WICKETS

Lancashire beat **Gloucestershire** at Old Trafford	11 August

WINNING BY 100 RUNS

127	**Surrey** beat **Nottinghamshire** at Guildford	23 July
103	**Surrey** beat **Warwickshire** at Whitgift School	9 August

WINNING BY ONE WICKET

Glamorgan beat **Derbyshire** at Derby	27 August
Essex beat **Durham** at Chester-le-Street	27 August

WINNING BY 1 RUN

Middlesex beat **Durham** at Southgate	16 July
Durham beat **Derbyshire** at Derby	17 September

NO PLAY POSSIBLE

Kent v. **Lancashire** at Canterbury	30 April
Surrey v. **Midddlesex** at The Oval	17 May
Kent v. **Sussex** at Tunbridge Wells	8 May
Surrey v. **Essex** at The Oval	29 May

NATIONAL LEAGUE AVERAGES

DERBYSHIRE

Batting	M	Inns	NO	HS	Runs	Av	100	50	ct/st
ME Cassar	13	13	1	126	405	33.75	1	1	2
MJ di Venuto	16	16	0	84	372	23.25	-	1	5
RJ Bailey	11	11	0	64	243	22.09	-	1	3
SD Stubbings	15	14	1	59	284	21.84	-	1	-
DG Cork	9	8	0	64	169	21.12	-	2	8
JP Pyemont	8	8	0	50	163	20.37	-	1	5
LD Sutton	10	9	1	53*	133	16.62	-	1	8/2
KJ Dean	13	11	8	8*	48	16.00	-	-	1
T Lungley	3	3	0	15	45	15.00	-	-	-
SP Titchard	4	4	0	33	57	14.25	-	-	-
MP Dowman	14	14	1	33	164	12.61	-	-	2
PJ Aldred	10	8	2	25	57	9.50	-	-	2
KM Krikken	9	9	1	34*	76	9.50	-	-	7/5
KZ Shah	4	4	0	20	32	8.00	-	-	1
SJ Lacey	11	9	0	40	60	6.66	-	-	3
TM Smith	3	3	0	12	19	6.33	-	-	-
TA Munton	15	12	3	18	54	6.00	-	-	3

Also batted: BJ Spendlove (1 match) 4;LJ Wharton (7 matches) 0*, 0*, 7*, 1*, 2ct.

Bowling	Overs	Mds	Runs	Wkts	Av	Best	4/inns
P Alfred	84	5	348	19	18.31	3-31	-
T Lungley	26	1	104	5	20.80	2-26	-
DG Cork	80	4	315	15	21.00	4-40	1
ME Cassar	74.4	1	347	16	21.68	4-29	1
TM Smith	21	2	119	5	23.80	3-45	-
MP Dowman	29	0	149	6	24.83	2-16	-
KJ Dean	97.2	7	461	15	30.73	4-30	1
LJ Wharton	46	2	216	6	36.00	3-29	-
TA Munton	133	16	446	12	37.16	3-24	-

Also bowled: RJ Bailey 18-0-94-0;SJ Lacey 60-2-309-3;KZ Shah 32-1-145-2.

DURHAM

Batting	M	Inns	NO	HS	Runs	Av	100	50	ct/st
PD Collingwood	15	15	2	86	607	46.69	-	7	11
SM Katich	16	16	3	70*	598	46.00	-	6	8
JM Daley	8	8	0	105	261	32.62	1	2	1
JJB Lewis	16	16	4	60	322	26.83	-	2	3
MA Gough	5	5	1	36	92	23.00	-	-	1
S MAli	4	4	0	36	87	21.75	-	-	2
N Killeen	13	5	2	21	60	20.00	-	-	3
NJ Speak	12	12	1	53*	212	19.27	-	1	1
J Wood	11	9	4	28*	75	15.00	-	-	3
MP Speight	12	11	0	55	144	13.09	-	1	12/3
NC Phillips	16	10	3	29*	90	12.85	-	-	5
N Peng	4	4	0	36	46	11.50	-	-	-
ID Hunter	14	7	3	14*	30	7.50	-	-	2
MJ Symington	5	5	0	16	23	4.60	-	-	3
A Pratt	7	6	2	10	17	4.25	-	-	2/2
R Robinson	4	4	0	7	10	2.50	-	-	1

Also batted: MM Betts (6matches) 4, 2*, 16, 2ct; SJ Harmison (6 matches)1*,2;
SJE Brown (1 match) and AM Davies (1 match) did not bat.

Bowling	Overs	Mds	Runs	Wkts	Av	Best	4/inns
N Killeen	104.5	8	415	29	14.31	6-31	3
NC Phillips	119.3	6	517	24	21.54	4-30	1
ID Hunter	93.5	3	430	17	25.29	4-29	1
SJ Harmison	50.5	2	258	8	32.25	3-45	-
PD Collingwood	85.5	2	395	12	32.91	3-29	-
J Wood	87	6	345	8	43.12	2-29	-

Also bowled: MM Betts 43-3-165-3; SJE Brown 7-0-22-0; AM Davies 6-0-15-3; MA Gough
5-0-30-0; SM Katich 17-1-94-2; R Robinson 6.1-0-30-1; MJ Symington 13-0-68-1.

ESSEX

Batting	M	Inns	NO	HS	Runs	Av	100	50	ct/st
N Hussain	6	6	0	60	256	42.66	-	3	3
WI Jefferson	3	3	0	65	117	39.00	-	2	1
SG Law	13	13	1	104*	413	34.41	1	2	1
JS Foster	6	6	3	22*	81	27.00	-	-	6/1

NATIONAL LEAGUE AVERAGES

ESSEX (CONT)

Batting	M	Inns	NO	HS	Runs	Av	100	50	ct/st
AP Grayson	15	15	3	64	309	25.75	-	1	5
SD Peters	15	15	1	73*	340	24.28	-	2	3
RC Irani	15	15	1	52	329	23.50	-	1	4
GR Napier	11	10	0	78	212	21.20	-	2	4
DDJ Robinson	5	5	0	51	101	20.20	-	1	2
DR Law	15	13	2	37	193	17.54	-	-	4
PJ Prichard	9	9	0	24	113	14.12	-	-	1
TJ Mason	14	10	4	12	51	8.50	-	-	9
AP Cowan	13	11	1	29*	76	7.60	-	-	4
BJ Hyam	9	6	1	16*	27	5.40	-	-	6/3

Also batted: RSG Anderson (3 matches) 1, 1; JE Bishop (2 matches) 1*, 16*;
MC Ilott (7 matches) 0*, 2*, 10, 2ct; AC McGarry (4 matches) 0*.

Bowling	Overs	Mds	Runs	Wkts	Av	Best	4/inns
MC Ilott	46	5	197	11	17.90	3-13	-
AP Cowan	103	9	433	22	19.68	4-39	2
AP Grayson	90.2	2	394	19	20.73	3-21	-
DR Law	95	4	442	18	24.55	3-41	-
RC Irani	106	18	354	14	25.28	3-10	-
TJ Mason	77.1	0	390	6	65.00	2-14	-

Also bowled: RSG Anderson 23-2-109-1; JE Bishop 4-0-29-1; SG Law 3-0-10-0;
AC McGarry 17-2-63-2; GR Napier 12-0-58-1.

GLAMORGAN

Batting	M	Inns	NO	HS	Runs	Av	100	50	ct/st
MTG Elliott	11	11	2	88	429	47.66	-	4	5
MP Maynard	14	14	2	88*	501	41.75	-	4	10/1
SP James	16	15	4	88*	439	39.90	-	5	5
MJ Powell	16	16	3	86	396	30.46	-	2	1
A Dale	16	15	3	76*	309	25.75	-	1	3
IJ Thomas	4	4	0	36	100	25.00	-	-	2
K Newell	16	14	0	78	317	22.64	-	2	2
RDB Croft	14	12	2	24	139	13.90	-	-	4
SD Thomas	12	7	0	21	72	10.28	-	-	2
AD Shaw	9	6	0	24	55	9.16	-	-	5/1
DA Cosker	6	5	2	17	26	8.66	-	-	-
MA Wallace	4	3	1	8*	15	7.50	-	-	3/1
OT Parkin	16	8	4	5*	20	5.00	-	-	6
AG Wharf	11	5	0	20	20	4.00	-	-	2
SL Watkin	4	4	2	2	3	1.50	-	-	2

Also batted: AW Evans (2 matches) 5, 6, 1ct; DS Harrison (3 matches) 2*, 4, 2, 1ct;
WL Law (1 match) 0.

Bowling	Overs	Mds	Runs	Wkts	Av	Best	4/inns
K Newell	45.5	3	222	10	22.20	3-32	-
SD Thomas	93.4	4	438	18	24.33	4-42	1
SL Watkin	37	2	162	6	27.00	2-28	-
DA Cosker	48	1	229	8	28.62	3-36	-
OT Parkin	126	10	636	20	31.80	3-39	-
A Dale	96	2	434	13	33.38	2-20	-
RDB Croft	106.3	1	446	11	40.54	2-22	-
AG Wharf	79	5	350	8	43.75	2-37	-

Also bowled: 3-1-10-0; DS Harrison 14-1-96-0.

GLOUCESTERSHIRE

Batting	M	Inns	NO	HS	Runs	Av	100	50	ct/st
RC Russell	16	15	6	55*	310	34.44	-	1	17/8
IJ Harvey	14	14	1	66	400	30.76	-	3	4
KJ Barnett	13	13	0	62	316	24.30	-	2	2
DR Hewson	5	4	0	45	85	21.25	-	-	1
THC Hancock	13	12	0	50	238	19.83	-	1	5
Snape	16	15	1	71	265	18.92	-	1	5
MW Alleyne	14	12	3	44*	168	18.66	-	-	8
MGN Windows	16	15	1	61	195	13.92	-	1	2
MJC Ball	10	6	1	30*	65	13.00	-	-	5
RJ Cunliffe	5	4	0	34	49	12.25	-	-	1
CG Taylor	13	8	1	37*	75	10.71	-	-	4
MJ Cawdron	5	4	0	26	38	9.50	-	-	1

NATIONAL LEAGUE AVERAGES

GLOUCESTERSHIRE (CONT)

Batting	M	Inns	NO	HS	Runs	Av	100	50	ct/st
JMM Averis	16	10	3	23*	65	9.28	–	–	1
AM Smith	16	10	6	3*	15	3.75	–	–	1

Also batted: J Lewis (2 matches) 0,16; RCJ Williams (2 matches) 2, 0, 1ct.

Bowling	Overs	Mds	Runs	Wkts	Av	Best	4/inns
IJ Harvey	112.1	11	372	34	10.94	5–19	4
JMM Averis	126.2	6	537	29	18.51	5–20	2
AM Smith	133	24	370	18	20.55	3–20	–
MW Alleyne	102	3	415	14	29.64	3–36	–
MCJ Ball	73	2	347	9	38.55	2–28	–
MJ Cawdron	34	1	166	4	41.50	2–37	–
JN Snape	48	0	228	5	45.60	1–19	–

Also bowled: KJ Barnett 6–0–24–1; THC Hancock 7.1–0–39–1; J Lewis 16–1–78–1.

HAMPSHIRE

Batting	M	Inns	NO	HS	Runs	Av	100	50	ct/st
WS Kendall	13	13	5	85*	388	48.50	–	3	3
RA Smith	15	15	2	88*	464	35.69	–	4	2
LR Prittipaul	6	4	1	61	87	29.00	–	1	1
JP Stephenson	10	10	2	83*	228	28.50	–	1	2
DA Kenway	12	12	0	90	330	27.50	–	3	7/4
JS Laney	15	15	0	69	286	19.06	–	1	2
SRG Francis	5	4	3	8*	17	17.00	–	–	2
DA Mascarenhas	15	12	1	33	166	15.09	–	–	4
SD Udal	16	11	4	51*	97	13.85	–	1	6
SK Warne	13	13	1	34	151	12.58	–	–	5
GW White	13	12	0	27	147	12.25	–	–	4
L Savident	3	3	0	25	34	11.33	–	–	–
PJ Hartley	5	3	1	14	18	9.00	–	–	–
AN Aymes	11	8	1	17	51	7.28	–	–	11/5
AD Mullally	11	7	2	7	21	4.20	–	–	1

Also batted: AC Morris (5 matches) 0, 16*, 1ct; SJ Renshaw (3 matches) 1, 0;
CT Tremlett (5 matches) 30*, 0, 1ct.

Bowling	Overs	Mds	Runs	Wkts	Av	Best	4/inns
SK Warne	113	15	438	25	17.52	4–23	2
AD Mullally	93	11	341	17	20.05	4–30	2
PJ Hartley	42	8	161	8	20.12	3–41	–
AD Mascarenhas	120	13	540	21	25.71	3–21	–
JP Stephenson	42.4	1	185	6	30.83	4–40	1
AC Morris	42	2	223	7	31.85	3–59	–
SD Udal	122.2	3	500	14	35.71	2–18	–

Also bowled: SRG Francis 27–4–118–1; LR Prittipaul 1–0–14–0; SJ Renshaw 17–1–75–2;
L Savident 7–1–20–0; CT Tremlett 41–0–185–4; GW White 1.4–0–9–0.

KENT

Batting	M	Inns	NO	HS	Runs	Av	100	50	ct/st
R Dravid	13	13	3	104	437	43.70	1	2	6
JB Hockley	9	8	2	64	236	39.33	–	1	3
MV Fleming	14	12	2	79	302	30.20	–	2	2
MJ McCague	7	5	1	56	120	30.00	–	1	1
AP Wells	11	11	1	90	284	28.40	–	2	1
MA Ealham	12	10	1	49*	175	19.44	–	–	3
PA Nixon	14	11	2	30*	170	18.88	–	–	22/4
DP Fulton	6	6	0	69	104	17.33	–	1	3
MJ Walker	14	13	0	63	224	17.23	–	1	5
MJ Saggers	6	4	3	10*	13	13.00	–	–	2
SA Marsh	8	7	0	38	78	11.14	–	–	3
RWT Key	5	5	0	16	41	8.20	–	–	–
DD Masters	14	9	2	10*	33	4.71	–	–	2
MM Patel	8	5	1	14*	18	4.50	–	–	2
K Adams	6	5	3	6*	8	4.00	–	–	–

Also batted: JM Golding (3 matches) 0, 0; DA Scott (2 matches) 27, 1ct; ET Smith (1 match) 14.
BJ Phillips (1 match) did not bat.

Bowling	Overs	Mds	Runs	Wkts	Av	Best	4/inns
DA Scott	14	0	61	5	12.20	3–21	–
MJ Saggers	46.4	3	187	13	14.38	3–22	–
MJ McCague	46.2	4	206	11	18.72	3–29	–

NATIONAL LEAGUE AVERAGES

KENT (CONT)

Bowling	Overs	Mds	Runs	Wkts	Av	Best	4/inns
MV Fleming	86.4	7	306	16	19.12	3–7	–
MM Patel	65	8	282	12	23.50	2–13	–
K Adams	44	2	195	8	24.37	4–19	1
MJ Walker	33	1	178	6	29.66	2–27	–
MA Ealham	91.4	7	313	10	31.30	3–38	–
DD Masters	99.1	8	433	9	48.11	2–10	–

Also bowled: R Dravid 11–0–56–0; JM Golding 13–2–38–1; BJ Phillips 7–0–25–4.

LANCASHIRE

Batting	M	Inns	NO	HS	Runs	Av	100	50	ct/st
SC Ganguly	13	13	2	102	569	51.72	2	4	4
MA Atherton	6	6	0	105	258	43.00	1	1	1
NH Fairbrother	15	14	3	75	354	32.18	–	3	5
A Flintoff	9	9	0	64	191	21.22	–	1	1
JP Crawley	13	13	2	71*	208	18.90	–	1	1
CP Schofield	12	9	2	34	125	17.85	–	–	1
GD Lloyd	14	12	3	46	157	17.44	–	–	2
MJ Chilton	7	7	1	37	95	15.83	–	–	–
WK Hegg	14	10	1	33	133	14.77	–	–	10/2
G Chapple	14	8	3	15*	62	12.40	–	–	1
JC Scuderi	6	4	1	14	30	10.00	–	–	1
ID Austin	12	8	3	9	23	4.60	–	–	1
G Yates	5	2	0	4	7	3.50	–	–	2
MP Smethurst	8	3	1	3*	6	3.00	–	–	2

Also batted: RJ Green (1 match) 3*; JJ Haynes (2 matches) 12, 2ct,1st; G Keedy
(6 matches) 1, 0*, 1ct; PD McKeown (1 match) 1; M Watkinson (3 matches) 33, 9, 1ct.
PJ Martin (4 matches) did not bat.

Bowling	Overs	Mds	Runs	Wkts	Av	Best	4/inns
G Keedy	33.3	0	149	9	16.55	5–30	1
ID Austin	92.5	5	313	15	20.86	4–14	1
A Flintoff	53	5	218	10	21.80	3–39	–
G Chapple	108	11	454	17	26.70	3–23	–
SC Ganguly	55	2	242	7	34.57	3–22	–
CP Schofield	89.5	2	439	11	39.90	2–37	–

Also bowled: MJ Chilton 1–0–12–0; RJ Green 4.5–1–24–0; PD McKeown 0.2–0–4–0;
PJ Martin 30–4–113–3; JC Scuderi 30–2–165–4; MP Smethurst 48–1–238–2; M Watkinson
24–1–122–3; G Yates 22–0–103–2.

LEICESTERSHIRE

Batting	M	Inns	NO	HS	Runs	Av	100	50	ct/st
BF Smith	16	15	2	90	508	39.07	–	4	2
DL Maddy	16	15	3	87*	393	32.75	–	2	4
Aftab Habib	15	14	2	70	384	32.00	–	2	1
JM Dakin	9	8	3	68*	130	26.00	–	1	1
VJ Wells	15	14	0	81	303	21.64	–	2	3
TR Ward	14	13	0	61	219	16.84	–	2	4
DI Stevens	12	11	2	332	121	13.44	–	–	4
PAJ DeFreitas	13	10	0	40	115	11.50	–	–	3
CC Lewis	10	9	2	26	77	11.00	–	–	4
ND Burns	16	11	1	29	105	10.50	–	–	28/2
D Williamson	6	4	0	12	27	6.75	–	–	2
J Ormond	12	8	5	5*	19	6.33	–	–	4
A Kumble	12	7	1	13	31	5.16	–	–	6

Also batted: SAJ Boswell (4 matches) 5*; CD Crowe (1 match) 5*; WF Stelling (1 match) 10*; IJ
Sutcliffe (3 matches) 18, 53, 2ct. AA Khan (1 match) did not bat.

Bowling	Overs	Mds	Runs	Wkts	Av	Best	4/inns
DL Maddy	47.3	2	203	13	15.61	4–16	1
D Williamson	24.2	0	121	7	17.28	3–32	–
SAJ Boswell	27	1	109	6	18.16	3–38	–
CC Lewis	76	13	238	13	18.30	4–34	1
A Kumble	99.5	11	346	16	21.62	3–26	–
J Ormond	96.3	11	384	15	25.60	3–43	–
VJ Wells	99.1	8	396	14	28.28	3–32	–
PAJ De Freitas	100	10	374	11	34.00	2–24	–
JM Dakin	67.3	7	348	9	38.66	2–36	–

Also bowled: CD Crowe 1–0–10–0; AA Khan 1.1–0–14–0; WF Stelling 9–2–35–3.

NATIONAL LEAGUE AVERAGES

MIDDLESEX

Batting	M	Inns	NO	HS	Runs	Av	100	50	ct/st
EC Joyce	5	5	3	40*	110	55.00	–	–	1
MR Ramprakash	12	12	2	61	408	40.80	–	3	5
BL Hutton	7	4	1	49	97	32.33	–	–	1
MA Roseberry	6	6	0	72	193	32.16	–	2	2
JL Langer	15	15	1	93	374	26.71	–	3	11
AJ Strauss	12	12	0	90	263	21.91	–	1	3
PN Weekes	13	12	2	43	204	20.40	–	–	7
OA Shah	9	9	0	39	174	19.33	–	–	–
D Alleyne	11	11	0	58	179	16.27	–	1	10/5
SJ Cook	13	9	1	28*	107	13.37	–	–	4
AW Laraman	8	7	4	11*	30	10.00	–	–	2
ARC Fraser	13	7	4	7	28	9.33	–	–	2
RMS Weston	6	6	0	28	56	9.33	–	–	2
KP Dutch	7	6	1	17	32	6.40	–	–	2
RL Johnson	12	8	1	16	40	5.71	–	–	1
JP Hewitt	5	3	0	12	17	5.66	–	–	2

Also batted: CJ Batt (2 matches) 3*, 1*, 1ct; TF Bloomfield (4 matches) 3*, 1*;
DC Nash (4 matches) 25*, 2ct/2st. – J Dalrymple (1 match) did not bat.

Bowling	Overs	Mds	Runs	Wkts	Av	Best	4/inns
RL Johnson	81.5	7	338	21	16.09	3–26	–
AW Laraman	63.1	4	275	17	16.17	6–42	2
ARC Fraser	92.5	14	322	18	17.88	4–18	1
PN Weekes	63.5	4	308	15	20.53	4–26	1
SJ Cook	83.5	7	315	14	22.50	3–22	–
BL Hutton	25	2	134	5	26.80	4–32	1
KP Dutch	50	4	211	6	35.16	1–18	–

Also bowled: CJ Batt 13–0–50–3; TF Bloomfield 20–1–65–3; J Dalrymple 7–1–37–1;
JP Hewitt 24–1–115–1; MR Ramprakash 17–2–56–0; OA Shah 8–0–54–1

NORTHAMPTONSHIRE

Batting	M	Inns	NO	HS	Runs	Av	100	50	ct/st
DJG Sales	15	15	5	84*	547	54.70	–	5	5
ML Hayden	15	15	2	96*	462	35.53	–	2	6
MB Loye	14	14	0	75	371	26.50	–	4	5
KJ Innes	12	9	2	55	181	25.85	–	1	2
AL Penberthy	15	13	3	39*	197	19.70	–	–	6
GP Swann	16	13	0	57	201	15.46	–	1	4
D Ripley	15	12	3	30	126	14.00	–	–	6/4
JW Cook	14	14	0	45	186	13.28	–	–	5
AS Rollins	6	6	0	28	71	11.83	–	–	3
DM Cousins	14	9	4	18	40	8.00	–	–	2
RJ Warren	5	5	1	10	23	5.75	–	–	5
JP Taylor	6	3	0	11	14	4.66	–	–	2
JF Brown	12	5	2	4	10	3.33	–	–	4
DE Malcolm	8	6	1	6	16	3.20	–	–	1

Also batted: MK Davies (2 matches) 0*, 4; RJ Logan (2 matches) 0, 17;
MR Strong (4 matches) 1, 1*, 0, 1ct. – TMB Bailey (1 match) did not bat but held 3 catches.

Bowling	Overs	Mds	Runs	Wkts	Av	Best	4/inns
AL Penberthy	110	8	437	22	19.86	5–29	2
KJ Innes	73	5	327	16	20.43	4–36	1
DM Cousins	100	6	415	19	21.84	3–27	–
GP Swann	69.5	1	345	14	24.64	4–14	1
JP Taylor	43	2	164	6	27.33	2–32	–
JF Brown	94.3	5	378	13	29.07	2–28	–

Also bowled: MK Davies 12–0–57–3; ML Hayden 11–0–73–1; RJ Logan 9.5–0–82–0;
DE Malcolm 51–4–243–4; DJG Sales 4–0–17–0; MR Strong 27.4–1–138–4.

NOTTINGHAMSHIRE

Batting	M	Inns	NO	HS	Runs	Av	100	50	ct/st
PJ Franks	16	11	8	32*	146	48.66	–	–	4
DJ Bicknell	16	15	2	115	537	41.30	1	5	3
Usman Afzaal	13	11	3	95*	292	36.50	–	2	6
JER Gallian	15	14	0	84	439	31.35	–	2	3
P Johnson	11	9	1	62	224	28.00	–	1	–
JE Morris	13	12	0	73	323	26.91	–	3	3
GE Welton	8	8	0	42	154	19.25	–	–	4

NATIONAL LEAGUE AVERAGES

NOTTINGHAMSHIRE (CONT)

Batting	M	Inns	NO	HS	Runs	Av	100	50	ct/st
CM Tolley	13	10	2	38	134	16.75	–	–	3
MN Bowen	4	3	0	31	48	16.00	–	–	–
PR Reiffel	8	4	1	18	41	13.66	–	–	1
CMW Read	16	13	3	29*	124	12.40	–	–	25/2
AJ Harris	13	4	2	9	21	10.50	–	–	4
DS Lucas	11	4	0	5	9	2.25	–	–	1

Also batted: GR Haywood (2 matches) 8, 16*; DJ Millns (4 matches) 4*, 8*, 13, 1ct;
RD Stemp (13 matches) 5, 4*, 2ct.

Bowling	Overs	Mds	Runs	Wkts	Av	Best	4/inns
PJ Franks	130.3	4	562	25	22.48	6–27	1
PR Reiffel	59	11	223	8	27.87	3–8	–
RD Stemp	99	3	404	14	28.85	4–36	1
DS Lucas	90.3	3	475	15	31.66	4–27	1
CM Tolley	88.1	3	352	9	39.11	2–27	–
AJ Harris	102	8	520	11	47.27	5–35	1

Also bowled: Usman Afzaal 13–0–81–4; DJ Bicknell 1–0–6–0; MN Bowen 25–0–119–3;
JER Gallian 10–0–73–0; GR Haywood 8.5–3–34–2; DJ Millns 33–2–185–4.

SOMERSET

Batting	M	Inns	NO	HS	Runs	Av	100	50	ct/st
ME Trescothick	11	11	1	92*	464	46.40	–	5	3
KA Parsons	16	15	2	69	436	33.53	–	3	1
J Cox	16	16	0	110	485	30.31	1	3	10
M Burns	16	15	0	97	387	25.80	–	3	4
PD Bowler	14	13	0	69	321	24.69	–	2	1
MN Lathwell	9	9	0	53	194	21.55	–	1	3
RJ Turner	15	14	4	44	210	21.00	–	–	14/3
ID Blackwell	16	15	2	50*	267	20.53	–	1	8
PS Jones	16	10	6	27	54	13.50	–	–	1
GD Rose	13	12	3	20	89	9.88	–	–	3
PCL Holloway	9	9	1	15	58	7.25	–	–	3
JID Kerr	3	3	1	13	14	7.00	–	–	1
AR Caddick	5	3	0	16	19	6.33	–	–	–
PW Jarvis	11	7	1	18	33	5.50	–	–	1

Also batted: MPL Bulbeck (1 match) 1, 1ct; ARK Pierson (2 matches) 31*, 8, 1ct;
PD Trego (3 matches) 0, 14, 1ct.

Bowling	Overs	Mds	Runs	Wkts	Av	Best	4/inns
ME Trescothick	68	2	329	16	20.56	4–50	1
PS Jones	127.4	11	620	28	22.14	4–32	3
PW Jarvis	88.2	2	475	14	33.92	3–23	–
KA Parsons	46	1	249	7	35.57	2–25	–
ID Blackwell	105.3	2	478	13	36.76	4–36	1
GD Rose	100	13	397	9	44.11	2–18	–

Also bowled: MPL Bulbeck 6–1–23–1; M Burns 15–1–90–2; AR Caddick 35.2–8–98–4;
J Cox 9–0–54–0; JID Kerr 17–0–97–3; ARK Pierson 18–0–84–3; PD Trego 20–0–95–0.

SURREY

Batting	M	Inns	NO	HS	Runs	Av	100	50	ct/st
GP Thorpe	8	8	3	126*	344	68.80	1	2	7
N Shahid	7	7	2	109*	239	47.80	1	1	6
AJ Stewart	5	5	1	72*	164	41.00	–	1	3/1
AJ Hollioake	14	13	4	111	346	38.44	1	–	7
IJ Ward	14	13	1	90*	429	35.75	–	3	5
AD Brown	14	14	0	51	330	23.57	–	1	6
JD Ratcliffe	13	9	4	42*	107	21.40	–	–	5
BC Hollioake	8	5	0	42	93	18.60	–	–	3
Saqlain Mushtaq	9	4	3	7*	15	15.00	–	–	2
MA Butcher	10	10	0	47	138	13.80	–	–	2
MP Bicknell	11	4	1	15*	37	12.33	–	–	3
IDK Salisbury	14	4	1	13	23	7.66	–	–	6
AJ Tudor	10	6	2	7	22	5.50	–	–	1

Also batted: GJ Batty (2 matches) 26*, 20, 2ct; JN Batty (9 matches) 8,6,4, 5ct/1st; GP Butcher
(2 matches) 14, 37, 1ct; CG Greenidge (6 matches) 3*, 3ct; TJ Murtagh (2 matches) 0;
PJ Sampson (2 matches) 4.
IE Bishop (2 matches) did not bat.

NATIONAL LEAGUE AVERAGES

SURREY (CONT)

Bowling	Overs	Mds	Runs	Wkts	Av	Best	4/inns
AJ Hollioake	59.4	1	263	23	11.43	5–29	3
IDK Salisbury	36.4	2	141	11	12.81	4–32	1
Saqlain Mushtaq	77	10	260	18	14.44	3–25	–
MP Bicknell	87	11	241	15	16.06	3–14	–
BC Hollioake	47.4	0	181	11	16.45	4–42	1
AJ Tudor	68	10	281	14	20.07	4–26	1
JD Ratcliffe	89	3	354	10	35.40	3–39	–

Also bowled: GJ Batty 11–0–64–0; IE Bishop 12–1–48–1; AD Brown 11–0–57–4;
GP Butcher 8–0–56–0; CG Greenidge 34.2–1–185–4; AJ Murtagh 17–1–102–1;
PJ Sampson 12–0–67–0.

SUSSEX

Batting	M	Inns	NO	HS	Runs	Av	100	50	ct/st
MG Bevan	12	12	6	89*	706	117.66	–	9	10
CJ Adams	14	14	0	100	483	34.50	1	4	11
RR Montgomerie	15	15	1	89	419	29.92	–	2	5
WJ House	14	13	4	80*	259	28.77	–	1	2
B Zuiderent	7	6	0	68	127	21.16	–	1	3
JR Carpenter	4	4	1	29	49	16.33	–	–	3
UBA Rashid	15	11	0	34	147	13.36	–	–	6
PA Cottey	13	12	1	47	134	12.18	–	–	3
RJ Kirtley	15	8	4	13*	35	8.75	–	–	3
MA Robinson	15	6	3	15*	16	5.33	–	–	1
RSC Martin-Jenkins	14	10	0	20	43	4.30	–	–	5
BV Taylor	11	5	2	5	9	3.00	–	–	1
NJ Wilton	10	7	1	3*	8	1.33	–	–	4/3

Also batted: AD Patterson (5 matches) 12, 20, 4ct/1st.
MH Yardy (1 match) did not bat.

Bowling	Overs	Mds	Runs	Wkts	Av	Best	4/inns
RJ Kirtley	106	6	499	26	19.19	4–32	3
WJ House	55.5	2	254	10	25.40	3–34	–
MA Robinson	116	7	460	18	25.55	4–23	1
BV Taylor	73	4	340	13	26.15	2–30	–
RSC Martin-Jenkins	102	7	438	16	27.37	2–30	–
UBA Rashid	94	2	446	15	29.73	3–38	–

Also bowled: CJ Adams 10–0–62–0;MG Bevan 8.1–0–51–4;MH Yardy 3–0–15–0.

WARWICKSHIRE

Batting	M	Inns	NO	HS	Runs	Av	100	50	ct/st
NV Knight	9	9	1	82	378	47.25	–	4	2
KJ Piper	15	7	6	44	44	44.00	–	–	15/7
DP Ostler	16	16	3	79*	385	29.61	–	2	7
TL Penney	15	14	4	51	291	29.10	–	1	8
A Singh	8	8	0	74	195	24.37	–	1	3
M A Sheikh	9	5	2	36	72	24.00	–	–	1
DR Brown	15	12	2	45*	226	22.60	–	–	4
GF Welch	11	10	0	55	201	20.10	–	1	4
AF Giles	13	11	0	45	221	20.09	–	–	7
MA Wagh	3	3	0	31	58	19.33	–	–	–
MJ Powell	12	11	1	44	181	18.10	–	–	3
NMK Smith	16	14	2	75*	171	14.25	–	1	9
D Hemp	9	8	0	45	106	13.25	–	–	1
AA Donald	7	5	3	11	19	9.50	–	–	–

Also batted: CE Dagnall (5 matches) 1, 1ct; T Frost (1 match) 18; ESH Giddins
(9 matches) 0, 0*, 3ct; A Richardson (3 matches) 0.

Bowling	Overs	Mds	Runs	Wkts	Av	Best	4/inns
CE Dagnall	42	1	142	12	11.83	4–34	1
AA Donald	52	8	148	11	13.45	3–9	–
DRBrown	117	14	447	25	17.88	3–13	–
NMK Smith	83.3	3	345	18	19.16	3–10	–
AF Giles	115	9	435	22	19.77	3–32	–
MJ Powell	27	1	124	6	20.66	2–13	–
MA Sheikh	70.3	4	280	8	35.00	2–24	–
ESH Giddins	57.4	4	182	5	36.40	2–15	–
GF Welch	87	10	304	7	43.42	2–32	–

Also bowled: A Richardson 23.2–1–109–4; MA Wagh 4–0–15–0.

NATIONAL LEAGUE AVERAGES

WORCESTERSHIRE

Batting	M	Inns	NO	HS	Runs	Av	100	50	ct/st
KR Spiring	4	4	0	71	135	33.75	–	1	3
PR Pollard	13	12	0	89	353	29.41	–	2	–
SJ Rhodes	16	15	4	48*	300	27.27	–	–	18/5
GA Hick	7	6	0	101	148	24.66	1	–	7
DJ Pipe	6	5	0	45	106	21.20	–	–	–
DA Leatherdale	16	15	0	43	314	20.93	–	–	6
WPC Weston	7	6	0	47	100	16.66	–	–	2
RC Driver	8	8	0	52	128	16.00	–	1	1
VS Solanki	16	15	1	59*	226	16.14	–	1	1
EJ Wilson	12	12	1	38	131	11.90	–	–	4
SR Lampitt	14	11	1	39	128	9.84	–	–	5
RK Illingworth	16	14	1	30	102	7.84	–	–	3
Kabir Ali	11	7	4	7	14	4.66	–	–	4
GD McGrath	14	7	3	1	1	0.25	–	–	1

Also batted: DC Catterall (3 matches) 2, 9*, 1ct;Kadir Ali (1 match) 20; CG Liptrot (4 matches)
1*, 15*, 2*; MJ Rawnsley (3 matches) 4*, 5*, 4, 1ct; A Sheriyar (3 matches) 1*, 1*.

Bowling	Overs	Mds	Runs	Wkts	Av	Best	4/inns
GD McGrath	112.4	30	244	30	8.13	4–9	2
MJ Rawnsley	21.5	2	90	5	18.00	3–31	–
CG Liptrot	17.1	0	117	5	23.40	3–44	–
Kabir Ali	63.3	4	318	13	24.46	3–19	–
DA Leatherdale	71.2	2	345	13	26.53	3–30	–
RK Illingworth	91.5	3	388	14	27.71	3–26	–
SR Lampitt	114.1	17	426	13	32.76	3–32	–

Also bowled: DC Catterall 9–0–61–0; RC Driver 6–0–42–1; GA Hick 19–0–126–1;
A Sheriyar 20–2–98–1; VS Solanki 3–0–14–0.

YORKSHIRE

Batting	M	Inns	NO	HS	Runs	Av	100	50	ct/st
A McGrath	10	9	4	85*	224	44.80	–	1	6
DS Lehmann	16	16	3	89	564	43.38	–	4	3
GM Hamilton	14	10	3	57*	222	31.71	–	1	1
RJ Blakey	16	12	1	62	290	26.36	–	1	21/5
GM Fellows	15	12	0	65	232	19.33	–	2	7
D Byas	12	12	0	52	230	19.16	–	1	10
MJ Wood	6	4	0	31	73	18.25	–	–	3
MP Vaughan	9	9	2	39	108	15.42	–	–	4
VJ Craven	5	5	0	28	77	15.40	–	–	5
S Widdup	4	4	0	38	49	12.25	–	–	2
RJ Sidebottom	7	6	2	21	36	9.00	–	–	–
C White	7	5	1	14	36	9.00	–	–	1
ID Fisher	7	4	0	20	29	7.25	–	–	1
JD Middlebrook	10	6	1	15*	30	6.00	–	–	–
CEW Silverwood	8	5	0	12	26	5.20	–	–	1
MJ Hoggard	15	7	4	2*	4	1.33	–	–	1

Also batted: D Gough (3 matches) 15*, 15*, 6*, 1ct;R J Harden (1 match) 2*; PM Hutchison
(5 matches) 0*, 1*, 1ct.
CJ Elstub (2 matches) and G Ramsden (1 match) did not bat.

Bowling	Overs	Mds	Runs	Wkts	Av	Best	4/inns
C White	44.5	4	126	14	9.00	4–14	1
MJ Hoggard	121.3	20	458	37	12.37	5–28	2
MP Vaughan	14.5	1	70	5	14.00	4–27	1
GM Hamilton	76.5	4	319	20	15.95	5–34	1
CEW Silverwood	51.5	7	194	12	16.16	4–11	1
ID Fisher	44.3	2	171	10	17.10	3–20	–
D Gough	47	8	136	7	19.42	3–19	–
JD Middlebrook	73	0	320	11	29.09	3–16	–
PM Hutchison	41.4	1	178	6	29.66	2–13	–

Also bowled: CJ Elstub 12.2–0–67–0;GM Fellows 13–1–54–2;G Ramsden 4–0–26–2;
RJ Sidebottom 43–4–183–2.

BENSON AND HEDGES CUP
GROUP A

15 April 2000
at Derby
Leicestershire 86 (37 overs)
Derbyshire 22 for 3 (8 overs)
Match abandoned – 1 pt each

at Chester-le-Street
Durham 178 for 4 (40 overs)(NJ Speak 72)
Yorkshire 168 for 9 (40 overs)
Durham (2 pts) won by 10 runs
Gold Award: NJ Speak

at Old Trafford
Nottinghamshire 164 for 7 (50 overs)
Lancashire 165 for 2 (46.5 overs)(MA Atherton 81*)
Lancashire (2 pts) won by eight wickets
Gold Award: MA Atherton

Free admission kicked off the season at Old Trafford, and Lancashire duly thrashed Nottinghamshire by eight wickets to give themselves an early advantage in the northern group. The Benson and Hedges Cup, reintroduced in full after a year's gap, was being played initially as a three-group league, with six counties in each regional section. The top two in each group were to receive automatic entry into the quarter-finals, and in addition the best two third-placed teams would also move into the knock-out stage.

Ian Austin was the most successful Lancashire bowler, claiming 3 for 26 from his ten-over stint. Peter Martin took 2 for 15 from eight overs and Andy Flintoff confirmed his recovery from the foot injury that forced him home early from England's winter tour of South Africa with a ten-over spell costing just 23 runs. Usman Afzaal fought his way to 45 but Notts' 50-over total of 164 for 7 was made to look wholly inadequate by Mike Atherton and John Crawley, who put on 115 for the second wicket. Atherton finished 81 not out, and Crawley scored 61, but Lancashire's new overseas signing Saurav Ganguly was caught at slip off Andy Harris for a sixth-ball duck.

At Chester-le-Street a match reduced to 40 overs per side was won, narrowly, by Durham. Nick Speak, the new captain, hit 72 from 98 balls and added 102 in 19 overs with Jon Lewis, who remained 55 not out as Durham totalled 178 for 4. In reply, Yorkshire could reach only 168 for 9 despite 45 from Craig White and 40 from Darren

Lehmann. Paul Collingwood picked up 4 for 31 with his medium-pacers as Durham pegged Yorkshire back doggedly following the visitors' comfortable progress to 122 for 1.

In bitterly cold conditions at Derby there was only frustration for the home side. A four-pronged seam attack of skipper Dominic Cork (3 for 27), Trevor Smith (3 for 14), Paul Aldred (2 for 18) and canny new signing Tim Munton (2 for 15) reduced Leicestershire to 86 all out. But then, with Derbyshire 22 for 3 in reply, rain arrived. With only eight overs bowled, and not the minimum of ten required for the Duckworth/Lewis calculations to come into force, the match was declared a 'no result'!

16 April 2000
at Leicester
Leicestershire 187 (49.3 overs)(J Wood 4 for 28)
Durham 167 for 9 (50 overs)(J Ormond 4 for 27)
Leicestershire (2 pts) won by 20 runs
Gold Award: J Ormond

at Trent Bridge
Nottinghamshire 44 (33.3 overs)
Derbyshire 98 for 1 (11.4 overs)(MJ di Venuto 61*)
Derbyshire (2 pts) won by nine wickets
Gold Award: DG Cork

at Headingley
Lancashire 166 for 9 (50 overs)(C White 5 for 25)
Yorkshire 167 for 6 (45.3 overs)
Yorkshire (2 pts) won by four wickets
Gold Award: C White

Chris Lewis' allegations of a match-fixing scandal provided the unfortunate backdrop to the match at Leicester, which, ironically, was decided in Leicestershire's favour in no small measure by a tenth-wicket stand of 47 between Lewis and James Ormond. Lewis, batting at number 11 because of stitches in a finger wound, hit 29 and boosted Leicestershire's total to 187. Vince Wells had earlier made 40, with John Wood bowling with hostility for Durham to pick up 4 for 28. In reply Nick Speak (49) and Paul Collingwood (35) did their best with the bat, but Durham could only reach 167 for 9 from their 50 overs as Ormond took 4 for 27 and Anil Kumble, the Indian leg-spinner and the county's new overseas signing, 3 for 26.

Derbyshire, denied by the weather the previous day, produced another fine bowling performance in seaming conditions at Trent Bridge to hammer Nottinghamshire by nine wickets. Dominic Cork's

Chris Lewis' allegations of English match-fixing made the headlines during the early season.

3 for 17 and Paul Aldred's 3 for 12 contributed heavily to Notts' plunge to 94 all out. Michael di Venuto, the Australian batsman signed from Sussex, then smashed 61 not out from 42 balls, and in the process broke seamer Andy Harris' left index finger with one fierce straight drive.

The first Roses clash of the new season was won by Yorkshire, at Headingley, with an unbroken seventh-wicket stand of 64 between Richard Blakey (33 not out) and Gavin Hamilton (28 not out) ultimately proving the difference. Blakey, in particular, showed the grit traditionally required in such meetings between the White and Red Rose, batting with a finger dislocated earlier in the field. The ball swung prodigiously all day, as is evident in Lancashire's tally of 26 wides and Yorkshire's 17, but Andy Flintoff found the middle of the bat often enough to make 35 from 50 balls, while John Crawley's 45 also helped Lancashire to a 50-over total of 166 for 9. Craig White was the outstanding bowler on display, with 5 for 25, while Hamilton picked up 3 for 24. In the Yorkshire reply, which initially slumped to 103 for 6, Saurav Ganguly showed just how useful his medium-pacers can be by taking 3 for 31.

18 April 2000
at Chester-le-Street
Durham 53 for 8 (10 overs)
Lancashire 55 for 1 (6.5 overs)
Lancashire (2 pts) won by nine wickets
Gold Award: SC Ganguly

At 5:00 p.m., after five pitch inspections, the umpires decreed that conditions would allow a ten-over thrash at Chester-le-Street – which Lancashire duly won after fine all-round contributions from Saurav Ganguly. The Indian captain took 3 for 7 from his two allotted overs, as Durham totalled just 53 for 8, and then struck 22 not out as Lancashire romped home by nine wickets with 3.1 overs to spare.

19 April 2000
at Headingley
Leicestershire 191 for 5 (50 overs)(Aftab Habib 70*, WF Stelling 50*)
Yorkshire 192 for 5 (45.5 overs)(D Byas 71)
Yorkshire (2 pts) won by five wickets
Gold Award: D Byas

Yorkshire produced an efficient win against Leicestershire at Headingley, spearheaded by a fiery new-ball spell by Darren Gough in which he removed both openers and finished with figures of 10–4–19–2. An unbroken stand of 122 between Aftab Habib (70 not out from 104 balls) and Billy Stelling (50 not out) rallied Leicestershire to 191 for 5 from their 50 overs, but Yorkshire eased home by five wickets with more than four overs unused. David Byas, the captain, scored 71 from 116 balls and Gary Fellows ended 26 not out. Stelling, a 30-year-old born in Johannesburg and a former Western Province and Boland player, qualifies as 'British' because of his Dutch ancestry.

20 April 2000
at Derby
Lancashire 218 for 6 (50 overs)(A Flintoff 70)
Derbyshire 219 for 4 (49 overs)(MP Dowman 65, RJ Bailey 50*)
Derbyshire (2 pts) won by six wickets
Gold Award: MP Dowman

at Trent Bridge
Durham 174 for 8 (28 overs)(SM Katich 50)
Nottinghamshire 172 for 7 (28 overs)
(DJ Bicknell 71*)
Durham (2 pts) won by 2 runs
Gold Award: DJ Bicknell

Matthew Dowman and Rob Bailey were the main heroes as Derbyshire upset Lancashire with a determined six-wicket win at Derby. Dowman, signed from Nottinghamshire, first took 2 for 28 from seven overs of medium pace in support of Tim Munton (10–3–20–2) as Lancashire were pegged to

218 for 6 from their 50 overs. Then Dowman struck 65 from 74 balls, with 11 fours and some eye-catching cover driving, and his lead was seized by Bailey with 50 not out from 59 deliveries. Matt Cassar (43) also contributed, but 39 were still required from five overs when Dominic Cork – by then Bailey's partner – was dropped on seven. Cork went on to reach 26 not out and the victory was all but sealed when Bailey pulled Peter Martin for six in the 48th over. For Lancashire, Ian Austin bowled his ten overs for 1 for 21, Andy Flintoff smote 70 off just 75 balls, and 84 were added in only 14 overs by Joe Scuderi (42) and Graham Lloyd (35 not out).

A tense finish at Trent Bridge left Durham the winners by just two runs against Nottinghamshire. Paul Franks needed to score two from the final ball of an exciting 28-over match, but was bowled as Neil Killeen produced a perfect delivery – straight and full – to defeat a lusty swing. The result was rough luck on Darren Bicknell, who remained 71 not out from 75 balls, with two sixes and six fours, and Jason Gallian (47), but perhaps the most decisive spell of bowling in the match came from John Wood who, though taking only one wicket, conceded a mere 16 runs from his six-over stint. Earlier, in Durham's 174 for 8, Simon Katich made 50, Nick Speak 34 and Paul Collingwood a rapid 31.

22 April 2000
at Derby
Yorkshire 82 for 2 (21.2 overs)
Derbyshire did not bat
Match abandoned – 1 pt each

at Leicester
Leicestershire v. Nottinghamshire
No play possible – 1 pt each

Yorkshire reached 82 for 2 from 21.2 overs, with Richard Blakey hitting 40, before rain ruled out any more play in the match against Derbyshire at Derby. At Leicester, meanwhile, no play at all was possible between Leicestershire and Nottinghamshire.

24 April 2000
at Chester-le-Street
Durham 245 for 9 (50 overs)(R Robinson 68, RJ Bailey 5 for 45)
Derbyshire 107 (40.4 overs)
Durham (2 pts) won by 138 runs
Gold Award: R Robinson

at Old Trafford
Leicestershire 172 (47.3 overs)(BF Smith 64*)
Lancashire 176 for 9 (46.3 overs)(A Kumble 4 for 28)
Lancashire (2 pts) won by one wicket
Gold Award: ID Austin

at Trent Bridge
Nottinghamshire 129 for 8 (35 overs)(D Gough 4 for 17)
Yorkshire 119 for 4 (28.2 overs)
Yorkshire (2 pts) won by six wickets
(DL Method: Yorkshire target 119 from 35 overs)
Gold Award: D Gough

The poor weather did ease enough, at least, for the final round of games to be played with few interruptions around the country. Durham clinched their qualification for the quarter-finals by thrashing Derbyshire at Chester-le-Street. A total of 245 for 9 was inspired by Ryan Robinson, released from the Yorkshire Academy two years earlier and now including four sixes and six fours in a bludgeoning 68 off 38 balls. No fewer than 86 runs came during his ten-over stay, although Derbyshire did not help their own cause with 25 wides. Rob Bailey's 5 for 45 was the best bowling analysis of his 18-year first-class career but Derbyshire badly missed their captain, Dominic Cork, who was laid up with gastric flu. Only Michael di Venuto (46) made any sort of impact as they were tumbled out for 107 in reply.

Lancashire crept into the last eight thanks to an unlikely last-wicket stand of 28 between Ian Austin (24 not out) and Mike Smethurst (10 not out). Last man Smethurst had a previous top score of just four, in any form of senior cricket, and after Anil Kumble had taken 4 for 28 (including Andy Flintoff stumped, charging him) Leicestershire looked favourites. But Austin and Smethurst inched Lancashire home and Leicestershire were made to pay for their failure to use up their entire 50 overs, Ben Smith remaining 64 not out when they were dismissed for 172 with 15 deliveries still to be bowled.

Rain reduced affairs at Trent Bridge initially to a 35-overs-per-side contest, but Darren Gough virtually assured Yorkshire of victory with a new-ball burst of 7–1–17–4 that reduced Nottinghamshire to 21 for 5. They eventually reached 129 for 8, with Chris Tolley unbeaten on 49, but Yorkshire were already cruising to their target at 119 for 4 when more rain necessitated their win, and quarter-final qualification, be confirmed under the Duckworth/Lewis regulations.

GROUP B

15 April 2000
at Cardiff
Gloucestershire 148 for 6 (25 overs)(MW Alleyne 50)
Glamorgan 150 for 7 (24.4 overs)
Glamorgan (2 pts) won by three wickets
Gold Award: SL Watkin

at Northampton
Northamptonshire v. Worcestershire
No play possible – 1 pt each

at Edgbaston
Somerset 48 for 2 (14 overs)
Warwickshire did not bat
Match abandoned – 1 pt each

The only match completed in this group was a
25-over contest at Cardiff. Gloucestershire's
148 for 6 was reached thanks largely to Mark
Alleyne, the captain, who made 50. Simon Jones'
five overs cost 47; by contrast, Steve Watkin
returned an analysis of 5–2–7–3. A consistent
batting display, headed by Steve James with 34,
saw Glamorgan home by three wickets, and with
just two balls to spare.
   At Edgbaston, Somerset had made 48 for 2 from
14 overs when rain arrived, and at Northampton no
play was possible at all between Northamptonshire
and Worcestershire.

16 April 2000
at Bristol
Warwickshire 94 (35.4 overs)(JMM Averis 4 for 8)
Gloucestershire 96 for 5 (28.1 overs)
Gloucestershire (2 pts) won by five wickets
Gold Award: JMM Averis

at Taunton
Somerset 257 for 7 (50 overs)(PCL Holloway 78, J Cox 59)
Northamptonshire 190 for 3 (40.1 overs)
(DJG Sales 64*, MB Loye 57)
Northamptonshire (2 pts) won by seven wickets
(DL Method: Northamptonshire target 190 from 41 overs)
Gold Award: DJG Sales

at Worcester
Glamorgan 147 (46.4 overs)(Kabir Ali 4 for 29)
Worcestershire 148 for 1 (GA Hick 55*, PR Pollard 54*)
Worcestershire (2 pts) won by nine wickets
Gold Award: Kabir Ali

James Averis, who took 4 for 8, picked up the Gold Award as
Gloucestershire defeated Warwickshire.

Gloucestershire sped to a five-wicket victory against
Warwickshire, dismissing their visitors for just 94 and
then being helped to their target by Allan Donald's
nine wides in seven wicketless overs. Trevor Penney's
25 was the only score of note in Warwickshire's
innings as James Averis (7.4–2–8–4) and Michael
Cawdron (3 for 30) enjoyed themselves. Ed Giddins
took 3 for 22 for Warwickshire but Dominic Hewson
saw Gloucestershire home with an unbeaten 30.
   Northamptonshire were perhaps fortunate to
triumph under the Duckworth/Lewis formula at
Taunton, although they were making good progress
at 183 for 3 from 39.3 overs (in reply to Somerset's
257 for 7) when rain came. A brief resumption later
allowed them to reach 190 for 3, before more rain
left Duckworth/Lewis to confirm the result. David

Sales, with 64 not out from 72 balls, had added 64 with Tony Penberthy (28 not out) when play was called off, and Mal Loye hit 57. For Somerset, Piran Holloway's 78 was the basis of a challenging score, with Jamie Cox (59) and Michael Burns (40) also contributing usefully.

An impressive 4 for 29 by 19-year-old paceman Kabir Ali, on his one-day county debut, was at the heart of Worcestershire's emphatic nine-wicket beating of Glamorgan at New Road. Stuart Lampitt also bowled well, taking 2 for 16 from his ten overs, but only Adrian Dale (49 not out) and Matthew Maynard (31) could make much headway. In contrast, the Worcestershire innings was a breeze, Graeme Hick hitting 55 not out and finishing the match with four successive boundaries off Alex Wharf. Paul Pollard was left unbeaten on 54.

18 April 2000
at Worcester
Gloucestershire 57 for 1 (10 overs)
Worcestershire did not bat
Match abandoned – 1 pt each

Gloucestershire reached 57 for 1 from just ten overs at Worcester before rain intervened. The match between Warwickshire and Northamptonshire at Edgbaston was totally washed out.

19 April 2000
at Taunton
Somerset v. Glamorgan
No play possible – 1 pt each

Somerset and Gloucestershire, denied a West Country championship derby by the split into two divisions, had the consolation of a Benson and Hedges group derby at Taunton washed away by more rain.

20 April 2000
at Northampton
Northamptonshire v. Gloucestershire
No play possible – 1 pt each

Gloucestershire continued their wretched luck with the weather when their match against Northamptonshire was abandoned.

21 April 2000
at Taunton
Somerset v. Worcestershire
No play possible – 1 pt each

Somerset and Worcestershire had to settle for one point apiece as rain ruled out their Taunton meeting.

22 April 2000
at Cardiff
Glamorgan v. Warwickshire
No play possible – 1 pt each

As heavy rain continued to sweep the western side of the country, the scheduled Glamorgan v. Warwickshire match at Cardiff also bit the dust (not that there was any dust at soggy Sophia Gardens!).

24 April 2000
at Bristol
Somerset 225 (49.5 overs)(JMM Averis 4 for 48)
Gloucestershire 154 for 5 (32 overs)
Gloucestershire (2 pts) won by 10 runs (DL Method: When rain stopped play Gloucestershire should have reached 145 from 32 overs)
Gold Award: IJ Harvey

at Northampton
Glamorgan 238 for 8 (50 overs)
Northamptonshire 199 (46 overs)(ML Hayden 67)
Glamorgan (2 pts) won by 39 runs
Gold Award: RDB Croft

at Edgbaston
Worcestershire 91 for 4 (10 overs)
Warwickshire 92 for 3 (9.5 overs)
Warwickshire (2 pts) won by seven wickets
Gold Award: G Welch

The Duckworth/Lewis formula smoothed Gloucestershire's passage into the Benson and Hedges Cup quarter-finals, although they would argue they were making good progress towards Somerset's 225 at Bristol when rain arrived with the home county on 154 for 5 from 32 overs. Matt Windows was still 42 not out, but Ian Harvey had just gone for 35, struck crucially off 29 balls as the bad weather closed in. For unlucky Somerset, Piran Holloway was the anchor with 72 off 97 balls while Ian Blackwell hit 41. James Averis was the most successful Gloucestershire bowler with 4 for 48.

Glamorgan clinched their qualification from this group by overcoming Northamptonshire by 39 runs at Wantage Road. Matthew Maynard's 48 from 55 balls gave the Glamorgan innings vital impetus, and at the end Adrian Dale and Steve James added 73 from the final ten overs. Michael Powell and Robert Croft also contributed to a solid batting effort and only Matthew Hayden (67) looked capable of threatening Glamorgan's final total of 238 for 8.

But the lottery of the qualification round was most apparent at Edgbaston where Worcestershire would have gone into the last eight had their match against Warwickshire been abandoned because of rain. Instead, after five inspections spanning six hours, it was decided that a ten-over match could be played – and Worcestershire lost! Paul Pollard's 20-ball 30 and Elliott Wilson's unbeaten 25 pushed the Worcestershire total to 91 for 4 but Nick Knight and Graeme Welch then added 53 for the Warwickshire first wicket, Knight clobbering 30 from 18 balls, and victory for the home side eventually arrived with one ball to spare. Allan Donald and Glenn McGrath, opposing world-class fast bowlers, were clattered for 46 runs from their combined four overs.

GROUP C

15 April 2000
at Chelmsford
Essex v. Surrey

at Southampton
Hampshire v. Middlesex

at Canterbury
Kent v. Sussex
All three matches, no play possible – 1 pt each

Rain hit this group hard on the opening day, with all three matches – at Canterbury, Chelmsford and Southampton – abandoned without a ball being bowled. In fact, the weather was to make qualification from this group in particular something of a lottery, leading several county officials to demand that the competition be scheduled for later in the season from 2001 onwards.

16 April 2000
at Lord's
Middlesex v. Essex

at the Oval
Surrey v. Kent
Both matches, no play possible – 1 pt each

Matches at Lord's and the Oval, respectively between Middlesex and Essex and Surrey and Kent, became the latest victims of the weather in one of the wettest Aprils on record.

18 April 2000
at Canterbury
Essex 175 for 8 (39 overs)(MA Ealham 4 for 17)
Kent 173 for 5 (39 overs)(MA Ealham 61)
Essex (2 pts) won by 2 runs
Gold Award: MA Ealham

at Hove
Sussex 97 (44 overs)
Surrey 61 for 1 (20 overs)
Surrey (2 pts) won by 35 runs (DL Method: When rain stopped play Surrey should have hit 27 from 20 overs)
Gold Award: IE Bishop

Action finally got under way in this group with wins for Essex and Surrey, putting them at an immediate advantage in the race for quarter-final qualification.

At Canterbury a magnificent all-round performance by Mark Ealham just failed to bring Kent the victory he, for one, deserved. First, Ealham took 4 for 17 as Essex reached 175 for 8 from their 39 overs in a match reduced in duration by rain. Then, after Kent themselves had stuttered, Ealham led the fightback with a powerful 61, aided by Alan Wells' sensible 36. A six off Mark Ilott from the penultimate ball seemed to have clinched Ealham the role of matchwinning hero but, with two runs now required off the last ball, he stepped back to swing to the off side, missed – and was bowled. The Essex innings had followed a similar pattern of early struggle and later freedom, with Danny Law (34) and Stephen Peters (42) providing the acceleration.

At Hove there was misery for Sussex, who were tumbled out for 97 in 44 overs with just two batsmen reaching double figures – and that after moving to 30 without loss after ten overs! Jason Ratcliffe took 3 for 15 from nine overs and Surrey then strolled to 61 for 1 from 20 overs before rain meant their victory had to be confirmed by the Duckworth/Lewis method.

19 April 2000
at Chelmsford
Essex 201 for 9 (50 overs)(RC Irani 50)
Hampshire 202 for 5 (47.3 overs)(AN Aymes 63, RA Smith 56)
Hampshire (2 pts) won by five wickets
Gold Award: AN Aymes

A stand of 120 between Robin Smith and Adrian Aymes swept Hampshire to a fine five-wicket victory over Essex at Chelmsford. Shane Warne, on his first appearance for Hampshire, was smashed over mid-wicket for six by Ronnie Irani (50) and later reverse-swept for four by Stephen Peters (43) as Essex totalled 201 for 9. Warne went wicketless, and conceded 44 runs, from his 10 overs. Aymes (63) and Smith (56), however, made sure Warne ended up on the winning side and mention must also be made of Chelmsford groundsman Stuart Kerrison who somehow managed to spirit up a dry and excellent pitch, which greatly added to the enjoyment of a 3,000-strong crowd.

20 April 2000
at Lord's
Middlesex v. Sussex

at Southampton
Hampshire v. Kent
Both matches, no play possible – 1 pt each

The games between Hampshire and Kent, at Southampton, and between Middlesex and Sussex, at Lord's, were further victims of the bad weather that was decimating the qualifying rounds.

21 April 2000
at Southgate
Middlesex v. Surrey
No play possible – 1 pt each

Middlesex had yet to bowl a ball in the competition, their frustration growing still deeper as the meeting with Essex, at Southgate, was abandoned.

23 April 2000
at Hove
Hampshire 168 for 9 (50 overs)
Sussex 170 for 8 (49.2 overs)
Sussex (2 pts) won by two wickets
Gold Award: MG Bevan

at Canterbury
Kent 204 for 9 (50 overs)
Middlesex 127 (36.2 overs)(J L Langer 66*, MA Ealham 4 for 32)
Kent (2 pts) won by 77 runs
Gold Award: PA Nixon

Glory be! Some cricket, at last, in this group as Michael Bevan expertly steered Sussex past Hampshire's 50-over total of 166 for 9 at Hove. Bevan, fresh from his exhilarating 185 not out for a Rest of the World XI against an Asian XI in the ICC Cricket Week extravaganza in Bangladesh, only hit

three fours in his innings. But his mastery of the match situation, the conditions, and the Hampshire bowlers was a joy to behold as Sussex eventually got home with four balls to spare. From 29 for 5, Sussex were initially rallied by Bevan and Robin Martin-Jenkins (45) in a stand of 97, but it was the Australian's coolness under pressure that finally hauled Sussex up to a match-winning 170 for 8. Peter Hartley, the veteran seamer who recently turned 40, was the Hampshire star: from number ten he struck 32 not out, and then picked up 5 for 20 from his ten overs. Adrian Aymes injured his knee midway through the Sussex innings, and handed the wicketkeeping gloves to Derek Kenway before leaving the field.

24 April
at the Oval
Hampshire 87 for 7 (10 overs)
Surrey 85 for 5 (10 overs)
Hampshire (2 pts) won by 2 runs
Gold Award: SK Warne

Nothing better summed up the farce that, thanks to the appalling weather, the qualifying groups had become than the situation on the final day of this group in which it was mathematically possible for Middlesex to reach the last eight simply by dint of having all five of their matches abandoned. In the end, thanks to the weather relenting, it did not happen – especially as Middlesex were beaten in their one venture out into the middle!

Their conquerors at Canterbury, Kent, were ironically the most unlucky team of a frantic day. With Mark Ealham taking 4 for 32, and James Golding 3 for 20, they overwhelmed Middlesex by 77 runs after battling themselves to 204 for 9 in unsurprisingly unhelpful batting conditions. Only Justin Langer, with 66 not out, prevented a total rout but – later in the early evening – it emerged that Kent's victory was not enough to put them into the final eight. After losing on the last ball to Essex, they had endured three total wash-outs, and so this win was not sufficient to earn them the requisite points to grab one of the two best third-placed spots in the three group tables.

Kent's fate was, in fact, sealed when Hampshire managed to squeeze out Surrey in a ten-over thrash at the Oval. Derek Kenway made 47 from 29 balls in Hampshire's 87 for 7 but Surrey were seemingly cruising at 60 for 3 from six overs when Shane Warne was brought on to bowl. Immediately removing Graham Thorpe to a top-edged sweep,

Warne finished with 2–0–6–2, which, in the context of the match, was decisive. Surrey still required ten from the final over, and could only manage seven. They, however, had already been assured of qualification – so it wasn't just the Hampshire players who were pleased with the outcome.

At Chelmsford, meanwhile, Sussex had breezed into the last eight by outscoring Essex on another fine pitch. Michael Bevan (157 not out) and Chris Adams (122, including four sixes) put on 271 in 41 overs as Sussex reached 316 for 3, and Essex could only reply with 254 for 8. Nasser Hussain made 40, but Will House enjoyed himself by taking 4 for 41 with his underused medium-pacers.

QUARTER-FINALS
9 May 2000

at Cardiff
Glamorgan 182 for 6 (50 overs)(A Dale 63*)
Hampshire 69 (34.2 overs)
Glamorgan won by 113 runs
Gold Award: A Dale

at Old Trafford
Durham 154 (46.5 overs)(SM Katich 62,
CP Schofield 4 for 34)
Lancashire 158 for 7 (45 overs)(NH Fairbrother 57*,
J Wood 4 for 26)
Lancashire won by three wickets
Gold Award: NH Fairbrother

at Hove
Gloucestershire 237 for 7 (50 overs)(IJ Harvey 88)
Sussex 208 for 9 (50 overs)(MG Bevan 71,
JR Carpenter 53*)
Gloucestershire won by 29 runs
Gold Award: IJ Harvey

at Headingley
Surrey 198 for 6 (50 overs)(AJ Stewart 97*,
MJ Hoggard 4 for 39)
Yorkshire 191 (49.5 overs)(MJ Wood 59,
DS Lehmann 50)
Surrey won by 7 runs
Gold Award: AJ Stewart

Surrey, Gloucestershire, Glamorgan and Lancashire won through to the semi-finals of the Benson and Hedges Cup after a day of drama.

A controversial match at Headingley ended with Surrey pipping Yorkshire by just seven runs, umpire Tony Clarkson upsetting the locals by giving Darren

Lehmann out at a crucial stage of the Yorkshire innings. Lehmann had made 50 from 73 balls in a stand of 109 for the fourth wicket with Martyn Wood (59) when Clarkson upheld an appeal for a leg-side catch at the wicket. Wood was then bowled off an inside edge with 33 needed, and Carl Greenidge struck another blow by running out Gary Fellows with a direct hit. Surrey, however, bowled and fielded zealously after Alec Stewart had defied the Yorkshire pace attack, in helpful conditions, with a magnificent 97 not out. Matthew Hoggard took 4 for 39 but Ben Hollioake accelerated Surrey to a defendable 198 for 6 with a hard-hitting 44.

Hampshire were humbled at Cardiff, being bowled out for only 69 on a pitch rendered almost grassless as a result of a marquee being erected over the entire square during the previous autumn's Rugby World Cup. Robin Smith, the Hampshire captain, said 'I'm very disappointed and almost speechless' after watching Owen Parkin, Steve Watkin and Adrian Dale rip through his side's

Darren Lehmann was the victim of a controversial umpiring decision as Yorkshire lost to Surrey.

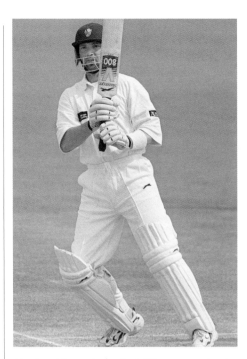

Matthew Maynard scored a brilliant century but it was not enough to deny Gloucestershire their hat-trick of victories in Lord's finals.

SEMI-FINALS
27, 28 and 29 May 2000

at Cardiff
Glamorgan 251 (49.1 overs)(MP Maynard 109, MJ Powell 67)
Surrey 212 (43 overs)(AJ Stewart 83, OT Parkin 4 for 60)
Glamorgan won by 32 runs
(DL Method: Surrey target 245 from 46 overs)
Gold Award: MP Maynard

at Bristol
Gloucestershire 220 for 6 (50 overs)(RJ Cunliffe 71)
Lancashire 205 for 9 (50 overs)(NH Fairbrother 74, AM Smith 4 for 27)
Gloucestershire won by 115 runs
Gold Award: RJ Cunliff

Big-name counties Surrey and Lancashire took a heavy fall in the Benson and Hedges Cup semi-finals over the bank holiday weekend, providing further fuel for those who believe the dividing up of first-class counties in both championship and one-day cricket to be a confusing, if not dangerous, nonsense.

The victors, at Cardiff and Bristol, were home teams Glamorgan and Gloucestershire, both of whom play in the championship's second division; Glamorgan play Division Two National League cricket as well.

The Welsh county made it through to the Lord's final first, reaching 99 for 2 on the rain-affected Saturday and then on Sunday seeing their third-wicket pair, Matthew Maynard (109 from 115 balls) and Michael Powell (67), boost their stand to 133 in 27 overs. Glamorgan's final total of 251 always looked to be too much for Surrey, despite Alec Stewart's fighting 85 from 111 balls, and one vital moment was the brilliant catch taken by Matthew Elliott to get rid of Alistair Brown for nought. Surrey were finally bowled out for 212 and Glamorgan could celebrate reaching their first knock-out final for 23 years.

After a rained-off Sunday, there was a good crowd at Bristol on bank holiday Monday to see Gloucestershire see off Lancashire by 15 runs. Both counties were without their overseas players – Ian Harvey injured and Saurav Ganguly away playing in the Asia Cup – but any theories that Lancashire, with all their international stars, would suffer less from the absences than Gloucestershire were soon laid to rest. Gloucestershire's 50-over total of 220 for 6 was a solid affair, Rob Cunliffe top-scoring with 71 from 114 balls, but other significant contributions came from Tim Hancock, Matt Windows and Mark Alleyne. In

batting line-up. Earlier Glamorgan had totalled 182 for 6 with Dale remaining unbeaten on 63 and Keith Newell scoring an invaluable 49.

John Wood had Lancashire reeling at 35 for 5, in reply to Durham's 154 at Old Trafford, before Neil Fairbrother steered his side out of the choppy waters. Fairbrother, joined by Warren Hegg (36) in a stand of 73 in 18 overs, finished 57 not out as Lancashire battled their way to victory by three wickets. For Durham, Simon Katich (62) and Martin Speight (36) added 87 for the second wicket before Chris Schofield (4 for 34) and Peter Martin, with 2 for 16 from his ten overs, reasserted control.

Gloucestershire withstood another fine one-day innings from Michael Bevan to march into the last four at Hove, their winning margin of 29 runs in no small measure due to a superb all-round performance by Bevan's compatriot Ian Harvey. The Australian first hit 88 from just 70 balls to push Gloucestershire's total up to 237 for 7. Mark Alleyne made 42 and Robin Martin-Jenkins included five maidens in his ten-over spell of 2 for 24. Harvey then stepped in with 3 for 28 from his ten overs as Bevan and James Carpenter (53 not out) did their best to take the game away from the visitors. Bevan's one-day run tally for the season stood at 404 from five innings after this match.

reply, Lancashire make a tentative start, sliding to 19 for 3 against a new ball wielded effectively by Mike Smith and Jon Lewis, and Mike Atherton laboured through 79 balls for 27 as he tried to redress the balance. In the end, however, even Neil Fairbrother's total of 74 from 102 deliveries could not rescue Lancashire's innings and left-arm seamer Smith, perhaps the most underrated cricketer in England, took most of the honours with figures of 4 for 27.

BENSON AND HEDGES CUP FINAL
10 June 2000

at Lord's
Glamorgan 225 for 10 (49.3 overs)(MP Maynard 104)
Gloucestershire 226 for 3 (46.5 overs)
(THC Hancock 60)
Gloucestershire won by seven wickets
Gold Award: MP Maynard

Matthew Maynard won the Man of the Match award for his classy 104 from 118 balls, but otherwise there was little cheer for Glamorgan on their first Lord's cup final day out for 23 years.

Gloucestershire, with the ruthless efficiency that is fast becoming familiar, won their third domestic one-day trophy inside 11 months. Teamwork, once again, was the key to their seven-wicket triumph, but Australian Ian Harvey's 5 for 34 left him unlucky not to pick up the individual award instead of Maynard.

Harvey included both Glamorgan openers in his haul, and the Welsh county's total of 225 was perhaps 20 short of a par figure on a true pitch and on one of the hottest days of a so-far miserable summer. Maynard did his very best but Michael Powell was a little too one-paced in the 48 from 97 balls that he contributed to the stand of 137 the pair added in 30 overs.

Kim Barnett, in his entertaining and unorthodox way, made sure Gloucestershire were quickly out of the blocks and, when 21, the veteran former Derbyshire captain overtook Mike Gatting to go into second place in the list of Benson and Hedges Cup run-scorers with 2,940. The leader? Well, Graham Gooch will take some catching on 5,176!

Tim Hancock, an unsung cog in the well-oiled Gloucestershire one-day wheel, scored a composed 60 and Rob Cunliffe also batted well on Barnett's eventual dismissal for a 42-ball 39. At 131 for 3, though, Gloucestershire still had much to do – which makes the 95-run unbroken fourth wicket partnership between skipper Mark Alleyne and the combative Matt Windows even better than it looks on paper.

Windows finished with 53 not out from 59 balls while Alleyne's unbeaten 40 took him 56 deliveries.

Victory was sealed with 19 balls to spare – the image of Jack Russell amid Gloucestershire's Lord's balcony celebrations is an enduring one. Benson and Hedges afterwards confirmed a two-year extension to its sponsorship of the competition (up to the end of the 2002 season), which is worth an extra £1.85 million to English cricket. It was a pity then, for the sponsors as much as anyone, that the exorbitant ticket prices charged for this cup final (£45 for an average seat, and no concessions for juniors) were a significant factor in the low crowd of only 20,000.

There were more Welsh fans than West Country ones, clearly because for many Glamorgan supporters it was new (if expensive) experience – whereas their Gloucestershire counterparts had already coughed up for two Lord's visits in 1999. Why no family tickets on offer? Why no realistic ticket pricing? If the atmosphere was a touch muted, then the ECB have to shoulder their share of the blame – and be a little more imaginative next time!

An unprecedented achievement: Gloucestershire celebrate their fourth successive one-day trophy on the balcony at Lord's.

NATWEST TROPHY

FIRST ROUND
2 May 2000

at Chester Boughton Hall
Cheshire 204 (50 overs)(I Cockbain 65)
Lincolnshire 204 for 9 (50 overs)(SG Plumb 48)
Lincolnshire won by losing fewer wickets
Man of the Match: RJ Chapman (Lincolnshire)

at Truro
Cornwall 170 for 6 (50 overs)(SC Pope 56)
Norfolk 171 for 6 (47.5 overs)(CJ Rogers 83*)
Norfolk won by four wickets
Man of the Match: CJ Rogers

at Gateshead Fell
Leicestershire Cricket Board XI 192 for 9 (50 overs)
(A Wright 112)
Durham Cricket Board XI 195 for 7 (49.5 overs)
(S Chapman 64, I Pattison 48*)
Durham Cricket Board won by three wickets
Man of the Match: A Wright

at Cheltenham
Nottinghamshire Cricket Board XI 125 for 9
(50 overs)
Gloucestershire Cricket Board XI 126 for 2
(28.5 overs)(Imraan Mohammed 53)
Gloucestershire Cricket Board XI won by eight wickets
Man of the Match: Imraan Mohammed

at Cove
Huntingdonshire 148 for 8 (50 overs)
Hampshire Cricket Board XI 120 (46 overs)
Huntingdonshire won by 28 runs
Man of the Match: B Young (Huntingdonshire)

at Colwall
Sussex Cricket Board XI
215 for 7 (50 overs) (K Ibrahim 63)
Herefordshire 209 for 9 (50 overs)
Sussex Cricket Board XI won by 6 runs
*Man of the Match: K Ibrahim (Sussex Cricket
Board XI)*

at Welwyn Garden City
Hertfordshire 114 (47.1 overs)
Cambridgeshire 115 for 6 (46 overs)(SA Kellett 42)
Cambridgeshire won by four wickets
Man of the Match: MJG Mason (Cambridgeshire)

at Clontarf
Ireland 140 (44.3 overs)(AR Dunlop 56,
AB Bryam 4 for 24)
Shropshire 141 for 5 (49 overs)(T Parton 51*)
Shropshire won by five wickets
Man of the Match: AB Bryam

at Northampton
Northamptonshire 173 for 8 (50 overs)(RE Falkner 46,
AJ Swann 40)
Northumberland 175 for 4 (48.2 overs)(AT Heather 79,
B Parker 50)
Northumberland won by six wickets
Man of the Match: AT Heather

at Walsall
Somerset Cricket Board XI 124 (45.4 overs)
Staffordshire 127 for 3 (29 overs)
Staffordshire won by seven wickets
Man of the Match: L Potter

at Mildenhall
Suffolk 145 (49.4 overs)(S Dearden 4 for 31)
Lancashire Cricket Board XI 146 for 6 (38.2 overs)
Lancashire Cricket Board XI won by four wickets
Man of the Match: S Dearden

at Pontarddulais
Wales Minor Counties 212 for 6 (50 overs)
(PV Simmons 82)
Buckinghamshire 201 for 9 (50 overs)
(KLT Arthurton 48, KJ Locke 41)
Wales Minor Counties won by 11 runs
Man of the Match: PV Simmons

at Bemerton, Salisbury
Scotland 93 (29.5 overs)
Wiltshire 94 for 3 (31.1 overs)
Wiltshire won by seven wickets
Man of the Match: JL Taylor (Wiltshire)

at Kidderminster
Kent Cricket Board XI 239 for 9 (50 overs)
(JDP Bowden 98)
Worcestershire Cricket Board XI 189 (44.2 overs)
(DJ Pipe 56, GR Hill 40)
Kent Cricket Board XI won by 50 runs
Man of the Match: JDP Bowden

SECOND ROUND
16 May 2000

at March
Cambridgeshire 123 (45.1 overs)(NT Gadsby 42, DB Pennett 4 for 20)
Cumberland 126 for 1 (32.2 overs)(AA Metcalfe 51*, ST Knox 40*)
Cumberland won by nine wickets
Man of the Match: MA Sharp (Cumberland)

at Heanor
Derbyshire Cricket Board XI 222 for 8 (50 overs) (AJ Marsh 53)
Gloucestershire Cricket Board XI 172 (43.3 overs) (CRJ Budd 52, AN Bressington 44)
Derbyshire Cricket Board XI won by 50 runs
Man of the Match: AJ Marsh

at Torquay
Devon 238 (49.5 overs)(RI Dawson 61, AJ Pugh 41, L Potter 4 for 9)
Staffordshire 46 (20.5 overs)(MC Theedom 5 for 18)
Devon won by 192 runs
Man of the Match: MC Theedom

at Bournemouth
Dorset 181 for 8 (50 overs)
Norfolk 71 (33.2 overs)(VJ Pike 5 for 10)
Dorset won by 110 runs
Man of the Match: VJ Pike

at Hartlepool
Denmark 218 (50 overs)(A Ahmed 94)
Durham Cricket Board XI 223 for 5 (38.3 overs) (MJ North 69*, SJ Chapman 60)
Durham Cricket Board XI won by five wickets
Man of the Match: MJ North

at Chelmsford
Essex Cricket Board XI 266 (50 overs)(GR Napier 79, A Hibbert 59)
Lancashire Cricket Board XI 251 for 9 (50 overs) (N Bannister 62, SE Dearden 44)
Essex Cricket Board XI won by 15 runs
Man of the Match: GR Napier

at Godmanchester
Huntingdonshire 204 for 8 (50 overs)(VP Winn 50)
Yorkshire Cricket Board XI 207 for 5 (45 overs) (M Doidge 54*, E McKenna 43)
Yorkshire Cricket Board XI won by five wickets
Man of the Match: M Doidge

at Grantham
Lincolnshire 210 for 8 (50 overs)(PC Trend 52, RP Lefebvre 4 for 37)
Holland 115 (37.2 overs)(SG Plumb 4 for 16)
Lincolnshire won by 95 runs
Man of the Match: PC Trend

at Southgate
Middlesex Cricket Board XI 203 for 8 (50 overs) (RK Rao 49)
Wiltshire 200 for 9 (50 overs)(JL Taylor 49, RJ Rowe 47)
Middlesex Cricket Board XI won by 3 runs
Man of the Match: AGJ Fraser (Middlesex Cricket Board XI)

at Jesmond
Bedfordshire 164 (48 overs)(JR Page 61)
Northumberland 167 for 3 (33.2 overs)(W Falla 64)
Northumberland won by seven wickets
Man of the Match: SJ Foster (Northumberland)

at Shifnal
Surrey Cricket Board 233 for 9 (50 overs) (Z de Bruyn 43)
Shropshire 239 for 4 (49.2 overs)(JBR Jones 76, JV Anders 51)
Shropshire won by six wickets
Man of the Match: JBR Jones

at Hastings
Sussex Cricket Board XI 206 (49.4 overs) (GRA Campbell 59, K Ibrahim 57)
Berkshire 207 for 5 (47.2 overs)(LH Nurse 81, SS Patel 53*)
Berkshire won by five wickets
Man of the Match: LH Nurse (Berkshire)

at Cardiff
Oxfordshire 120 (49.1 overs)
Wales Minor Counties 122 for 2 (35.3 overs) (AJ Jones 43*)
Wales Minor Counties won by eight wickets
Man of the Match: AJ Jones

at Stratford-upon-Avon
Kent Cricket Board XI 208 for 8 (50 overs)
Warwickshire Cricket Board XI 163 (47.3 overs)
Kent Cricket Board XI won by 45 runs
Man of the Match: SL Williams (Kent Cricket Board XI)

THIRD ROUND
21 June 2000

at Finchampstead
Durham 140 (49.4 overs)(SM Katich 40,
JE Emburey 4 for 13)
Berkshire 97 (28.5 overs)(MM Betts 4 for 34)
Durham won by 43 runs
Man of the Match: JE Emburey

at Carlisle
Cumberland 140 (48.1 overs)(JM Lewis 65,
K Adams 6 for 24)
Kent 141 for 4 (39 overs)(R Dravid 54)
Kent won by six wickets
Man of the Match: K Adams

at Derby
Derbyshire 356 for 2 (50 overs)(MJ di Venuto 173*,
DG Cork 93, LD Sutton 45)
Derbyshire Cricket Board XI 133 for 9 (50 overs)
(IJ Darlington 58)
Derbyshire won by 223 runs
Man of the Match: MJ di Venuto

at Exmouth
Devon 194 for 6 (50 overs)(DF Lye 56, MJ Wood 43)
Surrey 198 for 2 (44 overs)(AJ Stewart 70*, AD Brown
59, GP Thorpe 46*)
Surrey won by eight wickets
Man of the Match: DF Lye

at Bournemouth
Glamorgan 333 for 4 (50 overs)(MTG Elliott 156,
K Newell 129)
Dorset 194 (48.5 overs)(MG Miller 81, VJ Pike 45,
SD Thomas 4 for 27)
Glamorgan won by 139 runs
Man of the Match: MTG Elliott

at Chester-le-Street
Durham Cricket Board XI 167 (49.5 overs)
Northamptonshire 169 for 2 (32.2 overs)
(ML Hayden 77*)
Northamptonshire won by eight wickets
Man of the Match: ML Hayden

at Billericay
Warwickshire 214 for 8 (50 overs)(TL Penney 45*,
G Welch 41)
Essex Cricket Board XI 203 for 8 (50 overs)(N Carlier 56)
Warwickshire won by 11 runs
Man of the Match: TL Penney

at Canterbury
Kent Cricket Board XI 149 (50 overs)(SL Williams 45*,
SK Warne 4 for 34)
Hampshire 150 for 2 (36.5 overs)(AD Mascarenhas 67*,
JP Stephenson 40)
Hampshire won by eight wickets
Man of the Match: AD Mascarenhas

at Cleethorpes
Lincolnshire 190 for 9 (50 overs)(RWJ Howitt 52)
Lancashire 193 for 0 (30 overs)(SC Ganguly 120*,
MA Atherton 52*)
Lancashire won by ten wickets
Man of the Match: SC Ganguly

at Lord's
Middlesex 274 for 5 (50 overs)(JL Langer 100,
AJ Strauss 56, OA Shah 49)
Nottinghamshire 146 (37 overs)(AW Laraman 4 for 39)
Middlesex won by 128 runs
Man of the Match: JL Langer

at Southgate
Middlesex Cricket Board XI 153 (50 overs)
(BV Taylor 4 for 26)
Sussex 154 for 1 (27.1 overs)(RR Montgomerie 68*,
CJ Adams 64)
Sussex won by nine wickets
Man of the Match: BV Taylor

at Jesmond
Leicestershire 328 for 9 (50 overs)(DI Stevens 133,
VJ Wells 60, SJ Foster 6 for 52)
Northumberland 102 (33.3 overs)(A Kumble 5 for 27)
Leicestershire won by 226 runs
Man of the Match: DI Stevens

at Telford
Somerset 262 for 6 (50 overs)(ME Trescothick 87)
Shropshire 235 for 9 (50 overs)(JT Ralph 102,
JV Anders 43)
Somerset won by 27 runs
Man of the Match: JT Ralph

at Swansea
Essex 154 (48.1 overs)(SD Peters 58, RC Irani 45)
Wales Minor Counties 51 (21 overs)
Essex won by 103 runs
Man of the Match: SD Peters

at Harrogate
Yorkshire 240 for 5 (50 overs)(MP Vaughan 70, DS
Lehmann 48*, RJ Blakey 41)

Yorkshire Cricket Board XI 110 (38.5 overs)
(D Gough 5 for 30)
Yorkshire won by 130 runs
Man of the Match: MP Vaughan

There were no upsets in cricket's equivalent of the FA Cup first-round day, although Warwickshire just managed to hold off the Essex Cricket Board side by 11 runs at Billericay, and John Emburey, now nearly 48, took 4 for 13 from 9.4 overs for Berkshire against Durham, who were bowled out for 140 but still won.

James Ralph, a 24-year-old batsman, earned the Man of the Match award at Telford for hitting 102 not out off just 81 balls for Shropshire against Somerset, including three sixes and 11 fours. But Shropshire, finishing on 235 for 9 from their 50 overs were nevertheless beaten by 27 runs.

In one of the two matches played between first-class counties, Worcestershire beat Gloucestershire by three wickets with Ryan Driver's unbeaten 61, and a stand of 89 with David Leatherdale (53) rallying the home side after a slump to 68 for 4 in reply to Gloucestershire's 211 for 8. It was only a week or so later that this match was ordered to be replayed because it was discovered that Kabir Ali, the young Worcestershire fast bowler, had already played in the competition for the Worcestershire Board and was therefore ineligible.

The other 'all first-class' encounter was at Lord's, where Middlesex beat Nottinghamshire largely due to a fine hundred from Justin Langer, the Australian left-hander.

Two counties played against their own county board XI, Darren Gough taking 5 for 30 to dispatch the Yorkshire Cricket Board at Harrogate, and Michael di Venuto smashing a merciless 173 not out off 152 balls to lead home Derbyshire in the derby against the Derbyshire Cricket Board at Derby!

There were hundreds too for Keith Newell and Matthew Elliott, who put together an opening partnership of 246 for Glamorgan against Dorset, Lancashire's Saurav Ganguly (120 not out from 98 balls against Lincolnshire) and Darren Stevens, whose 133 spearheaded Leicestershire's crushing 226-run win against Northumberland.

Elsewhere, left-arm seamer Kristian Adams took 6 for 24 as Kent made short work of Cumberland, Alec Stewart's unbeaten 70 helped Surrey cruise past Devon's 194 for 6 at Exmouth, Matthew Hayden hit 77 not out as Northamptonshire saw off the Durham Cricket Board, and Shane Warne's wizardry (4 for 34) predictably proved too potent for the Kent amateurs.

Wales gave Essex a scare, reducing them to 15 for 4 at Swansea before Ronnie Irani and Stephen Peters rallied the county side to 154 all out. Irani and Mark Ilott then got to work with the new ball and Wales were soon dismissed for just 51.

4 July 2000

Replayed match – Worcestershire had fielded an ineligible player in the original fixture played at Worcester on 21 June.

Gloucestershire 163 (49.3 overs)(GD McGrath 4 for 23)
Worcestershire 158 (49.3 overs)(PR Pollard 55,
SJ Rhodes 43, JMM Averis 4 for 36)
Gloucestershire won by 5 runs
Man of the Match: MCJ Ball (Gloucestershire)

Worcestershire were left to regret the selection of Kabir Ali against Gloucestershire.

There was a thrilling climax to this controversial, replayed third-round tie, with Worcestershire losing by just five runs to a Gloucestershire side they had beaten in the original match. Ordered by the ECB to restage the game, due to the presence in the original tie of Kabir Ali, who had already played in the competition for the Worcestershire Board, Worcestershire looked like repeating the scoreline after Glenn McGrath's 4 for 23 had helped to restrict Gloucestershire to 163 all out. But the Benson and Hedges Cup and NatWest Trophy holders are a tough one-day nut to crack twice in succession, and slowly but surely Gloucestershire's bowlers began to exert pressure on a pitch that made stroke-play difficult. Paul Pollard made 55, but Ian Harvey added figures of 1 for 15 from ten overs to his earlier 32, and with James Averis taking 4 for 36 it all came down to Worcestershire needing six runs from the final two overs – but with their final-wicket pair at the crease. Last man McGrath played out a maiden to increase the tension but then Steve Rhodes, who had battled his way to 43, was bowled by off-spinner Martyn Ball after failing to score from the first two deliveries of the final over. Bill Athey, the Worcestershire coach, overcame his natural feelings of disappointment (and, probably, even resentment) by walking down the pavilion steps to shake the hand of each Gloucestershire player as they left the field of play.

FOURTH ROUND
5 July 2000

at Chester-le-Street
Durham 91 (42.4 overs)
Hampshire 92 for 5 (24.3 overs)
Hampshire won by five wickets
Man of the Match: JP Stephenson (Hampshire)

at Old Trafford
Lancashire 251 for 5 (50 overs)(SC Ganguly 97, MA Atherton 70, A Flintoff 43)
Essex 183 (42.3 overs)(DR Law 45, CP Schofield 4 for 34)
Lancashire won by 68 runs
Man of the Match: SC Ganguly

at Leicester
Gloucestershire 210 for 8 (50 overs)(KJ Barnett 86, CG Taylor 41)
Leicestershire 200 (48.1 overs)(DL Maddy 72, DI Stevens 55, IJ Harvey 4 for 40)
Gloucestershire won by 10 runs
Man of the Match: KJ Barnett

at Northampton
Northamptonshire 252 (50 overs)(DJG Sales 65, ML Hayden 63, D Gough 4 for 36)
Yorkshire 183 (43.5 overs)(A McGrath 64)
Northamptonshire won by 69 runs
Man of the Match: MR Strong (Northamptonshire)

at Edgbaston
Warwickshire 257 for 8 (50 overs)(AF Giles 107)
Derbyshire 217 (46.5 overs)(MJ di Venuto 84, AA Donald 4 for 42)
Warwickshire won by 40 runs
Man of the Match: AF Giles

5 and 6 July 2000

at Canterbury
Kent 121 (48.4 overs)
Glamorgan 122 for 5 (37.1 overs)(K Newell 62*, MA Ealham 4 for 36)
Glamorgan won by five wickets
Man of the Match: K Newell

at Southgate
Middlesex 223 for 4 (50 overs)(PN Weekes 71*, MR Ramprakash 42)
Somerset 58 (28.3 overs)(TF Bloomfield 4 for 17)
Middlesex won by 165 runs
Man of the Match: TF Bloomfield (Middlesex)

at the Oval
Sussex 192 for 9 (50 overs)(MG Bevan 60, RR Montgomerie 53)
Surrey 196 for 3 (47.4 overs)(MA Butcher 87*)
Surrey won by seven wickets
Man of the Match: MA Butcher

Gloucestershire, winners of the controversial replayed third-round tie against Worcestershire the day before, made it a golden 48 hours by seeing off Leicestershire by 10 runs in a remarkable finish at Grace Road.

All the qualities that have made Gloucestershire into such an effective one-day unit were on display as they tenaciously defended a score of 210 for 8 from their 50 overs. That total, about par on a slow pitch, was mainly the work of Kim Barnett, who repeatedly engaged his favourite smear through the off side on his way to 86, and a perky 41 from 39 balls by Chris Taylor.

After an uncertain start, Leicestershire rallied through a stand of 55 between Darren Stevens and Darren Maddy. When Stevens (55) flicked Martyn

Nick Speak upset the Durham fans with a poor decision to bat first under bad weather conditions, which left Durham defeated by five wickets.

Derbyshire bowlers for 107, after being promoted to number three, and then taking two wickets and a brilliant catch to send back Dominic Cork as the visitors could muster only 217 in reply to Warwickshire's 257 for 8.

A near full-strength Yorkshire side went down surprisingly meekly to Northamptonshire at Wantage Road, only Darren Gough and Gavin Hamilton making an impact with the ball as Northants ran up 252, thanks to powerful half-centuries from Matthew Hayden and David Sales. But the real surprise packet, as Yorkshire replied by sliding to 183 all out, was 26-year-old seamer Michael Strong who took three key wickets in just 20 deliveries with the new ball in what was only his fifth one-day match for the county since transferring from Sussex.

Nick Speak's decision to bat first in damp conditions, and under a heavy cloud at Chester-le-Street, left the Durham faithful speechless. That emotion became anger when they watched the home side subside to 91 all out and defeat by five wickets to Hampshire. Speak himself battled bravely to remain unbeaten on 15 in Durham's innings – but that made little difference to the match, or to the mood of the county's followers.

Saurav Ganguly and Michael Atherton shared their second NatWest Trophy partnership of more than 150 as Lancashire overwhelmed Essex at Old Trafford by 68 runs. Ganguly hit four sixes and six fours in his 97, while Atherton made 70 and Andy Flintoff a 29-ball 43 as Lancashire piled up 251 for 5. In reply, Essex were never in the hunt and leg-spinner Chris Schofield cashed in with 4 for 34.

Three matches went to a second day because of rain. At Canterbury a collapse to 121 all out on a seamer-friendly pitch condemned Kent to an eventual five-wicket defeat, despite a superb spell on the second morning from Mark Ealham who took 4 for 15 in six overs. Keith Newell's steady 62 not out, however, saw the Welsh county home.

Extraordinary events occurred at Southgate, where Somerset crumbled on the second day to 58 all out, their lowest score in the competition, and thus to a record 165-run defeat. Middlesex had totalled 223 for 4 from their 50 overs the previous day, a score in which Paul Weekes made a valuable 71 not out. There was no reason for Somerset's collapse, other than that the ball swung late for Tim Bloomfield (4 for 17) and Angus Fraser. Perhaps the Somerset batsmen were guilty of going for their shots too early; whatever, Aaron Laraman enjoyed his mopping-up exercise and Middlesex were through.

Ball's off-spin to mid-wicket Maddy responded to the extra responsibility and featured next in a partnership of 53 for the sixth wicket with Chris Lewis.

But, when Maddy went for 72 to a low catch at mid-wicket, it was the start of a collapse that saw the home side, needing 20 at the time from five overs, lose their last five wickets for nine runs in just 18 balls. Taylor held a steepler from Anil Kumble and the catch that sealed the match came from Ball, diving in the gully to dismiss Lewis.

At Edgbaston, Ashley Giles restated his claims for further England recognition by hitting the

At The Oval only two overs had been possible on the first scheduled day. Now, Sussex let things slip after reaching 143 for 2 in the 38th over and, with Adam Hollioake their main tormentor, struggled to 192 for 9 before the overs ran out. In reply, Surrey were anchored by Mark Butcher who went serenely to 87 not out from 146 balls and guided his side to a comfortable seven-wicket victory.

QUARTER-FINALS
25 July 2000

at Lord's
Middlesex 127 (44 overs)(AD Mascarenhas 4 for 25)
Hampshire 128 for 3 (34.5 overs)
Hampshire won by seven wickets
Man of the Match: AD Mascarenhas

at Edgbaston
Warwickshire 273 for 7 (50 overs)(NV Knight 118, DP Ostler 63, TL Penney 42)
Glamorgan 192 (44.4 overs)
Warwickshire won by 81 runs
Man of the Match: NV Knight

26 July 2000

at Bristol
Gloucestershire 280 for 8 (50 overs)(THC Hancock 110, KJ Barnett 51)
Northamptonshire 218 for 9 (50 overs)
(AL Penberthy 54, JW Cook 48, IJ Harvey 4 for 37)
Gloucestershire won by 62 runs
Man of the Match: THC Hancock

at The Oval
Surrey 210 for 7 (50 overs)(GP Thorpe 55, AJ Stewart 49, CP Schofield 4 for 41)
Lancashire 214 for 2 (36 overs)(A Flintoff 135*, SC Ganguly 51)
Lancashire won by eight wickets
Man of the Match: A Flintoff (Lancashire)

Nick Knight's superb 118, from 143 balls, provided the highlight of the two games played on 25 July. His innings took Warwickshire out of sight against Glamorgan at Edgbaston, a 50-over total of 273 for 7 being built on a second-wicket partnership worth 123 in 25 overs between Knight and Dominic Ostler (63 off 78 balls). Trevor Penney improvised effectively towards the end, hitting 42, and then Allan Donald's 3 for 29 undermined the Glamorgan reply, which eventually struggled on to 192.

At Lord's a pitch quite out of keeping with the demands of a domestic cup quarter-final condemned Middlesex to a heavy defeat against Hampshire, who cruised to a seven-wicket success after bowling out the home side for just 127. Dimitri Mascarenhas made the most of the seaming conditions to take 4 for 25 with the new ball, his best return in the competition, earning him the Man of the Match award. Shane Warne, promoted up to number three, hit 20 off 19 balls to enliven proceedings but, just after 4:30 p.m., it was all over. Mick Hunt, the MCC groundsman, was hampered, however, by the relaying work being done on part of the square – which was why the same strip used for the Lord's Test between England and the West Indies was called upon again. Could this tie have been played at Southgate, though?

The second two quarter-final games, played on 26 July, were a triumph for holders Gloucestershire – and for Lancashire's Andrew Flintoff. A century by Tim Hancock, his first limited-overs ton, in his 156th match, led the way for Gloucestershire at Bristol as Northamptonshire were steamrollered by 62 runs. Hancock, with 110 from 131 balls, added 121 in 22 overs for the second wicket with Kim Barnett (51 from 63 deliveries), and an eventual total of 280 for 8 was truly forbidding. Northants, despite a stand of 66 in 14 overs between Jeff Cook (48) and Mal Loye, never looked like mounting a serious challenge. Tony Penberthy's gallant 54 was mere defiance as Ian Harvey (4 for 37) again underlined his one-day bowling prowess.

It was at The Oval, however, where the headlines of the day were made. Flintoff, criticised in the national media for being overweight as he struggles to make an impact at international level, crushed Surrey's hopes with an awesomely powerful 135 not out. The big all-rounder needed only 110 balls for those runs, hitting clean and straight for the most part and striking four sixes and 19 fours in a brutal exhibition. Flintoff was joined in a second-wicket partnership of 190 by Saurav Ganguly, with the Indian captain, no slouch himself, content to sit back and play a supporting role with 51. All this, too, after Surrey had totalled 210 for 7, with Alec Stewart scoring 49 and Graham Thorpe 55, and after Mike Atherton had lost his off-stump to Alex Tudor in the first over of Lancashire's reply. Surrey, however, might not have lost by such a devastating margin of eight wickets if Flintoff, on 67, had not survived a leg before appeal by Ian Salisbury when a vicious googly had struck him on the back pad and seemingly right in front of his stumps.

SEMI-FINALS
12 and 14 August 2000

at Edgbaston
Warwickshire 262 for 4 (50 overs)(NV Knight 100, A Singh 85)
Hampshire 243 for 7 (50 overs)(RA Smith 61, JS Laney 43)
Warwickshire won by 19 runs
Man of the Match: NV Knight

at Bristol
Gloucestershire 248 for 7 (50 overs)(KJ Barnett 80, RC Russell 55)
Lancashire 150 (45.2 overs)(JP Crawley 41)
Gloucestershire won by 98 runs
Man of the Match: MW Alleyne (Gloucestershire)

Gloucestershire remained on course for an unprecedented fourth successive domestic cup success by proving to Lancashire that lightning really can strike twice. After beating them at Bristol in the Benson and Hedges Cup semi-final back at the end of May, Gloucestershire repeated the dose, at the same venue, when the second NatWest Trophy semi-final finally got under way 24 hours late due to rain. By the time Gloucestershire were underlining their supremacy as the new one-day kings of English cricket, of course, they already knew that their opponents in the final at Lord's would be Warwickshire. At Edgbaston, Neil Smith's team saw off the challenge of a Hampshire side badly missing the inspiration of Shane Warne.

Warwickshire totalled 262 for 4 from their 50 overs on a rare, sun-baked day, with openers Nick Knight and Anurag Singh providing the bulk of those runs with a magnificent stand of 185. The elegant Singh, at last fulfilling the promise of his youth on the big stage, stroked 85 while Knight's 100 off 128 balls confirmed that there are few better limited-overs openers in the game. In reply, Hampshire captain Robin Smith promoted himself to open in the belief that he, in the enforced absence of Warne, could fire his side to greater heights. It almost worked. Smith, who seven years previously had mauled Australia's attack for 167 in a one-day international on the same ground, reached 61 from 67 balls before his dismissal in the 23rd over. Jason Laney (43) and Will Kendall tried manfully to resuscitate Hampshire with a 53-run stand in 11 overs, but then Michael Powell ran out Kendall with a direct hit before, moments later, pulling off a stunning catch to get rid of Laney. Adrian Aymes' 33 not out took Hampshire to 243 for

7, but in the end Warne's constant phone calls of encouragement from his home in Melbourne (he was in Australia taking part in the indoor series against South Africa) proved to be in vain.

In the 1990s Lancashire were the undoubted domestic rulers of one-day cricket, winning eight titles. No more. A joyous Bristol crowd gloried in Lancashire's 98-run thrashing as Mark Alleyne's Gloucestershire displayed more desire, superior mobility in the field, more discipline in their bowling, and a better tactical awareness. Lancashire made a rapid exit from the ground afterwards, with several players even skipping the presentation ceremony, and their sour attitude could not have been helped by the knowledge that they had been outplayed despite having the better of the bowling conditions, and that Gloucestershire had been without absent Australian all-rounder Ian Harvey. Predictably put in, Gloucestershire's openers Tim Hancock and Kim Barnett capitalised on some ill-directed new ball bowling, and some shaky fielding, to give their side a solid start. Barnett (80) and Jack Russell, with a typically urgent 55 from 69 balls, then added 125 for the second wicket, and the veterans with a combined age of 76 drove their opponents to distraction with their fidgety, unorthodox but highly effective batting techniques. When skipper Alleyne strode in to thrash an unbeaten 36, from 27 balls, Gloucestershire's total had been pushed up to 248 for 7, and quick wickets with the new ball from Mike Smith and Jon Lewis confirmed Gloucestershire's ascendancy. Smith's opening burst brought him figures of 5–3–9–1, and later he returned with equal success to finish with 2 for 18 from his ten overs. Brilliant fielding backed up Gloucestershire's bowlers and, although John Crawley hit 41 from 56 deliveries, Lancashire were soon down and out. Alleyne, defying a long-term back complaint, took 1 for 20 from a 10-over spell in the middle of the innings and Lancashire, squeezed remorselessly, were finally all out for 150.

NATWEST TROPHY FINAL
26 (no play) and 27 August 2000

A Duckworth/Lewis calculation brought Gloucestershire an historic triumph in the NatWest Trophy final at Lord's, their 22-run success clinching for Mark Alleyne's tight-knit side an unprecedented fourth consecutive cup final win.

Seduced by the emotion of Allan Donald's final big game appearance for Warwickshire, however, in what was also NatWest's 20th and last final as sponsors of the competition, Man-of-the-Match adjudicator David Gower gave his award to the South African for his superb burst of 6–2–7–2 as Gloucestershire reached 122 for 3 in reply to Warwickshire's 205 for 7.

In truth, the real match-winner was Gloucester's left-arm seam and swing bowler Mike Smith, who took 2 for 16 in a skilful new ball spell and also returned to good effect towards the latter end of the Warwickshire innings to finish with the outstanding figures of 10–3–18–3. Tim Hancock, too, produced an excellent display with the ball after Gloucestershire captain Alleyne had won an important toss.

Some would point to the good fortune enjoyed by Gloucestershire in the competition, right from the moment they were beaten by Worcestershire in the original third round tie, but then won the replay because the home side had fielded an ineligible player. But, in fighting back in the field to defeat Leicestershire against the odds in the fourth round, and by then blowing away Lancashire in the semi-final, Gloucestershire earned the right to achieve this final crowning glory after two sensational years of limited-overs achievement.

And, although the result looked a hollow victory, there was no doubt that Gloucestershire were well ahead on points when the rain came in the 30th over of their reply. Indeed, Ian Harvey's belligerent 47 had ended just moments before play was abandoned – the Australian's concentration possibly affected by the perimeter commotion that inevitably accompanies an impending downpour. Harvey had added 53 for the second wicket with Kim Barnett (45) and Donald alone had looked capable of slowing up the Gloucestershire march towards a target that was always 20 or 30 runs light of being competitive.

What was a real shame about the occasion was that it could not take place 24 hours earlier on the allotted day. Instead of the full house that had assembled on the Saturday, merely to watch rain fall, barely 10,000 or so turned up on the Sunday morning – hardly surprising because so many spectators have lengthy journeys into London for this event and cannot possibly afford an overnight stay or a second day's travel costs in addition to outrageously high ticket prices. To compound the misery of many, an unsympathetic ruling meant that ticket-holders unable to return on the Sunday (or financially unable to) could get no refund for Saturday's wash-out.

Smith's dismissal of Nick Knight with his third ball was a key moment for Gloucestershire and, bravely though Ashley Giles batted for his 60 after being

FINAL – GLOUCESTERSHIRE v. WARWICKSHIRE
26 (no play) and 27 August 2000 at Lord's

WARWICKSHIRE

Batting			Bowling	O	M	R	W
NV Knight	c Russell, b Smith	1	Harvey	10	0	47	1
A Singh	b Smith	10	Smith	10	3	18	3
AF Giles	c Barnett, b Hancock	60	Averis	10	1	50	1
DP Ostler	c Harvey, b Averis	19	Alleyne	6	0	28	–
TL Penney	c Alleyne, b Smith	20	Hancock	10	1	34	2
MJ Powell	b Harvey	21	Ball	4	0	16	–
DR Brown	c Barnett, b Hancock	4					
NMK Smith (capt)	not out	28	**Fall of Wickets**				
*KJ Piper	not out	8	1-40, 2-93, 3-122				
AA Donald							
ESH Giddins							
	lb12, w22	34					
	45 overs (for 7 wickets)	**205**					

GLOUCESTERSHIRE

Batting			Bowling	O	M	R	W
THC Hancock	b Donald	18	Brown	5.4	0	38	1
KJ Barnett	b Donald	4	Giddins	7	0	20	–
IJ Harvey	c Powell, b Brown	4	Donald	6	2	7	2
*RC Russell	not out	6	Smith	4	0	23	–
MGN Windows		–	Giles	7	0	29	–
CG Taylor							
MW Alleyne (capt)							
JN Snape			**Fall of Wickets**				
MCJ Ball			1-9, 2-32, 3-81, 4-129, 5-134,				
JMM Averis			6-147, 7-170				
AM Smith							
	lb5, w1	6					
	29.4 overs (for 3 wickets)	**122**					

Umpires: JH Hampshire & R Julian
Toss: Gloucestershire
Man of the Match: AA Donald
(DL Method: Gloucestershire target 101 from 29.4 overs)

Gloucestershire won by 22 runs

promoted to number three, he took 104 balls to score those runs. Trevor Penney, too, laboured 50 balls for just 20 before becoming Smith's third victim and only some desperate hitting at the end by Warwickshire captain Neil Smith hauled them above 200.

So, while Gloucestershire's players celebrated their unique four-pronged assault on the record books, neutrals were left to admire again the winning formula that Alleyne and coach John Bracewell have instilled in their men. It is based on firm discipline in the field, flexibility of thought and approach with the bat, a determination not to be overawed by any opponent, and a team ethic in which unselfishness is tangible and real and not merely an ideal.

Left: Jack Russell congratulates Ian Harvey on catching Dominic Ostler.
Below: Gloucestershire celebrate with the trophy.

OXFORD AND CAMBRIDGE UNIVERSITIES
By Mark Baldwin

7, 8 and 9 April 2000 at Cambridge
Lancashire 364 for 3 dec. (JP Crawley 126,
A Flintoff 80*, NH Fairbrother 69*, J Scuderi 51) and
106 for 5 dec.
Cambridge University 168 (MP Smethurst 4 for 34)
and 132 (CP Schofield 5 for 48)
Lancashire won by 170 runs

7, 8 and 9 April 2000 at Taunton
Somerset 362 for 4 dec. (M Burns 160,
PD Bowler 157*) and 260 for 2 dec. (J Cox 100,
ME Trescothick 78, MN Lathwell 54*)
Oxford Universities 144 (S W Weenink 72*,
ID Blackwell 4 for 18) and 74 (PW Jarvis 4 for 21)
Somerset won by 404 runs

11, 12 and 13 April 2000 at Trent Bridge
Nottinghamshire v. Cambridge University
Match abandoned without a ball bowled

11, 12 and 13 April 2000 at Oxford
Oxford Universities v. Hampshire
Match abandoned without a ball bowled

26, 27 and 28 April 2000 at Cambridge
Essex 173 for 6 dec. (DR Law 55*) and 99 for 7 dec.
Cambridge University 50 for 1 dec.
Match drawn – no play was possible on the first day

26, 27 and 28 April 2000 at Oxford
Warwickshire 356 for 5 dec. (TL Penney 100*,
DL Hemp 96, DP Ostler 75)
Oxford Universities 10 for 3
*Match drawn – no play was possible on the first and
third days*

2, 3 and 4 May 2000 at Cambridge
Worcestershire 254 for 6 dec. (EJ Wilson 77,
PR Pollard 7) and 130 for 2 dec. (EJ Wilson 50 ret hurt)
Cambridge University 109 for 8 dec. (GD McGrath 4
for 10) and 105 for 4 (OJ Hughes 50*)
Match drawn

3, 4 and 5 May 2000 at Bristol
Gloucestershire 541 for 6 dec. (MGN Windows 166,
KJ Barnett 118*, THC Hancock 85, RJ Cunliffe 74,
JN Snape 69)
Oxford Universities 243 (RG Smalley 83, JJ Porter 67)
and (following on) 70 for 6
Match drawn

12, 13 and 14 May 2000 at Cambridge
Cambridge University 84 (KJ Dean 5 for 18) and 208
for 7 (AR Danson 117*)
Derbyshire 337 for 5 dec. (MP Dowman 94,
SD Stubbings 92, ME Cassar 77*)
Match drawn

16, 17 and 18 May 2000 at Cambridge
Cambridge University 218 for 9 dec. (RWJ Howitt
118*, AW Laraman 4 for 33) and 95 for 6
Middlesex 296 for 2 dec. (MA Roseberry 139rh)
Match drawn

16, 17 and 18 May 2000 at Oxford
Oxford Universities 160 (JRS Redmayne 68) and 112
(JJ Porter 50, OT Parkin 4 for 14, SD Thomas 4 for 14)
Glamorgan 475 for 6 dec. (AG Wharf 100*, WL Law 85,
MP Maynard 71, KNewell 64, AW Evans 58)
Glamorgan won by an innings and 203 runs

VARSITY MATCH

11, 12 and 13 July 2000 at Lord's
Cambridge University 382 for 4 (dec.)
(*JP Pyemont 124, OJ Hughes 119)
Oxford University 71 for 0 (RG Smalley 42,
JA Claughton)
Match drawn

The end of an old order fizzled out like a damp
squib at Lord's, with the final day of the 155th
University Match being lost to an outfield and parts
of the square soaked by torrential overnight rain.
Negotiation between the two captains, James
Pyemont of Cambridge and Tom Hicks of Oxford,
would have been needed anyway to achieve a
positive result, but it was still a sad end to an era.

Student cricket in England has been reorganised
in a radical way, and the Oxbridge universities are
part of this new deal. Oxford had already accepted
change, merging this year with Oxford Brookes and
playing under the name Oxford Universities.
Pyemont, however, was the last captain to lead an
independent Cambridge University in first-class
cricket. Next year it, too, will amalgamate in
cricketing terms with nearby Anglia Polytechnic
University and will therefore take the field as
Cambridge Universities.

The change to both institutions has arisen because
Oxford and Cambridge will now form two of the six
new University Centres of Cricketing Excellence
(UCCE), with the other four sites being at Durham,

Cardiff, Leeds/Bradford and Loughborough.

In 2001, each of the six centres will field teams to play three first-class matches against county sides, but the real focus of their season will be the five two-day grade-style matches that will form the UCCE Championship. In addition, the six will play a number of 50-over games in the BUSA Premier League.

Durham will, from next season, join Cambridge and Oxford in having first-class status and John Carr, the ECB's director of cricket operations, anticipates that the other three centres of excellence will achieve full first-class status too by 2003.

So, how do the Oxbridge traditionalists view such change? Actually, they have welcomed it, and are genuinely excited about the opportunities the new system will give to future generations of 17-to-21-year-old cricketers.

Ken Siddle, the senior executive officer of Cambridge University CC, said: 'We have welcomed the ECB's initiative in broadening the remit of university cricket. We did not need a crystal ball to realise that Oxbridge cricket would not endlessly enjoy the status it has had in the past, even though we have continued to produce good cricketers and people who go on to contribute fully in other areas of English cricket.

'It is right and proper that young cricketers going through the county ranks, from age-group teams, do not have to sacrifice their studies to become professionals. In the past, I think some players have been discouraged from attending further education by counties.

'It is vitally important now that the counties react positively to what is happening. They can forge real partnerships with the UCCE centres, both by encouraging certain promising young cricketers on their staffs to take advantage of these new courses and by enjoying the better early-season competition they will get from games against us.'

Pyemont added: 'Some might see this as a bitter pill to swallow because, in six or seven years' time, a Cambridge centre side might contain a majority of players who are based at Anglia and only a few actually attending Cambridge University.

'But if that happens, then so be it. I believe there is only one way to go, and that is what we are doing. It will lift the standards of university cricket, and Cambridge cricket, and it can only be good for the English game as a whole. I haven't looked at this season as the final nail in the coffin. I view it as a door opening, a new lease of life for Cambridge. I think the extra opportunities created for people to combine a high level of cricket with their studies will definitely produce more good English cricketers.'

Pyemont himself had the distinction of marking the University Match with a century, his 124 and Quentin Hughes' 119 providing the bulk of Cambridge University's 382–4 declared. Pyemont and Hughes put on 188 for the third wicket. But there had been a heavily rain-affected opening day, too, and Cambridge's declaration did not arrive until 4:50 p.m. on day two. Nevertheless, with Oxford replying with 71 for no wickets by the close, the scene was set for a double declaration and a meaningful last day. Yet, while eras come and go, the British weather stays maddeningly unpredictable.

Oxford Universities, however, could look back on the 2000 season with some pride – and especially their remarkable victory against Northamptonshire in early June. Hicks, the skipper, took 4 for 63 and 5 for 54 with his off-spin but the match belonged to Salman Khan, the fast bowler, who hit 87 after going in at number 11 in the Oxford first innings and then 39 not out when promoted to number nine second time around. Khan, in fact, added 134 in 205 balls with Alan Gofton (47 not out) for the last wicket as Oxford recovered from 87–9 to reach 221 all out. And then, in the second innings, as Oxford's batsmen chased 88 from the last 20 overs, and 44 from the final ten, Khan emerged to strike a succession of vital blows to bring victory by three wickets and Oxford's first win over Northants for 26 years. Their previous first-class win had come against Kent in 1998.

MINOR COUNTIES
by Mike Berry

Dorset, a county more renowned for past idiosyncrasies than present-day achievements, rid themselves of that reputation when they lifted the first Minor Counties title of the new millennium.

A five-wicket win over Cumberland, the defending champions, in the three-day play-off ensured it was third time lucky for the Western Division winners. They had lost out in the two previous finals, to Staffordshire in 1998 and to Cumberland in 1999.

Dorset's previous claim to fame had been a bizarre disposition for notoriety. There was the time the Reverend Andrew Wingfield-Digby, their ex-captain, and former spiritual adviser to the England team, instructed Graeme Calway to bowl 14 consecutive wides that were all allowed to run to the boundary (56 of the 60 runs off one over) to liven up a dying run-chase against Cheshire. And the unforgettable occasion when Ian Sanders was 'timed-out' while stuck in the lavatory during a batting collapse against Oxfordshire. But the 2000 season was all about fulfilling the rich potential that has been bubbling under in recent years. Their first title in 99 years of trying was achieved with a small squad of mostly locally-nurtured players, with the average age of the team who took part in the final just 24. Cumberland's, in contrast, was 31.

The performances of Toby Sharpe and David Kidner, a brace of talented teenage seam bowlers, were particularly gratifying for skipper Stuart Rintoul, as was the contribution of Darren Cowley, the son of first-class umpire Nigel and now domiciled back on the South Coast after a spell in South Africa. His uncomplicated hitting yielded crucial play-off innings of 75 and 63. That said, the cornerstone of Dorset's success was laid by Vyvian Pike, a 31-year-old leg-spinner whose talismanic presence couldn't be overstated. His 57 wickets took his tally in the last three seasons to an astonishing 166.

Dorset, who won six of their nine regional games, pipped Oxfordshire for the Western Division pennant with a record 140 points. Oxfordshire's challenge was built around the performance of a bowler of even more advancing years in 40-year-old paceman Keith Arnold.

Arnold decided to step down from the top tier of Birmingham League club cricket on the eve of the season, severing his ties with Walsall to join Leamington. Those Western Division batsmen who hoped he was winding down towards his pipe and slippers were sadly misguided. Arnold, as charming off the field as he can be cantankerous on it, celebrated his 21st season with Oxfordshire with a best-ever yield of 62 championship wickets, and his 500th career victim. His nine for 19 against Herefordshire at Thame, part of a match return of 15 for 76, was the best analysis of the season.

Herefordshire also harboured realistic title dreams, but the crushing 10-wicket defeat by Oxfordshire left them to concentrate on the one-day competition, the ECB 38-County Cup. Their 42-run victory over Cheshire in the Lord's final, as well as atoning for their 1995 defeat by Cambridgeshire, was notable for three prized personal performances. Paul Lazenbury, a 22-year-old former Gloucestershire left-hander who had scored three championship centuries in four days during July, hit 118 in a third-wicket stand of 203 with Chris Boroughs (94), and Kevin Cooper, the former Nottinghamshire and Gloucestershire veteran, collected five for 29.

An eventful year for Herefordshire, who dismissed 1990s giants Devon for 59 in an innings and 90-run victory at Kington, also included a hat-trick from John Shaw during his six for 44 against Dorset. Four other bowlers to collect the treasured three-in-three during the year were Richard Bates (Wiltshire v. Wales), Gary Kirk (Suffolk v. Hertfordshire), Chris Brown (Cheshire v. Wales) and Paul Newman (Norfolk v. Cambridgeshire).

Cumberland finished at the head of the Eastern Division for the second successive season. Though a potent force, the manner of their last-match win over Northumberland at Jesmond that terminated the challenge of Lincolnshire might have come straight out of the Wingfield-Digby charter of cricketing chicanery.

Collusion at tea on day one – instigated by what Cumberland captain Simon Dutton called his 'brainstorm' – resulted in Northumberland declaring at 10 for two off 13 overs in reply to 293 for two off 67, Cumberland forfeiting their second innings and Northumberland resuming with a target of 284, and with more than a day to get them!

Cumberland, having successfully taken the prospect of a draw out of the equation, completed a 155-run win soon after lunch on day two as seamers David Pennett (32 wickets) and Marcus Sharp (29) wielded their considerable influence. Dutton, recognised as one of the championship's most creative captains, said: 'It was my idea and I consulted the umpires to make sure I was doing nothing wrong. A lot of Minor Counties games have some sort of agreement and it was something that just came to me at tea.' Lincolnshire were less than impressed and Tony North, the secretary, said: 'We felt cheated.'

That Lincolnshire were even in a challenging position was all the more creditable given they suffered grievously from the inclement weather that plagued the campaign. They had four days out of a possible six in their opening three matches (including three days of a festival week at Sleaford) washed out without a ball bowled.

The season's two individual awards went to Eastern Division players. Richard Dalton, the Bedfordshire captain, took the Frank Edwards Trophy for topping the national bowling averages, his 23 victims costing only 10.17 runs apiece. The Wilfred Rhodes Trophy for the best batting average

went to Cambridgeshire's Simon Kellett, with 572 runs at 63.55. The former Yorkshire player featured in three double-century opening stands with Nigel Gadsby, two of them – 241 and 265 – in the same game against Suffolk at Saffron Walden.

Gadsby's 561 runs made him Cambridgeshire's all-time record scorer but Hertfordshire's David Ward, the former Surrey strokemaker, was the championship leading runmaker with 835, a tally enhanced by the highest innings of the summer, an awesome 202 not out against Norfolk at Lakenham. It came in what was the last championship fixture staged at the Norwich-based venue. After over 100 years at Lakenham, Norfolk are relocating their base to Horsford CC, a club ground five miles north-west of Norwich. Just like Dorset, they will be treading new territory in 2001.

MINOR COUNTIES FINAL TABLES

Eastern Division	P	W	L	D	NR	Ba	Bo	Pts
Cumberland	9	5	0	2	2	8	14	112
Lincolnshire	9	3	0	4	2	10	22	90
Suffolk	9	2	3	4	0	15	21	73 (b)
Northumberland	9	2	2	3	2	3	18	63
Bedfordshire	9	1	2	5	1	23	19	63
Buckinghamshire	9	2	3	4	0	11	19	62
Cambridgeshire	9	1	1	6	1	12	24	57
Norfolk	9	1	3	3	2	7	21	54
Staffordshire	9	0	0	7	2	10	22	42
Hertfordshire	9	0	3	4	2	12	16	36 (a)

Western Division	P	W	L	D	NR	Ba	Bo	Pts
Dorset	9	6	0	2	1	22	19	140 (a)
Oxfordshire	9	5	2	2	0	19	25	124
Shropshire	9	4	2	3	0	17	20	106 (b)
Herefordshire	9	3	3	2	1	18	24	95
Devon	9	2	3	2	2	21	25	88
Wiltshire	9	3	3	2	1	8	19	80
Berkshire	9	2	1	4	2	19	16	77
Cornwall	9	2	4	2	1	9	28	74
Cheshire	9	0	5	3	1	10	21	41 (b)
Wales	9	0	4	4	1	4	13	27 (b)

(a) 2pts deducted for slow over rate
(b) 5pts gained in lost one-day match

Championship play–off
10, 11, 12 September
at Bournemouth Sports CC
Cumberland 282-5 (DJ Pearson 108, JM Lewis 60, ST Knox 59) & 152 (TJ Sharpe 4-19)
Dorset 242-9 (DJ Cowley 75, M Swarbrick 52) & 196-5 (DJ Cowley 63, NJ Thurgood 62)
Dorset won by five wickets

ECB 38–County Cup Final
30 August
at Lord's
Herefordshire 291-6 (PS Lazenbury 118, CW Boroughs 94);
Cheshire 249-9 (PRJ Bryson 73, KE Cooper 5-29)
Herefordshire won by 42 runs

MATCH-FIXING by Jonathan Agnew

A trip to Cape Town – even in the depths of a South African winter – should always provoke excitement and anticipation. A beautiful city, sprawling beneath one of the most recognisable landmarks in the world, Cape Town is both so pretty and so vibrant that one can never tire of visiting. However, as I came in to land over the bay on the morning of 20 June, not even the spectacular sight of Table Mountain, standing rugged and proud against a crystal-clear blue sky, could lift either the depression or the anger that I was feeling that day.

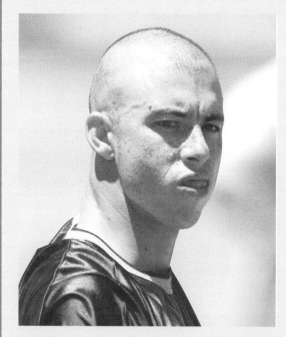

Herschelle Gibbs, who was exploited by the devious Cronje.

Barely two months before, I was still innocent: happy in my belief that Test cricket was a beautiful, unsullied game. Sure, there had been rumours about match-fixing in one-day cricket for some years. I have witnessed two games in Sharjah that I would swear on oath were deliberately rigged by one or more members of the Pakistan team, but that only strengthened the impression held by most of us that match-fixing and betting was an Asian problem.

But now, almost on a daily basis, the world's newspapers were full of allegations and counter-allegations. Even if only half were true, a murky picture of deceit and corruption was rapidly being exposed: an unfamiliar cricketing world in which matches could be thrown for $100,000 and players' performances set not by form or ability, but by a Bombay bookie's line.

Even so, when the Indian police announced that they had stumbled, by chance, upon evidence clearly incriminating the South African captain, Hansie Cronje, no one believed it. It seemed so totally out of the question that it was dismissed out of hand by many, including myself. Perhaps that was one reason for my feeling of anger as I waited, the day after my arrival in Cape Town, for Cronje to take the stand before the King Commission: it seemed that I, like so many others, had been duped. I had even hailed his declaration at Centurion Park as 'a great move forward for cricket'. What fools this devious, money-grabbing, manipulating liar had made of us.

Suddenly, amidst a scramble of dark-suited, hired muscle, Cronje appeared. It was no longer some kind of cruel dream: this was really happening. Behind me Cronje's father visibly stiffened, his face twisted in anxiety. Ewie did not deserve this: a kinder, more charming gentleman you could never wish to meet, yet how his son – once the nation's sporting hero – had let him down. 'It's been tough', Ewie admitted to me as we chatted in the sunshine during one of the breaks in proceedings. What an understatement!

Cronje's performance in the witness box only served to illustrate quite how haughty and contemptuous he had become. He deliberately sought to exploit the weakest and most vulnerable members of his team – Herschelle Gibbs, a Cape coloured, and the black Henry Williams. This was not lost on the public or, as it later demonstrated, the United Cricket Board of South Africa when it imposed only minimal punishment on the two youngsters. Cronje spoke back to the judge, Edwin King, and displayed a total lack of respect for the prosecutor, Shamila Batohi. He volunteered no information whatsoever and I have no doubt that he is withholding evidence. This, however, will only be proven if, and when, the Commission can get its hands on verifiable copies or

The disgraced Cronje, who will never play professional cricket again.

Dropped catches, crazy run-outs, the missing of a perfectly straight ball: pre-Cronje, these were perfectly acceptable and innocent passages of play. Now it is impossible not be cynical and because of that, this once highly respected, quietly spoken, gracious and apparently wonderful ambassador of cricket has raped and ruined the game we all love. It will take years for cricket to recover from his greed and exploitation.

Cronje will be banned for life and there must be the chance that others, on the subcontinent, will follow him. It should now be clear to each and every international cricketer that any future attempt by bookmakers to corrupt the game will not be tolerated. And yet, nothing has been done to remove the source of temptation by cutting the number of meaningless one-day internationals that are played around the world. Toronto, Singapore, Kenya: these tournaments are cropping up all over the place, and while we should welcome the globalisation of cricket, the fact is that the constant merry-go-round has trivialised these matches. Batsmen are much more likely to be tempted by a bookie's approach to fail one day if he knows he can redeem himself, in order to stay in the team, the next. Captains, too, are more approachable for precisely the same reason.

An international one-day league could be one way of raising the importance of each match, with the top four teams involved in a lucrative play-off at the end of each year. If the players, rather than the administrators and governing bodies, were allocated a realistic share of the revenue that the television rights for such a tournament would raise, this might avert temptation.

It is a sad fact, however, that cricket has now been exposed as being an easy target for corrupt, illegal bookmakers. If any good at all has come from the saddest year in the sport's history, it is that we are now painfully aware of that. At least we have a place from which to start cleaning up a game that remains fundamentally honest but has been tainted by the actions of a few devious, greedy men. Through their selfishness, these individuals have seriously jeopardised the popular perception of cricket as being a fair and decent game. Thanks to the likes of Hansie Cronje, watching cricket will never be the same again. ■

transcripts of telephone conversations between Hansie and an Indian bookmaker, Sanjay. Cronje's use of the word 'playing' in these conversations appears to allude to which of his players were playing along – bought, in other words – in his attempts to fix matches and rig line betting, which is similar to what we know as spread betting. Without these tapes, the Commission might never get to the bottom of Cronje's true involvement with the shady world of illegal bookmaking on the subcontinent, which has been estimated to be worth a staggering billion dollars per day.

Whatever the King Commission finally uncovers, Cronje's greatest crime has already been exposed, and the effects of it have quickly been felt across the world. He has sown seeds of doubt in the minds of all of us – professional cricket viewers, spectators and armchair followers of the game alike – who now find ourselves questioning the credibility of events on the field.

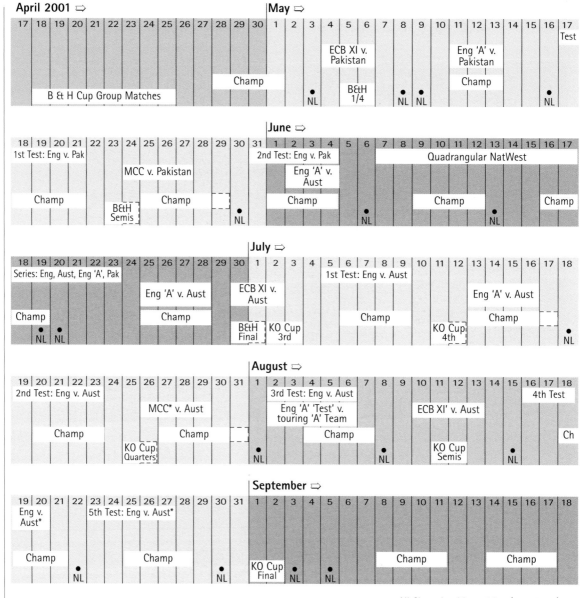

April 2001 ⇨

| 17 | 18 | 19 | 20 | 21 | 22 | 23 | 24 | 25 | 26 | 27 | 28 | 29 | 30 |

May ⇨

| 1 | 2 | 3 | 4 | 5 | 6 | 7 | 8 | 9 | 10 | 11 | 12 | 13 | 14 | 15 | 16 | 17 Test |

B & H Cup Group Matches — Champ — ECB XI v. Pakistan — B&H 1/4 — Eng 'A' v. Pakistan — Champ
● NL ● NL ● NL ● NL

June ⇨

| 18 | 19 | 20 | 21 | 22 | 23 | 24 | 25 | 26 | 27 | 28 | 29 | 30 | 31 | 1 | 2 | 3 | 4 | 5 | 6 | 7 | 8 | 9 | 10 | 11 | 12 | 13 | 14 | 15 | 16 | 17 |

1st Test: Eng v. Pak — MCC v. Pakistan — 2nd Test: Eng v. Pak — Eng 'A' v. Aust — Quadrangular NatWest
Champ — B&H Semis — Champ — Champ — Champ — Champ
● NL ● NL ● NL ● NL

July ⇨

| 18 | 19 | 20 | 21 | 22 | 23 | 24 | 25 | 26 | 27 | 28 | 29 | 30 | 1 | 2 | 3 | 4 | 5 | 6 | 7 | 8 | 9 | 10 | 11 | 12 | 13 | 14 | 15 | 16 | 17 | 18 |

Series: Eng, Aust, Eng 'A', Pak — Eng 'A' v. Aust — ECB XI v. Aust — 1st Test: Eng v. Aust — Eng 'A' v. Aust
Champ — Champ — B&H Final — KO Cup 3rd — Champ — KO Cup 4th — Champ
● NL ● NL ● NL

August ⇨

| 19 | 20 | 21 | 22 | 23 | 24 | 25 | 26 | 27 | 28 | 29 | 30 | 31 | 1 | 2 | 3 | 4 | 5 | 6 | 7 | 8 | 9 | 10 | 11 | 12 | 13 | 14 | 15 | 16 | 17 | 18 |

2nd Test: Eng v. Aust — MCC* v. Aust — 3rd Test: Eng v. Aust — Eng 'A' 'Test' v. touring 'A' Team — ECB XI' v. Aust — 4th Test
Champ — KO Cup Quarters — Champ — Champ — KO Cup Semis — Ch
● NL ● NL ● NL

September ⇨

| 19 | 20 | 21 | 22 | 23 | 24 | 25 | 26 | 27 | 28 | 29 | 30 | 31 | 1 | 2 | 3 | 4 | 5 | 6 | 7 | 8 | 9 | 10 | 11 | 12 | 13 | 14 | 15 | 16 | 17 | 18 |

Eng v. Aust* — 5th Test: Eng v. Aust*
Champ — Champ — KO Cup Final — Champ — Champ
● NL ● NL ● NL ● NL

* or touring 'A' team   NL= National League   All Championship matches (except one) start on either Friday or Saturday.

Yes, so it's only an exercise – an exercise in futility probably – but the aim of this imaginary 'fixture list' for 2001 is to illustrate just what is possible in terms of a structured, layered cricket season. It features:

● Test programme: the real dates of next summer's Tests v. Australia and Pakistan.
● Quadrangular NatWest Series (instead of a triangular), also involving England 'A'. Twelve round-robin matches, with the top two contesting a Lord's final.

● Additional first-class matches for England 'A', against the Pakistanis and Australians, climaxing with a 'Test' against next summer's touring 'A' team.
● A one-league county championship, maximising the amount of weekend play.
● Two-division National League; dates shown here can be flexible, especially to accommodate the staging of floodlit matches.
● Benson and Hedges Cup, and the former NatWest Trophy, to continue much as now.

An expanded England 'A' programme would act as a natural bridge between the championship and the Test arena, quality county venues like Taunton, Hove or Oakham would get to stage more representative cricket, and far more of the public would actually be able to watch cricket when it suited them! In the meantime...good luck deciphering the real 2001 fixture list! See you next year...

Mark Baldwin

SOUTH AFRICA

England Tour of South Africa
Standard Bank One-Day Series
Zimbabwe in South Africa
South Africa Domestic First-Class Season
South Africa Domestic One-Day Season
Australia in South Africa One-Day Series
First-Class Averages

ENGLAND TOUR OF SOUTH AFRICA
By Jonathan Agnew

Y ou do not need to gaze into a crystal ball to predict the outcome of England's winter tours these days. Throughout the 1990s, they managed to beat only one team away from home – New Zealand – and this trip to South Africa promised to be as tough and uncompromising as any other they had faced in that time.

Not only did South Africa look superior, particularly in the bowling and fielding departments, but Hansie Cronje's men also harboured an additional and powerful motivating ingredient: revenge. Anyone who was at Headingley in 1998 and witnessed South Africa's defeat there knew that they could not wait to line up against England again. Javed Akhtar's cavalier umpiring made such a mockery of the deciding match that it seriously muted the nation's celebrations and although, publicly, the South Africans came across as the best of losers, privately they were seething – and rightly so. Add to that their demise in the semi-final of the World Cup and it was clear that the South Africans, who are renowned for their fighting qualities at the best of times, were ready for a scrap.

England, meanwhile, appeared to be in a right old mess and languished below Zimbabwe at the very bottom of the unofficial world rankings. The previous summer had gone horribly wrong with an early exit from the World Cup followed by a two-to-one defeat against unfancied and unglamorous New Zealand in the Test series. Casualties lay strewn in England's wake: Alec Stewart was fired as captain after the World Cup and David Lloyd, the coach, jumped before he was pushed. Before the summer had ended, Graham Gooch and Mike Gatting, the selectors, had also been sacked. Nasser Hussain and Duncan Fletcher – who had never met each other before their appointments as captain and coach – now had the chance to forge a relationship over four long months in South Africa.

The decision was taken to restore Stewart as the wicketkeeping all-rounder, with Chris Read chosen as his understudy. In looking ahead, the selectors (or, at least, those who remained) went for batsmen Michael Vaughan, Chris Adams and Darren Maddy, and the two all-rounders Andrew Flintoff and Gavin

Previous page: South Africa celebrate at Pretoria after winning the series two-one.

Hamilton, while the Northamptonshire off-spinner was selected to support Phil Tufnell. There was nothing particularly wrong with any of the selections, but the most notable absentee, Mark Ramprakash, seemed to have been hard done by. There was a lack of experience, particularly since England's most dependable middle-order player – Graham Thorpe – had made himself unavailable for the tour in order to spend some time with his family and also to concentrate on his benefit.

As is now becoming the norm, the Test series was followed by a one-day tournament, which necessitated some changes in personnel. Alec Stewart had already let it be known that he was far from chuffed to be flying home at the end of the Tests.

Nicky Oppenheimer's XI v. England
1 Nov at Randjesfontein
England 203 for 7 dec. (66.3 overs)(MA Atherton 72, MP Vaughan 59)
Nicky Oppenheimer's XI 207 for 4 (37.2 overs) (M van Jaarsveld 40, DM Benkenstein 40)
Nicky Oppenheimer's XI won by 6 wickets

The traditional tour curtain-raiser went horribly wrong for the visitors as they became the first ever to lose this fixture. Amongst the champagne-swillers, Mike Atherton reached a patient 72 from 143 balls and Michael Vaughan, in his first innings for England, scored an unbeaten 59 before Hussain declared setting the home team 204 to win. Van Jaarsveld and Benkenstein, who both made 40, set up the reply but the vital injection came from Pothas, whose 39 not out came from only 24 deliveries. A poor start to the tour but not, we were assured, a crisis.

Easterns v. England
2 Nov at Benoni
England 234 for 9 (50 overs)(*N Hussain 64, Flintoff 54)
Easterns 215 for 7 (50 overs)(DJ Smith 75)
England won by 19 runs

England were able to make amends for their slip-up the following day with a comfortable victory against one of the least formidable state teams in South Africa. Hussain scored 64 and Flintoff a beefy 54 from only 56 balls as England reached 234 for 9 from 50 overs.

Tidy bowling then managed to restrict Easterns to 215 for 7.

England coach Duncan Fletcher talks to Test possible Darren Maddy in the nets.

Western Province/Boland v. England
5, 6, 7 and 8 Nov at Cape Town
Western Province/Boland 358 for 9 dec. (136.2 overs) (*LJ Koen 96, KC Jackson 80, SJ Palframan 72)
England 203 for 7 dec. (66.3 overs)(MA Atherton 72)
Match drawn

When the fixtures for the tour were first announced, it appeared that the combination of two states would provide the best possible opposition for England with the locals desperate to be chosen for this representative team. Sadly not. This was, at best, a second-rate line-up and the fact that they were able to outscore England quite so easily on first innings justified all the pre-tour concerns about England's batting line-up. Mike Atherton and Chris Adams apart – they scored 172 of England's 249 between them – it was a feeble exhibition as the last six wickets were lost for only 15 runs.

A declaration set England 250 in 47 overs but a draw was called after 41 with England having limped to 82 for 2. Dean Headley, who suffered a back spasm in the opening match, should be fit to bowl in the next couple of days. Flintoff was also unable to bowl.

Free State/Griqualand West v. England
12, 13, 14 and 15 Nov at Bloemfontein
England 358 for 9 dec. (118 overs) (CJ Adams 72, A Flintoff 65) and 211 for 1 dec. (50 overs) (MA Butcher 87, MA Atherton 81)
Free State/Griqualand West 194 (88 overs) (GFJ Liebenberg 92) and 222 (77.1 overs)(FC Brooker 56, LL Bosman 40)
England won by 153 runs

Chris Silverwood became one of the earliest replacements England have called up as worries grew over the fitness of Flintoff, in particular. Curiously, Flintoff played as a batsman and scored 65 as England's middle-order batsmen found some form. Darren Gough made his first impression on the tour, taking four wickets to give England a first-innings lead of 164.

Butcher and Atherton then put on 141 for the first wicket, enabling Hussain to set the home team an unlikely 376 to win. Tufnell claimed 3 for 27 as England romped to an easy victory.

Northerns/Gauteng v. England
18, 19, 20 and Nov at Centurion
England 303 (112.4 overs)(MA Atherton 81, MP Vaughan 85) and 195 for 8 dec. (61 overs)(MA Butcher 39, MA Atherton 39)
Northerns/Gauteng 201 (67.1 overs)(ND McKenzie 62, S Elworthy 43) and 195 (48.1 overs)(ND McKenzie 87)
England won by 102 runs

England's victory over the strongest team they had faced on the tour so far was overshadowed by the news that Dean Headley's spasm was, in fact, a fracture and his tour was over after bowling just ten deliveries in anger. There was better news of Flintoff, however, who bowled with genuine pace to give England victory in the last game before the first Test.

Atherton (81) and Vaughan (85) continued their run of form as England led by 102 on first innings. Declaring on 195 for 8 in their second, England set the home team 298 to win off a minimum of 83 overs.

They lost six wickets for 38 runs in 15 overs as Flintoff took 3 for 6, and although England had won two of their three first matches, Hussain warned that the real stuff now lay ahead. How right he was!

The uncompromising Allan Donald, whose bowling devastated the English side in Johannesburg.

FIRST TEST
25, 26, 27 and 28 Nov at Wanderers, Johannesburg
South Africa won by an innings and 21 runs

Within only 15 minutes of play, in which England lost their first four wickets for only two runs, all the early tour optimism had been blown away. Even in their worst nightmares, neither Nasser Hussain nor Duncan Fletcher – in his first Test match as England's coach – could have dreamed up such a ghastly start to the series. There was no coming back from such devastation, and South Africa took the opening match by an innings and 21 runs, a shade over one hour into the fourth day.

However, while those are the bare statistics, they do not illustrate England's wretched luck when, for the ninth consecutive overseas Test, they lost the toss. How crucial this was to prove.

The pitch at the Wanderers started damp, bordering on wet, and was clearly not fit for Test cricket. With heavy cloud cover hanging over the ground, Hansie Cronje had no hesitation in putting England into bat: Allan Donald and Sean Pollock did the rest.

As England's openers, Mike Atherton and Mark Butcher strode out to the middle, the umpires were involved in a lengthy discussion about the light. Certainly, it was not ideal, but Messrs Venkat and Orchard decided that play could begin. Six balls later, Donald delivered a spiteful off-cutter that ripped back and exploded into Atherton's off-stump. It was the key wicket and the effect in the England dressing room was shattering.

Hussain received a snorter from Pollock in the next over that slammed into his gloves and gave Lance Klusener a simple catch in the gully: 2 for 2. It was 2 for 3 when Butcher edged Donald to Mark Boucher in the third over and when Donald immediately trapped Stewart leg before first ball, an irate listener – who had just switched on his radio – telephoned the BBC to complain that I was giving the score the wrong way round, as in Australia! Sadly, he was mistaken.

Given the choice, Chris Adams probably would not have opted for the scenario that now awaited him in his first innings in Test cricket. Donald, the finest fast bowler in the world, was on a hat-trick in tailor-made conditions. England were 2 for 4, and another debutant, Michael Vaughan, was standing, open-mouthed, at the non-striker's end. However, the inexperienced pair added 32 for the fifth wicket, before Adams gloved Donald down the leg side for 16: 34 for 5.

Pollock and Donald were now rested, giving Vaughan and Andrew Flintoff the opportunity to rebuild the innings against the less threatening bowling of Lance Klusener and Cronje. Fifty-six priceless runs were accumulated in differing styles: Vaughan was watchful and technically correct while Flintoff preferred the uncomplicated approach. It was only a matter of time before the strike bowlers returned and, in the second over after lunch, Pollock flicked Vaughan's inside edge. The floodgates opened once again. Gavin Hamilton's first Test innings was brief – he edged Donald to third slip and departed for a duck; Flintoff was also caught by Boucher off Pollock for 38 – the top score of the innings – and Caddick became Boucher's fifth victim to leave England floundering on 103 for 9.

The only moment of light relief came when Allan Mullally hooked Donald for 6 – the batsman claimed it came off the middle of the bat when, in fact, it was a frantic top edge – but the innings came to an end after an unlikely last-wicket stand of 18 was snuffed out by Pollock. Donald finished with 6 for 53, but Pollock, with 4 for 16 from 14.4 overs had been every bit as awkward.

To remain in contention, England urgently needed wickets but, in the 30 overs that remained on the opening day, they managed to claim only one. And when South Africa then batted comfortably throughout the second day, it was becoming increasingly difficult to defend England's bowlers, who were disappointingly off-target.

Herschelle Gibbs and Daryll Cullinan dominated the early part of the day in a partnership of 96. Gibbs appeared to lose concentration within 15 runs of what was a certain century, but Cullinan was not to be denied. He made 108 in two and a half hours before Caddick finally pierced his defence. South Africa's lead, which stood at 162, was already unassailable. Cronje made 42 but the fireworks were provided by Klusener, who thrashed an uncompromising 72. He struck 11 boundaries before falling to Darren Gough early on the third morning. Pollock edged Gough to Stewart in the Yorkshireman's next over and when Donald lost his middle stump first ball, Gough found himself with the unusual possibility of claiming a hat-trick in consecutive Tests (the Sydney Test in January having been the previous match). However, as Paul Adams walked reluctantly to the middle, rain so slight it was barely discernible began to fall and the umpires took the players off the field. When the conditions improved one hour later, Cronje promptly declared, denying Gough his opportunity. South Africa's lead stood at 281.

Lance Klusener hits out during his innings of 61 not out on the second day of the first Test.

FIRST TEST SOUTH AFRICA v. ENGLAND
25, 26, 27 and 28 November 1999 at Wanderers, Johannesburg

ENGLAND

	First Innings		Second Innings	
MA Butcher	c Boucher, b Donald	1	lbw b Donald	32
MA Atherton	b Donald	0	c Boucher, b Pollock	0
N Hussain (capt)	c Klusener, b Pollock	0	b Pollock	16
MP Vaughan	c Boucher, b Pollock	33	lbw b Donald	5
*AJ Stewart	lbw b Donald	0	c Rhodes, b Donald	86
CJ Adams	c Boucher, b Donald	16	c Boucher, b Donald	1
A Flintoff	c Boucher, b Pollock	38	c & b Adams	36
GM Hamilton	c Pollock, b Donald	0	c Pollock, b Donald	0
AR Caddick	c Boucher, b Donald	4	b Pollock	48
D Gough	not out	15	not out	16
AD Mullally	lbw b Pollock	10	c Kallis, b Pollock	0
	lb3, w2	5	b4, lb10, w6	20
		122		**260**

	First Innings				Second Innings			
	O	M	R	W	O	M	R	W
Donald	15	3	53	6	23	7	74	5
Pollock	14.4	6	16	4	24.4	11	64	4
Cronje	5	2	15	-	6	3	22	-
Klusener	6	1	30	-	19	3	55	-
Adams	1	0	5	-	11	1	31	1

Fall of Wickets
1-1, 2-2, 3-2, 4-2, 5-34, 6-90, 7-91, 8-91, 9-103
1-0, 2-31, 3-41, 4-145, 5-147, 6-166, 7-166, 8-218, 9-260

SOUTH AFRICA

	First Innings	
G Kirsten	lbw b Mullally	13
HH Gibbs	b Mullally	85
JH Kallis	c Stewart, b Gough	12
DJ Cullinan	b Caddick	108
WJ Cronje (capt)	b Gough	44
JN Rhodes	lbw b Mullally	26
L Klusener	b Gough	72
SM Pollock	c Stewart, b Gough	2
*MV Boucher	not out	4
AA Donald	b Gough	0
PR Adams	not out	0
	b7, lb18, w2, nb10	37
	(for 9 wickets dec.)	**403**

	First Innings			
	O	M	R	W
Gough	30	8	70	5
Caddick	34	12	81	1
Mullally	34	7	80	3
Flintoff	14	5	45	-
Hamilton	15	1	63	-
Vaughan	11	1	39	-

Fall of Wickets
1-37, 2-79, 3-175, 4-284, 5-299, 6-378, 7-398, 8-403, 9-403

Umpires: DL Orchard & S Venkataraghavan
Toss: South Africa
Test Debuts: CJ Adams, GM Hamilton & MP Vaughan

South Africa won by an innings and 21 runs

It was on this ground four years ago, and in not dissimilar circumstances, that Atherton played the innings of his life. For more than a day and a half he blunted the South African attack to earn an unlikely draw. For history to repeat itself, he would need to bat for two and a half days. In fact, he was out first ball, edging a deadly delivery from Pollock, to complete a pair. Bearing in mind the quality of the two deliveries that claimed him in the match, this was no disgrace at all. Hussain was bowled by a scuttler for 16 and when Vaughan fell leg before to another ball that kept low, England were 41 for 3 and in danger of losing within three days.

Alec Stewart had barely scored a run on the tour and came out to bat on a king pair. However, chancing his arm rather too freely for some people's liking, he took the attack to the South Africans to the extent that Donald bowled to him with no fewer than three fielders set for the hook shot. Stewart and Butcher put on 104 before Butcher was given out leg before to Donald for 32 to start a slide of four wickets for 11 runs in 15 balls. Adams drove loosely and was caught behind for a single, Stewart carved Donald straight to Rhodes at cover for 86, of which 62 came in boundaries, and poor Hamilton completed the most miserable of debuts by bagging a pair. At the close of play on the third day, England were on the brink of certain defeat: 93 runs behind with only three wickets in hand.

At this point, every one of England's 17 wickets had been taken by either Donald or Pollock but Adams broke that sequence by tempting Flintoff to knock back a return catch. Flintoff and Caddick had resisted bravely, adding 52 on the fourth morning, but when Caddick was bowled for his Test best score of 48, Mullally's almost obligatory duck condemned England to their miserable defeat.

Donald was Man of the Match. He finished with match figures of 11 for 127 while Pollock's 8 for 80 confirmed his rapidly growing status in world cricket.

Gauteng Invitation XI v. England
1 Dec at Lenasia
England 274 for 5 (50 overs)(A Flintoff 79,
DL Maddy 60)
Gauteng Invitation XI 236 for 9 (50 overs)
(Z de Bruyn 82)
England won by 38 runs

It had all the potential to be the most slippery of banana skins, but England regrouped and dealt with this combined team on the little township ground. Darren Maddy scored his first runs of the tour and

despite some excellent hitting from Ndima, whose 52 included two sixes, England's total of 274 was never threatened as Gough and Silverwood claimed three wickets each.

KwaZulu Natal v. England
3, 4, 5 and 6 Dec at Durban
KwaZulu Natal 310 (93.3 overs)(JC Kent 103,
KP Pietersen 61) and 152 for 2 (61 overs)(AM Amla 53,
DJ Watson 52)
England 421 (164.2 overs)(*N Hussain 103,
A Flintoff 89)
Match drawn

A lacklustre match was not helped by the weather and more injuries to England's bowlers. This time it was Mullally and Silverwood who were forced to miss out, but that gave Tudor the chance to impress before the second Test. Having begun well, reducing the home team to 136 for 5, England were then frustrated by 20-year-old Kent, who scored 103, and 19-year-old Pieterson, whose unbeaten 61 helped the number 11, Gilder, add 69 runs for the tenth wicket.

Hussain lifted the gloom by scoring England's first century of the year – well, it was December, after all – as the match drifted towards stalemate.

SECOND TEST
9, 10, 11, 12 and 13 Dec at Port Elizabeth
Match drawn

After South Africa's fully justified unhappiness with the standard of umpiring during their tour of England 18 months ago, this was payback time. No fewer than five crucial decisions clearly went against England over the five days at St George's Park: a catalogue of errors that very nearly cost the visitors the match. That they managed to cling on to a draw – despite being reduced to 5 for 2 in their second innings – was no mean achievement under the circumstances. The wisdom – or, as I have always vehemently maintained, the folly – of umpires referring to television replays was exposed yet again.

However, while one can all too easily criticise the umpires, who are all thoroughly honourable and honest men trying to do an impossible and certainly thankless job, it is the players who are largely to blame. Both teams in this series appeal forcibly for anything that might be given out – both Alec Stewart and Mark Boucher are particularly guilty in this regard – with the result that the umpires are placed under enormous pressure. Wicketkeepers have now developed highly

Nasser Hussain and Michael Atherton leave the pitch at close of play on the first day of the second Test.

convincing and theatrical appeals for catches when the ball has clearly missed the edge of the bat. These would have been considered embarrassing only ten years ago. Sadly the success rate of these appeals, which can only be described as attempts to cheat the opposing batsman, is rising rapidly, with the inevitable consequence that the appeals are becoming more and more frequent.

The first error was, arguably, the most crucial. South Africa, having been put into bat on a warm and muggy morning, were soon reduced to 146 for 5 and this despite Darren Gough bowling well below his best. South Africa's approach was surprisingly cavalier: Gibbs was run out for 48, Kallis caught at mid-on and Cronje caught, driving, by short extra cover. Cullinan and Rhodes restored the innings with a stand of 55 before Cullinan was stumped for 58, and when Pollock was caught in the gully in the fourth over of the second day, South Africa were 268 for 7. With only Donald and Hayward to follow, the dangerous Klusener was joined by Boucher who, almost immediately, appeared to glove a catch to Stewart off the bowling of Caddick. Television replays supported England's obvious show of disappointment when Rudi Koertzen gave Boucher the benefit of the doubt. It might have been quite a different match.

The result was a record stand for the eighth wicket of 119 as South Africa escaped thanks to Klusener, who played one of the most remarkable lower-order innings in modern Test cricket. He finally lost Boucher to a catch by Stewart off Tufnell, but the arrival of the tail-enders merely caused him to go up a gear. His straight hitting was awesome and only when England's bowlers went round the wicket and aimed at his body did the left-hander appear even the slightest bit inconvenienced. He should have been run out attempting his 150th run, but Stewart dropped the ball and when Klusener was the last man out, caught at midwicket, he had batted for five and a half hours. England, understandably, were thoroughly deflated.

Further question marks were raised about Butcher's suitability as opener when he dragged a wide delivery from Pollock into his stumps with a firm-footed drive in only the second over, but Atherton and Hussain then added 155 for the second wicket. It was vintage Atherton. His last four innings in overseas Tests had been ducks, but he relished this challenge and when he flicked Donald for a fourth boundary in a single over, his face lit up. After nearly six and a half hours, Hayward snared him with a short ball that kept low for a highly prized first Test wicket, but England pressed on to record a first-innings score in excess of 300 for the first time in ten matches. However, they were still 77 runs behind with all but 15 minutes less than two days' play remaining.

Armed with that lead, South Africa's plan was to press on and declare with a short session remaining on the fourth evening, but they were denied by a combination of England's tenacity and their own customary lack of enterprise.

This was exacerbated by Kallis' obvious guilt in surviving a catch at silly point when he had scored only 12. Tufnell was the bowler and although the ball travelled quickly and low, Adams, the fielder, clearly knew he had taken the catch cleanly. Kallis, who must have seen this, stood his ground and umpire Koertzen called for the third umpire to reach a decision from the television replays.

Initially, none were convincing and Kallis who, in an era that appears to be lost forever, would have accepted the fielder's word, was reprieved. It was then that the pictures from Sky Television found their way on to the screens around the ground and, indeed, around the world. These replays, which were not available to the third umpire, did more than suggest that Adams had taken the catch. This situation was not the first of its kind. There have been several similar instances when additional cameras, other than those belonging to the host broadcaster, have shed new and critical evidence on decisions that had already been taken by an umpire who was denied access to them.

Once again, England were incensed. The pitch microphones picked up a series of foul exchanges between Stewart, Adams and Kallis, who initially gave the appearance of attempting to give his wicket away before grinding out an unbeaten 85. The sight of Adams and Kallis leaving the field together, all smiles, at the close of play merely confirmed that modern players appear to be quite happy with today's environment in which they do little more than cheat each other. There is very little respect for one's opponents in Test cricket nowadays.

Left 79 overs in which to score 302 to win or, at least, to survive, England quickly lost both Atherton and Butcher. Hussain and Vaughan negotiated 42 overs before Vaughan was adjudged by umpire Koertzen to have edged a catch down the leg side. When Stewart fell to a leg-before decision, in which the ball would surely have missed leg stump, alarm bells were ringing loudly in the England dressing room. As Hussain defended stoutly at one end, he could only watch as Adams, with nine overs left, fell to the cruellest decision of the match. A delivery from Cronje thumped into his pad and the ball ballooned up in the off side for the diving Rhodes to catch. The fielder, to his credit, did not appeal, but Cronje's hysterical celebrations, in which he jumped

Jacques Kallis attempts a big hit off Phil Tufnell on the fourth day of the second Test. Kallis remained at the crease following a controversial umpire's decision during this innings, which TV footage clearly revealed was wrong.

SECOND TEST SOUTH AFRICA v. ENGLAND
9, 10, 11, 12 and 13 December 1999 at St George's Park, Port Elizabeth

SOUTH AFRICA

	First Innings		Second Innings	
G Kirsten	c Hussain, b Caddick	15	c Vaughan, b Gough	2
HH Gibbs	run out (Flintoff)	48	c Flintoff, b Caddick	10
JH Kallis	c Caddick, b Silverwood	1	not out	85
DJ Cullinan	st Stewart, b Tufnell	58	b Caddick	18
WJ Cronje (capt)	c Flintoff, b Tufnell	2	c Vaughan, b Flintoff	27
JN Rhodes	c Atherton, b Flintoff	50	not out	57
L Klusener	c Adams, b Gough	174		
SM Pollock	c Vaughan, b Flintoff	7		
*MV Boucher	c Stewart, b Tufnell	42		
AA Donald	c Hussain, b Tufnell	9		
M Hayward	not out	10		
	b10, lb5, w1, nb18	34	b4, lb11, w1, nb9	25
		450	(for 4 wickets dec.)	260

	First Innings				Second Innings			
	O	M	R	W	O	M	R	W
Gough	21.1	1	107	1	19	6	52	1
Caddick	31	5	100	1	18	4	29	2
Silverwood	24	4	57	1	10	1	24	-
Tufnell	42	9	124	4	35	9	71	-
Vaughan	3	0	16	-	2	0	9	-
Flintoff	7	0	31	2	8.5	2	24	1

Fall of Wickets
1-28, 2-57, 3-87, 4-91, 5-146, 6-252, 7-268, 8-387, 9-401
1-5, 2-17, 3-50, 4-98

ENGLAND

	First Innings		Second Innings	
MA Butcher	b Pollock	4	lbw b Hayward	1
MA Atherton	b Hayward	108	b Pollock	3
N Hussain (capt)	c Boucher, b Donald	82	not out	70
MP Vaughan	b Hayward	21	c Boucher, b Kallis	29
*AJ Stewart	b Donald	15	lbw b Pollock	28
CJ Adams	c Kallis, b Pollock	25	c Rhodes, b Cronje	1
A Flintoff	b Pollock	42	c Boucher, b Kallis	12
AR Caddick	b Hayward	35	not out	4
D Gough	b Donald	6		
CEW Silverwood	c Klusener, b Hayward	6		
PCR Tufnell	not out	7		
	b1, lb8, nb13	22	lb2, nb3	5
		373	(for 6 wickets)	153

	First Innings				Second Innings			
	O	M	R	W	O	M	R	W
Donald	34	9	109	3	13	4	37	-
Pollock	34	7	12	3	17	8	18	2
Hayward	28.1	7	75	4	20	8	55	1
Klusener	25	9	48	-	14	9	17	-
Cronje	16	5	20	-	6	4	2	1
Kallis					7	1	22	2

Fall of Wickets
1-5, 2-160, 3-228, 4-229, 5-264, 6-281, 7-336, 8-349, 9-364
1-5, 2-5, 3-80, 4-125, 5-137, 6-149

Umpires: RE Koertzen & SA Bucknor
Toss: England
Test Debuts: M Hayward

Match drawn

all over the startled Rhodes, had the desired effect: Koertzen's finger was raised again and a distraught Adams first gestured in sheer disbelief, then slowly walked away, head bowed.

Flintoff soon followed, legitimately caught behind, but Hussain and Caddick ensured that, with two overs left, Cronje called off his hunt for victory.

The ill-tempered match left a nasty taste and suggested that the Boxing Day encounter in Durban would be played in anything but a festive spirit.

Eastern Province/Border v. England
16 Dec at Alice
England 309 for 8 (50 overs)(DL Maddy 133, MA Atherton 51)
Eastern Province/Border 156 (36.4 overs) (MR Benfield 58)
England won by 153 runs

Another new venue – near East London – as England continued to assist the United Cricket Board of South Africa with its township development programme. Maddy's 133 from 117 balls was enormous fun and helped to ease his frustrations. It also ensured that the combined 11 were never in the hunt as another forgotten man, Graeme Swann, took three wickets to bowl the opposition out in less than 37 overs.

Eastern Province/Border v. England
18, 19, 20 and 21 Dec at East London
Eastern Province/Border 384 (111.1 overs) (*PC Strydom 86, JDC Bryant 72, W Wiblin 63)
England 113 for 2 (28 overs)(CJ Adams 59)
Match drawn

A match ruined by the weather, but notable for Butcher's continued run of poor form. He scored nought, driving the last ball of a session into the gully. Vaughan was hit on the right hand and, although there was no break, it was to rule him out of the third Test.

THIRD TEST
26, 27, 28, 29 and 30 Dec at Durban
Match drawn

After much speculation about the spiteful behaviour of Kingsmead's notorious 'Green Mamba', the pitch was, in fact, so docile that two of the longest innings ever recorded in Test cricket dominated the match. Nasser Hussain made the third-slowest Test century by an Englishman: he ground out an unbeaten 146

in all but nine overs of two days' play. In return, and in blistering heat, Gary Kirsten – whose place was under threat at the start of the second innings – batted for 14 and a half hours: the second-longest Test innings of all time. His 275 equalled the highest Test score by a South African and unquestionably denied England a series-levelling victory.

At the end of the first day, the South African press had a field day. England had crawled to 135 for 2, having lost Atherton for a single and Butcher for 48. It was, indeed, torpid cricket – not helped by an extremely slow outfield – but the headline 'Boring, boring England!' was followed by the observation that the visitors had done 'cricket a disservice'. Strong stuff, which required some frantic back-pedalling by the correspondent in question later in the game.

The match came to life with the arrival of Alec Stewart at the crease early on the second day. Always fluent, but sometimes frustratingly casual, 'the

Shaun Pollock walks off disappointed in the background as Alec Stewart embraces Nasser Hussain after his 100 on the second day of the third Test.

Gary Kirsten is applauded off the field by the England team after scoring 275 on the final day of the third Test.

Gaffer' lifted the tempo in a rousing innings of 95 from only 145 balls. He and Hussain added 156 for the fourth wicket, 121 of them before lunch of which Stewart's share was 72. It was precisely what the match needed and, although the lower order fell away in typical fashion from 336 for 4 to 366 for 9, England at least had something to bowl at. Time, though, was always going to beat them, unless the bowlers produced something spectacular.

The third day began in high farce. A torrential overnight storm had flooded Kingsmead to the extent that the start of play was delayed; first for the ground to dry out and then, quite ridiculously, because the rain had got under the bonnet of the heavy roller. It simply would not start. Hussain, at this point, declared and Hansie Cronje announced that he wanted the pitch flattening by the heavy roller. While negotiations were taking place, an enormous, mauve road-roller – at least the size of a combine harvester – lumbered into view from a neighbouring building site and began to make its laborious, but nonetheless spectacular journey towards the pitch. Seeing this, the umpires – Doug

Cowie and David Orchard – immediately raced from the pavilion to halt its progress, ruling (quite rightly) that this particular roller had not been available at the start of the game. Suddenly, from nowhere, the light roller, which was no more than a cocoa tin, was produced and as it bounced, pointlessly, over the pitch, an enraged Cronje insisted on the heavy roller being used. Effectively, the South Africans were on strike.

The stalemate was eventually broken when a bare-chested Afrikaner, brandishing a large spanner, managed to fire up the original machine, and the result was that a further half hour was lost.

It may be that this nonsense had an effect on the South Africans. Perhaps Andy Caddick was all the more motivated as a result. We will never know. However, within 32 overs South Africa were 84 for 8, and 83 runs from avoiding the follow-on. Caddick was in devastating form, discovering sharp lift from a pitch that had offered nothing for any other bowler in the game. He claimed the first three wickets and then returned to bowl at a crucial time mid-innings, to expose South Africa's error in dropping Jonte Rhodes.

However, Sean Pollock – batting at number 7 – played an extraordinary innings. In a partnership of 70 with Paul Adams (of which Adams contributed 7) Pollock steered South Africa to within 13 runs of avoiding the follow-on and, therefore, out of danger. However, having batted so brilliantly, Pollock played a wild drive at Caddick and dragged the ball into his stumps for 64. It was Caddick's seventh wicket of the innings at a cost of 46, and when Adams lofted Gough to Silverwood at mid-on in the next over, Hussain had no hesitation in making South Africa bat again, 210 runs behind. The question was: could England – and Caddick in particular – do it again?

South Africa needed to bat for at least a day and a half to be safe. In the eighth over of the fourth morning, Herschelle Gibbs popped up a catch to short leg, but that was the only wicket to fall for 69 overs. Kirsten and Jacques Kallis took South Africa to within 17 runs of making England bat again when Gough, armed with the second new ball, found the edge of Kallis' bat for 69. Cullinan and Kirsten added a further 49 and just as the day was drifting towards its end, Hussain called up Andrew Flintoff. In fading light, Cullinan edged to Stewart to be replaced, most surprisingly, by Cronje. Given that South Africa, in the absence of Rhodes, were already a batsman down it was an extraordinary decision not to prefer a nightwatchman. When Flintoff despatched him in his next over – minutes before the close – England had real hope of wrapping up their victory on the final day.

This, however, was when Kirsten took over. The effect of the energy-sapping heat and humidity on England's bowlers – who were now into their third consecutive day in the field – cannot be over-emphasised, but Kirsten's was a magnificent effort. He did not offer a single chance in 14 and a half hours at the crease and it was his partnership of 192 with Mark Boucher, which lasted well into the afternoon, that thwarted England. Boucher's century was his third in Test cricket and he paved the way for a typically thuggish effort by Klusener, who made 45.

There was one final twist. Needing just a single to beat the watching Cullinan's record score of 275 – and facing Mark Butcher's alleged off-spin (which, even charitably, can only be described as optimistic), Kirsten completely missed a low, full delivery which knocked off his leg bail. Perhaps it was meant to be because since tea, England's attack comprised the likes of Hussain, Maddy, Butcher and Adams. With the fourth Test only three days away, we were left wondering how England's first-string bowlers would recover from their ordeal.

THIRD TEST SOUTH AFRICA v. ENGLAND
26, 27, 28, 29 and 30 December 1999 at Kingsmead, Durban

ENGLAND

	First Innings	
MA Butcher	c Klusener, b Adams	48
MA Atherton	b Hayward	1
N Hussain (capt)	not out	146
DL Maddy	c Adams, b Donald	24
*AJ Stewart	lbw b Hayward	95
CJ Adams	b Adams	19
A Flintoff	lbw b Cronje	5
AR Caddick	lbw b Cronje	0
D Gough	c Klusener, b Donald	9
CEW Silverwood	c Boucher, b Pollock	0
PCR Tufnell	not out	0
	b1, lb14, w3, nb1	19
	(for 9 wickets dec.)	366

	First Innings			
	O	M	R	W
Donald	23.4	3	67	2
Pollock	33	14	55	1
Hayward	20	3	74	2
Kallis	23	9	38	-
Klusener	17	5	38	-
Adams	43	17	74	2
Cronje	7	5	5	2

Fall of Wickets
1-7, 2-82, 3-138, 4-294, 5-336, 6-345, 7-345, 8-362, 9-362

SOUTH AFRICA

	First Innings		Second Innings	
G Kirsten	c Stewart, b Caddick	11	b Butcher	275
HH Gibbs	c Stewart, b Caddick	2	c Maddy, b Caddick	26
JH Kallis	c Stewart, b Caddick	0	c Stewart, b Gough	69
DJ Cullinan	b Gough	20	c Stewart,b Flintoff	16
WJ Cronje (capt)	c Stewart, b Caddick	28	c Sewart, b Flintoff	1
L Klusener	c Maddy, b Tufnell	15	(7) b Butcher	45
SM Pollock	b Caddick	64	(8) not out	7
*MV Boucher	b Caddick	0	(6) c Stewart, b Adams	108
AA Donald	b Atherton, b Caddick	0		
PR Adams	c Silverwood, b Gough	9		
M Hayward	not out	0		
	b4, lb1, w1, nb1	7	b5, lb13, w2, nb5	25
		156	(for 7 wickets)	572

	First Innings				Second Innings			
	O	M	R	W	O	M	R	W
Gough	15.5	6	36	2	28	5	82	1
Caddick	16	4	46	7	36	12	70	1
Silverwood	6	1	38	-	30	6	89	-
Tufnell	10	1	24	1	45	6	117	-
Flintoff	3	0	7	-	30	9	67	2
Hamilton	15	1	63	-				
Adams					13	3	42	1
Maddy					14	1	40	-
Butcher					8.2	0	32	2
Hussain					5	1	15	-

Fall of Wickets
1-11, 2-11, 3-24, 4-57, 5-74, 6-84, 7-84, 8-84, 9-154
1-41, 2-193, 3-242, 4-244, 5-436, 6-537, 7-572

Umpires: DL Orchard & DB Cowie
Toss: England
Test Debuts: nil

Match drawn

FOURTH TEST
2, 3, 4 and 5 Jan at Cape Town
South Africa won by an innings and 37 runs

After the gradual, yet definitive signs of progress made at Port Elizabeth and in the Christmas match at Durban, England chose the first Test of the new millennium to remind everyone of the frailties that had blighted them in the previous decade. Their batting at Cape Town was irresponsible and reckless and while the PR machine constantly reminds us, with some justification, that ups and downs must be expected while the team is rebuilt, the inescapable truth was that three of the most experienced batsmen – Atherton, Stewart and Butcher – were the chief culprits on this occasion.

The first innings was a disaster from which England could not recover and which handed the series to South Africa. Having won the toss and, with great relief, elected to bat first, the openers put on 115 for the first wicket: the first century opening partnership in 14 tests. Atherton was most fortunate on 15, surviving a straightforward chance to Rhodes, of all people, now reinstalled at cover point. From that moment, Atherton blossomed and produced one of his most fluent innings until, on 71, he fell for the bait, and hooked a gleeful Donald to deep square leg. Ten runs later, Butcher slashed the same, disbelieving bowler to Kirsten at third man! It was

Jacques Kallis hits out against Tufnell and is nearly caught in the deep by Caddick on the second day of the fourth Test.

FOURTH TEST SOUTH AFRICA v. ENGLAND
2, 3, 4 and 5 January 2000 at Newlands, Cape Town

ENGLAND

	First Innings		Second Innings	
MA Butcher	c Kirsten, b Donald	40	c Boucher, b Pollock	4
MA Atherton	c Kirsten, b Donald	71	c Cullinan, b Pollock	35
N Hussain (capt)	c Boucher, b Adams	15	lbw b Klusener	16
MP Vaughan	c Kirsten, b Donald	42	c Boucher, b Klusener	5
*AJ Stewart	c Kirsten, b Donald	40	b Adams	5
AR Caddick	c Cullinan, b Donald	0	(7) c Gibbs, b Donald	14
CJ Adams	c Pollock, b Kallis	10	(6) b Adams	31
A Flintoff	c Rhodes, b Klusener	22	absent injured	
D Gough	c Boucher b Klusener	4	(8) c Donald, b Kallis	8
CEW Silverwood	not out	1	(9) not out	5
PCR Tufnell	b Kallis	2	(10) c Cullinan, b Adams	0
	lb6, w2, nb3	11	lb3	3
		258		**126**

	First Innings				Second Innings			
	O	M	R	W	O	M	R	W
Donald	26	13	47	5	10.4	2	35	1
Pollock	27	8	59	–	14	8	19	2
Kallis	20	4	61	2	9.2	2	19	1
Klusener	16	5	42	2	7	4	8	2
Cronje	3	2	5	–				
Adams	21	9	38	1	19.3	5	42	3

Fall of Wickets
1–115, 2–125, 3–141, 4–213, 5–213, 6–218, 7–231, 8–253, 9–255
1–4, 2–40, 3–59, 4–62, 5–66, 6–105, 7–113, 8–125, 9–126

SOUTH AFRICA

	First Innings	
G Kirsten	c Stewart, b Silverwood	80
HH Gibbs	c Vaughan, b Silverwood	29
JH Kallis	c Atherton, b Gough	105
DJ Cullinan	c Vaughan, b Tufnell	120
WJ Cronje (capt)	c Vaughan, b Caddick	0
JN Rhodes	c Adams, b Silverwood	16
L Klusener	b Gough	3
SM Pollock	c Adams, b Caddick	4
*MV Boucher	lbw b Silverwood	36
AA Donald	c Adams, b Silverwood	7
PR Adams	not out	3
	b1, lb7, nb10	18
		421

	First Innings			
	O	M	R	W
Gough	37	6	88	2
Caddick	31	6	95	2
Silverwood	32	6	91	5
Flintoff	4	0	16	–
Tufnell	39.4	10	97	1
Butcher	3	0	9	–
Adams	7	2	17	–

Fall of Wickets
1–43, 2–201, 3–246, 4–247, 5–279, 6–290, 7–307, 8–397, 9–405

Umpires: CJ Mitchley & BC Cooray
Toss: England
Test Debuts: nil

South Africa won by an innings and 37 runs

too appalling for words: 115 without loss became 141 for 3 when Hussain was dismissed for the first time in three innings, caught by Boucher as a ball from Adams brushed his glove.

Stewart, fresh from his wonderful innings at Durban, was soon into his stride. He raced to 40 from only 65 balls in a partnership with the increasingly composed Vaughan when he became the third batsman to give his wicket away. Once again the hook trap was set and once again he picked out Kirsten with commendable accuracy. For Stewart to argue that the hook shot brings him plenty of runs is not good enough: far too often England's batsmen do not play according to the situation in hand and this, with the close of play fast approaching, should have been the time for restraint and responsibility. In fact Caddick, the nightwatchman, was dispatched from the dressing room and instantly dismissed by Donald to leave England on 215 for 5.

This was indeed the moment for the new generation of England's batsmen to stand up and make their mark. Vaughan began the day on 40, Adams nought and with Andrew Flintoff the next man in, the scene was set. But within 22 overs they had all gone. Vaughan added only two before becoming Donald's fifth victim, Adams edged a

The Test match (and the series) ends as Tufnell is caught out by Cullinan off the bowling of Adams.

drive to slip for 10 and, having scored 22 from 47 balls, Flintoff charged Klusener's first delivery and skied a catch to point to give the seam bowler his first wicket of the series. Klusener and Kallis wrapped it up as England lost five for 43 in the morning. All ten wickets had gone down for only 143 runs. By the close of the second day, England were already heading for defeat. Kirsten and Kallis enjoyed the serene batting conditions, taking South Africa to 200 for 1 with an unbeaten stand of 157.

With only a 58-run advantage, England needed to strike quickly, and Silverwood broke through in the first over of the third day when Kirsten nicked a catch to Stewart for 80. Kallis, who had been dropped by Stewart the previous day on only 11, reached a glorious century on his home ground before Atherton held on to an excellent, face-high slip catch off Gough. Cronje failed again, and when Rhodes, Klusener and Pollock all fell cheaply, England were back in the hunt. Once again, they could not complete the job. This time it was Cullinan, the most attractive South African batsman in the match, who took the game away from them. He received excellent support from the redoubtable Boucher, who is fast becoming as aggravating a thorn in England's side as Ian Healy in the Ashes Tests of the 1990s. The pair added 90, stretching the lead to 140 before Boucher found himself on the wrong end of a leg-before decision that beggared belief. Cullinan was the last man out for 120 when

he mowed Tufnell to mid-wicket. Given the extent of their exertions in Durban, England's bowlers kept going manfully. Silverwood recorded his first five-wicket haul in Test cricket, and the blame for England's predicament lay firmly with their batsmen.

England began the fourth day with all their second-innings wickets intact and a deficit of 159. Conditions remained favourable for batting and clearly what was required was a cautious start. Butcher's gruesome firm-footed drive at a wide, good-length delivery in the second over, therefore, was hugely disappointing. Hussain and Atherton took the score to 40, at which point the England captain received the worst umpiring decision of the series. He edged a full-length ball from Klusener along the ground towards the slip cordon and was adjudged leg before wicket. At no point did the ball strike either his pad or his boot, yet BC Cooray raised his finger in response to an optimistic appeal from the bowler. In the circumstances, Hussain's restraint was admirable.

England were now sliding down the slippery slope and towards the abyss. Vaughan essayed a cut to a delivery too close to him and edged to Boucher, Atherton fell to a brilliant catch to Cullinan's left at first slip and Stewart was bowled, hitting across the line at Adams. That was 66 for 5 and South Africa scented victory within four days. They were not to be disappointed as England, without Flintoff whose tour was ended by a fractured bone in his left foot through bowling, capitulated to 126 all out. South Africa's victory, by an innings and 37 runs, was the heaviest they had ever inflicted on England and it secured the series with one Test match still to play.

SA Invitation XI v. England
9, 10 and 11 Jan at Port Elizabeth
SA Invitation XI 253 (86.5 overs)(PJR Steyn 93, JDC Bryant 69)
England 331 (90.2 overs) (NV Knight)
Match drawn

This match should never have been in England's schedule. Dragged east to Port Elizabeth en route to Pretoria for the final Test, all the players who lost in Cape Town were rested and replaced by the one-day specialists, who had recently arrived for the triangular series that followed. Graeme Hick led England for the first time and scored 57, while Knight warmed up with a very good century. The game fizzled out into a dull draw.

FIFTH TEST
14, 15, 16, 17 and 18 Jan at Centurion Park
England won by 2 wickets

Sadly, and after an historic final day in which both captains agreed to forfeit an innings in order to set up an exciting finale to the series, this match was soon to be exposed as a sham. This was through no fault of England's, but entirely of the disgraced captain of South Africa, Hansie Cronje, whose decision to declare was rewarded by a bookmaker. He paid Cronje £5,000 and gave him a leather jacket.

The news of the declaration and double forfeiture was greeted rapturously by the strong contingent of English supporters who had paid something in the region of £3,000 to make the trip and who had spent the previous three days mooching around in the Sandton Shopping Centre. Suddenly the journey had been worthwhile and the fact that England won the thrilling run chase was merely the icing on the cake.

On a drizzly, grey opening day, play was delayed and interrupted to the extent that only 63 overs were possible. In this period – Hussain having put South Africa into bat – the ball nipped about off the seam quite alarmingly, but England's bowlers simply wasted the conditions. It was not impossible to imagine an experienced county attack dismissing the opposition for less than 100, but South Africa reached 155 for 6 at the close of the first day and the scoreboard did not change for another four days.

The problem was the bowlers' run-ups at the River Henopps end. A large, boggy patch refused to dry out and was made worse by overnight downpours. That being said, there was a general feeling in the media centre that if either team had been desperate to play in order to win the series, they might well have made an appearance on the fourth day when the wet patch was little more than an inconvenience. Indeed, the groundstaff were of the opinion that the ground was fit for play.

It was on that fourth morning that the other alternative – declaring the Test a draw and playing an unofficial one-day game – was ruled out. This followed a discussion between Dr Ali Bacher, the managing director of the United Cricket Board of South Africa, and the match referee, Barry Jarman. Rightly, they concluded that this would have been a step too far.

The first indication of unusual developments came before play started on the final day. A South African journalist announced that Cronje had declared immediately and that a deal had already been struck.

This seemed unlikely because Hussain could not have accepted a run chase until he had seen how the pitch would behave having been under a plastic sheet for three days but, nonetheless, our spirits were raised. They positively soared when, a few overs into the day, Hussain left the field for a while and then a succession of messages were relayed to South Africa's batsmen by the 12th man. Something was definitely cooking!

Klusener carefully negotiated the losses of Pollock, brilliantly run out by Hussain from mid-on for 30 and then Boucher for 22 to finish with 61 not out. The ball had barely moved off the straight and when Cronje called his batsmen in, setting England 249 to win from 76 overs, it seemed the South African captain had been extraordinarily generous.

To cheers from the rapidly swelling crowd, both teams took the field with 20 minutes to play before lunch. England's openers safely weathered this tricky period and in the absence of Allan Donald – who was forced out of the match due to an attack of gout – it was already clear that South Africa might miss their leading fast bowler. This was compounded later in the afternoon when Paul Adams badly dislocated a finger on his left hand while fielding and could not bowl a single ball in the game.

Early English optimism was dented when Mike Atherton edged Pollock to Boucher for 7: 28 for 1

Pieter Strydom, whose debut for South Africa was marred after his naming in the King Commision. Fielding at deep point, Strydom appeared not to see the ball and conceded a vital boundary.

became 102 for 4 with the losses of Butcher, Hussain and Adams – who had been promoted above the more obdurate Michael Vaughan. The manner in which Stewart and Vaughan approached their innings suggested that England had shut up shop and suddenly their partnership began to blossom. Stewart had reached 73 – and taken England to within 21 runs of victory – when Boucher snapped him up off the bowling of Hayward. Eight runs later, Maddy was run out for 3, attempting an unlikely second, and in the same over Caddick was caught by Boucher off Pollock for a duck. Suddenly, England were 236 for 7, still 13 runs short and with time running out.

With nine runs required from 11 balls, Vaughan's inexperience caught up with him and, backing away, he was bowled by Hayward for 69. Now, as Silverwood joined Gough – and with only Mullally to come – England were up against it.

Pollock bowled a brilliant penultimate over but was let down by Strydom – repeatedly named in the King Commission – who was fielding on the cover boundary. Silverwood carved the final delivery

The shamed face of South Africa's captain Hansie Cronje, who accepted a bribe from a bookmaker to declare on the fifth day of the final Test.

FIFTH TEST SOUTH AFRICA v. ENGLAND
14, 15, 16, 17 and 18 January 2000 at Supersport Park, Centurion

SOUTH AFRICA

	First Innings	
G Kirsten	c Adams, b Gough	0
HH Gibbs	c Adams, b Caddick	3
JH Kallis	b Caddick	25
DJ Cullinan	c & b Mullally	46
WJ Cronje (capt)	c Maddy, b Gough	0
PC Strydom	c Stewart, b Silverwood	30
L Klusener	not out	61
SM Pollock	run out (Hussain)	30
*MV Boucher	b Mullally	22
PR Adams	not out	4
M Hayward		
	b2, lb11, w3, nb11	27
	(for 8 wickets dec.)	248

	First Innings			
	O	M	R	W
Gough	20	2	92	2
Caddick	19	7	61	2
Mullally	24	10	42	2
Silverwood	7	1	45	1
Vaughan	2	0	9	–

Fall of Wickets
1–1, 2–15, 3–50, 4–55, 5–102, 6–136, 7–196, 8–243,

South Africa forfeited their second innings and England forfeited their first innings

ENGLAND

	Second Innings	
MA Butcher	lbw b Klusener	36
MA Atherton	c Boucher, b Pollock	7
N Hussain (capt)	c Gibbs, b Pollock	25
*AJ Stewart	c Boucher, b Hayward	73
CJ Adams	c Boucher, b Hayward	1
MP Vaughan	b Hayward	69
DL Maddy	run out (Kirsten)	3
AR Caddick	c Boucher, b Pollock	0
D Gough	not out	6
CEW Silverwood	not out	7
AD Mullally		
	b4, lb9, w4, nb3	24
	(for 8 wickets)	251

	Second Innings			
	O	M	R	W
Pollock	20	7	53	3
Hayward	17.1	3	61	3
Klusener	14	4	38	1
Kallis	13	2	44	–
Cronje	5	3	15	–
Strydom	6	0	27	–

Fall of Wickets
1–28, 2–67, 3–90, 4–102, 5–228, 6–236, 7–236, 8–240

Umpires: RE Koertzen & DB Hair
Toss: England
Test Debuts: PC Strydom

England won by two wickets

TEST MATCH AVERAGES
South Africa v. England

SOUTH AFRICA

Batting	M	Inns	NO	HS	Runs	Av	100	50
L Klusener	5	6	1	174	370	74.00	1	2
G Kirsten	5	7	0	275	396	56.57	1	1
DJ Cullinan	5	7	0	120	386	55.14	2	1
JN Rhodes	3	4	1	57*	149	49.66	–	2
JH Kallis	5	7	1	105	297	49.50	1	2
MV Boucher	5	6	1	108	212	42.40	1	–
HH Gibbs	5	7	0	85	203	29.00	–	1
SM Pollock	5	6	1	64	114	22.80	–	1
PR Adams	4	4	3	9	16	16.00	–	–
WJ Cronje	5	7	0	44	102	14.57	–	–
AA Donald	4	4	0	9	16	4.00	–	–

Also batted: M Hayward (3 Tests) 10*, 0*;PC Strydom (1 Test) 30

Fielding
19 – MV Boucher;4 – G Kirsten, L Klusener.3 – DJ Cullinan, SM Pollock, JN Rhodes.
2 – PR Adams, HH Gibbs, JH Kallis.1 – AA Donald

Bowling	Overs	Mds	Runs	Wkts	Av	Best	10m	5/inn
AA Donald	145.2	41	422	22	19.18	6–53	1	3
SM Pollock	184.2	69	396	19	20.84	4–16	–	–
M Hayward	85.2	21	265	10	26.50	4–75	–	–
PR Adams	95.3	32	190	7	27.14	3–42	–	–
JH Kallis	72.2	18	184	5	36.80	2–22	–	–
L Klusener	118	40	276	5	55.20	2–8	–	–

Also bowled: WJ Cronje 48 – 24 – 84 – 3;PC Strydom 6 – 0 – 27 – 0

ENGLAND

Batting	M	Inns	NO	HS	Runs	Av	100	50
N Hussain	5	8	2	146*	370	61.66	1	2
AJ Stewart	5	8	0	95	342	42.75	–	3
MP Vaughan	4	7	0	69	204	29.14	–	1
MA Atherton	5	8	0	108	225	28.12	1	1
A Flintoff	4	6	0	42	155	25.83	–	–
MA Butcher	5	8	0	48	166	20.75	–	–
D Gough	5	7	3	16*	64	16.00	–	–
AR Caddick	5	8	1	48	105	15.00	–	–
CJ Adams	5	8	0	31	104	13.00	–	–
CEW Silverwood	4	5	3	7*	19	9.50	–	–
PCR Tufnell	3	4	2	7*	9	4.50	–	–

Also batted: GM Hamilton (1 Test) 0, 0; DL Maddy (2 Tests) 24, 3;
AD Mullally (2 Tests) 10, 0

Fielding
14 – AJ Stewart (13ct/1st); 6 – CJ Adams, MP Vaughan. 3 – MA Atherton, DL Maddy.
2 – A Flintoff, N Hussain. 1 – AR Caddick, AD Mullally, CEW Silverwood

Bowling	Overs	Mds	Runs	Wkts	Av	Best	10m	5/inn
AD Mullally	58	17	122	5	24.40	3–80	–	–
AR Caddick	185	51	468	16	29.25	7–46	–	1
D Gough	171	34	527	14	37.64	5–70	–	1
A Flintoff	66.5	16	190	5	38.00	2–31	–	–
CEW Silverwood	109	19	344	7	49.14	5–91	–	1
PCR Tufnell	171.4	35	433	6	72.16	4–124	–	–

Also bowled: CJ Adams 20–5–59–1;MA Butcher 11.2–0–41–2; GM Hamilton 15–1–63–0;
N Hussain 5–0–15–0; DL Maddy 14–1–40–0; MP Vaughan 18–1–73–0

towards Strydom, who claimed not to see the ball and ran in the wrong direction! One run became four, which meant that just two were needed from the last over of the match. Gough heaved the first ball through mid-wicket and England began their celebrations, cruelly unaware of Cronje's devious motives. Unfortunately, one of the many sad conclusions to have been drawn, in retrospect, is that connivance of this nature between captains for the good of the game will never happen again. Test cricket lost its innocence at Centurion Park.

Gary Kirsten turns in time to see the ball he has edged going into the hands of Chris Adams at second slip.

STANDARD BANK ONE-DAY SERIES
By Jonathan Agnew

England's heartening victory in the final Test match gave them a welcome boost as the emphasis of the tour now switched to one-day cricket. Six 'specialists' – Mark Alleyne, Mark Ealham, Graeme Hick, Nick Knight, Vikram Solanki and Craig White – were added to the party but, controversially, Alec Stewart was one of the Test players sent home. Considering the innings of 73 that helped England to their win at Centurion Park, his reputation and his all-round ability, it did seem a curious decision. However, this was not a tournament of any enormous significance – far from it – and Stewart did need a minor operation on an injured hand that had been troubling him for a number of seasons.

A friendly 'pipe-opener' was staged at Potchefstroom, deep in Afrikaner country, where England successfully dealt with one of the weaker first-class teams in the country, North West. Of interest was that England omitted Chris Read – Stewart's replacement. Instead, Alleyne kept wicket, suggesting that the England management also recognised a potential weakness. Hick and White both completed half-centuries and North West never threatened to eclipse England's total of 264 for 9.

South Africa and Zimbabwe began the tournament proper at the Wanderers. Zimbabwe were restricted to 226 with Goodwin scoring 73. South Africa were steered to victory with 11 balls to spare by Cronje, who made an unbeaten 83.

Two days later, a huge crowd gathered on a blustery stormy morning in Bloemfontein to witness England's first encounter with South Africa. It was quickly silenced as South Africa subsided to 23 for 4 and then, in the 15th over, 53 for 5. The match was already effectively over as Gough claimed four of the first five wickets to fall. The only stand of any note was that of 69 between Kallis, who made 57, and Strydom – 34. That, and a few lusty blows from Klusener and Pollock, set England 185 to win. Any thoughts the crowd might have had about seeing wickets tumbling against the new ball were scuppered most emphatically by Hussain and Knight, who put on 165 and took England to within 20 of victory off their own bats. Hick finished it off and the spectators, who had spent most of the afternoon tending to the barbecues rather than watching the contest, left the ground early and most disgruntled.

Then it was on to Cape Town where England had the prospect of an enjoyable week in the only South African city worth a visit, and floodlit matches against both South Africa and Zimbabwe. England have never been as successful under lights as they would like, although their defeat by South Africa was, after a predominately boring match, a one-run classic.

Gough, again, bowled well, taking 3 for 36 as South Africa were restricted to only 204 for 7. England quickly found themselves behind the rate on a slow, increasingly damp pitch and, with two overs to go, required an unlikely 26 to win. Up stepped Read, who smashed 26 from only 23 balls. Nine were required off the final over, and four off the last ball to give the game some instant excitement. Gough could manage only two.

Two days and a trip to Robben Island later, it was time for England to make amends in the first match of the tournament against Zimbabwe. Again, the conditions made fast scoring extremely difficult but, even so, Zimbabwe's 211 for 7 seemed vulnerable. Henry Olonga, the opera-singing pace bowler with the extraordinary hairdo, then produced the spell of his life. In eight overs, he claimed 5 for 18 which left England with nowhere to go. Of the top six, only Hussain and Solanki reached double figures and when England were 47 for 6, the game was over. England stumbled on to reach 100, but were bowled out for 107 with Olonga finishing with 6 for 19.

England bounced back with a thorough annihilation at Kimberly two days later when Mark Ealham claimed the best figures ever recorded by an Englishman in limited-overs cricket. He took 5 for 15 – all of them lbw – as Zimbabwe crawled to 161

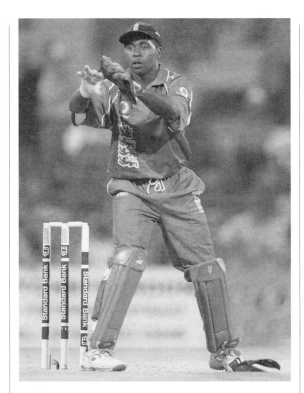

Mark Alleyne – a jack of all trades – who was added to the England side for the one-day series.

for 9. Hick's poor run against his native Zimbabwe continued – he made only 9 – but Knight's unbeaten 72 from 94 balls saw England home with eight wickets and nearly 18 overs in hand.

At this stage in the tournament, England and South Africa appeared to be heading comfortably towards the final. However, every one-day tournament throws up a surprise and this was provided at Durban where Zimbabwe, chasing 223 to beat South Africa, recovered from 107 for 6 to win off the last ball of the match. This also gave Zimbabwe the highest net run-rate of the three teams and every game was vital from now on. England had a week kicking their heels in East London – in fact, that is just about the most interesting thing to do there! – before meeting South Africa under lights. It was a good game, for once, with England setting the home team 232 thanks to another half-century from Knight and Alleyne's first fifty for England. South Africa were soon 126 for 5. McKenzie and Rhodes added 37, with Rhodes batting brilliantly until he was superbly caught by Alleyne at mid-off for 42. Eight were needed from the last over and, from the first two

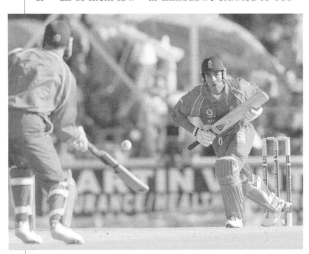

Vikram Solanki, one of the six specialists added to the England side, going for runs at Potchefstroom.

Zimbabwe celebrate the run-out of Mark Ealham at Cape Town.

balls, only one was scored. Pollock then swept an Ealham full toss for four and slogged the next to the boundary to give South Africa the points and leave England facing a make or break game against Zimbabwe in order to reach the final.

This was confirmed when South Africa defeated Zimbabwe by 53 runs at Port Elizabeth, but torrential rain – being part of the dreadful storms that brought chaos to neighbouring Mozambique – moved into the region. The first effect was to wash out the match at Centurion Park which enabled England to qualify for the final by virtue of their now superior net run-rate. Next, the storms caused the first day of the final to be obliterated – there was even talk of moving the game to Cape Town – prompting Ali Bacher to throw our tour plans into chaos by adding a third day to the showpiece. In the end this was not needed as both teams showed a refreshing determination to play in less than ideal conditions. Frankly, England's players were so heartily sick of Johannesburg by now they would have played in absolutely anything in order for them to move out.

When South Africa were bowled out for 149, with Caddick taking 4 for 19, it seemed that England would leave the country in high spirits. But that dream was destroyed by Pollock, who produced a spell of high-quality seam bowling in helpful conditions to take 5 for 20. He was helped by some superb catching – Kallis's effort at second slip to dismiss Hick was absolutely breathtaking – as England slipped to 64 for 6 and were bowled out in 38 overs for 111. Pollock was named not only Man of the Match, but also man of an unremarkable and easily forgettable series.

Match One – South Africa v. Zimbabwe
21 January 2000 at New Wanderers Stadium, Johannesburg (floodlit)
Zimbabwe 226 (49.5 overs)(MW Goodwin 73)
South Africa 229 for 4 (48.1 overs)(WJ Cronje 83*, HH Gibbs 65)
South Africa (2 pts) won by six wickets
Man of the Match: WJ Cronje

Match Two – South Africa v. England
23 January 2000 at Goodyear Park, Bloemfontein
South Africa 184 (49.5 overs)(JH Kallis 57, D Gough 4 for 29)
England 185 for 1 (39.3 overs)(N Hussain 85, NV Knight 71*)
England (2 pts) won by nine wickets
Man of the Match: D Gough

Match Three – South Africa v. England
26 January 2000 at Newlands, Cape Town (floodlit)
South Africa 204 for 7 (50 overs)
England 203 for 9 (50 overs)
South Africa (2 pts) won by 1 run
Man of the Match: L Klusener

Dale Benkenstein turns to see he has been bowled by Darren Gough at Bloemfontein.

Match Four – England v. Zimbabwe

28 January 2000 at Newlands, Cape Town (floodlit)
Zimbabwe 211 for 7 (50 overs)(NC Johnson 97)
England 107 (34.2 overs)(HK Olonga 6 for 19)
Zimbabwe (2 pts) won by 104 runs
Man of the Match: HK Olonga

Match Five – England v. Zimbabwe

30 January 2000 at De Beers Diamond Oval, Kimberley
Zimbabwe 161 for 9 (50 overs)(MA Ealham 5 for 15)
England 162 for 2 (32.1 overs)(NV Knight 72*,
N Hussain 64)
England (2 pts) won by eight wickets
Man of the Match: MA Ealham

Match Six – South Africa v. Zimbabwe

2 February 2000 at Kingsmead, Durban (floodlit)
South Africa 222 for 7 (50 overs)(L Klusener 65*,
JH Kallis 52)
Zimbabwe 223 for 8 (50 overs)(A Flower 59)
Zimbabwe (2 pts) won by two wickets
Man of the Match: A Flower

Match Seven – South Africa v. England

4 February 2000 at Buffalo Park, East London (floodlit)
England 231 for 6 (50 overs)(NV Knight 64,
MW Alleyne 53)
South Africa 233 for 8 (49.4 overs)
South Africa (2 pts) won by two wickets
Man of the Match: MW Alleyne

Match Eight – South Africa v. Zimbabwe

6 February 2000 at St George's Park, Port Elizabeth
South Africa 204 for 7 (50 overs)(JH Kallis 98*)
Zimbabwe 151 (46 overs)(NC Johnson 56)
South Africa (2 pts) won by 53 runs

Match Nine – England v. Zimbabwe

9 February 2000 at Supersport Park, Centurion
(floodlit)
Match abandoned without a ball bowled – 1 pt each

STANDARD BANK FINAL–SOUTH AFRICA v. ENGLAND
12 (no play) and 13 February 2000 at New Wanderers Stadium, Johannesburg (floodlit)

SOUTH AFRICA

Batting				Bowling	O	M	R	W
H Gibbs	c Knight, b Gough	8		Caddick	9	1	19	4
ND McKenzie	b Caddick	4		Gough	9	2	18	3
JH Kallis	b Gouhh	0		Mullally	9	3	22	1
WJ Cronje (capt)	c Knight, b Mullally	56		White	7	0	38	–
JN Rhodes	c Hick, b Caddick	5		Ealham	5	0	24	–
SM Pollock	c White, b Caddick	0		Alleyne	6	0	23	1
*MV Boucher	c Hick, b Alleyne	36						
L Klusener	c Hussain, b Gough	10		**Fall of Wickets**				
PC Strydom	c Maddy, b Caddick	3		1–14, 2–14, 3–14, 4–21, 5–21,				
S Elworthy	not out	8		6–95, 7–129, 8–132, 9–134				
HS Williams	run out (Gough)	7						
	lb5, w6, nb1	12						
	45 overs	**149**						

ENGLAND

Batting				Bowling	O	M	R	W
N Hussain (capt)	c Boucher, b Pollock	8		Pollock	9	1	20	5
NV Knight	c Boucher, b Pollock	10		Kallis	8	0	25	2
GA Hick	c Kallis, b Pollock	12		Elworthy	6	0	19	–
DL Maddy	c Kallis, b Pollock	0		Williams	6	0	18	1
MW Alleyne	c Cronje, b Pollock	6		Klusener	9	1	28	2
C White	b Klusener	16						
MA Ealham	c Boucher, b Klusener	4		**Fall of Wickets**				
*CMW Read	lbw b Williams	9		1–16, 2–22, 3–23, 4–41, 5–45,				
AR Caddick	c Boucher, b Kallis	7		14 6–64, 7–72, 8–83, 9–87				
D Gough	c Boucher, b Kallis	1						
AD Mullally	not out							
	lb1, w21, nb2	24						
	38 overs	**111**						

Umpires: RE Koertzen & DL Orchard
Toss: England
Man of the Match: SM Pollock
Man of the Series: SM Pollock

South Africa won by 38 runs

ZIMBABWE IN SOUTH AFRICA
By Neil Manthorp

Bloemfontein's inaugural Test match was dominated by South Africa, from the moment Hansie Cronje won the toss to shortly after lunch on the fourth day when Henry Olonga was superbly caught by Jonty Rhodes at mid-off.

Olonga's demise, for his highest Test score of 24, in the fifth over of the second session saw South Africa surge to victory by an innings and 13 runs. It was a harsh introduction to Test cricket on South African soil for the losers, their only previous engagement with their southern neighbours at that stage being the match South Africa won by seven wickets in Harare in 1995–96.

The South African players' attention was diverted from the match on the first two days by important developments further afield. On the first day, news filtered through that Makhaya Ntini's way back into the game had been paved by the success of his appeal against his conviction and six-year sentence for rape. The second day's third session was overshadowed by South Africa's Rugby World Cup semi-final against Australia at Twickenham, and the dressing room television was tuned accordingly. Had South Africa been playing more formidable opponents in Bloemfontein such laxity would no doubt have been frowned on. But at tea on the second day South Africa were in control at 183 for 3 in reply to Zimbabwe's first innings of 192.

Cronje began his innings needing 12 runs to surpass Gary Kirsten and become South Africa's most prolific run-scorer. He duly did so, but it proved a temporary honour as Kirsten reclaimed the record. Cronje's decision to insert the tourists paid early dividends when they stumbled to 47 for 3 at lunch on a lively though far from unfair pitch that was out of character with the batsman-friendly surfaces normally prepared in the Free State capital. Shaun Pollock, who bowled with perfect rhythm, completed a memorable day for him with figures of 5 for 39, his tenth five-wicket haul in Test cricket.

His father Peter enjoyed nine such successes, but in 28 matches.

'He did it in fewer games, so if I bring it up he's sure to remind me of that,' Pollock junior said. South Africa's total of 417 was built on weighty scores from Jacques Kallis, Cronje, Rhodes and Mark Boucher, whose unbeaten 55 at number nine sapped whatever resolve the Zimbabweans had left. Olonga's return of 4 for 93 had more to do with doggedness than penetrative bowling. The home side's last wicket fell 20 minutes before the scheduled tea interval on the third day and by the close Zimbabwe had slumped to 123 for 5 with Kallis swinging the ball wickedly to claim four wickets, three of them in the space of ten deliveries and at a cost of two runs.

It was all downhill for Zimbabwe after Pollock trapped Neil Johnson in front offering no stroke with the second ball of what became the final day, and Paul Adams did a textbook job of cleaning up the tail in taking 4 for 31. Whittall spent two courageous hours at the crease for his 51, but that was never going to be enough.

Shaun Pollock following in his father's footsteps. His consistent form took its toll on the Zimbabwean batsmen.

TEST MATCH SOUTH AFRICA v. ZIMBABWE
29, 30, 31 October and 1 November 1999 at Goodyear Park, Bloemfontein

ZIMBABWE

	First Innings		Second Innings	
GJ Rennie	lbw b Pollock	0	b Kallis	8
TR Gripper	run out (Dippenaar)	16	lbw b Kallis	11
MW Goodwin	c Boucher, b Pollock	7	c Boucher, b Kallis	0
ADR Campbell (capt)	c Klusener, b Pollock	27	c Cronje, b Pollock	33
*A Flower	lbw b Pollock	13	lbw b Kallis	39
NC Johnson	c Boucher, b Donald	6	lbw b Pollock	23
GJ Rennie	c Cullinan, b Kallis	14	c Boucher, b Adams	10
GJ Whittall	c Boucher, b Kallis	85	b Adams	51
BC Strang	c Cronje, b Pollock	9	lbw b Adams	0
HK Olonga	b Kallis	1	c Rhodes, b Adams	24
M Mbangwa	not out	0	not out	0
	lb6, w3, nb5	14	lb4, w5, nb4	13
		192		**212**

	First Innings				Second Innings			
	O	M	R	W	O	M	R	W
Donald	18	5	58	1	15	6	25	-
Pollock	21	6	39	5	19	5	62	2
Klusener	16	5	40	-	4	0	22	-
Kallis	17	4	44	3	21	3	68	4
Adams	3	1	5	-	12.1	5	31	4

Fall of Wickets
1-1, 2-14, 3-41, 4-63, 5-78, 6-79, 7-117, 8-140, 9-183
1-11, 2-19, 3-24, 4-77, 5-115, 6-123, 7-166, 8-166, 9-202

SOUTH AFRICA

	First Innings	
HH Dippenaar	lbw b Olonga	20
AM Bacher	c Goodwin, b Mbangwa	42
JH Kallis	lbw b Whittall	64
DJ Cullinan	c GW Flower, b Whittall	27
WJ Cronje (capt)	c A Flower, b Mbangwa	64
JN Rhodes	lbw b Olonga	70
SM Pollock	c Campbell, b Strang	8
L Klusener	lbw b GW Flower	19
*MV Boucher	not out	55
AA Donald	b Olonga	2
PR Adams	c Gripper, b Olonga	20
	lb3, w1, nb22	26
		417

	First Innings			
	O	M	R	W
Olonga	33.1	7	93	4
Strang	27	6	99	1
Johnson	2	0	8	-
Flower GW	23	5	44	1
Mbangwa	35	9	75	2
Whittall	30	9	95	2

Fall of Wickets
1-43, 2-72, 3-128, 4-218, 5-266, 6-278, 7-310, 8-342, 9-363

Umpires: DL Orchard & RS Dunne
Toss: South Africa
Test Debut: HH Dippenaar

South Africa won by an innings and 13 runs

SOUTH AFRICA DOMESTIC FIRST-CLASS SEASON
By Telford Vice

South Africa's provincial teams encountered their first season split into two divisions, and there can be no indication at this stage whether the move will be a success. Attendances at first-class matches are negligible, so that is no gauge; the cricket played seemed no more nor less competitive; and overall it was hardly noticeable that anything had changed.

The 11 teams were seeded on the basis of their results from the previous three seasons, with Easterns and North West bringing up the rear as new entries to the top flight. The seedings for 2000–2001 will be determined by 1999–2000's performances alone. The six Pool 'A' sides played five matches each, and the Pool 'B' teams four each. At the end of the league stage the top four teams from each pool contested the Super Eight series, and the remaining three were left to fight over the scraps offered in the Shield series.

The top two sides after the Super Eight stage, in which each team played four matches, met in a five-day final. Pool 'A', then, consisted of Border, Gauteng, Eastern Province, Northerns, Griqualand West and Easterns, with Pool 'B' made up of Natal, Free State, Boland, Western Province and North West. The three unfortunates who limped all the way to the Shield series were Griqualand West, North West and Easterns, while Gauteng topped the Super Eight series standings followed by Border.

Border, bridesmaids in both the first-class and limited-overs competitions a summer before after enduring more than a century as an unfashionable province, came to the Wanderers for the final determined to etch their name on the honours board. They had won three of their five pool matches and four of their seven Super Eight games with one loss. Border had clearly grown weary of their unfashionable status and their cricket was driven by the positive energy of a team whose time had come.

Gauteng, though, had played like a team used to winning. They had an identical Super Eight record to Border, but lost one match in the pool stage. So the final was all set to be an unfolding drama of old money versus the impoverished upstarts from down south. It did not disappoint. Gauteng captain Clive Eksteen won the toss and, on the advice of the groundsman, Chris Scott, asked Border to bat. It seemed an odd decision as the pitch did not look as if it would bother diligent batsmen unduly.

Then Border's sixth wicket tumbled with just 113 on the board, and Scott was hailed as a wise man. Not that his pitch had been entirely to blame for Border's spiral – injudicious batting had earned its share. As had accurate, aggressive bowling, particularly by Andrew Hall who would end the innings with 5 for 67. Captain and number six Pieter Strydom kept his attacking instincts in check to prop up an end, and after tea on the first day he was supplied with a sabre for his foil. Tyron Henderson, a brawny fast bowler who makes up with a keen eye and frightening power what he sacrifices to a somewhat wanting technique, joined his skipper and employed his idea of the drive to great effect in smashing 43 not out off 24 balls.

Strydom looked on his charge with something approaching awe as they left the field having ushered Border to the relative safety of 260 for 8. And well the captain might have – he had spent four unflinching hours on his unbeaten 78. The partnership was ended at 78 in the tenth over of the second day's play when Strydom was bowled by Kenny Benjamin having added ten runs to his score.

The Border tail had one more kink, however, as Makhaya Ntini helped Henderson add 63 for the last wicket before the innings ended at 346 in the second hour. Henderson played far more conservatively than a day earlier and his eventual 81 was the product of 87 balls and included nine fours and three sixes. By the close, Gauteng had scored an ominous-looking 221 for 3 with Daryll Cullinan well set on 55. Border had been significantly hampered by a thigh muscle injury their exemplary overseas player, Vasbert Drakes, had sustained while batting. Drakes soldiered on bravely, but without the pace and bounce that had made him a perennial threat in the league rounds.

Supported mostly by Geoff Toyana, who scored 63, in a partnership that stretched to 135, Cullinan was able to keep the innings together before being eighth out for an innings of 120 that was almost six hours in the making. Gauteng were dismissed before tea on the third day with a lead of 41, and by the close Border had slumped to 130 for 5 – four of them to the immaculate Benjamin – as the match tilted towards the home side. Mark Boucher, though, was in defiant mode on 70 not out having shared 78 for the fourth wicket with Steven Pope.

Boucher continued on the fourth day, adding 79 with Ian Mitchell for the sixth wicket before being bowled by who else but Benjamin for 112 and having spent four and a half hours at the crease. Border were dismissed 222 after lunch, with

Benjamin taking 6 for 48 to earn match figures of 10 for 150. Gauteng were left a target of 182 with ample time and a still sound pitch on which to reach it. However, the injured Drakes summoned the strength from somewhere and, in cahoots with Piet Botha, reduced them to 74 for 6. But the home side were not about to falter at the final hurdle and Hall stepped into the breach with a pugnacious unbeaten half-century to lead Gauteng to victory by three wickets.

Natal's Errol Stewart was by far the domestic season's most successful batsman with 553 runs scored at an average of 92.16 with two centuries and three half-centuries, prompting calls for his recall to the national team. Drakes, named Man of the Series, broke Mike Procter's record for first-class wickets in a Currie Cup, Castle Cup or Supersport series season with 60 wickets at 16.25. Procter dismissed 59 men in 1976–77.

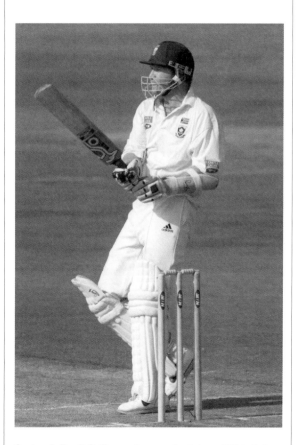

Gauteng's Daryll Cullinan, who scored a 6-hour 120 to help his team win the first-class final.

SOUTH AFRICA DOMESTIC ONE-DAY SEASON
By Telford Vice

Boland earned a workmanlike win over Eastern Province in the final at Paarl to celebrate their first major trophy. To the strains of the St George's Park band, which had been specially imported from Port Elizabeth for the occasion, Boland totalled a barely moderate 209 for 6 in their 45 overs in the face of tight bowling by the visitors on a none too straightforward pitch. Happily for the home side, whose supporters made ample use of the surrounding winelands' bounty in cheering their team to victory, Boland were able to restrict Eastern Province to 173 for 8.

Boland won the toss, but Meyrick Pringle's devilish away swing kept the score from climbing. Frustration set in and by the 27th over the score was 89 for 4. However, Justin Ontong, aged just 19, proved to be a batsman beyond his years in scoring an accomplished 67 off 73 balls. This was no wham bam knock, but a finely crafted innings in which just three deliveries were dispatched for four and one for six.

There was a spot of one-day bashing, but it came from Steven Palframan in a fifth-wicket stand of 90 that put Boland back on track for a decent total. However, the end product fell at least 20 runs short of that mark and it seemed Eastern Province, marshalled by veterans Mark Rushmere and Dave Callaghan and sparked by the youthful talent of Kevin Duckworth, Justin Kemp and Murray Creed, would have the measure of the Bolanders. That they didn't came down to a plucky effort by an attack that was deprived of the services of stalwarts Charl Willoughby and Henry Williams. Willoughby was with the South African team in Sharjah and Williams was forced out by injury. Their roles were admirably filled on the night by 18-year-old Con de Lange, Neil Carter and Charl Langeveldt. Not that the fates didn't attempt to conspire against the eventual champions: Kenny Jackson dropped two catches, and the second of these – Callaghan, in the slips – seemed certain to play into Eastern Province's hands. With the visitors reduced to 26 for 3 in the 11th over, it was clear they would have to rely on the old firm of Rushmere and Callaghan to dig them out of the ditch. And when Jackson grassed Callaghan, Boland's hopes of victory plunged. However, Rushmere and Callaghan had put on just 27 runs when De Lange removed the former.

Six overs later the same bowler accounted for Callaghan and at 125 for 6 in the 36th over Eastern Province's chances were plainly dwindling. Kemp and Creed attempted to coax the embers back into flame. However, Boland tightened their grip on the game and the trophy, and they were not letting go. Boland had finished second to Gauteng in the league rounds, with Eastern Province fourth behind Easterns.

The Eastern Province–Gauteng semi-finals turned out to be the better contests, with Callaghan scoring an epic century in the second leg to force a deciding match. Callaghan was in the thick of it again with a half-century in the third leg and Pringle swung the ball beautifully to take 2 for 12 off seven overs as Eastern Province won by 62 runs to book their berth in the final.

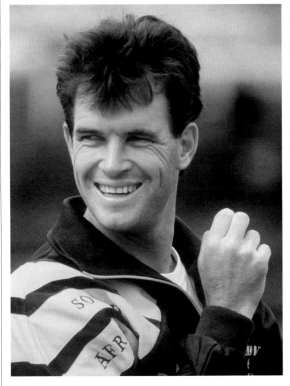

Mark Rushmere of Eastern Province, whose experience could not prevent Boland from lifting the trophy.

AUSTRALIA IN SOUTH AFRICA
ONE-DAY SERIES

Match One – South Africa v. Australia
12 April 2000 at Kingsmead, Durban (floodlit)
Australia 240 for 9 (50 overs)(DR Martyn 74,
AC Gilchrist 51, M Ntini 4 for 56)
South Africa 241 for 4 (48 overs)(GKirsten 97,
JH Kallis 61)
South Africa won by six wickets
Man of the Match: G Kirsten

Match Two – South Africa v. Australia
14 April 2000 at Newlands, Cape Town (floodlit)
South Africa 144 for 9 (50 overs)
Australia 145 for 5 (24.3 overs)(DR Martyn 50)
Australia won by five wickets
Man of the Match: DR Martyn

Match Three – South Africa v. Australia
16 April 2000 at New Wanderers, Johannesburg
Australia 205 (49.5 overs)(SR Waugh 51,
SM Pollock 4 for 37)
South Africa 209 for 6 (47.5 overs)(MV Boucher 55*,
L Klusener 52*)
South Africa won by four wickets
Man of the Match: L Klusener
Man of the Series: L Klusener

FIRST-CLASS AVERAGES

BATTING

	M	Inns	NO	HS	Runs	Av	100	50
D Jordaan	7	13	3	106	648	64.80	1	5
PC Strydom	10	14	2	125	759	63.25	2	7
L Klusener	9	11	2	174	545	60.55	1	3
DJ Cullinan	12	17	1	135	916	57.25	5	1
JDC Bryant	11	19	2	149	928	54.58	4	3
KR Rutherford	10	18	2	195*	818	51.12	3	3
N Hussain	9	14	3	146*	559	50.81	2	2
ML Bruyns	10	16	2	144	708	50.57	3	3
MV Boucher	10	14	2	112	598	49.83	2	3
G Kirsten	9	13	1	275	590	49.16	1	3
ND McKenzie	12	19	1	175	861	47.83	2	4
GM Hewitt	7	13	3	151	476	47.60	1	3
DJ Watson	10	16	2	220	659	47.07	1	3
JN Rhodes	6	9	1	124	375	46.87	1	3
JH Kallis	8	12	1	105	508	46.18	1	4
N Pothas	8	13	4	109*	415	46.11	1	2
DM Benkenstein	10	14	3	84	499	45.36	–	5
LJ Koen	9	16	2	113	634	45.28	1	4
JM Arthur	6	12	1	128	498	45.27	2	2
A Flintoff	7	11	2	89*	396	44.00	–	2
M van Jaarsfeld	11	18	5	238*	568	43.69	1	1
C Light	6	9	1	108*	347	43.37	1	1
MI Gidley	8	16	1	136	641	42.73	2	2
HH Dippenaar	9	17	1	200*	653	40.81	2	2
PJR Steyn	10	17	1	145	650	40.62	1	4
AM Bacher	11	19	0	195	768	40.42	2	2
MA Atherton	9	15	0	108	603	40.20	1	4
AG Prince	11	17	1	117	623	38.93	1	5
AM Amla	8	12	3	104	347	38.55	1	1
SJ Palframan	9	14	3	96	424	38.54	–	3
N Boje	9	18	4	76*	536	38.28	–	4
WJ Cronje	11	18	1	151*	650	38.23	2	1
PH Barnard	6	12	1	94	389	35.36	–	4
AC Hudson	8	12	1	106*	378	34.36	2	–
HD Ackerman	9	15	0	119	504	33.60	1	3
HH Gibbs	7	10	0	119	336	33.60	1	1
MP Vaughan	10	15	2	85	435	33.46	–	2
AJ Stewart	9	13	1	95	399	33.25	–	3
AC Dawson	7	10	2	57*	259	32.37	–	2
AJ Hall	10	15	4	62*	343	31.18	–	4
DJ Callaghan	9	15	1	118	434	31.00	2	2
I Mitchell	9	16	2	84	433	30.92	–	2
SC Pope	10	18	2	81*	493	30.81	–	3
MW Rushmere	9	15	2	94	400	30.76	–	3
PJ Botha	10	18	0	71	548	30.44	–	5
G Dros	9	13	1	94	361	30.08	–	2
PV Simmons	6	10	1	122	267	29.66	1	2
GFJ Liebenberg	10	20	0	126	584	29.20	1	3
CJ Adams	10	14	1	89	376	28.92	–	3
GL Brophy	8	15	1	73	404	28.85	–	3
SM Pollock	9	11	1	64	286	28.60	–	3
OD Gibson	6	12	1	62	313	28.45	–	2
SG Koenig	12	22	1	104	595	28.33	1	1
AI Gait	8	16	0	101	444	27.75	1	3
W Wiblin	11	19	1	81	490	27.22	–	5
MR Benfield	9	17	2	90	408	27.20	–	4
G Toyana	7	13	1	63	326	27.16	–	2
SI Fernando	5	9	0	55	242	26.88	–	2
DN Crookes	8	14	1	126	345	26.53	1	1
JF Venter	7	14	1	85	345	26.53	–	1
JG Myburgh	9	14	2	55	298	24.83	–	1
CC Bradfield	12	22	2	154*	496	24.80	1	2
PK Amre	7	12	2	71*	244	24.40	–	1
A Jacobs	7	13	2	66	268	24.36	–	2
QR Still	6	11	1	84	235	23.50	–	2
KC Jackson	9	15	2	106	305	23.46	1	2
JL Ontong	9	15	0	78	349	23.26	–	2
MA Butcher	10	16	1	87*	348	23.20	–	1
S Abrahams	9	12	3	63*	206	22.88	–	1
VC Drakes	10	15	1	71	319	22.78	–	2
W Bossenger	10	17	2	80*	341	22.73	–	1
HC Bakkes	9	14	3	62	250	22.72	–	1

FIRST-CLASS AVERAGES

BATTING

	M	Inns	NO	HS	Runs	Av	100	50
TT Samaraweera	5	9	1	69	177	22.12	–	2
LL Bosman	8	14	0	59	308	22.00	–	2
AG Botha	7	13	2	79	242	22.00	–	1
DJ Smith	7	10	0	58	217	21.70	–	2
MJ Lavine	6	10	0	59	213	21.30	–	1
FC Brooker	7	14	1	59	269	20.69	–	2
GT Love	11	15	6	52	186	20.66	–	1
LL Gamiet	11	17	1	44	327	20.43	–	–
T Henderson	11	16	3	81	257	19.76	–	1
PL Symcox	5	10	0	42	194	19.40	–	–
JM Henderson	9	16	0	70	308	19.25	–	2
RJ Peterson	9	11	2	42	173	19.22	–	–
CR Wilson	5	9	1	60	149	18.62	–	1
MW Pringle	8	11	1	83	179	17.90	–	1
S Elworthy	10	12	0	43	213	17.75	–	–
R Magiet	5	9	0	46	158	17.55	–	–
R Telemachus	9	12	3	50*	151	16.77	–	1
BM White	10	17	0	76	280	16.47	–	1
LD Ferreira	7	12	1	50	168	15.27	–	1
DW Murray	9	15	2	40	198	15.23	–	–
AG Lawson	5	9	0	35	132	14.66	–	–
P de Bruyn	6	9	0	34	124	13.77	–	–
AM van den Berg	5	8	9	41	110	13.75	–	–
AR Caddick	8	12	2	48	137	13.70	–	–
M Strydom	7	13	0	30	152	11.69	–	–
CE Eksteen	11	14	1	35	144	11.07	–	–
BT Player	8	12	0	46	127	10.58	–	–
MN van Wyk	4	8	0	31	83	10.37	–	–

Qualification: 8 complete innings, average 10.00

BOWLING

	Overs	Mds	Runs	Wkts	Av	Best	10/m	5/inns
HS Williams	261.5	73	551	42	13.11	6–27	–	3
JM Kemp	95.1	17	246	16	15.37	4–30	–	–
KCG Benjamin	250	79	594	38	15.63	6–48	1	3
HC Bakkes	250.4	74	617	39	15.82	6–33	–	3
VC Drakes	319.2	53	975	60	16.25	5–26	–	3
CM Willoughby	404.4	134	878	50	17.56	5–87	–	1
M Hayward	330.1	100	854	46	18.56	6–31	2	4
PC Strydom	105	30	281	15	18.73	3–8	–	–
DJ Terbrugge	396	120	870	44	19.77	5–45	–	1
S Elworthy	292.1	74	735	37	19.86	7–105	1	1
JF Venter	162	48	377	18	20.94	6–78	–	1
PJ Botha	203.2	60	453	21	21.57	4–27	–	–
AA Donald	272.3	82	693	32	21.65	6–53	1	4
AJ Hall	333.4	96	890	40	22.25	5–20	–	2
A Nel	200.5	70	424	19	22.31	5–61	–	1
JH Kallis	176.2	47	447	20	22.35	6–60	–	1
F Erasmus	132	33	392	17	23.05	3–27	–	–
SM Pollock	356.3	125	757	32	23.65	5–39	–	1
A Flintoff	98.3	23	285	12	23.75	3–6	–	–
RE Veenstra	333.3	91	832	35	23.77	5–95	–	1

FIRST-CLASS AVERAGES

BOWLING

	Overs	Mds	Runs	Wkts	Av	Best	10/m	5/inns
AR Caddick	298.2	88	690	29	23.79	7–46	–	2
BT Player	211.1	60	464	19	24.42	4–19	–	–
WB Masimula	136	30	391	16	24.43	4–35	–	–
D Pretorius	151.3	34	399	16	24.93	5–58	–	1
AD Mullally	182	64	390	15	26.00	3–31	–	–
PR Adams	344.5	81	836	32	26.12	6–78	–	3
OD Gibson	172.5	23	604	23	26.26	7–141	–	2
M Ntini	186.4	32	586	22	26.63	4–55	–	–
T Henderson	261.1	66	649	24	27.04	3–14	–	–
MJ Lavine	186	43	578	21	27.52	5–44	–	1
EAE Baptiste	224.3	75	497	18	27.61	4–18	–	–
PV Mpitsang	253	76	663	24	27.62	4–41	–	–
G Kruger	279.5	48	864	31	27.87	7–64	1	1
GM Gilder	241.5	62	654	23	28.43	6–61	–	1
RJ Peterson	297.2	76	881	30	29.36	6–67	–	2
AJ Tudor	128	24	444	15	29.60	3–61	–	–
AC Dawson	234.4	71	538	18	29.88	6–61	–	1
GJ Smith	296.2	56	885	29	30.51	5–81	–	1
JN Dreyer	227.4	52	764	25	30.56	5–81	–	2
R Telemachus	260.3	47	831	27	30.77	4–56	–	–
GT Love	304.2	70	878	28	31.35	5–124	–	1
D Gough	263.5	56	849	27	31.44	5–70	–	1
N Boje	320.3	110	668	21	31.80	5–38	–	1
CE Eksteen	482.4	162	1095	34	32.20	5–54	–	1
JC Kent	132	34	361	11	32.81	2–45	–	–
MW Pringle	228.4	64	566	17	33.29	4–103	–	–
MJG Davis	151.3	35	417	12	34.75	3–51	–	–
CK Langeveldt	157.1	49	387	11	35.18	2–22	–	–
GM Hamilton	130	30	394	11	35.81	3–28	–	–
KR Pietersen	192.1	50	516	14	36.85	4–141	–	–
WJ Cronje	152.1	51	370	10	37.00	2–5	–	–
DN Crookes	224.4	59	587	15	39.13	3–20	–	–
DH Townsend	184.5	33	610	15	40.66	4–102	–	–
CW Henderson	282	106	614	15	40.93	4–72	–	–
S Abrahams	299	91	680	15	45.33	4–67	–	–
AG Botha	250.3	56	692	14	49.42	4–89	–	–
L Klusener	250	73	658	12	54.83	3–47	–	–
PCR Tufnell	258.4	61	619	11	56.27	4–124	–	–

Qualification: 10 wickets in 8 innings

The following players took 10 wickets in fewer than 8 innings:–

	Overs	Mds	Runs	Wkts	Av	Best	10/m	5/inns
DJJ de Vos	71.4	18	166	12	13.83	6–32	1	2
JA Morkel	105.4	33	280	11	25.45	6–36	–	1
KR Pushpakumara	78	15	295	10	29.50	5–51	–	1
KSC de Silva	101.5	16	327	11	29.72	3–51	–	–
GJ Kruis	137.4	32	417	10	41.70	4–56	–	–

LEADING FIELDERS

37 – MV Boucher, N Pothas (36ct,1st); 34 – I Mitchell (33ct, 1st), SJ Palframan; 31 – GL Brophy (29ct,2st); 27 – ELR Stewart (26ct,1st); 25 – W Bossenger (23ct,2st); 24 – M Street (21ct,3st); 21 – LJ Koen, GFJ Liebenberg, DW Murray (18ct,3st), EG Poole, AJ Stewart (20ct,1st); 20 – TL Tsolekile; 19 – DJ Smith (18ct,1st); 18 – DN Crookes; 16 – W Wiblin; 15 – M van Jaarsveld; 13 – JDC Bryant, DJ Cullinan; 12 – SM Pollock; 11 – CJ Adams, DM Benkenstein, KC Jackson, MP Vaughan; 10 – CC Bradfield.

ZIMBABWE

Australia in Zimbabwe
Sri Lanka in Zimbabwe
England in Zimbabwe
Zimbabwe Domestic
First-Class Averages

AUSTRALIA IN ZIMBABWE
By Neil Manthorp

TEST MATCH
14, 15, 16 and 17 October 1999 at
Harare Sports Club

Alistair Campbell's bold decision to bat first on a cheeky pitch backfired horribly but, as both captains agreed afterwards, it need not have done so but for a couple of dropped catches and momentary lapses in concentration by the home side. In other words, if Zimbabwe had played a bit better, they wouldn't have been thrashed.

Colin Miller: three second-innings wickets for Australia against Zimbabwe.

Previous page: Zimbabwe celebrating during the one-dayer against England at Cape Town.

Glenn McGrath put a flaccid tour of Sri Lanka firmly behind him and bowled with more pace and spit than the local top order could handle. He removed opener Gavin Rennie (18) after Damien Fleming, with fabulous control, had found the edge and shoulder of the respective bats of Grant Flower (1) and Campbell (5).

The key wicket of Zimbabwe-born former WA batsman Murray Goodwin (0), who was buzzing at the prospect of playing his ex-countrymen, took a single ball to claim. Lunging forward and squeezing it to cover, Goodwin spluttered out of his crease in search of a non-existent single only to see Greg Blewett lob the ball to Justin Langer at short leg who removed the bails.

From 37 for 4 there was never likely to be a way back although Andy Flower and Neil Johnson did their best with a fifth-wicket stand of 70 either side of lunch. Then McGrath removed them both with a swish of his right arm and a pair of catches by Mark Waugh at second slip. Johnson's 75 was patient and clever, with long periods of defence, eight boundaries and a straight six off Shane Warne.

As heretical as it sounds to say it, the most memorable innings in Australia's reply of 422 came from Fleming who concocted his second Test half-century from 55 balls with great fun and ten boundaries. Steve Waugh, though, laid the platform with ruthless and metronomic efficiency during his unbeaten 151, an innings that saw him inaugurated as the 17th member of the '20 Test Century Club'. The Australian captain was, however, dropped by Henry Olonga on 39 and by Grant Flower on 94. He was at the crease for over seven hours and struck 18 fours, but it was the sight of the home side grovelling that kept him interested as much as the time or the runs.

Mark Waugh, too, made a significant contribution of 90 before patting a slower ball from left-arm spinner Grant Flower straight back to the bowler. He was suitably disgusted, and might even have exacerbated the situation with injury such was the force with which he slammed his bat into the ground.

Facing a deficit of 228, Zimbabwe's top order were much, much better second time around before collapsing with what seemed rude haste from 200 for 2 to 232 all out. Each member of the Zimbabwean top four loitered with the serious intention of doing not much for a very long time, and it took some some tremendously

TEST MATCH – ZIMBABWE v. AUSTRALIA
14, 15, 16 and 17 October 1999 at Harare Sports Club

ZIMBABWE

	First Innings		Second Innings	
GJ Rennie	c Ponting, b McGrath	18	(4) c McGrath, b Miller	23
GW Flower	c Ponting, b Fleming	1	lbw b McGrath	32
MW Goodwin	run out (Blewett/Langer)	0	c SR Waugh, b Warne	91
ADR Campbell (capt)	c Slater, b Fleming	5	(5) run out (Slater/Healy)	1
*A Flower	c ME Waugh, b McGrath	28	(6) c Healy, b McGrath	0
NC Johnson	c ME Waugh, b McGrath	75	(7) c ME Waugh, b McGrath	5
TR Gripper	lbw b Warne	4	(1) lbw b Miller	60
HH Streak	c ME Waugh, b Warne	3	(9) lbw b Warne	0
GJ Whittall	c Healy, b Warne	27	(8) c ME Waugh, b Warne	2
BC Strang	run out (Blewett)	17	c Langer, b Miller	0
HK Olonga	not out	0	not out	0
	b2, lb4 nb10	16	b9, lb2, w1, nb6	18
		194		**232**

	First Innings				Second Innings			
	O	M	R	W	O	M	R	W
McGrath	23	7	44	3	31	12	46	3
Fleming	15	6	22	2	21	6	31	–
Miller	19	6	36	–	34	10	66	3
Warne	23	2	69	3	30.1	11	68	3
Ponting	1	1	–	–	1	1	–	–
Waugh SR	4	1	17	–				
Blewett					5	1	10	–

Fall of Wickets
1–6, 2–6, 3–22, 4–37, 5–107, 6–119, 7–125, 8–165, 9–190
1–56, 2–154, 3–200, 4–208, 5–211, 6–220, 7–227, 8–227, 9–232

AUSTRALIA

	First Innings		Second Innings	
MJ Slater	c A Flower, b Strang	4	(2) not out	0
GS Blewett	c Campbell, b Streak	1	(1) b Cairns	4
JL Langer	run out (Olonga)	44		
ME Waugh	c & b GW Flower	90		
SR Waugh (capt)	not out	151		
RT Ponting	c Johnson, b Streak	31		
*IA Healy	c A Flower, b Strang	5		
SK Warne	c A Flower, b Streak	6		
DW Fleming	lbw b Strea	65		
CR Miller	c Johnson, b Streak	2		
GD McGrath	c Johnson, b Whittall	13		
	lb5, w4, nb1	10	w1	1
		422	(for 0 wicket)	**5**

	First Innings			
	O	M	R	W
Olonga	17	1	83	–
Streak	34	8	93	5
Strang	44	14	96	2
Johnson	2	0	14	–
Whittall	21.4	3	74	1
Flower GW	18	3	38	1
Gripper	3	0	19	0

Fall of Wickets
1–6, 2–7, 3–96, 4–174, 5–253, 6–275, 7–282, 8–396, 9–398

Umpires: ID Robinson & G Sharp
Toss: Zimbabwe
Test Debut: TR Gripper

Australia won by ten wickets

Zimbabwe captain Andy Flower knocked up 99-not out in the third one-dayer at Harare.

aggressive spin bowling from Colin Miller to unclamp two of them, Trevor Gripper (60) and Gavin Rennie (23).

McGrath picked a couple of late wickets to finish with respectable numbers but Warne, who was much too smart for everyone all day without luck, grabbed the last three wickets – including last man Goodwin for a dour 91 that began with 25 dot balls – without conceding a run to win the match.

ONE-DAY INTERNATIONALS

Mark Waugh continued his productive tour with a 96-ball innings of 106 against a weakened and intimidated attack, which he belted and prodded as he deemed fit. Waugh added 159 with Ricky Ponting (67) before running himself out in the 36th over. Damien Martyn (57* from 38 balls) thrashed the bowling around like a Zambeze crocodile to push the tourists to 303 for 6.

A capacity and raucous crowd returned home happy, however, and it was not just the gallons of cold beer. Neil Johnson continued his love affair with Australian bowling making a second successive century (110) following his unbeaten 132 at Lord's in the World Cup. Good as his effort was, though, it could not prevent the home side losing by 83 runs.

It can be difficult for a dominant captain to have 'fun' without appearing arrogant and without humiliating the opposition. Steve Waugh just about got away with it in this match, however, when he lined all nine fielders up alongside wicketkeeper Adam Gilchrist as Zimbabwe's number 11, David Mutendera, took strike with the total reading 98 for 9.

The last man to be called into the cordon, Adam Dale, trotted up from third man with a sheepish grin on his face as the photographers scurried to record the moment. It certainly did make a good picture, and probably one-day history, too, as the only time in recent memory the scene had presented itself was when Greg Chappell used six slips and three gulleys to the bowling of Dennis Lillee in a Test against New Zealand in 1976.

Only Trevor Madondo and Andy Blignaut reached the 20s in the home side's final score of 116 while Mark Waugh probably embarrassed Zimbabwe more than his brother had by playing the too-friendly bowling with exaggerated respect during a stodgy 56 not out from 95 balls.

Home captain Andy Flower gave the locals some prospect of respect in the final game with an unbeaten 99 that included two sixes in a final over

Even the Australian bowlers struggled with Neil Johnson, who made his second successive century against Australia.

that cost 20 and was bowled by Andrew Symonds after Steve Waugh got his sums wrong with Glenn McGrath and Adam Dale.

Sadly, even Flower's 109-ball effort could not prevent another messy thrashing as Australia reached 201 for 1 with Ricky Ponting (87*) leading the way in the absence of Mark Waugh, who was resting after making a century and a half in the first two matches. Michael Bevan pushed his stratospheric average up yet another couple of notches with a fiddly, unbeaten 77.

Match One
21 October 1999 at Queen's Sports Club, Bulawayo
Australia 303 for 6 (50 overs)(ME Waugh 106)
Zimbabwe 220 (43.4 overs)(NC Johnson 110)
Australia won by 83 runs
Man of the Match: ME Waugh

Match Two
23 October 1999 at Harare Sports Club
Zimbabwe 116 (37.3 overs)(TN Madondo 29)
Australia 117 for 1 (28.3 overs)(ME Waugh 54)
Australia won by 9 wickets
Man of the Match: DW Fleming

Match Three
24 October 1999 at Harare Sports Club
Zimbabwe 200 for 9 (50 overs)(A Flower 99)
Australia 201 for 1 (39 overs)(RT Ponting 87, MG Bevan 77)
Australia won by 9 wickets
Man of the Match: A Flower

Damien Fleming of Australia, who made his second Test half-century from 55 balls.

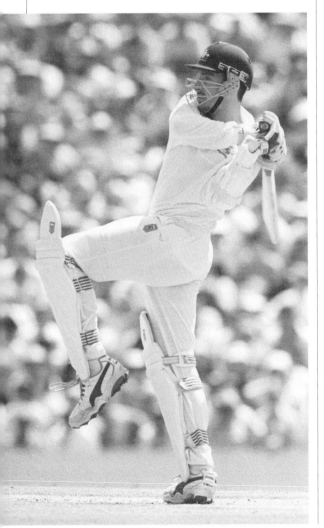

SRI LANKA IN ZIMBABWE
By Neil Manthorp

Almost three and a half days' worth of play were lost to the elements during the series, enough to ensure that the hoped-for engaging contest between two of Test cricket's emerging entities never materialised. That said, Sri Lanka played better cricket, and Zimbabwe worse, than the tourists' eventual one-nil victory suggests. Not only did the Sri Lankans deliver the superior performance as a team – the Zimbabweans seemed caught up in some sort of post-World-Cup funk – they also dominated the individual highlights of the series.

Top of that list must be Marvan Atapattu's double century in the first Test at Bulawayo and Nuwan Zoysa's hat-trick in the second match at Harare. The two feats could not have been more starkly contrasting. Atapattu's was an epic performance which saw him at the crease for ten hours in compiling his 216, and he was on the field for the duration of the match. Zoysa rooted out any hope Zimbabwe had of piecing together a decent first-innings score with the first three deliveries of the second over of the second Test – as explosive a start to a match as could be imagined.

Zimbabwe's Man of the Series would without doubt have been Andy Flower, who not only scored his team's only century of the rubber and added to it three half-centuries but, most importantly, stepped manfully into the breach after Alistair Campbell resigned the captaincy two days before the Harare Test against South Africa.

So there was Flower once more, leading the team, keeping wicket and filling the major batsman's berth: the same recipe for unhappiness that led him to relinquish the reins after the 1996 World Cup.

But there were simply no other viable captaincy candidates in the wake of Campbell's decision, though Neil Johnson's name came up in numerous conversations, and it was back to the tried and trusted Flower. Under the circumstances, he made an admirable fist of it.

The low point in the series had to be the manner of Murray Goodwin's dismissal on the fourth day of the second Test. Goodwin played forward defensively to a delivery from Chaminda Vaas, who kicked the ball back up the pitch. Known to suffer from the effects of the odd cloud of red mist, Goodwin seemed irritated by the bowler's act and walked down the pitch to launch his own kick at the approaching ball. He missed, and the ball trickled through to the slip cordon where Tillekaratne Dilshan picked it up and threw down the stumps with Goodwin out of his ground.

Shamefully, instead of castigating or even calming his young charge, Sanath Jayasuriya led the appeal and Goodwin had to be given out.

Marvan Attapatu produced an outstanding double century during a 10-hour knock in the first Test at Bulawayo.

Two other Sri Lankans, Dilshan and Russel Arnold, scored centuries in the series, while Ravindra Pushpakumara and Pramodya Wickremasinghe were the only bowlers to bag five-wicket hauls. Flower's aggregate of 388 runs was more than double that of Johnson, who scored the second most runs for Zimbabwe. The home side, still crippled by the absence of Heath Streak through injury, also struggled on the bowling front, where Henry Olonga's 4 for 103 in the first innings of the opening Test was the best of an ordinary set of performances.

In fact, ordinary would not be an inaccurate description of much of the series itself.

Murray Goodwin of Zimbabwe, whose outburst at the crease on the penultimate day of the second Test might have cost him his innings.

FIRST TEST – ZIMBABWE v. SRI LANKA
18, 19, 20, 21 and 22 November 1999 at Queen's Sports Club, Bulawayo

ZIMBABWE

	First innings		Second innings	
GW Flower	c Arnold, b Wickremasinghe	17	c Dilshan, b Muralitharan	48
GJ Rennie	lbw b Wickremasinghe	16	c Kaluwitharana, b Vaas	2
MW Goodwin	c Arnold, b Wickremaisnghe	61	c Dilshan, b Vaas	2
NC Johnson	c Arnold, b Vaas	17	not out	52
*A Flower (capt)	c Muralitharan, b Wickremasinghe	86	not out	15
ADR Campbell	run out (Dilshan)	0		
GJ Whittall	run out (Kaluwitharana)	11		
GB Brent	c Jayawardene, b Muralitharan	0		
BC Strang	c Kaluwitharana, b Wickremasinghe	41		
AR Whittall	c Kaluwitharana, b Wickremasinghe	8		
HK Olonga	not out	1		
	lb5, nb23	28	b1, lb4, nb2	17
		286	(for 3 wickets)	136

	First innings				Second innings			
	O	M	R	W	O	M	R	W
Vaas	28	3	88	1	13	4	27	2
Gallage	14	1	53	-	11	4	24	-
Wickremasinghe	21.2	6	60	6	8	1	20	-
Muralitharan	20	3	61	1	14	3	50	1
Arnold	6	3	8	-	2	-	9	-
Jayasuriya	7	1	11	-	1	-	1	-

Fall of Wickets
1-37, 2-38, 3-68, 4-167, 5-167, 6-212, 7-214, 8-250, 9-275, 1-8, 2-27, 3-72

SRI LANKA

	First Innings	
MS Atapattu	not out	216
ST Jayasuriya (capt)	lbw v AR Whittall	49
RP Arnold	c A Flower b Olonga	7
DPMD Jayawardene	lbw b Brent	17
TM Dilshan	lbw b Olonga	9
*RS Kaluwitharana	c A Flower, b Olonga	30
SI de Saram	c A Flower, b Brent	39
WPUJC Vaas	c Campbell, b Strang	9
IS Gallage	c GW Flower, b Strang	3
GP Wickremasinghe	c A Flower, b Strang	13
M Muralitharan	c GW Flower, b Olonga	6
	b12, lb11, w1,nb6	30
		428

	First innings			
	O	M	R	W
Olonga	32	6	103	4
Strang	30	9	91	3
Brent	32	12	55	2
Whittall AR	35	6	105	1
Whittall GJ	14	3	48	-
Flower GW	4	2	3	-

Fall of Wickets
1-85, 2-98, 3-141, 4-159, 5-238, 6-345, 7-372, 8-390, 9-417

Umpires: KC Barbour & EA Nicholls
Toss: Sri Lanka
Test Debuts: GB Brent, SI de Saram, TM Dilshan and IS Gallage

South Africa won by an innings and 219 runs

FIRST TEST
18, 19, 20, 21 and 22 November 1999 at Bulawayo

Marvan Atapattu's second Test double century, an undefeated 216, will remain the abiding memory of an otherwise unsatisfactory match. Rain prevented any further progress an hour before the scheduled close on the fourth day, having also put paid to play an hour after lunch a day earlier. A single giant yellow cover protected the entire table and a significant portion of the outfield.

However, the rain was nothing short of torrential and the Queen's Sports Club oval, thirsty though it was, was soon saturated.

The disruptions left Sri Lanka wondering what might have been. Thanks largely to Atapattu's sterling effort they had earned a lead of 142 when they were dismissed 20 minutes after lunch on the fourth day. Zimbabwe found the backbone to limit the damage to three wickets in the 49 overs they faced in their second innings, but there was little doubt Sri Lanka had the better of the draw.

The home side's first innings had as its apex a stand of 99 between Andy Flower and Murray Goodwin. The partnership featured a wicketless second session after Grant Flower, Gavin Rennie and Neil Johnson had all been sent packing before lunch on the first day that started with Sanath Jayasuriya inserting his opposition. Flower and Goodwin were separated 15 minutes after tea when Goodwin gently pulled a delivery from Pramodya Wickremasinghe to mid-on to go for 61. At 167 for 4 Zimbabwe's hopes of reaching respectability were somewhere between possibility and probability. But they took a serious blow with the next delivery when Alistair Campbell was run out having turned the ball behind backward square and set off without waiting for Flower's call. The captain's dismissal for 86 six overs before the close, when he cut Wickremasinghe to short third man, ended almost four and a half hours at the wicket in which he showed admirable resolve despite a dearth of decent support. Zimbabwe were dismissed 40 minutes into the second day, Wickremasinghe's career-best return of 6 for 60 a just reward for a fine display of old-fashioned fast bowling in which he made the batsmen play and waited for the error.

The rest of the match belonged entirely to Atapattu. He offered a solitary chance, on 58 with the total 135 for 2, when he edged Andy Whittall, the off-spinner, into the body of wicketkeeper Flower. Atapattu found his most reliable support in debutant Indika de Saram, who shared in a sixth-

wicket partnership of 138 of which the latter scored 39. The tall, shaven-headed opener with an intellectual bearing chose his words as carefully as he had chosen his strokes as he watched the rain ruin what was to have been the fifth day.

'Patience matters a lot when you are batting against Zimbabwe, because while they might not have the most threatening attack they bowl a tight line outside the off-stump,' Atapattu said. 'I concentrate by breaking my batting into small bits, like from drinks break to drinks break. You have an hour to concentrate, then you can switch off for a few minutes. Also, I don't have big shots like many other batsmen do. I recognise my strengths, play accordingly and wait for the loose ball to come. I don't look at the number of runs I've scored, but I do get a bit nervous in the nineties.' Question is, which nineties did he mean?

SECOND TEST
26, 27, 28, 29 and 30 November 1999 at Harare

The only conclusive match of the series could have been over almost before it began when Nuwan Zoysa took the first Test hat-trick by a Sri Lankan in the second over of the game. Sanath Jayasuriya won the toss and asked Zimbabwe to bat. His decision took on divine proportions when left-arm paceman Zoysa, who was returning from a back injury to play his eighth Test, shattered the home side's aspirations by removing Trevor Gripper, Murray Goodwin and Neil Johnson without a run on the board. Gripper was trapped in front offering no stroke, Goodwin edged a high bouncing delivery to be caught behind and Johnson was leg before to a ball which hit him low on the front pad. Bizarrely, a power failure interrupted the television broadcast as Johnson was walking out to become the third element of the hat-trick, so the spectacle was not beamed live back to Sri Lanka or anywhere else.

The calamity would in all likelihood have sunk Zimbabwe without trace had it not been for another granite innings from their captain, Andy Flower, who spent just on six hours at the crease for his 74. Grant Flower proved a brother in temperament as well as in the flesh as he and his skipper salvaged what they could from the morning session.

However, five overs after lunch Grant Flower was yorked by Muttiah Muralitharan to make it 53 for 4 and Sri Lanka looked on the verge of the conclusive breakthrough. It was not to be as Alistair Campbell summoned the discipline to stay with the remaining Flower until 40 minutes after tea, when his attacking

SECOND TEST – ZIMBABWE v. SRI LANKA
26, 27, 28, 29 and 30 November 1999 at Harare Sports Club

ZIMBABWE

	First Innings		Second Innings	
GW Flower	b Muralitharan	19	c Kaluwitharana, b Muralitharan	13
TR Gripper	lbw b Zoysa	0	c Arnold, b Vaas	4
MW Goodwin	c Kaluwitharana, b Zoysa	0	run out (de Saram)	48
NC Johnson	lbw b Zoysa	0	(5) c Atapattu, b Zoysa	14
*A Flower (capt)	lbw bVaas	74	(6) c Atapattu, b Jayasuriya	129
ADR Campbell	lbw b Wickremasinghe	36	(7) lbw b Muralitharan	5
GJ Whittall	b Muralitharan	1	(8) not out	53
GB Brent	c Kaluwitharana, b Vaas	3	(9) lbw b Jayasuriya	0
BC Strang	c Dilshan, b Vaas	4	(10) c Jayawardene, b Jayasuriya	3
HK Olonga	not out	10	(11) lbw b Jayasuriya	0
E Matambanaadzo	c Jayawardene, b Muralitharan	6	(4) run out (de Saram)	0
	b2, lb8, nb11	21	b3, lb15, nb5	23
		174		**292**

	First Innings				Second Innings			
	O	M	R	W	O	M	R	W
Vaas	27	8	8	3	35	7	78	1
Zoysa	13	4	22	3+	11	2	24	1
Wickremasinghe	18	7	31	-	28	10	51	-
Muralitharan	29.5	11	44	3	43	15	71	2
Jayasuriya	3	1	7	0	12.4	3	40	4
Arnold	5	2	10	-	1	0	3	-
Jayawardene					4	2	7	-

+ Hat Trick

Fall of Wickets
1-0, 2-0, 3-0, 4-53, 5-133, 6-134, 7-152, 8-153, 9-161
1-5, 2-28, 3-28, 4-51, 5-152, 6-159, 7-284, 8-284, 9-292

SRI LANKA

	First Innings		Second Innings	
MS Atapattu	run out (Johnson/Campbell)	37	run out (Goodwin)	6
ST Jayasuriya (capt)	c A Flower, b Olonga	6	c Gripper b Brent	7
RP Arnold	c Campbell, b Strang	49	c A Flower, b Brent	1
DPMD Jayawardene	c A Flower, b Strang	91	not out	6
TM Dilshan	not out	163	lbw b Brent	0
*RS Kaluwitharana	run out (Olonga)	19	not out	14
SI de Saram	c Goodwin, b Matambanadzo	17		
WPUJC Vaas	c Gripper, b Matambanadzo	5		
GP Wickremasinghe	c A Flower, b Whittall	7		
M Muralitharan	c GW Flower, b Olonga	5		
DNT Zoysa	c Gripper, b GW Flower	5		
	b1, lb10, w7,nb10	28	lb1, w2, nb1	4
		432	**(for 4 wickets)**	**38**

	First Innings				Second Innings			
	O	M	R	W	O	M	R	W
Olonga	30	5	88	2	5	1	14	-
Brent	22	4	68	-	7.2	3	21	3
Matambanadzo	31	6	95	2				
Strang	37	13	70	2	3	1	2	-
Gripper	1	0	6	-				
Whittall	19	2	60	1				
Flower GW	9.3	2	34	1				

Fall of Wickets
1-17, 2-97, 3-105, 4-283, 5-323, 6-371, 7-381, 8-403, 9-408
1-10, 2-15, 3-19, 4-20

Umpires: RB Tiffin & SA Bucknor
Toss: Sri Lanka
Test Debuts: nil

Sri Lanka won by six wickets

THIRD TEST – ZIMBABWE v. SRI LANKA
4, 5, 6, 7 and 8 December 1999 at Harare Sports Club

ZIMBABWE

	First Innings		Second Innings	
GW Flower	c Dilshan, b Pushpakumara	13	c Dilshan, b Vaas	13
CB Wishart	lbw b Vaas	1	b Vaas	9
MW Goodwin	b Pushpakumara	11	c Jayawardene, b Muralitharan	38
NC Johnson	lbw b Wickremasinghe	70	c Dilshan, b Wickremaisnghe	9
*A Flower (capt)	c Arnold, bVaas	14	not out	70
ADR Campbell	lbw b Pushpakumara	9	c Jayawardene, b Vaas	27
GJ Whittall	c Arnold, b Pushpakumara	37	c Arnold, b Muralitharan	9
RW Price	lbw b Pushpakumara	2	run out (Jayasuriya)	4
EA Brandes	b Vaas	9	not out	1
BC Strang	c Atapattu, b Vaas	28		
HK Olonga	not out	3		
	lb4, w15, nb2	21	b3, lb5, nb9	17
		218	**(for 7 wickets dec.)**	**197**

	First Innings				Second Innings			
	O	M	R	W	O	M	R	W
Vaas	29.4	10	56	4	22	5	48	3
Pushpakumara	25	5	56	5	21	5	39	-
Wickremasinghe	16	6	41	1	21	6	30	1
Muralitharan	24	6	51	-	35	12	52	2
Jayasuriya	4	1	10	-	8	4	8	-
Jayawardene					2	0	12	-

Fall of Wickets
1-5, 2-24, 3-33, 4-67, 5-82, 6-143, 7-174, 8-175, 9-196
1-14, 2-28, 3-51, 4-93, 5-151, 6-174, 7-184

SRI LANKA

	First Innings		Second Innings	
MS Atapattu	c Johnson, b Olonga	0	c A Flower, b Brandes	6
RP Arnold	not out	104	(3) not out	14
DPMD Jayawardene	c Goodwin, b Brandes	2		
ST Jayasuriya (capt)	c A Flower, b Brandes	4	(2) not out	16
TM Dilshan	c A Flower, b Strang	37		
*RS Kaluwitharana	c A Flower, b Whittall	7		
SI de Saram	c GW Flower, b Whittall	38		
WPUJC Vaas	c Campbell, b Brandes	0		
KR Pushpakumara	lbw b Strang	7		
GP Wickremasinghe	c A Flower, b Olonga	18		
M Muralitharan	b Olonga	5		
	lb2, w2,nb5	9		
		231	**(for 1 wicket)**	**36**

	First Innings				Second Innings			
	O	M	R	W	O	M	R	W
Olonga	22.4	2	54	3	4	1	11	-
Brandes	17	5	45	3	4	0	20	1
Strang	24	8	71	2	1	0	5	0
Whittall	17	9	37	2				
Price	8	3	22	0				

Fall of Wickets
1-1, 2-4, 3-29, 4-82, 5-90, 6-158, 7-159, 8-178, 9-208
1-7

Umpires: ID Robinson & S Venkataraghavan
Toss: Sri Lanka
Test Debut: RW Price

Match drawn

instincts took over and he swatted across the line to Wickremasinghe to be palpably leg before. The rest of Zimbabwe's resistance crumbled rapidly, and they were dismissed in the sixth over of the second day. By the close Sri Lanka had eased to a lead of 62 with seven wickets in hand.

A stand of 178 for the fourth wicket between Mahela Jayawardena and Tillekaratne Dilshan had much to do with the tourists' batting success, and it ended 40 minutes before lunch on the third day when Jayawardena was caught behind off Bryan Strang for 91. Dilshan's seamless batting on a flat pitch enabled him to reach 163 not out, his maiden Test century in only his second innings, in virtually eight hours when Sri Lanka were dismissed with a lead of 258 an hour before the scheduled close.

Zimbabwe stumbled to 34 for 3 in the 20 overs they faced, and the significant question of whether they would be thrashed or merely beaten was again left to their captain to answer. Flower's reply was his sixth Test century, as gutsy an innings as he will ever play. In the process he had to overcome the distraction of Murray Goodwin being run out by a throw from the slips after he had ventured up the pitch in the midst of a mild altercation with the bowler. But when the dust settled on the fourth day Zimbabwe had lost just three more wickets and were 23 runs short of dismissing the spectre of following on. They reached that goal without further loss, but 20 minutes before lunch on the final day Sanath Jayasuriya struck for the first time in a lethal burst of left-arm spin that would earn him career-best figures of 4 for 40 and dismiss Zimbabwe on the stroke of the interval.

Jayasuriya's first victim was Andy Flower, whose uppish slash backward off point ended a brave innings of 129 compiled in seven hours. Sri Lanka emerged from lunch needing 35 for victory. It was too easy for a team which is not often able to enjoy such dominance, and they wobbled to 20 for 4 before the winning runs streaked off Romesh Kaluwitharana's bat in the 16th over of the second session.

THIRD TEST
4, 5, 6, 7 and 8 December 1999 at Harare

Bad light curtailed the third day's play to 47 overs and the fourth day was washed out without a ball bowled, this ruining a match of considerable expectation. The first day belonged to Ravindra Pushpakumara, who took 5 for 44 as Zimbabwe slipped to 178 for 8 after Sanath Jayasuriya again

TEST AVERAGES
Sri Lanka v. Zimbabwe

SRI LANKA

Batting	M	Inns	NO	HS	Runs	Av	100	50
TM Dilshan	3	4	1	163*	209	69.66	1	–
MS Atapattu	3	5	1	216*	265	66.25	1	–
RP Arnold	3	5	2	104*	175	58.33	1	–
DPMD Jayawardene	3	4	1	91	116	38.66	–	1
SI de Saram	3	3	0	39	94	31.33	–	–
RS Kaluwitharana	3	4	1	30	70	23.33	–	–
ST Jayasuriya	3	5	1	49	82	20.50	–	–
GP Wickremasinghe	3	3	0	18	38	12.66	–	–
M Muralitharan	3	3	0	6	16	5.33	–	–
WPUJC Vaas	3	3	0	9	14	4.66	–	–

Also batted: IS Gallage (1 Test) 3; KR Pushpakumara (1 Test) 7; DNT Zoysa (1 Test) 5

Fielding
8 – RP Arnold; 6 – TM Dilshan, RS Kaluwitharana; 4 – DPMD Jayawardene; 3 – MS Atapattu; 1 – M Muralitharan

Bowling	Overs	Mds	Runs	Wkts	Av	Best	10m	5/inn
KR Pushpakumara	46	10	95	5	19.00	55–56	–	1
WPUJC Vaas	154.4	37	347	14	24.78	4–56	–	–
GP Wickremasinghe	112.2	36	233	9	25.88	6–60	–	1
M Muralitharan	165.5	50	329	9	36.55	3–44	–	–

Also bowled: RP Arnold 14–5–30–0; IS Gallage 25–5–77–0; ST Jayasuriya 35.4–10–77–4; DPMP Jayawardene 6–2–19–0; DNT Zoysa 24–6–46–4

ZIMBABWE

Batting	M	Inns	NO	HS	Runs	Av	100	50
A Flower	3	6	2	129	388	97.00	1	3
NC Johnson	3	6	1	70	162	32.40	–	2
GJ Whittall	3	5	1	53*	111	27.75	–	1
MW Goodwin	3	6	0	61	160	26.66	–	1
GW Flower	3	6	0	48	123	20.50	–	–
BC Strang	3	4	0	41	76	19.00	–	–
ADR Campbell	3	5	0	36	77	15.40	–	–
HK Olonga	3	4	3	10*	14	14.00	–	–
GB Brent	2	3	0	3	3	1.00	–	–

Also batted: EA Brandes (1 Test) 9, 1*; TR Gripper (1 Test) 0, 4; ET Matambanadzo (1 Test) 6, 0; RW Price (1 Test) 2, 4; GJ Rennie (1 Test) 16, 2; AR Whittall (1 Test) 8; CB Wishart (1 Test) 1, 9

Fielding
13 – A Flower; 4 – GW Flower; 3 – ADR Campbell, TR Gripper; 2 – MW Goodwin; 1 – NC Johnson

Bowling	Overs	Mds	Runs	Wkts	Av	Best	10m	5/inn
GB Brent	61.2	19	144	5	28.80	3–21	–	–
HK Olonga	93.4	15	270	9	30.00	4–103	–	–
BC Strang	95	31	239	7	34.14	3–91	–	–

Also bowled: EA Brandes 21–5–65–4; G Flower 13.3–4–37–1; TR Gripper 1–0–6–0; ET Matambanadzo 31–6–95–2; RW Price 8–3–22–0; AR Whittall 35–6–105–1; GJ Whittall 50–14–145–3

won the toss. Pushpakumara had played his last Test 18 months previously and was included in the XI for this match only after the hat-trick hero from the second Test, Nuwan Zoysa, returned home with a groin injury. However, Pushpakumara looked anything but a last resort against the Zimbabwean batsmen, rarely straying from his off-stump line and obtaining just enough movement off the seam to cause them problems.

Neil Johnson and Guy Whittall stopped the rot for almost two hours either side of tea in putting on 60 for the sixth wicket after Zimbabwe had crashed to 83 for 5. But their patience was the exception and Zimbabwe were dismissed 11 overs into the second day's play for 218 – well shy of what the sound pitch was worth. Pushpakumara finished with 5 for 56, while Chaminda Vaas' ability to keep the pressure on from the other end earned him 4 for 56.

By the close, which came 11 overs early due to bad light, another recalled medium pacer had made his mark. At 36, Eddo Brandes showed that what he may have lost in terms of pace in the three years in which he had not played a Test, he had gained in guile. Brandes ended the day with 3 for 29, among his victims Mahela Jayawardena and Jayasuriya, as Sri Lanka drooped to 159 for seven. Russel Arnold, 65 not out at the close, held together an otherwise fractious innings. His only real support came from Tillekaratne Dilshan, with whom he shared 53 runs for the fourth wicket, and Indika de Saram, who helped the opener add 68 for the sixth wicket. Sri Lanka were dismissed 45 minutes before lunch on the third day with a deficit of 13 runs, but Arnold was still there on 104 – his second Test century. It was a chanceless innings in which he simply kept his head, played sensibly and spent just more than six hours at the crease.

The close came with Zimbabwe having extended their lead to 61 for the loss of two wickets, thus leaving the match nicely poised. But the washed out fourth day effectively ended the Test as a contest.

Andy Flower delivered another memorable batting performance on the final day, scoring an unbeaten 70 of the highest quality. A token declaration left the Sri Lankans an unlikely target of 185 in 18 overs, and they reached 36 for 1 before bad light ended proceedings after nine overs.

ONE–DAY INTERNATIONALS

As they did in the Test series, Sri Lanka proved their superiority over Zimbabwe in the shorter format of the game and deservedly took the series three-one after the first match, in Bulawayo, was ended inconclusively by rain. Mercifully, considering the damage done to the Test matches by the elements, it was the only match afflicted in this way. In addition, all five one-day internationals were played on surfaces which were a credit to the Queen's Sports Club and Harare Sports Club groundsmen, no mean feat in a country where water as well as funds to spend on such relative non-essentials as pitch preparation are in desperately short supply.

In the doomed first match, Zimbabwe had reached 65 for 1 in the 15th over in reply to Sri Lanka's 284 for 9 when the weather intervened. Half-centuries by Sanath Jayasuriya, Romesh Kaluwitharana and Russel Arnold and steady scoring down the order took Sri Lanka to their imposing total. Jayasuriya's innings was a glorious blaze of 54 runs struck off 44 balls with six fours and three sixes. Seamer Gary Brent took 4 for 53, still his best figures in one-day international cricket, and his perfect throw from fine-leg accounted for Kaluwitharana.

Promodya Wickremasinghe supported Arnold in an eighth-wicket stand of 53 in the second one-day international.

Quite how Zimbabwe managed to lose the second match, played at the same venue a day after the first game, remains a mystery. With ten overs to go and six wickets in hand, the home side needed a moderate 64 runs to better Sri Lanka's 213. However, they were dismissed for 200 with five balls left in the match. The bowler who made all the difference for Sri Lanka was Jayasuriya, who brought himself on in the 29th over and took 4 for 41. Zimbabwe seemed to have set a course for victory when Alistair Campbell and Grant Flower put on 91 for the first wicket. The partnership ended in the 23rd over when Upul Chandana had Flower caught at long-on for 48. Campbell went on to make 56 before becoming Jayasuriya's first victim when he was caught at mid-wicket in the 38th over. Andy Flower, Murray Goodwin and Guy Whittall were the only other Zimbabweans to reach double figures as the Sri Lankan spinners, Jayasuriya, Chandana and Muttiah Muralitharan, tightened their grip on the match. Russel Arnold's maiden one-day international century held together an otherwise lacklustre Sri Lankan batting performance. Arnold was out to the last ball of the innings for 103 off 124 balls with seven fours and three sixes, helping Sri Lanka recover well after they had been reduced to 66 for 5. The left-handed number five was soon Sri Lanka's last recognised batsman, and he was forced to rely on the limited batting talents of number nine Wickremasinghe for his most sturdy support in an eighth-wicket stand of 53. Whittall claimed 4 for 35, taking all his wickets in the middle- and lower-order. Zimbabwe, who won the toss, too often strayed from the straight and narrow with the ball, but delivered a committed fielding performance in an innings which featured the 29 extras as the second-highest score.

In the third match played in Harare three days later, Muralitharan ripped through the heart of the Zimbabwean order to take 4 for 16 and guide Sri Lanka to victory by 98 runs. Zimbabwe badly lost their way – and their last nine wickets for 50 runs – in replying to Sri Lanka's 248 for 7 with 150. The collapse followed a brisk opening stand of 81 off 90 balls between Campbell and Grant Flower, which ended in the 16th over. Four overs later Flower, on 47, top-edged a delivery to short fine-leg to become

Muralitharan's first victim. The off-spinner turned the ball sharply on a surface that did not respond significantly to the other slow-bowlers' efforts, and the Zimbabweans were mesmerised by him. A stand of 94 between Marvan Atapattu, who scored 69, and Arnold rebuilt a Sri Lankan innings that slipped to 59 for 3 in the 16th over. The Zimbabwean bowlers sent down 17 wides between them and failed to stem the flow of runs in the final 15 overs. The last five overs yielded 60 runs. Despite those impediments, Henry Olonga took his career-best one-day international figures of 4 for 51.

Kaluwitharana's blistering 99 launched Sri Lanka to their series-clinching six-wicket win in the fourth match. The diminutive wicketkeeper-batsman hammered his runs off 86 balls with eleven fours and a six, and he had much to do with his team cruising past Zimbabwe's useful 260 for 4 with 32 balls to spare. The match turned on a third-wicket stand of 144 off 140 balls between Kaluwitharana and Mahela Jayawardena, who scored 63.

Zimbabwe also had a batsman to cheer, Man of the Match Stuart Carlisle, who endured a shaky first fifty to surge to his maiden international century with a flurry of attacking strokes. Carlisle's undefeated 121, which included chances on 31 and 83, was the product of 138 balls faced, of which he hit 8 for 4 and 4 for 6. Zimbabwe's best batting of the series came in a partnership of 131 off 77 deliveries, shared by Carlisle and captain Andy Flower, who scored 53 off 30 balls with eight fours before being caught on the cover boundary off Pramodya Wickremasinghe with the last ball of the innings.

The academic fifth match saw Zimbabwe manage a consolation six-wicket win. The uninterested Sri Lankans slumped to a total of 202 and the home side bettered that with 22 balls remaining. Zimbabwe's win was sealed in an unbroken partnership of 78 between Goodwin and Whittall, who came together with the score 128 for 4 in the 28th over after Zimbabwe had lost those four wickets for 34 runs in the space of ten overs. The partial collapse came after Campbell and Grant Flower had put on 94 for the first wicket. Tillekaratne Dilshan's maiden one-day international half-century brightened an otherwise dowdy Sri Lankan batting display.

Match One
11 December 1999 at Queen's Sports Club, Bulawayo
Sri Lanka 284 for 9 (50 overs)(RP Arnold 56,
ST Jayasuriya 54, RS Kaluwitharana 54,
GB Brent 4 for 53)
Zimbabwe 65 for 1 (14.5 overs)
Match abandoned

Match Two
12 December 1999 at Queen's Sports Club, Bulawayo
Sri Lanka 213 (50 overs)(RP Arnold 103,
GJ Whittall 4 for 35)
Zimbabwe 200 (49.1 overs)(ADR Campbell 56,
ST Jayasuriya 4 for 41)
Sri Lanka won by 13 runs
Man of the Match: RP Arnold

Match Three
15 December 1999 at Harare Sports Club
Sri Lanka 248 for 7 (50 overs)(MS Atapattu 69,
HK Olonga 4 for 51)
Zimbabwe 150 (37 overs)(M Muralitharan 4 for 16)
Sri Lanka won by 98 runs
Man of the Match: UDU Chandana

Match Four
18 December 1999 at Harare Sports Club
Zimbabwe 260 for 4 (50 overs)(SV Carlisle 121*,
A Flower 53)
Sri Lanka 262 for 4 (44.4 overs)(RS Kaluwitharana 99,
DPMD Jayawardene 63)
Sri Lanka won by six wickets
Man of the Match: SV Carlisle

Match Five
19 December 1999 at Harare Sports Club
Sri Lanka 202 (48.2 overs)(TM Dilshan 53)
Zimbabwe 206 for 4 (46.2 overs)(GW Flower 52)
Zimbabwe won by six wickets
Man of the Match: GJ Whittall

ENGLAND IN ZIMBABWE
By Jonathan Agnew

Coming at the end of such a long tour and with heavy storms still lashing southern Africa, a further two weeks in Zimbabwe and four more one-day internationals promised to be a serious challenge to the motivational skills of Messrs Hussain and Fletcher. That Zimbabwe also appeared to be descending into political uncertainty did not help matters, either. However, since it was because of England's appalling attitude three years ago that this short, relations-building trip had been organised in the first place, nothing but beaming smiles were displayed – in public, at least.

That the opening game in Bulawayo was played at all was a miracle. With storm clouds all around, it became a Duckworth-Lewis nightmare to the extent that Hick, who made an excellent 87, was reduced to consulting his printed calculations – which he kept in his trouser pocket – between every over. In fact, he got it spot on as he and Ealham put on 88 for the fifth wicket.

Allan Mullally, who edged a boundary to give England victory over Zimbabwe in Bulawayo.

A day off, on which it rained unrelentingly, followed before the most exciting one-day match of the winter was clinched by the unlikely batting prowess of Mullally. Chasing only 132 to win, England were 125 for 9, having lost four wickets for five runs, when the tall left-armer strode to the middle to join Gough. The force was with Zimbabwe, but Mullally managed to edge a boundary through third man (he later claimed to have run it off the face of the bat quite deliberately!) to give England victory with 22 balls to spare.

Up to Harare and more rain but, between the storms, Hick's revenge over his old team continued as England won the third match by 85 runs. Hick scored 80 and Maddy 53; but the most entertainment came in a five-over thrash involving Caddick and White who added 41. Zimbabwe lost early wickets and by the time they had staggered to 112 for 6 in the 36th over, the match was over.

This brought the record between the two countries to six apiece, but the decider had to wait as more rain caused the abandonment of the final encounter at Harare Sports Club thus bringing an end to a tour that had begun some four months earlier.

Match One
Zimbabwe 194 for 7 (48 overs)
(GW Flower 55, SV Carlisle 30)
England 199 for 5 (46.3 overs)(GA Hick)
England won by 5 wickets
Man of the match: GA Hick

Match Two
Zimbabwe 131 (47.3 overs)(SV Carlisle 31, NC Johnson 30)
England 134 for 9 (44.2 overs)
(MA Ealham 32, C White 26, VS Solanki 24)
England won by one wicket
Man of the Match: C White

Andy Caddick helped maintain England's superiority over Zimbabwe's batsmen.

Coach Duncan Fletcher gives advice to Graeme Hick in the nets. Hick was later named Man of the Match in two of the three one-dayers.

Match Three
England 248 for 7 (50 overs)(GA Hick 80, DL Maddy 53)
Zimbabwe 163 (46.5 overs)(SV Carlisle 41, MW Goodwin 28)
England won by 85 runs
Man of the Match: GA Hick

Match Four
Match abandoned without a ball bowled

Craig White made rapid progress in the winter one-day series, both in South Africa and in Zimbabwe.

ZIMBABWE DOMESTIC
By Telford Vice

Zimbabwean cricket took a great leap forward in 1999–2000 with the dramatic expansion of its first-class programme. The previous season's domestic first-class cricket amounted to three teams playing two matches, while another fixture was washed out without a ball bowled. A year later the programme featured five teams and 11 three-day matches. That may not seem a major advancement seen from the perspective of cricketers in countries where playing the game is at best an inevitable part of every summer weekend and at worst an expensive but still accessible sport. But in Zimbabwe the acquisition of a bag of second-hand equipment is cause enough to celebrate, so the extension of the first-class structure and programme was a dramatic development indeed. Previously, the Logan Cup had been the preserve of the Matabeleland XI, centred in Bulawayo, and various versions of Mashonaland teams, who were all drawn from in and around Harare. Accordingly, the 1998–99 season's line-up consisted of Mashonaland, Mashonaland 'A' and Matabeleland. In 1999–2000 that veritably ballooned to Mashonaland, Matabeleland, the Academy XI, Manicaland and Midlands. Not only that, Manicaland played competitive cricket throughout to deservedly reach the final against Mashonaland, at Harare Sports Club from April 7 to 9. Mashonaland began as favourites, not least because Manicaland were weakened by the absence of four established players. Gary Brent and Guy Whittall were on national service in the West Indies, Jon Brent was overseas and Andrew Whittall was out with an injured finger. Dirk Viljoen, also in the West Indies, was Mashonaland's only significant absentee.

Manicaland captain Mark Burmester won the toss and inserted his opposition, no doubt mindful of the fact that the only life his threadbare attack could expect at HSC would be there on the first morning. Overcast skies served only to strengthen that argument. However, the visitors wasted whatever advantage they may have held with some woefully wayward bowling and by dropping four catches before lunch. Openers Trevor Gripper and Gavin Rennie, neither of them among the more free-scoring of batsmen, had ample time to play themselves in.

By the time they were parted shortly before lunch, when Rennie was caught in the covers off Burmester for 52, Mashonaland had put 126 runs on the board.

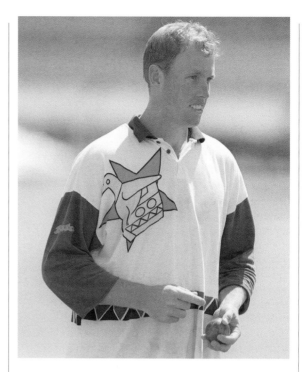

The absence of four of Manicaland's established players, such as Gary Brent (above) and Guy Whittall (below), due to national service in the West Indies may have jeopardised their success in the final against Mashonaland.

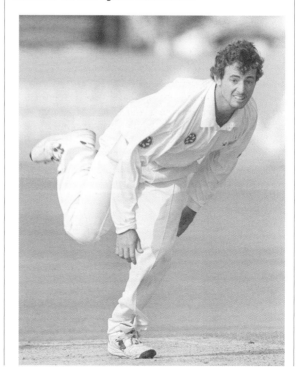

Gripper was caught behind off the most wayward of the bowlers, Leon Soma, for 86 after lunch, and just more than an hour later Mashonaland had let their concentration slip to the tune of 197 for five. That the home side were able to reach a total of 345 from that position had much to do with a sixth-wicket stand of 85 between Brad Robinson and Don Campbell, who brought contrasting approaches to the crease. Campbell scored his fifty in an hour, Robinson his 61 in two hours. Manicaland blocked out seven overs before bad light ended play an over early, but they showed less resolve on the second day by being dismissed for 123 to effectively end the match as a contest. Bryan Strang, who obtained movement through the air and off the seam, proved their undoing in taking seven for 20 off 21 overs. The only noteworthy defiance came from debutant opener Hamilton Masakadza, who ably picked his way through the ruins of the innings before being eighth out for 53. Strangely, given that he had a lead of 222, Mashonaland captain Gus Mackay declined to enforce the follow-on and instead batted out the day to close on 275 for five. Rennie and Gripper, who scored 87 and 78 respectively, shared an opening stand of 155. Mackay declared before play on the third morning, setting Manicaland a victory target of 498. The visitors made rather a better fist of it than in the first innings, with Neil Ferreira's 55 and Stuart Matsikenyeri's 73 particular highlights. However, Manicaland were again blown away by one bowler. This time it was Rennie, who resurrected the left-arm spin he had all but stopped bowling before this season because of back problems to take seven for 66 off 23.5 overs. Manicaland held out until just after tea, when they were dismissed for 240 to hand Mashonaland victory by 257 runs. Several of the 10 league matches also ended in emphatic victories, but an exception was the game between Midlands and Matabeleland at Kwekwe Sports Club played from 17 to 19 March. Doug Marillier scored 133 in an otherwise undistinguished Midlands first innings of 204, to which the visitors replied with 292 that consisted for the most part of Mark Vermeulen's 197. Half-centuries from Ray Price and David Mutendera lent a more balanced look to Midlands' second innings of 282, leaving Matabeleland to chase 195 for victory. But Ferreira got among the middle order to take 5 for 45 as the men from Bulawayo were dismissed for 180 to leave Midlands the winners by 14 runs. The season also threw up the oddity of Midlands being dismissed for 31 in their first innings by Mashonaland on a poor pitch at Harare Sports Club. Gus Mackay and Brighton Watambwa took 6 for 16 and 4 for 15 respectively as the innings imploded in the space of 12.5 overs. Manicaland's Neil Ferreira was the most respected batsman in 1999–2000 with three centuries and a half-century in his 501 runs scored at 72. Marillier of Midlands and Matabeleland's Vermeulen scored two centuries and a 50 each in averaging 68 and 63 respectively.

The season's most feared bowler was spirited Mashonaland captain Mackay, who took 18 wickets at 9.16 with a best analysis of 6 for 16, two five-wicket hauls and one 10-wicket masterpiece. Manicaland's Gary Brent dismissed 17 batsmen at 14.41, while the Academy's Greg Lamb and Dirk Viljoen of Mashonaland each sent 16 on their way. It will take some time before Zimbabwe's cricket fraternity will be able to see the fruits of their expanded first-class set-up, and the decisions of Murray Goodwin and Neil Johnson to leave the country has not helped the mood of those in the game. The volatile political situation, too, is a continuing worry to cricket as it is to every other sector of Zimbabwean society. But the good news is that cricket, thanks to the lifeblood supplied by sponsors with vision, is standing up for itself in Zimbabwe.

FIRST-CLASS AVERAGES

BATTING

	M	Inns	NO	HS	Runs	Av	100	50
MS Atapattu	5	7	1	216*	353	58.83	1	-
JA Young	4	6	2	89*	228	57.00	-	1
NR Ferreira	6	10	1	133	511	56.77	3	1
A Flower	5	10	2	129	438	54.75	1	3
RP Arnold	5	7	2	104*	268	53.60	1	1
DP Viljoen	5	7	1	173*	321	53.50	1	1
TM Dilshan	5	6	1	163*	256	51.20	1	-
GJ Rennie	9	14	0	152	666	47.57	2	3
MA Vermeulen	6	12	1	197	473	43.00	2	1
A Maregwede	4	7	1	59	246	41.00	-	2
DPMD Jayawardene	5	6	1	91	204	40.80	-	2
JA Rennie	3	5	1	63	161	40.25	-	2
DA Marillier	6	11	0	149	430	39.09	2	1
S Matsikenyeri	5	7	3	73*	134	33.50	-	1
GA Lamb	7	11	2	100*	299	33.22	1	1
CN Evans	5	8	0	153	262	32.75	1	-
TR Gripper	5	10	0	86	320	32.00	-	4
TJ Friend	4	6	0	48	188	31.33	-	-
SI de Saram	5	5	0	49	154	30.80	-	-
NC Johnson	5	10	1	75	271	30.11	-	3
GJ Whittall	6	11	2	85	257	28.55	-	2
MG Burmester	5	8	0	89	227	28.37	-	2
MW Goodwin	5	10	0	91	275	27.50	-	2
DJR Campbell	5	6	0	50	158	26.33	-	1
TN Madondo	4	5	0	59	130	26.00	-	1
DD Ebrahim	5	10	2	76*	196	24.50	-	1
ST Jayasuriya	4	6	1	49	121	24.20	-	-
BI Robinson	3	4	0	61	94	23.50	-	1
AJ Mackay	5	7	0	51	162	23.14	-	1
RS Kaluwitharana	4	5	1	30	91	22.75	-	-
C Delport	3	5	0	36	113	22.60	-	-
DJ Peacock	5	8	1	42	150	21.42	-	-
WT Siziba	4	8	1	54	144	20.57	-	1
MJ Vaughan-Davies	4	6	0	61	120	20.00	-	1
AP Hoffman	5	6	2	37*	73	18.25	-	-
DR Matambanadzo	4	7	0	50	123	17.57	-	1
CK Coventry	4	8	0	42	133	16.62	-	-
W Gilmour	5	8	1	33*	115	16.42	-	-
GW Flower	5	10	0	48	161	16.10	-	-
PK Gada	5	8	0	44	131	16.37	-	-
RW Price	7	14	0	82	223	15.92	-	2
DD Yatras	5	7	2	32	78	15.60	-	-
GR Savory	4	8	0	35	121	15.12	-	-
GD Ferreira	3	6	0	46	89	14.83	-	-
ER Marillier	3	6	1	46*	74	14.80	-	-
GH Haakonsen	4	4	0	45	59	14.75	-	-
LJ Soma	5	5	1	24	58	14.50	-	-
AR Whittall	4	4	0	42	57	14.25	-	-
RJ King	3	6	0	38	85	14.16	-	-
ADR Campbell	5	9	0	36	123	13.66	-	-
GP Wickremasinghe	4	4	0	18	54	13.50	-	-
GB Brent	8	11	0	55	148	13.45	-	1
BC Strang	6	9	0	41	118	13.11	-	-
DT Mutendera	6	11	2	51	111	12.33	-	1
LS Malloch-Brown	2	4	0	27	48	12.00	-	-
NR van Rensburg	2	4	0	16	47	11.75	-	-
IA Engelbrecht	4	7	0	28	79	11.28	-	-
SP Lawson	5	7	0	24	76	10.85	-	-
EZ Matambanadzo	7	11	4	31*	75	10.71	-	-
WPUJC Vaas	4	4	0	28	42	10.50	-	-
CA Grant	4	8	0	39	82	10.25	-	-

Qualification: 4 completed innings, average 10.00

FIRST-CLASS AVERAGES

BOWLING

	Overs	Mds	Runs	Wkts	Av	Best	10/m	5/m
SM Pollock	33	16	55	7	7.85	4-32	-	-
AJ Mackay	93.5	34	213	18	11.83	6-16	1	2
GD McGrath	86.3	25	163	13	12.53	5-36	-	1
CN Evans	51	21	77	6	12.83	4-5	-	-
BT Watamba	34	12	77	6	12.83	4-15	-	-
GJ Rennie	49.3	12	130	10	13.00	7-66	-	1
DW Fleming	62	23	110	8	13.75	3-16	-	-
GA Lamb	69.4	16	227	16	14.18	7-73	-	1
K Dabengwa	21.2	2	76	5	15.20	5-76	-	1
DP Viljoen	127.4	28	283	17	16.64	6-73	-	1
GP Wickremasinghe	129.2	45	255	15	17.00	6-60	-	1
TG Denyer	32.1	3	124	7	17.71	3-27	-	-
AP Hoffman	45.1	17	89	5	17.80	2-20	-	-
GB Brent	251.1	84	536	30	17.86	6-84	-	1
DNT Zoysa	42	7	92	5	18.40	3-22	-	-
GD Ferreira	66.5	10	240	13	18.46	5-45	-	1
HH Streak	34	8	93	5	18.60	5-93	-	1
KR Pushpakumara	46	10	95	5	19.00	5-56	-	1
TJ Friend	84	28	215	11	19.24	3-33	-	-
LJ Soma	95	22	251	13	19.30	4-43	-	-
WPUJC Vaas	176.4	44	404	19	21.26	4-43	-	-
IS Gallage	42	6	137	6	22.83	6-60	-	1
SK Warne	92.1	22	238	10	23.80	3-50	-	-
M Muralitharan	182	58	358	15	23.86	4-24	-	-
MG Burmester	109.2	39	288	12	24.00	3-45	-	-
GH Haakonsen	77.4	23	173	7	24.71	2-41	-	-
JA Rennie	79.5	23	249	10	24.90	5-70	-	1
BC Strang	212.4	73	479	19	25.21	7-20	-	1
M Abrams	51.2	10	204	8	25.50	4-46	-	-
IA Engelbrecht	122	27	338	13	26.00	3-52	-	-
JA Young	47.5	8	145	5	29.00	3-30	-	-
CJ Sanders	89	23	264	9	29.33	3-56	-	-
AR Whittall	158	33	491	16	30.68	6-151	-	2
MW Townshend	62.2	11	191	6	31.83	2-37	-	-
DJ Peacock	111.3	22	320	10	32.00	4-8	-	-
RW Price	213.2	55	596	18	33.11	3-14	-	-
HK Olonga	143.4	23	460	12	38.33	4-103	-	-
EZ Matambanaadzo	131	26	392	10	39.20	2-41	-	-
TR Gripper	51.1	7	198	5	39.60	2-42	-	-
EA Brandes	47	8	202	5	40.40	3-45	-	-
SP Brown	71	15	249	6	41.50	2-1	-	-
M Mbangwa	63	11	215	5	43.00	2-64	-	-
DT Mutendera	138.5	30	475	10	47.50	2-23	-	-
SP Lawson	141.5	27	483	10	48.30	3-14	-	-
SR Commerford	85	19	253	5	50.60	2-23	-	-

Qualification: 5 wickets

LAEDING FIELDERS

20 – NR Ferreira (17ct,1st); 18 – DJR Campbell (16ct,2st), A Flower; 14 – W Gilmour (13ct,1st); 11 – TM Dilshan (10ct,1st); 9 – ER Marillier (8ct,1st); 8 – RS Kaluwitharana; 7 – C Delport, DPMD Jayawardene; 6 – GW Flower, TR Gripper, MA Vermeulen; 5 – ADR Campbell, CA Grant, NC Johnson, AJ Mackay, WT Siziba, MJ Vaughan-Davies, DD Yatras

AUSTRALIA

Pakistan in Australia
India in Australia
Carlton and United One-Day Series
Sheffield Shield/Pura Milk Cup
Mercantile Mutual Cup
First-Class Averages

PAKISTAN IN AUSTRALIA
By Jim Maxwell

Bounce. Too much bounce. That's been the undoing of most down under visitors since the days of Lillee and Thomson in the 1970s. Ironically, in his 50th year and final competitive appearance, it was Lillee who embarrassed the Pakistanis in their opening tour match. Playing for an ACB Chairman's XI at the picturesque Lilac Hill Ground in Perth, Lillee and his son Adam, a local club player, took three wickets apiece, as Pakistan were thrashed by seven wickets.

In the lead-up to the Test series, Pakistan lost two more matches: a one-dayer against Western Australia by three runs, and more decisively, the first-class match against Queensland by 121 runs. They needed another four-day game to tune up for Test cricket, their preparation marred by another meaningless one-day tournament, in Sharjah, when their board, and the pundits, were talking up the approaching contest as a World Championship. Australia's selectors have never been sentimental. Their decision to replace record-holding wicketkeeper Ian Healy with Adam Gilchrist drew a barrage of criticism, particularly in Queensland. However, Healy's poor batting – and signs that the daily grind was becoming wearisome – forced his surprise announcement to retire barely a week before the first Test. His farewell was a lap of honour of the Gabba, not as the player who yearned for a last hurrah, but in his new role as a television commentator and, therefore, analyst of his successor. Healy's departure coincided with the appointment of John Buchanan as the replacement for Geoff Marsh as Australian coach. Buchanan's reputation had been built on taking Queensland to two Sheffield Shield titles, and his methods had won the support of Steve Waugh. That endorsement probably tilted the ACB's decision in Buchanan's favour over well-qualified rivals such as Steve Rixon, Greg Chappell and Wayne Clark.

As the series unfolded, Pakistan's mercurial talent could not match the relentless commitment and organisation of their opponents. They were certainly unlucky in Hobart, where an extraordinary partnership between Langer and Gilchrist won the match. Controversially Langer was given not out to a catch-behind appeal at a crucial stage, but he was

also glaringly dropped in the slips in the same over. Like a mantra that became a favoured Steve Waugh cliché, the contest was all about taking your chances, which Australia did better than Pakistan. Waugh's mental toughness has become a byword, and akin to the significance of a Kublai Khan or any great dynastic leader, his influence will be most apparent when he is no longer playing. He set the goal of winning all home Tests during the summer, knowing that he had the ammunition and the positive team attitude to achieve it.

The series was magnificently entertaining, both sides committed to the challenge of meeting attack with counter-attack. Australia, through McGrath, Fleming and Warne, were more disciplined with the ball, and the batting of Slater, Langer and Ponting, plus the sting of Gilchrist at number seven, proved superior. Another decisive factor in Australia's eventual three-nil win was their fielding. They were more athletic. Pakistan's pre-match routines were more like the neighbour who takes the dog for a walk than practice sessions that could create a brilliant dismissal that swings a match.

FIRST TEST
5, 6, 7, 8 and 9 November 1999 at Brisbane

Cramming in six Tests over two months meant an early start to the series, and Brisbane turned on a fine spring day for Steve Waugh's first outing at home as Test captain. The weather, and no doubt Australia's status as World Cup champions, drew a crowd of more than 15,000 to the renovated Gabba, which had taken on the look of a stadium with its circular surrounds of concrete and coloured plastic seats.

Adam Gilchrist and Scott Muller made their Test debuts for Australia, and Pakistan introduced all-rounder Abdur Razzaq. Gilchrist, who had already established himself with 76 one-day appearances, was expected to receive a lukewarm, maybe hostile reception from the Brisbane crowd, because he had replaced local hero Ian Healy. Healy's publicly generous support for his successor made for a smooth transition, and Gilchrist was warmly applauded after Waugh had won the toss and elected to bowl. Perhaps the fans were also cheering Muller, a Queensland fast bowler who made a shock rise to stardom following Gillespie's horrific injury in Sri Lanka. Reiffel's retirement, and a combination of wavering form and injuries among the alternatives, particularly Kasprowicz, had given Muller an opportunity. He was preferred to Colin Miller, another case of potential nudging out experience.

Previous page: Australian players celebrating with their winners' cheque following the three-nil whitewash in the Australia v. Pakistan Test series.

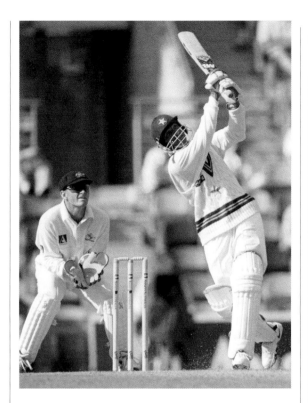

Yousuf Youhana of Pakistan hits a Shane Warne delivery for 4 on the way to 95 runs during Pakistan's first innnings.

Anwar's flashing off-side shots enlivened the early sparring, on an evenly grassed and true Gabba pitch. The pace trio was off-line, and Muller's nervousness served up the too full, too short, four balls. Switched ends, Fleming flicked the outside edge of Mohammad Wasim's bat with the first ball after drinks, giving Gilchrist a straightforward debut catch. Ijaz, who could pass for the national wood-chopping champion, David Foster, whooshed at his third ball from Fleming, and Warne consumed the deflection as smartly as his first-slip predecessor, Mark Taylor, had done habitually. Anwar's wristy, polished innings was worth 61 when he was deceived by Warne's straighter leg break, edging to Mark Waugh at slip, just after lunch. The languid Inzamam and aggressive Yohanna batted serenely, carrying the total to 265 for 3. McGrath trapped Inzamam leg before on the crease, and armed with a new missile, Fleming's out-swinger dismissed Yohanna five short of a well-deserved hundred. Nightwatchman Mushtaq succumbed to another out-swinger, after a blow amidships had the mob guffawing unkindly, and at 280 for 6 a vibrant opening day had just tilted to Australia in the last hour.

FIRST TEST – AUSTRALIA v. PAKISTAN
5, 6, 7, 8 and 9 November 1999 at Woolloongabba, Brisbane

PAKISTAN

	First Innings		Second Innings	
Saeed Anwar	c ME Waugh, b Warne	61	c Gilchrist, b McGrath	119
Mohammad Wasim	c Gilchrist, b Fleming	18	lbw b Fleming	0
Ijaz Ahmed	c Warne, b Fleming	0	c Gilchrist, b McGrath	5
Inzamam-ul-Haq	lbw b McGrath	88	c Ponting, b Fleming	12
Yousuf Youhana	c Gilchrist, b Fleming	95	c ME Waugh, b Muller	75
Azhar Mahmood	c Slater, b McGrath	13	(8) st Gilchrist, b Warne	0
Mushtaq Ahmed	c Gilchrist, b Fleming	0	(10) not out	1
Abdur Razzaq	c ME Waugh, b Muller	11	(6) c Ponting, b Warne	2
*Moin Khan	run out (Ponting/Gilchrist)	61	(7) c Muller, b Fleming	17
Wasim Akram (capt)	c & b Muller	9	(9) b Fleming	28
Shoaib Akhtar	not out	0	b Fleming	5
	b4, lb2 nb5	11	b6, lb6,nb5	17
		367		**281**

	First Innings				Second Innings			
	O	M	R	W	O	M	R	W
McGrath	28	4	116	2	21	9	63	2
Fleming	31	5	65	4	14.1	2	59	5
Muller	19	4	72	2	10	1	55	1
Warne	28.1	11	73	1	25	8	80	2
Blewett	5	1	22	–				
Ponting	5	1	12	–	4	0	12	–
Waugh SR	1	0	1	–				

Fall of Wickets
1–42, 2–42, 3–113, 4–265, 5–280, 6–280, 7–228, 8–334, 9–356
1–3, 2–8, 3–37, 4–214, 5–223, 6–225, 7–227, 8–273, 9–276

AUSTRALIA

	First Innings		Second Innings	
MJ Slater	c Yousuf Youhana, b Azhar Mahmood	169	(2) not out	32
GS Blewett	lbw b Mushtaq Ahmed	89	(1) not out	40
JL Langer	c Abdur Razzaq, b Mushtaq Ahmed	1		
ME Waugh	c Wasim Akram, b Mushtaq Ahmed	100		
SR Waugh (capt)	c Moin Khan, b Shoaib Akhtar	1		
RT Ponting	lbw b Shoaib Akhtar	0		
*AC Gilchrist	b Shoaib Akhtar	81		
SK Warne	c Mushtaq Ahmed, b Wasim Akram	86		
DW Fleming	lbw b Shoaib Akhtar	0		
GD McGrath	c Yousuf Youhana, b Wasim Akram	1		
SA Muller	not out	6		
	b 3, lb 12, nb 26	41	lb 2	2
		575	(for 0 wicket)	**74**

	First Innings				Second Innings			
	O	M	R	W	O	M	R	W
Wasim Akram	31.1	6	87	2	4	0	14	–
Shoaib Akhtar	32	2	153	4	5	0	25	–
Abdur Razzaq	17	3	66	–				
Azhar Mahmood	19	2	52	1	3.2	0	13	–
Mushtaq Ahmed	38	3	194	3	2	0	20	–
Ijaz Ahmed	2	0	8	–				

Fall of Wickets
1–269, 2–272, 3–311, 4–328, 5–342, 6–465, 7–485, 8–486, 9–489

Umpires: DJ Harper & EA Nicholls
Toss: Australia
Test Debuts: AC Gilchrist, SA Muller & Abdur Razzaq

Australia won by ten wickets

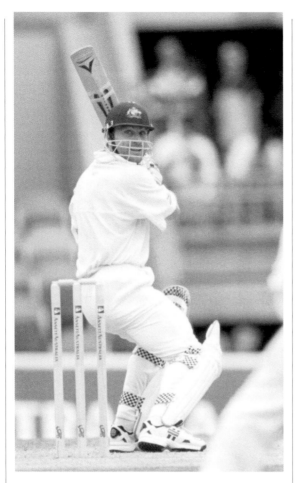

Michael Slater of Australia hits Abdur Razzaq for four on his way to his 13th Test century (first innings).

Next morning Moin mowed nine fours and a six in a thrilling tail-end swashbuckle. Moin was out when he could not beat Ponting's long return, while attempting to shield Shoaib from the strike. Defending a total scored at better than three runs an over, Pakistan went close to an early breakthrough, with both openers surviving Wasim Akram's swing as the ball thudded into their pads, missing leg, just, in his first over. The battle with Shoaib Akhtar was lively. The 'Rawalpindi Express' had come into the match under a cloud about his action. Secretively a video had been sent to the ACB after several express deliveries in Perth had raised an umpire's eyebrow. Alas there had been a leak in the process, and word got out that Shoaib was under suspicion. Curiously none of the Australian players had a concern about his action, and Shoaib had the full support of his captain. He was very quick, propelling the ball from

a tremendous explosion of his shoulder at the point of delivery. But he was inaccurate, and Slater took to him like a punter who thought the favourite was a certainty. Without Saqlain, who was having knee surgery, the attack was predictable. Mushtaq's spin lacked zip and control and he was pummelled. Slater was dropped twice, on 78 and 99, an edged cut sizzling to Mohammad Wasim in the slips, and Slater celebrating his let-off with a quick single that notched his 13th Test century. At stumps Australia had reached 233 for no wicket from only 62 overs.

The partnership had zoomed to a record 269 when Blewett padded up to Mushtaq. Eddie Nicholls, the Guyanese policeman who stood as the ICC umpire, raised his finger, but, as the story goes, he sidled over to his mate at square leg, Daryl Harper, as the batsmen changed over, and saw the big-screen replay of a slightly turning leg break to Blewett. Looking a little bemused he said to Harper: 'and Mushie told me it was his wrongun'. It did not faze Slater, who clouted 25 fours and a six out of 169. The innings had a few setbacks before the ever elegant Mark Waugh was joined by Gilchrist at 342 for 5 just after lunch. What a debut innings! The left-hander pounded 81 off 88 balls, as Waugh, his one-day opening partner, went to his 17th Test hundred. Shoaib at last pitched a classic in-swinging yorker, going around the wicket to Gilchrist, and Australia closed out the third day with a lead of 148 at 515 for 9.

Warne had often looked like the budding all-rounder, and as Muller held up his end, Warne lashed out. He hit three sixes from one Mushtaq over and by the time he had made 86 from 90 balls, 60 had been added for the last wicket, and Australia were 208 in front.

There was nothing in the pitch to suggest batting difficulty, but the pressure was quickly applied when Fleming trapped Wasim in front in the second over, and Ijaz whooshed ridiculously off McGrath. Anwar, missed by Mark Waugh on four, carried the fight with Yohanna, adding 177, Anwar playing brilliantly for his ninth Test century. A typical Brisbane downpour washed out the last session, but the ground was dry when Razzaq resumed with Anwar on the fifth day. And first ball he was deceived by a misdirected Warne full toss, which he hit straight to Ponting standing under his nose at silly point. Pakistan were all out in just over an hour thanks mainly to Fleming's swing bowling, and McGrath, who shifted Anwar. Chasing the next flight out of Brisbane, Slater and Blewett banged off the required runs in 14.2 overs. Slater was named Man of the Match.

SECOND TEST
18, 19, 20, 21 and 22 November 1999 at Hobart

Hobart has a rich historical significance. Its settlement in 1803 pre-dates all Australian capital cities other than Sydney, and Tasmanians are proud of who and where they are, gloriously isolated from the mainland. So isolated that they were left off the map for the 1982 Commonwealth Games opening ceremony. Hobart first hosted a Test match in 1989, 12 years after Tasmania were granted Sheffield Shield status. For the state that produced the first inter-colonial match, against Victoria, in 1851, an underpopulated Tasmania had struggled to keep up with the other wealthier mainland states. And now on 22 November, 1999, Hobart's place in Test history was put on the map forever.

An hour and a half before stumps on the fourth day Pakistan were certain to win the game when Australia had slid to 126 for 5, chasing a target of 369. Steve Waugh had just chipped a catch straight back to Saqlain, and Ponting was becoming a latter-day Tassie devil, when Wasim hit him in front for his third successive duck. Gilchrist confidently strode out to join Langer, whose longer term tenure was looking insecure. By stumps the two left-handers had kept the innings alive at 188 for 5.

Speculation about the result going into the fifth day hinged as much on the weather forecast as the remote chance Australia had of winning. After all, Saqlain had destroyed the tail in the first innings, and Pakistan had three lethal fast bowlers, and a second new ball up their sleeve. Propitiously, we could see Mount Wellington from the unfortunately positioned commentary box above the toilets at the River Derwent end of beautiful Bellerive. Beautiful one minute, and, in November, cold and wet the next. A light wind blew the clouds away, and the batsmen resumed the chase aggressively. In their favour the pitch had flattened out, now devoid of the moisture that helped Saqlain gain grip and bounce in his earlier deadliness. And the combination of two left-handers became a handful for frustrated bowlers, who were being driven on the rise, or cut or pulled, especially by Gilchrist at one-day momentum. Pakistan muffed a chance to break through when Mohammad Wasim dropped Langer in the slips off Wasim Akram when the score was 237, and in the same over a confident appeal for caught behind against Langer was turned down by umpire Parker. Psychologically this was a critical moment, and the Pakistanis' dejection was palpable. Langer and Gilchrist imposed their will, and the

runs rushed without blemish. Gilchrist's hundred arrived off 110 balls, the second-fastest for his country, and the extraordinary partnership was worth 238, when Langer slog/skied Saqlain to mid-wicket, with only five runs needed. Langer's steeliness and constant encouraging rapport sustained the partnership, giving Gilchrist the confidence to play his game, which already had him pencilled in as the most exciting number seven in Test cricket. He scored the winning runs in the third-highest fourth-innings total to win a Test, and even the disappointed Wasim was full of praise in defeat. 'They batted like champions. We were beaten by one of the greatest partnerships ever.' And certainly the result vindicated Steve Waugh's decision to bowl first, sensing, correctly, that the pitch would get better for batting.

In the first half hour of the match, McGrath moved past Richie Benaud's mark of 248 Test wickets with the quick disposal of Anwar and Ijaz, caught in the slips. Only Mohammad Wasim batted authoritatively, and a poor effort had Australia launching their assault before stumps. Another busy, confident start from Slater, Blewett and Langer made Pakistan look bedraggled at 191 for 1. Slater miscued from the toe his bat to mid-wicket, his seventh Test 90, and Saqlain started an amazing collapse when he won a dicey bat pad verdict from umpire Parker on Langer. Australia lost nine for 55, mesmerised by Saqlain's well-concealed over spinner, narrowly missing out on a hat-trick. At the other end Waqar revived memories of his swinging years by whacking Mark Waugh's pads, and then bowling Ponting with a prodigious late in-swerver, that he let go.

Saeed Anwar reproduced his scintillating Brisbane form as Pakistan built a solid position around some entertaining stroke-play from Ijaz and Inzamam.

The Bellerive Oval, Hobart.

Saqlain Mushtaq of Pakistan has Glenn McGrath stumped for 7 runs (first innings).

SECOND TEST – AUSTRALIA v. PAKISTAN
18, 19, 20, 21 and 22 November 1999 at Bellerive Oval, Hobart

PAKISTAN

	First Innings		Second Innings	
Saeed Anwar	c Warne, b McGrath	0	b Warne	78
Mohammad Wasim	c Gilchrist, b Muller	91	c McGrath, b Muller	20
Ijaz Ahmed	c Slater, b McGrath	6	(4) c SR Waugh, b McGrath	82
Inzamam-ul-Haq	b Muller	12	(5) c ME Waugh, b Warne	118
Yousuf Youhana	c ME Waugh, b Fleming	17	(6) c Ponting, b Fleming	2
Azhar Mahmood	bWarne	27	(7) lbw b Warne	28
*Moin Khan	c McGrath, b Muller	1	(8) c Gilchrist, b Fleming	6
Wasim Akram (capt)	c Gilchrist, b Warne	29	(9) c Blewett, b Warne	31
Saqlain Mushtaq	lbw b Warne	3	(3) lbw b Warne	8
Waqar Younis	not out	12	run out (Gilchrist)	0
Shoaib Akhtar	c Gilchrist, b Fleming	5	not out	
	b 10, lb 6, w 3	19	lb 6, w 1, nb 7	14
		222		**392**

	First Innings				Second Innings			
	O	M	R	W	O	M	R	W
McGrath	18	8	34	2	27	8	87	1
Fleming	24.5	7	54	2	29	5	89	2
Muller	12	0	68	3	17	3	63	1
Warne	16	5	45	3	45.4	11	110	5
Blewett	2	1	5	–	2	0	5	–
Ponting	5	1	12	–	4	0	12	–
Waugh SR					4	1	19	–
Waugh ME					2	0	6	–
Ponting					2	1	7	–

Fall of Wickets
1–4, 2–18, 3–71, 4–122, 5–148, 6–153, 7–188, 8–198, 9–217
1–50, 2–100, 3–121, 4–258, 5–263, 6–320, 7–345, 8–357, 9–358

AUSTRALIA

	First Innings		Second Innings	
MJ Slater	c Ijaz Ahmed, b Saqlain Mushtaq	97	(2) c Azhar Mahmood, b Shoaib Akhtar	27
GS Blewett	c Moin Khan, Azhar Mahmood	35	(1) c Moin Khan, b Azhar Mahmood	29
JL Langer	c Mohammad Wasim, b Saqlain Mushtaq	59	c Inzamam-ul-Haq, b Saqlain Mushtaq	127
ME Waugh	lbw b Waqar Younis	5	lbw b Azhar Mahmood	0
SR Waugh (capt)	c Ijaz Ahmed, b Wasim Akram	24	c & b Saqlain Mushtaq	28
RT Ponting	b Waqar Younis	0	lbw b Wasim Akram	0
*AC Gilchrist	st Moin Khan, b Saqlain Mushtaq	6	not out	149
SK Warne	b Saqlain Mushtaq	0	not out	0
DW Fleming	lbw b Saqlain Mushtaq	0		
GD McGrath	st Moin Khan, b Saqlain Mushtaq	7		
S A Muller	not out	0		
	b 2, lb 6, nb 5	13	b 1, lb 4, nb 4	9
		246	**(for 6 wickets)**	**369**

	First Innings				Second Innings			
	O	M	R	W	O	M	R	W
Wasim Akram	20	4	51	1	18	1	68	1
Shoaib Akhtar	17	2	69	–	23	5	85	1
Waqar Younis	12	1	42	2	11	2	38	–
Saqlain Mushtaq	24	8	46	6	44.5	9	130	2
Azhar Mahmood	7	1	30	1	17	3	43	2

Fall of Wickets
1–76, 2–190, 3–205, 4–205, 5–212, 6–236, 7–236, 8–236, 9–246
1–39, 2–81, 3–81, 4–125, 5–126, 6–364

Umpires: PD Parker & P Willey
Toss: Australia
Test Debuts: AC Gilchrist, SA Muller & Abdur Razzaq

Australia won by four wickets

Warne's probing accuracy was respected, and the breakthrough ball that shifted Anwar was a typical example of the champion's skill. Anwar padded up and the ball pitched in the rough wide of the off-stump, spitting back into the leg stump. Unplayable! Ijaz scythed away through point and cover, Inzamam scoring his first Test hundred in Australia. Multan's monolith was out to a screaming Mark Waugh snare at slip from a fierce, fast back cut, and the innings burbled on with Akram hitting out as 34 were usefully added for the last wicket.

It was during Inzamam's innings that an unexpected side-show blew up. Muller, playing his second, and probably last, Test, threw the ball wildly in from the deep over Gilchrist's head, with Warne at the bowler's end. A subsequent audio-enhanced replay on a chat show, picked up the cryptic remark 'ca not bowl, ca not throw', allegedly from a pitch microphone. Warne was the immediate suspect, and Muller, despite protestations from Warne of his innocence, assumed that he had been humiliated by the vice-captain. A witch-hunt was conducted to find the culprit, and eventually one of the Channel Nine cameramen, Joe, confessed to slipping the comment near an effects mike. Muller was still disbelieving, and after taking six wickets against India for Queensland, he leant over a stump microphone and blurted, 'six for the match, Warnie'. From thereon the quickest sledge became 'oh, mate, what's your name? Joe!' Joe, Adam and Justin all had stories to tell.

THIRD TEST
26, 27 and 28 November 1999 at Perth

Rest days are as rare as Test matches without leg before wicket decisions, and players without helmets. Perth is the exception. Unless the pitch has been anaesthetised, or fast bowlers break down, you can bet, if you're allowed to, that a Test will be over in three days. Perth rarely gets a crunch match in a series, and the West Indies have come to regard playing there as the same home-ground advantage that Australia enjoys at Lord's. The pitch always bounces, often like a trampoline from a length, and if there's any sideways shift from grass or the legendary cracks, then batting becomes a terminal task.

Australia reintroduced a fit Michael Kasprowicz to replace the chastened Scott Muller, and introduced the country's fastest bowler, Brett Lee for Colin Miller, who had carried the towels in the first two Tests. Was it another win for experience over youth, or just timing, that influenced the final decision to play Kasprowicz ahead of the tyro, Lee? In the pre-match chats Steve Waugh's preference for Lee was apparent, but he went with the experience option, and the selectors' preference, knowing that Lee's time would come soon enough. Besides, Kasprowicz had a solid record at the WACA, and was useful into the breeze.

Pakistan were forced to replace the injured Mohammad Wasim with Wajahatullah Wasti, and included occasional Test cricketer Mohammad Akram, for Waqar Younis, who only bowled eleven overs in the second innings in Hobart. Backing up four days after an arduous match was another problem for Pakistan, as their coach Richard Pybus was soon to discover. The difference in fitness between the two sides had been obvious, affecting the basic elements like running, catching and concentration. Pybus took the rap for a seriously

Above: Michael Kasprowicz bowls out Shoaib Akhtar for no score in the first innings.
Below: Ricky Ponting clips Shoaib Aktar through midwicket on his way to 197 runs (first innings).

underprepared outfit, exiting through the revolving door that so many former players, managers and ex-coaches had discovered in the conflicting world of Karachi/Lahore cricket politics.

The match, as expected, was well on the way to an early finish by the end of an exciting first day. Wasim Akram won the toss and did exactly what Steve Waugh had half hoped he would do. He batted. Half hoped because although the pitch looked even, it would bounce, and any early wickets could be mortally wounding. And so it proved. Pakistan lost three for 26 in the opening salvos, were 85 for 5 at lunch, and all out before tea for an edgy 155. McGrath and Fleming bowled a full length, and the innings was a series of slips catching repetitions, plus a brilliant leg-side catch from Gilchrist to dismiss Yohanna. And the catching was not perfect; Azhar Mahmood was put down three times, on the way to a top score of 39. Kasprowicz played his part with four wickets, and was on a hat-

Justin Langer (Player of the Series) raises his baggy green cap to his home Western Australian crowd, following Australia's victory in the third Test.

trick after claiming the last two wickets off consecutive balls.

Australia's innings began badly for a change, Wasim Akram winning an early leg before verdict, second ball, on Slater. He would have swapped the decision for Brisbane or Hobart, someone jocularly offering that there was only a hair in it. It was Daryl's first Test of the series. Blewett and the Waughs were out quickly too, and at 54 for 4 Mohammad Akram had grabbed three good wickets. Enter Ponting, on his fourth potential duck. By stumps he was a solid, threatening 62, Langer missed at 19, 63, and Australia were already ahead at 171 for 4. Just another quiet day of Test cricket; 14 wickets for 326, and a crowd of over 15,000 urging local hero Langer towards another century.

Pakistan's bowlers failed to stick to the mandatory WACA discipline of keeping a fuller length, and the cross bat cuts and pulls thundered out a partnership of 327. Ponting clobbered 197, his Test best, and Langer enlivened the bar talk with another confident hundred. Pakistan were batting again before stumps, after Mohammad Akram shared the mixed experiences of his best Test figures, and a visit to the match referee for a collision with Shane Warne near the end of Australia's innings.

Resuming the third day at 40 for 2, Pakistan needed a miraculous Hanif Mohammad-style two-day innings. It was not in their nature. Ijaz cut, pulled, slogged, miscued, and made a lively hundred, his sixth against Australia. A great net for the one-dayers, runs smashed at four an over. The captain joined in the valedictory frenzy with 52 from 40 balls. Like free beer at the Gulargambone picnic race meeting, it could not last. At precisely 15:06 Shoaib edged to Warne at slip, and Australia were celebrating a three-nil series win, on a margin of an innings and 20 runs. Perth had hosted another three-day Test, and a lively one with 882 runs scored at 3.8 per over, and 52 runs per hour. No one seemed to care that it had taken four and a half minutes to bowl each over in the match, and that play was finishing up to an hour over time on some days in the series. Ponting was named Man of the Match, and Langer the Player of the Series.

THIRD TEST – AUSTRALIA v. PAKISTAN
26, 27 and 28 November 1999 at WACA Ground, Perth

PAKISTAN

	First innings		Second innings	
Saeed Anwar	c Ponting, b McGrath	18	c Gilchrist, b Fleming	6
Wajahatullah Wasti	c Ponting, b McGrath	5	c Fleming, b McGrath	7
Ijaz Ahmed	b Fleming	1	c Slater, b Kasprowicz	115
Inzamam-ul-Haq	c SR Waugh, b Kasprowicz	22	(5) c ME Waugh, b McGrath	8
Yousuf Youhana	c Gilchrist, b McGrath	18	(6) c SR Waugh, b McGrath	0
Azhar Mahmood	c Warne, b Fleming	39	(7) b Warne	17
*Moin Khan	c & b Fleming	28	(8) c Gilchrist, b McGrath	26
Wasim Akram (capt)	not out	5	(9) c McGrath, b Kasprowicz	52
Saqlain Mushtaq	c Blewett, b Kasprowicz	7	(4) lbw b Warne	12
Shoaib Akhtar	b Kasprowicz	0	c Warne, b Fleming	8
Mohammad Akram	c ME Waugh, b Kasprowicz	0	not out	10
	lb 4, nb 8	12	lb 6, nb 9	15
		155		**276**

	First innings				Second innings			
	O	M	R	W	O	M	R	W
McGrath	19	4	44	3	21	5	49	4
Fleming	19	7	48	3	19.4	3	86	2
Kasprowicz	12	2	53	4	16	3	79	3
Warne	2	0	6	–	13	1	56	1

Fall of Wickets
1–18, 2–26, 3–26, 4–50, 5–83, 6–135, 7–142, 8–155, 9–155
1–15, 2–25, 3–53, 4–56, 5–114, 6–168, 7–230, 8–256, 9–261

AUSTRALIA

	First innings	
MJ Slater	lbw b Wasim Akram	0
GS Blewett	c Inzamam-ul-Haq, b Mohammad Akram	11
JL Langer	c Moin Khan, b Shoaib Akhtar	144
ME Waugh	c sub (Ghulam Ali), b Mohammad Akram	0
SRWaugh (capt)	c Yousuf Youhana, b Mohammad Akram	5
RT Ponting	c Ijaz Ahmed, b Azhar Mahmood	197
*AC Gilchrist	b Mohammad Akram	28
SK Warne	c Moin Khan, b Saqlain Mushtaq	13
MS Kasprowicz	not out	9
DW Fleming	lbw b Saqlain Mushtaq	0
GD McGrath	c Azhar Mahmood, b Mohammad Akram	0
	b 9, lb 9, nb 26	44
		451

	First innings			
	O	M	R	W
Wasim Akram	17	2	55	1
Mohammad Akram	27.5	1	138	5
Shoaib Akhtar	16	2	74	1
Azhar Mahmood	23	2	91	1
Saqlain Mushtaq	26	7	75	2
Wajahatullah Wasti	1	1	–	–

Fall of Wickets
1–0, 2–28, 3–48, 4–54, 5–381, 6–424, 7–424, 8–448, 9–450

Umpires: DB Hair & P Willey
Toss: Pakistan
Test Debuts: nil

Australia won by an innings and 20 runs

TEST MATCH AVERAGES
Australia v. Pakistan

AUSTRALIA

Batting	M	Inns	NO	HS	Runs	Av	100	50
AC Gilchrist	3	4	1	149*	264	88.00	1	1
JL Langer	3	4	0	144	331	82.75	2	1
MJ Slater	3	5	1	169	325	81.25	1	1
GS Blewett	3	5	1	89	204	51.00	–	1
RT Ponting	3	4	0	197	197	49.25	1	–
ME Waugh	3	4	0	100	105	26.25	1	–
SR Waugh	3	4	0	28	58	14.50	–	–
GD McGrath	3	3	0	7	8	2.66	–	–

Also batted: DW Fleming (3 Tests) 0,0,0; MS Kasprowicz (1 Test) 9*;
SA Muller (2 Tests) 6*, 0*

Bowling	Overs	Mds	Runs	Wkts	Av	Best	10/m	5/inn
MS Kasprowicz	28	5	132	7	18.85	4–53	–	–
DW Fleming	137.4	29	401	18	22.27	5–59	–	1
GD McGrath	134	36	393	14	28.07	4–49	–	–
SK Warne	129.5	36	370	12	30.83	5–110	–	1
SA Muller	58	8	258	7	36.85	3–68	–	–

Also bowled: GS Blewett 9–2–32–0; RT Ponting 11–2–31–0; ME Waugh 2–0–6–0;
SR Waugh 5–1–20–0

Fielding Figures
13 – AC Gilchrist (12ct/1st); 7 – ME Waugh; 5 – RT Ponting; 4 – SK Warne; 3 – GDMcGrath, MJ Slater, SR Waugh; 2 – GS Blewett, DW Fleming, SA Muller

PAKISTAN

Batting								
Saeed Anwar	3	6	0	119	282	47.00	1	2
Inzamam-ul-Haq	3	6	0	118	260	43.33	1	1
Ijaz Ahmed	3	6	0	115	209	34.83	1	1
Yousuf Youhana	3	6	0	95	207	34.50	–	2
Mohammad Wasim	2	4	0	91	129	32.25	–	1
Wasim Akram	3	6	1	52	154	30.80	–	1
Moin Khan	3	6	0	61	139	23.16	–	1
Azhar Mahmood	3	6	0	39	124	20.66	–	–
Saqlain Mushtaq	2	4	0	12	30	7.50	–	–
Shoaib Akhtar	3	6	2	8	23	5.75	–	–

Also batted: Abdur Razzaq (1 Test) 11, 2; Mohammad Akram (1 Test) 0, 10*;
Mushtaq Ahmed (1 Test) 0, 1*; Wajahatullah Wasti (1 Test) 5, 7; Waqar Younis (1 Test) 12*, 0

Bowling								
Saqlain Mushtaq	94.5	23	251	10	25.10	6–46	–	1
Mohammad Akram	27.5	1	138	5	27.60	5–138	–	1
Azhar Mahmood	69.2	8	229	5	45.80	2–43	–	–
Wasim Akram	90.1	13	275	5	55.00	2–87	–	–
Shoaib Akhtar	93	11	406	6	67.66	4–153	–	–

Also bowled: Abdur Razzaq 17–3–66–0; Ijaz Ahmed 2–0–8–0; Mushtaq Ahmed 40–3–214–3;
Wajahatullah Wasti 1–1–0–0; Waqar Younis 23–3–80–2

Fielding Figures
7 – Moin Khan (5ct/2st); 3 – Ijaz Ahmed, Yousuf Youhana; 2 – Azhar Mahmood, Inzamam-ul-Haq; 1 – Abdur Razzaq, Mohammad Wasim, Mushtaq Ahmed, Saqlain Mushtaq, Wasim Akram

INDIA IN AUSTRALIA
By Jim Maxwell

Australia overwhelmed India in a series of matches that highlighted the home team's superiority in every critical aspect of the game. India's inability to compete for more than a session or an individual innings was a sad commentary on their preparation and mental toughness. That said, their opponents played with the confidence and skill of a team that expected to win, and did, as decisively as any Australian team in history.

Emphasising Australia's achievement and depth was the fact that Fleming, who took 30 Test wickets in six Tests, did not play one Test in the following series in New Zealand. Nor did their leading run-scorer, Ponting, who was injured, and adequately replaced by Damien Martyn.

India's batting relied too much on the brilliance of Tendulkar. Ganguly supported him, but Dravid was an abject failure. The elegant right-hander was worn down by the probing accuracy of Shane Warne in Adelaide, and he never regained confidence. Laxman played an extraordinary cameo innings in a lost cause in Sydney, but failed when it mattered. And Tendulkar was unluckily dismissed in Adelaide, in both innings, making amends in Melbourne with a superb batting exhibition, and the personal satisfaction of the century that he longed for at the legendary MCG. The bowling was unspectacular, lacking the menace and penetration to run through a talented line-up. And whoever heard of an Indian team with one specialist spinner? Yes, a good one in Kumble. But he took only five wickets in the series, and whether it was the pitch's predictable bounce, the Kookaburra ball, or just the quality of Australia's batting, Kumble needed some spin support. So much effort seems to have gone into producing fast bowlers, in Kapil Dev's wake, that there is now a dearth of spin bowlers.

The captaincy wore down Tendulkar. High expectations and the fierce combativeness of the Australian team eroded Indian confidence. Tendulkar wavered with his tactics, and with the manipulation of his bowlers, especially in Adelaide when Australia was a precarious 4 for 52 on the first day of the series. He was so focused on wanting to lead his side with dominant batting that a sense of team was lost, and their deficiencies were exposed by relentless opponents.

Australia's performance was invigorated by the introduction of express bowler Brett Lee. The fascination with pace had been a talking point during Shoaib Akhtar's lively spells, when the radar gun had him nudging 150 kph. Like the Nasdaq index pushing a new high, the speed of Lee's rockets became more interesting than the flow of the contest, and his impact was dramatic, taking seven wickets on his debut in Melbourne.

FIRST TEST
10, 11, 12, 13 and 14 December 1999 at Adelaide

Sachin Tendulkar's presence, and the expected tilt with Australia's premier bowlers, McGrath and Warne, had heightened everyone's expectations when Steve Waugh won the toss and batted on a friendly-looking Adelaide Oval pitch. An hour later the Australian innings was floundering. Blewett edged to the wicketkeeper, Langer's pads were thereabouts, Slater drove low to cover, and Mark Waugh played a typical pre-double-figures lunge. Steve Waugh and the in-form Ponting consolidated, and must have been relieved when Tendulkar kept his strike bowlers out of the attack in the hour after

Steve Waugh celebrates his century in the first innings.

Sachin Tendulkar, dismissed for 61 runs, caught by Justin Langer off the bowling of Shane Warne (first innings).

lunch. By then, Waugh's jaw was set like a monumental inscription, and in a flawless innings he became the first player to score a hundred against every Test-playing nation. Ponting hammered drives, and missed by Laxman in the slips on 90, reached his sixth Test hundred. The partnership produced 239, remarkably Australia's fourth successive double-hundred stand of the summer. Waugh also passed the milestone of 8,000 Test runs.

India could have restricted Australia's innings to less than 400. Gilchrist was caught and bowled from the second ball of day two for a duck, exposing the tail at 6 for 298. The irrepressible Waugh found support from the budding all-rounder, Shane Warne, who gave chances at 12 and 16, and then cut loose. He faced 100 balls, added 108 with Waugh, and equalled his highest Test score, 86. The thought of a hundred disturbed Warne's attacking rhythm, and a cute attempted sweep was plumb leg before to Kumble.

The Indian innings began sensationally when Greg Blewett pulled off the type of dismissal that had become almost habitual in a confident team. Gandhi drove McGrath, and Blewett chased towards that famous straight and long Adelaide boundary. As the batsmen turned for an obligatory fourth run, Blewett pivoted on his pick-up, and released a

powerful return that hit the stumps at the bowler's end on the full, with a desperate Ramesh scrambling to get home. The third umpire pressed the red button, and when Kasprowicz pocketed a simple leg-gully catch from Gandhi, India were 2 for 9. Besieged by Warne's accuracy, the innings limped to 123 for 4 at stumps, with Tendulkar in a totally absorbed, defensive mood.

The maestro started the third day belligerently, pounding Fleming's full-pitched straighter deliveries. The excitement of a big innings was building when another probing Warne spell accounted for Tendulkar. The crease shuffle is always dangerous if the length is not killed, padded or attacked. Warne's tactical sequence of wrist-spinners forced the indecisive prod, and a successful bat pad appeal from Langer at short leg. Gilchrist's sharp stumping of Ganguly at 229 for 6 meant 13 were still required to avoid the possibility of following on. Waugh probably would not have enforced it, given the renowned variable fourth and fifth day bounce of the drying pitch. Nerves tightened when Warne bowled Mannava Prasad around his legs at 240 for 7, but there was enough sting in a swishy tail to prevent a quick collapse, Fleming taking the last three wickets for a lead of 156.

Australia's second innings provided portentous evidence of the changing nature of the pitch. Blewett top-scored, his 88 sketched with miscues, inside edges and a determination to guide the team

FIRST TEST – AUSTRALIA v. INDIA
10, 11, 12, 13 and 14 December 1999 at Adelaide Oval

AUSTRALIA

	First innings		Second innings	
GS Blewett	c BKV Prasad, b Srinath	4	(2) b Agarkar	88
MJ Slater	c Ramesh, b Ganguly	28	(1) c Ganguly, b Srinath	0
JL Langer	lbw b BKV Prasad	11	c Gandhi, b Kumble	38
ME Waugh	c MSK Prasad, b BKV Prasad	5	c Laxman, b Agarkar	8
SR Waugh (capt)	c MSK Prasad, b Agarkar	150	c MSK Prasad, b Agarkar	5
RT Ponting	run out (Agarkar/MSK Prasad)	125	c MSK Prasad, b BKV Prasad	21
*AC Gilchrist	c & b Agarkar	0	c Laxman, b Srinath	43
SK Warne	lbw b Kumble	86	c Dravid, b Srinath	0
MS Kasprowicz	b Kumble	4	not out	21
DW Fleming	not out	12		
GD McGrath	c MSK Prasad, b BKV Prasad	4		
	b 1, lb 5, nb 6	12	b 3, lb 8, w 2, nb 2	15
		441	(for 8 wickets dec.)	**239**

	First innings				Second innings			
	O	M	R	W	O	M	R	W
Srinath	29	3	117	1	21.5	4	64	3
Agarkar	26	5	86	2	18	6	43	3
BKV Prasad	24.3	4	83	3	18	5	48	1
Ganguly	7	1	34	1				
Kumble	34	1	101	2	32	9	73	1
Tendulkar	2	0	12	–				
Laxman	3	1	2	–				

Fall of Wickets
1-8, 2-29, 3-45, 4-52, 5-291, 6-298, 7-406, 8-417, 9-424
1-1, 2-65, 3-95, 4-113, 5-153, 6-204, 7-205, 8-239

INDIA

	First Innings		Second innings	
D Gandhi	c Kasprowicz, b McGrath	4	c Gilchrist, b McGrath	0
S Ramesh	run out (Blewett)	2	lbw b Warne	28
VVS Laxman	c SR Waugh, b McGrath	41	b Fleming	0
R Dravid	c Langer, b Warne	35	c Gilchrist, b Warne	6
SR Tendulkar (capt)	c Langer, b Warne	61	lbw b McGrath	0
SC Ganguly	st Gilchrist, b Warne	60	c Gilchrist, b Fleming	43
*MSK Prasad	b Warne	14	c Langer, b Fleming	11
AB Agarkar	b Fleming	19	c SR Waugh, b Fleming	0
J Srinath	c SR Waugh, b Fleming	11	c Slater, b McGrath	11
A Kumble	not out	17	b Fleming	3
BKV Prasad	lbw b Fleming	0	not out	2
	lb 1, w 1, nb 19	21	lb 1, nb 5	6
		285		**110**

	First Innings				Second innings			
	O	M	R	W	O	M	R	W
McGrath	30	13	49	2	12	2	35	3
Fleming	24.4	7	70	3	9.1	2	30	5
Kasprowicz	11	2	62	–	6	0	23	–
Warne	42	12	92	4	10	6	21	2
Blewett	6	1	11	–				
Waugh ME					1	1	–	–

Fall of Wickets
1-7, 2-9, 3-90, 4-107, 5-215, 6-229, 7-240, 8-266, 9-275
1-0, 2-3, 3-24, 4-27, 5-48, 6-93, 7-93, 8-102, 9-108

Umpires: DJ Harper & RS Dunne
Toss: India
Test Debuts: nil

Australia won by 285 runs

to comfort. Miserly length bowling denied the aggressive expression of the batsmen, with Agarkar and Srinath sharing the toil and rewards, around the top-spinning steadiness of Kumble. Waugh's closure half an hour after tea meant India had a potential 116 overs to make 396. Dreams of a Tendulkar-inspired victory were quickly dashed by McGrath and Fleming, who rapidly dispatched Gandhi and Laxman, and then McGrath won the killer verdict over Tendulkar. Ducking a short ball that did not bounce as high as he had anticipated, Tendulkar was whacked on the arm somewhere in front of the bails. He was certainly, in the words of another shortie, Sunil Gavaskar, vertically challenged. But the decision had the look of, well, close, but not conclusively plumb. It smacked of a moral decision, understandably given by an umpire caught in that horrible moment of making an instant judgement, without the benefit of the sitting-room replays.

From 76 for 5 at stumps it was just a question of when the early lunch would be devoured. Fleming should have taken a hat-trick, but Warne dropped a simple chance at slip from Srinath. Fleming grabbed 4 for 7 in 23 balls, bagging five for the innings and nine for the match. Australia's winning run was now five, and the swiftness of their victory on the last day almost guaranteed wins six and seven.

SECOND TEST
26, 27, 28, 29 and 30 December 1999 at MCG

Brett Lee's explosive debut and a masterly Sachin Tendulkar century lifted the spirits during a somewhat dank holiday Test match. Rain and bad light forced a rearrangement of playing times on each day, which meant stumps were being pulled at half past seven. No wonder Tests are finishing within the apportioned time, when the flexibility in the playing conditions allows for seven and a half hours of play to catch up. Alas for India they were like a kid on a skateboard chasing a bus. When they caught up they realised that they did not have the right money for the fare, and were tipped off. Even if India's bowlers had been able to remove Australia cheaply, their batting looked suspect, and would have been overwhelmed, whether it was 200 or 300 to chase. They lost by a wide margin, having had hopes of a draw until Warne trapped Tendulkar leg before without offering on the last afternoon.

The sight of a grassy MCG pitch quickly made up Tendulkar's mind to bowl after winning the toss. Srinath ripped in, bursting through Blewett, and hitting Langer high on the pads, which was close

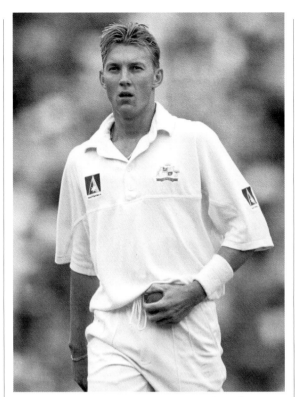

Brett Lee, the young fast bowler, making his debut for Australia at the MCG. Lee managed to take seven wickets in his first Test appearance.

enough for David Shepherd. Rain had delayed play until two o'clock, and a Boxing Day crowd of near 50,000 saw only four hours of cricket on a Melbourne day that did not quite encompass all four seasons. The pitch was more slow than menacing, and Mark Waugh put on 95 with the aggressive Slater. Agarkar, who, to quote my mate from Snake Gully, 'looks like he needs a good feed', whirred one into Waugh's pads, and when the light faded, Australia had scrounged out 3 for 138. India had rejected the artificial-light provision, and there's no doubt that the red ball can be hard to pick up against the lights. But if the ground has lights, common sense says that the game must go on for as long as possible. Maybe next year.

Another Slater hundred beckoned the next morning. He had reached 91 when his hook shot off Prasad went straight to Srinath at fine leg. Slater does not covet records, but his eighth Test 90 pushed him closer to the all-time tally for nervy 90s, and more happily, past 1,000 for the calendar year. Prasad celebrated enthusiastically, and was harshly treated in a subsequent hearing with the match

referee. A fine was excessive, and rough justice given some of McGrath's antics, which passed without censure.

At 197 for 5 Australia were even par for 300, when Gilchrist and Ponting got cracking. A sharp return catch to Kumble when Gilchrist was seven was ruled not out on referral to the eye in the box, and Gilchrist immediately took his belligerent cue. The effervescent Ponting raised 50 from 49 balls, the fastest Test half-century at the MCG, and when rain flooded the outfield, Australia were 332 for 5.

Fleming and debutant Lee knocked the bowling about on a ground that had dried out amazingly the following day. India were batting before lunch, and a confident Lee scythed through Ramesh's defence with his fourth ball, joining the exclusive club of bowlers who have taken a wicket in their first Test match over. Promoting himself to number four, Tendulkar soon had the measure of the bowling,

All elegance: Tendulkar stroking his first innings century.

SECOND TEST – AUSTRALIA v. INDIA
26, 27, 28, 29 and 30 December 1999 at Melbourne Cricket Ground

AUSTRALIA

	First innings			Second innings	
GS Blewett	b Srinath	2		(2) c Ganguly, b Kumble	31
MJ Slater	c Srinath, b BKV Prasad	91		(1) lbw b Agarkar	3
JL Langer	lbw b Srinath	8		c MSK Prasad, b Agarkar	9
ME Waugh	lbw b Agarkar	41		(5) not out	51
SR Waugh (capt)	c MSK Prasad, b BKV Prasad	32		(6) lbw b Agarkar	32
RT Ponting	lbw b Srinath	67		(7) not out	21
*AC Gilchrist	c Ganguly, b Agarkar	78		(4) c Srinath, b Kumble	55
SK Warne	c MSK Prasad, b Agarkar	20			
DW Fleming	not out	31			
B Lee	c & b Srinath	27			
GD McGrath	run out (Kanitkar)	1			
	b 1, lb 9, w 1, nb 14	25		lb 2, w 1, nb 3	6
		405		**(for 5 wickets dec.)**	**208**

	First innings				Second innings			
	O	M	R	W	O	M	R	W
Srinath	33.1	7	130	4	14	0	45	–
Agarkar	28	7	76	3	17	3	51	3
BKV Prasad	26	6	101	2	10	0	38	–
Ganguly	2	0	10	–				
Kumble	29	3	78	–	18	3	72	2

Fall of Wickets
1–4, 2–28, 3–123, 4–192, 5–197, 6–341, 7–343, 8–345, 9–404
1–5, 2–32, 3–91, 4–109, 5–167

INDIA

	First Innings			Second innings	
VVS Laxman	c ME Waugh, b McGrath	5		c McGrath, b Fleming	1
S Ramesh	b Lee	4		retired hurt	26
R Dravid	c Gilchrist, b Lee	9		c Gilchrist, b Lee	14
SR Tendulkar (capt)	c Langer, b Fleming	116		lbw b Warne	52
SC Ganguly	c ME Waugh, b McGrath	31		b Blewett	17
HH Kanitkar	lbw b Warne	11		lbw b Fleming	45
*MSK Prasad	b Lee	6		c Warne, b ME Waugh	13
AB Agarkar	lbw b Lee	0		c Blewett, b ME Waugh	0
J Srinath	c ME Waugh, b Lee	1		(10) c Warne, b Lee	1
A Kumble	not out	28		(9) run out (SR Waugh)	13
BKV Prasad	c ME Waugh, b McGrath	10		not out	6
	lb8, nb9	17		lb4, nb3	7
		238			**195**

	First innings				Second Innings			
	O	M	R	W	O	M	R	W
McGrath	18.1	3	39	3	17	8	22	–
Fleming	15	0	62	1	21.3	7	46	2
Lee	18	2	47	5	19	6	31	2
Warne	24	5	77	1	26	7	63	1
Waugh ME	1	0	5	–	3	0	12	2
Blewett					3	1	17	1

Ramesh retired hurt at 40–1 in the second innings

Fall of Wickets
1–11, 2–11, 3–31, 4–108, 5–138, 6–167, 7–167, 8–169, 9–212
1–5, 2–72, 3–110, 4–133, 5–162, 6–162, 7–184, 8–185, 9–195

Umpires: SJ Davis & DR Shepherd
Toss: India
Test Debuts: HH Kanitkar and B Lee

Australia won by 180 runs

respectfully waiting for the length to attack. Lee's shock spell after tea claimed three wickets in an over, and it was left to Kumble to partner Tendulkar past both a chanceless hundred, and the follow-on. Bad light intervened when most of the crowd had booked in for dinner, or retired to the bar, and India were 235 for 9, Tendulkar out for a majestic 116.

Around more rain breaks India were dislodged for 238, with Warne taking only one of the seven wickets required to break Lillee's Australian record of 355 dismissals, during the innings. Lee's pace and consistency created a five-wicket swag, and Australia pursued quick runs with a bank of 167. Accurate bowling kept the tempo more steady than sizzling. Gilchrist's promotion to number four was the answer, and his 55 out of 77 added with Mark Waugh gave Steve Waugh the opportunity to set a target of 376 from a possible 118 overs.

From 40 for 1 at stumps, India were still breathing at lunch with Tendulkar on 48 at 110 for 3. Ramesh had retired hurt at the start, the victim of a Lee thumb-crusher. Dravid's lack of shots dug another hole, and it was a shame to see a player of his class in such desperately poor form. Tendulkar, who had clearly won the first-innings battle with Warne, concentrated to preserve his wicket and keep his team afloat. Debutant Kanitkar fought doggedly, but Warne caused a misjudgement from the champion batsman when he padded up. In the mopping-up Mark Waugh was on a hat-trick, bowling his straight spinning, drifting occasionals, and the match ended with a run-out and almost a session to spare. India had been totally outplayed, and the debut pyrotechnics from Brett Lee, who took seven match wickets, were a sign that the dose could be repeated in Sydney in three days' time.

THIRD TEST
2, 3 and 4 January at Sydney

The third Test was a magnificent cricket occasion. Mark Waugh celebrated his one hundredth Test appearance, and received one of the most heart-warming receptions imaginable when he came out to bat just before lunch on the second day. In a burst of new millennium euphoria the fans rolled up in droves to fill the old ground. Over 42,000 shook off their New Year hangovers on the opening day, a total of 106,636 attending the three action-packed days that were needed for a massive Australian victory.

No one seemed to care whether the new millennium was starting in 2000 or 2001. Do you need an excuse for a party? Buoyed by this

Mark Waugh with a framed baggy green cap to commemorate his 100th Test appearance.

excitement the Australian players dipped their lids to history. Inspired by Steve Waugh's respect for traditions and the most powerful symbol in Australian cricket, the baggy green cap, the team wore replica caps of the model created for Joe Darling's side in England in 1899. They were black, and a much tighter fit than the design that became synonymous with all Australian elevens, featuring a green and gold, looser, baggy headpiece.

The match was never a contest after India was embarrassingly dismissed for 150 in their first innings. Tendulkar's positive decision to bat first backfired on an atypical grassy Sydney pitch. The strip was a revelation for the once-a-year frequenters of the SCG, who had become accustomed to dry, spinning surfaces. It certainly did not do any favours for Shane Warne, who needed five wickets to pass Lillee's Australian record, and ended up with none. Like Wyatt Earp in middle age, Warne was not as sharp out of the holster, and his old rivals had learned how to cope with, if not collar, his parabolic phenomena.

Tendulkar's decision was the more remarkable because he did not have an opening pair, entrusting wicketkeeper and number seven Mannava Prasad with the task of defying the new ball alongside Laxman. A prodding, pensive Prasad soon poked an out-swinger from McGrath to Mark Waugh in the slips, and Laxman, who would have heard his name

echoing with every snicked shot in a Caribbean crowd, was edging Lee to Slater. Tendulkar raised the quality of the contest for a while, whistling boundaries off his pads or past point. Just what the sell-out crowd wanted to see. The dice with McGrath after tea really enlivened the day. Several hooks and a cover drive produced 14 runs, McGrath responding to trap the maestro on the crease with the final ball of a memorable over. Not for the fans, who felt short-changed by the brevity of the confrontation that dazzled eight fours out of 45 from 53 balls. Bad light held up India's innings demise at 121 for 8, which included Agarkar's unwanted record of four consecutive primaries. McGrath's 16th five wickets in a Test innings swag took his overall tally to 271 wickets. Kumble's smart batting made sure India reached 150, which was about half a competitive total. Slater snicked, and Blewett played on, exposing Langer and Mark Waugh to a moving ball, as Srinath worked hard to keep his team competitive. Edges flew wide, there were several moral victories, and worst of all, Langer, on 45, was clean bowled by Srinath, who was mortified to see Ian Robinson's right arm outstretched. The standing ovation for Mark Waugh was reciprocated with some classy touches, but Ganguly's first ball burst through his defences, precipitating another Waugh. Steve's timing was unerringly crisp, cracking nine fours in a century-stand alongside a surging, cutting, pulling Langer. Srinath's first delivery with the second new ball hit Waugh's pads in front, but by the time stumps were pulled at seven o'clock, Langer had pillaged his third Test hundred of the summer, not out 167, and the bubbling Ponting was on 34.

From an early start, Australia quickly built on their overnight lead of 181 on the third, and extraordinary, final day. When Steve Waugh declared three-quarters of an hour after lunch, the lead was 402. Langer made a chanceless double century, his 223 became the highest individual score between the Border/Gavaskar Trophy antagonists. Ponting cracked a wonderful hundred, adding a scintillating 95 in an hour with Gilchrist either side of lunch.

The pundits speculated that India might get through the fourth day with a big innings from Tendulkar. The pitch had flattened out, so perhaps a serious fightback was possible. By tea the result had to come either tonight, or tomorrow quickly. McGrath knocked over Prasad and Dravid, struck Laxman on the grill of his helmet, and saw Langer take a catch between cover and mid-on to rob the

Justin Langer pulls Prasad as he scored a double century at Sydney.

crowd of Tendulkar's entertainment. Laxman's blow prompted a bewilderingly brilliant counter-attack. Waugh kept the field up, sensing an error at any moment, but a series of drives, pulls, smashes and dashes created a stunning hundred from 114 balls. At 258 for 7, and Laxman in command, the match was certain to carry over to another day. Lee returned and had the Axeman caught behind, and with Bhardwaj unable to bat because of an injured back, Venkatesh Prasad was run out by Gilchrist direct hit, attempting a quick bye to give Srinath the strike.

In the wash-up 482 runs had been scored in the day's play, McGrath took another five wickets, and was Man of the Match, and Australia's innings win meant that their goal of winning every Test of the season had been accomplished. Laxman's 167 was the third-highest innings percentage, 63.98 per cent, in Test cricket, and the kind of innings that was uniquely and blazingly representative of guns blasting on a sinking ship. Steve Waugh's team was earning its place in history, and at this moment was certainly the team of the new century.

THIRD TEST – AUSTRALIA v. INDIA
2, 3 and 4 January 2000 at Sydney Cricket Ground

INDIA

	First innings		Second innings	
*MSK Prasad	c ME Waugh, b McGrath	5	(2) c ME Waugh, b McGrath	3
VVS Laxman	c Slater, b Lee	7	(1) c Gilchrist, b Lee	167
R Dravid	c Ponting, b McGrath	29	c Warne, b McGrath	0
SR Tendulkar (capt)	lbw b McGrath	45	c Langer, b Fleming	4
SC Ganguly	c SR Waugh, b Blewett	1	c ME Waugh, b McGrath	25
HH Kanitkar	c Gilchrist, b Lee	10	c Slater, b Lee	8
VR Bharadwaj	c Gilchrist, b Lee	6	absent injured	
A Kumble	c Langer, b McGrath	26	(7) c Ponting, b McGrath	15
AB Agarkar	c ME Waugh, b Lee	0	(8) c Gilchrist, b McGrath	0
J Srinath	c Ponting, b McGrath	3	(9) not out	15
BKV Prasad	not out	1	(10) run out (Gilchrist)	3
	lb 12, w 1, nb 4	17	b 4, lb 2, w 1, nb 14	21
		150		**261**

	First Innings				Second Innings			
	O	M	R	W	O	M	R	W
McGrath	18.5	7	48	5	17	1	55	5
Fleming	13	7	24	–	13	2	47	1
Lee	21	9	39	4	11	2	67	2
Warne	12	4	22	–	13	1	60	–
Blewett	3	2	5	1	2	0	16	–
Ponting					1	0	8	–
Slater					1	0	2	–

Fall of Wickets
1–10, 2–27, 3–68, 4–69, 5–95, 6–118, 7–119, 8–119, 9–126
1–22, 2–26, 3–33, 4–101, 5–145, 6–234, 7–234, 8–258, 9–261

AUSTRALIA

	First Innings	
GS Blewett	b BKV Prasad	19
MJ Slater	c MSK Prasad, b Srinath	1
JL Langer	c BKV Prasad, b Tendulkar	223
ME Waugh	b Ganguly	32
SR Waugh (capt)	lbw b Srinath	57
RT Ponting	not out	141
*AC Gilchrist	not out	45
SK Warne		
DW Fleming		
B Lee		
GD McGrath		
	b 2, lb 21, nb 11	34
	(for 5 wickets dec.)	**552**

	First Innings			
	O	M	R	W
Srinath	28	4	105	2
Agarkar	19	3	95	–
BKV Prasad	28	10	86	1
Kumble	33.2	6	126	–
Ganguly	12	1	46	1
Bharadwaj	12	1	35	–
Tendulkar	7	0	34	1
Kanitkar	1	0	2	–

Fall of Wickets
1–9, 2–49, 3–146, 4–267, 5–457

Umpires: DB Hair & ID Robinson
Toss: India
Test Debuts: nil

Australia won by an innings and 141 runs

TEST MATCH AVERAGES
Australia v. India

AUSTRALIA

Batting	M	Inns	NO	HS	Runs	Av	100	50
RT Ponting	3	5	2	141*	375	125.00	2	1
JL Langer	3	5	0	223	289	58.80	1	–
AC Gilchrist	3	5	1	78	221	55.25	–	2
SR Waugh	3	5	0	150	276	55.20	1	1
ME Waugh	3	5	1	51*	137	34.25	–	1
SK Warne	3	3	0	86	88	29.33	–	1
GS Blewett	3	5	0	88	144	28.80	–	1
MJ Slater	3	5	0	91	123	24.60	–	1

Also batted: DW Fleming (3 Tests) 12*, 31*; MS Kasprowicz (1 Test) 4, 21*;
B Lee (2 Tests) 27; GD McGrath (3 Tests) 4, 1

Bowling	Overs	Mds	Runs	Wkts	Av	Best	10/m	5/inn
GD McGrath	113	24	248	18	13.77	5–48	1	2
B Lee	69	19	184	13	14.15	5–47	–	1
DW Fleming	96.2	25	279	12	23.25	5–30	–	1
SK Warne	127	35	335	8	41.87	4–92	–	–

Also bowled: GS Blewett 14–4–49–2; MS Kasprowicz 17–2–85–0; RT Ponting 1–0–8–0;
MJ Slater 1–0–2–0; ME Waugh 5–1–17–2

INDIA

Batting	M	Inns	NO	HS	Runs	Av	100	50
SR Tendulkar	3	6	0	116	278	46.33	1	2
VVS Laxman	3	6	0	167	221	36.83	1	–
SC Ganguly	3	6	0	60	177	29.50	–	1
A Kumble	3	6	2	28*	102	25.50	–	–
S Ramesh	2	4	1	28	60	20.00	–	–
HH Kanitkar	2	4	0	45	74	18.50	–	–
R Dravid	3	6	0	35	93	15.50	–	–
MSK Prasad	3	6	0	14	52	8.66	–	–
J Srinath	3	6	1	15*	42	8.40	–	–
BKV Prasad	3	6	3	10	22	7.33	–	–
AB Agarkar	3	6	0	19	19	3.16	–	–

Also batted: VR Bhardwaj (1 Test) 6; DJ Gandhi (1 Test) 4, 0

Bowling	Overs	Mds	Runs	Wkts	Av	Best	10/m	5/inn
AB Agarkar	108	24	351	11	31.90	3–43	–	–
J Srinath	126	18	461	10	46.10	4–130	–	–
BKV Prasad	106.3	25	356	7	50.85	3–83	–	–
A Kumble	146.2	22	450	5	90.00	2–72	–	–

Also bowled: VR Bhardwaj 12–1–35–0; SC Ganguly 21–2–90–2; HH Kanitkar 1–0–2–0;
VVS Laxman 3–1–2–0; SR Tendulkar 9–0–46–1

Fielding Figures
10 – AC Gilchrist (9ct/1st); 8 – ME Waugh; 6 – JL Langer; 4 – SR Waugh; 3 – RT Ponting,
MJ Slater, SK Warne. 1 – GS Blewett, MS Kasprowicz, GD McGrath

CARLTON AND UNITED ONE–DAY SERIES
By Jim Maxwell

The last laugh in the most one-sided one-day series ever staged in Australia was the decision to give the Player of the Series award to Pakistani all-rounder Abdur Razzaq. Australia lost only once on their way to absolute slaughter of the hapless Pakistanis in the second final by a margin of 152 runs. Razzaq, who scored 225 runs at 37.5 and took 14 wickets at 20.78, performed splendidly, but on any post-judgement of who made the most significant contribution to this series, the award had to go to either Ponting, Bevan or McGrath, or all three in a tie. Alas, the system of awarding progressive points always creates a distortion when a couple of individuals' match efforts score more heavily than a consistent series performance by a bunch of players in a hot team. The Australian team performance was exceptional, as the results indicate, and in a less humble moment they may have been tempted to say to Razzaq, and the tournament organiser, 'on ya bike, mate', when Razzaq took delivery of his $25,000 Honda motorcycle.

Cricket was kept alive during the series by the controversy surrounding Shoaib Akhtar, disgruntled Australian umpires, and the announcement of Australia's team of the century.

A ruling by the ICC's illegal action committee had banned Akhtar indefinitely from international matches. Pakistan appealed, and while Akhtar was cooling out in Perth as his team prepared for the opening match against Australia in Brisbane, the ICC granted him a last-minute reprieve. The decision reflected poorly on the cavalier leadership style of ICC Chairman Jagmohan Dalmiya, and the systems in place to deal with suspect bowlers. The wording of the announcement was just as bizarre. 'The panel...felt that Shoaib has a problem with his action while bowling a bouncer...since bouncers are not used in one-day cricket...it would be best to permit Shoaib to play.' So, by a convenient dispensation, Shoaib was one-day positive, and Test-match negative. In a superb act of subterfuge the Pakistani manager, Brigadier Mohammad Nazir, arranged for Shoaib to arrive in Brisbane just before the first match. Nazir hoped to disturb the Australian match plans with this deception, and a police escort ensured that Shoaib made his appointment. Nazir's tactics paid off. Pakistan won the match, with Shoaib taking three wickets, in what was Australia's most inept batting effort of the series.

Two days before the match the Australian umpires issued a joint statement to match referee Cammie Smith and team officials, expressing their disappointment with the constant criticisms of their performance. The ACB took a dim view of this protest, believing that the umpires should have dealt directly with them. Although the ACB's position was never made public, their decision to stand down leading umpire Daryl Hair from the finals series was a blunt reminder that employees must observe the appropriate protocols.

India's chances of edging out Pakistan for the big-cheque play-offs were dented with a two-wicket loss in the last over of their opening game. Defending 195, India were on top at 6 for 71 in Pakistan's innings, but Yohanna and the tail wobbled through. India did not win until the fifth of their eight matches against Pakistan in Adelaide, where Ganguly batted superbly for 141. By then India had to win all their remaining games to qualify, and they failed to win again. Tendulkar's mental state was apparent earlier in the series. After another late finish in Melbourne, and the trip to Sydney the next morning to prepare for a match the following day, he agreed that the programme was too demanding, with the diplomatic remark, 'one is looking at recovery'. Next day India were bowled out for 100 by Australia, Tendulkar out for one. India's best performance against Australia had come in their previous match. Chasing 270 on the back of a

Abdur Razzaq of Pakistan – Player of the Series and proud owner of a new Honda motorcycle.

glittering Ponting 115, Ganguly kept up the tempo, after Tendulkar had been brilliantly run out by a perfect flat throw from Brett Lee in the deep. Dravid contributed 60, the pursuit falling 28 runs short, and the match was disrupted by a crowd disturbance when Ganguly was red lighted on Symonds' throw-down.

Pakistan's eventful beginning at the Gabba, defending 184 to win by 45 runs, ignited Steve Waugh's men, and the closest Pakistan got to another win over Australia was in game eight at the MCG. Afridi's furious 45 from 48 balls launched the early assault on a 261-run target. Ijaz followed up, and was on 85 when Shane Lee started the 41st over with 60 needed off the last ten. Lee bowled Ijaz, and Pakistan fell apart, losing six for 44, including a direct hit run-out from Ponting at point. The margin was 15 runs, and Pakistan never looked like getting as close again.

In the verbal jousts leading into the finals, Wasim Akram unwisely suggested that Australia might fall apart under the big match pressure. Steve Waugh was cold-bloodedly dismissive, saying 'Wasim said the same thing before the World Cup Final, and we saw what happened there...all I want to say is he's talking rubbish'. The pressure was all on Pakistan. Their recycled coach Intikhab Alam claimed the team was superior to the victorious 1992 World Cup side captained by Imran Khan. The bowling was strong, but the batting could not cope with the sustained thrusts of McGrath and Brett Lee, nor the hungry outcricket that supported them.

In the first final Pakistan were 4 for 12, all out for 154, and lost by six wickets, with 7.2 overs to spare. In the second final Australia achieved their highest one-day total, 7 for 337. Gilchrist belted 51 from 42 balls, and Ponting's smooth 78 was supported by a spectacular run-a-ball 45 from Symonds. As Pakistan fell apart, 85 runs were whacked from the last ten overs. End of game. They went down swinging. 185 from 36.3 overs, and a huge margin of victory, 152 runs, which extended Australia's unbeaten run to nine matches. A quick look at the statistical leader board reveals Australia's quality and depth. Ponting totalled 404 runs, and number six specialist, Michael Bevan, was pushed up to four or five more often, scoring 388 for the series. McGrath led the attack with 19 wickets, ahead of Brett and Shane Lee, 16, and the burgeoning all-rounder Symonds, 12. And when Warne was injured MacGill stepped in, and took four wickets in the 81-run win over Pakistan in Sydney. As Wasim Akram concluded, 'Australia deserve to be World Champions'.

The controversial Shoaib Aktar of Pakistan – one-day positive and Test-match negative.

Match One – Australia v. Pakistan
9 January 2000 at Woolloongabba, Brisbane (floodlit)
Pakistan 184 for 8 (50 overs)
Australia 139 (39 overs)(Abdur Razzaq 4 for 23)
Pakistan (2 pts) won by 45 runs
Man of the Match: Abdur Razzaq

Match Two – India v. Pakistan
10 January 2000 at Woolloongabba, Brisbane (floodlit)
India 195 (48.5 overs)(SC Ganguly 61, RR Singh 50)
Pakistan 196 for 8 (49 overs)(Yousuf Youhana 63,
J Srinath 4 for 49)
Pakistan (2 pts) won by two wickets
Man of the Match: Yousuf Youhana

Match Three – Australia v. India
12 January at Melbourne Cricket Ground (floodlit)
Australia 269 for 7 (50 overs)(RT Ponting 115)
India 241 for 6 (50 overs)(SC Ganguly 100,
R Dravid 60)
Australia (2 pts) won by 28 runs
Man of the Match: RT Ponting

Match Four – Australia v. India
14 January 2000 at Sydney Cricket Ground (floodlit)
India 100 (36.3 overs)(GD McGrath 4 for 8,
A Symonds 4 for 11)
Australia 101 for 5 (26.5 overs)(J Srinath 4 for 30)
Australia (2 pts) won by five wickets
Man of the Match: A Symonds

Match Five – Australia v. Pakistan
16 January 2000 at Melbourne Cricket Ground
Pakistan 176 for 9 (41 overs)(Abdur Razzaq 51*)
Australia 177 for 4 (38.5 overs)(SR Waugh 81*)
Australia (2 pts) won by six wickets
Man of the Match: SR Waugh

Match Six – Australia v. Pakistan
19 January 2000 at Sydney Cricket Ground (floodlit)
Australia 286 (49.4 overs)(MG Bevan 77,
DR Martyn 50)
Pakistan 205 (45.2 overs)(SCG MacGill 4 for 19)
Australia (2 pts) won by 81 runs
Man of the Match: SCG MacGill

Match Seven – India v. Pakistan
21 January 2000 at Bellerive Oval, Hobart
Pakistan 262 for 7 (50 overs)(Abdur Razzaq 70*,
Ijaz Ahmed 67)
India 230 (46.5 overs)(SR Tendulkar 93,
Abdur Razzaq 5 for 48)
Pakistan (2 pts) won by 32 runs
Man of the Match: Abdur Razzaq

Match Eight – Australia v. Pakistan
23 January 2000 at Melbourne Cricket Ground
(floodlit)
Australia 260 for 9 (50 overs)(MG Bevan 83,
RT Ponting 53)
Pakistan 245 (48.5 overs)(Ijaz Ahmed 85,
S Lee 4 for 37)
Australia (2 pts) won by 15 runs
Man of the Match: MG Bevan

Match Nine – India v. Pakistan
25 January 2000 at Adelaide Oval (floodlit)
India 267 for 6 (50 overs)(SC Ganguly 141)
Pakistan 219 (44.4 overs)(Azhar Mahmood 67,
Ijaz Ahmed 54, A Kumble 4 for 40)
India (2 pts) won by 48 runs
Man of the Match: SC Ganguly

Match Ten – Australia v. India
26 January 2000 at Adelaide Oval (floodlit)
Australia 329 for 5 (50 overs)(ME Waugh 116,

Michael Bevan scored 71 against India at Perth.

SECOND FINAL – AUSTRALIA v. PAKISTAN
4 February 2000 at Sydney Cricket Ground (floodlit)

AUSTRALIA

Batting			Bowling	O	M	R	W
ME Waugh	run out (Saqlain Mushtaq)	53	Wasim Akram	10	1	65	1
*AC Gilchrist	c Moin Khan,		Shoaib Akhtar	9	0	61	–
	b Azhar Mahmood	51	Waqar Younis	4	0	38	–
RT Ponting	c Moin Khan,		Azhar Mahmood	7	0	51	1
	b Shahid Afridi	78	Saqlain Mushtaq	10	0	54	2
A Symonds	st Moin Khan,		Shahid Afridi	10	0	54	1
	b Saqlain Mushtaq	45					
MG Bevan	b Wasim Akram	3					
SR Waugh (capt)	run out (Saqlain Mushtaq)	37	**Fall of Wickets**				
S Lee	c Yousuf Youhana,		1-74, 2-170, 3-220, 4-224, 5-290,				
	b Saqlain Mushtaq	12	6-297, 7-308				
DR Martyn	not out	23					
SK Warne	not out	4					
B Lee							
GD McGrath							
	lb14, w12, nb5	31					
	50 overs (for 7 wickets)	337					

PAKISTAN

Batting			Bowling	O	M	R	W
Saeed Anwar	c Gilchrist, b McGrath	16	McGrath	9.3	2	49	5
Shahid Afridi	c Bevan, b B Lee	18	Lee B	9	0	51	3
Ijaz Ahmed	c Gilchrist, b McGrath	0	Warne	7	2	28	–
Yousuf Youhana	c Warne, b S Lee	41	Lee S	6	0	20	1
Mohammad Wasim	b B Lee	0	Symonds	5	0	30	–
Azhar Mahmood	c S Lee, b B Lee	27					
*Moin Khan	b McGrath	33	**Fall of Wickets**				
Wasim Akram (capt)	c SR Waugh, b McGrath	18	1-20, 2-21, 3-42, 4-43, 5-80,				
Saqlain Mushtaq	c Gilchrist, b McGrath	0	6-131, 7-149, 8-153, 9-177				
Waqar Younis	run out (Martyn/Gilchrist)	15					
Shoaib Akhtar	not out	1					
	lb7, w3, nb6	16					
	36.3 overs	185					

Umpires: SJ Davis & SJA Taufel
Man of the Match: RT Ponting
Toss: Australia
Man of the Series: Abdur Razzaq

Australia won by 152 runs

AC Gilchrist 92)
India 177 (46.5 overs)(R Dravid 63, B Lee 5 for 27)
Australia (2 pts) won by 152 runs
Man of the Match: ME Waugh

Match Eleven – India v. Pakistan
28 January 2000 at WACA Ground, Perth
Pakistan 261 for 8 (50 overs)
India 157 (46 overs)(RR Singh 51)
Pakistan (2 pts) won by 104 runs
Man of the Match: Wasim Akram

Match Twelve – Australia v. India
30 January 2000 at WACA Ground, Perth
India 226 for 6 (50 overs)(R Dravid 65)
Australia 230 for 6 (49.3 overs)(MG Bevan 71)
Australia (2 pts) won by four wickets
Man of the Match: MG Bevan

FIRST FINAL – AUSTRALIA v. PAKISTAN
2 February 2000 at Melbourne Cricket Ground (floodlit)

PAKISTAN

Batting				Bowling	O	M	R	W
Saeed Anwar	c Warne, b B Lee		7	McGrath	9	1	17	3
Shahid Afridi	c Gilchrist, b McGrath		0	Lee B	8.2	2	18	3
Ijaz Ahmed	c Warne, b McGrath		0	Warne	10	2	33	1
Inzamam-ul-Haq	lbw b McGrath		0	Lee S	10	1	37	1
Yousuf Youhana	lbw b S Lee		14	Symonds	7	1	24	1
Abdur Razzaq	c SR Waugh, b B Lee		24	Bevan	2	0	16	1
Azhar Mahmood	c SR Waugh, b Bevan		16	Waugh ME	1	0	7	–
*Moin Khan	c Martyn, b Warne		47					
Wasim Akram (capt)	b Symonds		15	**Fall of Wickets**				
Saqlain Mushtaq	b B Lee		16	1-1, 2-4, 3-4, 4-12, 5-28				
Shoaib Akhtar	not out		3	6-59, 7-78, 8-108, 9-147				
	lb2, w9, nb1		12					
	47.2 overs		154					

AUSTRALIA

Batting				Bowling	O	M	R	W
*AC Gilchrist	c Azhar Mahmood			Wasim Akram	6	0	26	–
	b Shoaib Akhtar		9	Shoaib Akhtar	7	1	26	2
ME Waugh	lbw b Shoaib Akhtar		10	Abdur Razzaq	5	0	19	–
RT Ponting	c Abdur Razzaq,			Azhar Mahmood	7	1	22	–
	b Shahid Afridi		50	Ijaz Ahmed	0.5	0	2	–
MG Bevan	c Abdur Razzaq,			Saqlain Mushtaq	10	0	27	1
	b Saqlain Mushtaq		54	Shahid Afridi	8	0	29	1
SR Waugh (capt)	not out		19					
DR Martyn				**Fall of Wickets**				
A Symonds				1-11, 2-27, 3-1104, 4-147				
S Lee								
SK Warne								
B Lee								
GD McGrath								
	lb4, nb		9					
	42.4 overs (for 4 wickets)		155					

Umpires: DJ Harper & SJA Taufel
Toss: Pakistan
Man of the Match: GD McGrath

Australia won by six wickets

SHEFFIELD SHIELD/PURA MILK CUP
By Jim Maxwell

Queensland's magnificent performance to win the domestic first-class competition was overshadowed by the controversy surrounding the change of the competition's name from the Sheffield Shield to the Pura Milk Cup. The timing of the decision to abandon 107 years of tradition added to the outrage felt by the game's spiritual believers. Six matches into the season the ACB announced that they had signed a four-year deal with National Foods, a major producer of dairy products, worth a reported two million dollars. The board had been looking for an appropriate sponsor for some time, knowing that the competition had been financially negative for years, and that the only other alternative was to reduce the number of matches. Several media organisations made a protest by refusing to use the new name in their reports, and recurring criticism was that tradition had again been sold out for a buck. In the business environment of commercial cricket the decision was understandable, but the suspicion lingered that Pura Milk was the first of many replacement names for an Australian sporting icon.

The Queensland Bulls fulfilled their ambitions with a stunning record of eight outright wins, and had the best of a drawn final against Victoria. All their wins were decisive, twice beating Victoria, South Australia and NSW for a massive 48-point haul at the top of the table. They lost to Western Australia by an innings late in the season, but by then their hosting of the final had been certain since January. The comparative statistics highlight the superb effort from the pace bowlers. Queensland averaged 32.5 runs per wicket, and dismissed their opposition at an average of 21 runs per wicket. Kasprowicz, Bichel and Dale shared 67 per cent of the dismissals, Kasprowicz taking a staggering 42 wickets at 11.64 in six appearances. Bichel played in every match, taking 53 wickets. In a bowlers' season, only two batsmen averaged over fifty. Andrew Symonds and Martin Love topped the list, Symonds' two centuries showing that he has the ability to play as a Test batsman. He scored at a phenomenal strike rate, 85, including 140 off 154 balls across a sodden outfield against South Australia. Wicketkeeper Wade Seccombe had another impressive year, with 408 runs and 54 dismissals.

In the final Stuart Law scored a match-securing 129, frustrating Victoria's bowlers. Bichel's lively pace bowling, 6 for 47, ensured a 103-run lead, and another solid Law innings, 84, plus a century from Love, left Victoria with an impossible fourth-innings chase. It was Queensland's third win in six seasons.

The mainstays of Victoria's challenging season were their captain, Paul Reiffel, and spurned Test opener Matthew Elliott. Reiffel took 59 wickets at 16.64, including nine in the final. Elliott was the only player to amass over 1,000 runs, 1,028 at 68.53 with four centuries, and was Player of the Season for a third time. The crunch match in Victoria's quest for the prize was against Western Australia at the MCG in early December. In a tight contest Victoria had set the Warriors a target of 176. At 2 for 129 the result seemed assured, when, inevitably, a run-out changed the flow of the innings, and Victoria miraculously grabbed 8 for 35 to win by 11 runs over the Shield holders. Ian Harvey's all-round form was impressive, totalling 543 runs at 49.36, and snaring 37 wickets at 22.27. Matthew Mott and Jason Arnberger helped Elliott at the top of the order, and left-arm pace bowler Matthew Inness returned a useful 31 wickets, including two swags of five in an innings. Wicketkeeper Darren Berry was a very effective team cajoler, collecting 54 dismissals.

In the West the continuing development of Michael Hussey as a potential Test batsman, and Brad Williams' re-emergence as a strike bowler, sustained the Warriors' claims on back-to-back titles. Hussey scored three centuries out of 874 runs at 51.41, and Williams, the former Victorian fast man, took 50 wickets at 23.02. The Warriors made a slow start, drawing two and losing their next four matches. In Adelaide they collapsed to lose by two runs, did the same ten days later against Victoria, lost to the Bulls in Brisbane by ten wickets, and, in a stirring contest, were beaten at home by NSW. They won their last four matches outright, including an innings win over Queensland. Opener Ryan Campbell finished off with scores of 111, 203 and 93 to head the aggregates at 885 runs, and Jo Angel, whose arm was broken by a Brett Lee scorcher midway through the season, returned the fire in Sydney with a career-best six for 64. Promising left-hander Simon Katich, who had toured Sri Lanka with the Australian team, took some time to recover from a debilitating virus, and scored only 328 at 29.81.

South Australia finished fourth, and were spiritedly led by Darren Lehmann. The dashing left-hander, discarded from the national team, made 995 runs at 58.52, and was usefully supported by David Fitzgerald, 817 runs at 40.85, and Ben Johnson, 599 at 46.07. The bowling relied on the hard work of paceman Paul Wilson, who lacked the penetrative supporting firepower to consistently bowl teams out. Jason Gillespie returned from his broken leg collision late in the season, and the spin of McIntyre and Young was occasionally effective. Tasmania have always produced batsmen: Boon, Ponting, and more currently di Venuto, the evergreen Cox, and all rounder Marsh. But bowlers are as scarce as Tassie tigers, and the performance of Mark Ridgway underscored the dearth of missing talent in the south land. At 38, Ridgway led the attack with 30 buzzing medium-quick wickets. And just above him on the averages list was Colin Miller, the 36-year-old off-spinner/medium pacer. The only team Tasmania could bowl out twice was NSW, a fact that was the source of more wisecracks about the Blues' bluest season.

Disaster. Undisciplined. Inept. NSW lost eight matches outright, make it nine, when the loss to the touring Indians is included. In the worst performance in their long and illustrious life, NSW tried 24 players, and finished with the wooden spoon for the second successive season. Administrators could no longer blame the poor results on the unavailability of top players representing their country. It was the same for every state, and besides NSW had won without their stars in 1993–94. The intense Michael Bevan scored 600 runs at over 60, but he could not get the best from the assorted mixture of youth and experience in the dressing room. An outright win over the Warriors in Perth was the kind of character-building effort that needed repetition. That team was led by Steve Waugh, who scored a hundred. Maybe the return of Steve Rixon to the coaching role next season will create a revival.

Incredibly, Mark Kasprowicz took 42 wickets in six appearances.

MERCANTILE MUTUAL CUP
By Jim Maxwell

Western Australia won a spectacular final over their highly performed rivals, Queensland. It was the Warriors' tenth win in the 31-year history of the domestic one-day competition. The final margin of 45 runs was remarkable, with Queensland capitulating, losing ten wickets for 70.

Ryan Campbell rediscovered his belligerent form, smashing 108 from 85 balls to inspire a solid Western Australian total of 6 for 301. Martin Love, 73, and Jimmy Maher, 102, slammed some wayward bowling to the tune of 186 in only 27 overs, and the Queensland Bulls were charging to victory as rampantly as they had for the bulk of the season. Langer's catch at wide mid-on to dismiss Love was the break that triggered the collapse, with Campbell leaping to his left behind the stumps to grab a prodding edge from a tired Maher. The combination of some undisciplined batting, and resurgent Warriors bowling and fielding, changed the direction of the game, five wickets falling for six runs at one stage.

Both teams deservedly played off in the final after finishing at the top of the points ladder. In the first semi-final the Warriors were pressed by South Australia, relying on a century from Simon Katich to overcome a poor start and create an impressive 7 for 246. Katich's Man-of-the-Match innings, and the talents of all-rounder Brad Hogg, who contributed 36 from 32 balls, and took three wickets bowling his left-arm spinners, underlined Western Australia's WACA superiority. Darren Lehmann sustained the Redbacks' chase, but when he was out for 85 in the 36th over, the tail, requiring six an over, succumbed.

At the Allan Border Field the Bulls always appeared to be in control of their semi-final against NSW. The Blues were pinned down by accurate pace bowling on a slow pitch, and battled to a marginally competitive 6 for 210, with Mark Higgs forcing 74 not out from 69 balls. Higgs had an amazing escape on one when he shouldered arms to Kasprowicz, and the ball hit the off bail, but somehow it was not dislodged.

Clinton Perren guided Queensland to victory with 22 balls and seven wickets to spare, making a tenacious Man of the Match 86 not out.

The one-round competition, involving each team in six matches, brought the brief life of the Canberra team to a close. In three seasons the Comets had only three meteoric matches, and lost all six matches last summer. Several imports, such as the massive Merv Hughes, and Rod Tucker, had improved Canberra's competitiveness and profile, but the shift of star locals Brad Haddin and Mark Higgs to NSW was inevitable for players wanting to develop first-class careers.

Simon Katich's impressive century earned him Man of the Match.

FIRST-CLASS AVERAGES

BATTING

	M	Inns	NO	HS	Runs	Av	100	50
RT Ponting	7	11	3	197	582	72.75	3	1
MTG Elliott	10	19	4	183*	1028	68.53	4	4
JL Langer	10	17	0	223	1108	65.17	5	3
DS Lehmann	10	20	2	149	1142	63.44	7	
AC Gilchrist	7	11	2	149*	537	59.66	1	3
DR Martyn	5	10	1	169	534	59.33	1	3
A Symonds	9	14	2	161	710	59.16	3	2
MG Bevan	7	14	3	132	613	55.72	2	2
J Cox	11	19	1	245	967	53.72	4	2
ME Hussey	10	18	1	172*	874	51.41	3	3
ML Love	12	18	2	238	792	49.50	3	2
IJ Harvey	9	15	4	107	543	49.36	1	4
RJ Campbell	10	18	0	203	885	49.16	2	5
SR Tendulkar	4	8	0	116	388	48.50	1	3
MP Mott	11	20	2	148	841	46.72	2	6
Saeed Anwar	5	9	0	119	402	44.66	1	3
DA Fitzgerald	11	22	1	159	935	44.52	5	3
Inzamam-ul-Haq	4	8	0	118	354	44.25	1	2
MJ di Venuto	11	18	0	136	793	44.05	1	7
JL Arnberger	11	22	2	214	869	43.45	2	5
SR Waugh	7	11	0	150	471	42.81	2	1
BA Johnson	11	22	7	104	637	42.46	2	1
VVS Laxman	6	12	0	167	502	41.83	2	2
DJ Marsh	11	18	1	157	698	41.05	3	1
MG Dighton	6	10	1	182*	369	41.00	1	1
Ijaz Ahmed	5	9	0	141	363	40.33	2	1
MJ Nicholson	6	10	4	39	240	40.00	-	-
SG Law	13	20	2	129	713	39.61	2	5
ML Hayden	10	18	3	128	573	38.20	2	2
MN Atkinson	11	15	6	62	342	38.00	-	1
MJ Slater	10	18	1	169	642	37.76	1	3
DF Hills	10	18	1	139	628	36.94	1	5
JA Dykes	10	16	0	153	589	36.81	2	1
MJ Phelps	5	10	0	192	360	36.00	1	2
Yousuf Youhana	5	9	0	95	314	34.88	-	3
GS Blewett	12	22	1	89	723	34.42	-	5
SC Ganguly	5	9	0	81	301	33.44	-	2
S Young	11	18	4	106	462	33.00	2	1
BJ Haddin	11	21	1	86	643	32.15	-	6
Moin Khan	5	9	0	70	284	31.55	-	3
LD Harper	10	16	1	92	465	31.00	-	1
Wasim Akram	4	8	2	52	181	30.16	-	1
DS Berry	11	16	3	106	390	30.00	1	1
SM Katich	7	12	1	76	328	29.81	-	3
WA Seccombe	13	18	2	151	472	29.50	1	-
SP Kremerskothen	10	15	6	82*	265	29.44	-	1
MJ North	4	5	1	60	117	29.25	-	1
GJ Mail	9	18	1	97	493	29.00	-	3
BP Julian	4	8	2	40	173	28.83	-	-
MJ Clarke	7	14	0	75	403	28.78	-	4
JP Maher	13	25	7	102*	508	28.22	1	2
S Ramesh	5	10	1	74	253	28.11	-	1
CJ Davies	7	14	0	69	378	27.00	-	3
ME Waugh	7	11	1	100	268	26.80	1	1
GI Foley	13	18	1	90	451	26.52	-	3
RS Dravid	6	12	1	107	288	26.18	1	-
MS Kasprowicz	8	10	3	50	183	26.14	-	1
Azhar Mahmood	4	8	0	83	208	26.00	-	1
GB Hogg	9	15	3	68	304	25.33	-	1
BJ Hodge	11	20	3	96	423	24.88	-	3
RM Baker	5	10	1	77*	204	22.66	-	1
JD Siddons	7	14	0	58	316	22.57	-	1
S Lee	7	14	0	98	312	22.28	-	1
AC Dale	10	13	2	48	245	22.27	-	-
CJ Richards	9	18	0	111	379	21.05	1	3
GJ Hayne	7	14	0	89	293	20.92	-	1
HH Kanitkar	4	8	1	58	145	20.71	-	1
A Kumble	5	10	3	28*	142	20.28	-	-
BE Young	11	20	3	114*	341	20.05	1	1
PR Reiffel	11	14	3	46*	217	19.72	-	-
DG Wright	8	12	2	45	177	17.70	-	-
GE Manou	11	19	4	78	261	17.40	-	1

FIRST-CLASS AVERAGES

BATTING

	M	Inns	NO	HS	Runs	Av	100	50
JM Vaughan	7	14	0	70	237	16.92	-	2
GR Robertson	6	11	1	67*	164	16.40	-	1
AB Agarkar	4	8	1	65*	112	16.00	-	1
DJ Saker	8	8	2	28	94	15.66	-	-
B Lee	8	12	3	34	138	15.33	-	-
BA Williams	10	15	4	28	142	12.90	-	-
SA Muller	11	12	6	20	73	12.16	-	-
SD Bradstreet	4	8	0	42	96	12.00	-	-
AJ Bichel	13	16	1	34*	170	11.33	-	-
P Wilson	11	15	4	32*	120	10.90	-	-
MW Ridgway	10	13	1	30	129	10.75	-	-
DJ Harris	4	8	0	31	85	10.62	-	-

Qualification: 8 completed innings, average 10.00

BOWLING

	Overs	Mds	Runs	Wkts	Av	Best	100/m	5/inns
MS Kasprowicz	247.3	69	706	49	14.40	5-32	1	4
PR Reiffel	425.2	118	982	59	16.64	5-65	-	1
GD McGrath	247	70	641	32	20.03	5-48	1	2
AJ Bichel	479.4	143	1207	60	20.11	6-45	1	2
B Lee	313.3	78	892	44	20.27	5-47	-	1
AC Dale	399.2	128	927	44	21.06	5-54	1	3
IJ Harvey	325.2	95	824	37	22.27	5-53	-	1
DW Fleming	234	54	680	30	22.66	5-30	-	2
B Williams	365.4	94	1151	50	23.02	6-74	-	5
P Wilson	428.4	123	1063	44	24.15	6-106	-	2
BA Swain	231.1	70	610	25	24.40	4-37	-	-
SA Muller	330	83	945	37	25.54	4-68	-	-
MW H Inness	229.4	77	829	31	26.74	6-70	1	2
J Angel	243.3	65	697	26	26.80	6-64	-	1
DA Nash	254	63	743	27	27.51	7-54	1	2
ML Lewis	118.1	20	427	15	28.46	4-101	-	-
S Lee	163.4	39	496	17	29.17	4-35	-	-
SR Cary	292.1	98	734	25	29.36	4-70	-	-
MA Anderson	221.4	60	658	21	31.33	4-50	-	-
DJ Saker	276.4	77	787	25	31.48	4-37	-	-
MJ Nicholson	166.5	32	554	17	32.58	4-42	-	-
AG Downton	250.3	65	786	24	32.75	6-56	-	2
MW Ridgway	331	85	1012	30	33.73	6-38	-	1
PE McIntyre	249.2	54	811	24	33.79	5-55	-	1
SK Warne	256.5	72	705	20	35.25	5-110	-	1
CR Miller	255.5	70	650	18	36.11	4-24	-	-
SCG MacGill	366.1	60	1351	36	37.52	4-42	-	-
GB Hogg	132.4	29	466	12	38.83	5-53	-	1
J Srinath	158	31	556	13	42.76	4-130	-	-
A Harrity	201	39	667	15	44.46	3-68	-	-
BE Young	463.4	114	1433	31	46.22	6-85	-	2
DG Wright	245.4	55	817	17	48.05	3-45	-	-
JM Heath	125.2	25	481	10	48.10	3-37	-	-
DJ Marsh	291.3	72	868	18	48.22	4-6	-	-
BKV Prasad	190.1	41	636	13	48.92	3-83	-	-
A Kumble	213	30	669	13	51.46	4-38	-	-

Qualification: 10 wickets in 8 innings

The following bowlers took 10 wickets in fewer than 8 innings:-

Saqlain Mushtaq	137.3	32	384	13	29.53	6-46	-	1
A B Agarkar	135	27	425	14	30.35	3-43	-	-
Mushtaq Ahmed	135	19	556	16	34.75	4-74	-	-

FIELDING

67 – WA Seccombe (65ct, 2st); 54 – DS Berry (52ct, 2st); 42 – GE Manou (34ct, 8st);
38 – RJ Campbell; 34 – MN Atkinson (26ct, 8st); 27 – AC Gilchrist (25ct, 2st);
26 – BJ Haddin (23ct, 3st); 20 – ML Love; 18 – Moin Khan (13ct, 5st); 15 – LD Harper, SG Law, ME Waugh; 14 – DJ Marsh; 13 – ME Hussey; 12 – ML Hayden, JL Langer; 11 – GI Foley; 10 – JP Maher

NEW ZEALAND

West Indies in New Zealand
Australia in New Zealand
Domestic First-Class Season
Shell Cup One-Day Competition
First-Class Averages

WEST INDIES IN NEW ZEALAND
by Bryan Waddle

Having suffered humiliation in South Africa 12 months earlier West Indies captain Brian Lara would have confidently embarked on the New Zealand tour with some belief that West Indies fortunes could be on the rise. Despite their early exit from the World Cup, they did have a drawn series at home with Australia to encourage them. Lara's magical deeds in the home series and the addition of the great Sir Vivian Richards' guiding hand as coach with Clive Lloyd as manager were enough to remind New Zealand that this West Indies side was a formidable opponent.

They had not played much cricket of any substance since the World Cup, with no Test matches since the Australian series. Many sides before them had come unstuck on the slow, low-bouncing wickets of New Zealand even if they had a squad of seasoned Test cricketers.

Previous West Indies tours of New Zealand had not provided the happiest memories but Lara's team made a genuine effort to cultivate a positive image and avoid any controversy that might tarnish their reputation as exciting, fun-loving cricketers. There was, as always, an imposing look about the side, a paper eleven that was capable of exploiting weakness and dominating ruthlessly any opposition not prepared to withstand them. Even without Curtly Ambrose and Carl Hooper, the bowling attack had reasonable balance. The indefatigable Courtney Walsh, who was searching for a world record in Test scalps, was supported by a useful quartet of pacemen, Reon King, Mervyn Dillon, Franklyn Rose and Pedro Collins.

While the batting lacked the overall class of previous sides, it included such well-performed players as Sherwin Campbell, Adrian Griffith, Shivnarine Chanderpaul and Jimmy Adams backed by the exciting potential of Ricardo Powell and Wavell Hinds. However, strength on paper has to be transformed into on-field performance and sadly this West Indian side with a quality leadership failed to deliver on its potential. Lara was unable to inspire his players and extract the commitment and discipline needed at international level after what was a promising start to the tour. By the end of the one-day series, the besieged captain was almost at breaking point, the pressure of carrying Caribbean expectations taking its toll on his playing skills and

Previous page: Chris Cairns, International Player of the Season.

Curtly Ambrose reflects on his missed opportunity.

his leadership. Twice after defeats in one-day internationals, an emotional Lara gave heartfelt personal feelings at press conferences, almost resigned to losing the captaincy he had coveted for so long. Rather than restoring pride in West Indian cricket, Lara's team had to endure the humiliation they had experienced 12 months earlier in South Africa.

New Zealand was not about to offer any consolation. Too often they had been on the receiving end and under new coach David Trist, who had inherited a solid professional unit from his predecessor Steve Rixon, there was a more ruthless attitude than before. Despite the positive signs and the quality displayed in the early stages of the tour, the West Indies went home beaten two-nil in the two-Test series and suffering a similar clean-sweep defeat in the five-match one-day series.

West Indies v. New Zealand 'A'

6, 7 and 8 December 1999 at Owen Delaney Park, Taupo
West Indies 450 for 5 dec. (S Chanderpaul 216*, RL Powell 86) and 64 for 4 dec.
New Zealand 'A' 140 and 58 for 2
Match drawn

Shivnarine Chanderpaul showed a liking for the lifeless Taupo pitch with a dominating innings of 216 not out as the West Indies settled in to the New Zealand lifestyle. The relaxed holiday resort area was almost like home for the tourists, who gained valuable pre-Test practice against New Zealand's second best. Ricardo Powell enjoyed his first taste of New Zealand with a rollicking innings of 86, while pace bowlers Dillon and Walsh issued a warning with some fiery pace bowling in even the most benign conditions.

West Indies v. Auckland
10,11,12 and 13 December 1999 at Eden Park, Auckland
West Indies 380 (SL Campbell 112, RD Jacobs 86*, JC Adams 65, RG Morgan 5 for 75)
and 228 for 1 (SL Campbell 109, D Ganga 100*)
Auckland 369 (JM Aiken 84, AC Barnes 52)
Match drawn

Sherwin Campbell scored successive hundreds in the final warm-up to the first Test on a batsman-friendly Eden Park No 2 pitch. Campbell followed his first-innings 112 with 100 off just 99 balls in the second innings before retiring hurt on 109. Darren Ganga joined the run feast with an unbeaten century after a first-innings duck while the Auckland attack gave the West Indians the best possible Test preparation. Auckland had one satisfaction – they got within 11 of the tourists' first-innings total with some solid top-order batting, and 51 extras.

First Test
16, 17, 18, 19 and 20 December 1999 at Westpac Trust Stadium, Hamilton

All-rounder Chris Cairns spent ten years trying to erase the 'potential' tag in an era when New Zealand was looking for a class player, a 'star' to assume the role carried by Sir Richard Hadlee and then Martin Crowe. Cairns is a naturally gifted player, but his career has been dogged by injury and an attitude that has not always conveyed positive vibes. With experience has come maturity and a consistency of performance that was not lost on the West Indies tourists.

While the loss of the first Test, by nine wickets, might have been a mystery for a West Indies side that opened the first day in perfect conditions with a record opening of 276, it was not for New Zealand. They would have been baffled though by a bowling performance which was below acceptable Test standard as Campbell and Griffith pounded 33 fours

and three sixes to reach 282 for 1 by stumps, which looked ominous for the home side. Campbell was the chief beneficiary, his hundred coming off 177 balls and he was dismissed just before stumps following the arrival of the second new ball. Griffith, the tall, rather awkward-looking left-hander, was more patient. His first Test hundred, in only his fourth Test, took 323 minutes and came from 261 balls.

Whatever happened between stumps and the start of the second day, it was enough to change the course of the Test and the series. Cairns embarked on what was a truly staggering performance to re-adjust the balance and ultimately secure New Zealand a nine-wicket win. He disposed of nightwatchman Ramnarine and later snared Powell, for a debut duck, and Franklyn Rose, in a second-day spell that gave him 3 for 14 from 15 overs as the West Indies lost nine wickets in the space of 76 runs.

New Zealand made a cautious start, openers Gary Stead and Matt Horne combining for the second half-century in successive Test innings after the 131 they produced in the third Test in India just over six weeks earlier. There has not been much continuity in

Chris Cairns celebrating another wicket in the first Test. His outstanding performance deservedly won him Man of the Match.

FIRST TEST – NEW ZEALAND v. WEST INDIES
16, 17, 18, 19 and 20 December 1999 at Westpac Trust Park, Hamilton

WEST INDIES

	First Innings			Second Innings	
AFG Griffith	c Parore, b Vettori	114		c Parore, b Cairns	18
SL Campbell	c Parore, b Nash	170		b Cairns	0
D Ramnarine	c Parore, b Cairns	8		(9) c & b Cairns	0
S Chanderpaul	c Fleming, b Astle	14		(3) c Parore, b Cairns	0
BC Lara (capt)	c Nash, b Vettori	24		(4) c Parore, b Nash	1
RL Powell	c Wiseman, b Cairns	0		(5) c Spearman, b Vettori	30
JC Adams	not out	17		(6) c sub (SB O'Connor), b Cairns	25
*RD Jacobs	c Spearman, b Vettori	5		(7) run out (Horne/Parore)	2
FA Rose	c Wiseman, b Cairns	4		(8) lbw b Cairns	3
RD King	b Nash	1		lbw b Cairns	0
CA Walsh	b Vettori	0		not out	5
	lb 6, nb 2	8		b 7, lb 3, nb 3	13
		365			**97**

	First Innings				Second Innings			
	O	M	R	W	O	M	R	W
Cairns	31	11	73	3	22.5	10	27	7
Nash	28	12	63	2	7	1	37	1
Vettori	34.1	9	83	4	22	12	20	1
Astle	16	2	67	1				
Wiseman	22	10	51	–	2	0	3	–
McMillan	4	1	22	–				

Fall of Wickets
1–276, 2–289, 3–311, 4–336, 5–336, 6–336, 7–345, 8–352, 9–362
1–0, 2–0, 3–1, 4–36, 5–78, 6–85, 7–90, 8–90, 9–90

NEW ZEALAND

	First Innings			Second Innings	
MJ Horne	c Rose, b King	32		(2) retired hurt	5
GR Stead	b Walsh	22		(1) b Walsh	16
CM Spearman	b Ramnarine	27		not out	30
SP Fleming (capt)	c Jacobs, b Ramnarine	66			
DL Vettori	c Adams, b King	29			
NJ Astle	c Ramnarine, b Walsh	48		(4) not out	7
CD McMillan	c Jacobs, b King	51			
CL Cairns	c Campbell, b Ramnarine	72			
*AC Parore	run out (Powell)	8			
DJ Nash	c Powell, b King	6			
PJ Wiseman	not out	0			
	b 4, lb 9, w 3, nb 16	32		b 4, lb 1, nb 7	12
		393		(for 1 wicket)	**70**

	First Innings				Second Innings			
	O	M	R	W	O	M	R	W
Walsh	29	4	81	2	8	1	33	1
Rose	27	4	103	–	6	0	28	–
King	26.2	2	81	4				
Ramnarine	36	10	82	3	1	0	4	–
Powell	5	2	13	–				
Adams	7	1	20	–				

Fall of Wickets
1–61, 2–67, 3–107, 4–162, 5–215, 6–258, 7–374, 8–379, 9–388
1–59

MJ Horne retired hurt at 16–0 in the second innings

Umpires: DB Cowie & DR Shepherd
Toss: West Indies
Test Debut: RL Powell

New Zealand won by nine wickets

opening partnership selections in New Zealand's recent Test history, and even less consistency of performance, making the partnership a noteworthy event. Spearman, Fleming, Vettori and Astle all made solid offerings against a lacklustre pace attack. It was only when New Zealand's reply was faltering at 258 for 6 that Cairns provided another sign of his class with an innings of 72 from 82 balls to help secure a lead of just 28. The partnership Cairns formed with Craig McMillan produced 116 runs although the belligerent all-rounder was lucky to survive a run-out ruling in his favour by the TV umpire.

New Zealand was hardly in a winning position with two days remaining, and a rain interruption on the fourth day that allowed only 29 overs did not help their cause. However, there was enough time for New Zealand to remove the best part of the Windies top order, leaving them 66 for 4. They had been three wickets down for one run before Powell flailed the attack for 30 of the 35 runs added for the fourth wicket with Griffith before conceding his wicket. Adams joined the left-hander as another 42 was added and there were increasing signs that a solid recovery could be achieved.

Cairns made the fifth day his own, removing any remaining doubts about his class. He took five of the six wickets to end the innings, with Ridley Jacobs avoiding the paceman being run out in an appalling misunderstanding with Jimmy Adams. The West Indies managed only 97, with Cairns taking career-best 7 for 27, including the figures of 11.5 overs 5 maidens, 5 for 16 on the final morning. In fact, his bowling figures were quite extraordinary. After the first day pummelling, Cairns had conceded 62 runs before he took his first wicket on the second day. His ten wickets had come at a cost of a further 38 runs. The 70 needed for victory was compiled easily, although opener Matt Horne suffered a broken finger from a delivery by Franklyn Rose that ended his series.

SECOND TEST
26, 27, 28 and 29 December 1999 at Basin Reserve, Wellington

If Brian Lara was searching history to achieve a series-squaring victory in the second Test, his decision to bowl first failed to offer a repeat. Lara would have recalled that the previous encounter between the two sides on the Basin Reserve produced the heaviest loss New Zealand has sustained in Test cricket: an innings and 322 runs. History would also have told him that his team

SECOND TEST – NEW ZEALAND v. WEST INDIES
26, 27, 28 and 29 December 1999 at Basin Reserve, Wellington

NEW ZEALAND

	First Innings	
CM Spearman	c Walsh, b King	24
GR Stead	c Campbell, b King	17
MS Sinclair	b King	214
SP Fleming (capt)	c Adams, b Chanderpaul	67
NJ Astle	run out (Rose/Walsh)	93
CD McMillan	c Jacobs, b King	31
CL Cairns	c Adams, b Rose	31
*AC Parore	b Rose	5
DJ Nash	not out	2
DL Vettori	c Campbell, b Rose	7
SB O'Connor		
	b 5, lb 12, w 1, nb 14	32
	(for 9 wickets dec.)	**518**

	First Innings			
	O	M	R	W
Walsh	41	5	112	–
King	36	11	96	4
Rose	32.3	5	113	3
Perry	32	5	120	–
Adams	26	9	45	–
Chanderpaul	6	1	15	1

Fall of Wickets
1–33, 2–76, 3–240, 4–429, 5–456, 6–507, 7–507, 8–514, 9–518

WEST INDIES

	First Innings		Second Innings	
AFG Griffith	c Fleming, b Nash	67	run out (Nash/Parore)	45
SL Campbell	lbw b Cairns	0	lbw b Cairns	3
NO Perry	c Parore, b Cairns	3	(7) lbw b Astle	0
S Chanderpaul	c Parore, b Cairns	5	(3) c Parore, b Nash	70
BC Lara (capt)	b Vettori	67	(4) c Parore, b Nash	75
JC Adams	c Stead, b Vettori	8	(5) c Parore, b Nash	4
*RD Jacobs	not out	19	(6) c Stead, b Vettori	20
FA Rose	c Parore, b Cairns	0	lbw b Cairns	10
RD King	run out (Vettori)	0	(10) not out	4
CA Walsh	b Cairns	0	(9) lbw b Nash	0
D Ganga	absent injured		absent injured	
	b 2, lb 4, w 2, nb 2	10	b 1, lb 1, w 1	3
		179		**234**

	First Innings				Second Innings			
	O	M	R	W	O	M	R	W
Cairns	19	5	44	5	13.1	4	25	2
Nash	18	8	23	1	16	4	38	4
Vettori	31	10	69	2	32	8	86	1
O'Connor	19	8	25	–	16	3	50	–
Astle	4	1	12	–	7	0	33	1

Fall of Wickets
1–1, 2–5, 3–17, 4–129, 5–141, 6–174, 7–175, 8–176
1–8, 2–83, 3–148, 4–154, 5–188, 6–204, 7–225, 8–225

D Ganga broke his right little finger fielding on 27 December and took no further part in the match

Umpires: EA Watkin & RB Tiffin
Toss: West Indies
Test Debut: MS Sinclair

New Zealand won by an innings and 105 runs

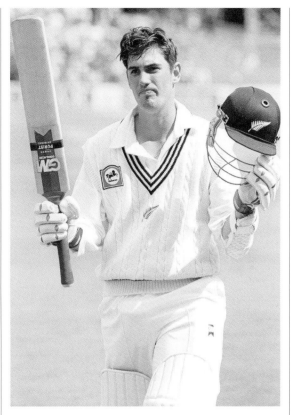

The young Matthew Sinclair acknowledges the applause following his remarkable Test debut of 214 in the second Test at Wellington.

batted first in that victory, compiling the highest-ever innings score against New Zealand.

A well-grassed pitch and a lush outfield provided enough encouragement to offer his bowlers first crack at the New Zealand top order. Courtney Walsh was closing in on Kapil Dev's world record of Test wickets, and history had been generous to the veteran Jamaican on the Basin – in that previous Test match he finished with a match analysis of 13 for 55. Without injured opener Matt Horne, New Zealand introduced 24-year-old Matthew Sinclair for his first Test and the confident Australian-born right-hander wasted little time writing his own history.

Stead was out before drinks in the first session, providing Sinclair with the stage to make a remarkable Test debut. His first scoring shot was not memorable, a French cut for four, but that did not diminish his confidence or desire to achieve something special. Australian-born, maybe, but now a proud New Zealander, Sinclair has many of the attributes that Australians boast: an unshakeable

Matthew Sinclair, Adam Parore, Dion Nash and Chris Cairns celebrate their successful Test victory.

self-belief, a hunger for runs and an intense desire to succeed combined with exciting natural skill and temperament. Sinclair joined an elite group of New Zealand cricketers by stumps when he was 123 not out. Jack Mills, Bruce Taylor, Rodney Redmond and Mark Greatbatch, all left-handers, had topped three figures on Test debut, but Sinclair had only just begun exploring new territory. He surpassed Mills' 117, the previous highest debut innings and proceeded to overhaul his personal-best innings of 203 not out before falling at 214, the equal second-highest score by a Test newcomer alongside West Indian Lawrence Rowe.

Sinclair added 164 with Stephen Fleming for the third wicket and 189 with Nathan Astle for the fourth wicket, a record for New Zealand against the West Indies. When he was fifth out at 456, bowled by Reon King, the West Indies were all but played out of the Test. Astle, who plays with such freedom and aggression in one-day internationals as an opener, has brought considerable discipline to his Test cricket batting down the order. While Sinclair was attracting much of the attention, Astle played with maturity, but was unfortunately run out for 93 after spending four hours in partnership with his younger colleague.

Curiously, New Zealand did not push the scoring rate in the latter stages of the innings, with Cairns and McMillan labouring through identical scores of 31. New Zealand were still able to declare at 518 for 9. King deserved his 4 for 96 from 36 overs, and Franklyn Rose repaid his captain's faith with three late wickets, while Walsh did not enjoy the previous rich pickings – 41 overs conceded 112 runs and no wickets. The West Indies' hopes were not helped by an injury to opener Darren Ganga while fielding that left him with a broken finger.

Facing five overs before stumps on the second day Sherwin Campbell was out in the first, and the quick dismissal of nightwatchman Nehemiah Perry and Shivnarine Chanderpaul left the West Indies in another battle for survival. Griffith and Lara painstakingly compiled a century-stand for the fourth wicket, 112, but Lara's dismissal by Vettori signalled another batting collapse. Cairns had been almost anonymous through the first two days, but it gave him the rest he needed to reach his irresistible best. The early wicket of Campbell set him up for his ninth five-wicket haul, leaving the West Indies 339 behind on the first innings.

The second innings did not start any better than the first. Campbell again failed, leg before for a

Brian Lara hits out at Wellington and puts wicketkeeper Adam Parore in danger.

second time to Cairns, and while there was greater resistance in the rest of the top order, the innings was ended in less than a day. Griffith played another dogged innings for 45, Chanderpaul produced a series-best 70, and Lara battled for three hours for 75 before falling to a dubious caught-behind decision. The dismissal of Courtney Walsh for his 35th Test duck also had an element of the unlucky, with TV replays indicating the leg before decision might have hit the bat first. Cairns collected the last wicket of the match when Rose was leg before, giving the all-rounder his 17th wicket of the series and his 150th in his 44th Test. It completed an outstanding calendar year 1999 for Cairns, his best in ten years of Test cricket – 47 wickets in ten Tests came at a cost of 20.51 each, while some inspirational batting had accumulated 548 runs at 39.14.

Cairns' success also showed in New Zealand's overall performance. The two-nil series win was their third in 1999, previously beating India one-nil in New Zealand and England in England. To win two-nil was sweet success as victories either home or away against the West Indies are very rare. It was only the sixth Test win in 30 outings between the two countries, and took captain Stephen Fleming to his tenth win since assuming the captaincy from Lee Germon.

TEST MATCH AVERAGES
New Zealand v. West Indies

NEW ZEALAND

Batting	M	Inns	NO	HS	Runs	Av	100	50
NJ Astle	2	3	1	93	148	74.00	–	1
SP Fleming	2	2	0	67	133	66.50	–	2
CL Cairns	2	2	0	72	103	51.50	–	1
CD McMillan	2	2	0	51	82	41.00	–	1
CJ Spearman	2	3	1	30*	81	40.50	–	–
GR Stead	2	3	0	22	55	18.33	–	–
DL Vettori	2	2	0	29	31	15.50	–	–
AC Parore	2	2	0	8	13	6.50	–	–

Also batted: MJ Horne (1 Test) 32, 5rh; DJ Nash (2 Tests) 6*, 2; MS Sinclair (1 Test) 214; PJ Wiseman (1 Test) 0*
SB O'Connor played in one Test but did not bat

Bowling	Overs	Mds	Runs	Wkts	Av	Best	10/m	5/inn
CL Cairns	86	30	169	17	9.94	7-27	1	2
DJ Nash	69	25	161	8	20.12	4-38	–	–
DL Vettori	119.1	39	258	8	32.25	4-83	–	–

Also bowled: NJ Astle 27-3-112-2; CD McMillan 4-1-22-0; SB O'Connor 35-11-75-0; PJ Wiseman 24-10-54-0

Fielding Figures
12 – AC Parore; 2 – SP Fleming, CJ Spearman, GR Stead, PJ Wiseman. 1 – CL Cairns, DJ Nash

WEST INDIES

Batting	M	Inns	NO	HS	Runs	Av	100	50
AFG Griffith	2	4	0	114	244	61.00	1	1
SL Campbell	2	4	0	170	173	43.25	1	–
BC Lara	2	4	0	75	167	41.75	–	2
S Chanderpaul	2	4	0	70	89	22.25	–	1
JC Adams	2	4	1	25	54	18.00	–	–
RD Jacobs	2	4	1	20	46	15.33	–	–
FA Rose	2	4	0	10	17	4.25	–	–
CA Walsh	2	4	1	5*	5	1.66	–	–
RD King	2	4	1	4*	5	1.66	–	–

Also batted: NO Perry (1 Test) 3, 0; RL Powell (1 Test) 0, 30; D Ramnarine (1 Test) 8, 0. D Ganga played in one Test but did not bat.

Bowling	Overs	Mds	Runs	Wkts	Av	Best	10/m	5/inn
RD King	62.2	13	177	8	22.12	4-81	–	–
D Ramnarine	37	10	86	3	28.66	3-82	–	–
CA Walsh	78	10	226	3	75.33	2-81	–	–
FA Rose	65.3	9	244	3	81.33	3-113	–	–

Also bowled: JC Adams 33-10-65-0; S Chanderpaul 6-1-15-1; NO Perry 32-5-120-0; RL Powell 5-2-13-0

Fielding Figures
3 – JC Adams, SL Campbell, RD Jacobs. 1 – RL Powell, D Ramnarine, FA Rose, CA Walsh

ONE-DAY INTERNATIONALS

The New Year started as the previous year had
ended for the West Indies, on a losing note. There
might have been a warmth about the welcome to the
first one-day international of 2000 but nothing
generous in New Zealand's on-field attitude. There
was an inescapable feeling that the West Indies
should have been able to defend 268 for 7 with the
bowling attack at their disposal.

Campbell and Jacobs opened up with a punishing
stand of 111, both scoring rapid half-centuries, and
with Lara's 76 New Zealand were facing a
formidable target. The innings lost momentum but
was still competitive in slow New Zealand
conditions. Man of the Match Nathan Astle and all-
rounder Chris Cairns provided the substance of the
chase, adding 136 for the fourth wicket. Cairns was

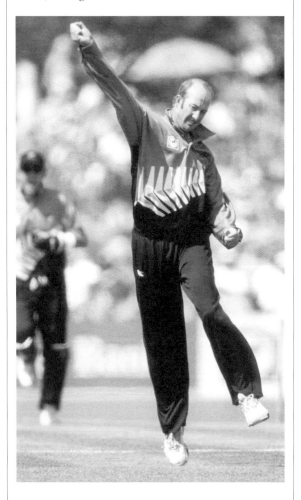

Chris Harris was typically dependable in the one-day series.

out for 75 with the score on 198 and Astle dismissed
the next ball for 77. Duckworth/Lewis scoring was
implemented to reduce New Zealand's target to 250
after rain robbed the game of four overs, Chris
Harris and Dion Nash completing the win off the
first ball of the 46th over.

Rain also reduced the second match at Taupo's
Owen Delaney Park but New Zealand achieved
their win much more comfortably than in Auckland.
Daniel Vettori was Man of the Match for his best-
ever one-day figures of 4 for 24 from eight overs,
with only Jimmy Adams able to play with any
assurance for 69. Captain Stephen Fleming led the
way with an unbeaten half-century as the 193 target
was reached with six overs to spare.

Batting was not quite as comfortable as New
Zealand sealed the series win in Napier. Set a
modest target of 160, New Zealand relied heavily on
a second-wicket partnership between Astle and
Fleming of 105 to guide them to victory. It was not a
certain victory when four wickets fell for 20 runs
until Harris and Fleming then Parore and Fleming
secured the win. Fleming's 66 not out was his
second successive half-century of the series.

Having settled the series, New Zealand embarked
on the clean sweep that captain Stephen Fleming had
urged from his side to prove its maturity. Wellington's
new stadium provided a stirring atmosphere for an
improved top-order batting effort. The West Indies
showed little improvement on their previous two
batting performances, reaching only 171 in 50 overs.
They had to resume their innings on the reserve day
after rain ended play after only 10.5 overs.

The lively medium pace of Scott Styris earned him
3 for 37 from ten overs but it was Chris Harris with
a miserly 1 for 15 from his ten overs that stifled any
attacking intent. Astle celebrated his 100th one-day
international with his 21st half-century from 72 balls
and with Roger Twose in sparkling form adding 68
not out the win came with ten overs to spare. They
were helped by some woeful West Indian fielding
with Astle dropped twice and Twose once in their
partnership of 149.

The same pairing of Twose and Astle were at the
forefront in the final encounter at Christchurch's
Jade Stadium, adding 170 for the third wicket – a
record against West Indies surpassing the 149
recorded three days earlier. Twose's highest one-day
score of 97 from just 90 balls was worthy of the Man
of the Match award, just ahead of Astle, who scored
85 in New Zealand's 302 for 6. It was his third half-
century of the series in which he scored 320 runs at
an average of 80. The West Indies batsmen showed

some spark for the first time in pursuit of the target, falling just 21 runs short of a win.

The two-nil Test series loss and the five-nil one-day series loss sent the West Indies team home with the worst record of any side to tour New Zealand. They played two first-class games at the start of the tour and both were drawn. That had followed a loss in an exhibition game of CricketMax, (a 20-over-a-side fixture) which opened the tour.

Match One

2 January 2000 at Eden Park, Auckland (floodlit)
West Indies 268 for 7 (50 overs)(BC Lara 76, RD Jacobs 65, SL Campbell 51)

New Zealand 250 for 7 (45.1 overs)(NJ Astle 77, CL Cairns 75)
New Zealand won by three wickets (DL Method: New Zealand target 250 from 46 overs)
Man of the Match: NJ Astle

Match Two

4 January 2000 at Owen Delaney Park, Taupo (floodlit)
West Indies 192 (41.3 overs)(JC Adams 69, DL Vettori 4 for 24)
New Zealand 194 for 3 (35.4 overs)(SP Fleming 59*)
New Zealand won by seven wickets
Man of the Match: DL Vettori

Match Three

6 January 2000 at McLean Park, Napier
West Indies 159 (49.5 overs)(NO Perry 52*)
New Zealand 160 for 6 (37.2 overs) (SP Fleming 66*, NJ Astle 50)
New Zealand won by four wickets
Man of the Match: SP Fleming

Match Four

8 and 9 January 2000 at WestpacTrust Stadium, Wellington
West Indies 171 for 9 (50 overs)
New Zealand 172 for 2 (36.3 overs) (NJ Astle 76*, RG Twose 68*)
New Zealand won by eight wickets
Man of the Match: CZ Harris

Match Five

11 January 2000 at Jade Stadium, Christchurch (floodlit)
New Zealand 302 for 6 (50 overs) (RG Twose 97, NJ Astle 85)
West Indies 282 (49.5 overs) (SL Campbell 71, SB Styris 4 for 57)
New Zealand won by 20 runs
Man of the Match: RG Twose

Captain Stephen Fleming on his way to securing victory for New Zealand.

AUSTRALIA IN NEW ZEALAND
By Jim Maxwell

Australia had not won a Test series in New Zealand for 23 years and Steve Waugh was on a mission. He was the only survivor from the 1986 tour, when an emotional Allan Border had threatened to resign the captaincy during a series of underwhelming Australian performances. Waugh was a comparative 'wet behind the ears' 20-year-old back then, needing the guidance of experienced men like the newly appointed coach, Bob Simpson. Fourteen years on Waugh had become one of the toughest players in the game. The failures of those seeking out tours had developed his desire for success, and he arrived in New Zealand determined to maintain Australia's omnipotent reputation.

The brutal power of Adam Gilchrist's left-handed batting delivered seven sixes at Christchurch in the one-day series.

Controversially Australia's tour strategy was made public when a copy of their game plan was inadvertently slipped under the wrong hotel room door in Wellington. The briefing notes analysed New Zealand's personnel, under the tour theme title 'never satisfied'. Unsurprisingly the plan referred to intimidation, with the rider of keeping everything under control, including sledging and body language. Control and discipline became the cornerstones of a highly successful tour, and apart from Damien Fleming momentarily snapping at Stephen Fleming in the Dunedin one-dayer, the team kept a high standard of composure on the field.

An early side-show between Shane Warne and two young fans, who had taken his photo while he was carelessly having a cigarette in the players' enclosure, in a non-smoking ground, eventually blew over, following an apology from Warne for his aggressive behaviour. The incident was an unfortunate reminder that the Australian vice-captain lacked discretion and maturity. New Zealand had reason to be confident following their clean sweep of Test and one-day wins over the West Indies. But the month's gap between series meant the Kiwis were underdone when Australia arrived fresh from their triangular triumph over India and Pakistan. Injuries to key bowlers Dion Nash and Geoff Allott also hindered the home side, who just didn't have the depth of their resourceful opponents.

The scoreboard suggests that Australia won both series easily. In Christchurch the team certainly hit a peak with one of the most explosively authoritative innings in memory from Adam Gilchrist, who hit seven sixes in a 98-ball 128. But the New Zealanders were always competitive, Astle's one-day batting and Cairns' refreshing audacity in the Tests providing spirited opposition.

All the matches were thrillingly played out, with a freneticism that underlined the impact of the 50-over game. Some quick-fingered umpiring may also have contributed to a sense of batting mortality, which triggered attack as the best means of prosperity. In Australia's case they had the firepower to overcome batting collapses. The Test series could well have been closer had New Zealand taken their chances in Auckland, and dismissed Gilchrist early on the third day. He capped off a strong series with a record ten catches in Hamilton, as Australia extended their run of Test wins to ten, and that elusive series victory in New Zealand.

ONE-DAY INTERNATIONALS

Steve Waugh's decision to change the batting order, and test the versatility of his team in the final match, went awry. Former New Zealand all-rounder Lance Cairns was typically blunt about Waugh's tactics, suggesting he was trying to take the mickey out of the Kiwis. Understandably Waugh wanted to challenge his players. And the loss was only Australia's third in 30 matches since their brilliant sequence started at the World Cup. The momentum had been amazing; coming into the last match in Auckland, a record 13 matches without defeat. And in terms of a build-up to the important Test series, Damien Martyn had the chance of playing an innings, carrying his bat for 116, instead of a 30-ball slash in the last ten overs.

The brutal truth of the series was that Australia had greater quality and depth in batting and bowling. New Zealand had some fine individual talent, but there were too many mediocre performers. The pressure fell back on Astle, Fleming, Twose and Cairns with the bat, and the medium pacers were clearly targeted by the Australian batsmen. Australia's run-rate was a rollicking 5.6 runs per over, and New Zealand's exactly five, statistics that confirmed the perfection of the pitches, and shorter boundaries than Australia's paddocks.

New Zealand lacked several key bowlers, who were injured, and Ricky Ponting's ankle injury in the final one-dayer in Sydney gave Matthew Hayden a renewed opportunity, and he grabbed it with three half-centuries, including a robust 64 not out in the washed-out opener in Wellington. Australia's pace attack destroyed the Kiwi batting in Auckland, McGrath and Lee scything three wickets apiece as the innings crumbled to 122 all out in 30.1 overs. The match finished with two and a half hours to spare, and the headbanging music that is a regular feature of the Kiwi one-day format was certainly more entertaining than a very one-sided contest.

Down south in Dunedin, rugby's house of pain at Carisbrook provided an unwanted headache for the officials, when the crowd on the terraces rioted. Reacting to a Parore helmet on wicket dismissal from a Lee bumper, the mob threw bottles on to the ground, in scenes reminiscent of the ugly disturbance in Barbados a year previously. How did the crowd get bottles? Why weren't they drinking from plastic cups? Where was the security team? Plenty of embarrassment for Chris Doig, the chief executive of New Zealand cricket, and his apology

Matthew Hayden's consistent batting helped take Australia to victory in four of the six one-dayers.

to the Australians was immediate. Batting first Australia had teed off, Gilchrist's 77 off 58 balls exciting a potent 4 for 310. The Kiwis' chase was on target at 2 for 169 in the 26th over. Waugh threw the ball to Martyn, who immediately trapped Twose leg before, prompting Astle to swing, and miss. New Zealand were all out for 260.

In Christchurch Australia were again sent in, and Gilchrist flayed the bowling in an innings that prompted Steve Waugh to suggest that the dazzling left-hander will score a double century one day! He hit seven sixes, most of them pulled or hooked, from deliveries barely short of a length. His hundred arrived from 78 balls, and he was on track for 200 when he was dismissed in the 28th over for 128 out of 189 for the first wicket. Steve Waugh smashed five sixes in a 44-ball 54, as Australia made their highest one-day total, at 6 for 349. It proved far too many.

In Napier New Zealand were sent in, and their 243 for 9 featured an excellent Astle hundred. Bevan, who had dropped Astle before he'd scored, made amends with a century that won the game with 4.2 overs and five wickets to spare.

Three up, with one to play, and Australia had a collapse with an altered batting order in Auckland. New Zealand won easily, despite a power failure that blacked out the lights for 15 minutes. Newcomer Chris Nevin, a wicketkeeper, was Man of the Match, making 74 in a seven-wicket win.

Match One
16 (no play) and 17 February 2000 at WestpacTrust Stadium, Wellington (floodlit)
Australia 119 for 1 (23 overs)
New Zealand did not bat
Match abandoned

Match Two
19 February 2000 at Eden Park, Auckland (floodlit)
New Zealand 122 (30.1 overs)
Australia 123 for 5 (24.4 overs)(ML Hayden 50)
Australia won by five wickets
Man of the Match: B Lee

Match Three
23 February 2000 at Carisbrook, Dunedin (floodlit)
Australia 310 for 4 (50 overs)(AC Gilchrist 77, ME Waugh 75, MG Bevan 52)
New Zealand 260 (45 overs)(NJ Astle 81, RG Twose 62)
Australia won by 50 runs

Match Four
26 February 2000 and Jade Stadium, Christchurch (floodlit)
Australia 349 for 6 (50 overs)(AC Gilchrist 128, ME Waugh 70, SR Waugh 54)
New Zealand 301 for 9 (50 overs)(SP Fleming 82, CZ Harris 59*)
Australia won by 48 runs
Man of the Match: AC Gilchrist

Match Five
1 March 2000 at McLean Park, Napier (floodlit)
New Zealand 243 for 9 (50 overs)(NJ Astle 104, DW Fleming 4 for 41)
Australia 245 for 5 (45.4 overs)(MG Bevan 107, ML Hayden 57)
Australia won by five wickets
Man of the Match: MG Bevan

Match Six
3 March 2000 at Eden Park, Auckland (floodlit)
Australia 191 (46.2 overs)(DR Martyn 116* (carried his bat)
New Zealand 194 for 3 (41 overs)(CJ Nevin 74, SP Fleming 60*)
New Zealand won by seven wickets
Man of the Match: CJ Nevin

FIRST TEST
11, 12, 13, 14 and 15 March at Auckland

Eden Park is a wonderful rugby venue. For the men in white, it's idiosyncratic, polygonal, misshapen. Its bizarre dimensions create a curious spectacle as the miscued shot shoots away to a 45-yard boundary. It's the pitch that makes the matches intriguing, and for Australia the results had been unfriendly since their last win in 1977. The groundsman's prediction that the pitch would turn square was New Zealand's best hope of winning again. Or so it seemed. The Kiwi spinners took 17 wickets, Vettori a record 12. But they couldn't quite deliver the result. Why? Well, as Steve Waugh explained with typical conciseness: they bowled too many four-balls.

Australia had tuned up for the big match with a five-wicket win over Northern Districts in Hamilton. Their team included Damien Martyn, who replaced the injured Ponting. Martyn hadn't played a Test for six years, but seemed a more relaxed, mature player at 29, and was in good form with hundreds in his last two innings. New Zealand reinstated Matthew Horne, who had recovered from a broken finger, and picked off spinner Paul Wiseman to support Daniel Vettori, with Simon Doull in for the injured Dion Nash from the side that had beaten the West Indies by an innings at the end of December.

The Test subscript was all about Shane Warne. Needing five wickets to go past Dennis Lillee's Australian record of 355 dismissals, Warne was glowingly endorsed by his captain. Waugh predicted 'he'll get 'em plus tax'. Was this Steve Waugh the psychologist, trying to ease the pressure of expectation that had been intensifying since the beginning of January, when Warne failed to take a wicket in the Sydney Test? Waugh's pre-match confidence camouflaged an anxiety about the contest, and much of Australia's batting was uneasily frantic. Warne, as it happened, broke the record, without tax.

Shane Warne breaks Lillee's Australian record of 355 dismissals in the first Test against New Zealand.

Waugh correctly called heads and his decision to bat looked marginal when Cairns hit Slater's off-stump without offer. Langer opted for the long handle to Vettori, carving eight fours and a six in a lightning 46 from 47 balls. Then he was stumped off Wiseman, and the innings was only kept afloat by a poised Mark Waugh. Eventually he ran out of support, 72 not out, as the spinners got the bite and turn that makes survival unlikely. Wiseman, who had taken three wickets to Vettori's five, was batting before the end of the day, and as the forlorn nightwatchman, was bowled by the last ball from Lee. New Zealand were 26 for 4 with one wicket to Warne and three to the pace attack.

Under artificial lighting, Fleming and Astle made a positive beginning on Saturday, moving the total to 80. If batsmen could determine the timing of drinks breaks, they would probably say no all day, going on the frequency of dismissals straight after the refreshment pauses. Sure enough Warne found the concentration fade from Astle, who snicked to slip after the first hour, and in Miller's next over Gilchrist created a brilliant dismissal, stumping Fleming as his back foot momentarily hovered over the crease. Warne got within one of the record when McMillan indecisively put his pad between the ball and the stumps, but it was McGrath who finished

off the innings, after Cairns gave notice of his attacking zeal.

Australia started their second innings 51 runs in front, and the frenzied approach continued with Slater holing out to mid-off in the third over. Langer's exuberant batting suggested he had been caught up in the party mood of Auckland's America's Cup celebrations, and he was third out for 47 from 64 balls, attempting another six off Vettori to one of Eden Park's short boundaries. Mark Waugh was caught at the wicket by the kind of bouncing, turning ball that tail-enders would have missed by a foot, and Steve Waugh hit a return catch to Wiseman, who had shared the new ball with Cairns. With 114 for 5 at stumps, the game should finish inside three days; the Australians were confident that another 50 would be enough.

Gilchrist could have been stumped by a sharper Parore early on the third morning, an escape that proved costly. Sixty-seven lively runs were whacked from the spinners, Martyn playing daringly until he was bowled, attempting an ambitious cut from Vettori. That was Vettori's hundredth Test wicket, and at 21 and 46 days, he became the youngest player to reach the milestone. Vettori finally removed the dangerous Gilchrist for 59, and his 7 for 87 added up to the best match return – 12

Daniel Vettori dismisses Mark Waugh in the first Test at Eden Park.

wickets – behind Hadlee's 15, in trans-Tasman matches. Wiseman had been less effective, and as one old-time Australian legend mistily remarked, 'if they were batting against Laker and Lock, they wouldn't have got a hundred'. They weren't and New Zealand needed 281 to win against Warne and Miller.

It was Miller who made the breaks, having Horne prodding to short leg, Sinclair misjudging the length on a quicker ball, and Fleming snapped up by Gilchrist down the leg-side. Warne bowled Astle, but the fight was sustained by a counter-attacking McMillan, supported by Cairns. At the end of the third day New Zealand were 151 for 5.

Heavy overnight rain made a section of the outfield unsafe, and the sight of Jeremy Coney doing his television preamble in flippers drew the only laugh on a cheerless fourth day. No play, and the pessimists scrambled to get on the draw at 20 to one, as more showers tipped in from the Waitakarei hills.

The damp outfield delayed a start until half past eleven, after umpires Venkatraghavan and Billy Bowden decided that the surface was marginally safe to resume. The fifth ball of Miller's first over ruined local anticipation of another win over Australia in Auckland. Cairns loosely lifted the ball to Steve Waugh at mid-wicket: 151 for 6. Parore rekindled hope, batting with the certainty of the pitch's truer character, and was still there at lunch, 6 for 183, including two hits for six off Miller. As the score tensely pushed towards 200, Brett Lee had Parore driving low to cover where Steve Waugh took the catch. McMillan, pinned down, lashed at a wider ball and was caught by Warne, who finally got the ball back and, in the flurry of a Wiseman sweep won the verdict for a catch that ended the match and gave the leg-spinner his record. The well-fought match proved that the best contests are played on pitches that allow the bowlers just enough expression to avoid the tag of 'predictable'.

FIRST TEST – NEW ZEALAND v. AUSTRALIA
12, 12, 13, 14 (no play) and 15 March 2000 at Eden Park, Auckland

AUSTRALIA

	First Innings			Second Innings	
MJ Slater	b Cairns	5		(2) c Horne, b Cairns	6
GS Blewett	c Astle, b Wiseman	17		(1) c Spearman, b Vettori	8
JL Langer	st Parore, b Wiseman	46		c Astle, b Vettori	47
ME Waugh	not out	72		c Parore, b Vettori	25
SR Waugh (capt)	c Spearman, b Vettori	17		c & b Wiseman	10
DR Martyn	c Astle, b Vettori	17		b Vettori	36
*AC Gilchrist	lbw b Wiseman	7		c Fleming, b Vettori	59
SK Warne	c Fleming, b Vettori	7		c Wiseman, b Vettori	12
B Lee	c Parore, b Vettori	6		not out	6
CR Miller	b Cairns	0		st Parore, b Vettori	8
GD McGrath	c Spearman, b Vettori	8		lbw b Wiseman	1
	b 7, lb 4, nb 1	12		b 7, lb 4	11
		214			**229**

	First Innings				Second Innings			
	O	M	R	W	O	M	R	W
Cairns	18	0	71	2	4	1	13	1
Doull	14	6	21	–	5	1	8	–
Vettori	25	8	62	5	35	11	87	7
Wiseman	14	2	49	3	33.5	6	110	2

Fall of Wickets
1–10, 2–77, 3–78, 4–114, 5–138, 6–161, 7–184, 8–192, 9–193
1–7, 2–46, 3–67, 4–81, 5–107, 6–174, 7–202, 8–214, 9–226

NEW ZEALAND

	First Innings			Second Innings	
MJ Horne	c Blewett, b McGrath	3		c Langer, b Miller	11
CM Spearman	c Martyn, b Lee	12		lbw b McGrath	4
MS Sinclair	lbw b Warne	8		lbw b Miller	6
PJ Wiseman	b Lee	1		(11) c Gilchrist, b Warne	9
SP Fleming (capt)	st Gilchrist, b Miller	21		(4) c Gilchrist, b Miller	8
NJ Astle	c ME Waugh, b Warne	31		(5) b Warne	35
CD McMillan	lbw b Warne	6		(6) c Warne, b Lee	78
CL Cairns	c Gilchrist, b McGrath	35		(7) c SR Waugh, b Miller	20
*AC Parore	c Gilchrist, b McGrath	11		(8) c SR Waugh, b Lee	26
DL Vettori	not out	15		(9) c Warne, b Miller	0
SB Doull	c Lee, b McGrath	12		(10) not out	5
	b 4, lb 1, nb 3	8		b 7, lb 7, nb 2	16
		163			**218**

	First Innings				Second Innings			
	O	M	R	W	O	M	R	W
McGrath	11.1	2	33	4	23	8	33	1
Miller	22	8	38	1	18	5	55	5
Warne	22	4	68	3	20.3	5	80	2
Lee	7	4	19	2	12	4	36	2

Fall of Wickets
1–5, 2–25, 3–25, 4–26, 5–80, 6–80, 7–102, 8–134, 9–143
1–15, 2–25, 3–25, 4–43, 5–121, 6–151, 7–195, 8–204, 9–204

Umpires: B Bowden & S Venkataraghavan
Toss: Australia

Australia won by 62 runs

SECOND TEST
24, 25, 26 and 27 March at Wellington

Cricket pundits and aficionados have a hankering for omens on the speculative days before a big match. Wellingtonians reminded confident visitors that the only time Australia had won at the Basin Reserve was in 1946. Yes, they won by an innings in two days, an inauspicious inaugural match that was not officially repeated for 27 years. Since then three draws and a New Zealand win formed the scorecard, and New Zealand had recently beaten the West Indies by an innings at the old ground, originally reclaimed from a swamp. Inquiries about trans-Tasman cricket helped to destroy a long-held belief that Australia had snubbed their neighbours after that one-sided 1946 contest. Second elevens, never the top team, were sent, until Kiwi administrator Bob Vance encouraged a more mature relationship in the early 1970s. It was New Zealand officials' fear of repeat thrashings that made them reluctant to invite the best teams, and in many ways that sense of inferiority was still manifest until Richard Hadlee bowled them to series win in Australia in 1985–86.

The damp weather was perfect for a Super 12 rugby game in the lead-up to the match, and the conditions looked ripe for bowling on the opening day. Not for Stephen Fleming, who won the toss and boldly decided to bat. The decision may have been a positive team move, but when your eleven includes three new-ball bowlers – Cairns, Doull and O'Connor – and a wonky top three, you have to bowl; one down, two to play. Poor batting and a couple of useful Lee out-swingers equated to 69 for 5 at lunch. Spearman drove wantonly off the edge, Horne slipsdrove, Sinclair was leaden-footed, Fleming hit to mid-on and McMillan snicked. Cairns, who had been itemised as 'fragile' in the Australian briefing notes, launched a thrilling assault on the bowling after lunch, his fifty coming from 54 balls, via a Mark Waugh dropped chance in the slips at 38. Astle, missed on 15, sturdily forced his front-foot presence, undone by Warne, whom he edged to slip. Parore kept calm; with Cairns selecting the right ball to pound away, he reached his third Test hundred. An excellent crowd, many on the free list to compensate for the one-day wash-out earlier in the tour, lapped up the clean hitting. Blewett's bouncy medium zippers dispatched Parore, and Cairns was going for another exocet into the Vance stand when Blewett somehow got his hands around a swirler at long on. In the tail swishing, Vettori was

Captain Steve Waugh on his way to 151 not out at Wellington.

out on a third-umpire referral when he edged a Warne spinner on to his boot. Langer just got under the deflection, with umpire Quested able to confirm only the carry, and not the edge, with the eye in the sky. Doull, requiring three wickets for the 100 Test landmark, had Blewett caught at second slip for a duck, and with nightwatchman Warne leg before to Vettori's last ball of the day, Australia were 2 for 29 chasing 298. What a fantastic day's entertainment.

Doull could have brought up number 99 in his first over on the second day, but the diminutively impassive Riazuddin gave Slater not out, missing... middle. Cairns, energised by his rampant batting and some zest in the pitch, picked up Langer on the outside edge, and surprised Mark Waugh, who couldn't keep a lifter out of short leg's clutches. At 51 for 4, Australia were a little shaky, and Steve Waugh was just finding his stride when a curler from Vettori went through, unsighting Parore, who missed an awkward stumping chance. Waugh was eight, and it was the last chance he offered in seven hours of remorseless dissection of the bowling. Slater was a purposeful, disciplined accomplice, and a partnership of 199 resulted. New Zealand were handicapped when Vettori retired with a back injury, and occasional medium pacer Craig McMillan

hurled down some Barlowesque bumpers. Slater gloved one of them to Parore, but Martyn measured off his best strokes and at the bad light cessation Australia led by 20 at 318 for 5. Waugh's 22nd Test century carried him to position six on the Test match run-scorers' list, and after Martyn had been caught by Parore for 78, Waugh became the first batsman to pass 150 against all Test-playing countries. He was aided by McGrath in a last-wicket partnership of 33, and the lead was 121 when New Zealand started again before lunch on the third day. Brett Lee produced deliveries that wrecked the stumps twice, and for those watching from afar, or on their evening news, they were missiles that spelt the cricket equivalent of the atom bomb. Matthew Horne missed a swinging full toss, and three balls later, the unfortunate Sinclair was spectacularly yorked. It was lethal bowling. Spearman saw off the new ball, and was in fine touch when Miller sorted out his footwork, and the obligatory bat pad went to Langer. Warne dismissed Astle for the fourth time in as many innings, and it was a beauty. A rarity in the later Warne period: the flipper which ripped through Astle's belated adjustment. McMillan injudiciously swept, top-edging to slip, and at 88 for 5, another pair of rest days was anticipated.

Chris Cairns' sturdy 109 in the first innings proved he wasn't the 'fragile' character the Australians had once labelled him.

Cairns, who batted so selectively in the first innings, went manic. He struck successive sixes off Warne, then when Lee came back from the Mount Victoria tunnel end, he hooked the ball violently out of the ground, on to a horticultural traffic island. In the same a drive over long off was played between front and back foot, as Cairns adjusted to a change of pace. Blewett tried a bumper and was hooked into oblivion. Fleming kept his head, and by the close for bad light, it was 189 for 5: 68 in front and fighting.

The fourth day speculation centred on a hundred for Fleming and continued mayhem from Cairns. McGrath, who was certain he had run Cairns out the previous evening with a direct hit, won a dubious leg-before decision from umpire Riazuddin on Cairns. The bludgeoner had contributed a brilliant double innings that saved New Zealand from a huge defeat. Miller had Fleming caught at mid-wicket, and some sensible hitting from Doull,

SECOND TEST – NEW ZEALAND v. AUSTRALIA
24, 25, 26 and 27 March 2000 at Basin Reserve, Wellington

NEW ZEALAND

	First Innings			Second Innings	
MJ Horne	c Warne, b Lee	4		b Lee	14
CM Spearman	c Gilchrist, b Lee	4		c Langer, b Miller	38
MS Sinclair	lbw b Miller	4		b Lee	0
SP Fleming (capt)	c Miller, b Warne	16		c Blewett, b Miller	60
NJ Astle	c ME Waugh, b Warne	61		b Warne	14
CD McMillan	c Gilchrist, b Lee	1		c ME Waugh, b Warne	0
CL Cairns	c Blewett, b Miller	109		lbw b McGrath	69
*AC Parore	c Gilchrist, b Blewett	46		run out (Blewett)	33
DL Vettori	c Langer, b Warne	27		c SR Waugh, b Lee	8
SB Doull	c Slater, b Warne	12		c SR Waugh, b Warne	40
SB O'Connor	not out	2		not out	4
	b 1, lb 8, nb 3	12		b 3, lb 8, nb 3	14
		298			**294**

	First Innings				Second Innings			
	O	M	R	W	O	M	R	W
McGrath	17	4	60	–	22.3	11	35	1
Lee	17	2	49	3	23	6	87	3
Miller	20	2	78	2	21	4	54	2
Warne	14.5	1	68	4	27	7	92	3
Blewett	8	1	24	1	3	0	15	–
Waugh SR	4	0	10	–				

Fall of Wickets
1-4, 2-9, 3-18, 4-53, 5-66, 6-138, 7-247, 8-282, 9-287
1-46, 2-46, 3-69, 4-88, 5-88, 6-198, 7-205, 8-222, 9-276

AUSTRALIA

	First Innings			Second Innings	
MJ Slater	c Parore, b McMillan	143		c Parore, b Vettori	12
GS Blewett	c Astle, b Doul	10		b Cairns	25
SK Warne	lbw b Vettori	7			
JL Langer	c Parore, b Cairns	12		(3) c Spearman, b O'Connor	57
ME Waugh	c Sinclair, b Cairns	3		(4) not out	45
SR Waugh (capt)	not out	151		(5) c Fleming, b O'Connor	15
DR Martyn	c Parore, b McMillan	78		(6) not out	17
*AC Gilchrist	c Parore, b O'Connor	3			
B Lee	lbw b O'Connor	0			
CR Miller	c & b McMillan	4			
GD McGrath	c & b Cairns	14			
	lb 1, nb 3	4		b 2, lb 1, w 3	6
		419		**(for 4 wickets)**	**177**

	First Innings				Second Innings			
	O	M	R	W	O	M	R	W
Cairns	26.3	2	110	3	13	2	45	1
Doull	19	3	78	1	10	2	35	–
Vettori	15	1	50	1	8	1	19	1
Astle	11	2	45	–	10.1	4	19	–
McMillan	23	10	57	3	2	0	13	–
O'Connor	26	2	78	–	11	3	43	2

Fall of Wickets
1-8, 2-29, 3-47, 4-51, 5-250, 6-364, 7-375, 8-375, 9-386
1-22, 2-83, 3-110, 4-144

Umpires: DM Quested & Riazuddin
Toss: New Zealand
Test Debuts: nil

Australia won by six wickets

40 from 34 balls, in association with Parore, created a final-innings target of 174.

Nursing a stress fracture in his back, Vettori bravely took the field, in the hope of a batting collapse. His first ball had Slater stumped, but he could only manage eight overs, as Australia efficiently mowed down the target score in the last session. Mark Waugh clipped the winning runs and Australia had won the series, achieving a record ninth successive victory, one more than Warwick Armstrong's team in 1921.

The fiery bowling of Brett Lee gradually took its toll on the New Zealand batsmen.

THIRD TEST
31 March and 1, 2 and 3 April at Hamilton

Going against the adage 'if it ain't broke, don't fix it', Australia took the line 'you can always improve a winning team', when Matt Hayden replaced Greg Blewett for the Third Test. In a weaker side, Blewett would have survived. Now his Test career was potentially over. Averaging 34 in 46 Tests was respectable, but he had been unconvincing as an opener, and Hayden appeared to be in good form. The left/right balance was restored, a factor that had made previous combinations, Slater/Taylor, Taylor/Marsh and Lawry/Simpson, successful.

The two-day gap between Wellington and Hamilton became three with the early finish at the Basin Reserve, and the home side had a difficult task to bolster their eleven with the back injury to Daniel Vettori. Northern Districts' left-arm spinner Bruce Martin was included in the squad, and tyro fast bowler Daryl Tuffey came in for the struggling Simon Doull. Playing two novices was considered too risky, so Tuffey and Wiseman played, with Martin heading off to the first-class final in Taupo. The greater push for change was in the top three, who had failed to provide any solid starts in four innings. Sinclair, who made a double hundred on debut against the West Indies, looked way out of his depth against higher-class bowling, and it was folly to believe that a player of his technical deficiencies should be sacrificed at number three. The final result may have been the same, but Fleming was the obvious choice to bat at three, and at least create the positive body language of a purposeful leader. The sense of déjà vu was overwhelming when Waugh won the toss and bowled. Spearman was clearly caught behind off Lee in his first over, but survived temporarily, until McGrath had him wafting decisively to Gilchrist. Horne looked like he was batting with a broken bat, or maybe without any bat, when he was mercifully caught behind, and Sinclair's footwork inevitably snicked into the cordon. Astle was still blinking when Lee hit his pads, second ball and, at 53 for 4, interest in Cairns' potential resurrective powers became the topic of lunchtime contemplation.

Fleming threatened another imposing total, finding excellent support from the aggressive McMillan. The pitch seemed true, and unsurprising, and at 4 for 131, the innings was building. Lee's in-swinger to the left-hander left Steve Dunne with no alternative, and Cairns powerfully coalesced with McMillan. They added 77. Lee, a bit full in length,

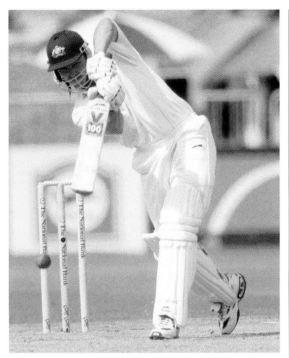

Damien Martyn just missed his maiden Test hundred at Hamilton.

THIRD TEST – NEW ZEALAND v. AUSTRALIA
31 March, 1, 2 and 3 April 2000 at Westpac Trust Park, Hamilton

NEW ZEALAND

	First Innings		Second Innings	
MJ Horne	c Gilchrist, b McGrath	12	run out (Miller)	0
CM Spearman	c Gilchrist, b McGrath	12	c Gilchrist, b Lee	35
MS Sinclair	c Warne, b Lee	19	lbw b Miller	24
SP Fleming (capt)	lbw b Lee	30	c Gilchrist, b Miller	2
NJ Astle	lbw b Lee	0	c Gilchrist, b Warne	26
CD McMillan	c Gilchrist, b Lee	79	c ME Waugh, b Warne	30
CL Cairns	c Martyn, b Lee	37	b McGrath	71
*AC Parore	not out	12	c Gilchrist, b McGrath	16
PJ Wiseman	b Warne	1	c Gilchrist, b Lee	16
DR Tuffey	c Gilchrist, b McGrath	3	not out	1
SB O'Connor	c Gilchrist, b McGrath	0	lbw b Lee	0
	b5, lb7, w2, nb13	27	lb4, nb4	8
		232		**229**

	First Innings				Second Innings			
	O	M	R	W	O	M	R	W
McGrath	21.5	8	58	4	20	7	50	2
Lee	23	8	77	5	18.4	2	46	3
Warne	20	5	45	1	25	11	61	2
Miller	11	4	28	–	20	5	58	2
Martyn	7	4	12	–				
Waugh SR	3	0	10	–				

Fall of Wickets
1-22, 2-42, 3-53, 4-53, 5-131, 6-208, 7-212, 8-224, 9-227
1-3, 2-49, 3-53, 4-71, 5-111, 6-130, 7-165, 8-220, 9-228

AUSTRALIA

	First Innings		Second Innings	
ML Hayden	c Parore, b O'Connor	2	(2) c Spearman, b Wiseman	37
MJ Slater	lbw b O'Connor	2	(1) bw b O'Connor	9
SK Warne	lbw b O'Connor	10		
JL Langer	b Cairns	4	(3) not out	122
ME Waugh	c Sinclair, b Wiseman	28	(4) c Sinclair, b Wiseman	18
SR Waugh (capt)	c Fleming, b Cairns	3	(5) retired hurt	18
DR Martyn	not out	89	(6) lbw b O'Connor	4
*AC Gilchrist	c Horne, b Wiseman	75	(7) not out	0
B Lee	c McMillan, b Cairns	8		
GD McGrath	b O'Connor	7		
CR Miller	c Tuffey, b O'Connor	2		
	b 4, lb 6, nb 12	22	lb 1, nb 3	4
		252	**(for 4 wickets)**	**212**

	First Innings				Second Innings			
	O	M	R	W	O	M	R	W
Cairns	22	7	80	3	10	1	60	–
O'Connor	15.5	5	51	5	11	1	53	2
Tuffey	9	0	75	–	11	1	52	–
Astle	4	3	5	–				
McMillan					0.3	0	4	–
Wiseman	11	3	31	2	9	1	42	2

Fall of Wickets
1-3, 2-16, 3-17, 4-25, 5-29, 6-104, 7-223, 8-233, 9-248
1-13, 2-96, 3-124, 4-190

Umpires: RS Dunne & AV Jayakaprash
Toss: Australia
Test Debut: DR Tuffey

Australia won by six wickets

was driven, until he tempted McMillan, who didn't plunder the apparent half-volley, and was caught by Gilchrist. New Zealand lost their five wickets quickly for 24, and Lee's five took his haul to 28 wickets inside five Tests.

In fading light Australia started badly, Hayden continuing his team's appalling run of opening partnerships when he was caught behind off the left-arm swing of O'Connor. In the last 11 innings the best beginning was 22, with nine under double figures. The light was very poor, and umpire Dunne later conceded that the batsmen should at least have been given the option of playing or leaving.

It was a break that set up the second day enticingly for the home side. A new ball, a nightwatchman, a gung-ho Slater, had wicket potential. O'Connor swung into action, with the complicity of Jayaprakash's finger. Screaming inswingers shifted Slater, then Warne, who got what the team fraternity describe as a 'shocker'. It was the start of a spate of poor decisions that had more to do with competence than partiality. The plumbest O'Connor leg before was on Mark Waugh, but to give three, when you have just given two, must have seemed excessive. Cairns knocked over Langer, and with a stare and a curse, Cairns had Steve Waugh caught at slip. Twenty-nine for 5, and the innings appeared to be ruined. Sadly for New Zealand, the support bowling was mediocre. Fledgling Tuffey had stage fright, and Cairns' second spell was a succession of tired half-pitches. Mark Waugh and Martyn added 75 in as many minutes; no risks, they just batted. Waugh's casual push at Wiseman popped up a close-in catch, and at 104 for 6, 200 looked like an optimistic outcome.

The hour after lunch produced a dazzling attack, mainly from Gilchrist, with 90 runs bursting from magic bats. In 80 balls Gilchrist pulled, drove, pulled, cut, 16 fours in an astonishing display. When he was caught off Wiseman he had scored 75 out of 119 for the seventh wicket. Martyn was heading for a maiden Test hundred, but not even the elevated McGrath could survive long enough for the eventful moment in Martyn's occasional Test career. O'Connor wrapped the innings at tea, leaving Martyn stranded on 89, and a slender lead of 20 for Australia.

Another horrible New Zealand start, this time a bad call from Spearman and Horne, was run out by Miller from mid-off. Sinclair made a better beginning against the pace, falling to Miller's off-spin, hit on the back pad. Spearman was more settled, but the dismissal of Fleming to a leg-side strangulation off Miller meant the Kiwis were only 38 ahead at stumps on the second day, at 3 for 58.

Gilchrist snapped up another edge from Spearman as Australia asserted their dominance before lunch, and the caterers started thinking about their own end-of-season picnic for day four. Warne deceived Astle again with his leg break, and McMillan was unceremoniously fired by umpire Dunne to Warne's last ball before lunch, having missed contact with the ball by a foot. It was left to Cairns to keep the match alive. The most amazing stroke, of many brutally struck blows, was a six driven off Warne over square leg. The omnipresent McGrath clean bowled the assailant, and when Gilchrist caught Wiseman off Lee, he became the first Australian wicketkeeper to complete ten dismissals in a Test. In his first nine Tests he had bagged 39 dismissals, and scored 629 runs at 57 per innings. Lee yorked O'Connor, and Australia needed 210 in just over two days for a clean sweep.

Langer assured a swift victory chase, scoring his first fifty from 42 balls. That was one better than Jack Gregory's Australian best 79 years ago, and a coincidental record alongside the achievement of eclipsing the winning sequence of Gregory and his team-mates. Hayden batted well enough to suggest that his openings might continue, and Steve Waugh

TEST MATCH AVERAGES
New Zealand v. Australia

NEW ZEALAND

Batting	M	Inns	NO	HS	Runs	Av	100	50
CL Cairns	3	6	0	109	341	56.83	1	2
CD McMillan	3	6	0	79	194	32.33	–	2
AC Parore	3	6	1	46	144	28.80	–	–
NJ Astle	3	6	0	61	167	27.83	–	1
SB Doull	2	4	1	40	69	23.00	–	–
SP Fleming	3	6	0	60	137	22.83	–	1
CJ Spearman	3	6	0	38	105	17.50	–	–
DL Vettori	2	4	1	27	50	16.66	–	–
MS Sinclair	3	6	0	24	61	10.16	–	–
MJ Horne	3	6	0	14	44	7.33	–	–
PJ Wiseman	2	4	0	16	27	6.75	–	–
SB O'Connor	2	4	2	4*	6	3.00	–	–

Also batted: DR Tuffey (1 Test) 3, 1*

Bowling	Overs	Mds	Runs	Wkts	Av	Best	10/m	5/inn
DL Vettori	83	21	218	14	15.57	7–87	1	2
SB O'Connor	63.5	11	225	11	20.45	5–51	–	1
PJ Wiseman	67.5	12	232	9	25.77	3–49	–	–
CL Cairns	93.3	13	379	10	37.90	3–80	–	–

Also bowled: NJ Astle 25.1–9–69–0; SB Doull 48–12–142–1; CD McMillan 25.3–10–74–3; DR Tuffey 20–0–127–0

Fielding Figures
10 – AC Parore (7ct/3st); 5 – CJ Spearman; 4 – NJ Astle, SP Fleming. 3 – MS Sinclair; 2 – MJ Horne, CD McMillan, PJ Wiseman. 1 – CL Cairns, DR Tuffey

AUSTRALIA

Batting	M	Inns	NO	HS	Runs	Av	100	50
DR Martyn	3	6	2	89	241	60.25	–	2
JL Langer	3	6	1	122*	288	57.60	1	1
SR Waugh	3	6	2	151*	214	53.50	1	–
ME Waugh	3	6	2	72*	191	47.75	–	1
AC Gilchrist	3	5	1	75	144	36.00	–	2
MJ Slater	3	6	0	143	177	29.50	1	–
GS Blewett	2	4	0	25	50	12.50	–	–
SK Warne	3	4	0	12	36	9.00	–	–
GD McGrath	3	4	0	14	30	7.50	–	–
B Lee	3	4	1	6*	20	6.66	–	–
CR Miller	3	4	0	8	14	3.50	–	–

Also batted: ML Hayden (1 Test) 2, 37.

Bowling	Overs	Mds	Runs	Wkts	Av	Best	10/m	5/inn
B Lee	100.4	26	314	18	17.44	5–77	–	1
GD McGrath	115.3	40	269	12	22.41	4–33	–	–
CR Miller	112	28	311	12	25.91	5–55	–	1
SK Warne	129.2	33	414	15	27.60	4–68	–	–

Also bowled: GS Blewett 11–1–39–1; DR Martyn 7–4–12–0; SR Waugh 7–0–20–0

Fielding Figures
18 – AC Gilchrist (17ct/1st); 4 – SK Warne, ME Waugh, SR Waugh. 3 – GS Blewett, JL Langer. 2 – DR Martyn; 1 – B Lee, CR Miller, MJ Slater

was shaken up by a bruising lifter from Tuffey that struck him on the left arm and forced his retirement. Langer batted like a tornado, reaching his sixth Test century from 102 balls, and cracking the winning runs just over an hour into the fourth day. Gilchrist was named Man of the Match, and in his valedictory series thank yous, Steve Waugh ominously said of the team's achievement: 'this is only the beginning'.

DOMESTIC FIRST-CLASS SEASON

While most aspects of the New Zealand game have produced positive results through successful development and marketing, the domestic first-class game is not one of them. There has been a strong emphasis on the international team and its programme, both Test and one-day, which has met with reasonable success but has been to the detriment of the overall domestic programme.

With New Zealand's season stretching from November to April, many cricketers did not play their opening first-class game until February. The elite players had a limited series of games early in the season playing for North or South in the round-robin Conference series with the touring England 'A'

Matthew Sinclair's consistent form labelled him not only as a potential Test match prospect but also brought him over 1000 runs through the season.

team. That series did at least identify some who were potential international players for the home series against the West Indies and Australia, the most notable being Matthew Sinclair, while others showed enough consistent form to achieve selection through other national teams. Sadly, once again, the public perception of the first-class game and the domestic one-day competition matched the reality, and much mediocre cricket was played in front of sparse crowds.

North won the Conference series with an outright victory over South and a tedious first-innings win over England 'A'. At least the emergence of Matthew Sinclair as a genuine Test match prospect started at this point. Sinclair touched up his resume with an outstanding innings of 182 against an England attack that was both lively and demanding, finishing the series with 44 in a meaningless second innings. Mark Richardson also grabbed his limited opportunity to complete another first-class hundred against North, his eighth century in a career that began ten years ago as a left spin bowler.

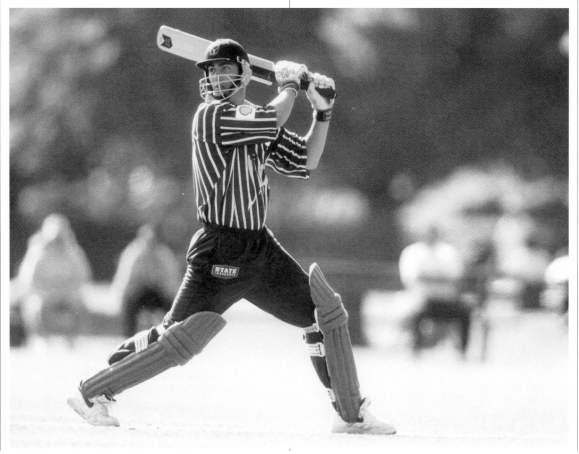

Both Sinclair and Richardson played significant parts in the Shell Trophy but their success wasn't enough to earn their respective sides – Central Districts and Otago – a place in the final. Sinclair was the only batsman in the first-class arena to score over 1,000 runs in the season from 26 innings for a respectable 41.75 average.

The other notable batting performers included Central Districts left-hander Glen Sulzberger, who headed the Shell Trophy aggregate with 550 runs, while long-serving Wellington batsman Jason Wells played just four games for 463 runs, an average of 94.60 and a purple patch that included three

Central Districts Glen Sulzberger – the left-hander headed the Shell Trophy aggregate with 550 runs.

successive centuries. Wells might not be the most aesthetically pleasing stroke player, but what he lacks in technique is more than made up for with his raw courage and unflinching determination.

Northern Districts' youthful top-order batting earned them the right to host the final against Auckland and an even younger left-arm spinner, Bruce Martin, displayed a maturity that had previously been the trademark of his team-mate, Daniel Vettori. Martin's first full season produced 37 wickets at 17.72, five times snaring five wickets in an innings, bagging ten in a match twice. His most impressive display came at Taupo against Auckland in the preliminary fixture between the ultimate finalists.

After a 14-over spell that ended with figures of 5 for 22, Martin finished off the match with career-best 7 for 33 from 18 overs to spearhead an innings and 65-run victory.

Defending trophy holders Central Districts gave themselves every chance of repeating their success, missing the final after an exciting eight-run loss to Auckland in the final round-robin match.

Central needed the maximum six points from the match to head Auckland for the second finals berth and at 246 for 6 chasing 280 on the final day they seemed to be coasting. Former Test batsman Mark Greatbatch was recalled to the Central team to add experience and with youthful captain Jacob Oram playing a commanding innings, it was flowing smoothly. Greatbatch was out for 30 at 246, wicketkeeper Sigley fell 4 runs later, and it was 250 for 7 before Andrew Penn and Oram scratched out a further 21 to put the target and the final within reach. But Auckland all-rounder Tama Canning had the dramatic final say, producing a hat-trick to dismiss Penn, then Tim Anderson and Lance Hamilton in his next over as Oram accumulated runs in between. Sadly, the captain was left 92 not out, and shattered that his side couldn't gain the victory it needed.

No such drama about the five-day final, which was won handsomely by Northern Districts just after lunch on the final day. Opener James Marshall and all-rounder Scott Styris gave the Northern first innings its substance before the punishing, if unorthodox, stroke-play of Simon Doull pushed the total to a respectable 292 that had hardly seemed possible at 210 for 9. Doull's audacious batting at number ten left him 63 not out from 59 balls including 12 fours in an 82-run partnership with Martin. Auckland batted in measured fashion on a very good batting pitch but they lacked the confident stroke-players that had given Northern such good service in the latter part of the season.

Northern were back batting before stumps on the second day with half the match over and three scheduled days remaining. They extended their 84-run lead by 40 without loss, which laid the foundation for the win. Contributions right through the order pushed the second-innings total to 367 and an overall lead of 451. Through rain delays Joseph Yovich produced a solid patient innings of 99, falling victim to nerves as his partners dropped at regular intervals.

As second qualifiers, Auckland needed to win the match outright to prevent Northern taking the trophy and attack was the plan as they faced what seemed an insurmountable target, even before the fourth innings started. Auckland didn't hold back, taking just 30 overs and 5 balls reaching 184, Stephen Lynch left 81 not out from just 59 balls in the madcap innings. Bruce Martin capped a successful first season with 5 for 75 from 11.5 overs.

The season ended as it had begun with a match that never created much excitement and left administrators to ponder a first-class programme that offered the players the competition many seek to improve their own personal standards.

SHELL CUP ONE-DAY COMPETITION

For a couple of days, the pretenders to Canterbury's crown as one-day champions could have considered the prospect of a seventh title in nine years to be just out of their grasp. A washed-out game and a surprise defeat at the hands of Wellington left Canterbury trailing Auckland by one point, and without their considerable international talent there was a growing confidence among the challengers. But such is the depth of one-day talent in Canterbury that when the internationals returned they had completed five straight wins and gained the advantage of two home ties in the best-of-three final series.

As Canterbury pressed on relentlessly only Auckland emerged as serious contenders when Northern Districts faltered in the second half of the series. Not only did Canterbury lose just one of their ten matches but the commanding way they achieved their victories ensured the other sides were playing only for second after the slight stumble in mid-competition.

Canterbury's domination coincided with the return of their international players after the West Indies series. Rebounding from the fifth round loss to Wellington, Canterbury beat Central Districts by four wickets and turned the tables on Wellington. Nathan Astle with a trademark century, 122, and Stephen Fleming's 60 gave them victory by 31 runs in a high-scoring game. Astle followed up with a century as Canterbury thrashed Otago.

Astle played seven of a possible 12 games in the Cup for 364 runs at 52, while Fleming played eight for the even better average of 58 from his 351 runs. Canterbury had two of the top five run-getters, with Brad Doody scoring 418, finishing behind Auckland's Aaron Barnes with 478 and Northern Districts' Mike Parlane with 476.

Auckland medium pacer Andre Adams was the top bowler. With a style similar to Gavin Larsen's, Adams collected 28 one-day wickets at the most impressive economy rate of 3.99, while Wellington seamer Paul Hitchcock achieved considerable success with 25 scalps while playing two games fewer than Adams. The format required a best-of-three final series for the first time since the Shell Cup's inception.

Canterbury needed only two of the three matches to secure the title, winning the first encounter at Eden Park and displaying their one-day strength by defending an innings of just 185. Double-figure scores were spread throughout the order but captain Gary Stead's 35 was the leading contribution.

Former Canterbury and New Zealand opener Lorne Howell gave Auckland every chance of a home victory. However, the experience of Cairns, 3 for 39 from ten, Astle and the miserly Chris Harris who conceded just 26 from his ten overs gave Canterbury an exciting two-run win. If any further evidence of Canterbury's strength was required it was supplied in the second final at Jade Stadium. All-rounder Dion Nash had given the Auckland innings its substance with 85 not out. It was needed after Auckland found itself 62 for 4 in the 17th over. Nash and Tama Canning added 112, with Canning contributing 58 in the total of 224.

Doody, Astle and Fleming organised the chase, 107 for the first wicket in 20 overs between Doody and Astle, and then Fleming joined Astle, adding 45 for the second wicket. The win and the title were achieved in the 42nd over, ensuring that the Canterbury one-day dynasty was maintained into the 21st century.

FIRST-CLASS AVERAGES

BATTING

	M	Inns	NO	HS	Runs	Av	100	50
JD Wells	4	6	1	143	473	94.60	3	1
SL Campbell	3	6	1	170	394	78.80	3	-
DR Martyn	5	9	3	109	430	71.66	1	3
JL Langer	5	9	1	155	538	67.25	2	2
CB Gaffaney	7	13	2	140*	624	56.72	1	4
SM Lynch	4	7	2	81*	280	56.00	-	1
CL Cairns	5	8	0	109	444	55.50	1	3
AFG Griffith	3	5	0	114	269	53.80	1	1
SJ Blackmore	4	6	0	91	320	53.33	-	3
S Chanderpaul	4	8	2	216*	319	53.16	1	1
KD Mills	6	9	3	81*	291	48.50	-	2
GP Sulzberger	7	13	0	159	628	48.30	2	2
SR Mather	8	8	2	117*	288	48.00	1	2
MW Alleyne	5	8	1	152*	327	46.71	1	1
VS Solanki	5	9	1	97	357	44.62	-	5
MHW Papps	4	8	1	84	305	43.57	-	3
MH Richardson	9	16	1	108	638	42.53	1	5
MS Sinclair	14	26	2	214	1002	41.75	3	2
DJG Sales	5	8	1	115	291	41.57	2	-
MD Bailey	7	12	0	100	497	41.41	1	1
JPD Oram	7	14	2	92*	496	41.33	-	4
SR Waugh	4	8	2	151*	243	40.50	1	-
NJ Astle	5	9	1	93	315	39.37	-	2
SP Fleming	6	10	0	78	386	38.60	-	4
JAH Marshall	9	16	1	81	569	37.93	-	5
BC Lara	3	5	0	75	189	37.80	-	2
SB Doull	4	7	2	63*	182	36.40	-	1
NR Parlane	7	12	1	147	391	35.54	1	2
CJ Nevin	6	9	1	72	284	35.50	-	1
TA Boyer	4	7	0	102	248	35.42	1	-
JC Adams	4	7	2	65	171	34.20	-	1
RG Petrie	5	7	1	72	203	33.83	-	1
AJ Redmond	7	13	2	72	363	33.00	-	3
DP Kelly	7	14	0	105	462	33.00	1	2
MA Gough	3	6	1	78	165	33.00	-	1
AC Gilchrist	5	9	3	75	185	32.50	-	2
BA Pocock	9	15	1	167	452	32.28	1	2
MD Bell	10	19	2	77	536	31.52	-	6
CD McMillan	6	10	0	79	307	30.70	-	3
CP Schofield	4	6	0	74	181	30.16	-	2
MW Douglas	7	13	2	64*	326	29.63	-	2
RL Powell	3	5	0	86	148	29.60	-	1
JI Englefield	7	14	0	76	407	29.07	-	5
ME Trescothick	4	7	1	45	170	28.33	-	-
ME Parlane	7	13	1	60	336	28.00	-	2
AC Barnes	8	14	1	65	361	27.76	-	3
MJ Horne	7	13	1	141	332	27.66	1	1
CJ Anderson	4	6	1	50	138	27.60	-	1
JAF Yovich	6	10	1	99	246	27.33	-	1
GS Blewett	4	8	1	83*	188	26.85	-	1
CM Spearman	9	16	1	61	400	26.66	-	1
BJK Doody	5	10	0	72	263	26.30	-	2
BGK Walker	10	15	2	107*	334	25.69	1	-
AJ Hore	4	7	0	102	176	25.14	1	-
IJ Ward	5	10	1	72	215	23.88	-	2
GR Stead	10	19	1	125	430	23.88	1	1
MJ Slater	4	8	0	143	186	23.25	1	-
RT King	7	12	0	104	274	22.83	1	1
HJH Marshall	7	12	1	58	248	22.54	-	2
CD Cumming	6	12	0	39	258	21.50	-	-
CJM Furlong	7	12	3	54*	189	21.00	-	2
JM Aiken	7	12	0	84	250	20.83	-	1
WA Wisneski	6	12	1	60	219	19.90	-	1
JEC Franklin	5	7	0	41	139	19.85	-	-
AC Parore	6	10	1	46	174	19.33	-	-
SB Styris	7	13	0	81	250	19.23	-	1
BP Martin	7	10	5	24	96	19.20	-	-
DR Tuffey	8	11	4	89*	129	18.42	-	1
TK Canning	6	10	1	53	162	18.00	-	-
MR Jefferson	5	7	0	35	124	17.71	-	-
GE Bradburn	7	11	1	63	176	17.60	-	1
GJ Hopkins	9	16	0	35	279	17.43	-	-

FIRST-CLASS AVERAGES

BATTING

	M	Inns	NO	HS	Runs	Av	100	50
GT Donaldson	5	9	0	60	149	16.55	-	1
DL Vettori	4	6	1	29	81	16.20	-	-
PJ Wiseman	10	16	4	39	193	16.08	-	-
PJ Franks	4	7	2	19	78	15.60	-	-
L Vincent	9	17	2	64	219	14.60	-	1
RG Hart	7	10	1	29	129	14.33	-	-
AJ Penn	7	12	3	27	126	14.00	-	-
MA Sigley	7	13	1	35	160	13.33	-	-
RA Lawson	7	13	0	46	162	12.46	-	-
J Hill	4	8	0	26	99	12.37	-	-
SK Warne	4	5	0	24	60	12.00	-	-
B Lee	5	6	1	39	59	11.80	-	-
RJ Turner	5	8	0	40	81	10.12	-	-

Qualification: 5 completed innings, average 10.00

BOWLING

	Overs	Mds	Runs	Wkts	Av	Best	10/m	5/m
BP Martin	237.3	52	656	37	17.72	7-33	2	5
A Sheriyar	153.4	33	409	22	18.59	6-70	-	2
PJ Franks	135.2	43	302	16	18.87	5-26	-	1
GD McGrath	150.2	52	346	18	19.22	4-33	-	-
TK Canning	281.3	105	577	30	19.23	5-47	-	2
LJ Hamilton	206.5	73	626	31	20.19	5-106	-	1
B Lee	161.4	37	486	24	20.25	5-77	-	1
GE Bradburn	176.1	55	405	20	20.25	4-37	-	-
CL Cairns	178.3	43	548	27	20.29	7-27	1	2
SB O'Connor	268.4	71	715	35	20.42	5-43	-	3
DL Vettori	202.1	60	476	22	21.63	7-87	1	2
JPD Oram	158.3	48	407	18	22.61	5-30	-	1
SB Styris	133.1	36	400	15	26.66	6-32	-	1
WC McSkimming	126.3	27	355	13	27.30	4-72	-	-
PJ Wiseman	394.4	102	988	34	29.05	7-113	1	2
JAF Yovich	176.1	27	581	20	29.05	4-19	-	-
CS Martin	264.2	74	686	23	29.82	4-54	-	-
DR Tuffey	265.5	62	763	25	30.52	4-31	-	-
SK Warne	158.2	38	519	17	30.52	4-68	-	-
CR Miller	205	53	582	19	30.63	5-55	-	1
WA Wisneski	217.5	48	621	20	31.05	5-98	-	1
KD Mills	215.2	59	622	20	31.10	3-16	-	-
JEC Franklin	115.5	15	395	12	32.91	4-41	-	-
KP Walmsley	181.2	42	568	17	33.41	4-43	-	-
DR Tuffey	265.5	62	763	22	34.68	4-31	-	-
BG K Walker	348.5	94	939	27	34.77	5-94	-	1
RG Petrie	152.5	49	375	10	37.50	3-53	-	-
J Patel	213	46	610	16	38.12	5-145	-	1
CJ Drum	158.5	53	428	11	38.90	3-34	-	-
AJ Penn	238.5	57	727	18	40.38	4-21	-	-
CJM Furlong	240.4	45	676	16	42.25	4-36	-	-
DG Sewell	137	27	453	10	45.30	3-58	-	-
AJ Redmond	187.2	41	554	12	46.16	4-72	-	-

Qualification: 10 wickets in 8 innings

The following bowlers took 10 wickets in fewer than 8 innings:-

GR Jonas	103.2	33	242	19	12.73	6-35	1	2
RJ Kirtley	105	31	289	15	19.26	5-54	-	1
MJ Mason	84.5	16	276	14	19.71	3-49	-	-
CP Schofield	117.1	36	290	12	24.16	5-107	-	1
RD King	95.2	26	251	10	25.10	4-81	-	-
AR Adams	115	30	399	15	26.60	5-64	-	1
TR Anderson	124.4	15	436	14	31.14	4-64	-	-
HJ Shaw	111	20	383	11	34.81	5-84	-	1

FIELDING

29 – AC Gilchrist (27ct, 2st); 26 – RA Young; 24 – AC Parore (21ct, 3st); 23 – GJ Hopkins (21ct, 2st), MA Sigley; 22 – RJ Turner (21ct, 1st); 21 – RG Hart (19ct, 2st); 15 – L Vincent; 14 – JAH Marshall, MS Sinclair; 13 – CJ Nevin (12ct, 1st); 12 – CM Spearman, PJ Wiseman; 11 – CB Gaffaney; 10 – MD Bailey, BB McCullum, SB Styris

INDIA

New Zealand in India
South Africa in India
India Domestic First-Class Season
India Domestic One-Day Season
First-Class Averages

NEW ZEALAND IN INDIA
By Bryan Waddle

Seldom does a touring team arrive in the subcontinent seemingly better prepared than the hosts for a cricket tour. New Zealand embarked on its three-Test tour after a semi-final place at the World Cup, followed by success, two-one over England, which gave a confidence rarely exhibited by New Zealand in India in the past.

While New Zealand enjoyed a short break after the England success, India had continued on its regular diet of meaningless one-day tournaments and at home faced a public unwilling to accept its poor showing at the World Cup. Mohammed Azharuddin paid the price that losing captains accept for defeat and made way for Sachin Tendulkar, who had missed over a month of cricket with a chronic back injury. After much private and media negotiating, Kapil Dev was appointed to take over as coach. The axe did not only fall heavily on Azharuddin: it also excised long-standing wicketkeeper Nayan Mongia.

The desire for change produced three new Test players, opener Devang Gandhi, allrounder Vijay Bhardwaj and new wicketkeeper MSK Prasad. New Zealand was able to avoid major disruption with only Roger Twose missing from the successful Test side in England. Twose, concerned about his form, made himself unavailable for the Test series, but specialising in the one-day form of the game was a certain selection for the one-dayers later in the tour.

Javagal Srinath, whose batting in the first innings of the first Test held India's head above water, while his bowling limited New Zealand's advantage.

Previous page: Anil Kumble celebrates with fellow teammates following a South African dismissal during the first Test at Mumbai.

New Zealand v. India 'A'
30 September, 1 and 2 October 1999 at Nehru Stadium, Poona
New Zealand 135 for 6 (44 overs)(NJ Astle 29, MD Bell 21)
India 'A' did not bat
Match drawn

Rain made the opening tour match little more than 44 overs' batting practice for New Zealand. Play was totally washed out on the first and third days and in conditions that offered nothing positive the New Zealand top order was delighted they had won the toss. Nathan Astle top-scored with 29 while number three Craig Spearman was the only batsman in the top six who did not achieve double figures.

New Zealand v. Indian Board Presidents XI
5, 6 and 7 October 1999 at Bakatullah Khan Stadium, Jodhpur
Indian Board Presidents XI 298 (97.3 overs) (HH Kanitkar 99, P Mullick 67) and 79 for 4 (29 overs) (GK Khoda 49)
New Zealand 444 for 5 (130 overs)(CD McMillan 168, MJ Horne 85)
Match drawn

Craig McMillan enjoyed the sun on his back as the New Zealand batsmen gained valuable practice in the lead-up to the first Test. In contrast to the Poona wash-out, Jodhpur was exceedingly hot – a fact not lost on McMillan, who blasted 168 not out from just 238 balls, including 20 fours and four sixes. Matt Horne, Craig Spearman and Adam Parore also passed 50 to provide New Zealand with all it required from the match.

Hrishikesh Kanitkar and Harbhajan Singh advanced their claims for Test selection with impressive performances, Kanitkar scoring 99 in the Board XI's first innings and Harbhajan taking four of the five wickets to fall in New Zealand's innings.

FIRST TEST
10, 11, 12, 13 and 14 October 1999 at Punjab CA Stadium, Mohali, Chandigarh

A green seamer is almost unheard of in India so New Zealand could not believe their hosts' generosity when they arrived in Mohali for the first Test with a seam-based attack. Winning the toss in those circumstances was vital for New Zealand, although captain Stephen Fleming is not noted for his mastery of calling correctly. Fleming could

The excellent Dion Nash claimed a career best 6 for 27 during the first Test at Mohali.

not conceal his delight, and also at the even more unlikely situation of damp spots on the pitch which ensured India would have a demanding first session.

At 42 for 7 at lunch, an early finish to the Test seemed inevitable and India's dismissal for 83 was only due to a ninth wicket stand of 30 between Mannava Prasad and the unorthodox stroke-play of Javagal Srinath. Dion Nash bowled superbly for a career-best 6 for 27 fully supported by Chris Cairns and Shayne O'Connor with two wickets each, ending the Indian innings in just 27 overs.

New Zealand should have had a greater lead than 132; Craig Spearman, Stephen Fleming and Nathan Astle all contributed solid innings as the pitch evened out and became increasingly more comfortable for batting. It was not so much the pitch, but in-swing movement and bounce that gave Srinath encouragement for his outstanding return of 6 for 45, and with it much of the credit for limiting New Zealand's advantage.

FIRST TEST – INDIA v. NEW ZEALAND
10, 11, 12, 13 and 14 October 1999 at Punjab CA Stadium, Mohali

INDIA

	First Innings		Second Innings	
D Gandhi	c Parore, b Nash	0	lbw b Astle	75
S Ramesh	b Nash	0	c & b Vettori	73
R Dravid	c Astle, b Cairns	1	b Vettori	144
SR Tendulkar (capt)	b O'Connor	18	not out	126
SC Ganguly	b Nash	2	not out	64
VR Bharadwaj	c Parore, b Cairns	0		
*MSK Prasad	not out	16		
SB Joshi	c Spearman, b O'Connor	0		
A Kumble	c Spearman, b Nash	7		
J Srinath	c Astle, b Nash	20		
BKV Prasad	c Fleming, b Nash	0		
	b 8, lb 5, nb 6	19	b 9, lb 7, nb 7	23
		83	**(for 3 wickets dec.)**	**505**

	First Innings				Second Innings			
	O	M	R	W	O	M	R	W
Cairns	9	4	23	2	24	3	76	–
Nash	11	3	27	6	37	16	79	–
O'Connor	7	1	20	2	18	3	73	–
Vettori					71	24	171	2
Astle					31	8	82	1
McMillan					2	0	8	–

Fall of Wickets
1–2, 2–3, 3–7, 4–10, 5–22, 6–38, 7–38, 8–53, 9–83
1–137, 2–181, 3–410

NEW ZEALAND

	First Innings		Second Innings	
MJ Horne	c Ganguly, b Srinath	6	c Ganguly, b Joshi	33
MD Bell	b Srinath	0	lbw b Srinath	7
CM Spearman	c & b Kumble	51	c Ganguly, b Joshi	35
SP Fleming (capt)	lbw b Srinath	43	c Ganguly, b Kumble	73
NJ Astle	c Kumble, b Srinath	45	c Prasad, b Srinath	34
CD McMillan	lbw b Joshi	22	c Ramesh, b Kumble	18
*AC Parore	not out	13	c Gandhi, b Kumble	7
CL Cairns	b BKV Prasad	7	not out	0
DJ Nash	c MSK Prasad, b Srinath	2		
DL Vettori	b Srinath	0		
SB O'Connor	c Gandhi, b Bharadwaj	2		
	b 5, lb 11, nb 8	24	b 24, lb 15, nb 5	44
		215	**(for 7 wickets)**	**251**

	First Innings				Second Innings			
	O	M	R	W	O	M	R	W
Srinath	22	9	45	6	31	9	63	2
BKV Prasad	19	6	56	1	16	7	24	–
Ganguly	1	0	1	–				
Kumble	18	3	49	1	41	19	42	3
Bharadwaj	14.1	4	26	1	13	3	34	–
Joshi	17	8	22	1	28	12	38	2
Tendulkar					6	2	11	–

Fall of Wickets
1–7, 2–8, 3–99, 4–156, 5–179, 6–181, 7–199, 8–207, 9–212
1–24, 2–95, 3–108, 4–186, 5–227, 6–246, 7–251

Umpires: PT Manuel & S Venkataraghavan
Toss: New Zealand
Test Debuts: D Gandhi, VR Bharadwaj, MSK Prasad

Match drawn

The improvement in conditions was more evident in India's second innings as they wiped off the deficit without loss. A sparkling partnership between Gandhi and Sadagopan Ramesh provided the foundation Tendulkar and Rahul Dravid needed to produce an emphatic 229-run third wicket stand which should have been a match-winner. Tendulkar took 215 balls to reach his hundred, having survived a close leg before decision first ball and took over three hours to achieve his half-century against some quality bowling from Nash. He was prepared to play a secondary role in the vital partnership with Dravid, who ended with 144. Daniel Vettori gained little reward for his 71 overs, taking 2 for 171, but the negative leg stump line to pitch in the bowler's footmarks limited his chances as much as it did India's capacity to score freely.

New Zealand's target of 374 in just over four sessions was demanding against Srinath and Anil Kumble, a master on a wearing pitch. However, Kumble was not the threat expected as New Zealand approached the last day needing 294 with nine wickets in hand. The leg-spinner was thwarted until the final 15 overs began and New Zealand had comfortably saved the Test. Fleming gave the innings its substance with a patient 73 from 250 balls, featuring in important match-saving partnerships with Astle and Craig McMillan before falling to the last ball of the match.

Kumble's three wickets moved him up to third on the all-time Indian list of Test-wicket-takers. However, India's inability to dismiss New Zealand in the 135 overs available said as much about the determination shown by the tourists as it did about the cautious attitude displayed by India.

New Zealand v. Ranji Trophy Champions (Karnataka)
17, 18 and 19 October 1999 at Chinnaswamy Stadium, Bangalore
New Zealand 249 for 6 (90 overs)(*SP Fleming) and 105 (47.5 overs)(NJ Astle 33, MD Bell 26)
Karnataka 269 for 9 (82 overs)(RV Bhardwaj 96) and 86 for 3 (20.4 overs)(RV Bhardwaj 33)

Not even the 12th first-class century by captain Stephen Fleming could prevent New Zealand from slumping to an embarrassing defeat in Bangalore – hardly the dress rehearsal New Zealand wanted for the second Test.

Fleming's innings and some quality bowling by Chris Cairns and Chris Drum gave New Zealand hopes of a draw after Vijay Bhardwaj had laboured over an innings of 96.

It seemed as though Karnataka's desire to give Bhardwaj a century had prevented the chance of a result but some insipid batting by New Zealand in the second innings and demanding spin bowling gave the home side the reward it deserved.

SECOND TEST
22, 23, 24 and 25 October 1999 at Green Park, Kanpur

If New Zealand was agreeably surprised at the pitch prepared for the first Test, there was nothing unexpected about the pitch in Kanpur for the second. A dry pitch, devoid of grass with worn spots on a good length greeted the teams before the toss, doubtless fair for both sides but sadly inadequate for international cricket teams. Neither side was

The precision bowling of Daniel Vettori troubled the Indian side during the second Test at Kanpur. He took 6 for 61 in 30 overs.

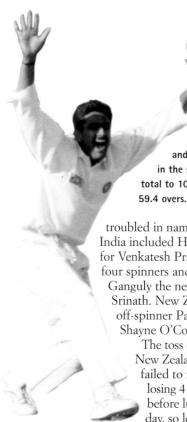

Anil Kumble pushed for the advantage on the poor pitch at Kanpur, taking 4 for 67 in the first innings and then a further 6 in the second, bringing his total to 10 for 134 from 59.4 overs.

troubled in naming their eleven. India included Harbhajan Singh for Venkatesh Prasad, opting for four spinners and giving Saurav Ganguly the new ball with Srinath. New Zealand included off-spinner Paul Wiseman for Shayne O'Connor.

The toss once again went New Zealand's way but they failed to fully capitalise, losing 4 wickets for 54 before lunch on the first day, so leaving the middle and lower order to provide a respectable total, although 256 with the batting strength New Zealand boasted was inadequate.

Kumble was the main beneficiary with 4 for 67, offering early signs that batting was going to be difficult on a pitch which was under-prepared and producing erratic bounce.

New Zealand did little to help itself when India batted as the openers raced to 162 before the first wicket fell. Some wayward bowling and missed chances allowed Gandhi and Ramesh to add 103 in the lunch to tea session, and by stumps on the second day India was only 44 behind with one wicket down. From that point the game was effectively over for New Zealand but they did not concede quite so easily over the next two days. The bowlers enjoyed spectacular success on the third morning, capturing four wickets for just 43 runs, Tendulkar and Ganguly with successive balls from Vettori, who also dispatched Dravid. All three had been troubled by Vettori, who bowled with great control on an unreliable pitch in a 30-over spell to take 6 for 61.

At 74 runs behind, New Zealand could have retrieved its position with India to bat last, but for the second time the batsmen lacked application on a demanding pitch and were knocked over for 155.

SECOND TEST – INDIA v. NEW ZEALAND
22, 23, 24 and 25 October 1999 at Green Park, Kanpur

NEW ZEALAND

	First Innings		Second Innings	
MJ Horne	c Prasad, b Ganguly	5	lbw b Kumble	3
MD Bell	lbw b Srinath	15	lbw b Kumble	7
CM Spearman	c Ramesh, b Kumble	12	(4) c Tendulkar, b Harbhajan Singh	1
SP Fleming (capt)	b Srinath	2	(5) c Dravid, b Harbhajan Singh	31
NJ Astle	lbw b Srinath	39	(6) c Bharadwaj, b Kumble	0
CD McMillan	c Ramesh, b Joshi	34	(8) lbw b Kumble	31
*AC Parore	c Dravid, b Kumble	35	b Harbhajan Singh	48
CL Cairns	c Tendulkar, b Kumble	53	(9) b Joshi	2
DJ Nash	not out	41	(3) b Kumble	0
DL Vettori	c Bharadwaj, b Harbhajan Singh	0	not out	8
PJ Wiseman	c Bharadwaj, b Kumble	0	lbw b Kumble	0
	b 7, nb 13	20	b 5, lb 9, nb 10	24
		256		**155**

	First Innings				Second Innings			
	O	M	R	W	O	M	R	W
Srinath	22	9	62	3	9	5	12	–
Ganguly	4	0	15	1	1	0	2	–
Kumble	32.5	12	67	4	26.5	6	67	6
Harbhajan Singh	17	6	30	1	15	3	33	3
Joshi	25	7	63	1	15	6	27	1
Bharadwaj	2	0	12	–				

Fall of Wickets
1–7, 2–33, 3–40, 4–50, 5–112, 6–130, 7–172, 8–255, 9–255
1–16, 2–16, 3–17, 4–28, 5–33, 6–71, 7–128, 8–138, 9–150

INDIA

	First Innings		Second Innings	
D Gandhi	c Fleming, b Astle	88	not out	31
S Ramesh	c Parore, b Astle	83	b Cairns	5
R Dravid	c Parore, b Vettori	48	lbw b Nash	1
SR Tendulkar (capt)	c Astle, b Vettori	15	not out	44
SC Ganguly	c & b Vettori	0		
VR Bharadwaj	c Spearman, b Wiseman	22		
*MSK Prasad	c Fleming, b Vettori	19		
SB Joshi	c Bell, b Vettori	19		
A Kumble	st Parore, b Vettori	5		
J Srinath	c Astle, b Wiseman	0		
Harbhajan Singh	not out	1		
	b 14, lb 6, nb 10	30	lb 1, nb 1	2
		330	(for 2 wickets)	**83**

	First Innings				Second Innings			
	O	M	R	W	O	M	R	W
Cairns	16	8	34	–	3	1	10	1
Nash	22	10	41	–	4	1	11	1
Vettori	55.1	11	127	6	6.2	2	22	–
Wiseman	29	0	81	2	5	0	39	–
Astle	26	12	27	2				

Fall of Wickets
1–162, 2–214, 3–243, 4–246, 5–255, 6–293, 7–311, 8–321, 9–326
1–5, 2–7

Umpires: DJ Harper & AV Jayaprakash
Toss: New Zealand
Test Debuts: nil

India won by eight wickets

Anil Kumble thrived in the conditions that had been skilfully prepared for him, adding six wickets to his first-innings 4 for 67, to complete a remarkable match analysis of 10 for 134 from 59.4 overs. He may well have been lucky with some of those wickets though, with umpire AV Jayaprakash – surprisingly referred to in some papers as 'Kumble's lucky umpire' after Kumble's ten wickets in an innings in Delhi – proving generous with his leg before decisions.

Cairns and Nash ensured India's victory was not completed without loss, dismissing Ramesh and Dravid, but Tendulkar smashed a blistering 44 from 39 balls to secure the win and the lead in the series.

THIRD TEST
29, 30 and 31 October, 1 and 2 November 1999 at Sardar Patel (Gujarat) Stadium, Motera Ahmedabad

Sachin Tendulkar kept the cricket world waiting for a long time for his first Test double century, but his 21st century in all, in his 71st Test match included a wide array of strokes that only Tendulkar could reveal. His batting on the first day, along with Ramesh and Dravid, had ensured India would produce a substantial total, and 331 for 3 at stumps on the first day was enough to settle the series. Tendulkar's audacious batting was not without blemish – he could have vanished in the 90s twice, offering chances New Zealand failed to accept.

On a pitch that had an element of Kanpur about it, dry and cracking, India set about confirming the series victory with confidence. Ramesh's maiden Test hundred off 155 balls was overshadowed by the Tendulkar gem. His century came off 157 balls, and his double off 319 as he proceeded to complete his longest innings in Test cricket. With New Zealand's bowlers battling in torrid conditions, Ganguly added to their misery with a restrained supporting century that secured the series.

Declaring at 583 for 7 should have been evidence enough to refute subsequent allegations that this Test was another in the long line of arranged matches. However, Tendulkar's curious refusal to enforce the follow-on when New Zealand fell for 308 aroused suspicions at his motive. There was patience and solid application about New Zealand batting, with Astle, Cairns and Fleming contributing handsomely to ensure India faced a prolonged period until after lunch on the fourth day in the field. Against an innings that contained three century-makers they fell 275 short, fully expecting to follow.

THIRD TEST – INDIA v. NEW ZEALAND
29, 30, 31 October, 1 and 2 November 1999 at Sardar Patel Stadium, Ahmedabad

INDIA

	First Innings		Second Innings	
D Gandhi	c Parore, b Cairns	6		
S Ramesh	c Spearman, b Harris	110	(1) c Parore, b Nash	16
R Dravid	c Parore, b Vettori	33	run out (Harris/Parore)	12
SR Tendulkar (capt)	c Nash, b Vettori	217	(2) b Cairns	15
SC Ganguly	c Nash, b Astle	125	(4) b Harris	53
AD Jadeja	b Vettori	13	(7) not out	12
*MSK Prasad	b Vettori	2	(5) c Parore b Astle	17
A Kumble	not out	27		
J Srinath	not out	33	(6) not out	19
BKV Prasad				
Harbhajan Singh				
	b 4, lb 7, nb 6	17	lb 4	4
	(for 7 wickets dec.)	583	(for 5 wickets dec.)	148

	First Innings				Second Innings			
	O	M	R	W	O	M	R	W
Cairns	24	5	82	1	6	1	29	1
Nash	28	6	86	–	8	0	35	1
Vettori	57	5	200	4	2	0	23	–
Astle	17	2	55	1	5	0	13	1
Harris	17	3	64	1	11	0	44	1
Wiseman	24	2	85	–				

Fall of Wickets
1–20, 2–102, 3–182, 4–463, 5–502, 6–518, 7–521
1–21, 2–35, 3–68, 4–114, 5–112

NEW ZEALAND

	First Innings		Second Innings	
GR Stead	c Ganguly, b Kumble	17	(2) c MSK Prasad, b Harbhajan Singh	78
MJ Horne	c Dravid, b Kumble	2	(1) c sub (Bharadwaj), b Kumble	41
DL Vettori	c sub (Bharadwaj), b Kumble	3		
CM Spearman	c Ramesh, b BKV Prasad	17	(3) not out	54
SP Fleming (capt)	c MSK Prasad, b Srinath	48	(5) not out	64
NJ Astle	c Ganguly, b BKV Prasad	74		
*AC Parore	lbw b Kumble	11		
CL Cairns	b Kumble	72		
CZ Harris	c Ramesh, b Srinath	12		
DJ Nash	not out	14		
PJ Wiseman	lbw b Harbhajan Singh	3		
	b 8, lb 14, nb 13	35	b 1, lb 5, nb 9	15
		308	(for 2 wickets)	252

	First Innings				Second Innings			
	O	M	R	W	O	M	R	W
Srinath	35	10	72	2	15	3	59	–
BKV Prasad	26	9	52	2	13	2	36	–
Kumble	48	21	82	5	31	16	57	1
Harbhajan Singh	30.4	8	78	1	26	8	55	1
Ganguly	2	1	2	–	4	–	20	–
Tendulkar					5	2	19	–
Dravid					1	1	–	–

Fall of Wickets
1–13, 2–29, 3–33, 4–65, 5–135, 6–166, 7–231, 8–284, 9–294
1–131, 2–131

Umpires: RE Koertzen & VK Ramaswamy
Toss: India
Test Debuts: nil

Match drawn

Tendulkar opted to bat again, suggesting his limited attack, just four specialist bowlers, was fatigued after a long stint in the field. With Tendulkar opening, the top order sought runs in rapid fashion, setting a target of 424 for victory, or of greater significance a minimum of 103 overs for New Zealand to survive. That task was never beyond the tourists, who had their best opening partnership of the series: 131 between Matt Horne and Gary Stead, who had only arrived in India two days prior to the Test as a replacement for the

Nathan Astle, whose 74 gave New Zealand's first innings some respectability in Ahmedabad.

TEST MATCH AVERAGES
India v. New Zealand

INDIA

Batting	M	Inns	NO	HS	Runs	Av	100	50
SR Tendulkar	3	6	2	217	435	108.75	2	–
SC Ganguly	3	5	1	125	244	61.00	1	2
DJ Gandhi	3	5	1	88	200	50.00	–	2
S Ramesh	3	6	0	110	287	47.83	1	2
R Dravid	3	6	0	144	239	39.83	1	–
J Srinath	3	4	2	33*	72	36.00	–	–
A Kumble	3	3	1	27*	39	19.50	–	–
MSK Prasad	3	4	1	19	54	18.00	–	–

Also batted: VR Bhardwaj (2 Tests) 0, 22; Harbhajan Singh (2 Tests) 1*; AD Jadeja (1 Test) 13, 12*; SB Joshi (2 Tests) 0, 19; BKV Prasad (2 Tests) 0

Fielding Figures
6 – SC Ganguly; 5 – MSK Prasad, S Ramesh; 3 – VR Bhardwaj, R Dravid; 2 – DJ Gandhi, A Kumble, SR Tendulkar

Bowling	Overs	Mds	Runs	Wkts	Av	Best	10m	5/inn
A Kumble	197.4	76	364	20	18.20	6–67	1	2
J Srinath	134	46	313	13	24.07	6–45	–	1
SB Joshi	85	33	150	5	30.00	2–38	–	–
Harbhajan Singh	88.4	25	196	6	32.66	3–33	–	–

Also bowled: VR Bhardwaj 29.1–7–72–1; R Dravid 1–1–0–0; SC Ganguly 12–1–40–1; BKV Prasad 74–24–168–3; SR Tendulkar 11–4–30–0

NEW ZEALAND

Batting	M	Inns	NO	HS	Runs	Av	100	50
SP Fleming	3	6	1	73	261	52.20	–	2
NJ Astle	3	5	0	74	192	38.40	–	1
CJ Spearman	3	6	1	54*	170	34.00	–	2
CL Cairns	3	5	1	72	134	33.50	–	2
AC Parore	3	5	1	48	114	28.50	–	–
DJ Nash	3	4	2	41*	57	28.50	–	–
CD McMillan	2	4	0	34	105	26.25	–	–
MJ Horne	3	6	0	41	90	15.00	–	–
MD Bell	2	4	0	15	29	7.25	–	–
DL Vettori	3	4	1	8*	11	3.66	–	–
PJ Wiseman	2	3	0	3	3	1.00	–	–

Also batted: CZ Harris (1 Test) 12; SB O'Connor (1 Test) 2

Fielding Figures
9 – AC Parore (8ct/1st); 4 – NJ Astle, CJ Spearman; 3 – SP Fleming; 2 – DJ Nash, DL Vettori; 1 – MD Bell

Bowling	Overs	Mds	Runs	Wkts	Av	Best	10m	5/inn
DJ Nash	110	36	279	8	34.87	6–27	–	1
NJ Astle	79	22	177	5	35.40	2–27	–	–
DL Vettori	191.3	42	543	12	45.25	6–127	–	1
CL Cairns	82	22	254	5	50.80	2–23	–	–

Also bowled: CZ Harris 28–3–108–2; CD McMillan 2–0–8–0; SB O'Connor 25–4–93–2; PJ Wiseman 58–12–205–2

injured Craig McMillan. Stead completed a valuable half-century and with Fleming and Spearman compiling unbeaten 50s the match ended in a tame draw with the final day a meaningless exercise. The series victory was important to India and to Tendulkar, his first back at the helm, although it might have been a more decisive victory had India shown more imagination and desire in Ahmedabad.

ONE-DAY INTERNATIONALS

The spectre of match-fixing and irregularities did not take long to surface as the quickfire series set off from Rajkot in the west to Gauhati in the east in the space of 13 days.

With the series tied at two all and the decider in Delhi, a prominent Indian official, Sunil Dev, a former vice-president of the BCCI, claimed the series was rigged and quoted a Delhi bookmaker as his source. Not surprisingly there was a string of denials but there was also plenty of evidence to arouse suspicion. That suspicion first emerged in the opening fixture at Rajkot where New Zealand savaged a strong Indian attack to reach 349 for 9 with Nathan Astle scoring 120.

India made a brilliant start to reach the 350 target, 90 for 2 after 13 overs and 171 for 3 when Dravid was out in the 27th over. Ajay Jadeja and Robin

Saurav Ganguly on his way to an unbeaten 153 not out in the third one-dayer at Gwalior against New Zealand. Ganguly's stand effectively won the game for India.

Singh had the New Zealand attack at their mercy adding 71 for the 4th wicket to leave them needing 110 off 12 and a bit overs. When Singh was out in the 38th over the wheels fell off and India lost 6 wickets for 66 in the space of nine overs.

In Hyderabad the stunning form-reversal produced another 350-plus target, after Tendulkar and Dravid had smashed a world-record second-wicket partnership of 331 runs on a stadium outfield that gave the appearance of a circus arena. Tendulkar surpassed his previous best of 143 in scoring 186 off 150 balls and ended just eight short of the highest individual one-day score created by Saeed Anwar. New Zealand could never match the class of the Indian pair and succumbed as easily as they had triumphed in Rajkot.

Surprisingly, key strike bowler Javagal Srinath was sent home before the third encounter in Gwalior. He was not needed anyway as Saurav Ganguly dissected New Zealand's attack, reaching 153 not out in India's total of 261 for 5. The real damage was done in the last ten overs with Ganguly and Robin Singh plundering 114 of their 119-run stand.

Astle and Spearman got New Zealand remarkably close with an opening stand of 99, Astle falling three short of another century. Even at 170 for 3 in the 37th over there was a faint hope of success for New Zealand but the ultimate task of scoring 23 from the last over was beyond them.

All-rounder Chris Cairns was the major influence on New Zealand winning the fourth encounter: his 80 off 111 balls and a partnership 96 with Roger Twose for the fourth wicket provided New Zealand with a respectable total of 236. India made a mess of the chase, losing in-form top-order trio Ganguly, Tendulkar and Dravid in the first seven overs for just 27. Joshi offered a spirited innings of 61 but New Zealand comfortably squared the series with one to play.

Batting first at Ferozshah Kotla in Delhi was New Zealand's undoing in the decider. With Srinath hastily recalled and newcomer Thiru Kumaran grabbing early wickets, New Zealand could not cope with the early seam movement and reached a disappointing 179 for 9. Ganguly was at his punishing best, posting 86 as India coasted to victory with six overs to spare and a three-two series win.

Match One

5 November 1999 at Municipal Stadium, Rajkot
New Zealand 349 for 9 (50 overs)(NJ Astle 120,
CM Spearman 68, RG Twose 56)
India 306 (47 overs)(AD Jadeja 95)
New Zealand won by 43 runs
Man of the Match: NJ Astle

Match Two

8 November 1999 at Lal Bahadur Shastri Stadium,
Hyderabad
India 376 for 2 (50 overs)(SR Tendulkar 186*,
R Dravid 153)
New Zealand 202 (33.1 overs)
India won by 174 runs
Man of the Match: SR Tendulkar

Match Three

11 November 1999 at Roop Singh Stadium, Gwalior
India 261 for 5 (50 overs)(SC Ganguly 153*)
New Zealand 247 for 8 (50 overs)(NJ Astle 97)
India won by 14 runs
Man of the Match: SC Ganguly

Match Four

14 November 1999 at Nehru Stadium, Guwahati
New Zealand 236 for 9 (50 overs)(CL Cairns 80)
India 188 (45.3 overs)(SB Joshi 61*)
New Zealand won by 48 runs
Man of the Match: CL Cairns

Match Five

17 November 1999 at Feroz Shah Kotla, Delhi
New Zealand 179 for 9 (50 overs)
India 181 for 3 (44 overs)(SC Ganguly 86)
India won by seven wickets
Man of the Match: SC Ganguly
Man of the Series: SC Gangul

The one-day series between India and South Africa brought
match fixing into the public eye. It was to lead to the
humiliation of Hansie Cronje.

SOUTH AFRICA IN INDIA
By Neil Manthorp

Match-fixing was to cast its deathly pall on the series in the weeks following this tour when Delhi Police released transcripts of taped telephone conversations between South African captain Hansie Cronje and bookmaker Sanjay Chawla during the five one-day internationals that followed the two-Test series.

The ghastly realisation that the transcripts were not a sick practical joke, which was how South Africans initially treated them, resulted in the formation of the King Commission of Inquiry into match-fixing. It subsequently emerged that Cronje had even spoken to four of his players before the Tests (the recorded conversations concerned the one-dayers) and offered them money to perform badly.

For Cronje's team the tour of India followed immediately after the five-Test home series against England and he was vociferous in his pronouncements on the importance of victory and the historical significance it would have.

Even before England arrived for their 14-week tour of South Africa, Cronje had said that victory in India was the most important target for the season. By the time Cronje led his team on to the tarmac of Mumbai airport, there was barely a South African supporter alive that didn't know India were unbeaten at home for 13 years.

The memory of South Africa's own foray into the spinners' den in 1996–97 was also an inspiration for

Herschelle Gibbs was to receive $15,000 for scoring below 20; in fact he scored 74.

revenge, apparently, after the tourists had suffered a crushing, morale-breaking defeat in the third Test in Kanpur with the series tied at one all. It was after that defeat that Cronje passed on an offer of $250,000 to his team to throw that final match of the tour, a one-off day/night international that was also a benefit match for Mohinder Armanath.

It was also during that Test match, when it was already patently lost on the third evening, that Cronje claims to have first taken money from a bookmaker – 'money for jam' as he told the King Commission. Unless it is proven otherwise, the version of events concerning the offers of money to underperform during this series must be accepted as they were subsequently confessed by Cronje and those of his players who were involved. The alternative is to disregard the tour and expunge it from the record books which, patently, would be an overreaction. Cronje made a 'light-hearted' offer of approximately £7,000 to Pieter Strydom to underperform in the first Test in Mumbai. He made a similar offer 'jokingly' to Jacques Kallis, Mark Boucher and Lance Klusener before the second Test in Bangalore.

Despite several players being mentioned in Cronje's illicit conversations during the one-day series, and charges being laid by the police against Cronje, Strydom, Herschelle Gibbs and Nicky Boje, the only offers that appear to have been made – and

accepted – were those of $15,000 to Gibbs and bowler Henry Williams before the fifth and final match. Gibbs was to score less than 20; he made 74. Williams was to concede more than 50; he broke down with a shoulder injury after ten deliveries. Neither was paid.

Ironically, there was some wonderful cricket played by the South Africans and, in the years to come, it may well emerge that Cronje's tragic collapse to temptation and greed inspired his team to their greatest effort.

South Africa v. Indian Board President's XI
19, 20 and 21 February 2000 at Brabourne Stadium, Mumbai

The tourists elected to bat and enjoyed the perfect start with the top five batsmen scoring between 56 and 33. Laudably, they declared overnight on 293 for 6 with a view to winning and Mornantau Hayward gave them a chance with a bruising 4 for 68 plus an injured finger which put Mohammad Azharuddin out of the match.

South Africa declared their second innings closed at 207 for 5 having dismissed the President's XI for 191 but they were thwarted the second time around by the last-wicket pair, who survived several overs surrounded by fielders. Debashish Mohanty blocked his way to a creditable 9 not out from 70 balls, steering the President's XI to 181 for 8, well short of their target of 329. Left-arm spinner Clive Eksteen took eight wickets in the match for South Africa.

FIRST TEST
24, 25 and 26 February 2000 at Wankhede Stadium, Mumbai

Sachin Tendulkar's penultimate Test as captain (this time around, anyway) started well with the toss and the obvious decision to bat first. Oddly and unpredictably, however, the steamy morning did not give way to a blaze of hot, dry sunshine and the energy-sapping humidity kept the ball swinging all day. Allan Donald, Shaun Pollock, Hansie Cronje and especially Jacques Kallis resembled Greek Orthodox priests with incense-burners as they moved the ball from left to right and back again as though it were on a string.

A mention should be made, too, of the exceptional ball maintenance and management skills of the whole South African side. They were all well aware of their good fortune and did everything in their power to preserve and protect the leather to keep it in optimum condition, either for conventional swing or, later, reverse swing.

Not too many sides take the trouble to identify their best 'polisher' and make sure the ball is relayed to him, even if he is not fielding at mid-on or mid-off. The sweatiest members of the side are strictly 'hands off' (unless catching!) in the early part of the innings but quite the opposite later on when one side of the ball needs to be soaked.

Tendulkar's 97, therefore, not only prevented the home side from being humbled before tea, but also showed – once again – why he is the best technically as well as aesthetically in the world.

The moving ball and the tumble of wickets forced him to attack anything short or full and the result was a dozen boundaries and a brace of hooked sixes that threatened to give the long-leg fieldsman a neck injury.

Particularly memorable, too, were a couple of cover drives played against outswingers that many a very good batsman would have edged, or missed. Tendulkar, though, moved the front foot further towards the pitch of the ball than most men a foot taller than him.

Ajit Agarkar helped stave off the South African attack with a first innings knock of 41 not out during the first Test.

Ajit Agarkar (41 not out) deserves mention for an effective bout of run-a-ball clubbing, mostly over backward point and cover, against an overconfident attack, but a total of 225 was all India could manage once Tendulkar was eighth man out, edging an away swinger to the wicketkeeper.

The tourists threatened to take total control of the match when Gary Kirsten (50) and Herschelle Gibbs (46) added 89 for the first wicket. Tendulkar, clearly desperate and apparently bereft of inspiration, played his last card – himself.

Bowling ripping off-spinners to the left-handers and fizzing leggies to the right-handers, he made the first breakthrough, took 3 for 10 in five overs and promptly disappeared to let Javagal Srinath (3 for 45) polish the innings off for 176 – an unexpected but potentially decisive lead of 49.

The tourists bounced straight back, though, with Allan Donald and Shaun Pollock making instant inroads in the second innings. Hansie Cronje then took three crucial wickets in the middle order including Tendulkar's with a fabulous, slow inswinger that the little maestro swished at, missed, and all but nodded at the bowler in acknowledgement.

Pollock's 4 for 24 did most towards India's slump to 113 all out but there was as much money on India as there was on South Africa with the tourists set 163 in the fourth innings. Another fine opening stand of 51 seemed to set South Africa on their way but then Anil Kumble started bowling mortar shells, explosive and dangerous enough for Nayan Mongia to summon his helmet.

Kirsten gloved a ball that would have hit him on the forehead to Mongia, Gibbs edged another snorter, Klusener sensed panic and drove loosely to mid-on while Pollock was hammered on the knee in front of middle stump by Kumble's flat topspinner. Cronje, also fidgety, ran himself out and Pieter Strydom nicked left-arm spinner Murali Karthik to slip. At 128 for 6 it seemed like India's match, with Jacques Kallis seemingly incapable of nudging even one single per over, not that his defensive skills were unappreciated as he concentrated on stopping the haemorrhage of wickets.

Cometh the hour cometh the man, however, and wicketkeeper Mark Boucher played Kumble with outrageous courage and skill, power-sweeping, pulling and late-cutting with such feisty determination it might have seemed arrogant. The South African dressing room betrayed the palpable tension as they sensed their chance of victory slipping away.

FIRST TEST – INDIA v. SOUTH AFRICA
24, 25 and 26 February 2000 at Wankhede Stadium, Bombay

INDIA

	First Innings		Second Innings	
W Jaffer	b Donald	4	c Klusener, b Pollock	6
VVS Laxman	c Eksteen, b Kallis	16	c Boucher, b Donald	0
R Dravid	b Donald	22	b Pollock	37
SR Tendulkar (capt)	c Boucher, b Kallis	97	lbw b Cronje	8
SC Ganguly	c Strydom, b Pollock	2	c Klusener, b Pollock	31
AD Jadeja	c Pollock, b Cronje	12	c Boucher, b Donald	1
*NR Mongia	c Boucher, b Cronje	0	(11) not out	19
A Kumble	run out (Donald/Boucher)	4	(7) c Boucher, b Cronje	4
AB Agarkar	not out	41	(8) c Boucher, b Cronje	3
J Srinath	b Kallis	0	(9) run out (Kallis/Cronje)	0
M Kartik	b Pollock	14	(10) c Boucher, b Pollock	2
	lb 7, w 1, nb 5	13	lb 1, nb 1	2
		225		**113**

	First Innings				Second Innings			
	O	M	R	W	O	M	R	W
Donald	16	6	23	2	14	6	23	2
Pollock	19.2	6	43	2	12.2	6	24	4
Klusener	10	0	53	–				
Kallis	16	8	30	3	5	1	21	–
Eksteen	6	0	26	–	7	3	21	–
Boje	5	0	17	–				
Cronje	7	1	26	2	12	5	23	3

Fall of Wickets
1–8, 2–39, 3–69, 4–86, 5–147, 6–151, 7–167, 8–173, 9–173
1–5, 2–13, 3–24, 4–73, 5–75, 6–80, 7–92, 8–92, 9–92

SOUTH AFRICA

	First Innings		Second Innings	
G Kirsten	b Tendulkar	50	c Mongia, b Kumble	20
HH Gibbs	c Ganguly, b Tendulkar	47	c Dravid, b Kumble	46
JH Kallis	c Laxman, b Kumble	5	not out	36
WJ Cronje (capt)	c Laxman, b Kumble	0	run out (Jaffer)	13
PC Strydom	c Agarkar, b Kartik	2	c Ganguly, b Kartik	3
L Klusener	c Laxman, b Srinath	33	c Srinath, b Kumble	1
SM Pollock	c Jadeja, b Tendulkar	0	lbw b Kumble	5
*MV Boucher	c Mongia, b Kartik	3	not out	27
N Boje	b Srinath	14		
CE Eksteen	b Srinath	4		
AA Donald	not out	1		
	b 8, lb 8, nb 1	17	b 4, lb 9	13
		176	(for 6 wickets dec.)	**164**

	First Innings				Second Innings			
	O	M	R	W	O	M	R	W
Srinath	12	2	45	3	11	3	26	–
Agarkar	7	1	15	–	4	1	15	–
Kumble	22	1	62	2	28	12	56	4
Kartik	18	6	28	2	19	5	50	1
Tendulkar	5	1	10	3	1	0	4	–

Fall of Wickets
1–90, 2–102 3–102, 4–105, 5–131, 6–131, 7–144, 8–169, 9–173
1–51, 2–76, 3–107, 4–110, 5–115, 6–128

Umpires: S Venkataraghavan & DR Shepherd
Toss: India
Test Debuts: N Boje, W Jaffer and M Kartik

South Africa won by four wickets

Kallis (36 not out from 129 balls) and Boucher (27 not out from 32, six fours) saw South Africa home, though in dramatically different styles, but they deserved their win, on the third day, as much because of the home side's insipidity – Tendulkar apart – as for their own grim, fighting qualities.

SECOND TEST
2, 3, 4, 5 and 6 March 2000 at Bangalore

A draw was all South Africa needed to create a little piece of history but they were all aware that, unless they won again, history would always record that their series win was achieved in 'only a two Test series'.

As it happened, there was none of the delicious drama of the first victory; this time, on a pitch that was clearly supposed to help the spinners but did not do so extravagantly, South Africa first bruised, then bullied and finally battered their hosts into brutal submission. Mornantau Hayward, who so terrorised the President's XI with his wide-eyed pace and aggression at the beginning of the tour, replaced spinner Clive Eksteen in the line-up, which was construed as a positive, attack-minded move.

Although protocol dictated that he bowl first change, he made the first breakthrough in his first over after India chose to bat first once again. He also drew Tendulkar (21) into an off-drive a fraction

Anil Kumble's 36 from 95 balls wasn't enough to stop the South African onslaught. Kumble was on fantastic all-round form, taking 6 for 143 from 68.4 overs.

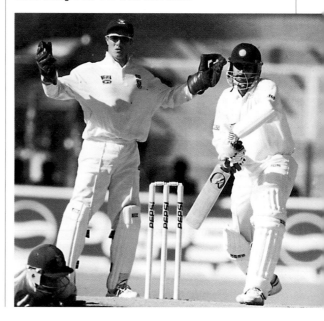

too early with a slower ball for the biggest prize of the day. All six of South Africa's bowlers enjoyed some success but Anil Kumble, who played with a straight bat and was notably happier than some of three top order to get behind the line, showed what was possible with an unbeaten 36 from 95 balls. Sadly it wasn't enough to prevent embarrassing disaster: 158 all out.

Allan Donald claimed his 295th Test wicket when he had Mohammad Azharuddin caught in the gully but, indicatively, his 1 for 31 was the worst return amongst six bowlers. Surprisingly, perhaps, the outstanding performance came from Nicky Boje, who showed fabulous control playing in this Test as the only left-arm spinner after Clive Eksteen's omission. He bowled 15 overs of well-flighted, sharply spinning deliveries and finished with 2 for 12. He is a confident cricketer at the worst of times but even he looked surprised at the lack of assertion attempted by the batsmen.

South Africa's own innings, they will justifiably claim, was as much a triumph of planning as of skill. Left-handers, they believed, held the key to nullifying Anil Kumble's threat and they all responded brilliantly. Gary Kirsten (79), nightwatchman Boje (85) and Lance Klusener (97) all played to the plan and, though it resulted in Cronje batting at number seven, the relentlessness of South Africa's approach, batting for 191.4 overs, crushed the spirit from the home side.

Jacques Kallis, too, batted himself to within a whisker of a century but, after 356 deliveries of granite-like obstinacy, Kumble had him snaffled off an inside edge at short leg for 95. Kirsten had gone the same way earlier while Klusener, frustrated and trying to reach three figures with one blow, lofted Murali Karthik to mid-off. Boje, in just his second Test, missed a 'jaffer' from Kumble and was bowled. Daryll Cullinan, the fifth man past 50, also popped one from Kumble to short leg.

Only one local man had anything to be proud of while South Africa, slowly but surely, won the series. Kumble bowled a staggering 68.4 overs for a return of 6 for 143. If anybody had been able to take wickets from the other end he, surely, would not have been forced to be both donkey and rapier for so long.

With a hopeless deficit of 321 facing their batsmen second time around, the scene was set for an individual marathon or two and a glorious rescue act. Rahul Dravid and Wasim Jaffer seemed to breathe noticeable sighs of relief after negotiating the new-ball spells of Donald, Pollock and Hayward but they made the understandable, if not forgivable, error of

The undisguised delight of Nicky Boje whose 7 for 94 deservedly won him Man of the Match at Bangalore.

relaxing completely when Boje was introduced.

Visibly buoyed by his first-innings performance, the spinner attacked with abandon (and lots of men around the bat). The result was startling and, once again, unexpected. He had both openers caught at slip and then trapped Saurav Ganguly leg before with an arm ball. From 47 for no wicket India were suddenly 71 for 3.

It was Donald's turn to claim the top prize although Tendulkar's fierce slash to cover took some catching by Herschelle Gibbs, who counted his fingers while Donald celebrated. With match and series now lost for sure, Azharuddin cut loose, crashing the seamers through the covers and flicking Boje from silly distances outside off-stump through mid-wicket. His 102, with 13 fours and two sixes, was his 22nd Test century and certainly ranked among the most meaningless.

Boje took some punishment during Azhar's charge but he returned later to claim another brace of victims – to his undisguised delight – and complete a dream Test worth 85 runs, 7 for 94 and the Man of the Match award.

Rarely have India been quite so badly beaten at home. No doubt if Tendulkar had not voluntarily decided to step down after the series he would have faced calls to do so. No more than one should expect as captain of India.

SECOND TEST – INDIA v. SOUTH AFRICA
2, 3, 4, 5 and 6 March 2000 at M Chinnaswamy Stadium, Bangalore

INDIA

	First Innings		Second Innings	
W Jaffer	c Boucher, b Hayward	13	(2) c Kallis, b Boje	23
R Dravid	c Boucher, b Cronje	17	(1) c Pollock, b Boje	18
SC Ganguly	lbw b Pollock	1	lbw b Boje	13
SR Tendulkar (capt)	c Cronje, b Hayward	21	c Gibbs, b Donald	20
M Azharuddin	c Klusener, b Donald	9	c Kirsten, b Pollock	102
M Kaif	lbw b Kallis	12	lbw b Kallis	23
*NR Mongia	lbw b Boje	20	absent ill	
A Kumble	not out	36	(7) lbw b Boje	28
N Chopra	c Pollock, b Boje	4	(8) c Boucher, b Donald	3
M Kartik	run out (Pollock/Boucher)	0	(9) c Gibbs, b Boje	2
J Srinath	c Gibbs, b Pollock	4	(10) not out	1
	b 8, lb 8, nb 5	21	b 8, lb 5, nb 4	17
		158		**250**

	First Innings				Second Innings			
	O	M	R	W	O	M	R	W
Donald	14	2	31	1	14	5	56	2
Pollock	17.3	5	26	2	24	14	40	1
Hayward	15	2	40	2	16	4	31	–
Cronje	12	6	17	1	3	0	17	–
Kallis	9	5	18	1	6	3	10	1
Boje	15	7	10	2	38	14	83	5

Fall of Wickets
1–29, 2–30, 3–58, 4–69, 5–77, 6–104, 7–114, 8–138, 9–139
1–47, 2–48, 3–71, 4–95, 5–144, 6–240, 7–244, 8–246

SOUTH AFRICA

	First Innings	
G Kirsten	c Jaffer, b Kumble	79
HH Gibbs	lbw b Kumble	4
N Boje	b Kumble	85
JH Kallis	c Jaffer, b Kumble	95
DJ Cullinan	c Jaffer, b Kumble	53
L Klusener	c Tendulkar, b Kartik	97
WJ Cronje (capt)	b Srinath	12
SM Pollock	c Tendulkar, b Kartik	1
*MV Boucher	b Kartik	15
AA Donald	lbw b Kumble	7
M Hayward	not out	0
	b 24, lb 3, nb 4	31
		479

	First Innings			
	O	M	R	W
Srinath	30	6	53	1
Kumble	68.4	15	143	6
Chopra	24	3	78	–
Kartik	50	11	123	3
Tendulkar	10	2	33	–
Ganguly	6	1	18	–
Kaif	3	0	4	–

Fall of Wickets
1–10, 2–171, 3–186, 4–271, 5–435, 6–441, 7–449, 8–468, 9–477

Umpires: AV Jayaprakash & RB Tiffin
Toss: India
Test Debuts: N Chopra and M Kaif

South Africa won by an innings and 71 runs

TEST MATCH AVERAGES
India v. South Africa

INDIA

Batting	M	Inns	NO	HS	Runs	Av	100	50
SR Tendulkar	2	4	0	97	146	36.50	–	1
A Kumble	2	4	1	36*	72	24.00	–	–
R Dravid	2	4	0	37	94	23.50	–	–
NR Mongia	2	3	1	20	39	19.50	–	–
SC Ganguly	2	4	0	31	47	11.75	–	2
W Jaffer	2	4	0	23	46	11.50	–	–
M Kartik	2	4	0	14	18	4.50	–	–
J Srinath	2	4	1	4	5	1.66	–	–

Also batted: AB Agarkar (1 Test) 41*, 3; M Azharuddin (1 Test) 9, 102; N Chopra
(1 Test) 4, 3; AD Jadeja (1 Test) 12, 1; M Kaif (1 Test) 12, 23; VVS Laxman (1 Test) 16, 0

Fielding Figures
3 – W Jaffer, VVS Laxman; 2 – SC Ganguly, NR Mongia, SR Tendulkar; 1 – AB Agarkar,
R Dravid, AD Jadeja, J Srinath

Bowling	Overs	Mds	Runs	Wkts	Av	Best	10m	5/inn
SR Tendulkar	16	3	47	3	15.66	3–10	–	–
A Kumble	118.4	28	261	12	21.75	6–143	1	–
J Srinath	53	11	124	4	31.00	3–45	–	–
M Kartik	86	22	201	6	33.50	3–123	–	–

Also bowled: AB Agarkar 11-2-30-0; N Chopra 24-3-78-0; SC Ganguly 6-1-18-0;
M Kaif 3-0-4-0

SOUTH AFRICA

Batting	M	Inns	NO	HS	Runs	Av	100	50
JH Kallis	2	3	1	95	136	68.00	–	1
G Kirsten	2	3	0	79	149	49.66	–	2
L Klusener	2	3	0	97	131	43.66	–	1
HH Gibbs	2	3	0	47	97	32.33	–	–
MV Boucher	2	3	1	27*	45	22.50	–	–
WJ Cronje	2	3	0	13	25	8.33	–	–
SM Pollock	2	3	0	5	6	2.00	–	–

Also batted: N Boje (2 Tests) 14, 85; DJ Cullinan (1 Test) 53; AA Donald (2 Tests) 1*, 7;
C E Eksteen (1 Test) 4; M Hayward (1 Test) 0*; PC Strydom (1 Test) 2, 3

Fielding Figures
10 – MV Boucher; 3 – HH Gibbs, L Klusener, SM Pollock; 1 – WJ Cronje, CE Eksteen,
JH Kallis, G Kirsten, PC Strydom

Bowling	Overs	Mds	Runs	Wkts	Av	Best	10m	5/inn
WJ Cronje	34	12	83	6	13.83	3–23	–	–
SM Pollock	73.1	31	133	9	14.77	4–24	–	–
N Boje	58	21	110	7	15.71	5–83	–	1
JH Kallis	36	17	79	5	15.80	3–30	–	–
AA Donald	58	19	133	7	19.00	2–23	–	–

Also bowled: CE Eksteen 13-3-47-0; M Hayward 31-6-71-2; L Klusener 10-0-53-0

ONE-DAY INTERNATIONALS

In the aftermath of Hansie Cronje's illegal dealings with bookmaker Sanjay Chawla, the result of the first match was placed firmly under the spotlight. South Africa's inability to defend a total of 301 for 3 at the Nehru Stadium was little short of astounding, particularly after the home side had stumbled to 101 for 4 with Tendulkar, Ganguly and Dravid all dismissed.

Mohammad Azharuddin (42) steadied the reply before Ajay Jadeja and Robin Singh launched a clinical assault in the closing overs to win the match with two deliveries to spare.

Both all-rounders tend to be slow starters but, when set, they are brutally effective. Jadeja's 92 came from 109 balls with eight fours and three late sixes while Singh's unbeaten 42 required just 43 balls.

Some badly conceived bowling and an injury to Mornantau Hayward after six overs cost South Africa the match, however, and rendered meaningless a brilliant opening stand of 235 earlier in the day between Gary Kirsten (115) and Herschelle Gibbs (111).

The match ended in farcical circumstances when Anil Kumble was awarded a four off the third ball of the final over even though Jacques Kallis had clearly fielded it inside the ropes at third man. The players charged off the field and the crowd on to it, only for the third umpire to reverse the decision and order everyone back again in order for Singh to score the winning single off the fourth ball, bowled at least ten minutes later.

India were in complete control of the second match played at the Keenan Stadium in Jamshedpur and had it not been for Hansie Cronje's 71 from 86 balls, in which he played the spinners with typical command, the result may have been even more emphatic.

Sunil Joshi finished with 4 for 38 from his ten overs and Saurav Ganguly finished the tourists off with an unbeaten 105 that included ten fours and four sixes. Rahul Dravid and Mohammad Azharuddin batted slowly, meaning victory, chasing just 200, came with just 17 balls remaining, but it was never remotely in doubt.

It was India's turn to struggle in Faridabad three days later as they limped to 248 for 8 in ideal batting conditions. Hansie Cronje used no fewer than eight bowlers and, oddly, brought himself on as first change and completed his ten overs despite conceding a weighty 69 runs.

Saurav Ganguly again looked in cracking form with 56 from 54 balls but Rahul Dravid failed to gain momentum during his 73 from 109. Gary Kirsten (93) and Cronje (66) dominated South Africa's reply but three late wickets for Tendulkar suddenly created a panic, which delayed a tense, two-wicket victory until the last ball of the penultimate over.

India's master batsmen, Mohammad Azharuddin (left) and Sachin Tendulkar.

The fourth match, in Baroda, in which India clinched the series, was even tenser as Robin Singh and wicketkeeper Saba Karim scrambled home with a single ball to spare chasing South Africa's 282 for 5.

Kirsten (72) continued his love affair with Indian pitches and Kallis weighed in with an undefeated 81 from 107 deliveries that some felt was scored more cautiously than was necessary. In a high-scoring match Anil Kumble's return of 1 for 32 displayed almost psychic cunning.

Tendulkar is almost guaranteed to score at least one century in a five-match series at home, though, and South Africa's bowlers had no answer to his velvety guillotine that brought him 122 from 141 deliveries, alternating soft touches with deadly cuts.

He was third man out at 256 and India were cruising, but the South African field tightened and Shaun Pollock struck twice more to make the Indians earn their win with sweaty palms and beating hearts. Unthinkably, South Africa almost failed to defend a total in excess of 300 for the second in the series during the final match, on the small but attractive Vidarbha Cricket Association ground in Nagpur.

Herschelle Gibbs, having apparently 'forgotten' about his agreement to score less than 20 in exchange for $15,000, smashed an extraordinary 74 off 53 balls that included a brace of boundaries off the first two balls he received. He was run out in just the 21st over, later admitting that thoughts of a world-record score were firmly in his head at the time.

Lance Klusener finally had the kind of platform on which he thrives, very nearly matching Gibbs' strike rate with an unbeaten 75 from 58 balls at the end of the innings, with South Africa closing at 320 for 7.

Tendulkar did his best to give India the flying start they needed with 93 from 89 balls and with Dravid (79) the reply reached 193 for 1 before both men were dismissed in the 28th over. The fight wasn't over, though, with Javagal Srinath's mid-innings pinch-hitting reaping 20, Robin Singh chipping 29 and Saba Karim 22. Extras mounted up to 30 and, somehow, India needed 18 off the last three overs with three wickets in hand. Two run-outs foiled their hopes and they finished ten runs short.

Match One
9 March 2000 at Nehru Stadium, Kochi
South Africa 301 for 3 (50 overs)(G Kirsten 115,
H Gibbs 111)
India 302 for 7 (49.4 overs)(AD Jadeja 92)
India won by three wickets
Man of the Match: AD Jadeja

Match Two
12 March 2000 at Keenan Stadium, Jamshedpur
South Africa 199 (47.2 overs)(WJ Cronje 71,
SB Joshi 4 for 38)
India 203 for 4 (47.1 overs)(SC Ganguly 105*)
India won by six wickets
Man of the Match: SC Ganguly

Match Three
15 March 2000 at Nahar Singh Stadium, Faridabad
India 248 for 8 (50 overs)(R Dravid 73,
SC Ganguly 56)
South Africa 251 for 8 (48 overs)(G Kirsten 93,
WJ Cronje 66,
SR Tendulkar 4 for 56)
South Africa won by two wickets
Man of the Match: WJ Cronje

Match Four
17 March 2000 at IPCL Sports Ground, Vadodara
South Africa 282 for 5 (50 overs)(JH Kallis 81*,
G Kirsten 72)
India 283 for 6 (49.5 overs)(SR Tendulkar 122,
SC Ganguly 87)
India won by four wickets
Man of the Match: SR Tendulkar

Match Five
19 March 2000 at Vidarbha CA Ground, Nagpur
South Africa 320 for 7 (50 overs)(L Klusener 75*,
HH Gibbs 74, MV Boucher 68)
India 310 (48.5 overs)(SR Tendulkar 93, R Dravid 79)
South Africa won by 10 runs
Man of the Match: L Klusener
Man of the Series: SR Tendulkar

INDIA DOMESTIC FIRST-CLASS SEASON
By Qamar Ahmed

In a season in which the master-batsman Sachin Tendulkar was so enraged with his players and the system that he gave up the national captaincy, Indian cricket was the loser in more ways than one. The poor showing in the Test series and a two-nil drubbing at home against South Africa showed that nothing seemed right with Indian cricket. This was reason enough for Tendulkar to hand over the reins to someone else. The Hansie Cronje controversy involving the Indian bookmakers was the last straw as Indian cricket went into a nosedive both on and off the field.

But there was no stopping Mumbai, who emerged as the winners of the prestigious first-class competition, the Ranji Trophy, essentially because of the performances of Sachin Tendulkar and his schoolmate Vinod Kambli. Tendulkar was so keen to play in the domestic competition that he even had the semi-finals postponed for two days so that he could play after appearing in the Dhaka Cricket Festival. His double century against Tamil Nadu steered his team into the final where his century against Hyderabad then contributed handsomely to Mumbai's 34th win in the 65-year history of the championship.

On dry and true pitches, it was a season for the batsmen. The charge was led by VVS Laxman, who scored eight centuries – a record in domestic cricket – and he achieved a remarkable aggregate of 1,415 runs, a new record for the Ranji Trophy. He also became the only batsman in its history to make two triple centuries.

Two Indian cricketers were not as keen as Tendulkar on supporting their state teams in the Ranji Trophy semi-final: Anil Kumble and Rahul Dravid both left for England, to join Leicestershire and Kent respectively, in contrast to the inspirational act by Tendulkar. Not surprisingly, Kumble and Dravid became the target of criticism and anger for their decision to skip the match against Hyderabad.

On heartbreaking pitches a couple of bowlers stood out. Off-spinner Kanwaljeet Singh of Hyderabad had a tally of 62 wickets (25.21) and the former Test spinner Venkatapathy Raju took 52 wickets in 11 matches at an average of 25.85. But, generally, the bowlers all struggled, and the runs came thick and fast. The highest team total was a massive 711 for 8 by Hyderabad against Karnataka in the semi-final, and there was a world record for endurance when Rajiv Nayyar, the Himachal Pradesh captain, batted for 1,015 minutes – nearly 17 hours – to make 271 against Jammu and Kashmir at Chamba. It was the longest innings in first-class cricket, passing the earlier record by former Pakistan opener Hanif Mohammad, who batted for 999 minutes against West Indies in the Barbados Test of 1958.

The Irani Cup match that features the previous season's Ranji Trophy winners was won by the Rest of India who beat Karnataka by an innings and 60 runs. Medium-pacer T Kumaran took 10 wickets for 86.

In the Duleep Trophy League, not a single match game produced an outright result. North Zone won the title by beating West Zone on first innings.

Generally, the season offered little in terms of talent and, once again, the statisticians found themselves loaded with calculators as batsmen gorged themselves. It has been the same for years in Indian domestic cricket: too many promises of sporting pitches, but none in sight anywhere in the country.

Rajiv Nayyar batted for almost seventeen hours for Himachal Pradash to record the longest-ever innings in first-class cricket.

INDIA DOMESTIC ONE–DAY SEASON
By Qamar Ahmed

With a superb all-round combination, North Zone annexed the Deodhar Trophy, beating West Zone by 29 runs. As in the Ranji Trophy, the batsmen dominated the bowlers but it was a tournament that produced immense interest throughout the length and breadth of the country.

North Zone warmed up for the final by scoring a seven-wicket victory against East Zone with the captain, Vikram Rathore, chipping in with a valuable 71, but it lost to Central Zone following a timid and complacent display by their batsmen. In a crucial match – a final of sorts – North Zone then defeated South Zone by seven wickets. South had done well to set a target of 278 with S Sarath, the best batsman of the competition, hitting 104. North, however, hit back through Rathore who made 106 and Ajay Jadeja who scored an unbeaten 60. It was well-contested match to bring the tournament to an end.

Sarath's other century (113) was made against Central Zone while the highest individual score of the contest was made by J Arun Kumar, who made an unbeaten 148 for South against East.

The Wills Trophy was won by Board President's XI which was led by Azharuddin. Chasing 263, Karnataka were bowled out for 165 with left-arm spinner Murali Kartik taking 4 for 17. For the President's XI Sanjay Bangar made an unbeaten 71. In the Challenger Trophy, the India Seniors defeated India 'A' by 52 runs and India 'B' by six wickets to meet India 'A' in the final. The India Seniors then piled up 320 for 9 with Laxman scoring 105 and SS Das 114. India 'A' could only manage 236 for 9 in reply.

A national inter-state tournament featuring all the teams participating in the Ranji Trophy may be a novel addition to the schedule next season. The Board has seen the commercial possibility for a national inter-state tournament with zonal winners coming to one venue to complete the competition.

Despite being caught for a duck, Mohammad Azharuddin captained Board President's XI to victory in the Wills Trophy.

FIRST-CLASS AVERAGES

BATTING

	M	Inns	NO	HS	Runs	Av	100	50
SR Tendulkar	7	14	2	233*	1008	100.08	4	2
S Sriram	9	12	0	288	1075	89.58	5	1
VVS Laxman	11	17	1	353	1432	89.50	8	–
AV Kale	7	10	1	248*	742	82.44	3	1
P Dharmani	13	18	3	305*	1194	79.60	4	5
M Azharuddin	10	15	3	200*	935	77.91	3	6
S Sharath	11	17	4	205	1012	77.84	3	6
R Nayyar	8	15	1	271	952	68.00	4	2
M Minhas	9	12	3	139	593	65.88	3	2
RR Parida	9	15	2	193	845	65.00	3	2
VG Kambli	12	17	1	154	1034	64.62	5	4
CC Williams	10	13	2	237*	698	63.45	3	1
V Shewag	12	18	1	274	1008	59.29	3	3
Sanjeev Sharma	7	10	2	117	472	59.00	2	3
R Puri	8	13	2	114*	646	58.72	3	4
D Mongia	11	15	1	179	790	56.42	3	3
SP Fleming	6	10	2	115*	428	53.50	1	2
RS Gavaskar	9	13	1	212*	637	53.08	2	3
MR Beerala	7	13	1	101*	617	51.41	1	4
AK Sharma	7	9	1	143	408	51.00	1	2
AA Muzumdar	13	20	4	131	814	50.87	1	6
LNP Reddy	5	10	2	101*	403	50.37	1	2
PV Paranjpe	9	15	2	185	652	50.15	3	2
VS Rathore	14	22	0	158	1103	50.13	3	6
SS Das	8	17	1	110	799	49.93	2	5
A Dani	12	19	1	140	892	49.55	2	6
W Jaffer	14	24	2	173*	1080	49.09	2	6
M Kaif	6	10	1	112	438	48.66	1	2
HK Badani	11	16	0	162	775	48.43	2	6
PL Mhambrey	7	8	1	117	337	48.14	1	2
SS Raul	8	14	1	120	608	46.76	2	4
Y Goud	8	14	2	182	559	46.55	1	4
RS Sodhi	12	19	1	114*	803	44.61	2	4
PJ Bhatt	8	14	0	158	619	44.21	2	3
Yuvraj Singh	7	10	1	149	397	44.11	1	2
H Jagnu	9	10	2	106*	350	43.75	1	1
Jasvir Singh	7	12	1	116	467	42.45	1	3
J Gokulakrishna	11	13	5	59*	337	42.12	–	2
V Pratap	12	19	3	100*	672	42.00	2	4
P Jai Chandra	7	12	3	72	377	41.88	–	4
DJ Gandhi	8	13	1	89	499	41.58	–	5
P Mullick	7	13	2	111*	455	41.36	2	1
M Saif	9	14	4	83	413	41.30	–	4
A Nandakishore	13	23	2	135	867	41.28	2	5
S Ramesh	6	12	1	110	454	41.27	1	3
R Dravid	7	14	0	149	577	41.21	2	1
AS Jain	8	12	0	114	490	40.83	1	4
TB Arothe	8	9	0	125	356	39.55	1	2
SH Kotak	9	15	0	126	586	39.06	2	2
Jitender Singh	10	15	0	125	575	38.33	3	1
R Shamshad	9	11	0	115	416	37.81	1	3
S Shukla	10	12	1	102	410	37.27	1	1
AA Pagnis	7	12	1	54	408	37.09	–	3
Sandeep Sharma	8	10	2	68*	290	36.25	–	3
N Haldipur	9	13	0	92	465	35.76	–	3
M Mudgal	10	11	1	74	357	35.70	–	1
Sunil Kumar	8	14	1	80	462	35.53	–	4
VST Naidu	13	22	4	93	628	34.88	–	5
SV Saravanan	6	9	0	126	314	34.88	1	1
N Chopra	9	13	3	132*	348	34.80	1	1
D Manohar	7	11	0	72	381	34.63	–	3
DV Kumar	10	17	1	93	554	34.62	–	4
PS Rawat	7	12	3	58	310	34.44	–	2
N Doru	7	11	0	105	378	34.36	1	2
GK Khoda	6	10	0	83	343	34.30	–	3
GK Pandey	9	11	0	163	377	34.27	2	–
S Verma	5	10	0	74	342	34.20	–	3
RLK Barrington	10	17	2	106	507	33.80	1	3
JR Madanagopal	12	18	0	85	601	33.38	–	6
S Oasis	5	8	0	76	262	32.75	–	2

FIRST-CLASS AVERAGES

BATTING

	M	Inns	NO	HS	Runs	Av	100	50
Rajiv Kumar	8	15	1	85	458	32.71	–	4
Jyoti P Yadav	10	13	1	70	389	32.41	–	4
RCV Kumar	8	15	0	131	482	32.13	1	1
J Arun Kumar	9	16	0	127	507	31.68	1	3
MS Dhoni	5	10	1	68*	283	31.44	–	1
SC Ganguly	6	11	1	125	313	31.30	1	2
N Ranjan	8	15	1	72	437	31.21	–	4
A S Kotecha	4	8	0	49	247	30.87	–	–
SB Joshi	10	13	1	75	370	30.83	–	3
SR Paul	11	15	1	47	431	30.78	–	–
CD Thomson	5	10	1	85*	276	30.66	–	2
AS Pathak	5	10	0	85	305	30.50	–	3
P Satwalkar	8	15	0	80	455	30.33	–	4
Parender Sharma	9	15	0	79	455	30.33	–	2
SS Dighe		7	11	0	73	330	30.00	–3
N Gaur	5	9	0	70	270	30.00	–	3
Kanwalkit Singh (JK)	5	10	1	62	267	29.66	–	2
B Akhil	7	9	0	80	267	29.66	–	2
P Das	5	8	0	69	237	29.62	–	2
D Mahajan	5	8	0	123	234	29.25	1	–
RJ Kanwat	7	10	0	143	289	28.90	1	1
Abhay Sharma	8	14	0	99	403	28.78	–	4
R Bali	5	9	0	80	259	28.77	–	1
S Bangar	8	13	0	130	370	28.46	1	1
TN Varsani	4	8	0	99	224	28.00	–	1
PK Krishnakumar	8	12	1	72	295	26.81	–	2
CM Spearman	6	10	1	56	240	26.66	–	3
S Shanker	5	9	1	52	212	26.50	–	1
RVC Prasad	5	10	0	79	262	26.20	–	1
V Sharma	5	8	0	54	207	25.87	–	1
A Ratra	8	12	2	75	257	25.70	–	2
Sangram Singh	5	9	0	103	229	25.44	1	–
RA Swaroop	8	9	0	88	228	25.33	–	2
S Mahesh	11	15	2	77	320	24.61	–	1
S Wankhade	7	11	1	139	234	23.40	1	–
Devendra Singh	8	13	2	87	249	22.63	–	1
A Vijay	12	18	0	122	402	22.33	1	1
V Dahiya	11	15	0	63	332	22.13	–	2
MM Parmar	8	13	1	71*	264	22.00	–	2
AR Kapoor	12	15	3	64	261	21.75	–	3
AA Rane	5	9	0	43	194	21.55	–	–
A Hashmi	5	10	0	58	214	21.50	–	2
PJ Rodrigues	4	8	0	68	172	21.50	–	1
MJ Horne	6	10	0	85	212	21.20	–	1
NR Mongia	9	12	2	65	208	20.80	–	1
U Chatterjee	9	9	0	34	184	20.44	–	–
R Naik	4	8	0	68	160	20.00	–	1

Qualification: 8 completed innings, average 20.00

BOWLING

	Overs	Mds	Runs	Wkts	Av	Best	10m	5/inn
S Oasis	85	31	190	10	19.00	5–27	–	1
Sarandeep Singh	273.5	71	719	37	19.43	6–41	1	3
DS Mohanty	137.4	38	361	18	20.05	5–28	–	1
BKV Prasad	238.5	72	568	28	20.28	6–60	1	3
U Chatterjee	573.1	186	1172	57	20.56	7–45	2	6
A Kuruvilla	229.2	39	660	32	20.62	5–47	–	2
RV Pawar	379.4	111	916	44	20.81	7–103	2	4
M Kartik	227.4	65	547	26	21.03	6–31	–	2
P Jain	157.1	37	431	20	21.55	5–143	–	1
J Srinath	245.3	73	578	26	22.23	6–45	–	2
PK Krishnakumar	172.4	40	558	25	22.32	6–84	–	2
PL Mhambrey	202.5	58	558	25	22.32	4–31	–	–
A Kumble	397.1	128	832	37	22.48	6–67	1	3
S Vidyuth	134.4	41	318	14	22.71	5–61	–	1
NR Odedra	290.4	75	841	37	22.72	6–52	2	3
DP Singh	195.4	48	485	21	23.09	4–44	–	–
GK Pandey	298	76	702	30	23.40	5–39	–	1

FIRST-CLASS AVERAGES

BOWLING

	Overs	Mds	Runs	Wkts	Av	Best	10m	5/inn
RS Sodhi	256.2	75	679	29	23.41	5–30	–	2
A Nehra	251.2	56	734	31	23.67	6–66	1	3
N Madhukar	163.1	37	522	22	23.72	6–109	–	–
NM Kulkarni	414	148	819	34	24.08	5–44	–	3
GN Umesh	156.2	33	470	19	24.73	5–61	–	1
Navdeep Singh	357.1	114	768	31	24.77	5–28	–	1
VN Buch	241.5	80	528	21	25.14	5–79	–	1
Kanwaljit Singh (Hyd)	644.2	167	1563	62	25.20	6–37	2	4
A Bhandari	224.4	52	688	27	25.48	5–75	–	1
SLV Raju	674	225	1535	59	26.01	6–57	–	4
V Jain	216.2	46	678	26	26.07	4–30	–	–
B Ramprakash	154.1	33	470	18	26.11	6–68	1	1
Harbhajan Singh	414	89	1207	46	26.23	5–69	–	3
S Mahesh	340.3	76	1014	38	26.68	4–37	–	–
T Kumaran	164.1	39	502	19	26.92	6–39	1	1
AW Zaidi	424.4	78	1316	48	27.41	9–45	1	3
F Ghyas	162	31	633	23	27.52	5–39	–	1
R Singh	279.5	62	803	29	27.68	7–80	–	1
S Satpathy	357.2	86	1053	38	27.71	6–86	–	3
Shakti Singh	283.2	57	777	28	27.75	6–85	1	3
SB Joshi	463.1	130	1229	44	27.93	6–48	–	2
AR Kapoor	503.2	102	1544	55	28.07	5–85	–	2
MA Khan	206	46	622	22	28.27	6–47	–	2
LR Shukla	189	53	516	18	28.55	6–86	–	1
HJ Parsana	174.1	38	517	18	28.72	6–68	–	1
DJ Nash	133.3	43	347	12	28.91	6–27	–	1
SS Raul	214.5	58	500	17	29.41	3–37	–	–
NP Singh	325.3	82	971	33	29.42	5–69	–	2
IR Siddiqui	246.4	69	752	25	30.08	8–72	1	2
H Singh	130.4	31	408	13	31.38	4–63	–	–
Z Khan	394.5	77	1321	42	31.45	5–43	1	3
P Satwalkar	143	37	416	13	32.00	4–41	–	–
MS Kadri	114.5	30	355	11	32.27	6–46	–	1
WP Majumdar	132.1	29	424	13	32.61	4–4	–	–
AR Yalvigi	200	54	596	18	33.11	5–43	–	1
S Sriram	172.2	50	399	12	33.25	2–4	–	–
AP Katti	136.4	36	366	11	33.27	4–29	–	–
J Gokulakrishna	289	70	859	25	34.36	5–42	–	1
YS Ranganath	228.3	46	528	15	35.20	5–69	–	1
S Sriwastava	199	36	599	17	35.23	6–82	–	1
SR Saxena	227.1	40	715	20	35.75	5–56	–	1
K Parida	277	56	790	22	35.90	6–84	–	1
D Ganesh	330.4	59	1051	29	36.24	5–115	–	1
P Thakur	219.4	68	523	14	37.35	3–32	–	–
RA Swaroop	312.5	72	748	20	37.40	4–161	–	–
Sanjeev Sharma	221	38	637	17	37.47	4–56	–	–
J Zaman	180.5	46	489	13	37.61	3–45	–	–
KN Ananthapad-manabhan	129.4	27	380	10	38.00	4–42	–	–
RB Patel	270	66	695	18	38.61	3–66	–	–
Sukhbinder Singh	225.4	44	663	17	39.00	5–113	–	2
RK Panta	123.1	12	513	13	39.46	6–103	–	1
A Barick	174	32	593	15	39.53	4–83	–	–
WD Balaji Rao	167.1	21	485	12	40.41	5–56	–	1
M Raza	313.5	59	836	23	40.69	5–49	–	1
Dhiraj Kumar	221.2	31	756	18	42.00	6–167	–	1
Sandeep Sharma	236.4	52	683	16	42.68	3–33	–	–
RJ Kanwat	155.4	26	497	11	45.18	4–65	–	–
V Shewag	152.4	24	498	10	49.80	4–87	–	–
N Chopra	234	60	613	12	51.08	3–65	–	–
Z Hussain	170	33	514	10	51.40	5–36	–	1
DN Chudasama	164	18	530	10	53.00	5–67	–	1
R Sanghvi	196	47	540	10	54.10	2–27	–	–

Qualification: 10 wickets in 8 innings

FIRST-CLASS AVERAGES

The following bowlers took 10 wickets in fewer than 8 innings:–

	Overs	Mds	Runs	Wkts	Av	Best	10m	5/inn
M Diwalkar	98.1	19	331	17	17.42	7–47	1	2
RR Powar	82.5	21	231	13	17.76	5–46	–	1
R Menon	90.2	21	253	14	18.07	6–70	–	2
MV Sane	94.4	28	218	12	18.16	7–83	1	1
Gagandeep Singh	129	39	332	18	18.44	5–49	–	1
G Dutta	96.3	22	259	14	18.50	8–23	1	1
AB Agarkar	91.4	17	222	12	18.50	4–83	–	–
H Wadekar	73.4	5	222	12	18.50	4–47	–	–
S Oasis	85	31	190	10	19.00	5–27	–	1
J Das (Orissa)	107.3	33	325	17	19.11	5–31	–	1
A Aware	51.4	8	222	11	20.18	6–97	–	2
A Piprode	81.5	23	212	10	21.20	3–80	–	–
MS Kumar	91	24	216	10	21.60	5–21	–	1
SK Vadiaraj	81.3	20	242	11	22.00	4–59	–	–
Avinash Kumar	244.3	55	485	22	22.04	6–43	1	2
KVP Rao	109	29	237	10	23.70	5–65	–	1
M Aslam	109.5	18	314	13	24.15	4–35	–	–
HS Sodhi	91	20	252	10	25.20	4–41	–	–
PV Gandhe	161.5	26	442	17	26.00	8–88	–	1
ND Hirwani	196	55	446	16	27.87	4–90	–	–
RK Chauhan	215	69	377	13	29.00	5–99	–	1
SH Jakati	121	26	360	12	30.00	3–41	–	–
FU Bambhaniya	91.5	20	300	10	30.00	5–54	–	1
Vijay Sharma	105	20	213	10	31.20	4–63	–	–
O Singh	150.3	22	456	13	35.07	5–81	–	1
MS Kulkarni	131	33	373	10	37.30	3–86	–	–
DL Vettori	235.3	52	645	16	40.31	6–127	–	1
Surendra Singh	171.1	31	446	11	40.54	4–67	–	–
Vikash Kumar	157	36	492	12	41.00	5–98	–	1
S Kulkarni	117	11	435	10	43.50	4–58	–	–
A Sukla	114.2	10	443	10	44.30	5–182	–	1
MV Rao	198	45	591	12	49.25	3–73	–	–

FIELDING FIGURES

33 – SR Paul (29ct, 4st); 30 – V Dahiya (28ct, 2st); 28 – SN Shiraguppi (22ct, 6st); 27 – VST Naidu (26ct, 1st); 24 – NR Mongia (22ct, 2st); 23 – MM Parmar (19ct, 4st); 21 – A Nandakishore; 20 – RB Jhalani (16ct, 4st), V Rathore; 19 – S Wankhade (17ct, 2st); 18 – SS Dighe (15ct, 3st), AA Mazumdar; 17 – W Jaffer, SS Karim (14ct, 3st), D Mongia; 16 – Dharmani, H Jagnu (13ct, 3st), VB Kamaruddin (12ct, 4st), M Mudgal (14ct. 2st); 15 – MS Dhoni (12ct, 3st), AC Parore (14ct, 1st), SLV Raju; 14 – B Akhil, MV Boucher, SS Das, Y Mohanty (11ct, 3st), AA Rane (13ct, 2st), A Ratra (11ct, 3st), VR Samant (12ct, 2st), R Sheikh (12ct, 2st), A Vijay; 13 – J Gokulakrishna, SM Kondhakar (12ct, 1st); 12 – HK Badani, D Dasgupta (9ct, 3st), NM Kulkarni, J Madanagopal, AA Pagnis, PH Patel (11ct, 1st), LNP Reddy; 11 – J Arun Kumar; 10 – S Dalal, SC Ganguly, N Haldipur, Kanwaljit Singh (Hyd), VVS Laxman, Sarabjit Singh, S Shanker, Youraj Singh (7ct, 3st)

PAKISTAN

Sri Lanka in Pakistan
Pakistan Domestic First-Class Season
Pakistan Domestic One-Day Season
First-Class Averages

SRI LANKA IN PAKISTAN
By Qamar Ahmed

Pakistan had come back home after a gruelling three-match Test series against Australia where they lost three–nil and, later, the Carlton & United one-day series to boot. They were hoping to salvage some pride against Sri Lanka at home, but there were more heartaches in store for them. Pakistan's rather weird policy of drastic changes to the make-up of the team and the captaincy bounced back on them embarrassingly as Sri Lanka had a clean sweep in the one-day series and also beat Pakistan in the first two Tests to win the series two–one. This was Sri Lanka's second win in a row in Pakistan after their 1995–96 success, and Pakistan's third defeat at home following visits by Australia and Zimbabwe.

Wasim Akram was replaced by Saeed Anwar as captain after Moin Khan had declined to lead the side. Anwar performed poorly as captain and was then injured after colliding with the umpire Mohammad Nazir in the second Test at Peshawar. Moin Khan then accepted the challenge and he immediately struck a chord with the team and won the final Test. By then it was too little too late.

Pakistan were also handicapped by the fact that their star bowler, Wasim Akram, suffered from a groin injury and could bowl only 13 deliveries in the first Test and was ruled out for the remaining two. Younis Khan, from Mardan in the North West Frontier, made a memorable debut in the first Test when he scored 107 in difficult circumstances while Inzamam's 86 and 138 in the final Test at Karachi were the highlights of Pakistan's inconsistent batting throughout the series. Waqar Younis, however, bowled superbly to finish with 13 victims, taking his tally to 292 Test wickets.

Meanwhile, Muttiah Muralitharan took 26 wickets in the three-match series – a record for a Sri Lankan – and he became the first bowler to pass 25 wickets in a series in Pakistan.

During the series Intikhab Alam was replaced by Javed Miandad as team coach. This created a huge controversy as Intikhab retaliated by criticising the Pakistan Cricket Board. 'I have been humiliated and my pride has been hurt,' he complained. 'My departure was announced in the middle of the series, which was very unceremonious for someone who has served the game and country for more than 35 years.'

Previous page: Atiq looks delighted as Youhana takes the catch to get rid of Arnold during the second Test at Peshawar.

Aravinda de Silva hitting a boundary off Saqlain Mushtaq during his 112 run knock against Pakistan on the second day of the first Test at Rawalpindi.

In all three one-day games that preceded the Test series, Saeed Anwar won the toss and put the visitors in: decisions that backfired on each occasion as Sri Lanka won the first match by 29 runs, the second by 34 runs and the final at Lahore by 104 runs. In the first game at Karachi, Sri Lanka notched up a massive 274 for 8 with the help of an unbeaten 119, with 7 fours by Marven Atapattu after Sanath Jayasuriya, opening the innings, making 54. Pakistan were given a 71 run first-wicket stand by Saeed Anwar and Aamir Sohail (now back in the fold) but they failed to capitalise and were dismissed for 245 in the 48th over. Younis Khan with 46 off 41 balls late in the order raised some hope, but it was in vain as Muttiah Muralitharan bagged 3 for 31 and Chaminda Vaas 2 for 32.

At Gujranwala, Pakistan failed to rise to the occasion as they were bowled out for 229 in the 46th over chasing 264 to win. Yousuf Youhana made 68 and Wasim Akram 34 off 29 balls with 4 sixes. For Sri Lanka, who made 263 for 6, Jayasuriya hit 65 off 78 balls with 9 fours and Atapattu 57. Vaas and Russel Arnold with 34 and 36 respectively rallied the late order.

In the third and final match at Lahore Pakistan fared even worse as they lost by 104 runs, giving Sri Lanka a clean sweep. After making 241 for 9, Sri Lanka bowled Pakistan out for 137 in the 40th over. The good work done by Wasim Akram (3–38) and Abdur Razzaq (4–36) was not supported by a weakened Pakistan batting line-up. Atapattu made 77 off 91 balls in Sri Lankan innings and was named Man of the Series. On their previous tour to Pakistan in 1995–96, Sri Lanka had won by an identical margin.

FIRST TEST
26, 27, 28 and 29 February and 1 March 2000 at Rawalpindi

Pakistan were unable to recover from the shock of being dismissed for 182 in the first innings – their lowest total against Sri Lanka at home – and lost the Test by two wickets at the 'Pindi Cricket Stadium. Having lost the toss and asked to bat, they were devastated on a seaming wicket by Chaminda Vaas and Pramodya Wickremasinghe. Five of the batsmen were caught either by the slips or the 'keeper, and their last seven wickets could contribute only 57 runs. There was little sign of the devastation to follow as Saeed Anwar and Wajahatullah Wasti put on 44 runs for the first wicket but, thereafter, only Inzamam-ul-Haq with 44 and Yousuf Youhana with 32 could provide some muscle to the batting.

Sri Lanka replied with 353, thanks to Aravinda de Silva's eighteenth Test century and his eighth against Pakistan. De Silva scored 112 and with Arjuna Ranatunga (49) he added 129 for the fifth wicket as Sri Lanka took a 108-run lead the second day. Late in the innings Vaas hit 53 useful runs to add 51 for the ninth wicket with Zoysa and Pakistan were soon trailing by 171 runs as they struggled to close the third day on 154 for 4. Younis Khan – aged only 22 – revived Pakistan's second innings on the fourth as he grafted a maiden Test century (107) on his debut. With Wasim Akram (79) he added a record 145 for the ninth wicket and became only the seventh Pakistani to make a century on debut. Out for 390, Pakistan left Sri Lanka a target of 220 to win on the final day.

Wasim Akram receiving treatment from Pakistani physio Riaz Ahmad during a drinks break. The other batsman with the bottle of water is Younis Khan. Both created a record partnership 9th wicket stand of 145.

FIRST TEST – PAKISTAN v. SRI LANKA
26, 27, 28, 29 February and 1 March 2000 at Rawalpindi Cricket Stadium

PAKISTAN

	First Innings		Second Innings	
Saeed Anwar (capt)	c Arnold, b Vaas	23	b Vaas	84
Wajahatullah Wasti	c Arnold, b Wickremasinghe	17	c Wickremasinghe, b Zoysa	1
Aamir Sohail	c Kaluwitharana, b Vaas	0	c Jayawardene, b Muralitharan	24
Inzamam-ul-Haq	c Arnold, b Wickremasinghe	44	c sub (UDU Chandana), b Zoysa	20
Yousuf Youhana	c Arnold, b Muralitharan	32	c Jayawardene, b Muralitharan	18
Younis Khan	lbw b Wickremasinghe	12	(7) c de Silva, b Muralitharan	107
*Moin Khan	c Kaluwitharana, b Wickremasinghe	21	(8) lbw b Vaas	10
Wasim Akram	c Vaas, b Muralitharan	0	(10) c Jayawardene, b Muralitharan	79
Abdur Razzaq	st Kaluwitharana, b Muralitharan	9	c Kaluwitharana, b Zoysa	3
Saqlain Mushtaq	not out	3	(11) not out	2
Waqar Younis	c Ranatunga, b Muralitharan	0	(6) c & b Vaas	8
	lb 9, nb 12	21	b 4, lb 12, nb 18	34
		182		**390**

	First Innings				Second Innings			
	O	M	R	W	O	M	R	W
Vaas	20	4	54	2	38	7	85	3
Zoysa	13	2	37	-	26	8	64	3
Wickremasinghe	20	5	37	4	24	4	76	-
Muralitharan	20.5	7	45	4	54.1	14	127	4
Arnold					1	1	0	-
de Silva					6	2	10	-
Jayasuriya					3	0	12	-

Fall of Wickets
1-44, 2-46, 3-59, 4-125, 5-135, 6-166, 7-167, 8-168, 9-179
1-9, 2-72, 3-136, 4-148, 5-169, 6-189, 7-224, 8-236, 9-381

SRI LANKA

	First Innings		Second Innings	
MS Atapattu	c Wajahatullah Wasti, b Waqar Younis	8	c Saqlain Mushtaq, b Waqar Younis	10
ST Jayasuriya (capt)	c Moin Khan, b Waqar Younis	17	c Aamir Sohail, b Abdur Razzaq	56
RP Arnold	c Moin Khan, b Waqar Younis	26	c Saqlain Mushtaq, b Waqar Younis	6
PA de Silva	lbw b Saqlain Mushtaq	112	c Moin Khan, b Abdur Razzaq	21
DPMD Jayawardene	run out (Younis Khan)	42	c Yousuf Youhana, b Saqlain Mushtaq	35
A Ranatunga	b Abdur Razzaq	49	not out	29
*RS Kaluwitharana	lbw b Abdur Razzaq	0	not out	36
WPUJC Vaas	not out	53	run out (Saqlain Mushtaq)	0
GP Wickremasinghe	c sub (Shahid Afridi), b Saqlain Mushtaq	0	(10) b Abdur Razzaq	0
N Zoysa	c Yousuf Youhana, b Waqar Younis	26	(9) c Wajahatullah Wasti, b Abdur Razzaq	13
M Muralitharan	c Moin Khan, b Aamir Sohail	7		
	b2, lb8, nb3	13	b1, lb11, nb2	14
		353	**(for 8 wickets)**	**220**

	First Innings				Second Innings			
	O	M	R	W	O	M	R	W
Wasim Akram	2.1	0	8	-				
Waqar Younis	30	3	103	4	24.5	6	78	2
Abdur Razzaq	32.5	7	99	2	26	6	56	4
Saqlain Mushtaq	34	9	78	2	33	7	74	1
Aamir Sohail	23.2	5	55	1				
Wajahatullah Wasti	1	1	0	-				

Fall of Wickets
1-9, 2-38, 3-69, 4-117, 5-246, 6-246, 7-280, 8-280, 9-331
1-16, 2-34, 3-73, 4-116, 5-144, 6-152, 7-177, 8-177

In the second innings A Ranatunga retired hurt (8*) at 145-6 and resumed at 177-8

Umpires: Athar Zaidi & DL Orchard
Toss: Sri Lanka
Test Debut: Younis Khan

Sri Lanka won by two wickets

Sri Lanka started the morning on 11–0, and lost three wickets in the pre-lunch session. However, skipper Jayasuriya made 56, his 15th fifty in Tests and later Kaluwitharana and Ranatunga fought stubbornly to add 43. Ranatunga was forced to retire hurt with a bruised thumb with 74 still required to win and when they lost four quick wickets after tea Sri Lanka were reduced to 177 for 8. Bravely, Ranatunga returned to the crease and steered his country past the target.

SECOND TEST
5, 6, 7, 8 and 9 March 2000 at Peshawar

With a 57-run win at the Arbab Niaz Stadium, Sri Lanka clinched the series. Muttiah Muralitharan took 10 wickets for 148 runs in the match to destroy Pakistan's batting and complete Sri Lanka's second series victory in Pakistan. It was Pakistan's third defeat in a row in a home Test.

After being put in, Sri Lanka were bowled out for 268 on the second day as Shoaib Akhtar – controversially restored to the team – captured 5 for 75. His first three wickets cost only 21 runs, but Atapattu held sway for nearly six hours with a defiant 75. Jayasuriya (30), de Silva (33) and Jayawardena (36) also played well as Shoaib – trying to prove a point, no doubt – bowled with fire and venom.

At 67 for 1 on the second day, Pakistan were well poised to make a sizeable score in reply, but their batting failed to come to terms with the guile of off-

Saeed Anwar made 74 against Sri Lanka on the third day of the second Test at Peshawar.

SECOND TEST – PAKISTAN v. SRI LANKA
5, 6, 7, 8 and 9 March 2000 at Arbab Niaz Stadium, Peshawar

SRI LANKA

	First Innings		Second Innings	
MS Atpattu	b Shoaib Akhtar	75	c Aamir Sohail, b Arshad Khan	29
ST Jayasuriya (capt)	b Shoaib Akhtar	30	lbw b Waqar Younis	6
RP Arnold	c Atiq-uz-Zaman	2	c Yousuf Youhana, b Arshad Khan	99
PA de Silva	lbw b Aamir Sohail	33	(7) c Waqar Younis, b Aamir Sohail	31
DPMD Jayawardene	c Shahid Afridi, b Aamir Sohail	36	(4) lbw b Waqar Younis	10
TM Dilshan	b Arshad Khan	13	(5) c Atiq-uz-Zaman, b Aamir Sohail	0
*RS Kaluwitharana	c Atiq-uz-Zaman, b Shoaib Akhtar	4	(6) lbw b Shoaib Akhtar	0
WPUJC Vaas	not out	17	c Yousuf Youhana, b Arshad Khan	5
GP Wickremasinghe	b Shoaib Akhtar	0	(10) c Younis Khan, b Shoaib Akhtar	5
KR Pushpakumara	c Atiq-uz-Zaman, b Abdur Razzaq	7	(9) c Atiq-uz-Zaman, b Waqar Younis	14
M Muralitharan	b Shoaib Akhtar	22	not out	2
	b 1, lb 8, nb 20	29	b 4, lb 7, nb 5	16
		268		224

	First Innings				Second Innings			
	O	M	R	W	O	M	R	W
Waqar Younis	5	0	20	-	16	3	38	3
Shoaib Akhtar	24.3	3	75	5	12.2	1	47	2
Arshad Khan	45	18	70	1	20	3	81	3
Abdur Razzaq	17	6	39	2	17	9	27	-
Shahid Afridi	7	0	31	-				
Aamir Sohail	11	1	24	2	8	3	20	2

Fall of Wickets
1-58, 2-67, 3-121, 4-186, 5-207, 6-209, 7-221, 8-223, 9-241
1-7, 2-69, 3-90, 4-108, 5-109, 6-188, 7-201, 8-206, 9-222

PAKISTAN

	First Innings		Second Innings	
Saeed Anwar (capt)	c Muralitharan, b Jayasuriya	74	c Wickremasinghe, b Vaas	36
Aamir Sohail	c de Silva, b Jayawardene	22	(4) c Jayawardene, b Jayasuriya	0
Yousuf Youhana	c Kaluwitharana, b Vaas	8	(5) lbw b Muralitharan	88
Inzamam-ul-Haq	not out	58	(3) c Jayawardene, b Muralitharan	9
Younis Khan	c Jayawardene, b Muralitharan	8	(6) c Arnold b Vaas	6
Shahid Afridi	c Arnold, b Vaas	4	(2) st Kaluwitharana, b Muralitharan	31
Abdur Razzaq	c Jayawardene, b Muralitharan	0	(7) lbw b Muralitharan	5
*Atiq-uz-Zaman	c Kaluwitharana, b Wickremasinghe	1	b Vaas	25
Waqar Younis	c Jayawardene, b Muralitharan	3	c Jayawardene, b Muralitharan	0
Arshad Khan	lbw b Muralitharan	0	c Jayawardene, b Muralitharan	0
Shoaib Akhtar	c Atapattu, b Wickremasinghe	5	not out	4
	lb 1, w 1, nb 14	16	b 9, lb 6, nb 12	27
		199		236

	First Innings				Second Innings			
	O	M	R	W	O	M	R	W
Vaas	20	3	44	2	16	3	69	3
Pushpakumara	11	2	36	-	10	1	31	-
Muralitharan	39	10	77	4	27.1	4	61	6
Jayawardene	5	3	7	1				
Jayasuriya	3	1	9	1	5	1	28	1
Wickremasinghe	10.5	4	25	2	12	5	22	-

Fall of Wickets
1-54, 2-82, 3-137, 4-154, 5-165, 6-166, 7-174, 8-177, 9-177
1-59, 2-77, 3-82, 4-103, 5-145, 6-208, 7-222, 8-222, 9-226

Umpires: Mohammad Nazir & JH Hampshire
Toss: Pakistan
Test Debut: Atiq-uz-Zaman

Sri Lanka won by 57 runs

spinner Muralitharan. In his post-lunch spell, Murali took 4 for 23 in eleven overs to finish with 4 for 77 as Pakistan were bundled out for 199. The last seven wickets had fallen for only 46 runs in the second session.

By the third evening, Sri Lanka had reached 129 for 5 and were already quite happy with a first innings lead of 198. They were finally dismissed for 224 at the stroke of lunch on the fourth day – with Russel Arnold missing his century by one run – to leave Pakistan an unlikely 294 to win.

They suffered a terrible start as their captain Saeed Anwar collided with umpire Mohammad Nazir while taking a single and injured his neck. Muralitharan began to chip away, picking up five wickets on the fourth day and setting up the victory that was clinched within only nine deliveries of the fifth.

THIRD TEST
12, 13, 15 and 16 March 2000 at Karachi

Pakistan completed an extraordinary turn-around to win the third and final Test by the emphatic margin of 222 runs with a day and 29 overs to spare. In the absence of the injured captain Saeed Anwar, Pakistan were led by their wicketkeeper Moin Khan, Javed Miandad having once again taken over as team coach. Anwar immediately declared that he would not like the job again.

Pakistan's victory came too late as Sri Lanka had already won the series, but they succeeded in keeping their unbeaten record in 34 Tests at the venue.

Put in to bat, Pakistan made 256 in the first innings with the help of two very fine innings by Shahid Afridi (74) and Inzamam-ul-Haq (86). Muralitharan claimed 4 more wickets for 89. Sri Lanka were dismissed for 227 as Arnold (48) and Kaluwitharana (42) made useful contributions but the tourists batting failed miserably against Waqar Younis and Shoaib Akhtar in particular. Pakistan capitalised on their marginal 29-run lead through some fine batting in the second innings as they mustered 421. Inzamam's 138, his ninth Test century with 17 fours and a six, was a brilliant innings which took him past 4,000 runs, while Younis Khan with 61 also impressed to add to his debut century in the first Test. Moin Khan thumped a blistering 70.

Sri Lanka were dismissed for 228 in only 46 overs. Jayasuriya fell in the seventh over to Waqar Younis, and then the wickets tumbled dramatically. Shahid Afridi, with 3 for 50, was Pakistan's most successful bowler.

ONE-DAY INTERNATIONALS

Match One
13 February 2000 at National Stadium, Karachi
Sri Lanka 274 for 8 (50 overs)(MS Atapattu 119*, ST Jayasuriya 54)
Pakistan 245 (48 overs)
Sri Lanka won by 29 runs
Man of the Match: MS Atapattu

Match Two
16 February 2000 at Jinnah Stadium, Gujranwala
Sri Lanka 263 for 6 (50 overs)(ST Jayasuriya 65, MS Atapattu 57)
Pakistan 229 (45.1 overs)(Yousuf Youhana 68)
Sri Lanka won by 34 runs
Man of the Match: ST Jayasuriya

Match Three
19 February 2000 at Gaddafi Stadium, Lahore
Sri Lanka 241 for 9 (50 overs) (MS Atapattu 77, Abdur Razzaq 4 for 36)
Pakistan 137 (39.3 overs)
Sri Lanka won by 104 runs
Man of the Match: MS Atapattu

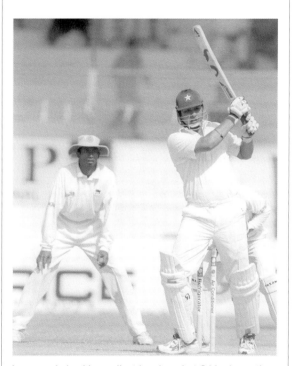

Inzamam during his excellent knock against Sri Lanka on the third day of the third Test at Karachi. He ran up an impressive 138 before being caught by Wickremasinghe.

THIRD TEST – PAKISTAN v. SRI LANKA
12, 13, 14 and 15 March 2000 at National Stadium, Karachi

PAKISTAN

	First Innings		Second Innings	
Naved Ashraf	b Pushpakumara	5	lbw b Muralitharan	27
Shahid Afridi	c Wickremasinghe, b Muralitharan	74	b Pushpakumara	34
Ijaz Ahmed	lbw b Vaas	7	c Dilshan, b Muralitharan	3
Inzamam-ul-Haq	run out (Pushpakumara/ Muralitharan)	86	c Wickremasinghe, b Muralitharan	138
Yousuf Youhana	c Wickremasinghe, b Muralitharan	7	(6) c Kaluwitharana, b Pushpakumara	11
Younis Khan	lbw b Vaas	7	(7) c Kaluwitharana, b Wickremasinghe	61
*Moin Khan	c de Saram b Wickremasinghe	6	(8) c Arnold, b Pushpakumara	70
Waqar Younis	c Dilshan, b Muralitharan	16	(9) c Dilshan, b Muralitharan	39
Shoaib Akhtar	c Pushpakumara, b Muralitharan	26	(5) lbw b Vaas	0
Irfan Fazil	not out	1	c Jayasuriya, b Pushpakumara	3
Mohammad Akram	c Atapattu, b Jayasuriya	0	not out	1
	lb 2, nb 19	21	lb 16, nb 18	34
		256		**421**

	First innings				Second innings			
	O	M	R	W	O	M	R	W
Vaas	18	4	49	2	34	8	107	1
Pushpakumara	16	4	37	1	20.5	3	66	4
Wickremasinghe	13	2	64	1	26	6	82	1
Muralitharan	32	11	89	4	40	6	107	4
Jayasuriya	6.5	2	15	1	9	1	28	–
Arnold					4	0	15	–

Fall of Wickets
1-38, 2-80, 3-111, 4-135, 5-152, 6-164, 7-197, 8-247, 9-255
1-70, 2-70, 3-84, 4-106, 5-159, 6-283, 7-320, 8-208, 9-419

SRI LANKA

	First Innings		Second Innings	
MS Atapattu	lbw b Waqar Younis	3	c Moin Khan, b Mohammad Akram	23
ST Jayasuriya (capt)	c Ijaz Ahmed, b Shoaib Akhtar	24	lbw b Waqar Younis	10
RP Arnold	c Younis Khan, b Irfan Fazil	48	c Moin Khan, b Waqar Younis	8
DPMD Jayawardene	c Moin Khan, b Waqar Younis	1	b Irfan Fazil	29
TM Dilshan	c Moin Khan, b Shahid Afridi	31	run out (Yousuf Youhana)	5
*RS Kaluwitharana	run out (Naved Ashraf)	42	b Shoaib Akhtar	33
IS de Saram	c Waqar Younis, b Shahid Afridi	5	lbw b Shahid Afridi	18
WPUJC Vaas	not out	25	c Shoaib Akhtar, b Shahid Afridi	28
KR Pushpakumara	c Moin Khan, b Shoaib Akhtar	1	c Irfan Fazil, b Shahid Afridi	44
GP Wickremasinghe	b Shoaib Akhtar	0	run out (sub Imran Nazir)	0
M Muralitharan	c Irfan Fazil, b Mohammad Akram	14	not out	5
	b 10, lb 2, nb 21	33	b 1, lb 7, nb 17	25
		227		**228**

	First innings				Second innings			
	O	M	R	W	O	M	R	W
Waqar Younis	10	2	39	2	11	4	32	2
Shoaib Akhtar	18	5	52	3	13	1	64	1
Mohammad Akram	14.1	2	49	1	10	1	44	1
Irfan Fazil	4	0	35	1	4	0	30	1
Shahid Afridi	12	3	40	2	8	1	50	3

Fall of Wickets
1-17, 2-41, 3-46, 4-100, 5-154, 6-164, 7-188, 8-206, 9-206
1-27, 2-41, 3-41, 4-59, 5-86, 6-121, 7-145, 8-191, 9-199

Umpires: Riazuddin & RB Tiffin
Toss: Sri Lanka
Test Debut: Irfan Fazil

Pakistan won by 222 runs

TEST MATCH AVERAGES
Pakistan v. Sri Lanka

PAKISTAN

Batting	M	Inns	NO	HS	Runs	Av	100	50
Inzamam-ul-Haq	3	6	1	138	355	71.00	1	2
Saeed Anwar	2	4	0	84	217	54.25	–	2
Shahid Afridi	2	4	0	74	143	35.75	–	1
Younis Khan	3	6	0	107	201	33.50	1	1
Yousuf Youhana	3	6	0	88	164	27.33	–	1
Moin Khan	3	6	0	70	107	26.75	–	1
Shoaib Akhtar	2	4	1	26	35	11.66	–	–
Aamir Sohail	2	4	0	24	46	11.50	–	–
Waqar Younis	3	6	0	39	66	11.00	–	–
Abdur Razzaq	2	4	0	9	17	4.25	–	–

Also batted: Arshad Khan (1 Test) 0, 5; Atiq-uz-Zaman (1 Test) 1, 25; Ijaz Ahmed (1 Test) 7, 3; Irfan Fazil 1*, 3; Mohammad Akram (1 Test) 0, 1*; Naved Ashraf (1 Test) 5, 27; Saqlain Mushtaq (1 Test) 3*, 2*; Wajahatullah Wasti (1 Test) 17, 1; Wasim Akram (1 Test) 0, 79

Fielding Figures
9 – Moin Khan (8ct/1st); 5 – Atiq-uz-Zaman; 4 – Yousuf Youhana; 2 – Aamir Sohail, Irfan Fazil, Saqlain Mushtaq, Wajahatullah Wasti, Waqar Younis, Younis Khan.
1 – Ijaz Ahmed, Shahid Afridi, Shoaib Akhtar.

Bowling	Overs	Mds	Runs	Wkts	Av	Best	10m	5/inn
Aamir Sohail	42.2	9	99	5	19.80	2–20	–	–
Shoaib Akhtar	67.5	10	238	11	21.63	5–75	–	1
Waqar Younis	96.5	18	310	13	23.84	4–103	–	–
Shahid Afridi	27	4	121	5	24.20	3–50	–	–
Abdur Razzaq	92.5	28	221	8	27.62	4–56	–	–

Also bowled: Arshad Khan 65–21–151–4; Irfan Fazil 8–0–65–2; Mohammad Akram 24.1–3–93–2; Saqlain Mushtaq 67–16–152–3; Wajahatullah Wasti 1–1–0–0; Wasim Akram 2.1–0–8–0

SRI LANKA

Batting	M	Inns	NO	HS	Runs	Av	100	50
PA de Silva	2	4	0	112	197	49.25	1	–
WPUJC Vaas	3	6	3	53*	128	42.66	–	1
RP Arnold	3	6	0	99	189	31.50	–	1
DPMD Jayawardene	3	6	0	42	153	25.50	–	–
MS Atapattu	3	6	0	75	148	24.66	–	1
ST Jayasuriya	3	6	0	56	143	23.83	–	1
RS Kaluwitharana	3	6	1	42	115	23.00	–	–
M Muralitharan	3	5	2	22	52	16.66	–	–
KR Pushpakumara	2	4	0	44	66	16.50	–	–
TM Dilshan	2	4	0	31	56	14.00	–	–
GP Wickremasinghe	3	6	0	5	5	0.83	–	–

Also batted: IS de Saram (1 Test) 5, 18; A Ranatunga (1 Test) 42, 29; DNT Zoysa (1 Test) 26, 13

Fielding Figures
10 – DPMD Jayawardene; 9 – R S Kaluwitharana (7ct/2st); 7 – RP Arnold; 5 – GP Wickremasinghe; 3 – TM Dilshan; 2 – MS Atapattu, PA de Silva, WPUJC Vaas; 1 – IS de Saram, ST Jayasuriya, KR Pushpakumara, M Muralitharan, A Ranatunga

Bowling	Overs	Mds	Runs	Wkts	Av	Best	10m	5/inn
M Muralitharan	213.1	52	516	26	19.84	6–71	1	1
WPUJC Vaas	146	29	408	13	31.38	3–69	–	–
KR Pushpakumara	57.5	10	170	5	34.00	4–66	–	–
GP Wickremasinghe	105.5	26	306	8	38.25	4–37	–	–

Also bowled: RP Arnold 5–1–15–0; PA de Silva 6–2–10–0; ST Jayasuriya 26.5–5–92–3; DPMD Jayawardene 5–3–7–1; DNT Zoysa 39–10–101–3

PAKISTAN DOMESTIC FIRST-CLASS SEASON
By Qamar Ahmed

In one of the longest domestic seasons in the country's history, a record number of 120 matches were played between 23 participating teams in the premier first-class competition, the Quaid-e-Azam Trophy. It could have been 122 had two matches not been washed out by rain! The number resulted from the participation of both the regional teams and those belonging to commercial organisations. The idea was introduced by a juvenile-minded chief of the Pakistan Cricket Board ad hoc committee, Mujeeb-ur-Rehman, who was placed in charge of the game after Pakistan's defeat in the final of the World Cup. Mujeeb, who also attempted to change the emblem of the Pakistan team, was ousted after the military takeover of the country and imprisoned along with the deposed prime minister Nawaz Sharif.

The Quaid-e-Azam Trophy, the only first-class championship, was won by PIA, who defeated Habib Bank in two days – the shortest-ever final. Allegations were made about the condition of the Iqbal Stadium at Faisalabad, as 22 wickets fell on the first day. PIA were two wickets down for 25 chasing 166, but their captain Asif Mujtaba and Ghulam Ali put on 141 off 29 overs for an unbroken stand to lead the team to victory.

The competition lasted four months with some entertaining cricket played along the way. The creation of Pakistan Reserves, a new side, meant that some of the teams lost their players and were understrength. Pakistan Reserves dominated Pool 'B' but a draw against REDCO put them in the back seat. Habib Bank had two outright wins against Faisalabad and Peshawar in their last three matches in addition to taking three points against Islamabad to go past Reserves with a 12-point lead.

PIA's nearest rivals in Pool 'A' were Lahore City Whites. REDCO, financed by Mujeeb-ur-Rehman, withdrew from the contest after his arrest, but later changed their mind and rejoined the tournament. PIA won five of their ten matches and remained unbeaten to get into the final.

The real champion of the competition was PIA's captain Asif Mujtaba. He scored 636 runs at 57.81 – including a career-best 240 against Lahore Division – and he bagged 50 wickets at only 13.74 apiece. Shoaib Mohammad scored 971 runs at 80.91 and Rizwan-uz-Zaman for PIA scored 768 at an average of 59.07. Both hit five hundreds each. Three bowlers reached the 50-wicket mark, National Bank's medium-pacer Athar Laeeq leading the bunch with a haul of 51 wickets at an average of 16.47.

Asif Mujtaba, captain of PIA, who amassed 636 runs through the season, which included a career best of 240 against Lahore Division.

PAKISTAN DOMESTIC ONE-DAY SEASON
By Qamar Ahmed

The 1999–2000 Pakistan domestic cricket season started and ended with one-day tournaments contested on a national level. In October, the schedule began with the Tissot Cup National One-Day Championship and, near the end of the season, the PCB gave permission to the National Bank of Pakistan to hold their own NBP Cup National One-Day Championship. The Bank hope that, alongside the Tissot Cup, their own competition will become a regular part of the Pakistan cricketing calendar.

The Pakistan International Airlines team flew away with the Tissot Cup, winning their seventh limited-over national title in 18 years. They beat newcomers REDCO by 38 runs in a high-scoring final under the lights of the Gaddafi Stadium in Lahore. PIA, captained by Wasim Akram, had several current national players in their ranks as wicketkeeper Moin Khan, all-rounder Azhar Mahmood and batsman Yousuf Youhana all supported their skipper in contriving a win over the opponents in the final.

The REDCO team was captained by Pakistan's pace spearhead Waqar Younis and included Test players Naved Ashraf and Mushtaq Ahmed, the leg-spinner. REDCO, a business concern run by the then-in-office PCB Chairman Mujeeb-ur-Rehman, had joined the national circuit the previous season by winning the Patron's Trophy Grade 2 Championship. They had proved their worth and ability by reaching the Tissot Cup final having improved with every match. However, in spite of the presence of a number of stars in the decider, it was Test discard Zahid Fazal who led PIA to victory with 85 off 93 balls that included a six and seven fours and was declared Man of the Match.

REDCO were missing from the NBP Cup event as, by then, Mujeeb had been removed as the PCB Chairman and Lt-General Tauqir Zia had taken over as the new chief. The company still exists, but its cricketing future appears doomed. The Khan Research Laboratories (KRL) team emerged as a new force in national limited-over cricket, but they were narrowly defeated by 19 runs by Habib Bank in the final at the Gaddafi Stadium. With the Pakistan team visiting the West Indies at the time, none of the national stars were available for the showpiece. However, Saleem Malik, who led Habib Bank, and his brother-in-law Ijaz Ahmed turned out, both failing to score and lasting a mere 12 balls between them. The star of the final was Imran Farhat, who captured four wickets for 37 runs with his leg-breaks as KRL crashed to 163 facing a modest Habib Bank total of 182.

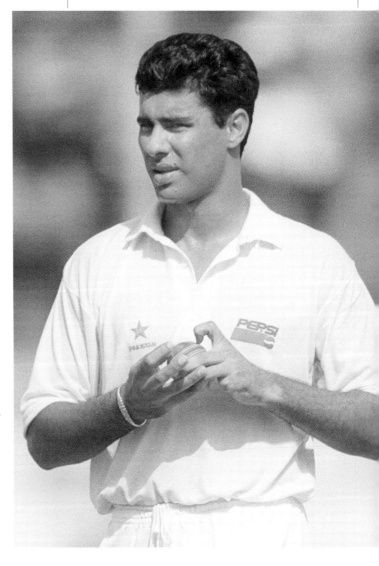

Waqar Younis – the REDCO captain – took his national team to within 38 runs of winning the Tissot Cup.

FIRST-CLASS AVERAGES

BATTING

	M	Inns	NO	HS	Runs	Av	100	50
Imran Abbas	9	14	3	204*	983	89.36	4	5
Shoaib Mohammad	11	15	3	180	971	80.91	5	1
Younis Khan	14	21	4	202*	1315	77.35	6	3
Naumanullah	8	11	2	171*	642	71.33	3	2
Rashid Latif	9	12	2	131*	674	67.40	2	3
Hasan Adnan	10	14	2	130	760	63.33	2	6
Shadab Kabir	9	11	2	137*	538	59.77	2	3
Rizwan-uz-Zaman	11	15	2	200*	768	59.07	5	-
Faisal Naveed	8	16	3	151*	761	58.53	4	3
Asif Mujtaba	11	13	2	240	636	57.81	1	4
Asim Kamal	10	17	4	122*	739	56.84	3	3
Hasan Raza	8	10	1	125	505	56.11	2	3
Yasir Hameed	9	16	0	154	895	55.93	3	3
Qaiser Abbas	6	9	1	168	447	55.87	1	3
Saeed Anwar, jr	11	16	4	177	669	55.75	2	2
Sajjad Akbar	9	10	1	99	493	54.77	-	5
Tariq Mohammad	7	12	3	165*	492	54.66	2	1
Asfar Nawaz	10	17	2	178	819	54.60	1	5
Saleem Mughal	9	15	2	193	699	53.76	3	3
Maqsood Raza	9	14	2	115	640	53.33	1	5
Mujahid Jamshed	9	14	0	158	729	52.07	3	4
Mohammad Ramzan	10	15	0	150	774	51.60	3	3
Akhtar Sarfraz	8	12	2	148	515	51.50	2	1
Hasnain Qayyum	10	13	1	161*	614	51.16	1	3
Sohail Jaffar	11	12	3	72	460	51.11	-	5
Shahid Anwar	10	15	0	160	761	50.73	3	1
Adil Nisar	10	15	1	158	703	50.21	2	1
Suleman Huda	10	17	1	166	792	49.50	2	4
Mansoor Rana	10	14	1	120	636	48.92	2	3
Saad Wasim	8	13	0	152	624	48.00	2	2
Shoaib Khan	9	15	2	127	623	47.92	1	3
Iqbal Imam	10	14	2	88	575	47.91	-	6
Azam Khan	10	13	2	93	526	47.81	-	5
Ali Naqvi	10	14	0	111	669	47.78	2	4
Aamir Sohail	10	16	0	164	759	47.43	3	2
Ijaz Ahmed, jr	10	16	1	188	706	47.06	1	3
Imran Nazir (Res)	6	11	1	164	469	46.90	1	3
Hanif-ur-Rehman	6	10	1	120	417	46.33	2	2
Intikhab Alam	7	8	0	106	368	46.00	1	1
Salim Elahi	6	9	0	140	412	45.77	2	1
Ashar Zaidi	6	10	0	127	455	45.50	1	2
Babar Zaman	8	12	0	108	536	44.66	1	4
Tariq Aziz	10	14	0	194	618	44.14	1	4
Taufiq Umar	7	9	0	176	392	43.55	1	2
Faisal Athar	9	13	0	122	560	43.07	1	4
Rafatullah	7	10	0	213	427	42.70	1	1
Naseer Ahmed	11	14	1	143	555	42.69	2	2
Mohammad Hussain	7	12	1	69	459	41.72	-	6
Majid Jahangir	7	10	1	90	375	41.66	-	2
Zia-ul-Hasan	5	9	1	79	327	40.87	-	2
Sajid Ali	10	15	0	149	609	40.60	2	3
Salman Shah	10	18	4	127*	558	39.85	1	2
Moin-ul-Atiq	5	9	1	91	315	39.37	-	2
Majid Majeed	7	11	0	132	433	39.36	1	2
Mohammed Masroor	10	17	1	150*	619	38.68	2	2
Aamer Hanif	7	12	4	129*	309	38.62	1	-
Rizwan Malik	7	14	1	169*	500	38.46	2	2
Ataullah Butt	6	11	0	150	413	37.54	1	1
Shahzad Malik	7	14	3	88	407	37.00	-	3
Iqbal Sheikh	4	8	0	140	296	37.00	1	1
Misbah-ul-Haq	11	21	0	129	770	36.66	1	4
Farooq Iqbal	7	13	4	55*	328	36.44	-	2
Zahoor Elahi	9	13	0	133	471	36.23	2	1
Nadeem Abbasi	9	11	2	91	326	36.22	-	1
Asadullah Butt	12	18	2	141	577	36.06	1	2
Bilal Asad	10	14	0	91	502	35.85	-	6
Aaley Haider	10	13	1	92	430	35.83	-	4
Arif Mahmood	7	13	1	75	429	35.75	-	3
Mohammad Nawaz	9	16	1	105	532	35.46	1	3
Iqbal Sheikh	6	9	0	67	317	35.22	-	4
Taimur Khan	10	16	2	139	492	35.14	1	2

FIRST-CLASS AVERAGES

BATTING

	M	Inns	NO	HS	Runs	Av	100	50
Atif Rauf	8	11	0	113	386	35.09	1	
2Nadeem Hussain	10	14	4	120*	349	34.90	1	
1Kamran Akmal	9	12	2	123*	347	34.70	1	1
Fida Hussain	7	13	1	141	415	34.58	1	2
Pervez Aziz	5	8	0	101	276	34.50	1	2
Zafar Jadoon	8	15	0	127	509	33.93	1	2
Ijaz Ahmed	6	11	0	141	373	33.90	2	1
Imran Farhat	7	11	1	100	338	33.80	1	1
Asif Mahmood	8	12	1	65	369	33.54	-	4
Saadat Gul	7	13	1	89	397	33.08	-	4
Zulfiqar Jan	7	11	1	63	329	32.90	-	2
ST Jayasuriya	4	8	0	60	263	32.87	-	3
Bazid Khan	10	14	1	119*	420	32.30	1	3
Mohammad Salim	6	11	0	123	355	32.27	1	1
Saboor Ahmed	6	10	2	76	257	32.12	-	1
Imran Khan	10	17	0	119	543	31.94	1	1
Haroon Raheem	8	15	2	135	412	31.69	1	1
Mohammad Hafeez	9	17	0	83	532	31.29	-	3
Zahid Fazal	11	12	2	75	311	31.10	-	1
Masroor Hussain	8	14	1	82	404	31.07	-	5
Basit Niazi	7	11	0	114	341	31.00	2	1
Irfan Bhatti	5	8	0	70	247	30.87	-	3
Manzoor Elahi	6	8	0	134	247	30.87	1	-
Salim Malik	6	8	0	77	247	30.87	-	1
Shahid Nawaz	5	8	0	83	246	30.75	-	3
Rehan Rafiq	10	17	2	90*	457	30.46	-	4
Ayaz Taifi	8	16	0	98	481	30.06	-	4
RP Arnold	4	8	0	99	239	29.87	-	1
Ahmer Saeed	8	12	1	105*	324	29.45	1	-
Mohammad Tariq	5	9	0	107	264	29.33	1	1
Akhtar Bangash	9	18	0	112	525	29.16	1	3
Sher Ali	5	9	1	62	227	28.37	-	2
Wasim Yousafi	7	9	1	98	226	28.25	-	1
Wasim Haider	5	8	0	89	221	27.62	-	1
Murtaza Hussain	10	10	2	53*	221	27.62	-	1
Riaz Sheikh	9	12	1	83	299	27.18	-	2
Babar Naeem	6	11	0	86	296	26.90	-	2
Saeed Azad	10	15	0	95	402	26.80	-	3
Azhar Hussain	7	13	0	50	344	26.46	-	1
Shahid Afridi	7	11	0	74	287	26.09	-	1
Inam-ul-Haq	8	13	0	55	339	26.07	-	1
DPMD Jayawardene	4	8	0	42	208	26.00	-	-
Asif Hussain	7	13	1	99	311	25.91	-	1
Asif Hussain	6	11	0	99	285	25.90	-	2
Ijaz Mahmood	5	8	0	47	207	25.87	-	-
Iftikhar Hussain	8	12	0	151	308	25.66	1	-
Naveed Ashraf	10	13	0	81	333	25.61	-	2
Khawar Ali	5	8	0	57	204	25.50	-	1
Naeem Ashraf	8	11	3	55*	203	25.37	-	1
Javed Sami	5	9	1	112	202	25.25	1	-
Khalid Mahmood	10	18	3	66*	378	25.20	-	1
Tahir Rashid	11	14	2	58*	302	25.16	-	1
Mutahir Ali Shah	10	15	4	50	275	25.00	-	1
Mohammad Shahbaz	10	13	1	91	299	24.91	-	2
Sajjad Ahmed	8	14	1	112*	319	24.53	1	-
Atiq-uz-Zaman	9	13	0	81	319	24.53	-	2
Ahmed Said	9	16	0	59	390	24.37	-	1
Usman Tariq	5	9	0	89	216	24.00	-	1
Sarfraz Ahmed	9	10	0	83	230	23.00	-	1
Inamullah Rashid	9	15	0	58	345	23.00	-	3
Faisal Iqbal	8	11	1	41	225	22.50	-	-
Javed Iqbal	7	13	0	56	292	22.46	-	3
Naveed-ul-Hassan	8	11	2	42	200	22.22	-	-
Mohammad Zaman	7	14	0	68	301	21.50	-	2
Mohammad Nawaz	6	12	1	47	236	21.45	-	-
Mohammad Shafiq	11	20	0	101	421	21.05	1	1
Yasir Ashfaq	10	15	1	42	294	21.00	-	-
Javed Hayat	11	16	0	60	336	21.00	-	3
Mohammad Wasim, jr	5	10	2	48	167	20.87	-	-
Tanvir Hussain	6	11	0	56	226	20.54	-	1
Babar Javed	5	8	0	59	164	20.50	-	1

FIRST-CLASS AVERAGES

BATTING

	M	Inns	NO	HS	Runs	Av	100	50
Imran Nazir (Lah)	6	8	0	44	162	20.25	-	-
Yasir Arafat	6	8	0	50	161	20.12	-	1
Bilal Marwat	6	10	1	40*	181	20.11	-	-

Qualification: 8 completed innings av 15.00

BOWLING

	Overs	Mds	Runs	Wkts	Av	Best	10/m	5/m
Asif Mujtaba	335.2	100	687	50	13.74	6-17	2	6
Aqib Javed	94.5	29	212	15	14.13	5-15	-	1
Athar Laiq	304.4	76	838	51	16.43	7-101	1	6
Kabir Khan	229	42	815	49	16.63	6-37	1	5
Nadeem Iqbal	285	56	808	47	17.19	7-25	1	3
Akram Raza	290.1	67	759	44	17.25	6-45	1	4
Arshad Khan	275.5	82	642	37	17.35	8-110	1	4
Zahid Saeed	195.5	30	614	34	18.05	6-86	1	3
Sajid Shah	220.3	50	585	32	18.28	6-28	-	3
Shahid Afridi	99.4	27	322	17	18.94	4-27	-	-
Kashif Shafi	181.3	44	493	26	18.96	5-105	-	1
Khawar Ali	72.3	17	198	10	19.80	3-26	-	-
Sarfraz Ahmed	308.3	85	744	37	20.10	7-50	1	2
Naveed-ul-Hasan	300.1	64	912	45	20.26	7-60	1	5
Saboor Ahmed	174.4	52	385	19	20.26	4-72	-	-
Shahid Aslam	138.4	20	366	18	20.33	4-37	-	-
Imranullah	205.2	45	632	31	20.38	5-53	-	2
Mohammad Aslam	298.5	102	673	33	20.39	6-49	-	2
Ali Gauhar	247.1	43	840	41	20.48	6-45	-	1
Nadeem Khan	400.1	131	845	41	20.60	5-78	-	1
Fahad Masood	172	26	600	29	20.68	7-45	-	2
Shahid Iqbal	227	57	581	28	20.75	8-52	-	3
Azhar Abbas	192.3	35	644	31	20.77	5-58	-	2
Shahid Nazir	186	30	572	27	21.18	5-60	-	1
Yasir Arafat	141	27	453	21	21.57	6-53	-	1
Naeem Akhtar	157.2	43	393	18	21.83	5-42	-	1
Farooq Hameed	164.5	38	415	19	21.84	5-127	-	1
Mohammad Hussain	360.2	99	832	38	21.89	6-97	1	4
Imran Tahir	333.4	71	955	43	22.00	8-76	2	4
Iqbal Imam	256.5	82	457	20	22.85	5-33	-	2
Farooq Iqbal	226.5	73	448	19	23.57	7-60	-	1
Saad Janjua	177.1	25	662	28	23.64	5-52	-	1
Aamir Wasim	279.5	69	687	29	23.68	5-25	-	1
Abdur Rehman	234.1	80	479	20	23.95	5-50	-	1
Ata-ur-Rehman	245.5	45	797	33	24.15	5-83	-	2
Murtaza Hussain	529.2	160	1214	50	24.28	6-58	1	5
Farhan Rasheed	398.3	103	1010	40	25.25	6-103	-	3
Haaris Khan	184.3	44	481	19	25.31	5-48	-	1
Aamer Mahmood	314.4	68	865	34	25.44	6-46	1	2
Yasir Ashfaq	271.2	68	770	30	25.66	6-45	-	1
Shakeel Ahmed	222.2	58	489	19	25.73	6-98	-	1
Irfan Bhatti	111.5	28	260	10	26.00	3-52	-	-
Saeed Anwar, jr	174.4	33	469	18	26.05	3-11	-	-
Waqas Ahmed	249.2	51	784	30	26.13	6-26	-	1
Ashar Zaidi	111.5	31	315	12	26.25	3-45	-	-
Maqbool Hussain	223	53	605	23	26.30	5-38	-	1
Naeem Khan	149.2	31	395	15	26.33	4-45	-	-
Javed Hayat	306.5	86	669	25	26.76	4-106	-	-
Rauf Akbar	145.2	32	437	16	27.31	4-36	-	-
Fazal-e-Akbar	311.1	62	965	35	27.57	4-60	-	-
Shakeel Nawaz	206.2	41	637	23	27.69	5-94	-	1
Kamran Hussain	206.5	27	723	26	27.80	5-30	1	2
Sarfraz Butt	183.4	34	537	19	28.26	7-84	-	1
Ahmed Hayat	203	29	679	24	28.29	6-74	-	1
Abdur Rauf	160.5	17	602	21	28.66	5-132	-	1
Jaffar Qureshi	374.3	101	1006	35	28.74	6-51	-	1
Nauman Habib	215.4	33	786	27	29.11	7-89	-	1
Shafiq Ahmed	333.1	80	935	32	29.21	6-46	-	2
Kashif Raza	158	32	529	18	29.38	4-52	-	-
Mohammad Sarfraz	201	37	738	25	29.52	4-33	-	-
Umar Rasheed	157	45	386	13	29.69	4-45	-	-

FIRST-CLASS AVERAGES

BOWLING

	Overs	Mds	Runs	Wkts	Av	Best	10/m	5/m
Aamer Nazir	375	68	1306	44	29.68	8-79	1	2
Nadeem Afzal	145.5	25	488	16	30.50	6-59	-	1
Stephen John	411.3	83	1252	41	30.53	5-53	-	2
Azhar Hussain	83.2	9	306	10	30.60	4-29	-	-
Sajid Ali	210.1	27	678	22	30.81	4-38	-	-
Mohammad Asif	168.5	35	435	14	31.07	4-37	-	-
Riaz Sheikh	280.3	58	840	27	31.11	6-58	1	1
Jaffar Nazir	225.5	32	750	24	31.25	5-87	-	1
Tahir Mahmood	270.3	29	974	31	31.41	5-45	-	1
Fahad Khan	83.2	10	315	10	31.50	3-15	-	-
Mohammad Hasnain	107	21	420	13	32.30	5-135	-	1
Rao Iftikhar	166.5	18	590	18	32.77	5-46	-	2
Naeem Ashraf	254	70	638	19	33.57	3-32	-	-
Naeem Tayyab	191.5	49	438	13	33.69	4-41	-	-
Saeed Amjal	317.4	65	879	26	33.80	5-109	-	1
Aamir Sohail	140.5	39	339	10	33.90	2-20	-	-
Fahim Fazal	157.2	26	519	15	34.60	3-27	-	-
Mohtashim Rasheed	181.4	57	382	11	34.72	4-43	-	-
Mohammad Javed	177.5	42	495	14	35.35	5-66	-	1
Mohammad Shafiq	261.1	48	789	22	35.86	55-80	-	1
Imran Amin	350	66	1176	32	36.75	4-76	-	-
Suleman Huda	161	44	457	12	38.08	2-28	-	-
Sheraz Haider	160.3	15	632	16	39.50	5-68	-	1
Mumtaz Ali	238	71	562	14	40.14	4-75	-	-
Tariq Munir	353.4	104	809	20	40.45	3-88	-	-
Kashif Ibrahim	277.4	76	722	17	42.47	3-66	-	-
Kashif Mahmood	114	13	529	12	44.08	4-40	-	-
Mohammad Zahid, jr	156	27	578	12	48.16	3-72	-	-

Qualification: 10 wickets in 8 innings

The following players took 10 wickets in fewer than 8 innings:

	Overs	Mds	Runs	Wkts	Av	Best	10/m	5/m
Mohammad Zahid	119.3	43	246	15	16.40	5-63	-	1
Danish Kaneria	154.3	49	418	24	17.41	7-101	1	4
Shoaib Malik	121.2	34	270	15	18.00	5-30	-	1
M Muralitharan	213.1	52	516	26	19.84	6-71	1	1
Mubashir Nazir	96	16	300	14	21.42	4-78	-	-
Shoaib Akhtar	67.5	10	238	11	21.63	5-75	-	1
Tabish Nawab	119	22	398	18	22.11	6-122	-	1
Usman Tariq	150	23	439	19	23.10	5-103	-	1
Waqar Younis	96.5	18	310	13	23.84	4-103	-	-
Sajjad Ali	123.3	20	460	19	24.21	5-40	-	2
Haider Ali	108.3	28	277	11	25.18	4-35	-	-
Iqbal Sheikh	94.3	22	282	11	25.63	5-79	-	1
Umair Hassan	67.2	7	310	12	25.83	4-166	-	-
Aqeel Ahmed	127.2	32	326	12	27.16	5-50	-	1
Shabbir Ahmed	106.4	17	462	17	27.17	6-72	-	1
Asad Ahmed	110	21	368	13	28.30	4-22	-	-
Mansoor Ahmed	78.5	8	285	10	28.50	6-123	-	1
Mohammad Akram	94.2	18	317	11	28.81	4-41	-	-
Salman Fazal	144.5	30	383	13	29.46	6-85	-	1
WPUJC Vaas	146	29	408	13	31.38	3-69	-	-
Zaman Haider	122	24	346	11	31.45	3-43	-	-
Tariq Aziz	105.1	15	388	11	35.27	4-50	-	-
Haider Raza	131.1	12	495	14	35.35	5-100	-	1
Sajjad-ul-Haq	123.5	16	504	11	45.81	5-112	-	1

FIELDING

20 – NR Ferreira (17ct,1st); 18 – DJR Campbell (16ct,2st), A Flower; 14 – W Gilmour (13ct,1st); 11 – TM Dilshan (10ct,1st); 9 – ER Marillier (8ct,1st); 8 – RS Kaluwitharana; 7 – C Delport, DPMD Jayawardene; 6 – GW Flower, TR Gripper, MA Vermeulen; 5 – ADR Campbell, CA Grant, NC Johnson, AJ Mackay, WT Siziba,; – MJ Vaughan-Davies, DD Yatras

WEST INDIES

Zimbabwe in the West Indies
Pakistan in the West Indies
Cable & Wireless One-Day Series
Busta Cup
Red Stripe Bowl
First-Class Averages

ZIMBABWE IN THE WEST INDIES
By Tony Cozier

Curtly Ambrose and Courtney Walsh proved yet again that when they are around the age of miracles is not over for West Indies cricket. The two phenomenal veterans were at the heart of the latest wonder as almost certain defeat was turned into incredible victory on the last day of the inaugural Test between the teams.

This time they were not alone in defying reality. Reon King and Franklyn Rose were their two accomplices, equally responsible for completing the unlikely mission of defending a winning target of 99. All four contributed to routing the Zimbabweans for 63, their lowest total in their 40 Tests.

The significance was unmistakable in the emotional outpouring among the eleven West Indians on the field and the thousand or so faithful scattered around the ground once Ambrose completed the result with the last three wickets for one run. There had been similar celebrations when Ambrose and Walsh instigated a comparable dramatic victory over South Africa in their initial Test in Bridgetown in 1992. The players gleefully grabbed souvenir stumps, hugged each other and assembled in a huddle before setting off on a lap of honour. It was in direct contrast to the depression of a year earlier when the West Indies were the ones dismissed for their lowest total, 51, by Australia and suffered a heavy defeat on the same ground.

Below: New West Indies captain Jimmy Adams tosses the coin, watched by opposition captain Andy Flower at the start of the first Test at Port-of-Spain.

FIRST TEST
16, 17, 18, 19 and 20 March 2000 at Queen's Park Oval, Port-of-Spain

As the Test kicked off, the gloom that had settled over West Indies cricket lifted in the space of four hours. Defeat and controversy were consigned to history by the never-say-die attitude of a revamped team under a new captain, coach and manager despite the absence of its one world-class batsman Brian Lara, who had resigned the captaincy and taken a break from the game only a few weeks earlier.

It was a shattering reversal for the Zimbabweans, seeking their second Test win overseas, and their fourth overall. They played disciplined, competitive cricket throughout, held the upper hand for four days but could not finally muster the resources to resist high-quality bowling.

A well-grassed pitch and steamy weather encouraged Andy Flower to bowl first on winning the toss. The West Indies were made to fight from Heath Streak's third ball of the match, which claimed Adrian Griffith leg before, to the last with which Ambrose plucked out Pom Mbangwa's off-stump. They were restricted to 59 for 2 off 28.1 overs by the time rain halted play ten minutes after lunch on the opening day. On resumption, they lost Chanderpaul to close at 79 for 3.

There was no recovery on the second day, the remaining seven wickets falling for 106 against disciplined Zimbabwean bowling that maintained a full length and direct line and was supported by sharp fielding. The only encouragement for the West Indies was the mature debut of Wavell Hinds, who was left stranded with 46 after two and a half hours. The other debutant, Chris Gayle, 20 and also left-handed and Jamaican, had the next best score, 33, before Brian Murphy's athletic fielding at cover ran him out. Zimbabwe overcame the loss of three early wickets to build a strong position going into the third day. Neil Johnson fell to Ambrose, first ball of the innings, Grant Flower to Walsh's sixth and Murray Goodwin, also to Walsh, in the 14th over. A lucky break and an unbroken partnership of 82 between Trevor Gripper and Andy Flower that occupied the remaining three and a quarter hours of the day revived them.

Captain Flower was yet to score when Walsh's first

Previous page: Curtly Ambrose and the West Indies team celebrate following the fall of the last wicket on the fifth day of the first Test against Zimbabwe.

West Indies debutant Chris Gayle drives Henry Olonga during his innings of 33 on the first day of the first Test.

ball passed him down the leg side. It brought a roared claim for a wicketkeeper's catch but umpire Steve Bucknor failed to detect the gloved deflection that was clear from the magnified, slow-motion TV replay. Flower also offered four slip chances of varying degrees of difficulty off the fast bowlers (at 38, 42, 52 and 60) on his way to his seventh hundred in his 40th Test.

Zimbabwe would have been nowhere without their captain's marathon effort, which lasted seven hours and ten minutes, included 12 boundaries (11 through the off side). He was still unbeaten when the last four wickets tumbled for four runs, three of them to Gayle's off-spin, coinciding with more rain that brought an early end to the day.

The importance of Flower's innings was obvious on the fourth day as Zimbabwe positioned themselves for the famous victory that never was. Their varied bowling and alert fielding reduced the West Indies to a lead of 98 at stumps with their last pair together.

Zimbabwe immediately took charge when Streak removed Griffith for his second duck with the third, and Gayle with the fourth, balls. Only a fourth-wicket stand of 78 between Shivnarine Chanderpaul and Jimmy Adams that occupied two and a half tense hours on either side of a lengthy lunchtime rain break delayed them for any time. Once they got rid of the pair in successive overs, the resistance ended and were it not for 28 extras (the second-highest contribution) Zimbabwe's task would have been even easier.

Zimbabwe captain Andy Flower sweeps Gayle in his undefeated 52 during the first Test.

Streak immediately dispatched the last man, King, in the first over of the final day, carrying his return to nine wickets in the match, so that Zimbabwe needed fewer than 100 runs to win. Only Australia, dismissed for 77 by England when set 85 at the Oval in 1882, had ever failed in such a situation.

The West Indies fast bowlers responded with unerring control, consistently probing around off-stump to capitalise on a pitch offering occasional movement and low bounce. In the face of such pressure, Zimbabwe collapsed, managing one, solitary edged boundary in the 47 overs it took to complete their demise. Zimbabwe's problems started in the fourth over when Johnson slapped Walsh to cover point and they were never offered any respite after that. Only Grant Flower passed double figures before he was undone by an unplayable off-cutter from Walsh that hit low on the off-stump.

By then, King and Rose had ripped the heart out of the middle order, leaving Ambrose to complete the job. He needed only 13 balls to dispatch the last three wickets.

FIRST TEST – WEST INDIES v. ZIMBABWE
16, 17, 18, 19 and 20 March 2000 at Queen's Park Oval, Port-of-Spain

WEST INDIES

	First innings		Second innings	
AFG Griffith	lbw b Streak	0	lbw b Streak	0
SL Campbell	lbw b Streak	24	run out (Murphy/Johnson)	23
CH Gayle	run out (Murphy/Johnson)	33	b Streak	0
S Chanderpaul	c A Flower, b Olonga	12	lbw b Streak	49
CEL Ambrose	c A Flower, b Streak	7	(8) c Johnson, b Murphy	1
JC Adams (capt)	lbw b Murphy	17	(5) c Murphy, b Olonga	27
WW Hinds	not out	46	(6) run out (Olonga/A Flower)	9
*RD Jacobs	c & b Murphy	10	(7) lbw b Olonga	0
FA Rose	b Johnson	1	c A Flower, b Streak	9
RD King	lbw b Streak	2	c A Flower, b Streak	1
CA Walsh	lbw b Murphy	11	not out	0
	b7, lb6, nb11	24	b11, lb6, w3, nb8	28
		187		**147**

	First innings				Second innings			
	O	M	R	W	O	M	R	W
Streak	24	9	45	4	17	8	27	5
Olonga	18	7	44	1	13	3	28	2
Mbangwa	10	3	21	–	15	10	15	–
Johnson	13	4	26	1	4	0	18	–
Murphy	13.4	7	32	3	15	3	23	1
Flower GW	2	0	6	–	9	4	13	–
Gripper					2	0	6	–

Fall of Wickets
1–4, 2–49, 3–72, 4–81, 5–87, 6–121, 7–136, 8–149, 9–161
1–0, 2–0, 3–37, 4–115, 5–115, 6–118, 7–119, 8–142, 9–146

ZIMBABWE

	First innings		Second innings	
NC Johnson	lbw b Ambrose	0	(2) c Adams, b Walsh	3
GW Flower	c Campbell, b Walsh	0	(1) b Walsh	26
TR Gripper	c Gayle, b Ambrose	41	lbw b King	3
MW Goodwin	c Gayle, b Walsh	20	c Jacobs, b Rose	8
*A Flower (capt)	not out	113	c Jacobs, b Rose	5
ADR Campbell	c Jacobs, b Ambrose	0	b Ambrose	6
SV Carlisle	b Ambrose	17	c Jacobs, b Rose	3
HH Streak	c Campbell, bGayle	20	lbw b Rose	0
BA Murphy	lbw b Rose	1	not out	0
HK Olonga	b Gayle	2	c Chanderpaul, b Ambrose	0
M Mbangwa	b Gayle	0	b Ambrose	0
	b2, lb6, w1, nb13	22	lb7, nb2	9
		236		**63**

	First innings				Second innings			
	O	M	R	W	O	M	R	W
Ambrose	25	13	42	4	11	6	8	3
Walsh	28	9	49	2	14	8	18	2
Rose	19	6	41	1	13	4	19	4
King	20	2	71	–	9	2	11	1
Gayle	15	2	25	3				

Fall of Wickets
1–0, 2–0, 3–27, 4–144, 5–144, 6–164, 7–232, 8–233, 9–236
1–4, 2–20, 3–37, 4–47, 5–51, 6–57, 7–57, 8–62, 9–63

Umpires: SA Bucknor & G Sharp
Toss: Zimbabwe
Test Debuts: CH Gayle, WW Hinds & BA Murphy

West Indies won by 35 runs

SECOND TEST
24, 25, 26, 27 and 28 March 2000 at Sabina Park, Kingston

A match of two distinct halves ended in a West Indies victory less one-sided than the margin indicated. It was embellished for a sizeable, expectant crowd by the achievement of Courtney Walsh, Jamaica's revered son of the soil, in surpassing Kapil Dev as Test cricket's highest wicket-taker and the vital, record eighth-wicket partnership between captain Adams and Rose, two more of the five Jamaicans in the eleven.

Walsh began the match five short of Kapil's record of 434. He and his hopeful countrymen were kept waiting until the last possible chance before he dismissed Zimbabwe's second-innings last man, Henry Olonga, to claim the record as his own. It immediately set off emotional celebrations that would continue for days and would include honours and gifts from a grateful government.

Zimbabwe had built a strong position when Rose joined Adams almost exactly midway through the match. They had totalled 308, principally through a fourth-wicket partnership of 176 between Goodwin, who passed his second Test hundred, and captain Flower and the 74 Stuart Carlisle raised for the last two wickets with Brian Strang and Olonga.

Severely handicapped throughout by the absence of their best bowler, Streak, with a back injury, Zimbabwe's grip was loosened, slowly but surely, first by Adams and Rose and then, almost as rapidly as in their second innings at Port-of-Spain, by their susceptible batting against penetrative fast bowling. Griffith's desperate blitz hastened their defeat on the final morning. Confronted by a completely different-looking surface from that in Port-of-Spain, Flower chose to bat, rather than bowl, on winning the toss. Basically slow, it offered even bounce, a little movement off the seam and turn, a bit for everyone.

Goodwin's hundred and his stand with his captain spurred Zimbabwe's revival from 40 for 3 to 220 for 5 when they were out to successive balls in the last ten minutes. Walsh made the early breakthrough, removing Grant Flower to a thin edge to the keeper, and King dismissed Gripper and Johnson just before lunch.

The next four hours were dominated by the positive batting of Goodwin, who survived a stinging chance to gully off Rose when 16, and his captain but the mood changed when Adams entrusted the second new ball to Rose and King instead of Ambrose and Walsh. Goodwin was run out at the non-striker's end one ball after a stay of 324 balls, with ten fours, and Flower so badly misjudged Rose's swing the next that he lost his off-stump offering no shot.

Zimbabwe's bowlers stifled the opposition with both bat and ball on the second day to seize the advantage by the close. They slumped to 234 for 8 before Carlisle, the recognised batsman, and Strang and Olonga, the numbers ten and eleven, added 72 between them, including a Zimbabwe last-wicket Test record 54. King returned his first five-wicket haul in his fifth Test.

The West Indies' reply could find no momentum and they needed 58 overs, 24 of them maidens, to inch to 106 for 4 by close. Only Campbell broke the shackles for a period after he was dropped by his namesake at second slip off Johnson when 26. Their problems continued into the third day as they declined to 171 for 7 before Adams and Rose came together half an hour after lunch and set about repairing the damage.

They took the West Indies to within 13 of the lead by the close when Adams had been going just over seven hours and 322 balls for 87 and Rose had notched his first half-century in his 15 Tests.

The fourth day was one of Bacchanalian celebration for a packed Sabina Park. First, Adams completed his fifth Test hundred, his first for four years, on the ground where he plays for club and country. Walsh then claimed his record-breaking 435th wicket and the West Indies ended on the verge of victory.

Both Adams and Walsh waited to the last moment to complete their goals. Adams scampered his 100th run with King as his last partner. Walsh's historic wicket was the last available, Olonga smartly caught by yet another Jamaican, Hinds, at forward short leg.

The West Indies owed their lead of 31 to the stand between Adams and Rose, a new eighth-wicket record, surpassing the 124 between Viv Richards and Keith Boyce against India at Calcutta that had stood since 1974. Adams needed 496 minutes to arrive at his hard-fought century. Of West Indian batsmen only Larry Gomes had ever taken nearly as long, with 425 minutes against Australia at Perth in 1984.

All attention shifted to Walsh when the West Indies bowled a second time. He quickly dispatched both openers to edged catches to draw level with Kapil but then had an agonising wait as King, Rose and Ambrose demolished the Zimbabwean middle order. Ambrose passed a landmark of his own when his dismissal of Campbell carried him past Malcolm Marshall's 376 Test wickets and behind only Walsh among West Indians. Time was running out for Walsh as Olonga entered with Streak unable to bat but the lion-hearted veteran was not to be denied the satisfaction of creating history in the city where he was born, raised and learned his cricket. As soon as Olonga prodded his catch to Hinds, it touched off bedlam on the field and emotional celebration in the stands. Walsh was enveloped by jubilant team-mates and his old partner, Ambrose, catching the mood, genuflected to him before he himself lay on the ground and kissed the pitch.

By then, the outcome of the match was virtually settled and Griffith and Campbell duly knocked off the required 102 early on the fifth day, leaving time for more celebrations and honours for Walsh as well as gifts from a grateful government.

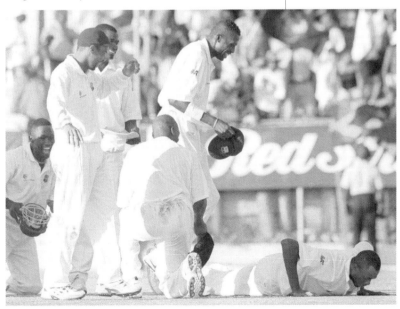

Courtney Walsh kisses the home turf following the dismissal of Olonga, to become the highest wicket-taker in the history of Test cricket.

SECOND TEST – WEST INDIES v. ZIMBABWE
24, 25, 26, 27 and 28 March 2000 at Sabina Park, Kingston

TEST MATCH AVERAGES
West Indies v. Zimbabwe

ZIMBABWE

	First innings			Second innings	
G Flower	c Jacobs, b Walsh	2	c Campbell, b Walsh	11
TR Gripper	c Walsh, b King	11	c Jacobs, b Walsh	0
MW Goodwin	run out (Hinds/Jacobs)	113	b King	9
NC Johnson	c Gayle, b King	0	(6) b Rose	29
*A Flower (capt)	b Rose	66	b King	10
BA Murphy	b Rose	0	(8) not out	0
ADR Campbell	lbw b King	1	(4) lbw b Amrose	22
SV Carlisle	c Jacobs, b Walsh	44	(7) lbw b Gayle	7
HH Streak	b King	2	absent injured	
BA Strang	c Jacobs, b King	13	(9) c Ambrose, b Rose	3
HK Olonga	not out	22	(10) c Hinds, b Walsh	2
	b4, lb12, w2, nb16	34	lb4, nb5	9
		308		**102**

	First innings				Second innings			
	O	M	R	W	O	M	R	W
Ambrose	25	8	36	–	16	9	14	1
Walsh	22.4	6	46	2	15.5	6	21	3
King	23	8	51	5	10	1	30	2
Rose	24	8	69	2	12	5	24	2
Gayle	10	0	46	–	6	3	9	1
Adams	9	2	32	–				
Chanderpaul	2	0	12	–				

Fall of Wickets
1–5, 2–40, 3–40, 4–216, 5–216, 6–223, 7–229, 8–234, 9–254
1–12, 2–14, 3–37, 4–48, 5–72, 6–90, 7–96, 8–100, 9–102

WEST INDIES

	First innings			Second innings	
AFG Griffith	b Johnson	6	(2) not out	54
SL Campbell	c Campbell, b Murrphy	48	(1) not out	16
CH Gayle	c A Flower, b Olonga	13		
S Chanderpaul	c A Flower, b Strang	12		
JC Adams (capt)	not out	101		
WW Hinds	c Campbell, b Murphy	14		
*RD Jacobs	c A Flower, b Olonga	27		
CEL Ambrose	c Carlisle, b Johnson	7		
FA Rose	c A Flower, b Johnson	69		
CA Walsh	c GW Flower, b Johnson	0		
RD King	b Olonga	4		
	b8, lb18, nb12	38	nb5	5
		339	(for 0 wicket)	**75**

	First innings				Second innings			
	O	M	R	W	O	M	R	W
Olonga	31.1	8	65	3	3	0	20	–
Strang	36	17	43	1	3	0	21	–
Johnson	37	15	77	4	5	1	27	–
Murphy	36	12	99	2				
Flower GW	18	9	14	–	1	1	0	–
Gripper	6	2	15	–	0.4	0	7	–

Fall of Wickets
1–37, 2–69, 3–85, 4–85, 5–122, 6–161, 7–170, 8–318, 9–318

Umpires: EA Nicholls & Athar Zaidi
Toss: Zimbabwe
Test Debuts: nil

West Indies won by ten wickets

WEST INDIES

Batting	M	Inns	NO	HS	Runs	Av	100	50
JC Adams	2	3	1	101*	145	72.50	1	–
SL Campbell	2	4	1	48	111	37.00	–	–
WW Hinds	2	3	1	46*	69	34.50	–	–
FA Rose	2	3	0	69	79	26.33	–	1
S Chanderpaul	2	3	0	49	73	24.33	–	–
AFG Griffith	2	4	1	54*	60	20.00	–	1
CH Gayle	2	3	0	33	46	15.33	–	–
RD Jacobs	2	3	0	27	37	12.33	–	–
CA Walsh	2	3	1	11	11	5.50	–	–
CEL Ambrose	2	3	0	7	15	5.00	–	–
RD King	2	3	0	4	7	2.33	–	–

Bowling	Overs	Mds	Runs	Wkts	Av	Best	10/m	5/inn
CEL Ambrose	77	36	100	8	12.50	4–42	–	–
CA Walsh	80.3	29	134	9	17.00	4–19	–	–
FA Rose	68	23	153	9	17.00	4–19	–	–
RD King	62	13	163	8	20.37	5–51	–	1

Also bowled: JC Adams 9–2–32–0; S Chanderpaul 2–0–12–0; CH Gayle 31–5–80–4

Fielding Figures
8 – RD Jacobs; 3 – SL Campbell, CH Gayle; 1 – JC Adams, CEL Ambrose, S Chanderpaul, WW Hinds, CA Walsh

ZIMBABWE

Batting	M	Inns	NO	HS	Runs	Av	100	50
A Flower	2	4	1	113*	194	64.66	1	1
MW Goodwin	2	4	0	113	150	37.50	1	–
SV Carlisle	2	4	0	44	71	17.75	–	–
TR Gripper	2	4	0	41	55	13.75	–	–
GW Flower	2	4	0	26	39	9.75	–	–
HK Olonga	2	4	1	22*	26	8.66	–	–
NC Johnson	2	4	0	29	32	8.00	–	–
HH Streak	2	3	0	20	22	7.33	–	–
ADR Campbell	2	4	0	22	29	7.25	–	–
BA Murphy	2	4	2	1	1	0.50	–	–

Also batted: M Mbangwa (1 Test) 0, 0; BC Strang (1 Test) 13, 3

Bowling	Overs	Mds	Runs	Wkts	Av	Best	10/m	5/inn
HH Streak	39	17	72	9	8.00	5–27	–	1
BA Murphy	64.4	22	154	6	25.66	3–32	–	–
HK Olonga	65.1	18	157	6	26.16	3–65	–	–
NC Johnson	59	20	148	5	29.60	4–77	–	–

Also bowled: GW Flower 30–14–33–0; TR Gripper 8.4–2–28–0; M Mbangwa 25–13–36–0; BC Strang 39–17–64–1

Fielding Figures
8 – A Flower; 2 – ADR Campbell, BA Murphy; 1 – SV Carlisle, GW Flower, NC Johnson

PAKISTAN IN THE WEST INDIES
By Tony Cozier

FIRST TEST
5, 6, 7, 8 (no play) and 9 (no play) May 2000 at Bourda, Guyana

Guyana's always threatening weather ended its grudging co-operation with cricket after two uninterrupted days and condemned a Test of intriguing possibilities to a watery end after the third truncated day.

As was the case in the earlier one-day internationals, the 210.3 overs available confirmed that the teams were evenly matched and stronger in bowling than the mainly inexperienced batting.

At 39 for 5 three quarters of an hour before lunch, against the perennial combination of Curtly Ambrose and Courtney Walsh after being sent in on a blameless pitch, Pakistan would have been nowhere without Inzamam-ul-Haq, their one proven world-class batsman. He duly responded with his tenth Test hundred, his second in successive Tests following his 138 against Sri Lanka in Karachi in March. He and young Abdur Razzaq batted through the remainder of the first day and into the second for a recuperative sixth-wicket partnership of 206. Both had escapes before they were parted early on the second day when Inzamam was leg before to King's in-swinger after a stay of 254 balls during which 20 fours were his main scoring strokes. He

Yousuf Youhana caught by Jacobs off the first ball from Ambrose on the first day of the first Test at Bourda, Guyana.

was missed by Campbell at second slip off King when 32, a high, fingertip chance at second slip. Razzaq might have been taken at the wicket by Jacobs off Adams when 74.

Once they were separated, Pakistan's last five wickets fell for 43 to the all-pace attack. Razzaq was so becalmed on the second day he spent 79 balls adding seventh before he was eighth out to a slip catch off McLean. He batted 320 balls for his highest Test score.

In the same way that Inzamam's presence was critical to Razzaq's success, so was Chanderpaul's to Nixon McLean's in a stand of 74 after the West Indies found themselves 139 for 6 early on the third day and struggling against Mushtaq Ahmed's guile.

After Campbell's early dismissal to Wasim Akram, Griffith and Hinds put on 67 with increasing confidence but both had gone by close of play and, when they were quickly joined by Adams, Gayle and Jacobs following a belated start next day, the West Indies were up against it.

Returning to the team after a month's lay-off from the triangular one-day series because of fatigue, Chanderpaul showed encouraging signs of getting back to his adhesive best and McLean dutifully curbed his inclination for big-hitting by scoring 46 in the remaining 130 minutes. Chanderpaul was stuck four away from his half-century when the weather set in and brought the contest to a halt.

SECOND TEST
18, 19, 20, 21 and 22 May 2000 at Kensington Oval, Barbados

Aided by a belated declaration, the West Indies held on for a draw, grimly, but comfortably in the end. Moin Khan kept his second innings going until after lunch on the last day, needlessly wasting valuable time that could have been better utilised by Mushtaq Ahmed and Saqlain Mushtaq, on a worn, if still easy-paced, pitch.

Pakistan had only four wickets in the bag, for 132, when Moin acknowledged failure and agreed to end the match with five overs still available. It was only the second draw in the 17 Tests at Kensington since 1977 when the West Indies' last pair kept Pakistan at bay. This was not as close but it was almost as tense.

At 41 for 3, another testing 43.4 overs remained but captain Adams and Hinds virtually guaranteed safety by holding firm for the next hour and three quarters and 28 overs. Hinds, the tall, upright 23-year-old Jamaican, whose first-innings 165 was his first hundred in his fourth Test and the highest of

FIRST TEST – WEST INDIES v. PAKISTAN
5, 6, 7, 8 (no play) and 9 (no play) May 2000 at Bourda, Georgetown

PAKISTAN

	First innings		
Mohammad Wasim	b Ambrose		4
Wajahatullah Wasti	b Walsh		8
Younis Khan	lbw b Ambrose		2
Inzamam-ul-Haq	lbw b King		135
Yousuf Youhana	c Jacobs, b Ambrose		0
*Moin Khan (capt)	c Adams, b King		6
Abdur Razzaq	c Gayle, b McLean		87
Wasim Akram	c Jacobs, b Walsh		16
Waqar Younis	b McLean		13
Saqlain Mushtaq	not out		8
Mushtaq Ahmed	c Gayle, b Ambrose		4
	lb2, nb3		5
			288

	First Innings			
	O	M	R	W
Ambrose	25.3	10	43	4
Walsh	28	10	46	2
McLean	26	5	93	2
King	26	7	57	2
Gayle	9	4	16	–
Adams	9	0	31	–

Fall of Wickets
1–12, 2–12, 3–21, 4–21, 5–39, 6–245, 7–262, 8–266, 9–277

WEST INDIES

	First innings		
SL Campbell	c Younis Khan, b Wasim Akram		1
AFG Griffith	lbw b Abdur Razzaq		34
WW Hinds	st Moin Khan, b Mushtaq Ahmed		34
JC Adams (capt)	c Younis Khan, b Mushtaq Ahmed		20
S Chanderpaul	not out		46
CH Gayle	c Wasim Akram, b Mushtaq Ahmed		13
*RD Jacobs	run out (Wajahtullah Wasti/ Mushtaq Ahmed)		6
NAM McLean	c Inzamam-ul-Haq, b Waqar Younis		46
CEL Ambrose	not out		2
RD King			
CA Walsh			
	lb2, nb18		20
	(for 7 wickets)		**222**

	First innings			
	O	M	R	W
Wasim Akram	20	6	46	1
Waqar Younis	15	3	46	1
Mushtaq Ahmed	32	5	91	3
Abdur Razzaq	10	2	13	1
Saqlain Mushtaq	10	1	24	–

Fall of Wickets
1–2, 2–69, 3–79, 4–106, 5–130, 6–139, 7–213

Umpires: SA Bucknor & RE Koertzen
Toss: West Indies
Test Debuts: nil

Match drawn

the three in a match that yielded 1,202 runs, again impressed with 52. It not only earned him the Man of the Match award but certified him as a genuine Test number 3.

Youhana's second Test century was vital to Pakistan on the first day while 18-year-old Imran Nazir's 131 in the second innings was a joyous exhibition of uninhibited stroke-play. Confronted by a grassless, pluperfect pitch similar to the batting paradises of the 1960s and stymied by the traditional lack of variety in their attack, the West Indies once more let Pakistan wriggle out of a tight bind on the first day.

Almost exactly mirroring the first morning in Georgetown, Pakistan found themselves 37 for 5 after an hour and a quarter, four to catches in the slips, one to short leg. They were revived by a chanceless 115 by Youhana, a first-ball victim in Georgetown, and the support he received from three successive partners, Moin with whom he added 73, Wasim Akram 69 and Saqlain 41. Youhana fell to a second slip catch off the second new ball, a tired shot that gave Walsh his fifth wicket and ended the innings.

Hinds dominated the second day, adding 133 for the second wicket with Campbell as the West Indies went ahead by 30 at close with five wickets intact, a distinct advantage. Ever eager to take on the experienced and varied bowling, Hinds used his bat

Wavell Hinds driving Mushtaq Ahmed during his maiden Test century of 165, in the second Test at Kensington Oval.

Sherwin Campbell is bowled by Saqlain Mushtaq for 58, as Moin Khan jumps for joy during the second Test at Kensington Oval, Barbados.

with such effect that his chanceless innings was embellished with 24 resounding boundaries before he fell near the end to a miscued hook to mid-on off Waqar, a stroke that had earned him three earlier fours in an over from the same bowler.

Campbell's 58 included four sixes, three hooked and one courtesy of overthrows, but Adams and Chanderpaul fell cheaply before Sarwan, the 11th teenager to represent the West Indies, showed class and character in remaining unbeaten 28 at stumps.

On the third day, it was the turn of three more young batsmen to enjoy the bounty provided by a placid pitch. Sarwan was denied the rare chance of a hundred on debut when he ran out of partners to be left unbeaten 84. Starting the previous afternoon, he batted five hours 20 minutes all told and guaranteed the West Indies a significant lead of 145. Nazir, in his second Test, similarly right-handed, small, boyish and precocious, set off with youthful disregard for either the reputations of the opposing bowlers or his team's situation. In the two hours 50 minutes he had on the third afternoon, he cracked 14 boundaries in 94, mostly with sweetly struck cuts of varying angles and handsome drives through the off side. He and Mohammed Wasim, 22, tall and orthodox, erased the deficit of 145, setting the match back on an even keel with a partnership not separated until it reached 219 next day when King dismissed both Imran Nazir and Younis Khan in quick succession before lunch. Nazir's 131 required only 180 balls and included 20 fours but no one followed his lead.

SECOND TEST – WEST INDIES v. PAKISTAN
18, 19, 20, 21 and 22 May 2000 at Kensington Oval, Bridgetown

PAKISTAN

	First innings		Second innings	
Mohammad Wasim	c Adams, b Walsh	4	lbw b King	82
Imran Nazir	c Campbell, b Ambrose	2	c Adams, b King	131
Younis Khan	c Chanderpaul, b Walsh	0	c Jacobs, b King	23
Inzamam-ul-Haq	c Adams, b King	8	c & b Walsh	29
Yousuf Youhana	c Campbell, b Walsh	115	c Adams, b McLean	19
Abdur Razzaq	c Hinds, b McLean	1	c sub (CH Gayle) b King	72
*Moin Khan (capt)	c Chanderpaul, b Walsh	38	b Adams	14
Wasim Akram	b Ambrose	42	c Hinds, b Adams	0
Saqlain Mushtaq	c Campbell, b Adams	12	b McLean	33
Waqar Younis	c Griffith, b Walsh	14	not out	1
Mushtaq Ahmed	not out	2		
	b2, lb9, nb4	15	lb4, w1, nb10	15
		253	**(for 9 wickets dec.)**	**419**

	First innings				Second innings			
	O	M	R	W	O	M	R	W
Ambrose	21	7	53	2	37	16	54	–
Walsh	13	4	22	5	36	6	102	1
King	17	1	56	1	29	9	82	4
McLean	16	3	63	1	23.4	4	112	2
Adams	17	1	45	1	26	9	52	2
Chanderpaul	2	0	3	–	2	0	13	–

Fall of Wickets
1–7, 2–7, 3–7, 4–34, 5–37, 6–110, 7–179, 8–220, 9–248
1–219, 2–232, 3–248, 4–294, 5–294, 6–341, 7–341, 8–411, 9–419

WEST INDIES

	First innings		Second innings	
SL Campbell	b Saqlain Mushtaq	58	c sub (Shahid Afridi), b Wasim Akram	8
AFG Griffith	c Moin Khan, b Waqar Younis	4	lbw b Waqar Younis	5
WW Hinds	c Inzamam-ul-Haq, b Waqar Younis	165	c Moin Khan, b Mushtaq Ahmed	52
S Chanderpaul	c Moin Khan, b Abdur Razzaq	9	c Mohammad Wasim, b Mushtaq Ahmed	16
JC Adams (capt)	c Younis Khan, b Saqlain Mushtaq	8	not out	34
RR Sarwan	not out	84	not out	11
CEL Ambrose	c Younis Khan, b Wasim Akram	22		
*RD Jacobs	b Saqlain Mushtaq	10		
NAM McLean	c Yousuf Youhana, b Wasim Akram	1		
RD King	c Mushtaq Ahmed, b Saqlain Mushtaq	2		
CA Walsh	c Moin Khan, b Saqlain Mushtaq	22		
	lb6, nb7	13	b1, lb1, nb4	6
		398	**(for 4 wickets)**	**132**

	First innings				Second innings			
	O	M	R	W	O	M	R	W
Wasim Akram	33	9	84	2	7	1	24	1
Waqar Younis	17	2	72	2	4	0	14	1
Mushtaq Ahmed	22	2	65	–	20	5	64	2
Abdur Razzaq	16	3	50	1				
Saqlain Mushtaq	51	10	121	5	21	12	28	–

Fall of Wickets
1–11, 2–144, 3–176, 4–213, 5–282, 6–321, 7–338, 8–339, 9–362
1–15, 2–15, 3–41, 4–113

Umpires: EA Nicholls & RE Koertzen
Toss: Pakistan
Test Debut: RR Sarwan

Match drawn

Pakistan's tactics once Younis was out were mystifying. With Inzamam, their leading batsman, and Youhana, the first-innings century-maker, occupying most of the time, they dawdled over 58 overs to add 92 over the last two sessions of the fourth day, losing four wickets, after compiling 101 off 25 overs in the first. On the last morning, they took 30.4 overs to add 74 before Moin timidly declared with nine wickets down once Razzaq was caught at long on for 72. By then, not enough time remained for a result.

THIRD TEST
25, 26, 27, 28 and 29 May 2000 at the Recreation Ground, St John's, Antigua

It was as close, tense and bizarre as they come and it took a captain's innings of nerveless, single-minded determination, combined with a healthy helping of necessary luck, to secure the West Indies victory by one wicket and the series one-nil.

Adams, in his fifth Test at the helm of a team his leadership had revitalised, kept his head and his wicket through three and a quarter hours of unrelenting pressure on the final day to marshal the remarkable triumph. Last man Walsh, unabashed holder of the record number of ducks in Test cricket but an old hand in such situations, stayed with Adams for an hour and a quarter and 13 overs, surviving 24 balls to the delight of the cheering, flag-waving stands as the final 19 runs were eked out in a match that remained in the balance throughout.

When they scampered the decisive run on Adams' bat-pad push into the covers off Wasim Akram half an hour after lunch, the captain raised his hands to the heavens, broke into a smile for the first time in the five and a half hours and, physically and emotionally drained by the effort, lay flat out on the grass. He was immediately smothered under a blanket of his jubilant players, celebrating a result that clinched the three-match series one-nil and kept intact the record of never losing a series in the Caribbean to Pakistan.

The Pakistanis trudged from the ground in the deep disappointment felt by all sportsmen in such circumstances. They, and everyone else, knew they would have won had not nervous fingers, of both umpires and of the fumbling Saqlain, failed to do what they should have done to reverse the outcome.

With 20 required, the ubiquitous television replay indicated that Adams had snicked Akram into Moin's gloves but umpire Billy Doctrove, the West Indian from Dominica in his first Test, did not agree.

Yousuf Youhana cuts while Hinds takes evasive action during Youhana's undefeated innings of 103 during the third Test at Antigua's Recreation Ground.

With 16 still needed, Walsh lunged forward to his second ball from Saqlain and the replays clearly showed an inside edge into pad and into the hands of Nazir at forward short leg. This time umpire Doug Cowie, of New Zealand, the ICC appointee, rejected demanding appeals. Twice, almost identical run-out chances were squandered with the batsmen – Ambrose and Adams in the first instance, Walsh and Adams in the second – standing in the same crease. Each time, the ball bounced from Saqlain's hands as it was returned to the bowler's end with a scrambling West Indian, and the match, at his mercy.

The Pakistanis took their defeat stoically, refusing to publicly condemn the umpiring and graciously congratulating their opponents. They entered the match with the shadow of Judge Qayyum's match-fixing report hanging over their four most senior players, Wasim Akram, Inzamam-ul-Haq, Mushtaq Ahmed and Waqar Younis. It was obvious they had something to prove, none more so than Akram, the 33-year-old veteran of 95 Tests, whose 11 wickets for 110 from 56.2 tireless overs were gained by high-quality left-arm swing bowling and earned him the Man of the Match award. As was the case in each of the first two Tests, they had to fight their way out of early trouble. They were 32 for 3 after being sent in on the liveliest pitch of the series before Youhana, as he had done in Barbados, revived them with 103 that was only ended when he ran out of partners after five and three quarter hours and 231 balls of unwavering concentration and flawless stroke selection.

He and Inzamam shared a partnership of 97 that steadied the innings and there was valuable later support from Moin and Akram. But, after Walsh collected yet another five-wicket return by polishing off the innings with the second new ball on the second morning, 269 seemed inadequate when the West Indies closed the day at 214 for 3 with Chanderpaul and Adams unbeaten in a partnership of 130.

It took Pakistan's tried and trusted campaigners to get them out of a couple of tight spots. Akram first turned the match on its head with a lengthy, unbroken spell of incisive bowling in the morning that brought him the last six West Indies wickets at the miserly personal cost of four runs from 28 balls. In the face of it, the home team collapsed to a meaningless lead of four runs, transforming the match into a straight second-innings contest.

When Pakistan went to tea 49 for 3, it was left to Inzamam and the consistent Youhana to ride the crisis with a stand of 80. Inzamam went for 68, showing such slow-moving dissent against umpire Doctrove's caught behind decision he was fined 20 per cent of his match fee by ICC referee Peter Burge.

Youhana held firm to the end of a day that, like so many others in the series, was prolonged to more than an hour's overtime because of the continuing sluggish over rate and a spate of interruptions and delays. He was 41 with Pakistan 157 for 5 going into the fourth day but he added only one more and it was left to the tail to carry the total past 200.

After shifting one way and then the next over the first three innings, the contest gradually tilted towards the West Indies before taking a wicked twist on what was the last ball of an intense fourth day. Going after 216 after completing Pakistan's second innings ten minutes after lunch, the West Indies were strongly placed at 144 for 3 with rain visibly approaching and Hinds and Adams entrenched when Hinds, obviously unsettled by the heightening tension after three and a half hours of batting excellence, dragged a short ball from Akram back into his stumps from a woeful pull shot.

All calm assurance, he led his team's charge with positive stroke-play until, suddenly and out of character, he was so overcome by the pressure that he needlessly barged into bowler Saqlain, with whom he had had an earlier, if inadvertent, physical clash, as he trotted down the pitch for a single.

It led to an exchange of words. Adams, his captain and partner, ushered him away from the confrontation and clearly tried to refocus him on the job at hand but Hinds had been terminally distracted. His dismissal in the next over was as predictable as it was untimely.

As he trudged towards the pavilion, the ground staff were dragging the covers on to the pitch from another direction and not another ball was bowled, leaving both teams starting the last day still even, the West Indies needing 72, Pakistan six wickets.

The loss of Sarwan in the day's sixth over, leg before for the second time to Akram, meant the responsibility rested almost solely on Adams. Not trusting his remaining partners to cope, he shielded them by taking as much of the strike as he could from Akram, who bowled 17.3 tireless overs, in three spells from either end, to add to his 12.3 of the previous day. Sticking unwaveringly to his calculated plan, Adams consistently refused blatant singles to deep-set fields to ensure Akram wouldn't get at the shaky tail. While he faced 141 balls on the day, the others had to deal with only 78, mostly from Mushtaq and Saqlain, who sent down 13 overs between them. Strangely, Moin didn't call on Waqar at all.

Adams could find no one to stay with him until Walsh entered and, with luck, obliged.

The West Indies cricket flag flies high as the jubilant captain Jimmy Adams and Courtney Walsh hail the thrilling one-wicket victory at the end of the third Test at Antigua.

THIRD TEST – WEST INDIES v. PAKISTAN
25, 26, 27, 28 and 29 May 2000 at Antigua Recreation Ground, St John's

PAKISTAN

	First innings		Second innings	
Mohammad Wasim	c & b Rose	13	b King	21
Imran Nazir	c Rose, b Ambrose	10	c Sarwan, b Walsh	0
Younis Khan	c Jacobs, b Ambrose	4	lbw b Ambrose	2
Inzamam-ul-Haq	c Griffith, b Walsh	55	c Jacobs, b Rose	68
Yousuf Youhana	not out	103	lbw b King	42
Abdur Razzaq	c Jacobs, b Walsh	2	(8) run out (Yousuf Youhana/ Moin Khan)	0
*Moin Khan (capt)	c Jacobs, b Rose	24	(6) c Hinds, b King	10
Wasim Akram	c Campbell, b King	26	(9) c Adams, b King	24
Saqlain Mushtaq	c Campbell, b Walsh	4	(7) c Campbell, b Ambrose	15
Waqar Younis	c Sarwan, b Walsh	4	c Adams, b Ambrose	16
Mushtaq Ahmed	c Jacobs, b Walsh	0	not out	3
	lb4, nb20	24	b2, lb4, nb12	18
		269		**219**

	First innings				Second innings			
	O	M	R	W	O	M	R	W
Ambrose	14	4	30	2	21	5	39	3
Walsh	26	2	83	5	20	4	39	1
Rose	19	4	48	2	20	2	69	1
King	16	3	48	1	23	6	48	4
Adams	14	2	40	–	6	1	18	–
Sarwan	2	0	16	–				

Fall of Wickets
1-21, 2-26, 3-33, 4-130, 5-132, 6-173, 7-209, 8-247, 9-268
1-0, 2-3, 3-49, 4-129, 5-150, 6-162, 7-163, 8-186, 9-213

WEST INDIES

	First Innings		Second innings	
SL Campbell	c Yousuf Youhana, b Mushtaq Ahmed	31	c Yousuf Youhana, Wasim Akram	6
AFG Griffith	b Mushtaq Ahmed	22	c Waqar Younis,	
Wasim Akram		23		
WW Hinds	run out (Mushtaq Ahmed/ Moin Khan)	26	b Wasim Akram	63
S Chanderpaul	b Wasim Akram	89	lbw b Abdur Razzaq	31
JC Adams (capt)	lbw Waqar Younis	60	not out	48
RR Sarwan	lbw b Wasim Akram	10	lbw b Wasim Akram	6
*RD Jacobs	lbw b Wasim Akram	0	run out (Yousuf Youhana/ Moin Khan)	5
FA Rose	c Abdur Razzaq, b Wasim Akram	15	c Wasim Akram, b Mushtaq Ahmed	4
CEL Ambrose	c Yousuf Youhana, b Mushtaq Ahmed	0	lbw b Saqlain Mushtaq	8
RD King	c & b Wasim Akram	3	b Wasim Akram	0
CA Walsh	not out	2	not out	4
	b1, lb10, nb4	15	b8, lb7, nb3	18
		273	(for 9 wickets)	**216**

	First innings				Second innings			
	O	M	R	W	O	M	R	W
Wasim Akram	26.2	7	61	6	30	2	49	5
Waqar Younis	21	8	41	1	11	0	39	–
Mushtaq Ahmed	24	3	68	2	17	3	61	1
Saqlain Mushtaq	23	4	48	–	22	7	38	1
Abdur Razzaq	12	1	44	1	11	3	14	1

Fall of Wickets
1-40, 2-73, 3-84, 4-215, 5-235, 6-243, 7-254, 8-258, 9-269
1-16, 2-31, 3-84, 4-144, 5-161, 6-169, 7-177, 8-194, 9-197

Umpires: B Doctrove & DB Cowie
Toss: West Indies
Test Debuts: nil

West Indies won by one wicket

TEST MATCH AVERAGES
Pakistan v. West Indies

PAKISTAN

Batting	M	Inns	NO	HS	Runs	Av	100	50
Yousuf Youhana	3	5	1	115	279	69.75	2	–
Inzamam-ul-Haq	3	5	0	135	295	59.00	1	2
Imran Nazir	2	4	0	131	143	35.75	1	–
Abdur Razzaq	3	5	0	87	162	32.40	–	2
Mohammad Wasim	3	5	0	82	124	24.80	–	1
Wasim Akram	3	5	0	42	108	21.60	–	–
Moin Khan	3	5	0	38	92	18.40	–	–
Saqlain Mushtaq	3	5	1	33	72	18.00	–	–
Waqar Younis	3	5	1	16	48	12.00	–	–
Younis Khan	3	5	0	23	31	6.20	–	–
Mushtaq Ahmed	3	4	2	3*	9	4.50	–	–

Also batted: Wajahatullah Wasti (1 Test) 8

Bowling	Overs	Mds	Runs	Wkts	Av	Best	10/m	5/inn
Wasim Akram	116.2	25	264	15	17.60	6-61	2	1
Waqar Younis	68	13	212	5	42.40	2-72	–	–
Saqlain Mushtaq	127	34	259	6	43.16	5-121	–	1
Mushtaq Ahmed	115	18	349	8	43.62	–	–	–

Also bowled: Abdur Razzaq 49-9-121-3

Fielding Figures
5 – Moin Khan (4ct/1st); 4 – Younis Khan, Yousuf Youhana; 3 – Wasim Akram; 2 – Inzamam-ul-Haq; 1 – Abdur Razzaq, Mohammad Wasim, Mushtaq Ahmed, Waqar Younis

WEST INDIES

Batting	M	Inns	NO	HS	Runs	Av	100	50
WW Hinds	3	5	0	165	340	68.00	1	2
JC Adams	3	5	2	60	170	56.66	–	1
RR Sarwan	2	4	2	84*	111	55.50	–	1
S Chanderpaul	3	5	1	89	191	47.75	–	1
CA Walsh	3	3	2	22	28	28.00	–	–
SL Campbell	3	5	0	58	104	20.80	–	1
AFG Griffith	3	5	0	34	88	17.60	–	2
CEL Ambrose	3	4	1	22	32	10.66	–	–
RD Jacobs	3	4	0	10	21	5.25	–	–
RD King	3	3	0	3	5	1.66	–	–

Also batted: CH Gayle (1 Test) 13; NAM McLean (2 Tests) 46, 1; FA Rose (1 Test) 15, 4

Bowling	Overs	Mds	Runs	Wkts	Av	Best	10/m	5/inn
CEL Ambrose	118.3	42	219	11	19.90	4-43	–	–
CA Walsh	123	26	292	14	20.85	5-22	–	2
RD King	111	26	291	12	24.25	4-48	–	–
NAM McLean	65.4	12	268	5	53.60	2-93	–	–

Also bowled: JC Adams 72-13-186-3; S Chanderpaul 4-0-16-0; CH Gayle 9-4-16-0; FA Rose 39-6-117-3; RR Sarwan 2-0-16-0

Fielding Figures
8 – RD Jacobs; 7 – JC Adams; 6 – SL Campbell; 3 – WW Hinds; 2 – S Chanderpaul, CH Gayle, AFG Griffith, FA Rose, RR Sarwan; 1 – CA Walsh

CABLE & WIRELESS ONE-DAY SERIES
By Tony Cozier

In an engaging preview to the Test series that followed, Pakistan overcame the West Indies in two of the best-of-three finals to secure the Cable & Wireless Trophy. It was the first triangular tournament of one-day internationals in the Caribbean and only the second time (after Australia, 1991) that the West Indies had lost a home series in the shorter game.

The teams were so evenly matched that the West Indies actually held a three-two advantage overall in their five matches, winning both in the preliminary round. Zimbabwe, their spirit diminished by their defeats in the preceding Tests, in both of which they held strong positions, and by the intensifying political crisis back home, lost all four matches, a disappointing end to their first tour of the Caribbean.

Throughout, the bowling was demonstrably stronger than the batting. Only in their meaningless second preliminary match, when the ever dangerous Wasim Akram was rested, did the West Indies come to terms with the varied Pakistan attack. Mushtaq Ahmed made the most significant impact with his leg-breaks and googlies that perplexed every batsman. He conceded an average of only three runs an over and his ten wickets included three in one over in the decisive third final in which he took 4 for 22. Only when Wavell Hinds got after him later in the second Test was his threat repelled.

For the West Indies, Reon King and Franklyn Rose confirmed their advances made in the Tests against Zimbabwe, rendering immaterial the absence of Courtney Walsh, whose turn it was, instead of Curtly Ambrose, to be rested in preparation for the more demanding contests ahead. King, fast and accurate, had 17 wickets, six more than anyone else on either side, at a cost of 11.52 each and an economy rate of 3.26 an over. Rose's figures of 5 for 23 that routed Pakistan for 117 in their first meeting in St Vincent were the best of the tournament.

On generally slow pitches that encouraged turn, the left-arm spin of captain Jimmy Adams and the flat off-spin of Chris Gayle were important, if surprising, adjuncts to the West Indies' pace. Both teams relied heavily on established players for their runs. Inzamam-ul-Haq, a new vice-captain for Moin Khan, was out for less than 30 only once in seven innings. In an order always prone to collapse (against the West Indies, 117 all out, 197 for 8, 148 all out and 116 for 6 off 45.1 overs in winning the decisive third final), his 295 runs at an average of 59 earned him the Man of the Series award. No other Pakistani averaged better than 30 as the 18-year-old Imran Nazir did not follow up his unbeaten 105 in their opening match against Zimbabwe until his century in the second Test against the West Indies.

Already without Brian Lara, the West Indies also missed Shivnarine Chanderpaul, who was given a month off after the Zimbabwe Tests, complaining of 'acute fatigue'. It placed additional responsibility on Adams and his vice-captain Sherwin Campbell, the only two remaining batsmen with more than 50 one-day internationals to their name. Campbell responded with 316 runs, average 45.14, that included his first hundred in limited-over cricket, 103 against Zimbabwe at Sabina Park. Adams started with scores of 60, 41 and 50 but tailed off sharply as he was run out four times in his seven innings. Refreshingly, the only free-scoring batting of the bowler-dominated tournament came from young players although none was consistent. At Sabina, the left-handed Wavell Hinds hit an unbeaten 116 off 125 balls for the West Indies in the tournament's

Wavell Hinds is bowled in the third final at Queen's Park Oval, which Pakistan won to take the series.

highest total, 280 for 3, against Zimbabwe. His all-Jamaican, all left-handed, unbroken fourth-wicket partnership of 125 with Gayle (53 off 45 balls) sent a packed home crowd of 12,000 into typically boisterous West Indian celebrations.

Another Jamaican, the shot-making Ricardo Powell, blazed 50 off 39 balls against Pakistan at the impressive new Queen's Park stadium in Grenada, Shahid Afridi lived up to his reputation with a run-a-ball 69, with three sixes and five fours, against Zimbabwe in Antigua, and Nazir's unbeaten 105 (135 balls, two sixes, ten fours) against Zimbabwe in Grenada confirmed the impression he first made in the triangular tournament a month earlier.

Ball so emphatically dominated bat throughout that there were only three individual hundreds in the ten matches, all against Zimbabwe, and seven completed totals of under 200. No result was closer than 17 runs or four wickets. It was hardly a memorable event.

Pakistan players Imran Nazir and captain Moin Khan celebrate the fall of Jacobs, who was caught by Nazir off the bowling of Mushtaq Ahmed in the third final.

Match One – West Indies v. Zimbabwe
1 April 2000 at Sabina Park, Kingston, Jamaica
West Indies 237 for 9 (50 overs)(SL Campbell 103, JC Adams 60)
Zimbabwe 150 (41.1 overs)(MW Goodwin 52)
West Indies (2 pts) won by 87 runs
Man of the Match: SL Campbell

Match Two – West Indies v. Zimbabwe
2 April 2000 at Sabina Park, Kingston, Jamaica
West Indies 280 for 3 (50 overs)(WW Hinds 116*, CH Gayle 58*)
Zimbabwe 239 for 8 (50 overs)(SV Carlisle 57, A Flower 52)
West Indies (2 pts) won by 41 runs
Man of the Match: WW Hinds

Match Three – Pakistan v. Zimbabwe
5 April 2000 at Antigua Recreation Ground, St John's, Antigua
Zimbabwe 199 for 9 (50 overs)
Pakistan 200 for 5 (47.1 overs)(Shahid Afridi 69)
Pakistan (2 pts) won by five wickets
Man of the Match: Shahid Afridi

Match Four – West Indies v. Pakistan
12 April 2000 at Arnos Vale Ground, Kingstown, St Vincent
West Indies 213 for 7 (50 overs)(JC Adams 50)
Pakistan 117 (41.3 overs)(Inzamam-ul-Haq 51*, FA Rose 5 for 23)
West Indies (2 pts) won by 96 runs
Man of the Match: FA Rose

Match Five – Pakistan v. Zimbabwe
15 April 2000 at Queen's Park, St George's, Grenada
Zimbabwe 204 for 7 (50 overs)
Pakistan 205 for 4 (43.1 overs)(Shahid Nazir 105*)
Pakistan (2 pts) won by six wickets
Man of the Match: Imran Nazir

Match Six – West Indies v. Pakistan
16 April 2000 at Queen's Park, St George's, Grenada
West Indies 248 for 6 (50 overs)(SL Campbell 56, RL Powell 50*)
Pakistan 231 (48.1 overs)(Inzamam-ul-Haq 69, Yousuf Youhana 56)
West Indies (2 pts) won by 17 runs
Pakistan were fined 1 over for slow bowling rate
Man of the Match: RD King

FIRST FINAL – WEST INDIES v. PAKISTAN
19 April 2000 at Kensington Oval, Bridgetown, Barbados

PAKISTAN

Batting		
Imran Nazir	c Wallace, b King	12
Shahid Afridi	c Jacobs, b Adams	17
Younis Khan	run out (Adams/Jacobs)	23
Inzamam-ul-Haq	c & b McLean	66
Yousuf Youhana	lbw b King	8
*Moin Khan (capt)	b Adams	0
Abdur Razzaq	run out (Gayle)	7
Wasim Akram	not out	42
Waqar Younis	c Jacobs, b Gayle	0
Mushtaq Ahmed	not out	11
Arshad Khan		
	lb2, w6, nb3	11
	50 overs (for 8 wickets)	**197**

Bowling	O	M	R	W
Ambrose	10	0	35	1
King	10	1	37	2
McLean	10	1	36	1
Rose	10	1	41	–
Gayle	6	0	26	1
Adams	4	1	20	1

Fall of Wickets
1-24, 2-32, 3-81, 4-100, 5-101,
6-137, 7-140, 8-144

WEST INDIES

Batting		
PA Wallace	c Yousuf Youhana, b Mushtaq Ahmed	47
SL Campbell	c Moin Khan, b Waqar Younis	11
WW Hinds	c Moin Khan, b Waqar Younis	35
CH Gayle	run out (Shahid Afridi/ Moin Khan)	8
JC Adams (capt)	b Abdur Razzaq	7
*RD Jacobs	c Younis Khan, b Arshad Khan	0
SC Joseph	b Shahid Afridi	28
FA Rose	b Shahid Afridi	11
NAM McLean	run out (Younis Khan/ Moin Khan)	1
CEL Ambrose	c sub (Shoaib Malik), b Shahid Afridi	11
RD King	not out	2
	b1, lb4, w12, nb2	19
	49.3 overs	**180**

Bowling	O	M	R	W
Wasim Akram	10	3	30	1
Waqar Younis	9	0	34	2
Abdur Razzaq	10	1	38	1
Mushtaq Ahmed	10	2	23	1
Arshad Khan	7	0	34	1
Shahid Afridi	3.3	0	16	3

Fall of Wickets
1-13, 2-99, 3-105 4-121, 5-122,
6-123, 7-145, 8-146, 9-175

Umpires: B Doctrove & EA Nicholls
Toss: Pakistan
Man of the Match: Wasim Akram

Pakistan won by 17 runs

SECOND FINAL – WEST INDIES v. PAKISTAN
22 April 2000 at Queen's Park Oval, Port-of-Spain, Trinidad

WEST INDIES

Batting		
PA Wallace	lbw b Wasim Akram	8
SL Campbell	c Waqar Younis, b Wasim Akram	77
WW Hinds	c Shahid Afridi, b Abdur Razzaq	24
JC Adams (capt)	run out (Moin Khan)	5
CH Gayle	run out (Mushtaq Ahmed)	33
RL Powell	c Arshad Khan, b Shahid Afridi	21
*RD Jacobs	b Abdur Razzaq	16
FA Rose	c Abdur Razzaq, b Wasim Akram	5
NAM McLean	not out	1
CEL Ambrose	not out	4
RD King		
	b2, lb4, w8	14
	50 overs (for 8 wickets)	**208**

Bowling	O	M	R	W
Wasim Akram	10	2	34	3
Waqar Younis	8	1	26	–
Mushtaq Ahmed	10	0	34	–
Abdur Razzaq	10	0	42	2
Arshad Khan	7	0	31	–
Shahid Afridi	5	0	35	1

Fall of Wickets
1-11, 2-69, 3-84, 4-134, 5-171,
6-189, 7-202, 8-203

PAKISTAN

Batting		
Imran Nazir	lbw b McLean	22
Shahid Afridi	c Jacobs, b McLean	21
Younis Khan	lbw b Gayle	31
Inzamam-ul-Haq	lbw b King	4
Yousuf Youhana	lbw b King	0
Abdur Razzaq	b Adams	6
*Moin Khan (capt)	c Hinds, b Adams	11
Wasim Akram	st Jacobs, b Gayle	4
Waqar Younis	run out (Hinds/Jacobs)	23
Mushtaq Ahmed	b Adams	3
Arshad Khan	not out	5
	b1, lb3, w8, nb6	18
	45 overs	**148**

Bowling	O	M	R	W
Ambrose	7	0	23	–
King	6	1	22	2
McLean	6	0	33	2
Rose	6	1	17	–
Adams	10	0	21	3
Gayle	10	0	28	2

Fall of Wickets
1-34, 2-72, 3-79, 4-79, 5-98,
6-98, 7-108, 8-124, 9-138

Umpires: B Doctrove & EA Nicholls
Toss: West Indies
Man of the Match: SL Campbell

West Indies won by 60 runs

THIRD FINAL – WEST INDIES v. PAKISTAN
23 April 2000 at Queen's Park Oval, Port-of-Spain, Trinidad

WEST INDIES

Batting		
PA Wallace	st Moin Khan,	
	b Mushtaq Ahmed	30
SL Campbell	c Inzamam-ul-Haq,	
	b Abdur Razzaq	26
WW Hinds	b Mushtaq Ahmed	7
JC Adams (capt)	b Shoaib Akhtar	9
CH Gayle	c Shahid Afridi,	
	b Mushtaq Ahmed	0
RL Powell	c Shahid Afridi,	
	b Mushtaq Ahmed	0
*RD Jacobs	c Imran Nazir,	
	b Saqlain Mushtaq	7
FA Rose	not out	9
CEL Ambrose	b Shoaib Akhtar	0
NAM McLean	c & b Saqlain Mushtaq	15
RD King	run out (Shahid Afridi)	0
	lb2, w6, nb3	11
	33.2 overs	114

Bowling	O	M	R	W
Wasim Akram	7	0	22	–
Shoaib Akhtar	7	0	31	2
Abdur Razzaq	6	1	17	1
Mushtaq Ahmed	8	1	22	4
Saqlain Mushtaq	5.2	0	20	2

Fall of Wickets
1–61, 2–61, 3–71, 4–71, 5–71,
6–83, 7–97, 8–97, 9–114

PAKISTAN

Batting		
Imran Nazir	c Jacobs, b King	4
Shahid Afridi	c Rose, b King	13
Younis Khan	c & b Adams	17
Abdur Razzaq	c Jacobs, b King	0
Inzamam-ul-Haq	not out	39
Yousuf Youhana	c Campbell, b Adams	4
*Moin Khan (capt)	c Jacobs, b King	10
Wasim Akram	not out	10
Shoaib Akhtar		
Mushtaq Ahmed		
Saqlain Mushtaq		
	lb7, w7, nb5	19
	45.1 overs	116

Bowling	O	M	R	W
Ambrose	10	4	15	–
King	10	1	25	4
Rose	10	0	30	–
McLean	8.1	2	20	–
Adams	5	0	17	2
Gayle	2	1	2	–

Fall of Wickets
1–13, 2–18, 3–19, 4–61, 5–73,
6–93

Umpires: B Doctrove & EA Nicholls
Toss: West Indies
Man of the Match: Mushtaq Ahmed
Man of the Series: Inzamam-ul-Haq

Pakistan won by four wickets

Chris Gayle: the most successful young batsman in West
Indian cricket, and the only player to pass 400 runs in the
Busta Cup.

BUSTA CUP
By Haydn Gill

Packed with West Indies players, Jamaica won the 2000 Busta Cup, their first first-class title in eight years, to complete their domination of the regional game following their triumph in the limited-overs Red Stripe Bowl and the under-19 Nortel championships.

Their success in the Busta Cup was overshadowed by the standard of cricket, which was again disappointing and of continuing concern to administrators and followers alike. Statistics can be misleading but they correctly revealed the quality of the batting. Only one batsman, the 20-year-old Jamaican left-hander Chris Gayle, passed 400 runs (623, average 56.63) and only another seven managed more than 300. Only three averaged above 40. There were two totals over 350 yet 12 fewer than 150 and a further 12 under 200. The previous season, when the figures were marginally better, Joey Carew, one of the Test selectors, bemoaned the situation. Now his chairman, Mike Findlay, made the same point. 'The standard of the cricket in the Busta Cup was very poor,' he said. 'We did not see much of the under-19 players who were in Sri Lanka [for the Youth World Cup] but what we have seen of the others who have been around the game for a while has not been encouraging.'

The inconsistency that has bedevilled the Test team was evident throughout and was best exemplified by the Leeward Islands. They passed 300 three times and matched it with a similar number of totals under 150. Five successive matches

typified their spasmodic form. In the third round, after all the West Indies players had returned from their ill-starred tour of New Zealand, they made 398 for 8 in the second innings after they had been routed for 85 in the first by the Windward Islands. They lost their next match to Guyana after leading on first innings but, in the final preliminary round, defeated Jamaica, who had just come off victories over Trinidad & Tobago and Barbados.

For all that, they qualified for the semi-final in fourth position and advanced to the final courtesy of more mediocre batting from Barbados, the defending champions. In the final, they reverted to their novice mode, folded for 142 in their first innings and could not recover as Jamaica protected their lead in a drawn match that was sufficient for the Cup.

Jamaica, with nine players of international calibre, managed to pull it together when it mattered most and duly deserved their success on the strength of their performances in the semi-final and final.

Once through, first-day hundreds in the respective matches by Gayle, 168 against Guyana in the semi, and his fellow left-hander Wavell Hinds, 127 against the Leewards in the final, set them on course for the championship that had eluded them since 1992. In his second season, Gayle distinguished himself almost every time he batted. Tall and somewhat heavy-footed, he compensated with powerful stroke-play, especially off the back foot, that made him almost 150 runs better than the next two in the aggregates, his Jamaican team-mate, all-rounder Laurie Williams (378) and the Barbados captain and opener, Philo Wallace (371). In the absence of any other genuine contender, he won the Most Valuable Player award.

Williams, 31 and a decade in the Jamaica team, enjoyed his best season, supplementing his runs with 20 wickets with his medium-pace swing bowling in an attack spearheaded by the pace of Franklyn Rose and Courtney Walsh and the off-spin of Nehemiah Perry once they were back from duty with the West Indies in New Zealand. Rose enjoyed one of the highlights of the season with a hat-trick of Test batsmen (Sherwin Campbell, Adrian Griffith and Philo Wallace) against Barbados. The Leewards were able to unearth one of the new batting prospects of the season, Runako Morton, 21, a tall, well-built right-hander from Nevis who impressed with his 110 against Jamaica and three half-centuries in two matches against Barbados. Curtly Ambrose had his first full home season in many years as he missed the New Zealand tour through injury. He proved his fitness and his enthusiasm by bowling an average of 20 overs an innings to claim 31 wickets at an average

of 12.03 that confirmed his class. Only Mahendra Nagamootoo, the Guyana leg-spinner, took as many.

The 1999 champions, Barbados, narrowly topped the standings after the qualifying rounds but were flattered by their position, losing to Jamaica, held to a draw by Guyana and the Leewards and defeating only the winless, eliminated teams, the Windwards and Trinidad & Tobago – and Trinidad & Tobago only by one run. Even in the absence of the left-arm spinner Winston Reid, retired after a long and notable career, and the injured fast bowler Corey Collymore, they still held their own with the ball. Leg-spinner Dave Marshall, for so long in Reid's shadow, was third among the wicket-takers with 28 and was well supported by fast bowlers Hendy Bryan and Dayne Maynard, back after three seasons. But their batsmen failed to repeat their successes of 1999.

Wallace joined Gayle as the only batsmen with two hundreds, while Campbell, Griffith, Roland Holder and Floyd Reifer, all West Indies players with creditable records at regional level, managed only two half-centuries between them. Reifer, a Test player a year earlier, was finally dropped.

Guyana were without two of their leading players, Carl Hooper and Clayton Lambert. Hooper's attempts to return from his club contract in Australia came to nothing and Lambert had retired. For the second successive season, Guyana played no home matches as the three that were scheduled had to be switched to other venues because of persistent rain.

Even though they fielded a young team, Guyana were once again good enough to advance to the semi-final, where they were put out by Jamaica's first-innings lead in a drawn match. Shivnarine Chanderpaul was one of the few batsmen from the New Zealand tour to get among the runs while Reon King bowled with pace and penetration in his three matches and Nagamootoo underlined his consistency of recent seasons.

Trinidad & Tobago were severely weakened by the retirement of stalwarts David Williams, Ian Bishop and Phil Simmons and of Daren Ganga, sidelined with a broken finger sustained in New Zealand. In addition, Brian Lara and Merv Dillon were in New Zealand for the first two rounds and, as it transpired, Lara would have had other matters occupying his mind, announcing his resignation from the West Indies captaincy soon after the last match.

The upshot was a shadow of the runners-up of the previous year. Trinidad & Tobago passed 200 only twice and crashed for under 150 four times. The season culminated with threats from the president of the Trinidad & Tobago Cricket Board (TTCB) to withhold match fees after defeat in two days by Jamaica. It did not materialise but six players were dropped for the next match, among them Suruj Ragoonath and Lincoln Roberts, Test players the previous season.

The Windward Islands showed some improvement over their weakness of recent years and were in contention for a place in the semi-finals before a miserable loss to Barbados in the first first-class match at the Botanical Gardens in Roseau, Dominica, for 20 years. Once more, they depended principally on their established players although the teenage opener, Devon Smith, confirmed his potential with a few promising innings. All-rounder Roy Marshall, 34, had another productive season with 289 runs (average 41.28) and 13 wickets, but the team lacked depth.

Prompted by reduced prices and the free admission of schoolchildren, attendances at almost every venue improved significantly, an encouraging development. This was counterbalanced by other negative aspects, such as the general behaviour of players and the standard of umpiring, which were inevitably related, and the sub-standard pitches and facilities at too many venues. They were all indicative of the overall malaise that has affected West Indies cricket at all levels.

Philo Wallace, captain of Barbados, who narrowly retained the title in 2000.

RED STRIPE BOWL
By Tony Cozier

Bitter experience, as well as the meteorological office, would confirm that it is always risky staging a cricket tournament in the Caribbean in November. Pressed for space in an increasingly packed programme and committed to the sponsors to host the semi-finals and final in Jamaica, the West Indies Cricket Board (WICB) went ahead all the same with the third Red Stripe Bowl at the tailend of the rainy season. Predictably, as the previous one-day championships outside of Guyana had been every November, it was again disrupted by the weather. Of all the cricketing countries in the region, only Guyana, situated on the South American mainland, with a different weather pattern, is then into its dry period and it was not used this time. For the first time the Leeward Islands hosted one zone, while as the home of the sponsors, Jamaica was guaranteed the other.

In 1995, two attempts at the final in what was then the Shell/Sandals Trophy had to be abandoned in Port-of-Spain. In each of the two previous Red Stripe Bowls, one semi-final was reduced to a no-decision by rain and so it was again, Barbados frustrated for the second year in succession.

On this occasion, the Bowl even had to contend with the aftermath of a hurricane as the zone held in the Leewards was delayed for two days to allow further ground preparation in Antigua and Anguilla in the wake of 'Lenny'. As it was, Canada had two of their three matches written off by more rain and inadequate pitch covering in Anguilla. It was a major disappointment, for a team that had travelled so far, for a chance of gaining experience.

Jamaica, unaffected by the interruptions, won all their matches on their way to the semi-final. Rain caused its abandonment and sent them through to the final without having to contend with a challenge from Barbados. The next day they defeated the Leewards to claim the limited-overs title for the first time in eight years. It was a satisfying victory and not only because of the lengthy wait. It was their first appearance in the final in the three years of the Red Stripe Bowl, named after 'the great Jamaican beer', and it was Courtney Walsh's announced last match as Jamaica captain. They topped Zone A where the totals were lamentably low, a reflection on both the character of the pitches and the quality of the batting.

The conditions at the Alpart Sports Club, in St Elizabeth, were clearly sub-standard for a tournament of such significance. The highest of the four totals there was Jamaica's 118 for 6 off 41 overs against Bermuda. The Windward Islands, as usual weak in batting, were routed for 76 from 35 overs by Guyana, yet the Guyanese only scraped home by three wickets. The returns were no more encouraging when the matches moved to Kingston. The Windwards were bowled out for 101 in 47.4 overs and Guyana for 146 in 49.5 by Jamaica at Sabina Park; Bermuda fell for 102 to Guyana and for 48 to the Windwards at Kensington Club, the lowest total since the regional one-day tournament was inaugurated in 1976.

Only two batsmen passed 50 in the six matches in the zone – the young Jamaican left-hander Chris Gayle with an unbeaten 75 against Guyana and the Windwards' new captain, Rawl Lewis, with 67 against Bermuda. The effects of Hurricane Lenny were evident in the slow, uneven pitch at the Antigua Recreation Ground where Barbados and the Leewards had to fight for runs in the opener and Canada were restricted to 88 for 7 from their reduced 41 overs by Barbados the next day.

As usual, Ronald Webster Park in Anguilla produced the best batting conditions and the totals there were more realistic. The Leewards' 260 for 6, built around a third wicket partnership of 159 between young Sylvester Joseph and the veteran Keith Arthurton, and Barbados' 291 for 7 – featuring Sherwin Campbell's first hundred in the one-day game – proved too much for Trinidad & Tobago.

The 21-year-old Joseph's 83 was the preface to an outstanding tournament that earned him the Most Valuable Player award. He followed it with 57 in the semi-final victory over Guyana and an even, unbeaten 100, his first for the Leewards, achieved off the last ball of the innings in the final.

Another Leeward Islander, fast bowler Goldwyn Prince, created such a favourable impression in his debut season he was included, like Joseph, in the West Indies 'A' team for the subsequent home series against India 'A'. Big and strong, he took a wicket with his first ball, removing Campbell, and had the first four against Trinidad & Tobago, among them Lara, who was also an early victim during a lively four-wicket burst from the left-armer Pedro Collins for Barbados. Franklyn Rose returned to regional cricket for the first time since his injury and suspension following the tour of South Africa and his incisive bowling made a definite impact on Jamaica's triumph.

The crowd for the final, once more held at the Kaiser Sports Club at Discovery Bay on Jamaica's north coast, was estimated at over 6,000 but facilities there, for players and spectators, are not up to standard. Yet WICB marketing director Chris Dehring stated it was a deliberate policy to use such informal venues to bring back the crowds and hinted at an expansion of the tournament for 2000. Given the realities of the regional and international programmes and the weather, it was a challenging task.

Sherwin Campbell scored his first one-day century for Barbados in the Red Stripe Bowl.

FIRST-CLASS AVERAGES

BATTING

	M	Inns	NO	HS	Runs	Av	100	50
ADR Campbell	4	6	2	158*	303	75.75	2	–
Inzamam-ul-Haq	3	5	0	135	295	59.00	1	2
Yousuf Youhana	5	9	1	115	438	54.75	2	2
A Flower	3	5	1	113*	207	51.75	1	1
CH Gayle	10	18	3	168	682	45.46	2	3
S Chanderpaul	9	15	2	112	579	44.52	1	2
RR Sarwan	11	20	3	111	752	44.23	2	5
WW Hinds	10	18	2	165	682	42.62	2	2
RA Marshall	5	8	1	70	289	41.28	–	2
Mohammad Wasim	5	9	0	111	366	40.66	1	2
D Ganga	5	9	1	63*	311	38.87	–	3
JR Murray	4	6	0	56	228	38.00	–	3
CM Tuckett	6	8	2	59*	226	37.66	–	2
SV Carlisle	4	6	0	86	226	37.66	–	2
JC Adams	10	17	3	101*	517	36.92	1	2
WD Phillip	5	7	2	45	177	35.40	–	–
MW Goodwin	4	6	0	113	207	34.50	1	–
LR Williams	7	12	1	135	378	34.36	1	1
PA Wallace	8	14	1	117	428	32.92	2	1
Abdur Razzaq	3	5	0	87	162	32.40	–	2
WW Cornwall	4	7	0	70	216	30.85	–	1
Imran Nazir	4	7	0	131	214	30.57	1	–
RS Morton	8	13	1	110	365	30.41	1	3
RIC Holder	6	10	1	66*	271	30.11	–	1
TM Dowlin	6	10	1	102	264	29.33	1	–
D Rampersad	6	10	0	107	279	27.90	1	–
SC Joseph	10	18	1	100	473	27.82	1	1
CO Browne	9	15	2	109*	356	27.38	1	–
SC Williams	4	7	0	84	191	27.28	–	2
A Haniff	8	15	1	84*	381	27.21	–	3
RG Samuels	7	13	1	73*	325	27.08	–	3
KLT Arthurton	7	11	0	88	296	26.90	–	2
KF Semple	7	12	0	67	301	25.08	–	4
TR Gripper	4	6	0	62	147	24.50	–	1
HR Bryan	6	10	2	76*	194	24.25	–	1
RAM Smith	5	8	0	65	184	23.00	–	1
RN Lewis	6	10	2	62	180	22.50	–	–
DS Smith	5	10	1	59	195	21.66	–	1
Wasim Akram	3	5	0	42	108	21.60	–	–
TO Powell	4	8	1	57	151	21.57	–	2
SL Campbell	9	17	2	58	322	21.46	–	1
NA de Groot	4	8	1	44	150	21.42	–	–
MV Nagamootoo	7	12	1	59	230	20.90	–	1
RL Powell	6	11	0	43	230	20.90	–	–
GW Flower	4	7	1	69	125	20.83	–	1
Younis Khan	5	9	1	103*	166	20.75	1	–
D Thomas	4	7	3	42	81	20.25	–	–
AFG Griffith	9	16	1	90	300	20.00	–	2
CD Cannonier	3	5	0	34	98	19.60	–	–
RO Hinds	4	7	0	32	135	19.28	–	1
KK Sylvester	5	10	2	51*	154	19.25	–	1
RD Jacobs	10	15	2	117*	245	18.84	1	–
IDR Bradshaw	3	5	0	39	92	18.40	–	–
Moin Khan	3	5	0	38	92	18.40	–	–
FA Rose	8	13	2	69	200	18.18	–	1
DRE Joseph	7	12	1	60	198	18.00	–	1
RO Hurley	6	10	0	55	173	17.30	–	1
Saq;ain Mushtaq	5	8	1	33	115	16.42	–	–
Mushtaq Ahmed	4	5	2	39	48	16.00	–	–
C DaC Wright	5	10	0	70	144	14.40	–	1
FA Adams	3	5	0	34	69	13.80	–	–

FIRST-CLASS AVERAGES

BATTING

	M	Inns	NO	HS	Runs	Av	100	50
NC McGarrell	6	10	0	54	125	12.50	–	1
CA Walsh	10	14	6	22	99	12.37	–	–
HK Olonga	3	5	1	23	49	12.25	–	–
MJ Morgan	5	6	2	30*	48	12.00	–	–
RJJ McLean	4	7	1	23*	71	11.83	–	–
Wajahatullah Wasti	3	5	0	26	59	11.80	–	–
I Jan	3	6	0	43	69	11.50	–	–
FL Reifer	4	6	0	37	68	11.33	–	–
NC Johnson	4	7	1	29	61	10.16	–	–
MG Sinclair	7	10	2	40	81	10.12	–	–
D Ramnarine	3	6	2	16	40	10.00	–	–

Batting: Qualification: 5 innings, average 10.00

BOWLING

	Overs	Mds	Runs	Wkts	Av	Best	100/m	5/inns
CEL Ambrose	443	188	692	50	13.84	5–39	–	2
LR Williams	142.1	45	315	20	15.75	6–45	–	1
DK Marshall	194.1	52	453	28	16.17	7–49	1	3
FA Rose	194.4	40	594	34	17.47	6–71	–	3
WW Cornwall	89	20	246	14	17.57	6–53	–	1
CA Walsh	325.2	90	687	39	17.61	5–22	–	2
RD King	310	78	755	42	17.97	5–24	1	3
KCB Jeremy	220.4	63	574	30	19.13	6–81	–	2
CM Tuckett	132.1	44	290	15	19.33	4–77	–	–
HR Bryan	217.1	69	496	25	19.84	5–38	–	1
DR Maynard	155.4	32	454	22	20.63	4–51	–	–
MV Nagamootoo	313.3	77	730	34	21.47	4–45	–	–
CE Cuffy	191.1	54	368	16	23.00	4–30	–	–
Saqlain Mushtaq	192.5	47	446	19	23.47	6–48	–	2
RO Hurley	203.4	55	470	18	26.11	3–15	–	–
NAM McLean	206.4	53	572	21	27.23	5–37	–	1
CEL Stuart	145.5	31	411	15	27.40	4–53	–	–
NO Perry	158.2	46	329	12	27.41	4–10	–	–
RA Marshall	149.3	26	368	13	28.30	4–84	–	–
KG Darlington	124	22	349	12	29.08	3–37	–	–
NC McGarrell	272.2	78	545	18	30.27	4–32	–	–
RN Lewis	149.1	28	372	12	31.00	4–66	–	–
PT Collins	131	29	363	11	33.00	3–36	–	–

Qualification: 10 wickets in 8 innings

The following bowlers took 10 wickets in fewer than 8 innings:

HH Streak	57	23	103	11	9.36	5–27	–	1
M Dillon	117	22	230	18	12.77	6–40	–	2
Mohammad Akram	53.4	18	151	11	13.72	5–16	–	1
Wasim Akram	116.2	35	264	15	17.60	6–61	1	2
M Persad	166	39	379	21	18.04	5–63	–	1
D Ramnarine	102.5	27	244	11	22.18	5–31	–	1
BA Murphy	130.1	37	316	13	24.30	4–71	–	–
HK Olonga	106.1	23	358	12	29.83	3–65	–	–
Mushtaq Ahmed	156	28	480	11	43.63	3–91	–	–

FIELDING

31 – RD Jacobs;25 – CO Brown (22ct,3st);18 – SL Campbell;17 – MS Sinclair;
15 – SC Joseph;14 – CH Gayle;13 –V Nagamootoo;10 – JC Adams, KF Semple,
PA Wallace

SRI LANKA

Australia in Sri Lanka
South Africa in Sri Lanka
Aiwa Cup Triangular Series

AUSTRALIA IN SRI LANKA
By Jim Maxwell

Collision! That is Australia's indelible memory from a series surprisingly won by the home side. Steve Waugh and Jason Gillespie collided in the outfield attempting to catch a Jayawardene sweep at a particularly tense stage of play in the first Test at Kandy.

They both wound up in hospital, Waugh with a smashed nose and Gillespie a broken leg that put him out of the game for six months. That incident, Muralitharan's spin bowling, and heavy rain strongly influenced Sri Lanka's ultimate one-nil win – their first against Australia in a Test series.

Following a disastrous performance in the World Cup, Sri Lanka's victories in both series were gratifying, and a cheerful distraction from the turmoil surrounding the local board upheavals and a court case.

Sri Lanka's fortunes were encouraged by Dav Whatmore's recall to the coaching position, and the retention of their two most experienced batsmen, Aravinda de Silva and Arjuna Ranatunga, both of whom had been dropped for the one-day tournament.

The Australian preference for separate international teams meant only six of the one-day squad stayed on, swelled by the arrival of eight others, four of whom had played a season of county cricket. The Test squad had two new inclusions since the last campaign in the Caribbean had concluded in April. Matthew Hayden was recalled to replace Matthew Elliott, and another left-hander, Simon Katich, carried the 'promising player' mantle.

Sri Lanka Board XI v. Australia at Colombo
3, 4, 5 and 6 September 1999 at P Saravanamuttu Stadium, Colombo
Sri Lanka Board XI 228 (79.3 overs)(SI de Saram 67, RP Arnold 63) and 271 (80.1 overs)(RP Arnold 79, LPC Silva 70
Australia 179 (57.5 overs)(*SR Waugh 42, RT Ponting 35) and 321 for 6 (101 overs)(GS Blewett 148, JL Langer 52, MJ Slater 51)
Australia won by 4 wickets

The warm-up four-day match in Colombo began bizarrely with a dispute about the toss. The board eleven captain Hashan Tillekeratne tossed casually

Previous page: National hero and Sri Lanka's favourite son, Arjuna Ranatunga bids farewell to Test-match cricket.

on the dressing-room steps, and as soon as the coin came down, Tillekeratne announced that he would bat. A bemused Steve Waugh, who had not even seen the result before Tillekeratne pocketed the coin, immediately insisted that the toss should be conducted properly, out in the middle. Reluctantly, a chastened Tillekeratne shuffled on to the pitch, where Steve Waugh called correctly, and then shocked his team-mates and Tillekeratne by suggesting a third toss. Waugh's fair-mindedness produced the inevitable conclusion: 'Board eleven won toss and will bat.' But they only did so for 20 overs on the first day as heavy storms washed out play.

Australia's weakness against spin was exposed on the second day, as they slumped to 175 in reply to the Board eleven's 228. Ominously, on a dry, turning pitch left-armer Rangana Herath took four wickets.

The conditions also suited Colin Miller, who produced a career-best five-wicket haul in the second innings. Russel Arnold boosted his test chances with two half-centuries, contributing to a lead of 320.

Aravinda de Silva's partnership with Arjuna Ranatunga helped to secure victory for Sri Lanka during the first Test at Kandy and won him Man of the Match.

In the chase, Blewett rose above previous inadequacies facing spin, and walloped a superb 148. He shared a century partnership with Slater, which indicated that Australia had at last discovered a reliable opening pair. Maybe. Australia romped in by four wickets, allowing plenty of time for the scenic bus trip up through the mountains to Kandy.

In the sidelight rivalry for leg-spin selection it was clear that Warne had reimposed his presence as the number one over MacGill. Warne's World Cup and recent form, against MacGill's total absence from the game, ensured that the selection was never going to be the issue that forced Warne's omission in the Caribbean.

FIRST TEST
9, 10 and 11 September 1999 at Asgiriya Stadium, Kandy

Sri Lanka achieved their first Test win over Australia before tea on the third day of a remarkable match. Ranatunga's replacement as captain, Sanath Jayasuriya, celebrated a surprise victory on his test leadership debut. Surprise because a combination of pace and spin, and a freak accident dramatically influenced the course of events. Steve Waugh's concern about the potentially destructive impact of Muralitharan's off-spin influenced his decision to bat first. It was a decision that backfired spectacularly when Australia crashed to 7 for 61 at lunch. The local candy was still sticky when Sri Lanka's sinistral pace duo, Vaas and Zoysa, bowled jaffas at the top order, starting with Slater leg before to the second ball of the match.

So when did two left-handers last open the bowling in a Test match? Before Ceylon became Sri Lanka, and before Ian Meckiff was called for throwing. Throwing? The appearance of Muralitharan at the crease didn't raise an eyebrow, at least officially, nor an umpire's arm. Who would have dared, given the guidelines about reporting on suspicion, rather than calling infringers of a badly worded law?

Besides, Muralitharan had taken over 200 Test wickets, a tally that seemed to guarantee his legitimacy. The unorthodox nature of his action accentuated his freakishness, and the amount of turn could be phenomenal. And now he had a top-spin for unpickable variation. His prodigious spin could make left-handers look idiotic, and after Vaas and Zoysa shared the first five wickets, he had Healy stumped off Kaliwitharana's pads.

The innings was saved from double-figure obliteration by the dextrous footwork of Ponting

The left-arm seam bowling of Chaminda Vaas accounted for six wickets in the first Test.

and Gillespie's straight bat. Ponting attacked skilfully, adding 107 with his patient partner, and was unlucky not to reach a hundred, last out, caught and bowled by Muralitharan for 96.

Aravinda de Silva excited Sri Lanka's reply, revealing classy touches against the spin of Miller and Warne. The partnership with Jayawardene was growing ominously when Miller tempted the new vice-captain to sweep.

Steve Waugh ran backwards from square leg, unaware that Gillespie was fast approaching from the boundary behind him. As Waugh neared the ball, Gillespie collided with him, the impact stirring the dust and incapacitating both players horrendously. Gillespie was prone, clutching his left leg, and Waugh's face bore the blood of a Mike Tyson knock-out punch. They were both taken by

FIRST TEST – SRI LANKA v. AUSTRALIA
9, 10 and 11 September 1999 at Asgiriya Stadium, Kandy

AUSTRALIA

	First innings		Second innings	
MJ Slater	lbw b Vaas	0	(2) lbw b Muralitharan	27
GS Blewett	lbw b Zoysa	0	(1) c Atapattu, b Muralitharan	14
JL Langer	c de Silva, b Vaas	7	lbw b Vaas	5
ME Waugh	c & b Vaas	6	b Vaas	0
SR Waugh (capt)	c de Silva, b Zoysa	19	absent injured	
RT Ponting	c & b Muralitharan	96	(5) c Jayasuriya, b Chandana	51
*IA Healy	st Kaluwitharana, b Muralitharan	11	(6) b Muralitharan	3
SK Warne	c Atapattu, b Zoysa	0	(7) run out (Jayasuriya)	6
JN Gillespie	lbw b Muralitharan	41	absent injured	
CR Miller	c Atapattu, b Muralitharan	0	(8) b Vaas	8
GD McGrath	not out	4	(9) not out	10
	nb 4	4	b6, lb5, w1, nb4	16
		188		**140**

	First innings				Second innings			
	O	M	R	W	O	M	R	W
Vaas	16	2	43	3	15	7	15	3
Zoysa	13	2	38	3	10	3	28	0
Muralitharan	25.1	4	63	4	26	5	65	3
Jayasuriya	5	0	5	-	4	1	7	-
Chandana	8	1	39	-	2.2	0	9	1
de Silva					3	0	5	-

Fall of Wickets
1-0, 2-4, 3-9, 4-16, 5-40, 6-59, 7-60, 8-167, 9-171
1-37, 2-49, 3-49, 4-49, 5-58, 6-75, 7-99, 8-140

SRI LANKA

	First innings		Second innings	
ST Jayasuriya (capt)	lbw b McGrath	18	c sub(ML Hayden), b Miller	18
MS Atapattu	c Langer, b Miller	25	c Blewett, b McGrath	0
RP Arnold	lbw b Miller	19		
PA de Silva	c Ponting, b Warne	78	not out	31
DPM D Jayawardene	c Ponting, b Warne	46	c Slater, b Miller	9
A Ranatunga	c Healy, b Warne	4	not out	19
*RS Kaluwitharana	b Miller	9	(3) b Miller	5
UDU Chandana	c sub (ML Hayden), b Warne	12		
WPUJC Vaas	not out	2		
DNT Zoysa	c Miller, b Warne	7		
M Muralitharan	c McGrath, b Miller	0		
	b4, lb7, nb3	14	b8, lb2, nb3	13
		234	**(for 4 wickets)**	**95**

	First innings				Second innings			
	O	M	R	W	O	M	R	W
McGrath	18	5	66	1	7	2	19	1
Gillespie	12	2	43	0				
Miller	20.3	6	62	4	13	2	48	3
Warne	16	4	52	5	6.5	3	18	0

Fall of Wickets
1-22, 2-69, 3-70, 4-177, 5-181, 6-197, 7-223, 8-226, 9-234
1-12, 2-24, 3-39, 4-60

Umpires: PT Manuel & S Venkataraghavan
Toss: Australia
Test Debuts: nil

<u>Sri Lanka won by six wickets</u>

helicopter to a Colombo hospital, where doctors repaired Waugh's badly broken nose and Gillespie's fractured left tibia. Waugh would recover for the next Test, but Gillespie's injury was long-term, out for up to six months.

Acting captain Warne, goaded by the heckling taunts of a crowd who remembered his sharp remarks about Ranatunga in Australia, bowled superbly, bagging his first five-wicket innings haul for 20 months, including Ranatunga's wicket for four. Miller spun the ball hard on a pitch offering serious turn and variable bounce. They held Sri Lanka to a 46-run lead.

An injury-depleted Australian line-up succumbed to the pace of Vaas and Muralitharan's deadly spin. Mark Waugh achieved his fifth duck in six Test innings in Sri Lanka, the innings in a heap at 6 for 89 at stumps on day two.

Thanks to Ponting's second skilful innings, and a 41-run stand with McGrath, Australia did well to lead by 94, without Steve Waugh and Gillespie. It wasn't enough to defend, but there were some fretful moments before the veteran de Silva/Ranatunga pairing scored the winning runs. Miller's claim for a caught-and-bowled was turned down by umpire Manuel, who should have at least deferred to the third umpire as the ball had clearly carried, and McGrath badly missed a catch off Ranatunga's skewed drive at mid-off. Ponting overthrows ended the match ten minutes before tea. In barely two and a half days Sri Lanka had recorded their 15th and most famous Test win, 14 years to the day since they first won a Test, against India in 1985. (Ponting and de Silva were joint Man of the Match.)

SECOND TEST
22, 23, 24, 25 and 26 September 1999 at Galle International Stadium

Steve Waugh's recovery from a badly broken nose was astonishing. Four fractures had pushed his nose under the socket of his left eye, after that horrendous collision with Jason Gillespie. Within a week of being discharged from hospital, Waugh was back in the nets. Underlining the toughness and determination that was so typical of him, he announced that he would play.

Between Tests Australia scored a morale-encouraging win over a Sri Lankan Board eleven in Colombo. Gillespie's replacement, Scott Muller, made an impressive debut taking 5 for 64, and then had the misfortune of splitting the webbing in his right hand, diving for a catch of his own bowling in the second innings. Michael Slater scored a ruthlessly impressive century, as Australia bowled out the Board eleven for 90 to win the three-day match by 247 runs. Sri Lanka introduced 21-year-old left-arm spinner Rangana Herath, replacing Chandana, and Australia substituted Damien Fleming for the injured Gillespie.

The Test began sensationally when Jayasuriya was caught in the slips off the first ball. At that moment his decision to bat first looked suspect, but the truer nature of the pitch was quickly revealed, as Arnold, then de Silva, dug in. De Silva was more restrained than at Kandy, and patiently acquired runs from a highly disciplined attack. Warne's accuracy was compelling, taking three wickets including that of the out-of-touch Ranatunga, holing out to mid-on. A surprise lifting ball from Fleming, the second brand-new version, accounted for de Silva fending to Steve Waugh in the gully. Vaas struck boldly in the tail-end entertainment, the innings wrapped up an hour into the second day for 296. Three dropped catches spoilt an impressive effort from all of Australia's bowlers.

Slater and Blewett set about Sri Lanka's spinners boldly, their opening stand the best for two years in a Test match. Slater's footwork can be pulsatingly destructive, and his calculated attack on Muralitharan's fuller-length deliveries was precise, and rewarding. But the unorthodox off-spinner kept probing, deceiving Blewett in flight to end the stand

Michael Slater made the highest score of the drawn second Test at Galle.

SECOND TEST – SRI LANKA V. AUSTRALIA
22, 23, 24, 25 (np) and 26 September 1999 at Galle International Stadium

SRI LANKA

	First innings		Second innings	
ST Jayasuriya (capt)	c ME Waugh, b McGrath	0	not out	21
MS Atapattu	c Healy, b Warne	29	not out	28
RP Arnold	c Warne, b Miller	50		
PA de Silva	c SR Waugh, b Fleming	64		
DPM Jayawardene	c Blewett, b Warne	46		
A Ranatunga	c Miller, b Warne	10		
*RS Kaluwitharana	b McGrath	25		
WPUJC Vaas	c Ponting, b Fleming	41		
R Herath	run out(Blewett)	3		
DNT Zoysa	c ME Waugh, b McGrath	1		
M Muralitharan	not out	7		
	b4, lb8, nb8	20	lb3, nb3	6
		296	**(for 0 wicket)**	**55**

	First innings				Second innings			
	O	M	R	W	O	M	R	W
McGrath	26.5	7	81	3	7	2	23	–
Fleming	23	6	74	2	4	0	15	–
Miller	23	1	72	1	3	1	9	–
Warne	25	11	29	3	3.2	1	5	–
Ponting	4	1	7	–				
Waugh ME	2	1	9	–				
Blewett	3	0	12	–				

Fall of Wickets
1–0, 2–80, 3–100, 4–193, 5–206, 6–226, 7–262, 8–288, 9–288

AUSTRALIA

MJ Slater	st Kaluwitharana, b Muralitharan	96
GS Blewett	b Muralitharan	62
JL Langer	c Ranatunga, b Muralitharan	7
ME Waugh	c Ranatunga, b Muralitharan	10
SR Waugh (capt)	c Kaluwitharana, b Herath	19
*IA Healy	c Jayawardene, b Muralitharan	4
RT Ponting	c Ranatunga, b Herath	1
SK Warne	c Atapattu, b Herath	0
DW Fleming	b Herath	16
CR Miller	run out (Jayasuriya/Kaluwitharana)	6
GD McGrath	not out	0
	b1, lb4, nb2	
		228

First innings	O	M	R	W
Vaas	9	3	31	–
Zoysa	6	1	9	–
Herath	34.3	6	97	4
Muralitharan	38	10	71	5
Jayasuriya	9	1	15	–

Fall of Wickets
1–138, 2–160, 3–179, 4–182, 5–188, 6–189, 7–189, 8–215, 9–228

Umpires: BC Cooray & DB Cowie
Toss: Sri Lanka
Test Debut: R Herath (SL)

Match draw

at 138. In his next 13 overs, Muralitharan took four more wickets, the prize swag including Slater, stumped for another Test score in the 90s, 96.

The left-handed Langer had an almost impossible task trying to attack the turning ball, and his nightmare of attempted sweeps and misses ended in Ranatunga's hands at slip. Mark Waugh went similarly, failing to read Muralitharan's topspinner. From 5 for 188 at stumps, Australia succumbed to the left-arm spin of debutant Rangana Herath, when play eventually resumed after tea on the third day.

Aravinda de Silva dug in during the second Test at Galle, patiently accumulating runs against a disciplined Australian attack. His steady dedication might have helped secure victory had rain not ended the Test.

Like Muralitharan, Herath possessed the variety to bamboozle. He mixed orthodox left-arm spinners with a straight-breaking ball akin to the effectiveness of an arm ball. He was too good for players unaccustomed to him, and took the last four innings wickets in 39 balls.

Sri Lanka were none for 44 at stumps, but the rain that washed out play earlier in the day returned overnight, washing out play on day four. Only 19 minutes of play was possible on the final day, heavy rain ruining a match that had looked loaded in favour of the home side.

THIRD TEST
30 September, 1, 2, 3 and 4 October 1999 at Sinhalese Sports Club, Colombo

Galle's gale swept on to Colombo, and the Sinhalese sports club ground was pounded in the intervening days between Tests. It was a miracle that play started only an hour after the scheduled time for 'play gentlemen', with Australia batting in extreme heat and humidity. The Australian team had been variously distracted by Simon Katich, who contracted chicken pox, forcing his quarantining in room 266, Ian Healy suffering a thigh-muscle strain that had Gilchrist being placed on standby, and Stuart MacGill copping a fine for swearing at a croupier in the Bally club casino in Colombo. A fine, US$975, that he publicly described as excessive. The moral of the story is that if you're winning, and you think the dealer is cheating, leave. It's more profitable than swearing!

Waugh's decision to bat was solidly supported by another century-opening partnership between Blewett and Slater. Poor catching allowed three escapes, runs coming slowly on a heavy ground that discouraged boundaries.

The pace was more accumulative than accelerated, 126 added from 53 overs when Slater was stumped off part-time spinner Arnold. Blewett miscued a drive to cover, and the innings again faltered in the final session, although Mark Waugh was adjudged caught in close when the 'seeing eye' of the replay concluded that the ball had hit his pads.

Waugh had totalled 29 in five Test innings on tour, prompting comparative *schadenfreude* for the pundits who recalled his four ducks in 1992. Overnight rain delayed play for an hour, and it was Ponting who took the initiative from the troublesome spinners. He lost Steve Waugh to a dubious caught-behind decision from Peter Willey, and Vaas quickly dispatched Healy and Warne with the second new ball.

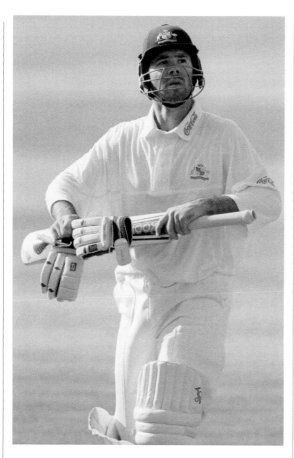

Despite Ricky Ponting's stand of 105 not out, Australia failed to clinch the Test, again due to rain.

A determined Damien Fleming kept the innings alive, as Ponting confidently moved to 90, when the heavens opened again an hour before tea, forcing play to be abandoned. Ponting achieved a notable fourth Test hundred on the third morning, extending the partnership with Fleming to 80. Vaas cleaned out the tail-enders, leaving Ponting not out on 105. More rain held up the start of Sri Lanka's innings, play washed out again, until day four. McGrath dramatically repeated his second Test opening blitz, by having a nonplussed Jayasuriya caught in identical fashion with his first ball. Fleming ripped out Atapattu and Arnold, and at 10 for 3 Australia sensed a chance of bowling out Sri Lanka to force the follow-on.

De Silva steadied the missile assault, adding 50 with Jayawardene. Fleming made the break, but as soon as the veteran pairing of de Silva and Ranatunga became associated, the rains tumbled down again, forcing another abandonment after lunch.

THIRD TEST – SRI LANKA v. AUSTRALIA
30 September, 1, 2, 3 and 4 (np) October 1999 at Sinhalese Sports Club, Colombo

AUSTRALIA

	First innings	
GS Blewett	c Atapattu, b Herath	70
MJ Slater	st Kaluwitharana, b Arnold	59
JL Langer	c Ranatunga, b Muralitharan	32
ME Waugh	c Arnold, b Muralitharan	13
SR Waugh (capt)	c Kaluwithrarana, b Herath	14
RT Ponting	not out	105
*IA Healy	c Jayawardene, b Vaas	7
SK Warne	lbw b Vaas	0
DW Fleming	c Atapattu, b Muralitharan	32
CR Miller	lbw b Vaas	0
GD McGrath	c Atapattu, b Vaas	0
	nb10	10
		342

	First innings			
	O	M	R	W
Vaas	23.4	5	54	4
Zoysa	10	4	23	–
Herath	35	10	98	2
Muralitharan	52	5	150	3
Jayasuriya	9	2	14	–
Arnold	7	4	3	1

Fall of Wickets
1-126, 2-147, 3-182, 4-183, 5-221, 6-253, 7-255, 8-335, 9-342

SRI LANKA

	First innings	
ST Jayasuriya (capt)	c Warne, b McGrath	0
MS Atapattu	c Healy, b Fleming	2
RP Arnold	lbw b Fleming	0
P A de Silva	not out	19
DPMD Jayawardene	c Healy, b Fleming	21
A Ranatunga	not out	1
*RS Kaluwitharana		
WPUJC Vaas		
R Herath		
DNT Zoysa		
M Muralitharan		
	b8, lb1, w5, nb4	18
	(for 4 wickets)	**61**

	First innings			
	O	M	R	W
McGrath	10	3	25	1
Fleming	5.5	0	14	3
Warne	5	1	11	–
Miller	1	0	2	–

Fall of Wickets
1-0, 2-7, 3-10, 4-60

Umpires: KT Francis & P Willey
Toss: Australia
Test Debuts: nil

Match drawn

TEST MATCH AVERAGES
Australia v. Sri Lanka

AUSTRALIA

Batting	M	Inns	NO	HS	Runs	Av	100	50
RT Ponting	3	4	1	105*	253	84.33	1	2
MJ Slater	3	4	0	96	181	45.25	–	2
GS Blewett	3	4	0	71	147	36.75	–	2
SR Waugh	3	3	0	19	52	17.33	–	–
GD McGrath	3	4	3	10*	14	14.00	–	–
JL Langer	3	4	0	32	51	12.75	–	–
ME Waugh	3	4	0	13	29	7.25	–	–
IA Healy	3	4	0	11	25	6.25	–	–
CR Miller	3	4	0	8	14	3.50	–	–
SK Warne	3	4	0	6	6	1.50	–	–

Also batted: DW Fleming (2 matches) 16, 32; JN Gillespie (1 match) 41

Bowling	Overs	Mds	Runs	Wkts	Av	Best	10/m	5/inn
SK Warne	56.1	20	115	8	14.37	5–52	–	1
DW Fleming	32.5	6	103	5	20.60	3–14	–	–
CR Miller	60.3	10	193	8	24.12	4–62	–	–
GD McGrath	68.5	19	214	6	35.66	3–81	–	–

Also bowled: GS Blewett 3–0–12–0; JN Gillespie 12–2–43–0; RT Ponting 4–1–7–0; ME Waugh 2–1–9–0

Fielding Figures
4 – IA Healy; 3 – RT Ponting; 2 – GS Blewett, CR Miller, SK Warne, ME Waugh; 1 – JL Langer, GD McGrath, MJ Slater, SR Waugh

SRI LANKA

Batting	M	Inns	NO	HS	Runs	Av	100	50
PA De Silva	3	4	2	78	192	96.00	–	2
DPMD Jayawardene	3	4	0	46	122	30.50	–	–
RP Arnold	3	3	0	50	69	23.00	–	1
MS Atapattu	3	5	1	29	84	21.00	–	–
ARanatunga	3	4	2	19*	34	17.00	–	–
ST Jayasuriya	3	5	1	21*	57	14.25	–	–
RS Kaluwitharana	3	3	0	25	39	13.00	–	–

Also batted: UDU Chandana (1 match) 12; R Herath (2 matches) 3; M Muralitharan(3 matches) 0, 7*; WPUJC Vaas (3 matches) 2*, 41; DNT Zoysa (3 matches) 7, 1

Bowling	Overs	Mds	Runs	Wkts	Av	Best	10/m	5/inn
WPUJC Vaas	63.4	17	143	10	14.30	4–54	–	–
M Muralitharan	141.1	24	349	15	23.26	5–71	–	1
R Herath	69.3	16	195	6	32.50	4–97	–	–

Also bowled: RP Arnold 7–4–3–1; UDU Chandana 10.2–1–48–1; PA de Silva 3–0–5–0; ST Jayasuriya 27–4–41–0; DNT Zoysa 39–10–98–3

Fielding Figures
7 – MS Atapattu; 5 – (2ct/3st) RS Kaluwitharana; 4 – A Ranatunga; 2 – PA De Silva, DPMP Jayawardene; 1 – RP Arnold, ST Jayasuriya, M Muralitharan, WPUJC Vaas

A saturated outfield, a frustrated Australian team, and finally more rain, ensured Sri Lanka's historic series victory, with only nine hours of play possible in the match. Jayasuriya described the win as the greatest achievement of his life. For a nation beset by political turmoil and civil war, the cricketers' success was a glorious moment, defeating the most powerful opponents in the world in both moods of the game. The match also bade farewell to umpire KT Francis and Australian coach Geoff Marsh.

SOUTH AFRICA IN SRI LANKA
By Neil Manthorp

FIRST TEST
20, 21, 22, 23 July 2000 at
Galle International Stadium

As much as South Africa knew they would struggle against specialist spinners on specially prepared wickets, and as much as they tried to prepare, there was nothing they could do to stop the onslaught of Muttiah Muralitharan in Galle.

A haul of 13 for 171 was richly deserved, a display of such control and variation that even Daryll Cullinan, who finished with an unbeaten century in South Africa's first innings, described his time against Murali as 'a bit of a lottery'. Murali, in turn, paid tribute to the batsmen for erecting a stage of Rolling Stones proportions for him to perform upon. Not only did Sri Lanka score 522, but they did so in under five sessions, which provided more time, and runs, than Murali could possibly need. To be fair,

The precision and finesse of Muttiah Muralitharan's bowling in the first Test devastated the South African side.

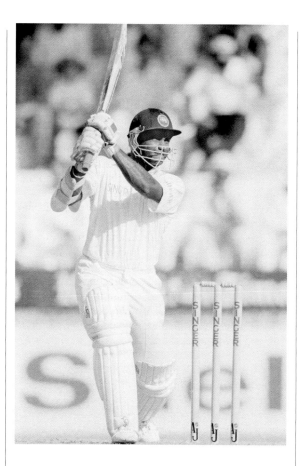

With captain Sanath Jayasuriya setting the scene (148) for a commanding Sri Lankan innings (522), the South Africans had little chance of catching up.

the match may have been very different had Sanath Jayasuriya not won the toss on a pitch that would have been ready for play at least three days earlier. The moment the coin landed, however, was the last time Sri Lanka needed any luck.

Jayasuriya lashed his opposite number, Shaun Pollock, high over backward point in no more than the third over of the innings and repeated the stroke just a couple of overs later. In his debut Test as captain, but his 43rd in all, Pollock was being double-dared. Once he had decided to keep his attacking field and leave third man and other boundaries unguarded, Pollock was committed. So was Jayasuriya, however, and by lunch the Sri Lankan captain was just four runs short of becoming only the fifth man to score a century before lunch on the first day of a Test. His team, at 145 for 0, had already taken control of the match. Like a gambler chasing his losses, Pollock continued to attack for

FIRST TEST – SRI LANKA v. SOUTH AFRICA
20, 21, 22 and 23 July 2000 at Galle International Stadium

SRI LANKA

MS Atpattu	c Boje, b Ntini	54
ST Jayasuriya (capt)	c McKenzie, b Adams	148
RP Arnold	c Boucher, b Adams	5
DPMD Jayawardene	c Boucher, b Pollock	167
*K Sangakkara	lbw b Boje	23
A Ranatunga	c Pollock, b Adams	13
HDPK Dharmasena	c Klusener, b Pollock	4
UDU Chandana	c Cullinan, b Kallis	8
WPUJC Vaas	b Pollock	54
DNT Zoysa	c & b Cullinan	10
M Muralitharan	not out	2
	b15, lb16, nb3	34
		522

	First innings			
	O	M	R	W
Pollock	30.4	8	73	3
Kallis	17	7	41	1
Ntini	19	1	73	1
Adams	45	6	184	3
Klusener	15	4	38	–
Boje	22	2	72	1
Cullinan	2	0	10	1

Fall of Wickets
1–193, 2–211, 3–216, 4–297, 5–318, 6–341, 7–365, 8–482, 9–500

SOUTH AFRICA

	First innings		Second innings	
G Kirsten	c Sangakkara, b Muralitharan	12	run out (Vaas/Sangakarra)	55
ND McKenzie	b Muralitharan	11	c Ranatunga, b Chandana	25
JH Kallis	c Arnold, b Muralitharan	29	c Muralitharan, b Chandana	40
DJ Cullinan	not out	114	c Arnold, b Muralitharan	12
JN Rhodes	b Muralitharan	12	not out	63
L Klusener	c Chandana, b Dharmasena	19	c Sangakkara, b Muralitharan	4
*MV Boucher	b Muralitharan	0	lbw b Muralitharan	7
SM Pollock (capt)	c Dharmasena, b Muralitharan	12	c Arnold, b Muralitharan	4
N Boje	c Atapattu, b Jayasuriya	12	lbw b Muralitharan	35
PR Adams	c Atapattu, b Chandana	4	b Muralitharan	2
M Ntini	c Ranatunga, b Chandana	8	b Muralitharan	0
	b2, lb1, nb10	13	b3, lb5, nb6	14
		238		**269**

	First innings				Second Innings			
	O	M	R	W	O	M	R	W
Vaas	12	2	16	–	7	2	18	–
Zoysa	4	1	12	–	5	2	11	–
Dharmasena	25	5	70	1	10	1	37	–
Muralitharan	41	8	87	6	35	5	84	7
Chandana	14	3	46	2	29	6	88	2
Jayasuriya	3	0	4	1	5	0	21	–
Arnold					1	0	2	–

Fall of Wickets
1–25, 2–30, 3–86, 4–119, 5–162, 6–168, 7–198, 8–213, 9–223
1–58, 2–112, 3–139, 4–141, 5–153, 6–163, 7–193, 8–263, 9–269

Umpires: PT Manuel & DJ Harper
Toss: Sri Lanka
Test Debut: K Sangakkara & ND McKenzie

Sri Lanka won by an innings & 15 runs

most of the day as the Test match crumbled around him. Paul Adams, whose first three deliveries had been dispatched by Jayasuriya to various boundaries, collected the second most expensive innings analysis for South Africa.

The Sri Lankan captain finally slogged Adams to deep mid-wicket but the spinner's victory was as hollow as a drum. Mahela Jayawardene never needed to assert his authority because his captain had done it before him and the tourists served up four balls per over for the rest of the innings. Nonetheless, he batted faultlessly and attacked with flair, particularly against the short ball. Cullinan's century, in fairness to Jayawardene, was even more skilful – but only because it had to be. Murali teased and teased, sometimes seeming arrogant and cruel as they lobbed his increasingly powerful grenades higher and higher. Only Cullinan knew where the bomb shelter was, and every time he received a 'dud' he thrashed it over mid-wicket. But he admitted that he couldn't read the ball from the hand – 'let's be honest,' he said afterwards, 'you need a lot of luck to survive against a bowler like him on a wicket like that.' You also make some of your own.

Jonty Rhodes made some for himself when South Africa followed on 284 runs behind but his unbeaten 63 wasn't even enough to make the home side bat again. It might have been had Nicky Boje's contribution to an eighth-wicket stand of 70 not been ended by an odd leg-before decision from Peter Manuel. Murali's delivery, from over the wicket to the left-hander, pitched 10 inches outside leg stump. Not that it made the slightest difference. Sri Lanka were superb. Rarely have South Africa been more outplayed.

SECOND TEST
30, 31 July, 1 and 2 August 2000 at Asgiriya Stadium, Kandy

South Africa's crushing defeat in the first Test was caused by their inability to cope with a single, brilliant bowler, which was excusable. Their lack of 'fight', however, the quality on which they pride themselves most, was not.

They made up for this in the second Test in tingling style, three times coming back from 'impossible' positions to finally steal a match from their hosts by just seven runs after almost four days of non-stop tension. Sri Lanka should have won, but 'should' plays for the same team as 'what if' and 'maybe'.

Sanath Jayasuriya chose to bowl first on a strange,

heavily cracked pitch that had nonetheless sweated profusely for two days under heavy tarpaulin covers and it looked like a decent decision with South Africa staggering to 34 for 5 after 90 minutes.

Lance Klusener and Mark Boucher, reasoning that conditions were unlikely to improve much when it dried out, embarked on a scintillating recovery during which they hit the spinners over the top at every opportunity and thrashed at anything with width. They added 124 for the sixth wicket before Muttiah Muralitheran scampered to gather a drive off his own bowling and ran Boucher out. Klusener squeezed another 80 unlikely but valuable runs from the last two wickets and finished unbeaten on 118 when the innings ended, surprisingly, on the right side of 250. That was the first comeback.

The second came at the end of the Sri Lankan first innings when Marvan Atappatu's straight-batted remorselessness and Arjuna Ranatunga's belligerence had led the reply to 286 for 4. The lead was 33, there were six wickets left and two batsmen were 'in' with a century and a half respectively. The series was beginning to look safe. Pollock, now desperate, came back and bowled as fast and as aggressively as he had for a couple of years to instigate a sickening collapse to 308, more so for the fact that it began when Ranatunga was given out leg before by Daryl Harper after a rising delivery had hit him in the box.

For South Africa, the deficit of 55 felt more like a lead after their fightback but at 50 for 3 the reality struck. Jacques Kallis (87) proved that he and

Marvan Atappatu, who, combined with Ranatunga, helped Sri Lanka to 286 for 4 during the second Test. Their lead was not enough and the South Africans went on to win by 7 runs.

Atapattu alone had the technique to survive for long periods with such uneven bounce and his four-hour vigil underpinned the second innings. Both captains believed a fourth innings target of 150-plus would be difficult and by the end of the third evening South Africa were 192 for 8, a lead of 137.

Critically, as it transpired, Nicky Boje was able to borrow and beg another 39 runs on the fourth morning with Paul Adams, once again, playing a part as unlikely as it was determined. The target was set: 177. Disaster greeted the run chase immediately when both openers were dismissed first ball and the scoreboard read 21 for 4 after ten overs. Ranatunga chose that moment to play one of the finest innings of his career.

From the moment he arrived, every ball he faced seemed drawn by a superior power to the middle of his bat. He cut, pulled and drove ten boundaries in his 38th Test 50, from just 36 balls, and South Africa had been transported almost instantly from elation to doubt. Russel Arnold did no more than take singles and admire during a stand of 109 that took Sri Lanka to within 47 of victory.

Then came South Africa's third, and decisive, comeback. Boje made the breach when Arnold padded up and was leg before. Klusener applied the pressure at the other end, bowling slow off-cutters off five paces that fully exploited the uneven bounce and worn surface. Ranatunga turned Boje off the face of the bat into Jonty Rhodes' hands at short leg and at tea the home side were 161 for 7 needing 16 runs.

Klusener yorked Upul Chandana with the first ball after the break, leaving Chaminda Vaas as the last realistic hope as the injured Nuwan Zoysa came to the crease with Jayasuriya as his runner, a wise head to make sure nothing silly happened. All three batsmen promptly choked, Vaas was run out and Muttiah Muralitheran was caught behind first ball, leaving South Africa to win the sixth closest Test, by runs, ever.

THIRD TEST
6, 7, 8, 9 and 10 August 2000 at Sinhalese Sports Club, Colombo

Arjuna Ranatunga's farewell to Test cricket overshadowed the fact that his successor, Sanath Jayasuriya, could win the series against South Africa with a victory on his mentor's home ground. Seasoned Sri Lankan cricket watchers seemed convinced that, after two almost rainless Tests, the weather would ensure Ranatunga's goodbye would be the highlight. And so it was, as the match

SECOND TEST – SRI LANKA v. SOUTH AFRICA
30, 31July, 1 and 2 August 2000 at Asgiriya Stadium, Kandy

SOUTH AFRICA

	First innings		Second innings	
G Kirsten	lbw b Vaas	0	b Dharmasena	13
ND McKenzie	c Jayawardene, b Zoysa	0	b Zoysa	1
JH Kallis	lbw b Muralitharan	16	b Muralitharan	87
DJ Cullinan	b Dharmasena	2	b Muralitharan	6
JN Rhodes	b Dharmasena	12	c Sangakkara, b Jayasuriya	33
L Klusener	not out	118	c Sangakkara, b Jayasuriya	4
*MV Boucher	run out (Muralitharan)	60	c Atappatu, b Muralitharan	15
SM Pollock (capt)	c Jayawardene, b Chandana	5	c Sangakkara, b Vaas	20
N Boje	lbw b Chandana	0	c sub (TM Dilshan), b Chandana	27
PR Adams	c Jayawardene, b Dharmasena	6	not out	14
M Hayward	b Muralitharan	13	lbw b Chandana	0
	b9, lb6, nb6	21	b7, lb1, nb3	11
		253		**231**

	First innings				Second Innings			
	O	M	R	W	O	M	R	W
Vaas	8	5	11	1	14	6	17	1
Zoysa	6	2	16	1	5	0	17	1
Dharmasena	30	3	58	3	16	2	47	1
Muralitharan	30.5	3	95	2	36	8	76	3
Chandana	20	2	58	2	9.5	0	21	2
Jayasuriya					13	1	45	2

Fall of Wickets
1–0, 2–4, 3–16, 4–34, 5–34, 6–158, 7–173, 8–173, 9–210
1–10, 2–37, 3–50, 4–121, 5–128, 6–153, 7–186, 8–186, 9–231

SRI LANKA

	First innings		Second innings	
MS Atapattu	lbw b Pollock	120	lbw b Pollock	0
ST Jayasuriya (capt)	c Kallis, b Hayward	28	lbw b Hayward	0
RP Arnold	run out (Kallis)	28	lbw b Boje	40
DPMD Jayawardene	c Cullinan, b Boje	18	c Boucher, b Hayward	1
*K Sangakkara	run out (McKenzie)	24	c Hayward, b Kallis	5
A Ranatunga	lbw b Hayward	54	c Rhodes, b Boje	88
HDPK Dharmasena	c Boucher b Pollock	3	c Rhodes, b Klusener	0
WPUJC Vaas	c Rhodes, b Pollock	4	(9) run out (Kallis/Klusener)	5
UDU Chandana	not out	1	(8) b Klusener	16
DNT Zoysa	b Kallis	3	not out	2
M Muralitharan	b Kallis	0	c Boucher, b Boje	0
	b6, lb12, nb7	25	b7, lb1, nb3	11
		308		**169**

	First innings				Second Innings			
	O	M	R	W	O	M	R	W
Pollock	24	5	83	3	11	4	38	1
Hayward	22	6	67	2	5	1	15	2
Kallis	11.4	4	18	2	8	1	25	1
Boje	15	2	50	1	10.1	4	24	3
Klusener	11	2	21	–	13	3	34	2
Adams	14	1	44	–	3	1	26	–
Cullinan	2	0	7	–				

Fall of Wickets
1–53, 2–109, 3–142, 4–182, 5–286, 6–296, 7–300, 8–303, 9–308
1–0, 2–5, 3–9, 4–21, 5–130, 6–133, 7–161, 8–161, 9–169

Umpires: G Silva & DJ Harper
Toss: Sri Lanka
Test Debuts: nil

South Africa won by 7 runs

finished in a draw and the series a tie. The national selectors even recalled Aravinda de Silva to be present at his great friend's final hurrah.

Jayasuriya once again won the toss and once again put South Africa in to bat at the venue most conducive to seam bowling in the country. The tourists also did their bit to continue the pattern of the series by collapsing miserably at the top of the order.

Ruchira Perera, a left-arm seamer called up as a direct replacement for the injured Nuwan Zoysa, struck with his first ball when Neil McKenzie edged a wide half-volley. Chaminda Vaas also enjoyed the overcast conditions and after little more than three hours South Africa were 117 for 6.

The eerie sense of déjà vu continued when Lance Klusener launched another rescue mission, initially in thrilling style but later becoming necessarily canny. He reached 50 from just 64 balls before the day was ended prematurely by rain with South Africa on 194 for 7. On day two he pushed, steered and cajoled his way to 95 not out from 175 balls before last man Nantie Hayward top-edged a full toss to leave him stranded within sight of another century.

Jayasuriya (85) produced another nerveless assault on South Africa's fidgety seamers when Sri Lanka replied, but left-arm spinner Nicky Boje, supposedly 'number two' to the more heralded Paul Adams, unhinged the top order with a couple of lengthy spells that contained every facet of attacking skill and variety. Upul Chandana (32) lashed out with a vital contribution towards the end of the innings to reduce the deficit from a probable 60 or 70 runs to a manageable 21 while Boje collected his second five-wicket haul in six months and only the third by a South African spinner since readmission.

Ruchira Perera made a memorable start to the third Test: he took a wicket first ball.

South Africa's second innings was dominated by caution with Gary Kirsten setting the tone in an innings of 40 from 150 balls. Jonty Rhodes made 14 more runs from a delivery more while Muttiah Muralitharan bowled and bowled, and bowled, finally collecting 5 for 68 to equal his own national record of 26 wickets in a series. Every time the home side felt they could win, however, more resistance arrived from the lower order, with Klusener (35), Mark Boucher (25) and finally Boje (29 not out) making the game safe.

Mahela Jayawardene completed his fourth century, and his second of the series, during Sri Lanka's theoretical pursuit of 263 in two sessions but he was hardly tested and needed to prolong the game in order to reach three figures, appreciably disgruntling the South Africans in the process.

The final hour of the match belonged to Ranatunga, however, who was cheered all the way to the wicket by an emotional crowd who had been given free access for the day to bid him farewell. He blocked a couple, launched a couple down the ground, exchanged highly amusing verbal bouncers with Pollock and Klusener, among others, and generally looked as good as he ever was.

Jayasuriya was not alone in wiping away a tear or two when the match ended. The stage was built, the marching bands arrived, the speeches started and the grand old man of Sri Lankan cricket walked away with his head held very high indeed.

Mahela Jayawardene, who completed two centuries during the South African series.

THIRD TEST – SRI LANKA v. SOUTH AFRICA
6, 7, 8, 9 and 10 August 2000 at Sinhalese Sports Club, Colombo

TEST MATCH AVERAGES
Sri Lanka v. South Africa

SOUTH AFRICA

	First innings		Second innings	
G Kirsten	c Ranatunga, b Perera	11	lbw b Muralitharan	40
ND McKenzie	c Arnold, b Perera	0	run out (Jayasuriya)	17
JH Kallis	c Sangakkara, b Vaas	19	b de Silva	0
DJ Cullinan	c Atapattu, b Vaas	38	c Arnold, b Muralitharan	3
JN Rhodes	b Muralitharan	21	c Jayawardene, b Muralitharan	54
L Klusener	not out	95	c Sangakkara, b Muralitharan	35
*MV Boucher	c Chandana, b Vaas	4	b Muralitharan	25
SM Pollock (capt)	b Muralitharan	33	c Sangakkara, b Jayasuriya	13
N Boje	c Sangakkara, b Vaas	21	not out	29
PR Adams	lbw b Muralitharan	15	c & b Jayasuriya	3
M Hayward	c de Silva, b Chandana	0	not out	3
	b2, lb8, nb12	22	lb4, nb15	19
		279	(for 9 wickets dec.)	**241**

	First innings				Second Innings			
	O	M	R	W	O	M	R	W
Vaas	36	9	85	4	10	2	22	–
Perera	18	3	60	2	2	0	13	–
de Silva	5	2	16	–	24.5	7	49	1
Muralitharan	39	14	70	3	45.5	14	68	5
Chandana	4.2	0	26	1	5	0	23	–
Jayasuriya	3	0	9	–	24	4	56	2
Arnold	3	1	3	–	2.1	0	6	–

Fall of Wickets
1-0, 2-23, 3-57, 4-89, 5-103, 6-117, 7-186, 8-240, 9-278
1-50, 2-50, 3-59, 4-107, 5-152, 6-169, 7-197, 8-220, 9-236

SRI LANKA

	First innings		Second innings	
MS Atapattu	b Hayward	10	c Kirsten, b Pollock	0
ST Jayasuriya (capt)	c Kirsten, b Boje	85	b Adams	17
RP Arnold	c Klusener, b Boje	28		
PA de Silva	st Boucher, b Boje	2	(5) lbw b Klusener	41
DPMD Jayawardene	c Kirsten, b Boje	34	(4) not out	101
WPUJC Vaas	lbw b Pollock	5		
A Ranatunga	b Boje	14	(6) not out	28
*K Sangakkara	c Boucher, b Hayward	25	(3) c Rhodes, b Hayward	6
UDU Chandana	c McKenzie, b Pollock	32		
PDRL Perera	c Boje, b Pollock	10		
M Muralitharan	not out	0		
	b3, lb1, w1, nb8	13	nb2	2
		258	(for 4 wickets)	**195**

	First innings				Second Innings			
	O	M	R	W	O	M	R	W
Pollock	22.2	10	40	3	6	3	13	1
Hayward	20	2	68	2	9	1	21	1
Kallis	13	3	48	–	4	2	4	–
Klusener	9	2	36	–	12.1	4	20	1
Boje	34	8	62	5	20	4	65	–
Adams					16	3	72	1

Fall of Wickets
1-19, 2-122, 3-130, 4-135, 5-170, 6-180, 7-201, 8-223, 9-257
1-6, 2-20, 3-37, 4-119

Umpires: BC Cooray & EA Nicholls
Toss: Sri Lanka
Test Debuts: nil

Match drawn

SRI LANKA

Batting	M	Inns	NO	HS	Runs	Av	100	50
DPMD Jayawardene	3	5	1	167	321	80.25	2	–
ST Jayasuriya	3	5	0	148	278	55.60	1	1
A Ranatunga	3	5	1	88	197	49.25	–	2
MS Atapattu	3	5	0	120	184	36.80	1	1
RP Arnold	3	4	0	40	101	25.25	–	–
UDU Chandana	3	4	1	32	57	19.00	–	–
WPUJC Vaas	3	4	0	54	68	17.00	–	1
K Sangakkara	3	5	0	25	83	16.60	–	–
DNT Zoysa	2	3	1	10	15	7.50	–	–
HDPK Dharmasena	2	3	0	4	8	2.66	–	–
M Muralitharan	3	4	2	2*	2	1.00	–	–

Also batted: PA de Silva (1 Test) 2, 41; PDRL Perera (1 Test) 10

Bowling	Overs	Mds	Runs	Wkts	Av	Best	10/m	5/inns
M Muralitharan	227.4	52	480	26	18.46	7-84	1	3
ST Jayasuriya	48	5	135	5	27.00	2-45	–	–
WPUJC Vaas	87	30	169	6	28.16	4-85	–	–
UDU Chandana	82.1	11	262	9	29.11	2-21	–	–
HPDK Dharmsena	71	11	212	5	42.40	3-58	–	–

Also bowled: RP Arnold 6.1-1-11-0; PA de Silva 29.5-9-65-1; PDRL Perera 20-3-73-2; DNT Zoysa 20-5-56-2

Fielding Figures
9 – K Sangakkara; 5 – RP Arnold; 4 – MS Atapattu, DPMD Jayawardene; 3 – A Ranatunga; 2 – UDU Chandana; 1 – PA de Silva, HDPK Dharmasena, ST Jayasuriya, M Muralitharan

SOUTH AFRICA

Batting	M	Inns	NO	HS	Runs	Av	100	50
L Klusener	3	6	2	118*	275	68.75	1	1
JN Rhodes	3	6	1	63*	195	39.00	–	2
DJ Cullinan	3	6	1	114*	175	35.00	1	–
JH Kallis	3	6	0	87	191	31.83	–	1
N Boje	3	6	1	35	124	24.80	–	–
G Kirsten	3	6	0	55	131	21.83	–	1
MV Boucher	3	6	0	60	111	18.50	–	1
SM Pollock	3	6	0	33	87	14.50	–	–
ND McKenzie	3	6	0	25	54	9.00	–	–
PR Adams	3	6	1	15	44	8.80	–	–
M Hayward	2	4	1	13	16	5.33	–	–

Also batted: M Ntini (1 Test) 8, 0

Bowling	Overs	Mds	Runs	Wkts	Av	Best	10/m	5/inns
SM Pollock	94	30	247	11	22.45	3-40	–	–
M Hayward	56	10	171	7	24.42	2-15	–	–
N Boje	101.1	20	273	10	27.30	5-62	–	1

Also bowled: PR Adams 78-11-326-4; DJ Cullinan 4-0-17-1; JH Kallis 53.4-17-136-4; L Klusener 60.1-15-149-3; M Ntini 19-1-73-1

Fielding Figures
7 – MV Boucher (6ct,1st); 4 – JN Rhodes; 3 – DJ Cullinan, G Kirsten; 2 – N Boje, L Klusener, ND McKenzie; 1 – M Hayward, JH Kallis, SM Pollock

AIWA CUP TRIANGULAR SERIES
By Qamar Ahmed

The World Cup champions of 1999, Australia, suffered a shock defeat in the final of the Aiwa Cup Triangular Series as they succumbed to Sri Lanka by the imposing margin of eight wickets. After their triumph against Pakistan in the final of the World Cup at Lord's only 72 days before, it was an embarrassment for the champions. Sri Lanka, who had failed to go past the league round of matches in the World Cup, had all the reasons to celebrate because it marked an end to their disappointing spell that had lasted more than year. The midnight sky in Colombo was lit up with fireworks as the jubilant fans danced in the streets.

Their experienced players, Arjuna Ranatunga and Aravinda de Silva, were dropped while Roshan Mahanama had announced his retirement. Dav Whatmore, their coach during their successful 1996 World Cup campaign, was back in the fold and Sanath Jayasuriya was made the new captain.

Australia sailed into the final by winning all their four matches in the preliminary round but performed poorly when it came to the crunch. Seeking to equal England's one-day record of 12 wins in a row, Australia were restricted to 202 as the Sri Lankan spinners, Muttiah Muralitharan, Russel Arnold, Upul Chandana and Sanath Jayasuriya took two wickets each. Mark Waugh (32) and Steve

Upul Chandana took 2 for 33 as Sri Lanka beat Australia in the final of the Aiwa series.

Waugh (43) played with any amount of confidence. Sri Lanka reached the target at a canter, in only the 40th over, losing Marvan Atapattu for 24 and Arnold for 47. Romesh Kaluwitharana hit a hurricane, unbeaten 95 with 12 fours as he punished Glenn McGrath and Jason Gillespie in particular. He put on 110 runs with Arnold for the second wicket to deny the Australians.

In the two opening games at Galle, Australia beat both Sri Lanka and India, by 51 runs and eight wickets respectively. Marred by rain, the results were achieved through the Duckworth/Lewis system. Sri Lanka, chasing 207, were out for 106 in the 38th over as Gillespie took a career-best 3 for 26. Shane Warne, with 2 for 39, became Australia's highest wicket-taker in one-day games with 204 in 126 matches. Adam Gilchrist, with 68 off 92 balls with seven fours, and Andrew Symonds, with an unbeaten 68 with as many boundaries, took Australia to an eight-wicket win over India, who had been contained to a modest 151 for 7 off 38 overs. Australia had no problem reaching the target in only 29.1 overs. Gilchrist and Symonds shared 132 runs for the second wicket in 147 balls to make things easy.

Sri Lanka's first win was against India by the huge margin of seven wickets. An opening stand of 83 off 115 balls between Atapattu and Jayasuriya helped Sri Lanka reach the target of 206 in 46.4 overs. Jayasuriya made 61 off 62 balls while Atapattu hit six fours in his unbeaten 71.

Australia breezed into the final when they beat Sri Lanka by 27 runs at Premadasa Stadium under lights. Mark Waugh's 84 in 94 balls steered them to 241 for 9 before Sri Lanka were reduced to 48 for 4. They were eventually dismissed for 214 in the 48th over. Debutant Chamara Silva, with 54 off 85 balls, was their highest scorer. Gillespie and McGrath destroyed India in the next match by sharing six wickets as India suffered a hat-trick of losses, losing the match by 41 runs. Sadagopan Ramesh and Robin Singh put on 123 for the sixth wicket in India's 211 in reply to Australia's 252 for 8, but it was in vain. Ramesh made 71 and Singh 75. Gilchrist, besides his 77 with nine fours, had completed his 100 dismissals in one-day games.

Australia finished at the top of the preliminary rounds with eight points from four games, leaving Sri Lanka and India to fight it out for the other place in the final. India won by 23 runs against Sri Lanka in their last match. They made 296 for 4 with the help of 120 by Tendulkar and 85 by Saurav Ganguly and restricted Sri Lanka to 247 for 9 but to no effect. Adam Gilchrist was the Man of the Series.

Match One – Sri Lanka v. Australia
22 August 1999 at Galle International Stadium
Australia 206 for 9 (43 overs)(ST Jayasuriya 5 for 28)
Sri Lanka 160 (37.4 overs)
Australia (2 pts) won by 52 runs
(D/L Method: Sri Lanka target 212 from 43 overs)
Man of the Match: JN Gillespie

Match Two – Australia v. India
23 August 1999 at Galle International Stadium
India 151 for 7 (38 overs)
Australia 159 for 2 (29.1 overs)(A Symonds 68*,
AC Gilchrist 68)
Australia (2 pts) won by eight wickets
Man of the Match: A Symonds

Match Three – Sri Lanka v. India
25 August 1999 at Premadasa Stadium, Colombo
India 205 for 8 (50 overs)
Sri Lanka 206 for 3 (46.4 overs)(MS Atapattu 71*,
ST Jayasuriya 61)
Sri Lanka (2 pts) won by seven wickets
Man of the Match: MS Atapattu

Match Four – Sri Lanka v. Australia
26 August 1999 at Premadasa Stadium, Colombo
Australia 241 for 9 (50 overs)(ME Waugh 84)
Sri Lanka 214 (47.1 overs)(PLC Silva 54)
Australia (2 pts) won by 27 runs
Man of the Match: ME Waugh

Match Five – Australia v. India
28 August 1999 at Sinhalese Sports Club, Colombo
Australia 252 for 8 (50 overs)(AC Gilchrist 77)
India 211 (48.3 overs)(RR Singh 75, S Ramesh 71,
JN Gillespie 4 for 26)
Australia (2 pts) won by 41 runs
Man of the Match: AC Gilchrist

Match Six – Sri Lanka v. India
29 August 1999 at Sinhalese Sports Club, Colombo
India 296 for 4 (50 overs)(SR Tendulkar 120,
SC Ganguly 85)
Sri Lanka 247 for 9 (42 overs)(ST Jayasuriya 71,
DPMP Jayawardene 62, MS Atapattu 55)
India (2 pts) won by 23 runs
Man of the Match: RR Singh

AIWA CUP FINAL – SRI LANKA v. AUSTRALIA
31 August 1999 at Premadasa Stadium, Colombo

AUSTRALIA

Batting			Bowling	O	M	R	W
*AC Gilchrist	c Jayawardene,		Zoysa	7	0	31	–
	b Wickremasinghe	21	Arnold	8	0	42	2
ME Waugh	b Muralitharan	32	Wickremasinghe	8	0	24	1
RT Ponting	run out (de Saram/		Muralitharan	10	0	36	2
	Kaluwitharana	28	Chandana	10	0	33	2
DS Lehmann	c & b Chandana	21	Jayasuriya	7	0	33	2
SR Waugh (capt)	b Muralitharan	43					
MG Bevan	b Chandana	0					
A Symonds	not out	22	**Fall of Wickets**				
SK Warne	c Silva b Arnold	21	1–37, 2–74, 3–75, 4–126, 5–126,				
JN Gillespie	b Arnold	14	6–144, 7–178, 8–197, 9–198				
DW Fleming	st Kaluwitharana,						
	b Jayasuriya	0					
GD McGrath	st Kaluwitharana,						
	b Jayasuriya	1					
	lb3, w3, nb3	9					
	50 overs	**202**					

SRI LANKA

Batting			Bowling	O	M	R	W
MS Atapattu	c Gilchrist, b Fleming	24	McGrath	7	0	47	–
+RS Kaluwitharana	not out	95	Gillespie	9	0	37	1
RP Arnold	b Gillespie	47	Fleming	7	1	28	1
ST Jayasuriya (capt)	not out	26	Warne	8	0	46	–
DPMD Jayawardene			Symonds	3	0	14	–
SI de Saram			Waugh SR	3	0	16	–
LPC Silva			Lehmann	1.3	0	13	–
UDU Chandana			Ponting	0	0	2	–
GP Wickremasinghe							
M Muralitharan			**Fall of Wickets**				
DNT Zoysa			1–64, 2–174				
	lb5, w5, nb6	16					
	38.3 overs (for 2 wickets)	**208**					

Umpires: BC Cooray & KT Francis
Toss: Australia
Man of the Match: RS Kaluwitharana
Man of the Series: AC Gilchrist

Sri Lanka won by eight wickets

SHARJAH

AND THE ONE-DAY INTERNATIONALS

Coca-Cola Champions Trophy
Coca-Cola Sharjah Cup
Super Challenge 2000
DMC Cup Toronto Cricket Festival
LG (Safari) Cup
Biman Millennium Cup
Singer Cup
Asia Cup

COCA-COLA CHAMPIONS TROPHY
By Qamar Ahmed

Pakistan was undoubtedly the better team in this triangular competition. In the four preliminary matches, they defeated the West Indies twice and beat Sri Lanka once with one match tied. This ensured that it was Sri Lanka who met Pakistan in the fifty-overs-per-side final. Pakistan's victory by 88 runs bagged them the title for the eleventh time in sixteen years of competitive cricket in Sharjah.

The final turned out to be a controversial affair with two dubious umpiring decisions in consecutive overs both counting against Sri Lanka, who were in pursuit of Pakistan's 211 for 9. Saeed Anwar (53) and Inzamam-ul-Haq (54) had made useful scores, but Pakistan were in trouble at 148 for 6 in the 40th over. Wasim Akram then blasted 30 off 26 balls as the late order put on 63 runs off the last 10 overs.

Sri Lanka quickly lost Jayasuriya for no runs, but were taken to 49 for 1 in the ninth over by de Silva and Kaluwitharana. Then their bad luck struck. First, umpire Steve Dunne gave de Silva out to a slip catch by Inzamam when the ball appeared, quite clearly, to have touched the ground. Such was the criticism of the decision by the television commentary team that Dunne left his post in the third umpire's room to berate the BBC's Jonathan Agnew, in particular. De Silva left, grudgingly, wondering whatever happened to batsmen receiving the benefit of the doubt.

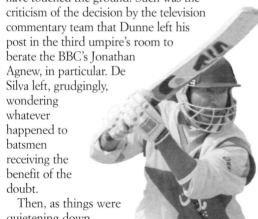

Then, as things were quietening down, David Shepherd dispatched Kaluwitharana, leg before, despite a thick inside edge. The match was effectively over, and Azhar Mahmood nabbed 5 for 28 as Sri Lanka, from 66 for 5, slumped to 123 all out.

In the opening match the West Indies were helped to victory by three wickets against Sri Lanka in the last over of the match. The West Indies made heavy weather of Sri Lanka's 178 before their win. Jimmy Adams' 1 for 23 – with an unbeaten innings of 74 – made the job easier, after Lara was out on the third ball of the innings for no runs. In the second match Pakistan had a convincing 130-run victory against the West Indies. It was Pakistan's fifth win in a row against the West Indies, having beaten them in the preliminary rounds of the World Cup and three times in a row in Toronto. Pakistan, having won the toss, scored 260 for 5 in 50 overs. Anwar made 72 with three fours and four sixes in 87 balls and Inzamam made 71, sharing 97 runs for the third wicket with Youhana, who made 48. The West Indies were out for 130 in the 35th over as Abdur Razzaq and off-spinner Shoaib Malik picked up two wickets each for 26 and 34 runs respectively.

In the next match Pakistan were brought back from the brink to tie the match through a career best by Razzaq, who took 5 for 31. Sri Lanka, chasing 197, were out for 196 as the game ended in a tie. Well-poised at 157 for 1 through a 115-run second-wicket-stand between Kaluwitharana (71) and Russel Arnold (61), Sri Lanka lost their last nine wickets for only 39 runs as Razzaq ran through the late order.

In the 150th one-day game at the venue in Sharjah, Sri Lanka had a nine-wicket win over the West Indies to recover from the shock of an earlier tied game against Pakistan. The West Indies – except for Wavell Hinds (58) – faltered badly, to be all out for 145 after deciding to bat first. Muralitharan with 3 for 22 had mesmerised them. An opening stand of 128 between Jayasuriya and Kaluwitharana then made the job easier as Sri Lanka reached the target in the 28th over. Jayasuriya's 88 off 80 balls was their highlight as he hit eight fours and three sixes.

Pakistan once again proved too strong for the Sri Lankans as they beat them by 118 runs in the following match, the fifth of the competition. The Sri Lankans, replying to Pakistan's 239 for 8, were shattered by young fast bowler Shabbir Ahmed, who dismissed Jayasuriya and Kaluwitharana to finish with 2 for 11 in six overs as Sri Lanka succumbed and were all out for 121 in the 34th over. Sri Lanka's last seven wickets were gone for 37 runs after a fourth-wicket stand of 69 between Aravinda de Silva and Atapattu. Pakistan's innings were studded by Shahid Afridi's 58 with five sixes and two fours and by an unbeaten 59 off 51 balls by Razzaq.

Saeed Anwar's 53 in the final helped earn Pakistan the trophy. Previous page: the Colonial Stadium, Melbourne.

In the last match before the final, Pakistan beat the West Indies by 138 runs allowing Sri Lanka in to the final. Pakistan rattled up 255 for 5 after they won the toss. Youhana scored an unbeaten 71 off 46 balls and Hasan Raza 77 to set the West Indies a formidable target. Azhar Mahmood took a career best 6 for 18 as the West Indies collapsed from 92 for 3 to 116 all out in the 32nd over. Pakistan continued in the same vein in the final against Sri Lanka.

Match One – Sri Lanka v. West Indies
13 October 1999 at Sharjah CA Stadium
Sri Lanka 178 (49.3 overs)
West Indies 181 for 7 (49.2 overs)(JC Adams 74*)
West Indies (2 pts) won by three wickets
Man of the Match: JC Adams

Match Two – Pakistan v. West Indies
14 October 1999 at Sharjah CA Stadium
Pakistan 260 for 5 (50)(Saeed Anwar 72, Inzamam-ul-Haq 71)
West Indies 130 (34.4 overs)
Pakistan (2 pts) won by 130 runs

Match Three – Pakistan v. Sri Lanka
15 October 1999 at Sharjah CA Stadium
Pakistan 196 (49.4 overs)
Sri Lanka 196 (49.1 overs)(RS Kaluwitharana 75, RP Arnold 61, Abdur Razzaq 5 for 31)
Match tied – 1 pt each
Man of the Match: Abdur Razzaq

Match Four – Sri Lanka v. West Indies
17 October 1999 at Sharjah CA Stadium
West Indies 145 (49.3 overs)(WW Hinds 58)
Sri Lanka 146 for 1 (28 overs)(ST Jayasuriya 88)
Sri Lanka (2 pts) won by nine wickets
Man of the Match: ST Jayasuriya

Match Five – Pakistan v. Sri Lanka
18 October 1999 at Sharjah CA Stadium
Pakistan 239 for 8 (50 overs)(Abdur Razzaq 59*, Shahid Afridi 58)
Sri Lanka 121 (33.4 overs)
Pakistan (2 pts) won by 118 runs
Man of the Match: Shahid Afridi

Match Six – Pakistan v. West Indies
19 October 1999 at Sharjah CA Stadium
Pakistan 255 for 5 (50 overs)(Hasan Raza 77, Yousuf Youhana 71*, Inzamam-ul-Haq 61)
West Indies 117 (31.3 overs)(AzharMahmood 6 for 18)
Pakistan (2 pts) won by 138 runs
Man of the Match: Azhar Mahmood

FINAL – PAKISTAN v. SRI LANKA
22 October 1999 at Sharjah CA Stadium

PAKISTAN

Batting			Bowling	O	M	R	W
Saeed Anwar	c Kaluwitharana, b Chandana	53	Vaas	8	0	20	1
Shahid Afridi	c Jayawardene, b Vaas	2	Zoysa	10	0	34	2
Abdur Razzaq	c Atapattu, b Zoysa	6	Wickremasinghe	4	0	31	–
Inzamam-ul-Haq	c Zoysa, b Jayasuriya	54	Muralitharan	10	0	39	–
Yousuf Youhana	b Chandana	5	Chandana	10	0	40	3
Hasan Raza	st Kaluwitharana, b Chandana	18	Jayasuriya	8	0	42	2
Wasim Akram (capt)	c Jayasuriya, b Zoysa	30					
*Moin Khan	run out (Chandana)	7	**Fall of Wickets**				
Azhar Mahmood	not out	13	1–12, 2–25, 3–96, 4–106, 5–145,				
Shoaib Malik	st Kaluwitharana, b Jayasuriya	12	6–148, 7–179, 8–194, 9–211				
Mohammad Akram							
	b1, lb4, w5, nb1	11					
	50 overs (for 9 wickets) 211						

SRI LANKA

Batting			Bowling	O	M	R	W
ST Jayasuriya	c Shahid Afridi, b Wasim Akram	0	Wasim Akram	8	2	21	2
+RS Kaluwitharana	lbw b Wasim Akram	10	Mohammad Akram	7	1	26	–
PA de Silva	c Inzamam-ul-Haq, b Abdur Razzaq	25	Abdur Razzaq	5	0	13	1
DPMD Jayawardene	c Moin Khan, b Azhar Mahmood	8	Azhar Mahmood	10	2	28	5
MS Atapattu	c Moin Khan, b Azhar Mahmood	3	Shoaib Malik	6	1	30	2
RP Arnold	not out	27					
UDU Chandana	c Moin Khan, b Azhar Mahmood	0	**Fall of Wickets**				
WPUJC Vaas	c Inzamam-ul-Haq, b Azhar Mahmood	9	1–0, 2–49, 3–50, 4–57, 5–66				
GP Wickremasinghe	b Azhar Mahmood	1	6–70, 7–85, 8–89, 9–117				
DNT Zoysa	c & b Shoaib Malik	22					
M Muralitharan	b Shoaib Malik	0					
	lb5, w9, nb4	18					
	36 overs	**123**					

Umpires: DB Cowie & DR Shepherd
Toss: Pakistan
Man of the Match: Azhar Mahmood
Man of the Series: Inzamam-ul-Haq

Pakistan won by 88 runs

COCA-COLA SHARJAH CUP
By Qamar Ahmed

The doom and gloom of their disastrous series at home against Sri Lanka was soon forgotten as Pakistan beat South Africa in the final of the three-nation Coca-Cola Sharjah Cup. Having lost their first two games against India and South Africa by five and three wickets respectively, Pakistan were able to raise their profile through some fine bowling by Waqar Younis, who was declared Man of the Series for his tally of 13 wickets.

Chasing 264 runs in the final, South Africa were sailing along nicely at 198 for 4 by the 40th over, but then lost three wickets within a space of three runs. Pakistan won by 16 runs. With successive deliveries of his seventh over, Waqar had Nicky Boje caught at the wicket and then bowled Lance Klusener to turn the game around. Shaun Pollock averted the hat-trick and Mark Boucher added 57 off 49 balls, but Waqar returned to bowl both of them and bring victory for Pakistan. Earlier, Imran Nazir and Shahid Afridi had put on 121 runs for Pakistan's opening stand and in the last five overs Pakistan rattled up 43 runs.

In the opening round Makhaya Ntini – who had been cleared of a rape charge – took 3 for 36 and Steve Elworthy picked up 3 for 17 as India tumbled for 164 in the 46th over. Gary Kirsten (71) and Herschelle Gibbs (87) knocked off the runs in 20.4 overs to record their first ten wicket win in one-day internationals.

In the second match Mohammad Azharuddin hit 54 off 89 balls to take India to a five-wicket win over Pakistan. Choosing to bat first Pakistan were bundled out for 146 in the 46th over, losing their last seven wickets for 38 runs. India reached the required target in the 44th having, at one stage, been 41 for 2 before Rahul Dravid and Azharuddin put on 70 runs for the third wicket.

South Africa then beat Pakistan by three wickets. Klusener took 5 for 47 to restrict Pakistan to 196 for 8 in 50 overs, and was twice on a hat-trick. South Africa survived early jitters to win the match in the 45th over.

Pakistan avenged their defeat, beating India in the following game by 98 runs. Pakistan scored 272 for 3, with 93 coming in the last 10 overs. Inzamam blasted 121 with nine fours and five sixes to post his seventh one-day century and his second against India, who were then shattered by Waqar and Wasim. Waqar took 5 for 31, with Wasim claiming Tendulkar.

India – who had a rotten tournament – were beaten again in the next game by South Africa to knock them out of the competition. They were bowled out for 164 as Nantie Hayward took 4 for 31 and South Africa cruised to victory with 7.2 overs remaining.

Pakistan reached the final by ending their 14-match losing streak against South Africa. Defending only 168, Shoaib took three wickets in one over to bowl South Africa out for 101 in the 27th over. He finished with 3 for 9 in 29 balls.

Pakistan's Waqar Younis, who took 13 wickets and was declared Man of the Series.

Match One – India v. South Africa

22 March 2000 at Sharjah CA Stadium (floodlit)
India 164 (45.2 overs)
South Africa 168 for 0 (29.2 overs)(HH Gibbs 87*,
G Kirsten 71*)
South Africa (2 pts) won by 10 wickets
Man of the Match: S Elworthy

Match Two – India v. Pakistan

23 March 2000 at Sharjah CA Stadium (floodlit)
Pakistan 146 (45.3 overs)
India 149 for 5 (43.3 overs)(M Azharuddin 54)
India (2 pts) won by five wickets
Man of the Match: M Azharuddin

Match Three – Pakistan v. South Africa

24 March 2000 at Sharjah CA Stadium (floodlit)
Pakistan 196 for 8 (50 overs)(Imran Nazir 71,
L Klusener 5 for 47)
South Africa 199 for 7 (44.3 overs)
South Africa (2 pts) won by three wickets
Man of the Match: L Klusener

Match Four – India v. Pakistan

26 March 2000 at Sharjah CA Stadium (floodlit)
Pakistan 272 for 3 (50 overs)(Inzamam-ul-Haq 121*,
Yousuf Youhana 56*)
India 174 for 9 (50 overs)(Waqar Younis 5 for 31)
Pakistan (2 pts) won by 98 runs
Men of the Match: Inzamam-ul-Haq & Waqar Younis

Match Five – India v. South Africa

27 March 2000 at Sharjah CA Stadium (floodlit)
India 164 (48.5 overs)(M Hayward 4 for 31)
South Africa 167 for 4 (42.4 overs)(JH Kallis 53*)
South Africa (2 pts) won by six wickets
Man of the Match: M Hayward

Match Six – Pakistan v. South Africa

28 March 2000 at Sharjah CA Stadium (floodlit)
Pakistan 168 (49.2 overs)(Yousuf Youhana 65)
South Africa 101 (26.5 overs)(HH Gibbs 59* – carried
his bat)
Pakistan (2 pts) won by 67 runs
Man of the Match: Shoaib Akhtar

FINAL – PAKISTAN v. SOUTH AFRICA
31 March 2000 at Sharjah CA Stadium (floodlit)

PAKISTAN

Batting			Bowling	O	M	R	W
Imran Nazir	st Boucher, b Crookes	69	Pollock	10	1	54	1
Shahid Afridi	c Kallis, b Klusener	52	Hayward	9	0	52	–
Younis Khan	lbw b Klusener	4	Kallis	10	0	57	2
Inzamam-ul-Haq	b Pollock	53	Elworthy	3	0	21	–
Yousuf Youhana	c Cronje, b Kallis	26	Klusener	10	1	27	2
*Moin Khan (capt)	lbw b Kallis	2	Crookes	5	0	20	1
Abdur Razzaq	not out	28	Cronje	3	0	22	–
Wasim Akram	not out	5					
Waqar Younis							
Arshad Khan			Fall of Wickets				
Mohammad Akram			1-121, 2-133, 3-137, 4-204, 5-209,				
	lb10, w10, nb4	24	6-256				

50 overs (for 6 wickets) 263

SOUTH AFRICA

Batting			Bowling	O	M	R	W
HH Gibbs	c Inzamam-ul-Haq,		Wasim Akram	9	2	23	1
	b Wasim Akram	5	Waqar Younis	10	0	62	4
ND McKenzie	c Mohammad Akram,		Mohammad Akram	9	0	42	1
	b Arshad Khan	58	Abdur Razzaq	9	0	33	1
JH Kallis	c Moin Khan,		Shahid Afridi	4	0	30	–
	b Mohammad Akram	11	Arshad Khan	8	0	51	3
WJ Cronje (capt)	c Younis Khan, b Arshad Khan	79					
DN Crookes	b Arshad Khan	3					
*MV Boucher	b Waqar Younis	57	Fall of Wickets				
N Boje	c Moin Khan,		1-12, 2-30, 3-135, 4-137, 5-198,				
	b Waqar Younis	0	6-199, 7-199, 8-224, 9-239				
L Klusener	b Waqar Younis	0					
SM Pollock	b Waqar Younis	14					
S Elworthy	not out	5					
M Hayward	b Abdur Razzaq	4					
	lb6, w4, nb3	13					

49 overs 247

Umpires: DJ Harper & PT Manuel
Toss: Pakistan
Man of the Match: Waqar Younis
Man of the Series: Waqar Younis

Pakistan won by 16 runs

SUPER CHALLENGE 2000
By Jim Maxwell

The first official international one-day series to be played in a covered stadium produced a tied result, ensuring at least a statistical relevance for this historic event. The marketing hype that promised a mouth-watering contest in a state-of-the-art venue was overdone, simply because this was not the World Cup, and all one-day series outside that special quadrennial occasion seem somewhat meaningless.

The credibility of the series was certainly enhanced by the two combatants, Australia and South Africa. The promoters were eager to cash in on their remarkable World Cup semi-final tie, and their reputations as the toughest opponents in the game. There was also a sense of renewal in the air, when Steve Waugh and Shaun Pollock spoke about how much the image of the game had been tarnished by match-fixing revelations, and how these indoor matches presented a chance to play cricket that people could believe in again.

South Africa were fresh from a tour of Sri Lanka, but were in a rebuilding phase without Cronje, Gibbs and Alan Donald, who was playing his final season with Warwickshire. Australia were at full strength, McGrath, Warne, Bevan and Harvey in prime county form, and Ponting recovered from a serious ankle injury. But apart from participation in two warm-up games against Queensland, most of the squad had been doing what the rest of the country's sports followers do in winter: watch football. And this series was being staged in direct competition to the football (as in Australian Rules and Rugby League) finals.

Designed specifically for football, the Colonial Stadium had begun its life prematurely. Recurrent problems with the condition of the playing surface had dogged the proprietors since the ground's christening in March, and there were understandable concerns about its suitability for cricket. The lighting was much lower than the usual tower structures at other cricket grounds. The hothouse pitch was another unknown factor, even though the concept had been successful during Packer's World Series.

In the event, the pitch played superbly. It looked like a slab from the old Sabina Park under the dim sepulchral pre-match lighting. Adelaide Oval curator Les Burdett was congratulated by both captains for his creation. Some spectacular outfield catching confirmed the light quality, and the only imperfection was an occasional slipperiness in the outfield.

Australia began confidently by posting their highest one-day score in the opening match, 5 for 295, swelled by a 222 partnership between century-makers Michael Bevan and Steve Waugh. Bevan pipped Waugh for the accomplishment of being the first player to reach an indoor hundred, and the craft of his innings was underscored by typically aggressive running between the wickets. Waugh is remarkable. Unlike Bevan, who'd been swotting hundreds for Sussex, Waugh hadn't had a serious hit for four months. He outpaced Bevan and was a tired 114 not out when Shane Lee was crashing Pollock for successive sixes over cover. The Proteas were quickly depowered by McGrath, and deflowered by Warne's spin and Harvey's subtle changes of pace.

South Africa's 8 for 226 in the second match seemed inadequate, and when Australia were 2 for 146 in the 33rd over, a two-nil series lead was looming. Lacking their customary aggression, the Australian batting fell away and a useful spell from all-rounder Andrew Hall meant Australia needed 13 from the last over, and then two off the final ball to win. Warne could score only one, and the result was, remarkably, a tie.

In the third contest, South Africa made a gritty recovery from 4 for 19 to 7 for 206, thanks to Klusener and McKenzie adding 98. Again the target appeared comfortably within Australia's range, and again their batting subsided, after Gilchrist thumped 63 from 67 balls. Nicky Boje, who'd slammed two sixes in making 28 not out, bowled his left-armers cleverly, and was rewarded with Man of the Match and of the Series. The margin was eight runs, and the sight of both captains holding the trophy provided a bizarre conclusion to an innovative event. More than 90,000 spectators attended the three games, but while most of them probably thought that the logo painted on the ground, Pentasoft, was advertising a new toilet paper, the sponsors, in reality an Indian software company, were happy that their television audience of over five million subscribers had enjoyed uninterrupted entertainment.

DMC CUP TORONTO CRICKET FESTIVAL

Match One – India v. West Indies

11 September 1999 at
Toronto Cricket, Skating & Curling Club
West Indies 163 (46.2 overs)(SL Campbell 62)
India 165 for 2 (37.3 overs)(S Ramesh 55*,
SC Ganguly 54*)
India won by eight wickets
Man of the Match: SC Ganguly

Match Two – India v. West Indies

12 September 1999 at
Toronto Cricket, Skating & Curling Club
West Indies 190 for 6 (50 overs)(SL Campbell 59)
India 120 (41.5 overs)
West Indies won by 70 runs
Man of the Match: SL Campbell

Match Three – India v. West Indies

14 September 1999
at Toronto Cricket, Skating & Curling Club
India 225 for 7 (50 overs)(R Dravid 77, M Dillon 5 for 51)
West Indies 137 (34.2 overs)(RL Powell 76,
N Chopra 5 for 21)
India won by 88 runs
Man of the Match: R Dravid

Match Four – Pakistan v. West Indies

16 September 1999
at Toronto Cricket, Skating & Curling Club
Pakistan 230 for 6 (50 overs)(Saeed Anwar 63)
West Indies 215 for 9(50 overs)(SL Campbell 69)
Pakistan won by 15 runs
Man of the Match: Saeed Anwar

Match Five – Pakistan v. West Indies

18 September 1999 at
Toronto Cricket, Skating & Curling Club
Pakistan 222 for 5 (50 overs)(Yousuf Youhana 104*,
Abdur Razzaq 55)
West Indies 180 (46.2 overs)(WW Hinds 65)
Pakistan won by 42 runs
Man of the Match: Yousuf Youhana

Match Six – Pakistan v. West Indies

19 September 1999 at
Toronto Cricket, Skating & Curling Club
West Indies 161 (44.4 overs)
Pakistan 162 for 3 (39.4 overs)(Abdur Razzaq 57,
Inzamam-ul-Haq 55*)
Pakistan won by seven wickets
Man of the Match: Abdur Razzaq

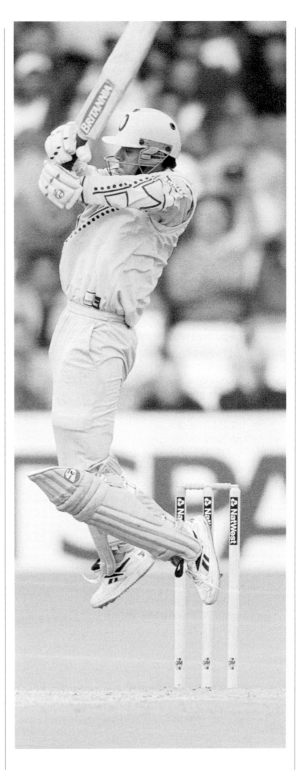

Rahul Dravid's 77 in the third match, which included six fours and two sixes, earned him Man of the Match.

LG (SAFARI) CUP

Match One – Kenya v. Zimbabwe
25 September 1999 at Gymkhana Club Gound, Nairobi
Kenya 199 for 8 (50 overs)(RD Shah 71)
Zimbabwe 200 for 7 (49.2 overs)(MW Goodwin 76*,
A Flower 55)
Zimbabwe (2 pts) won by three wickets
Man of the Match: MW Goodwin

Match Two – India v. South Africa
26 September 1999 at Gymkhana Club Ground, Nairobi
South Africa 117 (48 overs)(SB Joshi 5 for 6)
India 120 for 2 (22.4 overs)
India (2 pts) won by eight wickets
Man of the Match: SB Joshi

Match Three – South Africa v. Zimbabwe
28 September 1999 at Gymkhana Club Ground, Nairobi
Zimbabwe 216 (47.4 overs)(GW Flower 91)
South Africa 217 for 1 (35 overs)(L Klusener 101*)
South Africa (2 pts) won by nine wickets
Man of the Match: L Klusener

Match Four – Kenya v. India
29 September 1999 at Gymkhana Club Ground, Nairobi
India 220 for 7 (50 overs)(S Ramesh 50)
Kenya 162 (50 overs)
India (2 pts) won by 58 runs
Man of the Match: VR Bharadwaj

Match Five – Kenya v. South Africa
30 September 1999 at Gymkhana Club Ground, Nairobi
South Africa 220 for 7 (50 overs)
Kenya 196 (48.1 overs)(SO Tikolo 67)
South Africa (2 pts) won by 24 runs
Man of the Match: SO Tikolo

Match Six – India v. Zimbabwe
1 October 1999 at Gymkhana Club Ground, Nairobi
India 277 for 6 (50 overs)(SC Ganguly 139)
Zimbabwe 170 (38.3 overs)(NC Johnson 52,
N Chopra 4 for 33)
India (2 pts) won by 107 runs
Man of the Match: SC Ganguly

INDIA v. SOUTH AFRICA
3 October 1999 at Gymkhana Club Ground, Nairobi

SOUTH AFRICA

Batting			Bowling	O	M	R	W
HH Gibbs	b Bharadwaj	84	BKV Prasad	10	5	21	2
L Klusener	b Mohanty	0	Mohanty	10	2	36	2
JH Kallis	c Dravid, b BKV Prasad	9	Joshi	10	0	55	–
JH Rhodes	c Ganguly, b BKV Prasad	0	Chopra	9	0	48	1
WJ Cronje (capt)	b Chopra	39	Singh	2	0	18	–
DN Crookes	c MSK Prasad, b Mohanty	25	Ganguly	1	0	16	–
DM Benkenstein	b Bharadwaj	18	Bharadwaj	8	0	34	3
SM Pollock	not out	23					
*MV Boucher	c Jadeja, b Bharadwaj	10	**Fall of Wickets**				
AC Dawson	run out (Ganguly/Chopra)	6	1–2, 2–12, 3–18, 4–96, 5–149,				
S Elworthy	not out	9	6–187, 7–188, 8–212, 9–219				
	b2, lb5, w2, nb3	12					
	50 overs (for 9 wickets)	235					

INDIA

Batting			Bowling	O	M	R	W
S Ramesh	c Crookes, b Dawson	8	Pollock	9	0	28	2
SC Ganguly	c Boucher, b Pollock	10	Dawson	10	1	43	1
R Dravid	c Rhodes, b Crookes	30	Kallis	8.3	0	33	1
*MSK Prasad	run out (Kallis/Boucher)	63	Klusener	7	0	33	2
AD Jadeja (capt)	c sub (HH Dippenaar),		Crookes	9	0	47	3
	b Pollock	30	Elworthy	4	0	21	–
VR Bharadwaj	c Pollock, b Klusener	24					
RR Singh	b Crookes	6	**Fall of Wickets**				
SB Joshi	st Boucher, b Crookes	18	1–18, 2–25, 3–90, 4–141, 5–163,				
N Chopra	c Crookes, b Klusener	5	6–190, 7–196, 8–201, 9–208				
BKV Prasad	not out	3					
DS Mohanty	lbw b Kallis	0					
	lb4, w5, nb3	12					
	47.3 overs	209					

Umpires: EA Nicholls & G Sharp
Toss: India
Man of the Match: HH Gibbs
Man of the Series: VR Bharadwaj

South Africa won by 26 runs

Herschelle Gibbs' flawless 84 with six
fours and three sixes helped South Africa
make 235 for 9 in 50 overs in the final
against India, who were bowled out for
209 with 15 balls still remaining.

BIMAN MILLENNIUM CUP

Match One – Bangladesh v. West Indies
8 October 1999 at
Bangabandhu National Stadium, Dhaka
West Indies 292 for 6 (50 overs)(S Chanderpaul 92*,
JC Adams 56)
Bangladesh 219 for 5 (50 overs)
(Al Shahariar Rokon 62*, Khaled Masud 53*)
West Indies won by 73 runs
Man of the Match: JC Adams

Match Two – Bangladesh v. West Indies
9 October 1999 at
Bangabandhu National Stadium, Dhaka
West Indies 314 for 6 (50 overs)(BC Lara 117,
S Chanderpaul 77*)
Bangladesh 205 (49.1 overs)(Aminul Islam 66,
SL Campbell 4 for 30)
West Indies won by 109 runs
Man of the Match: BC Lara

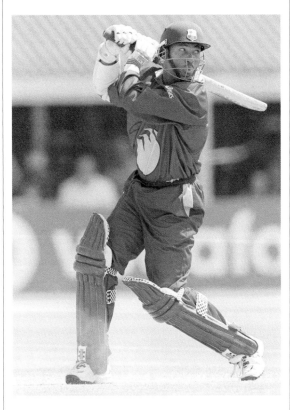

The West Indian captain Brian Lara proved to be the highlight of the Biman Millennium Cup, carving out a scintillating 117 with 18 fours and four sixes in the second match. He scorched past his hundred in only 45 balls.

SINGER CUP

Match One – Sri Lanka v. Pakistan
5 July 2000 at Galle International Stadium
Pakistan 164 for 8 (45 overs)(Inzamam-ul-Haq 83*,
DNT Zoysa 4 for 34)
Sri Lanka 166 for 5 (37.3 overs)(MS Atapattu 62)
Sri Lanka (2 pts) won by five wickets
Man of the Match: DNT Zoysa

Match Two – Sri Lanka v. South Africa
6 July 2000 at Galle International Stadium
Sri Lanka 249 for 7 (50 overs)(K Sangakkara 84,
RP Arnold 60*)
South Africa 212 (48.2 overs)(AJ Hall 81,
G Kirsten 59, UDU Chandana 4 for 44)
Sri Lanka (2 pts) won by 37 runs
Man of the Match: K Sangakarra

Match Three – Pakistan v. South Africa
8 July 2000 at
R Premadasa Stadium, Khetterama (floodlit)
South Africa 241 for 6 (50 overs)(JH Kallis 83,
G Kirsten 52)
Pakistan 223 for 9 (50 overs)(Imran Nazir 80,
N Boje 4 for 25)
South Africa (2 pts) won by 18 runs
Man of the Match: JH Kallis

Match Four – Sri Lanka v. Pakistan
9 July 2000 at
R Premadasa Stadium, Khetterama (floodlit)
Pakistan 240 for 6 (50 overs)(Younis Khan 59)
Sri Lanka 244 for 4 (49.2 overs)(ST Jayasuriya 54)
Sri Lanka (2 pts) won by six wickets
Man of the Match: ST Jayasuriya

Match Five – Sri Lanka v. South Africa
11 July 2000 at Sinhalese Sports Club, Colombo
South Africa 167 (49.2 overs)(JH Kallis 83*)
Sri Lanka 168 for 2 (27.3 overs)(DA Gunawardene 87)
Sri Lanka (2 pts) won by eight wickets
Man of the Match: DA Gunawardene

Match Six – Pakistan v. South Africa
12 July 2000 at Sinhalese Sports Club, Colombo
Pakistan 153 (44.1 overs)(DJ Terbrugge 4 for 20,
MV Boucher 5ct)
South Africa 156 for 3 (37.3 overs)
South Africa (2 pts) won by seven wickets
Man of the Match: DJ Terbrugge

ASIA CUP

Match One – Bangladesh v. Sri Lanka

28 (no play) and 29 May 2000 at
Bangabandhu National Stadium (floodlit)
Bangladesh 175 for 6 (Javed Omar 85*)
Sri Lanka 178 for 1 (PA de Silva 96*)
Sri Lanka (2 pts) won by nine wickets
Man of the Match: PA de Silva

Match Two – Bangladesh v. India

30 and 31 May 2000 at
Bangabandhu National Stadium (floodlit)
Bangladesh 249 for 6 (50 overs)(Akram Khan 64,
Habibul Bashar 57)
India 252 for 2 (40.1 overs)(SC Ganguly 135*)
India (2 pts) won by eight wickets
Man of the Match: SC Ganguly

Match Three – India v. Sri Lanka

1 June 2000 at Bangabandhu National Stadium (floodlit)
Sri Lanka 276 for 8 (50 overs)(ST Jayasuriya 105)
India 205 (45 overs)(SR Tendulkar 93)
Sri Lanka (2 pts) won by 71 runs
Man of the Match: ST Jayasuriya

Match Four – Bangladesh v. Pakistan

2 June 2000 at Bangabandhu National Stadium (floodlit)
Pakistan 320 for 3 (50 overs)(Imran Nazir 80, Yousuf
Youhana 80, Inzamam-ul-Haq 75*)
Bangladesh 87 (34.2 overs)
Pakistan (2 pts) won by 233 runs
Man of the Match: Imran Nazir

Match Five – India v. Pakistan

3 June 2000 at Bangabandhu National Stadium (floodlit)
Pakistan 295 for 7 (50 overs)(Yousuf Youhana 100*)
India 251 (47.4 overs)(AD Jadeja 93, Abdur Razzaq
4 for 29)
Pakistan (2 pts) won by 44 runs
Man of the Match: Yousuf Youhana

Match Six – Pakistan v. Sri Lanka

5 June 2000 at Bangabandhu National Stadium (floodlit)
Sri Lanka 192 (49 overs)(MS Atapattu 62)
Pakistan 193 for 3 (48.2 overs)(Yousuf Youhana 90*)
Pakistan (2 pts) won by seven wickets
Man of the Match: Yousuf Youhana

FINAL – PAKISTAN v. SRI LANKA
7 June 2000 at Bangabandhu National Stadium (floodlit)

PAKISTAN

Batting				Bowling	O	M	R	W
L Saeed Anwar	c Muralitharan, b Jayasuriya		82	BKV Prasad	10	5	21	2
Imran Nazir	c & b Zoysa		3	Vaas	8	0	52	–
Shahid Afridi	c Arnold, b Zoysa		22	Zoysa	8	1	44	2
Yousuf Youhana	c & b Chandana		25	Weeraratne	6	0	23	–
Inzamam-ul-Haq	not out		72	Muralitharan	10	0	42	–
*Moin Khan (capt)	not out		56	Chandana	10	0	43	1
Abdur Razzaq				Jayasuriya	8	0	63	1
Wasim Akram								
Azhar Mahmood				**Fall of Wickets**				
Arshad Khan				1–17, 2–56, 3–124, 4–173				
Mohammad Akram								
	b3, lb7, w2, nb5		17					
50 overs (for 4 wickets)			**277**					

SRI LANKA

Batting				Bowling	O	M	R	W
ST Jayasuriya (capt)	c & b Mohammad Akram		22	Wasim Akram	8	0	38	2
*RS Kaluwitharana	run out (Saeed Anwar/ Moin Khan)		0	Mohammad Akram	8	0	50	2
WPUJC Vaas	b Mohammad Akram		10	Abdur Razzaq	7.2	0	40	1
MS Atapattu	c Moin Khan, b Wasim Akram		100	Azhar Mahmood	10	0	40	–
PA de Silva	c Yousuf Youhana, b Arshad Khan		20	Arshad Khan	10	0	42	2
RP Arnold	c Shahid Afridi, b Arshad Khan		41	Shahid Afridi	2	0	20	–
DPMD Jayawardene	run out (Shahid Afridi)		0					
UDU Chandana	b Wasim Akram		24	**Fall of Wickets**				
DNT Zoysa	not out		6	1–6, 2–21, 3–46, 4–117, 5–196,				
M Muralitharan	c sub (Shoaib Maik), b Abdur Razzaq		0	6–202, 7–220, 8–237, 9–238				
K Weeraratne	absent injured							
	lb8, w5, nb2		15					
45.2 overs			**238**					

Umpires: SK Bansal & AV Jayaprakash
Toss: Pakistan
Man of the Match: Moin Khan
Man of the Series: Yousuf Youhana

Pakistan won by 39 runs

FORM CHARTS

Derbyshire
Durham
Essex
Glamorgan
Gloucestershire
Hampshire
Kent
Lancashire
Leicestershire
Middlesex
Northamptonshire
Nottinghamshire
Somerset
Surrey
Sussex
Warwickshire
Worcestershire
Yorkshire

DERBYSHIRE CCC

FIRST-CLASS MATCHES
BATTING

	MP Dowman	SD Stubbings	MJ Di Venuto	SP Titchard	RJ Bailey	DG Cork	ME Cassar	KM Krikken	P Aldred	TA Munton	TM Smith	KJ Dean	BJ Spendlove	LD Sutton	SJ Lacey	KZ Shah	LJ Wharton	T Lungley	M Saxelby	JP Pyemont	Extras	Total	Wickets	Result	Points
v. Leicestershire	8	21	70	8	118	8	11	51	36	4	2*										22	359	10	D	10
(Derby) 26–29 April	0*	2*	–	–	–	–	–	–	–	–	–										–	2	–		
v. Yorkshire	7	0	70	4	14		9	38	38	16*	15	0									28	239	10	L	2
(Headingley) 3–5 May	4	4	33	11	54*		24	0	0	4*	21	15									20	190	9		
v. Cambridge University	94	92		8			77*					–	0	18	2*	–	–	–			46	337	5	D	–
(Cambridge) 12–14 May	–	–																			–	–	–		
v. Yorkshire	16	49	30		29	43	47	9		2*	19	6*			25						28	303	9	D	10
(Derby) 17–20 May	20	84*	81*																		24	209	1		
v. Somerset	41*	41*	–	–	–	–	–	–	–	–	–										19	101	–	D	7
(Taunton) 24–27 May	–	–																			–	–	–		
v. Lancashire	4	42	15		12	1	22	7	22*	2	13			13							17	170	10	D	7
(Old Trafford) 31 May–3 June	5*	11	–	–	–	–	–	–	–	–	2										6	24	2		
v. Surrey	69	3	16	3	0	44*	5	17	0	1	0										33	191	10	W	15
(Derby) 7–9 June	10	0	92*	–	40*	–	4	–	–	–	–										21	167	3		
v. Leicestershire	1	0	26	16	11	1	30	24	5	0*		0									19	133	10	L	3
(Leicester) 14–17 June	28	8	13	38	24	0	40	27	10	0*		0									35	223	10		
v. Durham	12	6	49	23			0	0		0	22	3*		10			0				26	151	10	L	2
(Darlington) 28–30 June	61	0	11	87*			7	6		52	0	0		7			1				17	249	10		
v. Lancashire		64	1	32		52		25		12	53*			8	12	10			17		21	307	10	D	10
(Derby) 7–10 July		27	17	0		–		–		–	–			15*	9*	–			6		6	80	4		
v. Kent	21	72	0	4		58		0		11	1			10	0	0*					4	181	10	L	3
(Derby) 12–15 July	9	16	3	74				17		37	0			14	37	38*					24	269	10		
v. Kent	77	41	13	52					1	3		0		13	48	6*				4	21	279	10	D	9
(Canterbury) 28–31 July	–	135*		141*					–	–					–					17	17	293			
v. Hampshire	110	0	14	18	20				10	4		0		36	55*	7					36	310	10	D	10
(Derby) 2–5 August	4	20	78*	6	0				0	6*		22		79	5	33					40	293	9		
v. West Indians	39	7		5	112*		21*				–			34	–	–				4	20	242	5	L	–
(Derby) 9–11 August	1	23		0	65*		9					4		0	0	14	7			11	11	145	10		
v. Surrey	36	11	10		9		1		6	0		0		26	7*	0					12	118	10	L	3
(Oval) 16–17 August	9	41	0		0		0		4	13		0		23	0	0*					7	97	10		
v. Durham	2	9	0	54	45	28			3	2		3		2			1*				18	167	10	W	15
(Derby) 22–25 August	140	5	31	23	200*	1			14	21*		–		15							26	476	7		
v. Hampshire	1	36	52	90		0				1		0		77	2		0*			40	53	352	10	L	6
(Southampton) 6–9 September	4	19	0	53		5				0		0*		37	10		0			20	19	167	10		
v. Somerset	–	–	–	–	–	–	–	–	–	–	–	–		–	–	–	–	–	–	–	–	–	–	D	7
(Derby) 13–16 September	–	–	–	–	–	–	–	–	–	–	–	–		–	–	–	–	–	–	–	–	–	–		

	MP Dowman	SD Stubbings	MJ Di Venuto	SP Titchard	RJ Bailey	DG Cork	ME Cassar	KM Krikken	P Aldred	TA Munton	TM Smith	KJ Dean	BJ Spendlove	LD Sutton	SJ Lacey	KZ Shah	LJ Wharton	T Lungley	M Saxelby	JP Pyemont
Matches	17	18	16	11	13	10	14	10	11	16	10	12	1	10	11	5	7	1	1	4
Innings	29	32	25	19	19	11	20	13	14	22	13	15	1	16	17	6	9	–	2	5
Not Out	3	4	3	2	4	2	2	0	1	7	2	3	0	1	4	2	4	–	–	–
Runs	833	889	725	530	728	452	341	221	149	191	152	49	0	407	242	102	15	–	23	79
Highest score	140	135*	92*	141*	118	200*	77*	51	38	52	53*	22	0	79	55*	38*	7	–	17	40
Average	32.03	31.75	32.95	31.17	48.53	50.22	18.94	17.00	11.46	12.73	13.81	14.08	–	27.13	18.61	25.50	3.00	–	11.50	15.80
100s	2	1		1	2	1														
50s	4	4	6	3	5	2	1	1	–	1	1	–	–	2	1	–	–	–	–	–

DERBYSHIRE CCC

FIRST–CLASS MATCHES

BOWLING

	DG Cork	TA Munton	TM Smith	P Aldred	ME Cassar	KJ Dean	SJ Lacey	LJ Wharton	Overs	Totals	Byes/Leg-byes	Wickets	Run outs	
v. Leicestershire	26-8-60-3	18-2-83-0	15-2-54-2	17-2-60-1	9.5-5-16-2				94.5	309	18	10	1	A
(Derby) 26–29 April	–								–					
v. Yorkshire		43-6-117-0	26.3-4-102-1	33-7-97-4	24-8-72-0	19-2-74-0			152.3	508	24	5	–	ABC
(Headingley) 3–5 May		–							–					
v. Cambridge University					10-4-11-1	13-5-18-5			49.2	84	10	10	–	BDE
(Cambridge) 12–14 May					7-2-16-1	10-7-13-1	29-14-42-1	25-10-37-0	115	208	13	7	–	BCDE
v. Yorkshire	23-4-52-2		15-3-45-0		29.1-8-76-6	15-4-42-0	43-12-110-1		128.1	349	17	10	–	A
(Derby) 17–20 May	–				–				–					
v. Somerset	11-4-25-0	19-7-43-2	13-1-51-3	14-4-39-1	4.5-0-38-3	9-3-25-1			70.5	240	19	10	–	
(Taunton) 24–27 May														
v. Lancashire	17.5-6-52-2	16-4-41-1	11-3-43-0	9-2-20-1	11-6-25-2		6-2-18-2		70.5	213	14	9	–	
(Old Trafford) 31 May–3 June	–						–		–					
v. Surrey	22-4-62-2	19.5-7-34-7	2-0-11-0	4-2-13-1	4-0-11-0				51.5	138	7	10	–	
(Derby) 7–9 June	25-8-62-3	15-2-53-2	2-0-23-0	8.4-1-25-1	12-0-46-3				62.4	218	9	10	1	
v. Leicestershire	23-5-61-0		12.5-2-53-0		15-2-62-4	8.4-1-47-4			90.3	310	9	10	–	A
(Leicester) 14–17 June	3-0-13-0	5-3-13-0			3-0-19-0				11	47	2	–	–	
v. Durham		41-13-84-3	22-2-108-1			19-2-83-2	19-3-65-0	24-4-88-1	140	479	5	9	–	B
(Darlington) 28–30 June		–				–			–					
v. Lancashire	22-8-41-6	11-1-36-0	12-3-29-0				10-0-36-1		61	172	6	10	1	E
(Derby) 7–10 July	–								–					
v. Kent	32-11-77-1	35-14-54-6	23-5-63-2				16-4-40-1		116	280	14	10	–	E
(Derby) 12–15 July	11-2-33-0	17-5-44-1	2-0-14-0				18-3-34-1		60.3	171	21	2	–	EF
v. Kent		38.1-11-56-0			26-6-69-1		28-7-52-8	15-6-27-0	9-2-20-0	116.1	251	27	9	–	
(Canterbury) 28–31 July		–							–					
v. Hampshire		35-8-86-2			23-5-61-1		29-4-98-3	30.2-8-84-4	131.2	394	16	10	–	AE
(Derby) 2–5 August		–							–					
v. West Indians			5.3-1-28-0		15.3-5-39-1		22-12-47-0	31-7-96-5	106	390	7	9	1	ABEG
(Derby) 9–11 August			–		5-0-37-1		8-2-25-1	22-8-83-4	52	221	4	8	1	ABE
v. Surrey		20-3-69-2		21-8-68-1	11-2-44-1	19.3-5-51-6		8-1-13-0	79.3	260	15	10	–	
(Oval) 16–17 August		–		–					–					
v. Durham	11-2-28-0	13-4-27-2		–	9-2-35-2	14.5-4-52-6		–	47.5	144	2	10	–	
(Derby) 22–25 August	7-0-35-1	20-10-44-3		12-3-47-2	5-2-15-0	14-3-49-3		21-4-46-1	86	267	14	10	–	A
v. Hampshire		29-8-76-2			21-6-76-2	28-3-134-1	25.3-2-98-4	24-6-81-1	134.3	522	24	10	–	AG
(Southampton) 6–9 September		–							–					
v. Somerset	13-1-40-1	19.3-5-64-0		23-2-72-3	16-2-64-1	19-7-47-4			94.3	311	14	9	–	A
(Derby) 13–16 September	–								–					

	DG Cork	TA Munton	TM Smith	P Aldred	ME Cassar	KJ Dean	SJ Lacey	LJ Wharton
Overs	246.5	439.3	149	203.3	212.2	246	241.5	164
Maidens	63	122	24	44	54	57	68	42
Runs	641	1093	571	624	702	785	626	464
Wickets	22	35	9	17	30	44	16	12
Bowler's average	**29.13**	**31.22**	**63.44**	**36.70**	**23.40**	**17.84**	**39.12**	**38.66**

A   RJ Bailey 9-2-18-1; 3-0-11-0; 3-1-7-1; 6-2-9-0; 6-1-14-0; 1-1-0-0; 4-2-5-0; 7-1-17-0; 3-0-18-0; 4-0-10-0.
B   MP Dowman 2-1-7-0; 11-3-22-1; 13-6-23-0; 15-1-46-2; 10-0-41-0; 2-0-16-1.
C   SP Titchard 2-0-4-0; 3-2-1-0.
D   T Lungley 9.2-6-10-3; 14-5-31-3.
E   KZ Shah 6-1-13-0; 14-4-32-1; 6-0-24-2; 10-1-32-0; 4-2-6-0; 8-1-35-0; 17-1-112-2; 11-3-51-0.
F   MJ di Venuto 8.3-3-19-0.
G   JP Pyemont 4-0-20-0; 4-0-15-0.

FIELDING

21 – LD Sutton (20cfc/lsfc)	
20 – KM Krikken (18ct/2st)	
12 – MJ diVenuto	
11 – MP Dowman	
7 – DG Cork, TO Munton	
4 – P Aldred, RJ Bailey, TM Smith, SD Stubbings	
2 – BJ Spendlove, LJ Wharton	
1 – ME Cassar, SJ Lacey	

DURHAM CCC

FIRST–CLASS MATCHES

BATTING

	JJB Lewis	JA Daley	SM Katich	PD Collingwood	NJ Speak	N Peng	MP Speight	N Killeen	MM Betts	SJ Harmison	SJE Brown	ID Hunter	J Wood	NC Phillips	MJ Symington	SM Ali	MA Gough	A Pratt	GJ Pratt	Extras	Total	Wickets	Result	Points
v. Surrey	10	1	8	66	3	98	9	7	0	15	4*									13	234	10	W	16
(Chester-le-Street) 2–5 May	5	4	65	0	1	23	36	0	23	0	4*									25	186	10		
v. Lancashire	2	7	45	37	4	0	0	11	10	3	0*									45	164	10	L	3
(Chester-le-Street) 11–13 May	2	15	13	8	2	12	18	0	5	1	0*									16	92	10		
v. Leicestershire	25	16	137*	2	1	4	12		0*	–		63	26							16	302	8	D	10
(Chester-le-Street) 24–27 May																				–	–	–		
v. Kent	12	12	2	14	4	21	8		4*		0		1	0						3	81	10	L	3
(Tunbridge Wells) 31 May–3 June	3	14	41	12	4	0	22*		2		12		0	8						25	143	10		
v. Yorkshire	52	16	4	20	11	9	37		1	9		1			8*					21	189	10	L	3
(Chester-le-Street) 7–9 June	0	10	5	16	32	12	44		5	0*		3			36					38	201	10		
v. Hampshire	0		2	6	22	9	12		12	0*	1			11	1					7	83	10	L	3
(Basingstoke) 14–16 June	3	26	13	6	0	17			23	abs	2*			1	2					0	93	9		
v. Derbyshire	36		114	111	78	23	0	14	55	33*	10*					0				5	479	9	W	20
(Darlington) 28–30 June																				–	–	–		
v. Yorkshire	66		55	23	61*	6	2	5	10	19						0	24			43	314	10	D	10
(Headingley) 7–9 July																				–	–	–		
v. Leicestershire	33	4	43	22	18		18	0	0	0*				15		0				18	171	10	L	3
(Leicester) 12–14 July	5	7	18	8	9		0	0	9	0*				10		7				20	93	10		
v. Lancashire	25		129	60	10		38*			12				3	25		4	28	5	31	370	10	L	6
(Old Trafford) 19–22 July	47		23	3	38*		0			2				44	1		12	1	11	24	206	10		
v. Somerset	115		0				15		33*		10			4		18	9	3		44	292	10	D	9
(Chester-le-Street)	12	36*	17	1*														5		2	73	3		
v. Kent	0		6	28	89*	2	34				0	16	0					6	23	19	223	10	D	8
(Chester-le-Street) 9–12 August	59*	36	21	11*	18															12	157	3		
v. Somerset	31	34	20	74	78					15	2*	26		9			33	38		18	378	10	D	10
(Taunton) 16–19 August																				–	–	–		
v. Derbyshire	11	27	38	0	23					3*	0	1			30		9	0		2	144	10	L	3
(Derby) 22–25 August	0	14	70	66	39				2	1	3*	10					25	21		16	267	10		
v. Hampshire (Chester-le-Street)	70	50	60	12		55	1		8		0						0	27*		37	320	9	L	3
31 August–3 September	12*		16*															7		4	39	1		
v. Surrey	1	14	77	4			12	8	9	0*					29		28	36		23	241	10	L	2
(Oval) 6–9 September	8	2	0	4		48	14		0	0*							20	31		16	144	10		

	JJB Lewis	JA Daley	SM Katich	PD Collingwood	NJ Speak	N Peng	MP Speight	N Killeen	MM Betts	SJ Harmison	SJE Brown	ID Hunter	J Wood	NC Phillips	MJ Symington	SM Ali	MA Gough	A Pratt	GJ Pratt
Matches	16	10	16	16	14	8	11	10	11	11	14	3	10	5	2	3	7	7	2
Innings	28	17	28	27	24	14	18	15	18	15	21	4	15	9	3	4	12	10	3
Not Out	2	0	3	0	5	0	1	1	4	3	12	0	0	0	1	0	0	1	0
Runs	645	247	1089	681	552	231	354	144	192	104	82	83	181	76	44	25	176	191	39
Highest score	115	50	137*	111	89*	98	55	38*	55	33*	19	63	44	29	36	18	33	38	23
Average	24.80	14.52	43.56	25.22	29.05	16.50	20.82	10.28	13.71	8.66	9.11	20.75	12.06	8.44	22.00	6.25	14.66	21.22	13.00
100s	1	–	3	1	–	–	–	–	–	–	–	–	–	–	–	–	–	–	–
50s	4	1	5	4	4	1	1	–	1	–	–	1	–	–	–	–	–	–	–

DURHAM CCC

FIRST–CLASS MATCHES

BOWLING

	SJE Brown	MM Betts	N Killeen	PD Collingwood	SJ Harmison	ID Hunter	J Wood	NC Phillips	Overs	Totals	Byes/Leg-byes	Wickets	Run outs	
v. Surrey	18-7-29-3	15-7-19-1	13-4-19-3	2.5-1-3-1	7-0-24-1				55.5	104	10	10	1	
(Chester-le-Street) 2–4 May	8.4-6-8-3	10-1-36-2	10-5-14-3	1-0-6-0	12-4-19-2				41.4	85	2	10	–	
v. Lancashire	18-3-43-0	16-4-52-3	20-4-54-2	8-1-32-0	18-3-74-4				80	263	8	10	1	
(Chester-le-Street) 11–13 May	17.3-6-51-7	21-6-47-2	1.5-0-6-0	4-2-5-1	14-3-23-0				58.2	134	2	10	–	
v. Leicestershire		33-4-73-3		4-0-7-0	30.9-9-61-3	22-4-66-0	30-2-89-3		129.3	336	15	10	–	A
(Chester-le-Street) 24–27 May	–				–	–			–	–	–	–	–	
v. Kent	15-4-36-1	25-10-28-2		15-7-15-0			30.2-13-36-5	17-5-25-0	110.2	177	25	10	1	A
(Tunbridge Wells) 31 May–3 June	23-10-37-2	16-7-33-2		15-3-21-2			19.3-6-46-2	17-4-47-1	106.3	237	15	9	–	AB
v. Yorkshire		23-4-42-2		14-3-43-1	26-7-58-2	22.3-4-73-4			98.3	294	17	10	–	C
(Chester-le-Street) 7–9 June		13-3-30-2		7.3-1-12-1	14-4-27-0	7-2-11-1			45.3	97	11	4	–	C
v. Hampshire	22.1-3-62-4	32-9-76-2		15-5-34-2	19-6-33-1		24-4-94-1	13-4-23-0	128.1	340	16	10	–	A
(Basingstoke) 14–15 June	–	–		–	–		–	–	–	–	–	–	–	
v. Derbyshire	11-0-37-1	12-4-30-7	14-3-34-1	–	12-2-40-1				49	151	10	10	–	
(Darlington) 28–30 June	16.4-5-40-6	19-3-58-3	15-4-38-0	13-6-22-0	17-6-43-1				89.4	249	9	10	–	A
v. Yorkshire	15.4-5-33-4	12-2-32-2	14-5-36-1	5-3-5-1	14-4-21-2				60.4	129	2	10	–	
(Headingley) 7–9 July	27-6-80-0	25-3-71-2	37-14-70-2	25-11-58-0	23-5-50-0				148	386	26	4	–	AD
v. Leicestershire	21-7-41-1	23-7-40-2	15-7-34-1	10-2-24-1			21.4-4-60-5		94.4	222	9	10	–	A
(Leicester) 12–14 July	21-2-70-5	11-4-20-1	12.4-3-51-2	6-2-15-0			21-4-59-1		85.4	259	8	10	–	A
v. Lancashire	17-7-31-0		14-4-46-1	2-0-5-0			28.1-4-81-4	36-10-95-1	140.1	445	23	10	–	AE
(Old Trafford) 19–22 July	3-1-9-0		3-0-10-0	–			4-1-9-0	11-1-53-3	32.4	132	2	4	–	A
v. Somerset	35-8-69-3	12-5-22-1	32-9-52-1	9-0-17-0			28-4-88-5		126	280	15	10	–	E
(Chester-le-Street) 28–31 July	–		–	–			–		–	–	–	–	–	
v. Kent	16.4-3-59-5		19-4-53-3	–		5-1-15-1	16-4-32-0		56.4	170	11	10	1	
(Chester-le-Street) 9–12 August	29-3-96-2		20-7-46-1	12-6-29-0		13-1-63-0	28.2-8-81-3		118.2	354	9	7	–	A
v. Somerset	25-6-85-1			11-2-26-1	20-4-69-1		20.4-4-50-4	23-5-62-1	111.4	362	17	8	–	AE
(Taunton) 16–19 August	–			–	–		–	–	–	–	–	–	–	
v. Derbyshire	10-3-31-3	14-3-41-3		5-0-8-1	10.3-1-42-3		10-1-33-0		50.3	167	8	10	–	A
(Derby) 22–25 August	24-6-88-2	22-5-82-2		14-4-30-0	23.1-5-81-3		20-4-94-0		126.1	476	22	7	–	ABE
v. Hampshire (Chester-le-Street)	4-0-16-0		8-1-27-0	4-0-10-0			4-2-5-0		20	69	11	0	–	
31 August–3 September	18-2-80-2		21-6-47-1	2-0-4-0	14-0-42-0		14-2-61-0		77.1	292	18	4	–	AE
v. Surrey	26-7-77-1		19-4-60-0	14-2-53-0	26-6-105-2			39.5-7-110-1	128.5	453	30	4	–	AE
(Oval) 6–9 September	–		–	–	–				–	–	–	–	–	

	SJE Brown	MM Betts	N Killeen	PD Collingwood	SJ Harmison	ID Hunter	J Wood	NC Phillips
Overs	442.2	354	288.3	214.2	304.1	69.3	319.4	156.5
Maidens	110	91	84	61	69	12	66	36
Runs	1208	832	697	474	822	228	918	415
Wickets	56	44	22	12	26	6	33	7
Bowler's average	**21.57**	**18.90**	**31.68**	**39.50**	**31.61**	**38.00**	**27.81**	**59.28**

A   SM Katich 10-1-25-1; 8-2-12-1; 12-2-27-0; 3-1-2-0; 9-1-39-0; 8-0-22-0; 4-0-14-0; 14-1-36-1; 15-0-58-0; 4.4-0-10-0;
16-5-30-1; 6-0-29-0; 1-0-4-0; 2-0-15-0; 3-1-10-1; 2-0-9-0.
B   JA Daley 4-0-11-0; 3-0-9-0.
C   MJ Symington 13-1-61-1; 4-1-6-0.
D   SM Ali 3-0-9-0.
E   MA Gough 28-4-106-4; 7-1-39-1; 10-3-17-0; 6-0-24-0; 18-6-55-0; 5.1-0-30-0; 2-0-9-0.

FIELDING

29 – MP Speight
21 – SM Katich
19 – PD Collingwood
8 – JJB Lewis
7 – MM Betts, A Pratt
4 – JA Daley
3 – MA Gough, NC Phillips, NJ Speak
2 – SJE Brown, SJ Harmison, J Wood
1 – SM Ali, N Killeen, N Peng, GJ Pratt

ESSEX CCC

FIRST–CLASS MATCHES

BATTING

	AP Grayson	IN Flanagan	DDJ Robinson	SD Peters	TJ Mason	DR Law	BJ Hyam	AP Cowan	RSG Anderson	DDJ Thompson	PM Such	PJ Prichard	N Hussain	SG Law	RC Irani	MC Ilott	AC McGarry	GR Napier	WI Jefferson	JS Foster	Extras	Total	Wickets	Result	Points
v. Cambridge University (Cambridge) 26–28 April	11	23	37	1	10	55*	9	5*													22	173	6	D	–
	9	5	5*	25	0	8	21	4			3*										19	99	7		
v. Nottinghamshire (Chelmsford) 3–6 May	58			0	1							7*	4	120	16	11*					11	274	9	D	9
	28			0	5		8	39*	30			29	24	55	20	4					21	263	10		
v. Zimbabweans (Chelmsford) 11–14 May	15			22	22	7			19	15	6*	28	33	33	21						28	249	10	D	–
v. Warwickshire (Edgbaston) 17–20 May	15		32	34*			–					36		83	91*						7	298	4	D	8
	–		–	–								–		–	–						–	–			
v. Sussex (Chelmsford) 23–26 May	31	9	22	0	1	34			67*			7		6	46	10					22	255	10	D	8
	4*		–									13*		–							5	22	–		
v. Northamptonshire (Ilford) 31 May–3 June	47		31	22	0	0	1	2*				9		37	53	0					14	216	10	W	16
	4	93*	17*				18					20		9	55						12	228	5		
v. Gloucestershire (Bristol) 6–8 June	19		0	12	6	53	0					96	3	4	52	4*					14	263	10	W	17
	52		32*	9	0	0	21					1	0	28	42	3					11	199	10		
v. Glamorgan (Cardiff) 15–18 June	5	6	0	39	52*	36	6					59			168*	–					39	410	7	D	8
	13	0	28	0	2	2	10	3*				6			19	5					14	102	10		
v. Middlesex (Chelmsford) 28–30 June		18	9	54*			1	7	1		0	7		5	3	24					7	136	10	L	3
		3	5	9		12	25	8			14	25		6	12	14*					9	142	10		
v. Nottinghamshire (Trent Bridge) 7–10 July	144		9			68*	4	30			3*	19		165	26	4					33	505	9	D	10
	–		–									–		–	–						–	–			
v. Sussex (Arundel) 12–15 July	5	61	46	32*	9	4					2	4		40	21	1					52	277	10	D	9
	1	65	22*	49	10	5*						66		12	4						20	254	7		
v. Worcestershire (Chelmsford) 19–21 July	0	abs	23	2	0						6*	45		19	0	25	1				10	131	9	W	15
	69	–		0	4	0						20		133*	14*	–					12	287	6		
v. Middlesex (Lord's) 2–5 August	36	21	9			13	0	1			1	14		2	76			0*			27	200	10	D	8
	23	13	4			0	0	5*				26		26	25*			–			8	130	7		
v. Worcestershire (Kidderminster) 9–12 August	4		67		1	25	0				2	74	10	189	14			0*			76	462	10	W	20
	50*											62*									13	125			
v. Gloucestershire (Colchester) 16–19 August	56		18	24*	15	7	1				0	0		7	21			21			4	174	10	L	3
	47		16	3	29	2	6				2	12		58	33*			5			30	243	10		
v. Glamorgan (Southend) 30 August–2 September	0		27	3				30*	0		0	8		70	95				1	52	6	292	10	D	8
	9		8	1				67	17*			32		82	83*				4	34	13	350	8		
v. Northamptonshire (Northampton) 6–9 September	20	6	11	0				0	4		14	31		59	27					16*	45	233	10	D	8
	8	42	50*	–								0		119*	2						4	225	4		
v. Warwickshire (Chelmsford) 13–16 September	17	92	1									0		10	72*					7*	9	208	9	W	15
	7	5	77*									19		8	64*					–	22	202	4		

	AP Grayson	IN Flanagan	DDJ Robinson	SD Peters	TJ Mason	DR Law	BJ Hyam	AP Cowan	RSG Anderson	DDJ Thompson	PM Such	PJ Prichard	N Hussain	SG Law	RC Irani	MC Ilott	AC McGarry	GR Napier	WI Jefferson	JS Foster
Matches	17	4	12	16	10	15	15	14	9	2	12	17	4	16	17	10	3	1	1	3
Innings	31	8	19	28	14	23	24	20	8	1	13	31	6	27	29	13	3	2	2	4
Not Out	2	0	3	6	2	3	0	6	3	0	4	3	0	2	7	4	2	0	0	2
Runs	807	89	561	602	140	360	256	245	170	15	53	775	74	1385	1196	119	1	26	5	109
Highest score	144	23	93*	77*	52*	68*	53	67	67*	15	14	96	33	189	168*	25	1	21	4	52
Average	27.82	11.12	35.06	27.36	11.66	18.00	10.66	17.50	34.00	15.00	5.88	27.67	12.33	55.40	54.36	13.22	1.00	13.00	2.50	54.50
100s	1	–	–	–	–	–	–	–	–	–	–	–	–	5	1	–	–	–	–	–
50s	5	–	4	4	1	2	1	1	1	–	–	5	–	6	9	–	–	–	–	1

ESSEX CCC

FIRST-CLASS MATCHES

BOWLING

	AP Cowan	DR Law	RSG Anderson	TJ Mason	PM Such	AP Grayson	MC Ilott	RC Irani	Overs	Totals	Byes/Leg-byes	Wickets	Run outs	
v. Cambridge University	6-2-11-0	5-2-8-1	5-2-6-0	4-2-4-0	6-3-5-0	2-1-2-0			34	50	4	1	–	A
(Cambridge) 26-28 April	–	–							–	–	–	–	–	
v. Nottinghamshire	17.1-3-56-1		25-10-68-0	24-6-60-3		3-0-9-0	28-8-82-1	22-5-57-4	119.1	340	8	10	1	
(Chelmsford) 3-6 May	6-0-17-1		9-2-41-1	16-3-54-1		2-0-6-0	12-3-24-2	6-2-5-1	51	150	3	6	–	
v. Zimbabweans		25-8-66-1	26-5-69-5	14-2-54-0	14-5-37-2				105.3	315	13	10	–	A
(Chelmsford) 11-14 May				4-0-26-0	4-1-14-0				17	75	8	–	–	A
v. Warwickshire	25-7-60-1	21-5-78-5	25-3-105-1	31-7-82-0		2-0-5-0		24.3-7-63-1	128.3	400	7	8	–	
(Edgbaston) 17-20 May	–								–	–	–	–	–	
v. Sussex		13-2-38-0	18-3-59-1	25-5-93-1		21-6-48-2	24.2-6-64-2	16-2-62-1	117.2	374	10	7	–	
(Chelmsford) 23-26 May		–							–	–	–	–	–	
v. Northamptonshire		8-2-18-1	15-3-34-6	–		–	9-4-16-1	15-5-36-2	47	114	10	10	–	
(Ilford) 31 May-3 June		20-8-59-1	33.2-12-77-5	15-3-49-0		2-0-10-0	23-4-82-1	27-13-40-3	120	327	10	10	–	
v. Gloucestershire	18-3-36-2	20.3-1-70-3		21-7-42-1			19-6-67-3	16-5-47-1	94.3	268	6	10	–	
(Bristol) 6-8 June	7-3-15-2	4.4-0-15-4		2-0-6-0			7-2-17-1	11-5-30-3	31.4	85	2	10	–	
v. Glamorgan	21-6-56-3			25.2-9-65-1		6-0-21-0	20-7-37-3	15-5-34-0	94.2	263	15	8	–	
(Cardiff) 15-18 June	16-3-57-1	12-0-44-2		4-2-4-0		3-2-2-0	14-5-34-1	17-4-33-1	66	177	3	5	–	
v. Middlesex	15-3-40-3	12-0-41-0			24-4-51-5		12-4-26-0	15-3-50-2	78	222	14	10	–	
(Chelmsford) 28-30 June	20-2-39-1	4-0-8-0			41.2-7-167-7		17-7-38-2	10-6-11-0	93.2	293	19	10	–	B
v. Nottinghamshire	15.3-5-44-2	6-0-34-0			4-2-15-0		17-6-34-1	17-5-52-2	59.3	180	1	5	–	
(Trent Bridge) 7-10 July	–						–		–	–	–	–	–	
v. Sussex	14.4-2-61-4	15-2-74-3			23-4-41-0	–	20-5-50-2	14-4-29-1	86.4	265	10	10	–	
(Arundel) 12-15 July	14-4-37-0	7-1-38-0			41-7-113-2	15-5-55-3	13-3-30-1	16-6-35-2	106	321	13	8	–	
v. Worcestershire		15-5-37-1			36-11-61-1	5-2-10-0	19-4-47-2	18.4-4-47-3	109.4	240	9	10	–	C
(Chelmsford) 19-21 July		9-3-42-2			22.3-8-39-5	7-4-4-0	4-1-12-1	2-0-5-0	57.3	176	12	10	–	C
v. Middlesex	28-7-70-4	16-5-50-1			22-10-24-0	13-3-28-1		17-1-59-1	108	287	8	10	2	C
(Lord's) 2-5 August	18-5-55-2	10.3-1-39-1			9-1-29-1	14-1-38-2		5-3-5-1	56.3	174	8	9	2	
v. Worcestershire	20-8-69-4	22-1-85-2			6-0-36-0	17-6-34-1		19-11-24-2	92	302	10	10	1	C
(Kidderminster) 9-12 August	24-8-54-5	7-3-23-0			12-3-36-0	16-2-43-0		25-5-79-5	92	282	3	10	1	C
v. Gloucestershire	25-5-83-2	9-1-41-0		11-3-27-1	32-10-60-4	12-3-17-0		24.2-7-56-3	121.2	324	12	10	–	D
(Colchester) 16-19 August	15-0-66-5	4-0-17-0		15.1-3-38-3	11-5-22-0			18-2-53-2	63.1	197	10	10	–	
v. Glamorgan	31-9-83-2	19-0-82-1	29-8-109-2		41.5-8-95-3	25-3-72-0		17-3-60-1	162.5	507	6	9	–	
(Southend) 30 August-2 September	–	–	–			–			–	–	–	–	–	
v. Northamptonshire	13.3-2-51-1			14-0-47-2	28-3-106-3	45-5-127-3	13-1-39-1	7-2-18-0	120.3	410	22	10	–	
(Northampton) 6-9 September	–			–	–	–			–	–	–	–	–	
v. Warwickshire	29-6-115-1		30.2-6-107-1		28-7-83-3		25-10-64-2	13-5-18-0	125.2	400	13	8	1	E
(Chelmsford) 13-16 September	–				–		–		0.3	8	0	–	–	

	AP Cowan	DR Law	RSG Anderson	TJ Mason	PM Such	AP Grayson	MC Ilott	RC Irani
Overs	398.5	291.4	234.4	239.3	422.4	178	283.2	407.3
Maidens	98	50	56	55	101	39	85	120
Runs	1175	1042	729	710	1055	443	724	1008
Wickets	47	30	24	14	36	10	26	42
Bowler's average	**25.00**	**34.73**	**30.37**	**50.71**	**29.30**	**44.30**	**27.84**	**24.00**

A DJ Thompson 6-3-10-0; 26.3-8-76-2; 4-1-20-0.
B SG Law 1-0-11-0.
C AC McGarry 16-6-29-3; 13-1-62-2; 12-2-48-1; 8-1-44-0; 8-0-44-0.
D GR Napier 8-2-28-0.
E DDJ Robinson 0.3-0-8-0.

FIELDING

55 – BJ Hyam (49ct/6st)
19 – SG Law
12 – SD Peters
10 – AP Grayson, PJ Prichard
7 – IN Flanagan
6 – DR Law
5 – N Hussain, DDJ Robinson
4 – AP Cowan, JS Foster, MC Ilott, TJ Mason, GR Napier
3 – PM Such
2 – RC Irani
1 – WI Jefferson

GLAMORGAN CCC

FIRST–CLASS MATCHES
BATTING

	MTG Elliott	SP James	A Dale	MP Maynard	MJ Powell	WL Law	AD Shaw	RDB Croft	SD Thomas	SL Watkin	SP Jones	DA Cosker	AW Evans	K Newell	AG Wharf	OT Parkin	DS Harrison	MA Wallace	IJ Thomas	Extras	Total	Wickets	Result	Points
v. Worcestershire (Worcester) 26–29 April	–	–	–	–	–	–	–	–	–	–	–									–	–	–	D	6
	–	–	–	–	–	–	–	–	–	–	–									–	–	–		
v. Warwickshire (Edgbaston) 3–6 May	117	166	24	1	10	4	10	16	15	4*	0									33	400	10	D	10
	37	0	13	52	18	1	56*	2*												15	194	6		
v. Gloucestershire (Cardiff) 11–14 May	49	0	6	1	1	1	88*	0	26	51		7								20	250	10	D	9
	17	109	1	119*	19	17*	–*	–	–	–										18	300	4		
v. Oxford Universities (Oxford) 16–18 May				71	46	85	14		18*				58	64	100*					19	475	6	W	–
v. Warwickshire (Cardiff) 23–26 May	–	–	–	–	–	–	–	–	–	–	–									–	–	–	D	5
	–	–	–	–	–	–	–	–	–	–	–									–	–	–		
v. Sussex (Hove) 31 May–3 June	14	8	75	5	46	1	6	10	0	0*	0									20	185	10	L	2
	42	32	41	3	26	23	45	31	0	7*	13									21	284	10		
v. West Indians (Cardiff) 6–8 June	9	39	15		2	0	23	1*				1		27	1	0				22	140	10	L	–
	25	27	17		11	2	2	8				0*		12	0	0				9	113	10		
v. Essex (Cardiff) 15–18 June	32	6	10	98	2		80*		15*			0		0	1					19	263	8	D	8
	52	5	24*	44	34		3*		–	–				6	–					9	177	5		
v. Worcestershire (Swansea) 28 June–1 July	62	28	34	6	20		1		6	0		12*		5	20					24	218	10	W	16
	57	0	66	14	70		21		17	2*		8		38	3					15	311	10		
v. Northamptonshire (Northampton) 7–9 July	1	14	47		23		3		8	6		7	2	4	101*					18	234	10	W	16
	26	62	53		6		0		34*	11		14	19	17	5					8	255	10		
v. Middlesex (Southgate) 12–15 July	17	3	81		0		23		30			13	10	28	1	5*				21	232	10	W	16
	127	31	23		26		14		11			1*	17	26	5					26	307	8		
v. Northamptonshire (Cardiff) 19–22 July	76	8	6	6	2		36	19	6	2*		2		27						8	198	10	W	15
	117	15	35	1	53		37*	–	–	–					38*					14	310	5		
v. Gloucestershire (Bristol) 3–5 August	6	8	2	0	9				52			4		4	16	10*	0			11	122	10	L	3
	16	1	0	1	61				48*			0		3	31	2	27			20	210	10		
v. Nottinghamshire (Cardiff) 16–19 August		77	36	77	2	27	13	5				14*		3	1			11		22	288	10	D	9
		30	20*	0	33	0	1*	–	–	–		–		2	–			2		11	99	6		
v. Sussex (Colwyn Bay) 23–25 August	177	309*	48*	67	64		–	–	–	–		–		–	–					53	718	3	W	20
	–	–	–	–	–		–	–	–	–		–		–	–					–	–	–		
v. Essex (Southend) 30 August–1 September		30	48	102	128		22	12*	1*			5	8	13					82	56	507	9	D	12
		–	–	–	–		–	–	–			–	–	–					–	–	–	–		
v. Nottinghamshire (Trent Bridge) 6–8 September		3	14	37	13		56	26*						3	0			10	10	9	187	10	L	3
		24	41	0	4		7	4	28					35	0			59*	35	9	246	10		
v. Middlesex (Cardiff) 13–16 September		0	57	11	114		50	3	7					1			13*	34	5	30	325	10	D	10
		35*	–											–			–	–	45*	13	93	0		

	MTG Elliott	SP James	A Dale	MP Maynard	MJ Powell	WL Law	AD Shaw	RDB Croft	SD Thomas	SL Watkin	SP Jones	DA Cosker	AW Evans	K Newell	AG Wharf	OT Parkin	DS Harrison	MA Wallace	IJ Thomas
Matches	13	17	17	15	18	8	12	12	17	13	5	12	4	13	10	5	1	3	3
Innings	21	28	27	22	28	11	18	14	20	13	3	15	6	21	15	6	2	5	5
Not Out	0	2	3	1	0	1	5	3	7	6	0	4	0	1	2	3	0	1	1
Runs	1076	1070	837	716	843	161	462	236	336	125	13	88	114	356	285	30	27	116	177
Highest score	177	309*	87	119*	128	85	88*	56	52	51	13	14*	58	64	101*	13*	27	59*	82
Average	51.23	41.15	34.87	34.09	30.10	16.10	35.53	21.45	25.84	17.85	4.33	8.00	19.00	17.80	21.92	10.00	13.50	29.00	44.25
100s	4	3	0	2	2	–	–	–	–	–	–	–	–	–	–	2	–	–	–
50s	4	2	5	5	4	1	3	2	1	1	–	1	1	–	–	–	–	1	1

GLAMORGAN CCC

FIRST–CLASS MATCHES
BOWLING

	SL Watkin	SD Thomas	SP Jones	A Dale	RDB Croft	DA Cosker	OT Parkin	AG Wharf	Overs	Totals	Byes/Leg-byes	Wickets	Run outs	
v. Worcestershire	19–10–33–2	13–2–55–2	9.1–0–66–2	12–1–47–1					53.1	206	5	7	–	
(Worcester) 26–29 April	–	–	–	–			–	–	–	–				
v. Warwickshire	35–7–97–3	30–4–119–1	28–1–106–1	13–1–56–0	41–11–136–1				150	551	24	6	–	A
(Edgbaston) 3–6 May	–	–					–	–	–	–				
v. Gloucestershire	16–4–48–3	15.5–59–2		4–0–9–0	35–10–61–3	30–12–58–2			101.5	242	6	10	–	A
(Cardiff) 11–14 May	13–5–34–1	14–3–28–1			41–16–65–4	38–23–40–2			107	174	3	9	1	B
v. Oxford Universities		11–3–19–1	11–1–32–2			6.5–2–12–2	10–2–34–3	12–1–34–0	61.5	160	11	10	–	C
(Oxford) 16–18 May		8.2–2–14–4	12–5–23–1			15–6–35–1	10–4–14–4	7–1–25–0	52.2	112	1	10	–	
v. Warwickshire	16–6–32–0	20–3–76–1	14–1–47–4	7–0–27–0	34–6–85–0				92	280	6	5	–	A
(Cardiff) 23–26 May	–	–	–	–	–				–	–				
v. Sussex	36–8–102–4	27–5–103–2	29.3–4–97–0	21–4–63–2	27–6–85–0				140.3	463	13	9	–	
(Hove) 31 May–3 June	–	1–0–4–0	0.2–0–3–0						1.2	7	0	–	–	
v. West Indians				4–0–16–0	34–19–26–5	16.1–3–51–2	8–2–23–0	13–4–57–3	75.1	176	3	10	–	
(Cardiff) 6–8 June				–	22.1–8–44–3	7–1–15–0	11–5–23–3	10–4–9–4	50.1	97	6	10	–	
v. Essex	31–12–65–2	36–8–94–2		13–5–23–0		49–20–67–1		28–7–79–1	203	410	7	7	–	ABC
(Cardiff) 15–18 June	14.2–6–26–6	16–9–14–3		–		3–1–4–0		14–4–44–1	47.2	102	14	10	–	
v. Worcestershire	18–4–48–1	19.5–4–72–5		7–1–14–0		12–5–15–1		14–3–41–3	70.5	196	6	10	–	
(Swansea) 28 June–1 July	19–5–49–2	14.2–1–50–3		–		37–10–82–4		17–3–63–1	90.2	252	5	10	–	AC
v. Northamptonshire	17–5–45–2	18–7–35–1		11–3–29–3		5.4–2–13–1		11–3–37–3	62.4	167	8	10	–	
(Northampton) 7–9 July	11.4–2–31–3	9.5–0–48–3		7–3–9–1		12–5–24–1		11–0–64–2	51.3	178	2	10	–	
v. Middlesex		19–3–55–4		14–2–37–2		2–1–10–0		17.1–7–36–3	57.1	164	4	10	1	
(Southgate) 12–15 July		23–3–99–2		22.4–12–25–5		27–8–83–2	18–3–68–0	21–3–80–1	112.4	374	14	10	–	C
v. Northamptonshire	7.3–4–15–1	21–6–43–5		16–4–50–1	28.2–8–77–3	14–3–40–0			87.2	229	2	10	–	B
(Cardiff) 19–22 July		20.3–9–47–3		14–4–27–1	46–10–108–5	22–2–82–1			102.3	227	13	10	–	
v. Gloucestershire		14–2–52–1		9–3–21–1		19.1–8–34–2	20–7–29–3	23–5–102–3	95.1	308	25	10	–	D
(Bristol) 3–5 August		–		–		–	2–1–4–0	2.3–0–23–0	4.3	27	0	–	–	
v. Nottinghamshire		22–3–69–2		5–1–15–0	45–14–108–3	36–8–96–2		16–3–47–3	124	343	8	10	–	
(Cardiff) 16–19 August		–		–					–	–				
v. Sussex	26–7–76–4	21–25–69–0		2–1–4–0	25–5–77–0	18–9–43–1		16.5–3–68–5	108.5	342	5	10	–	
(Colwyn Bay) 23–25 August	15–4–45–2	15–2–72–0		16–4–46–5	14.5–2–42–1	7–0–27–0	–	9–0–65–2	76.5	316	19	10	–	
v. Essex	18–5–46–3	14.2–1–70–3		4–0–19–0	33–5–83–3	27–6–45–1			103.2	292	6	10	–	C
(Southend) 30 August–2 September	22–7–67–1	23–4–71–1		9–1–19–0	48–13–114–3	26–6–68–3	–		128	350	11	8	–	
v. Nottinghamshire	25–2–99–5	22–1–87–1		16–3–47–1	10–1–35–0			14–0–66–2	93	371	17	10	–	C
(Trent Bridge) 6–8 September	10.1–2–31–3			9–0–26–0			–		20.1	66	0	3	–	B
v. Middlesex	20–3–78–0	19–1–88–3		5–1–16–0	25.5–2–109–2		24–5–74–4		98.5	387	7	10	–	BC
(Cardiff) 13–16 September	–	–		–	–				–	–				

	SL Watkin	SD Thomas	SP Jones	A Dale	RDB Croft	DA Cosker	OT Parkin	AG Wharf
Overs	389.4	488	104	240.4	510.1	429.5	108	256.3
Maidens	108	93	12	54	136	141	30	51
Runs	1067	1612	374	645	1255	944	291	940
Wickets	47	56	10	23	37	29	17	37
Bowler's average	**22.22**	**28.78**	**37.40**	**28.04**	**33.91**	**32.55**	**17.11**	**25.40**

A   MTG Elliott 3-0-13-0; 1-0-1-0; 1-0-7-0; 13-4-20-0; 2-1-2-0.
B   MP Maynard 1-0-4-0; 12-5-14-0; 0.3-0-2-0; 1-0-9-0; 1-0-3-0.
C   K Newell 11-6-18-2; 21-14-21-1; 1-0-1-0; 1-0-5-0; 7-1-23-0; 6-1-20-1; 4-1-12-1.
D   DS Harrison 10-2-45-0

FIELDING

33 – A D Shaw (29cfc/4st)	
19 – MTG Elliott, MP Maynard (17ct/2st)	
11 – MJ Powell	
10 – MA Wallace	
9 – DA Cosker	
8 – A Dale	
5 – SP James, K Newell, AG Wharf	
4 – RDB Croft, WL Law	
3 – IJ Thomas	
2 – SD Thomas	
1 – SL Watkin	

GLOUCESTERSHIRE CCC

FIRST-CLASS MATCHES
BATTING

Match	THC Hancock	I Mohammed	MGN Windows	KJ Barnett	MW Alleyne	IJ Harvey	RC Russell	JN Snape	J Lewis	AM Smith	TP Cotterell	RJ Cunliffe	MJ Cawdron	JMM Averis	MCJ Ball	CG Taylor	MA Hardinges	RCJ Williams	DR Hewson	BW Gannon	AN Brassington	Extras	Total	Wickets	Result	Points
v. Sussex (Bristol) 26–29 April	–	–	–	–	–	–	–	–	–	–	–	–	–	–	–	–	–	–	–	–	–	–	–	–	D	5
v. Oxford Universities (Bristol) 3–5 May	85	–	166	118*	1	–	16	69	–	–	–	74	–	–								12	541	6	D	–
v. Glamorgan (Cardiff) 11–14 May	29	4	76	7	79	14*			0		0	19		4								10	242	10	D	8
	30	0	5	7	11	46		20		0*		22		25*	0							3	174	9		
v. Nottinghamshire (Trent Bridge) 17–20 May	4	9	3	126	0				38	11	5*	4		5								34	290	10	D	9
							38	18																		
v. Worcestershire (Bristol) 23–26 May	0	0	16	0	70	16	43	12	12*	1	7											22	199	10	D	6
v. Middlesex (Lord's) 31 May–3 June	0	3	18	33		15	52	5	0*		5		4			104						20	259	10	W	17
	23		54	82		1	12	16	1*		7		10			25						7	242	10		
v. Essex (Bristol) 6–8 June	4		107		8		54	1				2	27	7		18	0	28*				12	268	10	L	5
	26		0		4		16	0*				3	15	3		0	0	5				13	85	10		
v. Zimbabweans (Bristol) 16–19 June	abs	0	47				27		4		0*	0			25	14		27	9			14	167	9	L	–
	inj	4	25				28		0		1	19			7	3		11	1*			36	135	9		
v. Warwickshire (Edgbaston) 28 June–1 July			36	106		31	70	21	7	2*		36				0		0	6			35	350	10	D	11
			56	37			16*	20*	8			7				25		58	–			5	232	7		
v. Northamptonshire (Cheltenham) 12–15 July			15		6	0	15		0	0*	0	13	18			42		3				4	116	10	L	2
			24		8	52	110*		4	14	0	2	2			41		57				14	328	10		
v. Warwickshire (Cheltenham) 19–22 July	46	24	79	16	25	2			1						21	22		1	1*			16	254	10	D	9
	25	14	62*	37	5*			–							–	9			67			18	237	5		
v. Worcestershire (Worcester) 28–30 July	10	14	10	4	27	0	4		0		0				0			4	0*			14	87	10	L	3
	6	15	0	10	25	18	43	12							30*			4	8			13	184	10		
v. Glamorgan (Bristol) 2–5 August	1		82	11	38		10	40				12	7	53				1			2*	51	308	10	W	18
	4*		–	–	–		–	–				–	–	13*							–	10	27	0		
v. Essex (Colchester) 16–19 August	43		25	24	43	16	54*					6		35				12		28		38	324	10	W	18
	2		1	57	2	1	39	2				33	37					10	4*			9	197	10		
v. Middlesex (Bristol) 21–24 August	0		10	22			27	0	2*			16	2			43		43	13			10	188	10	W	15
	35		70*	0								–	32*			0		–				10	147	3		
v. Northamptonshire (Northampton) 30 August–1 September	22	2	5	4			40	15	22		0*	15	8					45				8	186	10	L	1
	9	36	13	18			41	23*	0		0	12	6					39				12	209	10		
v. Sussex (Hove) 7–8 September	3		49		4	60	0	0	4			21*	15					35	4			32	227	10	W	16
	–		–		–	–	–	–				–	–					–				–	–	–		
v. Nottinghamshire (Bristol) 13–16 September			18*	41*								–						3	–			11	73	1	W	15
			38	28	8	10	53	10	16*			–				38*		15				32	248	7		

	THC Hancock	I Mohammed	MGN Windows	KJ Barnett	MW Alleyne	IJ Harvey	RC Russell	JN Snape	J Lewis	AM Smith	TP Cotterell	RJ Cunliffe	MJ Cawdron	JMM Averis	MCJ Ball	CG Taylor	MA Hardinges	RCJ Williams	DR Hewson	BW Gannon	AN Brassington
Matches	15	4	18	11	16	10	16	14	16	9	8	8	5	5	9	11	1	2	11	8	1
Innings	22	6	29	16	24	14	23	19	22	10	10	13	7	7	14	20	2	3	21	10	1
Not Out	1	0	3	2	0	1	3	3	2	6	4	0	0	1	2	2	0	1	1	4	1
Runs	407	71	1028	640	410	395	593	560	160	54	7	201	93	60	244	476	0	76	448	74	2
Highest score	85	24	166	118*	126	79	110*	69	38	14	5*	74	27	25*	53	104	0	43	67	28	2*
Average	19.38	11.83	39.53	45.71	17.08	30.38	29.65	35.00	8.00	13.50	1.16	15.46	13.28	12.00	20.33	26.44	–	38.00	22.40	12.33	–
100s	–	–	2	1	1	–	1	–	–	–	–	–	–	–	–	1	–	–	–	–	–
50s	1	–	6	3	–	4	2	4	–	–	–	1	–	–	1	–	–	3	–	–	–

GLOUCESTERSHIRE CCC

FIRST-CLASS MATCHES

BOWLING

	AM Smith	J Lewis	IJ Harvey	MW Alleyne	MJ Cawdron	JN Snape	MCJ Ball	BW Gannon	Overs	Totals	Byes/Leg-byes	Wickets	Run outs	
v. Sussex	10-5-13-3	10-3-21-1	10-2-38-1	4-1-16-0					39	110	13	5	–	A
(Bristol) 26–29 April	–	–	–						–	–	–	–	–	
v. Oxford Universities		16-6-34-3		8-3-13-1	16-8-30-1	15-11-7-2			107.4	243	9	10	–	ABC
(Bristol) 3–5 May		2-2-0-1		5-1-6-0	6-1-12-1	14-9-11-2			51	70	4	6	1	AB
v. Glamorgan		28.4-6-73-6	21-9-38-2	2-1-5-0			9-1-25-0		102.4	250	18	10	1	AB
(Cardiff) 11–14 May		12-2-38-0	–	11-2-38-0			21-1-113-1		78	300	8	4	1	AB
v. Nottinghamshire	18.2-6-50-3	20-4-55-5	15-5-47-0	11-5-31-1		–			70.2	215	14	10	1	A
(Trent Bridge) 17–20 May	15-3-36-1	18-4-53-2	19-6-63-4			2-0-18-0			60	207	5	8	–	AC
v. Worcestershire	16-3-46-1	18-5-64-2	5-0-22-0	16-3-68-2		7-1-33-0			81	310	7	6	–	AC
(Bristol) 23–26 May	–			–		–			–	–	–	–	–	
v. Middlesex	21-7-52-5	22.2-7-51-2		13-1-51-1		–			79.2	204	5	9	–	BC
(Lord's) 31 May–3 June	15-2-40-2	22-6-45-1		20.5-6-49-6		2-0-5-0			73.5	212	6	10	1	BB
v. Essex		17-4-64-0		18-5-32-3	23-5-65-3	13-6-18-0			102.2	263	8	10	1	BCD
(Bristol) 6–8 June		22-10-47-6		12-4-29-0	10-5-24-0	6.3-2-18-2			79.3	199	7	10	–	BD
v. Zimbabweans		34.2-11-95-8			23-6-94-1		22-3-89-0	28-3-107-1	142.2	568	29	10	–	ACE
(Bristol) 16–19 June		10-2-33-1			16-2-66-0		3-0-29-0	9-4-36-1	57	258	8	2	–	A
v. Warwickshire	19-3-59-2	24-9-66-1	19.3-7-44-2			–		21-6-58-5	83.3	233	6	10	–	
(Edgbaston) 28 June–1 July	8-3-17-0	10-2-36-2	3-1-13-0			4-3-4-0		5-1-33-0	33	108	1	2	–	F
v. Northamptonshire	32-6-94-2	31-5-11-0	29-4-101-2	10-2-23-0	28-9-70-3				154.3	543	8	10	–	AF
(Cheltenham) 12–15 July	–								–	–	–	–	–	
v. Warwickshire		22-6-53-0	23-12-29-5	15-3-57-0			22-7-53-2	20.5-1-62-3	102.5	260	6	10	–	
(Cheltenham) 19–22 July		25-6-50-3	23.2-5-71-4	11-2-41-0			29-7-67-0	22-4-66-3	113.2	316	15	10	–	F
v. Worcestershire	17.2-8-16-4		18-7-37-3	5-2-9-0				10-4-35-3	50.2	98	1	10	–	
(Worcester) 28–30 July	23-8-39-1		30.3-8-100-6	7-3-22-0				14-4-53-3	74.3	225	11	10	–	
v. Glamorgan				–	13.3-5-45-5	–			40.3	122	5	10	–	BCG
(Bristol) 2–5 August				3-1-4-0	23.4-8-54-1		5-2-12-0		78.4	210	8	10	1	BCG
v. Essex		16.3-7-37-2		10-3-24-1			17-4-32-3	14-0-61-3	67.3	174	2	10	–	C
(Colchester) 16–19 August		18-9-40-2		14-4-44-3		5-0-21-1	29-10-52-1	14-0-66-3	84	243	16	10	–	
v. Middlesex	18-5-47-2	22-6-72-4		4-0-15-0			14.1-5-31-3	9-2-19-0	73.1	207	4	10	–	C
(Bristol) 21–24 August	12-6-32-2	15.1-6-36-4		–			19-4-35-2	5-1-19-1	51.1	124	2	10	1	
v. Northamptonshire		32-11-96-2		26-12-51-1		27-4-70-3	53-14-120-3		179	469	27	10	–	AC
(Northampton) 30 August–1 September		–							–	–	–	–	–	
v. Sussex		19-3-62-2	15-6-19-6	9-2-20-0				9-2-33-2	52	138	4	10	–	
(Hove) 7–8 September		6-1-20-3	10-2-13-4	7-3-10-3				2-0-16-0	25	71	12	10	–	
v. Nottinghamshire	21-5-52-2	23.1-8-45-3	13-5-23-1	13-3-26-3		11-4-15-0		15-6-47-1	96.1	216	8	10	–	
(Bristol) 13–16 September	5-0-30-0	9.5-1-50-3	–					4-0-21-0	18.5	104	3	3	–	

	AM Smith	J Lewis	IJ Harvey	MW Alleyne	MJ Cawdron	JN Snape	MCJ Ball	BW Gannon
Overs	250.4	526	254.2	254.5	159.1	106.3	243.1	201.5
Maidens	70	152	79	72	49	40	58	38
Runs	623	1447	658	684	460	220	658	732
Wickets	30	69	40	25	15	10	15	29
Bowler's average	20.76	20.97	16.45	27.36	30.66	22.00	43.86	25.24

A TP Cotterell 5-1-9-0; 27-4-69-2, 18-9-24-0; 31-13-54-1, 23-2-72-2; 6-2-18-0, 5-0-27-1; 15-4-49-1; 17-4-74-0, 19-0-86-0; 3-1-10-0; 33-8-90-1.

B JMM Averis 20.4-6-65-1, 6-1-13-1; 11-1-37-0, 11-5-31-0; 16-5-33-0, 14-1-67-0; 17.2-3-50-2, 16-5-58-0; 13-4-40-2, 20-5-72-1.

C THC Hancock 5-1-16-0; 1-0-5-0; 4-0-21-0; 7-4-12-1; 4-0-6-0; 13-2-50-0; 9-4-19-2, 12-2-24-3; 10-3-18-1, 4-3-4-0; 6-2-19-1; 8-2-15-0.

D MA Hardinges 10-3-20-1, 13-6-16-2.

E DR Hewson 5-1-30-0.

F CG Taylor 3-2-4-0; 21.3-1-126-3; 3-2-6-0.

G AN Brassington 5-3-13-1, 15-3-36-4.

FIELDING

60 – RC Russell (55ct/5st)	
20 – MW Alleyne	
15 – KJ Barnett	
8 – RJ Cunliffe, JN Snape	
7 – THC Hancock	
6 – IJ Harvey	
5 – MGN Windows	
4 – BW Gannon, AM Smith	
3 – DR Hewson	
2 – J Lewis	
1 – RI Dawson	

HAMPSHIRE CCC

FIRST-CLASS MATCHES
BATTING

	GW White	JS Laney	WS Kendall	RA Smith	DA Kenway	JP Stephenson	L Savident	AC Morris	SJ Renshaw	SRG Francis	CG van der Gucht	AD Mascarenhas	SK Warne	SD Udal	PJ Hartley	AN Aymes	AD Mullally	AJ Sexton	H Brunnschweiler	CT Tremlett	LR Prittipaul	Extras	Total	Wickets	Result	Points
v. Zimbabweans	10	4	27	6	48	0	7	1	12	1	0*											15	131	10	D	-
(Southampton) 27-30 April	28	44	56*	60	2	-	10*	-	-	-	-											34	234	4		
v. Somerset	34	14	11	6	93*	19		31	4			2	0	5								13	232	10	L	4
(Southampton) 3-5 May	78*	6	0	1	1	4		10	2			17	0	0								7	126	10		
v. Yorkshire	13	13	3	15	14	6		0				3	0	6	5*							23	101	10	L	3
(Headingley) 12-14 May	1	19	78*	22	7	6		4				25	0	0	22							14	198	10		
v. Leicestershire	0	8	4	26	30			26				8	16	7	7	74						23	229	10	D	8
(Southampton) 17-20 May	6	14	8	31	5				2*			10	11*	1		13						22	123	8		
v. Lancashire	45*	14	36	61	5	-										7*						7	175	4	D	7
(Southampton) 23-26 May	-																									
v. Surrey	96	0	7	0	12	6				2		2	19			44	8*					14	210	10	L	4
(Oval) 1-4 June	23	0	41	12	1	1				30*		59	50			2	4					40	263	10		
v. Lancashire	12	17	14	4	0	7		0	0			18*				10	8					5	95	10	L	3
(Liverpool) 6-8 June	9	6	18	6	35	0		23		1*			11			7	8					15	139	10		
v. Durham	29		42	43	47				5*			27	0	35		40	0	36				36	340	10	W	18
(Basingstoke) 14-16 June	-																									
v. Surrey	6		23	36	30			4				12	17	3*		2	12	5				17	167	10	L	3
(Southampton) 29 June-2 July	73		15	3	23					0*		2	23	24		50	10	5				44	272	10		
v. Somerset	44		29	6	0	0								2		11		2				14	142	10	D	7
(Taunton) 7-10 July	18		161	36	54	-								9*		3*		4				34	319	5		
v. New Zealand 'A'	14	49	2		20	8				15*		25		31			3	3	16			18	204	10	L	-
(Portsmouth) 12-15 July	3	28	92		0	4				5*			0	85			16	19	17			16	285	10		
v. Kent	9	81	21	13	35				1			7	69	31	23*	13						17	320	10	L	6
(Portsmouth) 19-22 July	80*	9	0	4	1				0			17	4	1	4	1						15	136	10		
v. Derbyshire	0	2	8	50	136	16						100	12	28*	14			6				22	394	10	D	11
(Derby) 2-5 August	-																									
v. Leicestershire	2	15	20	15	8	14	19					34	12			71	1*					17	228	10	L	4
(Southampton) 8-11 August	50	6	16	20	7	5	60					27*				6	0					19	217	10		
v. Kent	4	9	4	5			4*					0	45	21		1	3				52	8	156	10	L	3
(Canterbury) 22-25 August	29	43	72	14			0					12	4	28		18*	0				35	43	298	10		
v. Durham (Chester-le-Street)	23*	26*				-															20	20	69	0	W	15
30 August- 3 September	0	52	119*	41		-								4*							35	41	292	4		
v. Derbyshire	10	10	143	33				8				62	34	1	17*	20					152	32	522	10	W	20
(Southampton) 6-9 September	-																									
v. Yorkshire	11		73	20	13			13				0	65	14*	0	0					0	4	213	10	L	4
(Southampton) 13-16 September	37		13	6	58			4				17	4	12	0*	1					24	9	185	10		

	GW White	JS Laney	WS Kendall	RA Smith	DA Kenway	JP Stephenson	L Savident	AC Morris	SJ Renshaw	SRG Francis	CG van der Gucht	AD Mascarenhas	SK Warne	SD Udal	PJ Hartley	AN Aymes	AD Mullally	AJ Sexton	H Brunnschweiler	CT Tremlett	LR Prittipaul
Matches	18	14	18	17	15	10	1	8	4	9	1	16	15	12	9	13	8	4	1	1	4
Innings	32	25	31	29	27	15	2	12	7	13	1	24	22	21	11	22	12	7	2	2	6
Not Out	4	1	3	0	1	0	1	1	1	7	1	1	2	3	5	5	2	0	0	0	0
Runs	797	489	1156	595	685	96	17	154	69	64	0	473	431	346	103	398	60	71	22	33	298
Highest score	96	81	161	61	136	19	10*	60	26	30*	0*	100	69	85	23*	74*	12	36	19	17	152
Average	28.96	20.37	41.28	20.51	26.34	6.40	17.00	14.00	11.50	10.66	-	20.56	21.55	19.22	17.16	23.41	6.00	10.14	11.00	16.50	49.66
100s	-	-	3	-	1	-	-	-	-	-	-	1	-	-	-	-	-	-	-	-	1
50s	5	2	5	3	3	-	-	1	-	-	-	2	3	1	-	3	-	-	-	-	1

HAMPSHIRE CCC

FIRST-CLASS MATCHES
BOWLING

	AC Morris	SRG Francis	JP Stephenson	SK Warne	SD Udal	AD Mascarenhas	PJ Hartley	AD Mullally	Overs	Totals	Byes/Leg-byes	Wickets	Run outs	
v. Zimbabweans	24-9-56-0	15-2-62-2	9-1-27-0						106	364	8	7	–	ABCD
(Southampton) 27-30 April	–	–	–						–	–	–	–	–	
v. Somerset	20-2-80-3		8-2-24-0	33-10-83-1	23-6-51-2	13-2-41-0			111.1	319	17	10	1	A
(Southampton) 3-5 May	5-1-17-0		–						10.1	40	6	1	–	AD
v. Yorkshire	21-3-72-2		17-3-53-1	26.3-3-81-2	10-4-20-0	20-3-51-2	26-5-91-3		120.3	399	31	10	–	
(Headingley) 12-14 May	–		–	–	–	–	–		–	–	–	–	–	
v. Leicestershire				43-13-86-5	15-5-35-0	19-4-33-2	29-5-70-2		129	289	18	10	–	A
(Southampton) 17-20 May				–	–	–	–		–	–	–	–	–	
v. Lancashire		12.1-2-63-2	5-0-14-0	21-4-51-2		14.5-3-52-4	10.5-2-33-2		63.5	215	2	10	–	
(Southampton) 23-26 May		–	–	–		–	–		–	–	–	–	–	
v. Surrey		23-5-95-4	20-4-74-2	30.1-9-81-2		14-6-30-0		23-9-43-1	110.1	333	10	10	1	
(Oval) 6 June		10-0-58-1	9-4-16-0	21.1-7-31-5				17-5-31-4	57.1	142	6	10	–	
v. Lancashire		16-4-30-1	18-4-52-2	16.4-4-61-4				26-10-64-3	92.4	269	6	10	–	AD
(Liverpool) 6-8 June		–	–	–				–	–	–	–	–	–	
v. Durham		4-2-6-0		18.4-7-34-4	2-1-3-0	8-3-17-3		17-9-18-3	49.4	83	5	10	–	
(Basingstoke) 14-16 June		4-2-10-0		11-2-22-4	14.3-2-35-3	6-1-14-0		7-3-12-2	42.3	93	0	9	–	
v. Surrey		14-2-58-0		31-12-90-2	16-2-63-0	14-4-34-2		24.2-6-75-6	99.2	331	11	10	–	
(Southampton) 29 June-2 July		6-0-22-0		29.1-3-90-5	13-3-40-1	8-1-23-0		15-4-48-0	71.1	228	5	6	–	
v. Somerset		16-3-51-1	21-3-74-2	38-11-91-4		14-4-47-1	21.3-1-101-2		110.3	368	4	10	–	
(Tauton) 7-10 July		–		–		–	–		–	–	–	–	–	
v. New Zealand 'A'		15.1-3-53-2	5-1-19-0		10-5-8-2	16-3-47-2			59.1	153	10	10	–	EF
(Portsmouth) 12-15 July		20-6-53-1	21.1-5-68-4		40-15-65-0	20-5-51-1			128.1	339	13	8	–	DE
v. Kent		11-5-27-1		37-11-81-4	20.2-5-52-2	17-8-26-1	13-2-54-0		100.2	252	10	10	–	D
(Portsmouth) 19-22 July		4-1-14-0		31.4-13-69-0	20-8-42-4	10-5-11-0	18-5-56-0		84.4	205	9	4	–	D
v. Derbyshire			7-3-16-0	23-8-42-0	14-6-11-0	10-1-37-0	24-5-81-1	37.3-12-93-9	115.3	310	30	10	–	
(Derby) 2-5 August			9-2-29-0	36-9-63-2	27-8-60-2	3-1-6-0	4-0-16-0	33-8-95-5	112	293	24	9	–	
v. Leicestershire	18.3-2-54-2		13-1-49-1	4-0-16-0	20-4-59-2			28-6-84-5	83.3	266	4	10	–	
(Southampton) 8-11 August	11-3-22-0		10-0-51-1		15.3-5-36-2	23-5-65-2		37-15-59-4	96.3	240	7	10	1	
v. Kent	17.5-7-51-2			32-4-107-3	16-4-34-0	16-6-32-0		39-10-90-5	120.5	323	9	10	–	
(Canterbury) 22-25 August	7-0-21-2			20.2-10-34-6	3-0-17-0	5-2-13-1		16-5-46-1	51.2	146	15	10	–	
v. Durham (Chester-le-Street)	21.3-6-68-3			27-10-76-2		9-2-39-1	10-0-54-1	24-4-74-1	92.3	320	6	9	1	D
30 August-3 September	–			–		–	–	–	3	39	0	1	–	DGH
v. Derbyshire	13.2-3-48-3			41-14-103-4	31-8-81-2	15-6-28-1	10-0-44-0		113.2	352	33	10	–	D
(Southampton) 6-9 September	13-5-23-1			24.2-13-36-2	26-9-58-5	2-1-6-0	9-2-25-1		74.2	167	19	10	1	
v. Yorkshire	6-0-39-0			27-6-92-5	7.1-2-15-1	7-5-13-2	13-2-42-1		60.1	205	4	10	1	
(Southampton) 13-16 September	5-2-11-0			21-0-116-2	23-6-76-4	10-3-21-1	16-3-30-2		75	265	11	10	1	

	AC Morris	SRG Francis	JP Stephenson	SK Warne	SD Udal	AD Mascarenhas	PJ Hartley	AD Mullally
Overs	183.1	170.2	172.1	639.4	350.3	313.5	204.2	343.5
Maidens	43	37	33	183	104	88	32	105
Runs	562	602	566	1620	818	796	697	832
Wickets	18	15	13	70	30	28	15	49
Bowler's average	31.22	40.13	43.53	23.14	27.26	28.42	46.46	16.97

A   SJ Renshaw 25-5-86-2; 14.1-6-23-3, 5-0-13-1; 23-7-47-1; 15-4-50-0.
B   CG van der Gucht 22-7-75-3.
C   L Savident 8-0-39-0.
D   GW White 3-0-11-0; 0.1-0-4-0; 1-0-6-0; 2-0-13-0; 2-1-2-2, 1-0-4-0; 1-0-3-0; 3-0-15-0.
E   CT Tremlett 13-6-16-4, 24-8-75-2.
F   WS Kendall 1-0-1-0.
G   RA Smith 2-0-26-0.
H   AN Aymes 1-0-13-1.

FIELDING

38 – AN Aymes (32ct/6st)
17 – WS Kendall
14 – DA Kenway (13ct/1st), SK Warne, GW White
12 – JS Laney
8 – SD Udal
7 – JP Stephenson
4 – I Brunnschweiler, AC Morris
3 – AD Mascarenhas, AJ Sexton, RA Smith
1 – SRG Francis, LR Prittipaul, SJ Renshaw, L Savident

KENT CCC

FIRST-CLASS MATCHES

BATTING

	ET Smith	RWT Key	R Dravid	AP Wells	MA Ealham	PA Nixon	MV Fleming	JR Hockley	MJ Saggers	MM Patel	MJ McCague	DD Masters	JM Golding	DA Scott	DP Fulton	MJ Walkter	K Adams	RJ Trott	Extras	Total	Wickets	Result	Points
v. Lancashire	0	10*	17*	–	–	–	–	–	–	–	–	–	–	–	–	–	–	–	2	29	1	D	7
(Canterbury) 26–29 April	–	–	–	–	–	–	–	–	–	–	–	–	–	–	–	–	–	–	–	–	–		
v. Zimbabweans	4	4	182	58	–	54	38	74	–	–	–	0	18*	–	–	–	–	–	55	487	8	W	–
(Canterbury) 3–5 May	–	–	–	–	–	–	–	–	–	–	–	–	–	–	–	–	–	–	–	–	–		
v. Surrey	24	19	44*	22*	–	–	–	–	–	–	–	–	–	–	–	–	–	–	6	115	2	D	6
(Oval) 11–14 May	5	7	71	0	83	50*	7	2	–	7	–	0*	–	–	–	–	–	–	23	255	8		
v. Surrey	–	–	–	–	–	–	–	–	–	–	–	–	–	–	–	–	–	–	–	–	–	D	6
(Canterbury) 23–26 May	–	–	–	–	–	–	–	–	–	–	–	–	–	–	–	–	–	–	–	–	–		
v. Durham	8	6	–	7	9	19	39	–	2	26	–	1*	–	–	13	20	–	–	27	177	10	W	15
(Tunbridge Wells) 31 May–3 June	0	1	24	72*	8	40	–	–	–	40	–	9	–	–	5	21	–	–	17	237	9		
v. Somerset	–	27	90	10	28	16	25*	–	–	0	10	0	–	–	4	25	–	–	26	261	10	L	5
(Bath) 6–9 June	–	22	17	7	43	28*	23	–	–	1	0	1	–	–	4	61	–	–	16	223	10		
v. Yorkshire	–	–	3	46	2	0	27	29	0*	1	–	0	–	–	3	0	–	–	18	129	10	L	3
(Headingley) 14–16 June	–	–	12	6	7	8	7	0	6*	0	–	12	–	–	1	14	–	–	9	82	10		
v. Somerset	–	–	51	88	0	11	1	40	1	30	–	2*	–	–	5	15	–	–	17	261	10	D	8
(Maidstone) 28 June–1 July	–	–	54	95	60*	–	–	–	0*	–	–	–	–	–	115	–	–	–	14	338	3		
v. Derbyshire	–	–	83	55	4	4	47	24	13	–	–	12	–	–	9	5	–	0*	24	280	10	W	17
(Derby) 12–15 July	–	38	–	1	–	–	–	–	–	–	–	–	–	–	66*	41*	–	–	25	171	2		
v. Hampshire	–	0	137	7	–	17	15	–	0	15	–	0	–	–	33	0	–	0*	28	252	10	W	17
(Portsmouth) 19–22 July	–	60	73*	0	–	5*	–	–	–	–	–	–	–	–	42	4	–	–	21	205	4		
v. Derbyshire	2	37	2	–	4	80*	23	–	0*	60	–	0	–	–	16	0	–	–	27	251	9	D	9
(Canterbury) 28–31 July	–	–	–	–	–	–	–	–	–	–	–	–	–	–	–	–	–	–	–	–	–		
v. Leicestershire	40	14	32	–	6	2	18	–	1	8	–	0	–	–	11	48*	–	–	21	201	10	D	8
(Canterbury) 2–5 August	13	53	24	–	3	1	5	–	–	5*	–	–	–	–	21	24*	–	–	38	187	7		
v. Durham	19	4	7	–	–	0	35	0	6*	–	–	45	–	–	27	15	–	–	11	170	10	D	7
(Chester-le-Street) 9–12 August	175	11	47	–	11*	22*	33	–	–	–	–	4	–	–	17	19	–	–	15	354	7		
v. Lancashire	0	6	1	45	14	–	–	–	0	17	11	0*	–	–	2	46	–	–	13	155	10	L	3
(Old Trafford) 17–19 August	15	15	6	8	10	–	–	–	2	35	0	0*	–	–	1	16	–	–	17	125	10		
v. Hampshire	0	4	20	26	134*	–	–	–	18	–	8	21	–	–	20	47	–	–	23	323	10	W	18
(Canterbury) 22–25 August	21	–	10	9	8	–	–	–	0	–	24	5	–	–	48	2	–	–	15	146	10		
v. Yorkshire	46	18	72	–	7	23	23	–	12	–	14	2*	–	–	25	42	–	–	33	317	10	L	6
(Canterbury) 7–10 September	3	3	2	–	0	19	42	–	13	–	72	5*	–	–	8	6	–	–	24	197	10		
v. Leicestershire	40	–	77	–	19	29*	–	2	6	–	3	–	–	–	16	19	–	–	15	228	8	D	5
(Leicester) 13–16 September	–	–	–	–	–	–	–	–	–	–	–	–	–	–	–	–	–	–	–	–	–		
Matches	11	16	16	12	11	17	14	5	14	13	7	16	1	3	14	14	1	2					
Innings	18	27	25	19	14	24	18	5	17	15	11	20	1	3	24	23	–	2					
Not Out	0	1	3	2	1	7	2	0	5	1	0	7	1	2	1	3	–	2					
Runs	415	562	1221	297	293	567	471	111	91	258	191	71	18	8	512	490	–	0					
Highest score	175	83	182	60*	83	134*	47	74	24	60	72	21	18*	4*	115	61	–	0*					
Average	23.05	21.61	55.50	17.47	22.53	33.35	29.43	22.20	7.58	18.42	17.36	5.46	–	8.00	22.26	24.50	–	–					
100s	–	–	2	–	–	1	–	–	–	–	–	–	–	–	–	–	–	–					
50s	–	5	8	2	2	3	–	1	–	1	1	–	–	–	1	1	–	–					

KENT CCC

FIRST-CLASS MATCHES

BOWLING

	MA Ealham	MJ Saggers	MJ McCague	MV Fleming	MM Patel	DD Masters	Overs	Totals	Byes/Leg-byes	Wickets	Run outs	
v. Lancashire (Canterbury) 26-29 April	20-6-53-4	15-2-53-2	5-1-15-1	13-4-56-1	3.5-1-7-2	–	56.5	186	2	10	–	
	–			–	–		–	–	–	–	–	
v. Zimbabweans (Canterbury) 3-5 May				11-4-10-0	30.4-14-44-4	18-3-44-4	78.4	159	20	10	–	AB
				–	25.4-10-82-2	17-8-37-5	51.4	165	6	9	–	B
v. Surrey (Oval) 11-14 May	25-5-76-1	23-6-66-2		23-8-59-1	36-7-98-0	28-8-75-3	142.5	417	27	10	1	C
	–			–	–		0.4	17	0	–	–	D
v. Surrey (Canterbury) 23-26 May	29-8-91-2			22-5-60-1	20-4-49-0	23-8-74-2	118	348	6	8	–	CE
	–			–	–	–	–	–	–	–	–	
v. Durham (Tunbridge Wells) 31 May-3 June	15-4-24-2	12-4-18-2		7-3-6-0	11-8-3-0	19.2-6-27-6	64.2	81	3	10	–	
	11.4-6-9-1	15-5-32-1		15-9-14-3	30-15-38-4	12-4-21-0	84.4	143	25	10	–	F
v. Somerset (Bath) 6-9 June	26-8-68-2		17-3-56-0	18-6-42-1	30-9-59-1	23.5-9-55-5	118.5	295	8	10	–	F
	19.4-3-61-2		4-0-21-1	4-0-10-0	36-20-43-3	15-2-37-1	78.4	193	17	8	1	
v. Yorkshire (Headingley) 14-16 June	19-6-41-2	17-4-35-2		16-6-37-3	3-3-0-0	13-5-33-2	68	149	3	10	1	
	3.1-0-14-1	9-3-26-2		–	–	5-0-20-1	17.1	63	3	4	–	
v. Somerset (Maidstone) 28 June-1 July	12-1-43-0	29.4-3-112-2		23-5-68-2	54-16-118-4	26-6-88-1	154.4	475	17	10	1	F
	–			–	–	–	–	–	–	–	–	
v. Derbyshire (Derby) 12-15 July		21-3-62-4		6-0-17-0	26.5-13-31-2	14-4-24-3	81.5	181	2	10	–	G
		14-4-35-0		23-4-71-3	34.3-11-77-6	14-3-24-1	101.3	269	22	10	–	FG
v. Hampshire (Portsmouth) 19-22 July		22-4-63-2		6-0-22-0	39.3-10-118-4	17-5-60-1	93.3	320	13	10	1	G
		12-3-25-1		6.2-2-17-2	26-6-46-5	3-0-18-0	56.2	136	13	10	1	CG
v. Derbyshire (Canterbury) 28-31 July	28-9-55-1	25-6-72-4		15.5-4-41-2	26-10-44-1	12-1-35-1	115.5	279	17	10	1	CF
	10-1-36-0	10-2-32-0		4-1-15-0	17-4-45-0	15-3-30-0	108	293	7	0	–	CDFHIJ
v. Leicestershire (Canterbury) 2-5 August	22-6-56-1	33.5-10-70-4		13-1-54-2	20-6-65-1	32-7-92-1	133.5	375	19	10	–	CF
	–			–	–	–	–	–	–	–	–	
v. Durham (Chester-le-Street) 9-12 August		26.5-5-79-7	22-4-56-1	12-3-25-1		17-5-34-0	84.5	223	13	10	1	F
		17-3-44-2	8-1-22-0	10-2-26-1		13-2-37-0	58	157	12	3	–	CK
v. Lancashire (Old Trafford) 17-19 August		22-6-54-4	14-3-40-2		32.3-9-72-3	15-1-60-1	87.3	236	1	10	–	C
		14-3-47-2	12.4-2-29-3		25-7-47-1	15-3-49-3	76.4	198	6	10	–	CF
v. Hampshire (Canterbury) 22-25 August		17-3-47-5	6-1-19-1			12.1-3-31-4	51.1	156	6	10	–	BF
		30-11-53-3	19-4-52-5			27-5-69-0	115	298	27	10	1	BCF
v. Yorkshire (Canterbury) 7-10 September	19-5-41-0	26-5-78-2	13-0-74-0	23-3-77-4		25-3-74-3	115	401	9	10	–	CF
	12.2-0-35-5	14-3-45-4	9-1-28-0	7-2-22-1		4-0-13-0	46.2	145	2	10	–	

	MA Ealham	MJ Saggers	MJ McCague	MV Fleming	MM Patel	DD Masters
Overs	271.5	425.2	129.4	278.1	527.3	435.2
Maidens	67	98	21	72	183	104
Runs	703	1148	412	753	1086	1161
Wickets	24	57	14	28	43	48
Bowler's average	**29.29**	**20.14**	**29.42**	**26.89**	**25.25**	**24.18**

A   JM Golding 17-7-38-1.
B   DA Scott 2-1-3-1, 9-1-40-2; 12-4-28-0, 34-12-86-1.
C   R Dravid 7.5-3-16-2; 2-0-10-1; 1-0-2-0; 5-2-5-0, 10-1-18-0; 3-2-1-0; 7-1-16-0; 4-1-9-0, 6-1-11-0; 2-0-5-1; 6-0-35-0.
D   RWT Key 0.4-0-17-0; 9-1-17-0.
E   K Adams 22-4-58-2.
F   MJ Walker 1-0-4-1; 4-1-7-1; 10-1-29-0; 5-0-11-0; 4-0-10-0, 7-1-18-0; 10-3-18-1; 7-1-16-0; 4-0-9-1; 4-1-25-0, 3-0-6-0; 3-0-13-0.
G   BJ Trott 14-3-45-1, 11-2-29-0; 9-1-44-2, 8-3-15-1.
H   ET Smith 6-0-20-0.
I   DP Fulton 17-5-45-0.
J   PA Nixon 3-1-10-0.
K   JB Hockley 3-3-0-0.

FIELDING

46 – PA Nixon (44ct/2st)	
29 – DP Fulton	
15 – R Dravid	
13 – MM Patel	
12 – MJ Walkter	
6 – ET Smith	
4 – MV Fleming, RWT Key, DD Masters	
3 – MA Ealham, MJ Saggers, AP Wells	
2 – JR Hockley, MJ McCague, DA Scott	
1 – RJ Trott	

LANCASHIRE CCC

FIRST–CLASS MATCHES
BATTING

Match	JP Crawley	MA Atherton	J Scuderi	NH Fairbrother	A Flintoff	GD Lloyd	WK Hegg	CP Schofield	PJ Martin	G Chapple	MP Smethurst	MJ Chilton	SC Ganguly	S Keedy	G Yates	NT Wood	PD McKeown	ID Austin	JJ Haynes	RJ Green	Extras	Total	Wickets	Result	Points
v. Cambridge University (Cambridge) 7–9 April	126	8	51	69*	80*																30	364	3	W	–
		19				13	8	36	14*	0	3*										13	106	5		
v. Kent (Canterbury) 26–29 April		17	9		77	0	2	34	2	4	1*	38	0								2	186	10	D	4
																					–	–			
v. Leicestershire (Old Trafford) 3–6 May	1	1		138	119	24	29	66	16	25	0*		30								39	488	10	W	20
																					–	–			
v. Durham (Chester-le-Street) 11–13 May	5	25		2	10	31	3	50	40	0	2*		73								22	263	10	W	17
	7	4		41	18	1	26	18	0	7	1*		5								6	134	10		
v. Hampshire (Southampton) 23–26 May	33		17	7	5	28	6	39*	21	20		18		13							8	215	10	D	6
																					–	–			
v. Derbyshire (Old Trafford) 31 May–3 June	22	41*				22	0		5*	8		13		29	0	27	30				16	213	9	D	8
																					–	–			
v. Hampshire (Liverpool) 6–8 June	23		0	77*	73	29	5			0		18	18					0			26	269	10	W	17
																					–	–			
v. New Zealand 'A' (Liverpool) 13–16 June	156	12*			83							16	21				33		7*	–	24	352	5	D	–
		0		37*		26				0		6					2		27*	0	3	101	6		
v. Yorkshire (Old Trafford) 29 June–2 July	0			18	35	58	23		24	4*	35	44		2	3						23	269	10	W	17
	6			19*							22*										0	47	1		
v. Derbyshire (Derby) 7–10 July	37	0		28	28	26*			1	0		36	4				4			0	8	172	10	D	7
																					–	–			
v. Somerset (Taunton) 12–15 July	6	113	46	2		17	13	2		2	1*		21	0							16	239	10	D	7
	120	58	5	1		1	4	35		39*	13*		99	12							30	417	5		
v. Durham (Old Trafford) 19–22 July	117	64		8		86	38	2		12	13		65	6*	7						27	445	10	W	20
	17	64*		12		32	1*						4								2	132	2		
v. Yorkshire (Headingley) 28–31 July	23	21		5	28	12	75		19	0		28		7						29*	20	267	10	D	9
	46*	17		26*	25																13	127	2		
v. Surrey (Oval) 2–5 August	1		25	15	36	0	12	4		4	0*		0	2							21	120	10	L	3
	21		21	47	10	1	4	1		7	0		27	0*							6	145	10		
v. Kent (Old Trafford) 17–19 August	42		23	48	29		22	16	0		5	23	0	17*							11	236	10	W	16
	3		11	43	5		0	70*	27		2	1	5	17							14	198	10		
v. Leicestershire (Leicester) 22–25 August	139	48		100*	55		65*					21	87								59	574	5	D	12
																					–	–			
v. Somerset (Old Trafford) 8–10 September		57		17		126	128	6		41	15*	46	1	0							26	463	9	W	20
																					–	–			
v. Surrey (Old Trafford) 13–16 September		5		10		1	93*	24	4	0	17	30	54	34							52	324	10	D	10
		11		90		1	21*	9	5*	5	66	5	65	1							25	304	9		

	JP Crawley	MA Atherton	J Scuderi	NH Fairbrother	A Flintoff	GD Lloyd	WK Hegg	CP Schofield	PJ Martin	G Chapple	MP Smethurst	MJ Chilton	SC Ganguly	S Keedy	G Yates	NT Wood	PD McKeown	ID Austin	JJ Haynes	RJ Green
Matches	15	11	9	15	10	16	17	15	9	16	16	10	14	13	3	1	3	1	1	3
Innings	22	17	13	23	14	22	23	19	11	19	19	14	21	15	3	1	4	1	2	3
Not Out	1	1	2	5	1	1	5	2	3	1	10	1	0	3	0	0	0	0	2	1
Runs	951	532	261	823	570	608	639	461	134	218	161	286	671	144	10	27	69	0	34	29
Highest score	156	133	51	138	119	126	128	66	40	41	66	46	99	34	7	27	33	0	27*	29*
Average	45.28	33.25	23.72	45.72	43.84	28.95	35.50	27.11	16.75	12.11	17.88	22.00	31.95	12.00	3.33	27.00	17.25	–	–	14.50
100s	5	1	–	2	1	1	1	–	–	–	–	–	–	–	–	–	–	–	–	–
50s	–	4	1	3	4	2	4	3	–	–	1	–	6	–	–	–	–	–	–	–

LANCASHIRE CCC

FIRST–CLASS MATCHES

BOWLING

Match	PJ Martin	G Chapple	MP Smethurst	A Flintoff	J Scuderi	CP Schofield	G Keedy	G Yates	Overs	Totals	Byes/Leg-byes	Wickets	Run outs	
v. Cambridge University	20-9-31-0	20-11-22-3	20.1-9-34-4	7-4-8-0	12-2-42-2	9-3-14-1			88.1	168	17	10	–	
(Cambridge) 7-9 April	13-9-16-2	13-1-27-2	12-3-23-1	–	3-0-6-0	22.5-5-48-5			63.5	132	12	10	–	
v. Kent	5-3-10-0	4-0-17-1							9	29	2	1	–	
(Canterbury) 26-29 April	–								–	–	–	–	–	
v. Leicestershire	31.5-9-67-7	16-4-39-1	10-1-50-0	18-7-31-2		22-6-47-0			104.5	265	7	10	–	A
(Old Trafford) 3-6 May	26-9-44-1	12-1-43-3	6-2-13-1	8-4-8-1		27.1-6-82-4			79.1	198	8	10	–	
v. Durham	22.4-14-27-2	20-7-42-6	9-2-31-0	5-2-10-0		2-0-2-0			68.4	164	20	10	1	A
(Chester-le-Street) 11-13 May	9-4-12-1	12-7-14-2	15.3-3-50-7	4-1-3-0					42.3	92	6	10	–	A
v. Hampshire	15-5-22-2	10-3-26-0		5-1-20-0	8-4-23-0	17-4-42-1	14-3-41-1		69	175	1	4	–	
(Southampton) 23-26 May	–			–					–	–	–	–	–	
v. Derbyshire	20.5-5-44-5	20-3-53-2			12-2-29-0		27-13-30-2	1-0-3-0	80.5	170	11	10	1	
(Old Trafford) 31 May-3 June	–	5-2-8-0			4-0-9-0		6-3-3-1	1.4-1-0-1	16.4	24	4	2	–	
v. Hampshire		15-4-36-0	11-3-15-4	5-2-12-3	8-4-20-3				44	95	3	10	–	B
(Liverpool) 6-8 June		17-5-44-1	8-1-20-1	10.4-5-18-4	10-3-25-2				64.4	139	9	10	–	B
v. New Zealand 'A'			16-6-37-7	4-0-17-0	22.2-8-41-2	22-6-47-1			77.2	194	8	10	–	CD
(Liverpool) 13-16 June			8-3-25-1	5-1-17-1	10-0-49-1	11-4-8-0			37	114	2	3	–	C
v. Yorkshire		13-2-27-4	13.2-3-40-3			5-1-16-0	20-7-41-3	–	59.2	164	12	10	–	A
(Old Trafford) 29 June-2 July		10.2-4-24-1	13-5-29-2			5-1-11-0	27-8-47-4	17-4-31-2	72.2	151	9	10	1	
v. Derbyshire		22.4-5-58-2	25-4-87-1				32-9-62-3		106.4	307	9	10	2	AC
(Derby) 7-10 July		16-1-43-3	4-1-10-0				13-4-23-1		33	80	4	4	–	
v. Somerset		29-8-91-0	27-2-131-1		27-7-58-4	29-6-82-3	47-14-109-0		177	565	15	10	1	AE
(Taunton) 12-15 July		–	–						–	–	–	–	–	
v. Durham		13.5-1-59-2	15-3-62-1			13-1-59-1	46-15-99-4	22-7-67-2	111.5	370	17	10	1	A
(Old Trafford) 19-22 July		5-1-19-0	5-1-9-0			10-3-19-0	50-22-56-6	44-16-91-4	114	206	12	10	–	
v. Yorkshire		30-6-80-3	31-5-101-3	3.5-2-5-1			27-4-73-1		124.5	376	11	10	–	ACE
(Headingley) 28-31 July		–	–						–	–	–	–	–	
v. Surrey		32-8-78-1	29-12-63-6	4.5-1-14-1	21-5-65-2	11-2-35-0	13-3-38-0		110.5	310	17	10	–	
(Oval) 2-5 August		4-0-13-0	7-2-39-0	–	6-0-22-0	12.5-1-65-2	22-2-79-2		51.5	227	9	4	–	
v. Kent	19-5-42-5		11-2-27-2	4-2-6-0		9-3-31-2	12-2-36-1		55	155	13	10	–	
(Old Trafford) 17-19 August	11-3-18-1		11-1-36-1	9-0-20-0		11.4-4-25-4	16-9-13-3		58.4	125	13	10	1	
v. Leicestershire			19-4-54-3	21-3-72-2	13-3-43-2	27-3-78-3	16-3-49-0		109	372	22	10	–	ADE
(Leicester) 22-25 August			20-1-89-0	9-2-32-0	2-0-9-0	43-8-149-3	34-7-77-3		112	408	25	6	–	AF
v. Somerset	14-1-41-1	15-6-34-4	13-3-29-3			5.4-4-4-2			49.4	132	15	10	–	A
(Old Trafford) 8-10 September	17-6-39-2	12-2-56-2	13-3-58-3			11.3-4-36-1	2-0-14-1		55.3	222	19	10	1	
v. Surrey	12-1-51-1	26-4-79-3	17.1-4-53-2			30-5-94-4	21-4-60-0		106.1	359	22	10	–	
(Old Trafford) 13-16 September	–	–	–			–								

	PJ Martin	G Chapple	MP Smethurst	A Flintoff	J Scuderi	CP Schofield	G Keedy	G Yates
Overs	236.2	431.5	380.1	99.2	120	356	478	85.4
Maidens	83	101	90	34	28	78	142	28
Runs	464	1175	1176	207	333	1029	1005	192
Wickets	30	49	56	14	14	39	37	9
Bowler's average	15.46	23.97	21.00	14.78	23.78	26.38	27.16	21.33

A SC Ganguly 7-2-24-0; 10-2-32-1, 2-1-7-0; 8-0-28-0; 11-3-39-2; 17-0-79-1; 2-0-7-0; 12.4-2-33-0; 9-1-45-0, 3-0-8-0; 2-0-9-0.
B ID Austin 5-1-9-0, 19-13-23-2.
C RJ Green 11-2-42-0, 3-0-13-0; 16-3-52-0; 18-4-68-1.
D MJ Chilton 2-1-2-0; 1-0-3-0.
E NH Fairbrother 1-1-0-0; 2.2-1-5-1; 3-1-6-0.
F JP Crawley 1-0-19-0.

FIELDING

45 – WK Hegg (39ct/6st)
20 – GD Lloyd
16 – NH Fairbrother
11 – MA Atherton, A Flintoff
10 – MJ Chilton, SC Ganguly
6 – JP Crawley, CP Schofield
4 – G Chapple
3 – MP Smethurst, G Yates
2 – RJ Green, S Keedy, PJ Martin
1 – JJ Haynes, PD McKeown

LEICESTERSHIRE CCC

FIRST–CLASS MATCHES
BATTING

	VJ Wells	DL Maddy	TR Ward	BF Smith	Aftab Habib	DI Stevens	CC Lewis	ND Burns	PAJ deFreitas	A Kumble	J Ormond	JM Dakin	CD Crowe	SAJ Boswell	IJ Sutcliffe	D Williamson	P Griffiths	SJ Adshead	WF Stelling	Extras	Total	Wickets	Result	Points
v. Derbyshire (Derby) 26–29 April	0	4	1	38	33	78	15	37	79	1	1*									22	309	10	D	9
	–	–	–	–	–	–	–	–	–	–	–									–	–	–		
v. Lancashire (Old Trafford) 3–6 May	56	6	39	4	4	41	24	6	1	15	30*									39	265	10	L	4
	45	18	4	19	37	7	5	28	13	0	0*									22	198	10		
v. Somerset (Leicester) 11–14 May		5	2	3	172*	13		6	0	4	8	135	9							30	387	10	W	19
		39	0	45	9	3						19*								9	124	4		
v. Hampshire (Leicester) 17–19 May	2	22	1	32	66	19		67*	0	2	36			14						28	289	10	D	9
	–	–	–	–	–	–		–	–	–	–			–						–	–	–		
v. Durham (Chester-le-Street) 24–27 May	17	50	0	14	11	10	9	1	81*	20	89	21								33	336	10	D	9
	–	–	–	–	–	–	–	–	–	–	–	–								–	–	–		
v. Yorkshire (Headingley) 31 May–3 June	19	63	24	30	6	9			6	70	20			12*	14					23	296	10	D	7
	–	–	–	–	–	–			–	–	–			–	–					–	–	–		
v. Derbyshire (Leicester) 14–17 June	11	22	5	3	164		0	0*	37	0	0				43					25	310	10	W	18
	–	11*	34*	–	–		–	–	–	–	–				–					2	47	2		
v. Surrey (Oakham School) 7–9 July	13	10		3	0	6	3	30	38	10	5*				1					24	143	10	L	3
	9	0		20	4	68	24	8	25*	0	0				14					12	184	10		
v. Durham (Leicester) 12–14 July	12	0		111*	9	40		10	10	3	14		0	0						13	222	10	W	16
	10	77		8	52	19		36*	36	1	0		12	0						8	259	10		
v. Surrey (Guildford) 19–21 July	15	3		102	20	6		4	27	2	2*			37	47					53	318	10	L	6
	17	0		8	2	14		0	24	5	0			7	1*					9	87	10		
v. West Indians (Leicester) 28–30 July	84	48		76	0	12						11	3*	34	21*	–	–			44	333	7	D	
	–	1		–	–	11						–	–	2*	–	0	–			12	26	3		
v. Kent (Canterbury) 2–5 August	72	22		27	78			23	16	56	9*	10	12	15						35	375	10	D	11
	–	–		–	–			–	–	–	–	–	–	–						–	–	–		
v. Hampshire (Southampton) 8–11 August	22	8		5	61	12		0			60	26	5*	53	4					10	266	10	W	17
	20	18		15	13	24		23			8	2	20	37	43*					17	240	10		
v. Yorkshire (Leicester) 16–19 August	27	66		0	59	49		58	19	6*	6	30		2						29	351	10	D	11
	–	–		–	–	–		–	–	–	–	–		–						–	–	–		
v. Lancashire (Leicester) 22–25 August		26		10	93		0	15	97	28	0	50	0*	7						46	372	10	D	9
		9		44	73	16		30*	123*			18		52						43	408	6		
v. Somerset (Taunton) 1–4 September	98	102		69	72	0		57	0	35	16		0*	1						20	470	10	D	11
	–	–		–	–	–		–	–	–	–		–	–						–	–	–		
v. Kent (Leicester) 13–16 September	–	–		–	–			–	–	–	–		–	–						–	–	–	D	6

	VJ Wells	DL Maddy	TR Ward	BF Smith	Aftab Habib	DI Stevens	CC Lewis	ND Burns	PAJ deFreitas	A Kumble	J Ormond	JM Dakin	CD Crowe	SAJ Boswell	IJ Sutcliffe	D Williamson	P Griffiths	SJ Adshead	WF Stelling
Matches	15	17	7	17	17	15	5	16	14	12	12	9	8	5	12	3	1	1	1
Innings	19	25	10	23	23	22	7	21	18	16	15	12	8	7	17	5	–	1	–
Not Out	0	1	1	2	1	0	0	4	3	0	7	1	2	3	1	3	–	0	–
Runs	549	630	110	686	1038	457	80	445	677	181	95	458	103	63	319	116	–	0	–
Highest score	98	102	39	111*	172*	78	24	67*	123*	56	30*	135	30	20	53	47	–	0	–
Average	28.89	26.25	12.22	32.66	47.18	20.77	11.42	26.17	45.13	11.31	11.87	41.63	17.16	15.75	19.93	58.00	–	–	–
100s	–	1	–	2	2	–	–	–	1	–	–	1	–	–	–	–	–	–	–
50s	4	4	–	2	8	2	–	3	4	1	–	3	–	–	2	–	–	–	–

LEICESTERSHIRE CCC

FIRST–CLASS MATCHES

BOWLING

	J Ormond	CC Lewis	PAJ deFreitas	A Kumble	VJ Wells	JM Dakin	CD Crowe	SAJ Boswell	Overs	Totals	Byes/Leg-byes	Wickets	Run outs
v. Derbyshire	23-4-94-2	21-4-44-1	34-7-85-2	42-13-86-3	20.3-5-40-2				140.3	359	10	10	–
(Derby) 26-29 April	–								4	2	0	–	–	AB
v. Lancashire	34-6-122-4	20-0-108-2	34-13-84-2	36.1-11-93-2	17-3-59-0				143.1	488	13	10	–	A
(Old Trafford) 3-6 May													
v. Somerset	25-4-79-3		24.5-10-49-3	26-9-62-2		22-6-44-2	4-0-19-0		101.5	262	9	10	–
(Leicester) 11-14 May	21-4-58-0		27-11-48-3	38.2-12-61-5		18-7-27-0	5-1-12-0		113.2	246	30	10	–	A
v. Hampshire			20.3-6-36-3	27-4-53-2	11.3-4-30-1	18.4-4-49-1		12-3-40-1	95.4	229	9	10	–
(Leicester) 17-19 May			21-7-41-4	22-7-27-2	5-2-8-1	3-1-8-0		7-2-23-1	60	123	14	8	–	A
v. Durham		20-2-50-1	38-9-99-3		12-2-42-0	20-4-55-1	19.2-8-33-3		117.2	302	12	8	–	A
(Chester-le-Street) 24-27 May													
v. Yorkshire	24-11-50-1		23-6-40-0		6-1-25-1			9.4-3-18-1	64.4	146	9	4	1
(Headingley) 31 May-3 June	–				–			–						A
v. Derbyshire	14.5-2-50-6	4-1-7-0	23-8-39-2	12-5-21-2	2-1-4-0				56.5	133	11	10	–
(Leicester) 14-17 June	24-7-58-2	15.1-3-33-2	2-0-3-0	40-17-58-2	21-6-58-4				105.1	223	7	10	–	A
v. Surrey	34-4-92-3	18-2-60-1	29-6-115-3	35-5-101-0	17.5-1-65-2				148.5	505	13	10	–	A
(Oakham School) 7-9 July													
v. Durham	22.1-5-44-4		17-6-36-1	14-4-32-4	7-0-21-1			10-3-28-0	71.1	171	6	10	–
(Leicester) 12-14 July	11.1-0-34-5		6-0-14-1	10-5-23-4				5-0-18-0	32.1	93	4	10	–	A
v. Surrey	29-6-87-6		25-7-76-1	17-1-68-3	4-0-25-0				81	288	15	10	–	C
(Guildford) 19-21 July	3-1-14-0		15-2-30-0	3-1-5-0	4-1-13-0				39.3	119	9	0	–	ABCD
v. West Indians					11-2-32-0	25-3-90-2	37-14-89-3		123	414	16	10	–	ACE
(Leicester) 28-30 July													
v. Kent	22.2-10-57-3		10-5-13-0	32-9-61-4	4-0-15-0	7-1-20-2	13-5-26-1		88.2	201	9	10	–
(Canterbury) 2-5 August	10-3-28-0		10-3-34-0	33-13-44-6	–	7-4-7-0	25-6-56-1		85	187	18	7	–	A
v. Hampshire					20-6-39-3	21.3-7-70-2	14-3-28-1	15-4-39-3	81	228	3	10	–	AC
(Southampton) 8-11 August					20.4-4-54-4	7-1-29-1	27-2-55-4	12-3-30-0	79.4	217	7	10	–	C
v. Yorkshire	27-3-82-2			32-9-81-1	12-5-30-3	19-1-71-2	21.1-4-61-2		111.1	340	15	10	–
(Leicester) 16-19 August	–			–	–									A
v. Lancashire	29-3-76-1		47-7-112-2	45-9-140-1		30-2-112-1	20-2-74-0		177	574	39	5	–	A
(Leicester) 22-25 August	–													
v. Somerset			25-4-81-2	34-5-117-2	7-0-40-0	14-2-59-0		17-3-64-2	103	411	16	7	–	A
(Taunton) 1-4 September			8-1-24-1	–	4-1-20-0	–		6-0-18-1	27	90	1	2	–	ABF
v. Kent	27-2-91-2		20-4-46-0		16-5-28-1				92	228	7	8	–	AG
(Leicester) 13-16 September	–		–		–									

	J Ormond	CC Lewis	PAJ deFreitas	A Kumble	VJ Wells	JM Dakin	CD Crowe	SAJ Boswell
Overs	380.3	98.1	459.2	498.3	222.3	211.4	185.3	93.4
Maidens	75	12	122	139	48	39	50	21
Runs	1116	302	1105	1133	648	641	453	278
Wickets	44	7	33	45	23	14	15	9
Bowler's average	25.36	43.14	33.48	24.17	28.17	45.78	30.20	30.88

A   DL Maddy 2-1-2-0; 2-0-9-0; 4-2-10-2; 6-1-12-2, 2-1-2-0; 8-5-11-0; 2-1-4-0; 1-0-1-0, 3-6-0; 15-2-59-1; 1-0-4-0;
3-0-11-0; 10-1-57-1; 4-0-12-0; 6-1-21-0; 6-0-34-1, 6-1-15-0; 4-1-7-0.
B   DI Stevens 2-2-0-0; 3-0-8-0; 1-0-6-0.
C   D Williamson 6-0-17-0, 7-2-17-0; 7-0-37-1, 13-2-42-1; 18-3-65-3.
D   ID Sutcliffe 1.3-0-12-0.
E   P Griffiths 21-3-65-1.
F   BF Smith 1-1-0-0, 2-0-6-0.
G   WF Stelling 25-8-49-5.

FIELDING

37 – ND Burns (36ct/lst)
16 – DL Maddy
11 – IJ Sutcliffe
10 – BF Smith
8 – Aftab Habib, TR Ward, VJ Wells
6 – CC Lewis, DI Stevens
4 – CD Crowe
3 – A Kumble
2 – JM Dakin
1 – PAJ deFreitas, J Ormond

MIDDLESEX CCC

FIRST-CLASS MATCHES

BATTING

Match	AJ Strauss	MR Ramprakash	JL Langer	OA Shah	RMS Weston	PN Weekes	DC Nash	RL Johnson	ARC Fraser	PCR Tufnell	TL Bloomfield	BL Hutton	MA Roseberry	AW Laraman	KP Dutch	SJ Cook	CJ Batt	EC Joyce	Extras	Total	Wickets	Result	Points
v. Northamptonshire (Lord's) 3–6 May	28	93	120	76	12	39	17	8	3*	–	–								31	427	8	D	12
	111	38	37*	7	39	–	–	–	–	–	–								11	243	3		
v. Worcestershire (Worcester) 11–14 May	47	6	1	6	16	21	12	21	9*	0	4		139*						18	161	10	L	3
	37	14	73	0	15	5	3	14	4	0*	0		–						16	181	10		
v. Cambridge University (Cambridge) 16–18 May	–			43	32*	5*	–					31	–	–					46	296	2	D	–
	–																			–			
v. Northamptonshire (Northampton) 24–27 May	18	54	17	15	1		35	20	22*	16	4	4	26						11	217	10	D	8
	–	16*									4*	13							4	24	0		
v. Gloucestershire (Lord's) 31 May–3 June	0		41	30	32		14	13	8	8*		11	35						21	204	9	L	4
	36		49	33	19		2	2	9	10	4*	13	87						22	212	10		
v. Sussex (Horsham) 7–10 June	26	0	64	60		23	76*	9	26	4		0				21			26	370	10	D	11
	33	20	45	55		23	47*	7*		3						–			20	337	6		
v. Nottinghamshire (Lord's) 14–17 June	6		96	0	4	27	4	0	16	0*		47				0			13	166	10	L	3
	10		104	31	0	36	9	9	0*			5				6			15	223	10		
v. Essex (Chelmsford) 28–30 June	35	0	21		2	4	0	19	1*						55	10			28	222	10	W	16
	10	15	13		26	25	69	15	0*						91	5			19	293	10		
v. Worcestershire (Southgate) 7–10 July	90	101	23	8	3	18	4	9	19	0*			1						27	303	10	D	10
	–																			–			
v. Glamorgan (Southgate) 12–15 July	3	83	7	23	2	13	10	1	0*			11	1						10	164	10	L	3
	73	40	61	40	32	1	46*	30	9			4	8						30	374	10		
v. Sussex (Southgate) 28–31 July	39	110*	0	2		15	14	1	8			4			3	1			30	227	10	L	4
	3	112	48	11		5	52	2*	1			28			1	4			16	283	10		
v. Essex (Lord's) 2–5 August	45	84	5			22		4	17*	2		55	0		14			10	29	287	10	D	9
	29	49	0			1		22*	3	–		8	13		24			9	16	174	9		
v. Nottinghamshire (Trent Bridge) 9–11 August	43	1	108			48	23	19	0*			7	8			43		51	61	412	10	W	20
	13*	–	–			–	–	–	–	–		2*				–		–	12	27	0		
v. Warwickshire (Edgbaston) 17–20 August	19	120*	109			13	9*			0	5		62		23			0	20	380	8	D	9
	10	–	69*			–	–	–	–	–			47*		–			–	0	126	1		
v. Gloucestershire (Bristol) 21–24 August	4	5	77			11	31	7	0*			22	4			5		31	10	207	10	L	4
	10	3	20			10	6	1	4			0	3			16		49	2	124	10		
v. Warwickshire (Lord's) 5–8 September	75	88*	70				5			7*		23						45	37	350	5	D	11
	–						–			–		–						–		–			
v. Glamorgan (Cardiff) 13–16 September	9	51	213*	15		41	41	0	0	2		6						0	9	387	10	D	11
	–																			–			
Matches	17	13	16	12	6	8	17	15	15	16	10	10	11	1	5	7	2	6					
Innings	28	21	27	20	10	13	24	23	22	21	8	15	20	–	7	10	3	8					
Not Out	2	4	3	0	1	1	2	3	6	9	2	2	3	–	0	0	0	1					
Runs	862	1088	1472	489	170	244	446	413	227	100	16	188	549	–	160	145	27	195					
Highest score	111*	120*	213*	76	39	39	76*	69	30	19	4*	55	139*	–	91	43	21	51					
Average	33.15	64.00	61.33	24.45	18.88	20.33	20.27	20.65	14.18	8.33	2.66	14.46	32.29	–	22.85	14.50	9.00	27.85					
100s	1	4	5	–	–	–	–	–	–	–	–	–	1	–	–	–	–	–					
50s	3	6	7	3	–	–	1	2	–	–	–	1	2	–	2	–	–	1					

MIDDLESEX CCC

FIRST-CLASS MATCHES

BOWLING

	ARC Fraser	RL Johnson	TF Bloomfield	PCR Tufnell	PN Weekes	SJ Cook	KP Dutch	Overs	Totals	Byes/Leg-byes	Wickets	Run outs	
v. Northamptonshire	28-13-49-4	23.2-4-75-2	17-2-62-1	27-10-49-3	12-1-19-0			113.2	280	10	10		A B
(Lord's) 3-6 May	10-3-23-0	9-2-23-1	11.1-3-42-1	24-4-67-1	18-5-60-0			77.1	237	9	3	–	B
v. Worcestershire	20-9-29-4	21-5-63-2	13-1-57-4	11-6-21-0	–			65	182	12	10	–	
(Worcester) 11-14 May	10-2-30-1	14-4-49-2	6-1-29-0	6-1-35-0	1.4-0-15-0			37.4	161	3	3	–	
v. Cambridge University			21-3-58-3		13.4-0-45-2	16-5-29-0	9-1-27-0	84.4	218	9	9	–	C D
(Cambridge) 16-18 May			9-1-25-2		8-4-7-1	6-0-25-1	13-6-16-2	42	95	0	6	–	C
v. Northamptonshire	25-8-56-0	25-7-70-0	16-4-46-4	38-13-92-6				115	319	20	10	–	B D
(Northampton) 24-27 May	–	–	–	–				–	–	–	–	–	
v. Gloucestershire	17-2-50-2	23.4-9-83-5	13-4-47-0	23-9-35-2				85.4	259	6	10	–	A D
(Lord's) 31 May-3 June	21-10-49-3	24-6-66-4	9.4-1-61-2	24-8-50-0				80.4	242	5	10	–	A
v. Sussex	22-4-69-1	27-10-71-6		23-6-69-0	1-0-7-0			90	300	17	9	–	A E
(Horsham) 7-10 June	20-5-59-0	–											
v. Nottinghamshire	22.2-6-51-3	26-6-89-2		36-12-56-4	1-1-0-0			102.2	265	12	10	–	A E
(Lord's) 14-17 June	18-3-65-1	22-6-63-1		31-12-52-1	8-1-28-0			101	293	15	6	1	A E
v. Essex	20-7-31-4	14-5-33-1		34-15-39-4			16-6-28-1	84	136	5	10	–	
(Chelmsford) 28-30 June	4-0-6-0	3-0-17-0		16-4-46-3	1.1-0-2-1		16-5-62-6	40.1	142	9	10	–	
v. Worcestershire	9-6-8-1	21-10-39-3	3-0-15-0	33-9-48-4			17.1-8-24-2	83.1	141	7	10	–	
(Southgate) 7-10 July	4-2-5-0	9-6-8-0	3-0-7-1	15-3-39-3	8-4-17-0		10-5-15-1	49	95	4	5	–	
v. Glamorgan	19-3-46-2	21-3-83-3		16-5-40-1	2-1-10-1		14-3-31-1	77.2	232	13	10	–	D
(Southgate) 12-15 July	22-4-47-3	17-5-50-0		32-10-69-1	12-3-32-2			113	307	18	8	–	A D
v. Sussex	13-6-39-1	12-2-37-0		40-16-88-4		13.1-7-16-2	18-3-40-3	101.1	243	8	10	–	A
(Southgate) 28-31 July	20-5-59-0	–		29-8-75-2		12-1-39-1	13.3-3-74-0	77.3	270	7	3	–	B
v. Essex	24-11-45-3		18-4-56-0	35.2-19-48-6		10-2-25-0		97.2	200	5	10	–	B D
(Lord's) 2-5 August	13-3-28-0		11.4-1-37-0	31-14-45-3		14-9-13-4		73.4	130	6	7	–	B
v. Nottinghamshire	14-4-39-3	24-4-90-3		22-7-41-3		15.5-2-48-1		79.5	245	3	10	–	D
(Trent Bridge) 9-11 August	19.4-3-64-6	22-7-76-3		13-2-28-1		6-2-15-0		60.4	192	9	10	–	
v. Warwickshire		12-2-43-1	13-5-31-1	16-3-45-0		13-5-41-0		69	211	5	4	1	B D
(Edgbaston) 17-20 August		17-8-27-1	15-2-47-1	30-11-69-2		11-2-28-1		80	191	9	5	–	B
v. Gloucestershire	24-7-47-2	22-6-58-2		36.3-21-23-5		14-5-36-1		101.3	188	8	10	–	B
(Bristol) 21-24 August	19.3-12-23-1	12-4-22-2		27-12-53-0		6-1-20-0		73.3	147	8	3	–	B D F
v. Warwickshire	32-13-48-2	24-1-107-2	21-0-117-2	22.3-3-71-2				117.3	416	16	10	–	B D G
(Lord's) 5-8 September	5-0-31-0	2-0-11-0	5-1-15-0	6-1-18-0				23	109	5	1	–	F
v. Glamorgan	15-4-47-1	26-8-76-4	13-2-65-1	36.1-11-74-4				103.1	325	16	10	–	A B D
(Cardiff) 13-16 September	5-0-28-0	4-0-17-0	5-0-15-0					19	93	5	0	–	G H

	ARC Fraser	RL Johnson	TF Bloomfield	PCR Tufnell	PN Weekes	SJ Cook	KP Dutch
Overs	475.3	473	222.3	738.3	86.3	137	142.4
Maidens	150	130	35	255	20	41	45
Runs	1112	1429	834	1500	242	335	365
Wickets	48	50	23	65	7	11	17
Bowler's average	**23.16**	**28.58**	**36.26**	**23.07**	**34.57**	**30.45**	**21.47**

A   OA Shah 2-0-7-0; 6-1-21-1, 2-0-11-1; 5-0-23-1; 4-3-4-0, 6-2-21-0; 4-1-16-1; 5-1-15-0; 1-0-8-0.
B   MR Ramprakash 4-1-9-0, 5-0-13-0; 9-2-26-0; 3-0-16-0; 4-2-5-0, 4-3-1-0; 8-2-16-0, 7-3-11-0; 5-1-16-0, 5-1-6-0; 6-2-11-1; 7-1-17-0.
C   AW Laraman 15-4-33-4, 6-0-22-0.
D   BL Hutton 10-3-17-0; 2-1-9-0; 3-0-17-0; 5.2-3-9-2, 10-5-27-0; 6-0-16-1; 4-0-24-0; 7-2-30-1; 3-0-9-0; 11-3-37-1; 5-0-22-0.
E   CJ Batt 12-3-44-1; 13-5-53-1, 16-3-49-2.
F   JL Langer 1-0-6-0; 5-1-29-1.
G   EC Joyce 1-0-9-0; 4-1-15-0.
H   AJ Strauss 1-0-13-0.

FIELDING

36 – DC Nash (32ct/4st)	
25 – JL Langer	
13 – RL Johnson	
9 – KP Dutch, MR Ramprakash	
8 – BL Hutton, PN Weekes	
7 – EC Joyce, OA Shah	
6 – AJ Strauss	
4 – ARC Fraser, PCR Tufnell	
3 – MA Roseberry, RMS Weston	
2 – SJ Cook	
1 – CJ Batt, TF Bloomfield, AW Laraman	

NORTHAMPTONSHIRE CCC

FIRST–CLASS MATCHES

BATTING

	AS Rollins	ML Hayden	MB Loye	DJG Sales	RJ Warren	AL Penberthy	GP Swann	TMB Bailey	RJ Logan	DM Cousins	DE Malcolm	D Ripley	MK Davies	JW Cook	RA White	AJ Swann	KJ Innes	MR Strong	JAR Blain	JF Brown	JP Taylor	MJ Powell	Extras	Total	Wickets	Result	Points
v. Nottinghamshire	0	7	21	5	2	47*	25	4	15	4	8												15	153	10	D	7
(Trent Bridge) 26–29 April	–	–	–	–	–	–	–	–	–	–	–	–															
v. Middlesex	100	20	13	25	13	59	19		2*	0	3	6											20	280	10	D	8
(Lord's) 3–6 May	96	93	0*	3	32*	–	–																13	237	3		
v. Nottinghamshire	8	101	9	276		62	25		4	19*	6	39	10										26	585	10	W	20
(Northampton) 11–14 May	–	–	–	–		–	–		–	–	–	–	–														
v. Middlesex	21	69	47	1		23	43		2	7*	0	55	25										26	319	10	D	10
(Northampton) 24–27 May	–	–	–	–		–	–		–	–	–	–	–														
v. Essex	9	28	23	2			3		0	0	0	6	2	13*									28	114	10	L	3
(Ilford) 31 May–2 June	9	73	62	18			47		24	2*	4	0	25	39									24	327	10		
v. Oxford Universities				27		16	13					6		32	11	108	32*	10*					20	275	7	L	–
(Oxford) 6–8 June				6		57	38*					8	5		20	0	4	14	31*	1*			4	188	8		
v. Warwickshire	42	30	93	9		46	0		1	7	0	15*	1										22	266	10	L	4
(Northampton) 14–17 June	76	47	1	4		21	72		3	4	0*	12	2										7	249	10		
v. Glamorgan	6	4	47	15		0	1			29*	3	44						0		0			18	167	10	L	3
(Northampton) 7–9 July	0	41	10	61		2	19		7	0	5							27*		0			6	178	10		
v. Gloucestershire	63	75	39	76		26	40		15			48*		137						3	11		10	543	10	W	20
(Cheltenham) 12–15 July	–	–	–	–		–	–		–			–		–						–	–						
v. Glamorgan	0	40	0	2		26	48		1	27		53		18						8*			6	229	10	L	4
(Cardiff) 19–29 July	0	51	42	51		57	19		0			33		11						0	0*		13	277	10		
v. Warwickshire	19	122	2	18		22	58	21	10			27								0*	11		8	318	8	W	18
(Edgbaston) 28–30 July	8	72	25	17		18*	8	6	7			3								0	0		12	176	10		
v. Worcestershire	63	147	52	60		83	4		2			56		1						0	3*		48	519	10	W	19
(Northampton) 4–7 August	–	–	–	–		–	–		–			–		–						–	–						
v. Sussex	30	18	18		151	96	30		17			21		23						1*	13		42	460	10	W	19
(Northampton) 9–11 August	–	–	–		–	–	–		–			–		–						–	–						
v. Sussex	2	6		9	29	8	20		17*			5		4						0	0		10	110	10	W	15
(Eastbourne) 16–18 August	15	21		5	0	10	24		2			39*		116						0	8		30	270	10		
v. Gloucestershire	49	41		55	61	116	15					10		4		61*				2	20		35	469	10	W	18
(Northampton) 30 August–1 September	–	–		–	–	–	–					–		–		–				–	–						
v. Essex	20	164		61	10	15	6		16*			54		4						7	27		26	410	10	D	12
(Northampton) 6–9 September	–	–		–	–	–	–		–			–		–						–	–						
v. Worcestershire	0			11	48	2		96*		24*				9		19	5				14	1	31	260	10	D	8
(Worcester) 13–16 September	0			15	0	11	22	5						21		13	25				0	1	12	125	10		
Matches	16	15	12	13	9	15	16	4	6	16	7	13	5	11	1	3	2	4	1	10	7	1					
Innings	24	22	18	20	13	21	24	7	8	23	10	18	8	17	2	5	4	5	1	14	10	2					
Not Out	0	0	1	0	1	2	0	2	1	7	1	3	0	1	0	1	1	2	1	5	1	0					
Runs	636	1270	504	713	417	785	597	200	51	210	24	475	79	502	31	201	66	72	31	30	96	2					
Highest score	100	164	93	276	151	116	72	96*	24	29*	8	56	25	137	20	108	32*	27*	31*	11	27	1					
Average	26.50	57.72	29.64	35.65	34.75	41.31	24.87	40.40	7.00	13.12	2.66	31.66	9.87	31.37	16.50	50.25	22.00	24.00	–	3.33	10.66	1.00					
100s	1	4	–	1	1	1	–	–	–	–	–	–	–	2	–	1	–	–	–	–	–	–					
50s	4	6	3	5	2	5	3	1	–	–	–	3	–	–	–	1	–	–	–	–	–	–					

NORTHAMPTONSHIRE CCC

FIRST–CLASS MATCHES
BOWLING

	DE Malcolm	DM Cousins	RJ Logan	AL Penberthy	GP Swann	MK Davies	JF Brown	MR Strong	JP Taylor	Overs	Totals	Byes/Leg-byes	Wickets	Run outs	
v. Nottinghamshire	12-2-45-5	13-4-31-4	1-1-0-0							26	79	3	9	–	
(Trent Bridge) 26–29 April	–														
v. Middlesex	30-8-73-0	36-8-123-5	27.3-6-100-2	7-2-25-0	20-1-76-1					126.3	427	4	8	–	A
(Lord's) 3–6 May	7-2-31-0	13-4-41-0	15-2-65-0	5-1-25-1	12-0-72-2					52	243	9	3	–	
v. Nottinghamshire	18-5-39-2	23-7-78-2	31-13-68-3		17-3-47-0	31-9-83-3				120	333	18	10	–	
(Northampton) 11–14 May	6-1-13-1	16-4-41-4	5-1-26-0		8.1-3-11-2	19-11-25-3				54.1	128	12	10	–	
v. Middlesex	24-8-62-3	17-5-39-1	17.4-2-61-5		1-0-14-0	10-0-32-1				69.4	217	9	10	–	
(Northampton) 24–27 May	4.2-2-9-0	4-1-11-0			–	–				8.2	24	4	–	–	
v. Essex	16.5-5-53-4	25-9-44-4	14-5-50-0		4-0-6-0	16-4-33-1				82.5	216	8	10	1	A
(Ilford) 31 May–2 June	18-4-40-3	19.2-4-71-1	5-0-26-0		22-4-51-1	8-1-30-0				72.2	228	10	5	–	
v. Oxford Universities					6-1-24-0	19-7-40-1		12-5-31-2	12-2-41-1	80.4	221	6	10	–	B C
(Oxford) 6–8 June					16-2-49-0	5-1-26-0		15-3-46-4	12-2-29-1	64.5	243	5	7	–	B C
v. Warwickshire	25-4-89-0	41-8-132-2	17-3-57-1	23-5-54-5	28-2-116-0	25-12-70-0	23-3-60-3		22-6-51-1	161	568	42	9	–	A
(Northampton) 14–17 June	–	–					9.5-1-49-1		11-4-27-0	–					
v. Glamorgan	12-1-47-1	19-5-51-2		13-4-34-2	11-4-41-2			12.2-2-37-2	15-1-41-0	73.2	234	14	10	–	
(Northampton) 7–9 July	11-4-40-0	8-0-35-0		9-1-26-3	16.3-1-55-4			6-0-35-0	9-2-26-0	71.3	255	6	10	–	
v. Gloucestershire		15-5-28-4		15-5-41-2	9.1-8-13-2		6-2-10-1	5-0-17-0	18-4-42-4	59.1	116	2	10	–	
(Cheltenham) 12–15 July		14-3-27-1		5-0-17-0	49.5-12-118-6		21-2-58-3	8-1-18-0	15.3-7-27-6	131.5	328	12	10	–	
v. Glamorgan		21-8-45-2		9-0-26-0	7-2-21-0		15-8-15-2	17-4-50-4	20-4-59-1	85.2	198	0	10	–	
(Cardiff) 19–29 July		18-4-35-2		21-7-42-0	28.3-6-95-1		55-18-136-3	9-0-35-0	20-6-45-2	117.3	310	10	5	–	
v. Warwickshire		6-0-20-0			29-9-74-4		31.2-13-56-4		14-3-39-1	81.1	236	13	10	–	
(Edgbaston) 28–30 July		6-2-14-1			20.2-2-65-2		41-7-93-2		14-1-35-0	65.2	204	6	10	–	
v. Worcestershire		12-6-13-2			33-7-72-2		34.1-9-88-5		18-4-51-3	109	249	13	10	–	
(Northampton) 4–7 August		13-6-19-1			24-7-55-5		27-4-90-6		12-4-27-4	81	198	9	10	–	
v. Sussex		22-7-36-4		4-1-16-0	29-8-74-2		42-9-100-5			102.3	232	12	10	–	
(Northampton) 9–11 August		13-3-25-1		–	26-7-72-2		33-13-88-4			70.2	211	10	10	–	
v. Sussex		14.3-2-39-3		10-3-26-2	5-1-7-1		32.3-12-53-4			56.3	153	6	10	–	
(Eastbourne) 16–18 August		13-6-25-4		–	1-0-1-0		22.2-1-78-7			33.3	65	9	10	–	
v. Gloucestershire		20-10-41-4					9-1-33-0			80	186	6	10	–	D
(Northampton) 30 August–1 September		24.2-9-38-3					4-3-3-0			109.2	209	12	10	–	D
v. Essex		15-0-51-1		5-0-15-1	20-1-67-2		34-12-68-4			68.4	233	27	10	1	
(Northampton) 6–9 September		21-7-50-4		–	24-3-70-0		43-17-84-3			80	225	1	4	–	E
v. Worcestershire		18-4-61-3		–			14.4-4-34-4			37.3	124	4	7	–	C
(Worcester) 13–16 September		10.3-2-54-2		5-1-11-0			20-3-62-0			30.3	119	7	6	–	C

	DE Malcolm	DM Cousins	RJ Logan	AL Penberthy	GP Swann	MK Davies	JF Brown	MR Strong	JP Taylor
Overs	184.1	510.4	133.1	131	467.3	133	517.5	84.2	212.3
Maidens	46	143	33	30	92	45	142	15	50
Runs	541	1318	453	358	1366	339	1258	269	540
Wickets	19	67	11	16	41	9	61	12	24
Bowler's average	28.47	19.67	41.18	22.37	33.31	56.50	20.62	22.41	22.50

A ML Hayden 6-1-26-0; 7-1-22-0; 2-0-8-1.
B JAR Blain 13-1-37-1, 9-2-37-0.
C KJ Innes 7.4-1-23-3, 10-3-31-2; 1.3-0-8-1, 3-0-20-0.
D AJ Swann 6-2-12-1, 22-11-30-2.
E JW Cook 1-0-7-0.

FIELDING

42 – D Ripley (38ct/4st)
21 – ML Hayden
19 – AS Rollins
10 – AL Penberthy
9 – TMB Bailey (8ct/1st), DG Sales
8 – GP Swann
4 – JW Cook
3 – JF Brown, DM Cousins, JP Taylor, RJ Warren
2 – MK Davies, RA White
1 – JAR Blain, RJ Logan, MB Loye, MR Strong, AJ Swann

NOTTINGHAMSHIRE CCC

FIRST-CLASS MATCHES

BATTING

	DJ Bicknell	Usman Afzaal	JER Gallian	P Johnson	JE Morris	CMW Read	CM Tolley	PJ Franks	DJ Millns	DS Lucas	RD Stemp	MN Bowen	GE Welton	WM Noon	AJ Harris	PR Reiffel	SJ Randell	MJA Whiley	CJ Hewison	Extras	Total	Wickets	Result	Points
v. Northamptonshire	11	0	2	0	5	7	2	1	9	25*	6*									11	79	9	D	7
(Trent Bridge) 26–29 April	-																			-	-	-		
v. Essex	59	0	11	100	1	19	51	53	20*	6	4									16	340	10	D	10
(Chelmsford) 3–6 May	5	3	12	13	44	17	25*	22*	-	-										9	150	6		
v. Northamptonshire	33	33	45	12	88	9		9	50*	0	5	24								25	333	10	L	4
(Northampton) 11–14 May	3	15	1	26	46	8		2	1	10	0*	4								12	128	10		
v. Gloucestershire	2	0	11		0	20		26	36*	25	1		74	0						20	215	10	D	8
(Trent Bridge) 17–20 May	2	14	42		19	25		14	14*	10*	-		42	7						18	207	8		
v. Warwickshire	180*	-	-	-	-	-	-	-	-	-	-		200*							26	406	0	D	12
(Edgbaston) 2–5 June	-																			-	-	-		
v. Worcestershire	12	151*	23	10	4	0		27	4	6			3		39					34	313	10	L	6
(Trent Bridge) 7–10 June	43	13	0	6	26	13		60	25	7			60		0*					22	275	10		
v. Middlesex	11	28	28		67	45	12	5			2*	7	36		6					18	265	10	W	17
(Lord's) 14–17 June	34	127	16		5	56*	34				-	-	6		-					15	293	6		
v. Essex	64	65*	3	9	11	0*				-			13		-					15	180	5	D	6
(Trent Bridge) 7–10 July	-												-		-					-	-	-		
v. Worcestershire	16	86	45	0	8	50			35		3		32*		0	45*				38	358	10	D	11
(Worcester) 12–15 July	11*	-											9		-					4	24	0		
v. Sussex	45	43	44	1	76	38*			1		4		9		31	7				45	344	10	D	10
(Hove) 19–22 July	23	54	120	9	115	9			0		-		6		2*	9*				32	379	8		
v. Warwickshire	10	82	31	22	52	83	26		9				10		14	26*				63	368	10	D	11
(Trent Bridge) 3–6 August	25	0	2	19		45	14	20	-				9		12*	60*				26	232	8		
v. Middlesex	4	37	44		6	28	60	20		19*			8		6		0			13	245	10	L	4
(Trent Bridge) 9–11 August	20	11	0		4	17	2	50		46*			18		15		0			9	192	10		
v. Glamorgan	20	103	13	43	28	1		33			4*		74		3	4				17	343	10	D	10
(Cardiff) 16–19 August	-																			-	-	-		
v. Sussex	144	45	9		18	0		6			5*		2		19	74				29	351	10	D	11
(Trent Bridge) 30 August–2 September	35	0	110*	33*	30	-							11		-	-				19	238	4		
v. Glamorgan	20	29	150	6		20		32				13	4		2*	50			24	21	371	10	W	19
(Trent Bridge) 6–8 September	3	36*	15*										4						6	2	66	3		
v. Gloucestershire	19	7	19	21		0		41		21*	11	22	23		4					28	216	10	L	1
(Bristol) 13–16 September	4*	36	0*	23*								13	21		-					7	104	3		
Matches	16	16	16	12	13	16	6	13	8	10	11	4	13	1	11	7	1	1	1					
Innings	28	26	26	19	20	23	9	18	11	12	11	6	23	2	14	8	2	-	2					
Not Out	3	3	3	2	0	3	1	1	4	5	5	0	2	0	4	4	0	-	0					
Runs	858	1018	796	353	601	479	223	447	195	184	45	83	674	7	153	275	0	-	30					
Highest score	180*	151*	150	100	115	56*	60	60	50*	46*	11	24	200*	7	39	60*	0	-	24					
Average	34.32	44.26	34.60	20.76	30.05	23.95	27.87	26.29	27.85	26.28	7.50	13.83	32.09	3.50	15.30	68.75	-	-	15.00					
100s	2	3	3	1	1	-	-	-	-	-	-	-	1	-	-	-	-	-	-					
50s	2	4	-	-	3	3	2	3	1	-	-	-	3	-	-	3	-	-	-					

A   MJA Whiley (2 innings) did not bat

NOTTINGHAMSHIRE CCC

FIRST-CLASS MATCHES

BOWLING

	PJ Franks	DJ Millns	DS Lucas	RD Stemp	Usman Afzaal	AJ Harris	PR Reiffel	Overs	Totals	Byes/Leg-byes	Wickets	Run outs	
v. Northamptonshire	19.4-8-32-2	20-6-58-5	12-4-44-3					54.4	153	7	10	–	A
(Trent Bridge) 26–29 April	–	–						–	–	–	–	–	
v. Essex	24-4-91-3	17.2-5-64-2	19-3-61-4	14-5-37-0				79.2	274	5	9	–	A
(Chelmsford) 3–6 May	30-11-60-3	16-3-58-3	21-5-53-2	35.4-14-66-2	2-1-6-0			111.4	263	13	10	–	A
v. Northamptonshire	23-2-111-0	23.3-5-102-2	26-5-115-2	36-7-127-4	12-2-36-1			144.3	585	14	10	1	B
(Northampton) 11–14 May	–			–	–			–	–	–	–	–	
v. Gloucestershire	31.2-15-43-4	23-3-90-2	40-11-92-3	14-6-29-1				117.2	290	20	10	–	C
(Trent Bridge) 17–20 May	–		–	–				–	–	–	–	–	
v. Warwickshire	15.5-4-27-3	11-0-44-3	11-4-22-1	7-3-13-2	–			44.5	110	4	10	1	
(Edgbaston) 2–5 June	15-0-72-1	16-4-67-3	13-0-62-1	38-19-46-3	17-7-43-0			101	305	10	8	–	C
v. Worcestershire	25-4-85-0	24-6-92-4	25.5-5-86-3		15-3-45-1	18-2-58-1		112.5	402	18	10	–	C
(Trent Bridge) 7–10 June	23.4-5-81-1	5.2-2-17-1	3-1-12-0		16-6-33-1	25-3-85-4		84	292	15	7	–	C
v. Middlesex	17-3-56-7			20.4-5-58-3	–	9-2-36-0		53.4	166	1	10	–	A B
(Lord's) 14–17 June	18-5-45-1			39-10-103-3	7-2-24-0	20.4-8-34-5		94.4	223	3	10	–	A B
v. Essex			28-5-94-0		11-1-36-0	43-7-139-5	32-11-74-3	146	505	20	9	–	C D
(Trent Bridge) 7–10 July								–	–	–	–	–	
v. Worcestershire		21-3-58-3		26-12-45-0	10-4-9-0	25.4-5-84-3	25-4-59-3	122.4	284	12	10	–	C
(Worcester) 12–15 July		15-2-54-0		51-17-123-5	13-3-45-1	32-9-101-2	25-6-53-0	142.4	431	15	10	1	C E
v. Sussex		24-3-120-1		25-4-85-1	3-0-18-0	25-4-111-2	32-10-85-4	122	472	11	10	–	C
(Hove) 19–22 July		10-0-56-1		13-3-62-0	3.2-0-20-2	11-0-52-0	11-1-31-0	57.2	278	2	3	–	C
v. Warwickshire	24-1-102-1		19-4-52-0		2-2-0-0	21-1-76-1	26.3-8-62-5	108.3	324	10	10	–	A
(Trent Bridge) 3–6 August	11-2-41-0		9-1-33-2		2-0-7-0	13-2-35-1		41	132	6	4	–	A F
v. Middlesex	28-4-90-3		22-5-73-4		4-0-12-0	23.4-4-87-2		109.4	412	27	10	–	A C G
(Trent Bridge) 9–11 August	1.3-0-16-0		2-0-9-0		–			3.3	27	2	–	–	
v. Glamorgan	13-0-40-2			33-12-67-4	9-2-19-0	28.5-6-101-4	13-1-49-0	96.5	288	12	10	–	
(Cardiff) 16–19 August	3-1-6-0			33-21-34-3	21-11-26-3	5-0-18-0	5-4-4-0	68	99	11	6	–	H
v. Sussex	20-3-74-2			3-1-16-0		29.1-4-110-6	27-7-69-2	85.1	287	6	10	–	C
(Trent Bridge) 30 August–2 September	–			–		2-1-1-0	2.5-2-1-0	4.5	4	2	0	–	
v. Glamorgan	10-2-42-2				1-1-0-0	15.3-0-69-5	13-2-42-2	47.3	187	7	10	–	B
(Trent Bridge) 6–8 September	20-5-59-6				1-1-0-0	24-2-96-2	21.1-4-57-2	76.1	246	3	10	–	B
v. Gloucestershire	6.4-2-12-0		9-3-22-1			5-1-36-0		21.4	73	3	1	–	B
(Bristol) 13–16 September	14.3-0-67-1		12-1-58-1	10-1-35-2		8-1-29-1		57.3	248	12	7	–	B

	PJ Franks	DJ Millns	DS Lucas	RD Stemp	Usman Afzaal	AJ Harris	PR Reiffel
Overs	394.1	226.1	271.5	398.2	149.2	384.3	233.3
Maidens	81	42	57	140	46	62	60
Runs	1252	880	888	946	379	1358	586
Wickets	42	30	27	33	9	44	21
Bowler's average	29.80	29.33	32.88	28.66	42.11	30.86	27.90

A   CM Tolley 3-1-12-0; 5-1-16-0, 7-5-7-0; 2-1-3-0, 3-1-3-0; 16-10-22-3, 5-2-9-1; 11-1-35-0.
B   MN Bowen 24-4-80-0; 5-1-12-0, 7-4-11-1; 8-2-27-1, 10-2-31-0; 1-1-0-0, 13-2-47-2.
C   JER Gallian 9-6-16-0; 2-1-5-0; 5-1-18-1, 11-0-49-0; 10-1-33-0; 15-6-17-1, 4-2-14-0; 13-0-42-2, 9-1-55-0;
     8-4-17-1; 6-2-12-0.
D   SJ Randell 22-2-109-1.
E   JE Morris 2.4-0-26-1.
F   GF Welton 1-0-1-0.
G   MJA Whiley 13-2-71-0.
H   DJ Bicknell 1-1-0-0.

FIELDING

40 – CMW Read	
23 – JER Gallian	
10 – P Johnson	
9 – Usman Afzaal	
7 – JE Morris, RD Stemp, GE Welton	
5 – PJ Franks, CJ Hewison	
4 – AJ Harris	
3 – DJ Bicknell, DS Lucas	
2 – MN Bowen, DJ Millns, CM Tolley	
1 – WM Noon, MJA Whiley	

SOMERSET CCC

FIRST-CLASS MATCHES

BATTING

	J Cox	ME Trescothick	PD Bowler	MN Lathwell	M Burns	RJ Turner	ID Blackwell	GD Rose	MPL Bulbeck	PW Jarvis	PD Trego	PCL Holloway	AR Caddick	PS Jones	KA Parsons	ARK Pierson	JO Grove	JID Kerr	J Tucker	Extras	Total	Wickets	Result	Points
v. Oxford Universities	7	0	157*	4	160	15*														19	362	4	W	–
(Taunton) 7–9 April	100	78	–	54*	–	18*														10	260	2		
v. Surrey	2	85	37		81	0	2	37*	3*			0	19	–						36	302	8	D	10
(Taunton) 26–29 April	–	–	–		–	–	–					–		–						–	–	–		
v. Hampshire	153	3	56		1	56	15	13*	3			0	0	0						19	319	10	W	18
(Southampton) 3–5 May	4	15*	–									13*								8	40	1		
v. Leicestershire	8	105	8		4	0	58	1					17		20	16	8*			17	262	10	L	4
(Leicester) 11–14 May	24	43	48		6	15	19	2					27		25	1*	0			36	246	10		
v. Derbyshire	16	30	57		1	14	16	2					23	0	47	0*				34	240	10	D	5
(Taunton) 24–27 May	–	–	–										–		–					–	–	–		
v. Kent	52	24	5		0	16	45					50	12	10	62	5				14	295	10	W	17
(Bath) 6–9 June	43	0	11		17	27*	18					19	21*	0	18					19	193	8		
v. Surrey	34	45	0		17	3	16				0	1		0	1	12*				16	145	10	L	2
(Oval) 14–16 June	36	13	37		3	1	32*				4	24		9	12	1				18	190	10		
v. Kent	17	90	108		20	35	69				35	31	8*	25	18					19	475	10	D	11
(Maidstone) 28 June–1 July	–	–	–																	–	–	–		
v. Hampshire	26	16	25	56	14	18	4				6	113	0*	46						44	368	10	D	11
(Taunton) 7–10 July	–	–	–																	–	–	–		
v. Lancashire	171		95	43	108	75	8	6*				0	1		0	25				33	565	10	D	11
(Taunton) 12–15 July	–		–	–	–	–	–													–	–	–		
v. Yorkshire	10		15	1	14	38	16	2			27*	27		0	20					12	182	10	L	3
(Scarborough) 19–21 July	7		15	4	0	20	24	20			0	1		56*	38					27	212	10		
v. Durham	5	17	107		3	10	82*			1		14	3	1		8				29	280	10	D	9
(Chester-le-Street) 28–31 July	–	–	–																	–	–	–		
v. Yorkshire	4		34	8		36	11	124			62	15		6	32		5*			22	359	10	D	11
(Taunton) 2–5 August	27	139*	47								0				108*					47	368	3		
v. Durham	25	31	39	89	18	0	102								12	15*				31	362	8	D	11
(Taunton) 16–19 August	–	–	–																	–	–	–		
v. West Indians	41	47		55	6	25						1			193*	1	17	32	14	56	488	10	W	–
(Taunton) 23–26 August		11		78*	43	39						0			2		48				240	6		
v. Leicestershire	58	38*	0	23	47		109	5							48			19*		64	411	7	D	12
(Taunton) 1–4 September	40*	27*	7		3															13	90	2		
v. Lancashire	53	14	16	20	0	0	8						1*	0	1			4		15	132	10	L	3
(Old Trafford) 8–10 September	20	75	5	9	2	36	2						1	10	12*			27		23	222	10		
v. Derbyshire		117*	4	30	13	16	37							28	0	14	0*	34		18	311	9	D	7
(Derby) 13–16 September		–	–																					

	J Cox	ME Trescothick	PD Bowler	MN Lathwell	M Burns	RJ Turner	ID Blackwell	GD Rose	MPL Bulbeck	PW Jarvis	PD Trego	PCL Holloway	AR Caddick	PS Jones	KA Parsons	ARK Pierson	JO Grove	JID Kerr	J Tucker
Matches	17	9	18	9	15	18	18	15	3	2	7	13	3	15	15	6	10	4	1
Innings	26	14	26	14	20	26	23	18	2	1	8	20	4	16	22	9	10	5	1
Not Out	1	1	5	1	1	2	2	5	1	0	1	1	1	4	2	3	5	1	0
Runs	983	548	1305	257	775	492	582	510	6	1	134	377	52	122	745	126	56	116	14
Highest score	171	105	157*	54*	160	75	109	124	3*	1	62	113	21*	56*	193*	48	17	34	14
Average	39.32	42.15	62.14	19.76	40.78	20.50	27.71	39.23	6.00	1.00	19.14	19.84	17.33	10.16	37.25	21.00	11.20	29.00	14.00
100s	3	1	5	–	2	–	1	2	–	–	1	–	–	–	2	–	–	–	–
50s	3	3	4	1	5	2	2	1	–	–	1	1	–	1	1	–	–	–	–

SOMERSET CCC

FIRST-CLASS MATCHES

BOWLING

	GD Rose	PD Trego	M Burns	ID Blackwell	AR Caddick	PS Jones	JO Grove	KA Parsons	Overs	Totals	Byes/Leg-byes	Wickets	Run outs	
v. Oxford Universities	7-1-12-1	12-2-28-1	7-3-5-0	14-8-18-4					68	144	10	10	1	A B C
(Taunton) 7-9 April	8-2-10-1	7-4-19-1	–	–					30.1	74	1	9	–	A B C
v. Surrey	7-1-29-0				16-2-71-3	10-2-41-5			45	185	0	10	–	A
(Taunton) 26-29 April	–								–					
v. Hampshire	16-7-50-2			22-12-26-1	24.5-7-62-5	19-6-47-2			91.5	232	13	10	–	A C
(Southampton) 3-5 May	9-5-8-1			16-5-29-1	23.1-5-64-7	–			57.1	126	7	10	–	C
v. Leicestershire	34-11-74-5			29-9-78-0			30.5-7-90-5	12-3-41-0	139.5	387	14	10	–	C D
(Leicester) 11-14 May	9-1-28-2			2-0-15-0			7-0-26-0	5.5-0-28-1	29.5	124	9	4	–	D
v. Derbyshire	10-1-28-0			2-0-6-0		8-1-21-0	6-0-45-0		26	101	1	0	–	
(Taunton) 24-27 May	–								–					
v. Kent	14-2-39-1			7-2-27-0	25-6-57-6	18.5-3-63-2	13-3-53-1	4-1-14-0	81.5	261	8	10	–	
(Bath) 6-9 June	0.2-0-2-0			20-7-33-2	25-12-40-4	23-4-74-3	7-0-35-0	–	89.2	223	8	10	1	C E
v. Surrey		22-4-79-2	20-3-70-0	26.3-3-99-2		37-11-103-4	24-3-113-1	7-2-23-0	154.3	548	13	10	–	C E
(Oval) 14-16 June		–	–	–		–	–	–	–					
v. Kent		19-7-58-2	17-9-20-2	22-5-54-1		26-3-74-3		12-4-34-0	106.4	261	5	10	1	C D
(Maidstone) 28 June-1 July		16-2-69-2	11-3-32-1	23-5-77-0		14-3-22-0		16-6-36-0	114	338	4	3	–	C D F
v. Hampshire	17.1-3-47-4	9-0-42-2	–	–		15-3-45-4			41.1	142	8	10	–	
(Taunton) 7-10 July	21-8-61-0	9-1-56-0	11-2-25-2	17-5-35-0		22-3-92-3		15-4-38-0	95	319	12	5	–	
v. Lancashire	14-3-47-1	11-3-39-2	8-2-36-0	6-1-21-0		19-3-77-2	7.5-2-13-5		65.5	239	6	10	–	
(Taunton) 12-15 July	17-3-64-1	23-4-86-1	5-1-11-3	53-19-105-1		35-9-111-2	7-2-30-1		140	417	10	9	–	
v. Yorkshire	27-3-90-2	26.1-6-84-4	20-5-75-2	15-7-29-1		24-5-67-1		18-5-42-0	130.1	400	13	10	–	
(Scarborough) 19-21 July	–	–	–	–		–		–	–					
v. Durham	24-7-50-2			5-4-1-0		24-8-60-1	16-3-58-4	15-7-21-1	105	292	12	10	–	B C
(Chester-le-Street) 28-31 July	9-1-21-2			–		7-1-16-0	3-0-11-0	–	24.2	73	2	3	–	B
v. Yorkshire	16-2-47-2	11-1-43-1		32-7-77-2		18.4-6-56-2	15-1-54-0	4-0-29-2	98.4	327	8	9	–	E
(Taunton) 2-5 August	–	–		–		–	–	–	–					
v. Durham	22-8-58-1		9-1-29-0	21-7-50-1		27.1-4-112-1	19-4-53-3	8-1-25-0	127.1	378	10	10	1	D
(Taunton) 16-19 August														
v. West Indians			–	23-3-60-2			17.2-0-64-3	11-3-45-1	90.2	290	8	9	–	D G H
(Taunton) 23-26 August			6-1-28-1	10-3-20-1			17-3-59-3	–	55	169	1	9	–	G H
v. Leicestershire	25-4-69-1		7.2-0-28-1	21-4-78-1		28-5-116-2	18-3-72-1		122.2	470	10	10	–	G
(Taunton) 1-4 September	–		–	–		–	–		–					
v. Lancashire	26-6-74-0		11-3-28-2	25-7-72-3		28-8-97-3		8-1-24-0	127.2	463	16	9	–	D G
(Old Trafford) 8-10 September	–		–	–		–		–	–					

	GD Rose	PD Trego	M Burns	ID Blackwell	AR Caddick	PS Jones	JO Grove	KA Parsons
Overs	332.3	165.1	132.2	411.3	114	403.4	193.1	150.4
Maidens	79	34	33	123	32	88	27	41
Runs	908	603	387	1010	294	1294	733	443
Wickets	29	18	14	23	25	40	21	11
Bowler's average	31.31	33.50	27.64	43.91	11.76	32.35	34.90	40.27

A MPL Bulbeck 13-3-31-2, 8-2-23-3; 12-3-44-2; 4-1-11-0.
B PW Jarvis 7-2-17-0, 7.1-2-21-4; 18-1-80-2, 5.2-2-23-1.
C ME Trescothick 8-3-23-1; 6-1-23-0, 9-4-18-1; 8-0-50-0; 7-2-17-0; 13-1-40-1; 1-0-7-0, 6-2-17-0; 3-0-10-0.
D ARK Pierson 26-8-40-0, 6-0-18-1; 9.4-4-9-1, 26-2-77-0; 21-8-41-3; 14.2-3-59-1; 18-10-45-1, 8-2-24-0.
E J Cox 7-2-14-0; 5-1-8-0; 2-0-13-0.
F PCL Holloway 2-0-4-0.
G JID Kerr 23-3-97-4; 15-1-93-0; 13-3-40-1, 11-6-18-4.
H J Tucker 8-3-28-1, 3-0-19-0.

FIELDING

39	RJ Turner
17	KA Parsons
9	PCL Holloway
8	PD Bowler, ME Trescothick
6	ID Blackwell, J Cox
4	PS Jones, FIN Lathwell, GD Rose
3	M Burns, ARK Pierson, PD Trego
2	PW Jarvis
1	AR Caddick, J Tucker

SURREY CCC

FIRST-CLASS MATCHES
BATTING

Opponent / Venue	MA Butcher	IJ Ward	GP Thorpe	AJ Stewart	AD Brown	AJ Hollioake	BC Hollioake	MP Bicknell	IDK Salisbury	AJ Tudor	IE Bishop	JN Batty	RM Amin	CG Greenidge	JD Ratcliffe	Saqlain Mushtaq	N Shahid	GP Butcher	Extras	Total	Wickets	Result	Points
v. Somerset	4	1	0	16	47	59	20	18	2	16*	0								2	185	10	D	6
(Taunton) 26–29 April	–	–	–	–	–	–	–	–	–	–	–	–	–	–	–	–	–	–	–	–			
v. Durham	15	12	18		9	7	2	1	11*	5	12	0							12	104	10	L	3
(Chester-le-Street) 2–4 May	24	17	1		4	0	0	7	0	17*	2	7							6	85	10		
v. Kent	47	38	11	36	60	51	6	73	50	7*			3						35	417	10	D	8
(Oval) 11–14 May	17*	0*											–						0	17	0		
v. Kent	32	158*	3		28	17	29	27	5	33*		10	–						6	348	6	D	7
(Canterbury) 23–25 May	–	–	–	–	–	–	–	–	–	–	–	–	–	–	–	–	–	–	–	–			
v. Hampshire	32	5	58		24	37		59	1	64*		16			0	21			16	333	10	W	18
(Oval) 2–4 June	2	0	13		7	41		14	8*	0		9			26	10			12	142	10		
v. Derbyshire	3	41	0	14	12	16		7	4	16					0	8*			17	138	10	L	3
(Derby) 7–9 June	6	10	8	42	75	21		4	20*	7					2	12			11	218	10		
v. Somerset	82	0	115		0	39		34	23	27		100*				11	77		40	548	10	W	20
(Oval) 14–16 June	–	–	–	–	–	–	–	–	–	–	–	–	–	–	–	–	–	–	–	–			
v. Hampshire	34	15	44		71	47	1	56*	7	5		26				0			25	331	10	W	18
(Southampton) 29 June–2 July	116*	42	9		0	24	10					1*				17			9	228	9		
v. Leicestershire	0	6			295*	4	2	5	12	22		19				66	37		37	505	10	W	20
(Oakham School) 7–9 July	–	–	–	–	–	–	–	–	–	–	–	–	–	–	–	–	–	–	–	–			
v. Yorkshire	5	28			7	48	8	45	29*			1		3		1	36		15	226	10	W	16
(Oval) 12–15 July	0	39			140*	1	13	40	12			1					80		19	345	8		
v. Leicestershire	0				34	18	21	0	10*			3		6		1	47		41	288	10	W	17
(Guildford) 19–21 July	47*	61*																	11	119	0		
v. Lancashire	4	6			54	80	24	28	35	35		12				4*	1		27	310	10	W	18
(Oval) 2–5 August	95	20			19*	18	2*									62			11	227	4		
v. Derbyshire	78	57			15	42		3	24	0*		0				0	17	7	17	260	10	W	17
(Oval) 16–17 August	–	–	–	–	–	–	–	–	–	–	–	–	–	–	–	–	–	–	–	–			
v. Yorkshire	8	59			2	37	4		57*	24		47				12	29	27	50	356	10	D	11
(Scarborough) 30 August–1 September	49*	0			4*	13											13	–	10	89	3		
v. Durham	191	144			5*	20											33	10*	50	453	4	W	20
(Oval) 6–9 September	–	–	–	–	–	–	–	–	–	–	–	–	–	–	–	–	–	–	–	–			
v. Lancashire	0	28			23	49		79*	3	5		24				54	2	66	26	359	10	D	11
(Old Trafford) 13–16 September	–	–	–	–	–	–	–	–	–	–	–	–	–	–	–	–	–	–	–	–			

	MA Butcher	IJ Ward	GP Thorpe	AJ Stewart	AD Brown	AJ Hollioake	BC Hollioake	MP Bicknell	IDK Salisbury	AJ Tudor	IE Bishop	JN Batty	RM Amin	CG Greenidge	JD Ratcliffe	Saqlain Mushtaq	N Shahid	GP Butcher
Matches	16	16	8	3	16	16	10	15	16	14	2	13	1	3	2	12	9	4
Innings	25	25	12	4	23	23	14	18	19	16	3	16	1	2	4	14	12	4
Not Out	4	3	0	0	5	0	1	2	6	6	0	2	0	0	0	2	0	1
Runs	891	894	280	108	935	689	142	500	313	283	14	276	3	9	28	217	434	110
Highest score	191	158*	115	42	295*	80	29	79*	57*	64*	12	100*	3	6	26	66	80	66
Average	42.42	40.63	23.33	27.00	51.94	29.95	10.92	31.25	24.07	25.72	4.66	19.71	3.00	4.50	7.00	18.08	36.16	36.66
100s	2	3	1	–	2	–	–	–	–	–	–	1	–	–	–	–	–	–
50s	3	3	1	–	4	3	–	4	2	1	–	–	–	–	–	2	3	1

SURREY CCC

FIRST-CLASS MATCHES
BOWLING

	MP Bicknell	AJ Tudor	BC Hollioake	IDK Salisbury	Saqlain Mushtaq	Overs	Totals	Byes/Leg-byes	Wickets	Run outs
v. Somerset	19–5–48–2	21–5–81–1	15–3–66–0	24–6–56–3		95.2	302	4	8	–
(Taunton) 26–29 April	–	–	–	–		–	–	–	–	–
v. Durham	20–5–52–3	17–5–39–2	13.4–3–41–4	12–2–39–0		75.4	234	9	10	–
(Chester-le-Street) 2–4 May	27–6–85–5	19–4–45–3	13.1–6–27–2	–		65.1	186	8	10	–
v. Kent	9–3–19–1	8–4–18–0	6–2–14–0	10–3–33–1		45	115	0	2	–
(Oval) 11–14 May	25–7–53–3	18.5–2–67–3	2–0–9–0	35–10–81–2		92.5	255	5	8	–
v. Hampshire	29–12–52–4	16–5–52–3		13–4–33–0	34–10–65–3	92	210	8	10	–
(Oval) 2–4 June	26–8–60–1	19.3–8–57–5		16–7–31–1	44–15–89–3	105.3	263	26	10	–
v. Derbyshire	19.1–1–75–4	17–3–64–5			3–0–13–0	50.1	191	5	10	–
(Derby) 7–9 June	18.5–5–52–1	11–0–59–1			13–5–24–1	44.5	167	7	3	–
v. Somerset	10–3–24–0	6–3–25–0		17–6–31–4	25.2–11–47–6	63.2	145	10	10	–
(Oval) 14–16 June	7–2–21–0	7–3–25–1		30.4–9–60–8	30–7–75–1	75.4	190	6	10	–
v. Hampshire	10–2–25–2	9–1–26–0	3–0–24–0	19.3–7–40–2	22–4–51–6	63.3	167	1	10	–
(Southampton) 29 June–2 July	10–2–27–1	14–1–46–0	–	32–4–84–4	23.2–1–84–4	80.2	272	30	10	1
v. Leicestershire	11–3–41–3	16–4–34–3		18–8–29–1	17.2–8–25–2	57.2	143	14	10	1
(Oakham School) 7–9 July	15–4–44–3	–	15–4–48–2	14–4–41–0	15–4–35–5	60	184	8	10	–
v. Yorkshire	24.1–8–40–1		2–1–1–0	24.3–2–105–3	30–8–63–6	86.4	242	15	10	–
(Oval) 12–15 July	8–4–17–2		2–0–4–0	15–4–36–3	17.4–5–41–5	48.4	126	10	10	–
v. Leicestershire	28.1–5–72–7		19–5–74–0	6–1–9–0	39–9–93–2	108.1	318	27	10	–
(Guildford) 19–21 July	12.5–3–47–9			–	1–0–2–0	24.5	87	3	10	–
v. Lancashire	10–3–20–1	15.1–6–48–7	4–0–17–0	–	10–4–28–2	39.1	120	7	10	–
(Oval) 2–5 August	11–4–12–0	11–2–42–2	–	14–4–46–5	20–8–45–3	56	145	0	10	–
v. Derbyshire	19–7–36–3	15–4–34–1		–	7–2–12–1	53.3	118	8	10	–
(Oval) 16–17 August	7–2–16–0			8–1–25–3	9.3–5–11–7	33.3	97	5	10	–
v. Yorkshire		17–1–75–4	19–1–67–3	–	1.1–1–0–2	41.1	158	3	10	1
(Scarborough) 30 August–1 September		6–1–13–0	4–0–15–0	6–2–13–0	8–1–18–0	25	68	7	0	–
v. Durham	7–3–20–1	6–1–14–0		34.3–8–105–7	35–8–91–2	82.3	241	11	10	–
(Oval) 6–9 September	11–5–23–1	11–2–41–3		20.3–8–49–4	12–3–23–1	54.3	144	8	10	1
v. Lancashire	14–2–49–1	19–2–98–2		10.5–1–38–1	34–8–81–4	87.5	324	26	10	1
(Old Trafford) 13–16 September	6–1–22–1	5–1–41–1		–	–	85	304	21	9	–

	MP Bicknell	AJ Tudor	BC Hollioake	IDK Salisbury	Saqlain Mushtaq
Overs	413.2	304.3	117.5	380.3	451.2
Maidens	115	71	25	101	127
Runs	1052	1071	407	984	1016
Wickets	60	47	11	52	66
Bowler's average	17.53	22.78	37.00	18.92	15.39

NB: Surrey did not bowl v Kent (23–26 May)

A IE Bishop 12–5–24–1; 13–1–54–1, 4–2–20–0.
B AJ Hollioake 4.2–1–23–1; 2–1–1–0; 3–2–4–0; 4–1–13–0; 5–2–8–0; 4–2–8–1; 5–2–10–0; 6–0–21–1, 9–1–31–0.
C RM Amin 9–2–27–0, 12–2–40–0.
D JD Ratcliffe 7–2–21–1, 2.5–0–25–0.
E AD Brown 1–0–3–0; 1–0–1–0; 1–0–8–0; 1–0–2–0; 24–9–56–1.
F CG Greenidge 6–3–18–0, 6–2–18–0; 12–2–35–0, 11–6–35–1.
G GP Butcher 7.3–3–18–5, 4–0–13–0; 4–1–13–0; 4–0–11–0, 2–0–10–0.
H N Shahid 1–0–6–0.
I JN Batty 6–0–21–1.
J MA Butcher 27–7–86–5.
K IJ Ward 5–2–10–0.

FIELDING

36 – JN Batty (29ct/7st)
27 – AJ Hollioake
16 – AD Brown
13 – MA Butcher, N Shahid
8 – BC Hollioake, Saqlain Mushtaq, AJ Stewart
6 – IDK Salisbury, GP Thorpe
5 – MP Bicknell, AJ Tudor
4 – IJ Ward
2 – JD Ratcliffe
1 – RM Amin

SUSSEX CCC

FIRST-CLASS MATCHES
BATTING

	RR Montgomerie	MTE Peirce	MG Bevan	CJ Adams	PA Cottey	WJ House	RSC Martin-Jenkins	NJ Wilton	JD Lewry	RJ Kirtley	MA Robinson	S Humphries	AD Patterson	UBA Rashid	JJ Bates	BV Taylor	WG Khan	JR Carpenter	MH Yardy	Extras	Total	Wickets	Result	Points
v. Gloucestershire	0	2	46	16	21	0*	4*	–	–	–	–									21	110	5	D	4
(Bristol) 26–29 April	–																			–				
v. Warickshire	6	10	30	42	9	31		2	2	0*	4									18	224	10	L	3
(Hove) 11–14 May	51	8	36	23	26	35	0		39	14	7*	18								20	277	10		
v. Worcestershire	25	21	41	36	0		29		0	12	0*		5	37						52	258	10	L	4
(Hove) 18–21 May	24	2	26	8	21		6		18	0	1*		0	14						28	148	10		
v. Essex	5	86	10	0	154		17		7*	–	–		0	61*						34	374	7	D	11
(Chelmsford) 23–26 May	–								–				–							–				
v. Gloucestershire	71	60	107	90	7		25		7	2	8*		8	51*						27	463	9	W	20
(Hove) 31 May–3 June	1*	6*	–	–			–		–	–	–		–							0	7	–		
v. Middlesex	12	2	72	35	36		35		0	17*			8	51*	1					31	300	9	D	10
(Horsham) 7–10 June	–																			–				
v. Worcestershire	37	42	0	55	76				9	7	0*		4	15		2				30	277	10	W	17
(Worcester) 15–16 June	5	2	23*	32*	–				–	–	–		–			–				2	64	2		
v. New Zealand 'A'	41	34			15	14		0			14*		6	12		38	0		25	30	229	10	L	–
(Hove) 28 June–1 July	89	11			7	20		0*			5		19	9		20	8		0	17	205	10		
v. Warwickshire	7	41	13	38	36		4		7	2			1	3	0*					6	158	10	D	7
(Edgbaston) 7–10 July	–																			–				
v. Essex	14	0	0	11	83		86		12	0	1*		3	35						20	265	10	D	9
(Arundel) 12–15 July	18	13	151*	53	0		37		5	1*	–		8	16						19	321	8		
v. Nottinghamshire	133	18	166	55	17	24		6	7	0			0		1*					45	472	10	D	12
(Hove) 19–22 July	95	0	174	1*	–				–	–			–		–					8	278	3		
v. Middlesex	30	22	30	0	42		44	2*	1	21			6	15						30	243	10	W	16
(Southgate) 28–31 July	7	25	173*	20	–		–	–	26*	–										19	270	3		
v. Northamptonshire	10	21		11	22		27	2	7	0*			27	17		74				14	232	10	L	3
(Northampton) 9–11 August	10	14		16	112		0	2	2*	2			33	0		10				10	211	10		
v. Northamptonshire	7	6		84	17		5	14	4	0	0*		1			1				14	153	10	L	3
(Eastbourne) 16–18 August	1	0		24*	1		5	19	0	0			4			0				11	65	10		
v. Glamorgan	23			156	2	0	8	15	1*	4	0		110						4	19	342	10	L	3
(Colwyn Bay) 22–25 August	6			68	2	13		32*	4	12	2		54						9	37	316	10		
v. Nottinghamshire	129		26	9	3		14	46	8	5			25		0*				0	22	287	10	D	9
(Trent Bridge) 30 August–2 September	2*	–	–	–	–		–	–	–	–			–		–				0*	2	4	–		
v. Gloucestershire	30			1	11	9	5	12	8	19			17		0*				14	12	138	10	L	3
(Hove) 7–8 September	10			1	9	0	6	0	1*	0			0		6				12	26	71	10		

	RR Montgomerie	MTE Peirce	MG Bevan	CJ Adams	PA Cottey	WJ House	RSC Martin-Jenkins	NJ Wilton	JD Lewry	RJ Kirtley	MA Robinson	S Humphries	AD Patterson	UBA Rashid	JJ Bates	BV Taylor	WG Khan	JR Carpenter	MH Yardy
Matches	17	14	12	16	16	6	15	8	17	16	9	2	7	15	4	5	3	1	4
Innings	30	24	18	26	23	10	23	11	24	22	11	4	9	22	6	6	6	2	8
Not Out	2	1	3	3	0	1	1	2	5	4	8	1	0	3	4	0	4	0	1
Runs	899	446	1124	913	740	112	499	150	149	146	19	41	37	585	54	9	143	8	64
Highest score	133	86	174	156	154	35	86	46	39	26*	8*	18	8	110	17	6	74	8	25
Average	32.10	19.39	74.93	39.69	32.17	12.44	22.68	16.66	7.84	8.11	6.33	13.66	4.11	30.78	9.00	4.50	23.83	4.00	9.14
100s	2	–	5	1	2	–	–	–	–	–	–	–	–	1	–	–	–	–	–
50s	4	2	1	7	2	–	2	–	–	–	–	–	–	4	–	1	–	–	–

SUSSEX CCC

FIRST-CLASS MATCHES
BOWLING

	JD Lewry	RJ Kirtley	MA Robinson	RSC Martin-Jenkins	MG Bevan	UBA Rashid	JJ Bates	BV Taylor	Overs	Totals	Byes/Leg-byes	Wickets	Run outs	
v. Warwickshire	38–9–123–0	30–9–101–2	35–14–88–3	36–5–133–1	3–0–17–0				160	548	26	7	–	ABC
(Hove) 11–14 May	–								–					
v. Worcestershire	23–5–77–1	19.5–4–79–3	19–4–52–2	11–0–34–0		21–6–56–2			93.5	311	13	8	–	
(Hove) 18–21 May	6–0–27–0	5.1–1–19–0	6–1–18–2	7–1–26–1		–			24.1	96	6	3	–	
v. Essex	20–2–82–1	23–6–69–3	17–6–39–2	12–4–38–3		7–2–21–1			79	255	6	10	–	
(Chelmsford) 23–26 May	3.2–0–11–0	3–0–6–0				–			6.2	22	5	0	–	
v. Glamorgan	14–3–40–4	17–4–48–3	13–7–7–0	14–6–28–3	3–0–12–0	17–5–36–0			78	185	14	10	–	
(Hove) 31 May–3 June	13–1–46–0	21.2–8–52–1	23–9–44–1	31–7–94–5	3–1–5–0	16–7–28–2			108.2	284	15	10	1	D
v. Middlesex	29.4–7–84–3	30–8–75–0		24–6–66–4	15–2–54–1	6–2–19–1	17–3–51–0		122.4	370	19	10	1	A
(Horsham) 7–10 June	15–4–43–2	4–1–21–0		7–1–25–1	8–1–19–2	31–5–132–1	27–4–85–2		92	327	12	6	–	
v. Worcestershire	11.4–3–71–3	18–1–60–3	17–6–36–2			1–0–8–0		18–5–44–2	65.4	230	11	10	–	
(Worcester) 15–16 June	15.4–7–29–5	6–1–21–1	6–1–22–1			–		14–5–27–3	41.4	110	11	10	–	
v. New Zealand 'A'	30–15–62–2			25–4–67–1		46–11–102–0	47–21–120–2		191	491	22	5	–	CEF
(Hove) 28 June–1 July	–			–					–					
v. Warwickshire	24–9–66–6	21–5–57–3		11–2–40–0	1–1–0–0	13–3–35–1		12–3–37–0	84	252	9	10	–	A
(Edgbaston) 7–10 July	16–3–64–1	12–4–31–0		11.1–1–46–0	–	4–1–16–0		–	43.1	165	8	2	1	
v. Essex	22–11–35–1	29–7–85–6	25–9–37–0	21–4–56–3	2–0–7–0	8–1–19–0			107	277	38	10	–	
(Arundel) 12–15 July	8–3–18–0	14.4–3–38–1	10–6–13–0	17–4–75–3	–	6–0–28–0			72.4	254	8	7	–	
v. Nottinghamshire	28–7–57–2	29–10–90–6			24–3–65–1	17–5–45–0		16–5–42–0	119	344	24	10	1	AC
(Hove) 19–22 July	26.5–7–64–2	29–5–89–2			10–1–44–0	23–3–93–4		14–2–69–0	102.5	379	20	8	–	
v. Middlesex	13–1–59–1	15.5–5–50–5		16–2–55–3	5–0–23–0	3–1–7–0			57.5	227	16	10	–	A
(Southgate) 28–31 July	23.1–6–45–2	29–10–65–4		2–0–14–0	7–0–33–0	35–8–80–4	7–1–28–0		104.1	283	12	10	–	A
v. Northamptonshire	17–3–50–0	31–8–94–3		23–6–64–0		43.5–13–103–5	28–6–90–1		154.5	460	18	10	1	AF
(Northampton) 9–11 August	–			–					–					
v. Northamptonshire	15–6–38–3	15.2–4–41–6	7–3–12–1	8–5–17–0					45.2	110	2	10	–	
(Eastbourne) 16–18 August	19.4–4–57–4	17–8–52–2	20–7–58–2	20–3–55–1		9–2–24–1			85.4	270	24	10	–	
v. Glamorgan	29–3–131–0	40–5–169–2	30–4–111–0	22–2–117–0		24–3–111–0			162	718	25	3	–	ACE
(Colwyn Bay) 22–25 August	–			–					–					
v. Nottinghamshire	34.4–12–89–6	31–11–71–3		16–4–59–0	3–0–18–0	11–6–26–1		17–4–79–0	112.4	351	9	10	–	
(Trent Bridge) 30 August–2 September	13–2–50–1	11–2–23–0		7–0–42–1	2.4–0–29–0	2–0–5–0		9–1–45–1	50.4	238	5	4	–	A
v. Gloucestershire		16–4–51–3	19.3–8–53–4	19–8–51–3				18–3–62–0	72.3	227	10	10	–	
(Hove) 7–8 September		–		–					–					

	JD Lewry	RJ Kirtley	MA Robinson	RSC Martin-Jenkins	MG Bevan	UBA Rashid	JJ Bates	BV Taylor
Overs	524.4	521.4	228	360.1	103.4	343.5	126	118
Maidens	137	138	77	75	11	84	35	28
Runs	1569	1559	537	1202	400	994	374	405
Wickets	53	63	16	33	5	23	5	6
Bowler's average	**29.60**	**24.74**	**33.56**	**36.42**	**80.00**	**43.21**	**74.80**	**67.50**

Sussex did not bowl v. Gloucestershire (26–29 April)

A CJ Adams 4–1–16–0; 1–0–2–0; 2–0–8–0; 1–1–0–0; 5–1–17–1; 1–0–6–0; 5–0–19–0; 2–0–3–0; 6–0–39–1.
B MTE Peirce 11–3–17–1.
C WJ House 3–1–7–0; 16–5–42–0; 4–1–21–0; 10–0–34–1.
D PA Cottey 1–1–0–0.
E MH Yardy 24–7–67–0; 5–0–17–0.
F WG Khan 3–0–9–0; 7–0–22–0.

FIELDING

19 –	NJ Wilton
17 –	RR Montgomerie
15 –	CJ Adams, AD Patterson
8 –	PA Cottey
6 –	UBA Rashid
5 –	JJ Bates, RJ Kirtley, JD Lewry, S Humphries (4ct/lst)
4 –	RSC Martin-Jenkins
3 –	WJ House, MTE Peirce, MA Robinson
2 –	MG Bevan

WARWICKSHIRE CCC

FIRST–CLASS MATCHES
BATTING

Match	NV Knight	MJ Powell	DP Ostler	DL Hemp	TL Penney	NMK Smith	DR Brown	AF Giles	T Frost	AA Donald	ESH Giddins	G Welch	KJ Piper	A Richardson	MA Wagh	DA Altree	MA Sheikh	A Singh	CE Dagnall	Extras	Total	Wickets	Result	Points
v. Oxford Universities	2	40	75	96	100*	28	4*	–												11	356	5	D	–
(Oxford) 26–28 April	–																							
v. Glamorgan	233	73	24	32	85	31	–	4*			–	35*	–	–						34	551	6	D	12
(Edgbaston) 3–6 May	–																							
v. Sussex	38	19	13	90	7	0	203	128*				–								50	548	7	W	20
(Hove) 11–14 May	–																							
v. Essex	–	30	144	16	39	68*	42	7				0	12*	–	7					35	400	8	D	10
(Edgbaston) 17–20 May	–																							
v. Glamorgan	80	73	26	0	39*	0	54*	–												8	280	5	D	6
(Cardiff) 23–26 May	–																							
v. Nottinghamshire	–	0	28	4	37	1	11	10				0	0	9*	–	4				6	110	10	D	4
(Edgbaston) 2–5 June	7	93	38	43	0	51*	5					16	8	0*	–					44	305	8			
v. Northamptonshire	–	145	145	14	2	7	5	44				55	0	17*	–		58*			76	568	9	W	20
(Northampton) 14–17 June	–																							
v. Gloucestershire	96	10	18	–	58*	11	19			0		10	4	0	1					6	233	10	D	8
(Edgbaston) 28 June–1 July	6	11	36*												52*					3	108	2			
v. Sussex	4	13	5	4	87	1	98			9	0	13*			1					17	252	10	D	9
(Edgbaston) 7–10 July	70*	66*											13	2						14	165	2			
v. Gloucestershire	25	28	58	11	9	0	37			2	1*	12	59							18	260	10	D	9
(Cheltenham) 19–23 July	28	54	35	42	19	25	6			1*	0		69	18						19	316	10			
v. Northamptonshire	12	9	88	26	32	28	5	17		5		1	0*							13	236	10	L	4
(Edgbaston) 28–30 July	43	0	13	3	2	67	8	2		18		24	12*							12	204	10			
v. Nottinghamshire	29	11	41	70	6	0	37	37		10*	14		28							41	324	10	D	10
(Trent Bridge) 3–6 August	37	5	9	8	38*	–	19*													16	132	4			
v. Middlesex	8	29	78*	–	36*										40		13			7	211	4	D	7
(Edgbaston) 17–20 August	55	5	44	–	15*	30*									20		11			11	191	5			
v. Worcestershire	75	–	4	3	10	13		0				18	2*	4			0			13	142	10	L	3
(Worcester) 21–23 August	0	–	9	51	11	27		0				10	3*	25			79			16	231	10			
v. Worcestershire	69	88	10	–	5	4		16				11*	–		130		46			28	407	8	D	12
(Edgbaston) 30 August–2 September	–																							
v. Middlesex	92	52	129	–	22	36		8				20	0	14			0	5*		38	416	10	D	10
(Lord's) 5–8 September	–	9*											17	–	74*		–			9	109	9			
v. Essex	106	32	11	28*	13	15						0	–	137			7	6*		45	400	8	L	6
(Chelmsford) 13–16 September	0*											8*			–		–			0	8	–			

	NV Knight	MJ Powell	DP Ostler	DL Hemp	TL Penney	NMK Smith	DR Brown	AF Giles	T Frost	AA Donald	ESH Giddins	G Welch	KJ Piper	A Richardson	MA Wagh	DA Altree	MA Sheikh	A Singh	CE Dagnall
Matches	6	17	16	17	13	17	16	13	1	8	9	7	16	13	9	1	1	5	2
Innings	8	26	24	24	18	20	22	14	–	9	6	8	18	9	16	1	1	7	2
Not Out	0	2	2	2	4	2	6	3		2	1	1	3	7	3	0	1	0	2
Runs	474	1046	1096	834	569	464	622	444		69	15	116	260	43	592	4	58	156	11
Highest score	233	145	145	129	100*	87	203	128*		18	14	55	69	17*	137	4	58*	79	6*
Average	59.25	43.58	49.81	37.90	40.64	25.77	38.87	40.36		9.85	3.00	16.57	17.33	21.50	45.53	4.00	–	22.28	–
100s	1	2	2	1	1	–	1	1		–	–	–	–	–	2	–	–	–	–
50s	1	8	7	5	2	4	2	1		–	–	1	1	–	3	–	1	1	–

WARWICKSHIRE CCC

FIRST–CLASS MATCHES
BOWLING

	AA Donald	ESH Giddins	A Richardson	AF Giles	NMK Smith	DR Brown	CE Dagnall	Overs	Totals	Byes/Leg-byes	Wickets	Run outs
v. Oxford Universities	4-4-0-2	3-0-10-1						7	10	0	3	–
(Oxford) 26-28 April								–				
v. Glamorgan		24-4-92-2	25-7-57-1	42-17-89-5	14-3-36-0			130	400	11	10	–
(Edgbaston) 3-6 May		17-7-30-1	16-5-28-2	39-14-72-2	15-6-32-1			94	194	9	6	–
v. Sussex		18-12-37-2	20-3-69-4	16-4-48-1	–	14-2-55-3		68.2	224	15	10	–
(Hove) 11-14 May		23.3-9-50-3	17-3-53-1	33-13-61-3	26-5-80-3	7-2-22-0		106.3	277	11	10	–
v. Essex			23-4-74-2	21-3-58-0	7-2-25-0	18-3-85-2		89	298	5	4	–
(Edgbaston) 17-20 May			–	–				–				
v. Nottinghamshire			24-7-68-0	39-10-89-0	13-1-45-0			130.1	406	24	0	–
(Edgbaston) 2-5 June			–					–				
v. Northamptonshire			20-5-63-2	29-16-45-4	14.5-6-42-3			83.5	266	20	10	–
(Northampton) 14-17 June			13-5-23-0	44-17-90-8	25-4-80-2			105	249	5	10	–
v. Gloucestershire	22-4-59-4		26.5-8-72-2	34-9-65-1	9-0-34-1	16-4-46-2		116.5	350	29	10	–
(Edgbaston) 28 June-1 July	7-1-16-0		17-5-39-2	20-4-68-3	–	7-0-28-0		73	232	5	7	–
v. Sussex	14-8-26-1	13-4-38-0		27-10-58-6	13.5-7-21-3	4-0-13-0		71.5	158	2	10	–
(Edgbaston) 7-10 July	–	–						–				
v. Gloucestershire	17-3-39-1	26-7-77-3		21-10-49-2	7-2-29-2	18.2-5-52-2		89.2	254	8	10	–
(Cheltenham) 19-23 July	19-11-22-1	10-4-24-0		45-14-74-4	12-2-38-0			108	237	15	5	–
v. Northamptonshire	16-1-50-2		19-7-39-0	32.3-6-118-6	19-3-57-1	13-0-50-0		99.3	318	4	10	1
(Edgbaston) 28-30 July	2-0-6-0		2-0-14-0	25.4-3-78-5	26-3-66-5	–		55.4	176	12	10	–
v. Nottinghamshire	31.3-7-100-3	32-10-90-1		21.3-5-43-1		26-5-87-5		113	368	35	10	–
(Trent Bridge) 3-6 August	27-6-60-2	28-9-70-4		8-4-8-0		16-3-74-2		79	232	20	8	–
v. Middlesex			30-9-99-4	29-4-87-1	15-0-63-1	21-5-65-1		111	380	10	8	–
(Edgbaston) 17-20 August			–	–				13.5	126	0	1	–
v. Worcestershire		30.2-10-75-4	32-8-81-3		3-2-5-0	23-5-78-1		113.2	338	12	10	1
(Worcester) 21-23 August		2-0-13-0	2.3-0-19-0					5.3	36	4	1	–
v. Worcestershire	23-9-69-4	11-2-46-0	15-3-47-2		23-6-51-3	16-4-45-1		89	263	5	10	–
(Edgbaston) 30 August-2 September	7-1-18-0		11-5-12-0		17-6-41-1	10-3-24-0		72	181	15	1	–
v. Middlesex	16-6-65-0		25-7-69-0		19-5-44-0	18.4-4-55-3	24-6-76-2	111.4	350	13	5	–
(Lord's) 5-8 September	–		–		–	–	–	–				
v. Essex			20-4-57-1		20-3-49-2	17-3-49-1	19-8-48-1	77	208	1	5	–
(Chelmsford) 13-16 September			10-1-57-1		5-0-21-0	11-1-51-1	11.4-2-57-2	38.4	202	12	4	–

	AA Donald	ESH Giddins	A Richardson	AF Giles	NMK Smith	DR Brown	CE Dagnall
Overs	205.3	237.5	368.2	526.4	310.4	268.2	54.4
Maidens	61	78	96	163	70	49	16
Runs	530	652	1040	1200	875	917	181
Wickets	20	21	27	52	28	24	5
Bowler's average	26.50	31.04	38.51	23.07	31.25	38.20	36.20

NB: Warwickshire did not bowl v. Glamorgan (23-26 May)

A G Welch 22-3-97-1, 5-1-22-0; 18-6-41-0; 29-8-94-0; 12-0-60-0, 8-2-19-0; 8-0-41-0, 14-5-47-0; 16-2-56-1; 24-5-87-1.
B MJ Powell 3-0-18-1, 2-1-1-0; 2-0-10-0; 5-3-9-0; 1-0-4-0; 2-0-14-0; 1-1-0-1; 8-1-24-0.
C DA Altree 20.1-1-77-0.
D MA Sheikh 8-1-36-1, 15-6-32-0.
E DL Hemp 8-1-29-2; 2-0-13-0, 5-1-17-0; 1-0-4-0.
F MA Wagh 3-1-10-0; 1-1-0-0; 1-1-0-0, 14-6-30-0; 5-0-11-0; 1-0-4-0.
G DP Ostler 5-0-46-1.
H A Singh 6.5-0-66-0.

FIELDING

31 – KJ Piper (28ct/3st)	
19 – DP Ostler	
11 – DR Brown	
10 – MJ Powell	
9 – DL Hemp	
8 – TL Penney, MJK Smith	
4 – AF Giles, NV Knight, MA Wagh	
3 – AA Donald, A Richardson	
1 – ESH Giddins, A Singh, G Welch	

WORCESTERSHIRE CCC

FIRST-CLASS MATCHES

BATTING

	EJ Wilson	PR Pollard	GA Hick	VS Solanki	KR Spiring	DA Leatherdale	SJ Rhodes	SR Lampitt	RK Illingworth	A Sheriyar	GD McGrath	RC Driver	Kadeer Ali	Kabir Ali	WPC Weston	DN Catterall	CG Liptrott	MJ Rawnsley	DJ Pipe	Extras	Total	Wickets	Result	Points
v. Glamorgan	16	0	76	1	26	42	30*	5	3*	–	–	–	–	–	–	–	–	–	–	7	206	7	D	5
(Worcester) 26–29 April	–	–	–	–	–	–	–	–	–	–	–	–	–	–	–	–	–	–	–					
v. Cambridge University	77	72	–	0	–	11	4	15*	–	–	–	34*	3	–	–	–	–	–	–	38	254	6	D	–
(Cambridge) 2–4 May	50*	20	–	25	11*	–	–	–	–	–	–	8*	–	–	–	–	–	–	–	16	130	2		
v. Middlesex	104*	0	4	30	–	2	9	0	4	0	1	–	–	8	–	–	–	–	–	20	182	10	W	15
(Worcester) 11–14 May	19	3	115*	–	–	0*	–	–	–	–	–	–	–	–	–	–	–	–	–	5	161	3		
v. Sussex	22	–	–	98	38	35	34*	7	1	–	15	32	–	–	–	–	–	–	–	29	311	8	W	18
(Hove) 18–21 May	47	–	–	33	4*	0*	–	–	–	–	–	4	–	–	–	–	–	–	–	8	96	3		
v. Gloucestershire	4	7	14	161*	28	65	16	0*	–	–	–	–	–	–	–	–	–	–	–	15	310	6	D	10
(Bristol) 23–26 May	–	–	–	–	–	–	–	–	–	–	–	–	–	–	–	–	–	–	–	–	–	–		
v. West Indians	5	0	–	51	–	–	4	26	14	–	–	47	–	12	5	25	0*	–	–	43	232	10	D	–
(Worcester) 2–4 June	–	–	–	–	–	–	–	–	–	–	–	–	–	–	–	–	–	–	–	–	–	–		
v. Nottinghamshire	23	–	122	27	–	117	16	6	15	15*	8	16	–	–	1	–	–	–	–	36	402	10	W	20
(Trent Bridge) 7–10 June	54	–	26	80	–	11	7	34*	44*	–	–	0	–	–	13	–	–	–	–	23	292	7		
v. Sussex	14	8	–	0	–	56	4	20	10	11*	0	64	–	24	–	–	–	–	–	19	230	10	L	4
(Worcester) 15–16 June	36	3	–	8	–	2	14	2	1	14	0	0	–	15*	–	–	–	–	–	15	110	10		
v. Glamorgan	18	–	–	40	–	59*	4	1	15	–	2	18	0	9	–	–	–	18	–	12	196	10	L	3
(Swansea) 28 June–1 July	7	–	–	8	–	50	37	43	44	–	0*	35	0	5	–	–	–	16	–	7	252	10		
v. Middlesex	0	12	–	–	–	20	33*	4	–	–	5	12	8	12	0	–	–	18	–	17	141	10	D	7
(Southgate) 7–10 July	11	22	–	–	–	12	16*	–	–	–	–	22*	0	–	0	–	–	–	–	12	95	5		
v. Nottinghamshire	102	53	–	–	–	18	0	5	–	–	4	0	2	8*	52	–	–	8	–	32	284	10	D	9
(Worcester) 12–15 July	34	74	–	–	–	4	103	20	–	–	55	30	0	50*	15	–	–	7	–	39	431	10		
v. Essex	12	77	–	2	–	62	13	4	–	–	1*	1	–	13	27	–	–	5	–	23	240	10	L	4
(Chelmsford) 19–21 July	6	10	–	53	–	7	13	10	–	–	1*	0	–	43	0	–	–	7	–	26	176	10		
v. Gloucestershire	1	23	17	0	–	5	15	20*	–	0	6	–	–	–	5	–	–	3	–	3	98	10	W	15
(Worcester) 28–30 July	11	20	10	41	–	56	52*	7	–	7	7	–	–	–	0	–	–	3	–	11	225	10		
v. Northamptonshire	3	32	15	32	–	132*	4	7	3	4	–	–	–	1	3	–	–	–	–	13	249	10	L	2
(Northampton) 4–7 August	2	9	46	0	–	1	4	56*	0	17	–	–	–	12	40	–	–	–	–	11	198	10		
v. Essex	5	123*	1	55	–	52	8	6	–	1	–	–	–	0	11	–	0	–	–	40	302	10	L	6
(Kidderminster) 9–12 August	1	69	75	56	–	36	0	0	–	0*	–	–	–	1	5	–	10	–	–	29	282	10		
v. Warwickshire	–	5	0	160	–	18	46	25*	–	0	–	–	–	–	0	–	1	3	54	26	338	10	W	18
(Worcester) 21–23 August	–	–	0*	–	–	–	–	–	–	–	–	–	–	–	11*	–	–	–	17	8	36	1		
v. Warwickshire	34	–	–	71	–	42	39*	2	–	–	7	2	–	–	23	–	0	4	30	9	263	10	D	8
(Edgbaston) 30 August–2 September	51	–	–	57*	–	–	–	–	–	–	–	–	–	–	58*	–	–	–	–	15	191	1		
v. Northamptonshire	10	10	–	0	–	46	42	5*	–	–	–	0	–	–	–	–	–	–	5	6	124	7	D	7
(Worcester) 13–16 September	0	0	–	30	–	3	24	1*	–	–	–	47*	–	–	–	–	–	–	1	13	119	6		
Matches	17	14	8	16	3	17	18	18	10	11	14	11	4	10	10	1	4	9	3					
Innings	31	24	14	28	4	30	28	27	12	11	15	20	7	15	19	1	3	13	5					
Not Out	2	1	2	2	1	5	6	8	2	3	3	4	0	3	2	0	1	0	0					
Runs	779	652	521	1138	96	975	591	331	154	69	112	372	13	213	269	25	1	102	107					
Highest score	104*	123*	122	161*	38	132*	103	56*	44*	17	55	64	8	50*	58*	25	1	18	54					
Average	26.86	28.34	43.41	43.76	32.00	39.00	26.86	17.42	15.40	8.62	9.33	23.25	1.85	17.75	15.82	25.00	–	7.84	21.40					
100s	2	1	2	2	–	2	1	–	–	–	–	–	–	–	–	–	–	–	–					
50s	4	5	2	8	–	7	1	1	–	1	1	–	1	2	–	–	–	–	1					

WORCESTERSHIRE CCC

FIRST-CLASS MATCHES

BOWLING

Match	GD McGrath	A Sheriyar	SR Lampitt	DA Leatherdale	RK Illingworth	VS Solanki	Kabir Ali	MJ Rawnsley	Overs	Totals	Byes/Leg-byes	Wickets	Run outs
v. Cambridge University (Cambridge) 2–4 May	11-7-10-4	14.2-5-22-1	11-4-21-0	9-2-18-1	3-0-11-0	7-1-22-2			55.2	109	5	8	-
	-	10-4-16-0	11-3-39-2	8-4-17-2	12-7-11-0	6-1-13-0			47	105	9	4	-
v. Middlesex (Worcester) 11–14 May	15-6-30-2	10-1-55-4	13-3-44-4				8-1-26-0		46	161	6	10	-
	17-6-36-3	16.2-2-45-2	10-4-27-1		16-5-34-3		7-2-18-0		72.2	181	8	10	-
v. Sussex (Hove) 18–21 May	23.5-5-54-5	18-1-101-1	12-1-50-3		2-0-5-0	-	8-1-36-1		63.5	258	12	10	-
	14-5-30-4	17-2-69-2	10.2-3-35-3		3-2-1-0	2-0-7-1	-		46.2	148	6	10	-
v. Gloucestershire (Bristol) 23–26 May	18.1-7-50-2	21-8-51-4	12-5-41-2	4-0-28-0	7-1-19-2				62.1	199	10	10	-
	-	-	-						-	-	-	-	-
v. West Indians (Worcester) 2–4 June			13-4-24-1		18-8-24-2	-	13-2-50-2		62.2	164	3	10	1
			16-6-39-3		31-12-55-2	7-0-33-1	26-5-100-1		98	301	2	9	-
v. Nottinghamshire (Trent Bridge) 7–10 June	28.1-8-86-8	19-5-77-0	21-3-69-2	3-0-10-0	20-4-53-0	1-1-0-0			96.1	313	4	10	-
	20.4-6-57-2	16-2-71-0	19-7-42-4	11-3-52-3	11-5-32-1	-			78.4	275	16	10	-
v. Sussex (Worcester) 15–16 June	21.2-11-39-3	14-2-65-1	13-3-43-1	1-0-12-0	13-4-46-0		16-2-66-3		78.2	277	6	10	2
	6.2-1-20-0	5-1-29-2	-				1-0-15-0		12.2	64	0	2	-
v. Glamorgan (Swansea) 28 June–1 July	20-3-72-3		12-4-31-1	9-2-23-2	18.5-6-23-1	1-0-1-0	14-4-21-0		87.5	218	8	10	1
	24.1-8-70-3		19-7-40-2	7-3-17-3	22-9-51-0	3-0-13-0	14-1-42-1	19-2-71-1	108.1	311	7	10	-
v. Middlesex (Southgate) 7–10 July	23.2-8-43-2		19-5-58-2	6-0-22-0			21-5-52-1	39-8-125-5	108.2	303	3	10	-
	-		-				-	-	-	-	-	-	-
v. Nottinghamshire (Worcester) 12–15 July	23.2-5-70-3		17-4-63-0	13-4-46-2			23-3-81-3	20-7-57-0	104.2	358	10	10	1
	-						4-0-19-0	3-1-3-0	7	24	2	0	-
v. Essex (Chelmsford) 19–21 July	18-7-40-5		7-2-16-0			3.3-0-7-1	7-2-29-1	18-7-35-2	53.3	131	4	9	-
	18.5-4-75-3		4-0-23-0	3-1-10-1		18-0-75-1	11-3-38-1	26-7-64-0	80.5	287	2	6	-
v. Gloucestershire (Worcester) 28–30 July	16-9-29-7	13-3-51-1	2.5-0-5-2					-	31.5	87	2	10	-
	15-3-40-3		15-6-27-3	8-0-39-1				4-2-6-0	56	184	3	10	-
v. Northamptonshire (Northampton) 4–7 August		21-5-83-0	25-6-63-5	11-1-33-0	45-9-118-2	29-6-80-3	12-3-50-0		170	519	20	10	1
v. Essex (Kidderminster) 9–12 August		28.2-3-110-4	23-7-60-1	10-1-40-0			20-2-114-4	28-8-91-1	116.2	462	16	10	-
		2-0-22-0	10-3-34-0	-			15-4-36-0	8-2-24-0	35.1	125	5	-	-
v. Warwickshire (Worcester) 21–23 August		18.2-6-52-2	12-6-23-1	9-3-16-1				-	54.2	142	7	10	-
		21-6-60-1	18.4-3-45-7	16-6-36-1			4-1-16-0		75.4	231	6	10	-
v. Warwickshire (Edgbaston) 30 August–2 September	42.4-11-90-6		34-5-117-1	7-0-27-0		5-0-19-0		19-5-48-0	129.4	407	12	8	-
	-		-	-					-	-	-	-	-
v. Northamptonshire (Worcester) 13–16 September	25-10-75-4		22-3-58-3	14-3-44-2				2-1-12-0	73.2	260	9	10	-
	13.5-2-41-8		11-1-36-2	5-1-18-0					36.5	125	4	10	-

	GD McGrath	A Sheriyar	SR Lampitt	DA Leatherdale	RK Illingworth	VS Solanki	Kabir Ali	MJ Rawnsley
Overs	415.4	278.2	412.5	154	221.5	82.3	219	204
Maidens	132	59	108	34	72	9	41	55
Runs	1057	1048	1173	508	483	270	811	573
Wickets	80	28	56	19	13	9	20	9
Bowler's average	13.21	37.42	20.94	26.73	37.15	30.00	40.55	63.66

NB: Worcestershire did not bowl v. Glamorgan (26–29 April)

A   GA Hick 6-0-13-1; 4-0-14-0, 1-0-5-0; 27-6-72-0; 7-0-31-0.
B   DN Catterall 14.2-2-50-4, 11-3-42-2.
C   CG Liptrot 4-0-13-0, 7-1-30-0; 15-2-44-6, 16-3-68-1; 22-5-94-0; 7-0-49-0, 7-0-26-0.
D   RC Driver 8-2-31-1; 3.2-0-13-1.
E   PR Pollard 0.1-0-4-0.

FIELDING

55	SJ Rhodes (54ct/1st)
23	VS Solanki
13	SR Lampitt
9	DA Leatherdale, EJ Wilson
8	GA Hick
5	RK Illingworth, Kabir Ali, CG Liptrott, MJ Rawnsley
3	GD McGrath, PR Pollard
2	RC Driver
1	DN Catterall, Kadeer Ali, WPC Weston

YORKSHIRE CCC

FIRST-CLASS MATCHES

BATTING

	D Byas	MP Vaughan	RJ Blakey	DS Lehmann	C White	MJ Wood	GM Fellows	GM Hamilton	D Gough	RJ Sidebottom	MJ Hoggard	VJ Craven	JD Middlebrook	RJ Harden	PM Hutchison	G Ramsden	MJ Lumb	SM Guy	CJ Elstub	CEW Silverwood	S Widdup	A McGrath	ID Fisher	Extras	Total	Wickets	Result	Points
v. Derbyshire	49	155*	13	95	17	100*	37	10*	–	–	–	–												32	508	5	W	20
(Headingley) 3–5 May	–	–	–	–	–	–	–	–																–	–			
v. Hampshire	8	–	19	85	11	9	1	125	23		20*	29	1	0										68	399	10	W	19
(Headingley) 12–14 May	–	–	–	–	–	–	–	–																–	–			
v. Derbyshire	49		0	133		9	15		11			58	45	0	0	0*								29	349	10	D	10
(Derby) 17–20 May	–		–	–		–	–					–			1									–	–			
v. Zimbabweans	1				32	14	12			1		21	0	0			2	29*						12	124	10	L	–
(Headingley) 24–27 May	1				0	22	15			10		3	7					66*	10					12	147	10		
v. Leicestershire	44		9	39	17*	19*	–	–				1	–								–			17	146	4	D	7
(Headingley) 31 May–3 June	–		–	–	–	–															–			–	–			
v. Durham	29	94	21	79	9	3	6	5		1*		22	0											25	294	10	W	17
(Chester-le-Street) 7–9 June	6	7	34*	20	12	7*	–	–																11	97	4		
v. Kent	14	9	22	28	0	13	18			1	0	18								23*				3	149	10	W	15
(Headingley) 14–16 June	10	0	4	29*	4	11*	–													–				5	63	4		
v. Lancashire	2	56	38	6					0			6			0*					1	26	4	3	22	164	10	L	3
(Old Trafford) 29 June–2 July	30	32	2	0					0			31			3*					18	9	0	5	21	151	10		
v. Durham	6	34	3	28	1		0		4	0		9								6	29*			9	129	10	D	7
(Headingley) 7–10 July	18	118	15	136		48*	17*																	34	386	4		
v. Surrey	9	80	10	55	4	24*			0	0		14								1	26			19	242	10	L	4
(Oval) 12–15 July	7	10	0	17	5	18			6*	2		11								18	22			10	126	10		
v. Somerset	84	30	24	77		22				4*	7			0						48	44	27		33	400	10	W	20
(Scarborough) 19–21 July	–	–	–	–		–														–	–	–		–	–			
v. West Indians	41*	2										53	2		0					4		1		8	126	10	L	–
(Headingley) 24–25 July	30	0										10	8		inj					2		13		8	94	9		
v. Lancashire	81	31	0	83	10		46					14								34	16	17		40	376	10	D	11
(Headingley) 28–31 July	–	–	–	–	–		–													–	–	–		–	–			
v. Somerset	2*			56		11	3			6		42						42		4	5	74	68*	14	327	9	D	10
(Taunton) 2–5 August	–			–		–	–					–						–		–	–	–	–	–	–			
v. Leicestershire				115	0	16		66				15						17	17	38	1	24		29	340	10	D	10
(Leicester) 16–19 August				–	–	–		–										–	–	–	–	–		–	–			
v. Surrey (Scarborough)	19			66		16	23		10*			2							0	3	0	0		18	158	10	D	7
30 August–1 September	–			–		–	–						17*						–	38*				13	68	–		
v. Kent	7	69		116		4	28			2										7	3	133	16	13	401	10	W	20
(Canterbury) 7–10 September	7	14		42		12	0			1										10	6	21	28	2	145	10		
v. Hampshire	26	30		46		28	3		0			22								21*	9	4	4	12	205	10	W	16
(Southampton) 13–15 September	16	16		92		17		61	6			5								0	1	17	19*	15	265	10		

	D Byas	MP Vaughan	RJ Blakey	DS Lehmann	C White	MJ Wood	GM Fellows	GM Hamilton	D Gough	RJ Sidebottom	MJ Hoggard	VJ Craven	JD Middlebrook	RJ Harden	PM Hutchison	G Ramsden	MJ Lumb	SM Guy	CJ Elstub	CEW Silverwood	S Widdup	A McGrath	ID Fisher
Matches	17	9	12	16	3	11	14	13	3	6	15	8	11	2	7	1	1	6	4	9	9	10	6
Innings	26	15	18	23	3	17	20	16	2	7	17	11	15	3	8	1	2	9	4	11	14	14	10
Not Out	2	1	1	1	0	3	4	2	0	2	3	1	0	0	2	1	1	2	3	1	1	1	2
Runs	596	697	264	1477	38	256	341	402	28	15	91	251	201	1	3	0	68	136	6	173	201	375	181
Highest score	84	155*	56	136	17	100*	46	125	23	6*	20*	58	45	1	3*	0*	68	42	4*	48	44	133	68*
Average	24.83	49.78	15.52	67.13	12.66	18.28	21.31	28.71	14.00	3.00	6.50	25.10	13.40	0.33	0.50	–	68.00	19.42	6.00	17.30	15.46	28.84	22.62
100s	–	2	–	4	–	1	–	1	–	–	–	–	–	–	–	–	–	–	–	–	–	1	–
50s	2	3	1	9	–	–	–	2	–	–	–	2	–	–	–	–	1	–	–	–	–	1	1

A   SA Richardson 3 & 11
B   JW Inglis 2 & 2
C   LC Weekes 10 & 10
D   GA Lambert 1; 3* & 2*

YORKSHIRE CCC

FIRST-CLASS MATCHES
BOWLING

	D Gough	MJ Hoggard	RJ Sidebottom	GM Hamilton	C White	JD Middlebrook	PM Hutchison	CEW Silverwood	ID Fisher	Overs	Totals	Byes/Leg-byes	Wickets	Run outs	
v. Derbyshire	14-1-68-0	16-4-36-3	9-0-44-2	13-2-42-2	15-5-20-2					75	239	8	10	–	ABC
(Headingley) 3–5 May	17-4-34-3	15.5-8-25-1	6-2-22-0	12.1-1-41-2	11-2-47-3					67	190	2	9	–	
v. Hampshire	14.3-6-23-4			12-5-20-1	9-3-12-3	9-3-17-2				52.3	101	7	10	–	
(Headingley) 12–14 May	15-4-29-2	13-2-47-1		10.5-1-43-3	14-3-30-2	8-1-37-2				61.5	198	12	10	–	C
v. Derbyshire		23-4-72-1		18.1-5-42-2		23-4-61-0	18-1-74-3			100.1	303	5	9	–	CD
(Derby) 17–20 May		6-0-35-0		5-1-24-0		12-3-35-1	7-0-37-0			40	209	12	1	–	CD
v. Zimbabweans		21-9-40-1		20.1-11-24-2		29-5-89-4	15-5-38-1			98.1	235	20	10	1	A
(Headingley) 24–27 May		11-1-18-3		7.3-1-22-5		–	7-4-8-1			30.3	68	2	10	–	A
v. Leicestershire		21-6-55-1		21-6-80-2		22-9-39-3	15.5-3-62-3			101.5	296	9	10	–	CE
(Headingley) 31 May–3 June		–		–		–				–	–	–	–	–	
v. Durham	14-2-28-1	21.5-5-67-5		14-2-33-2		11-0-33-1	13-6-19-1			73.5	189	9	10	–	
(Chester-le-Street) 7–9 June	26.2-5-63-6	20-7-37-0		12-4-33-2		16-4-32-1	7-3-20-1			81.2	201	16	10	–	
v. Kent		17-10-16-2	18.2-8-27-5	18-9-27-2		5-1-12-0		17-7-31-1		75.2	129	16	10	–	
(Headingley) 14–16 June		13-6-22-2	12.5-7-16-6	12-3-27-1		1-1-0-0		15-9-12-1		53.5	82	5	10	–	
v. Lancashire			13-3-30-0			23-8-63-3	6-0-34-1	23.4-9-67-4	17-4-56-2	85.4	269	9	10	–	C
(Old Trafford) 29 June–2 July			1-0-5-0			–	5-1-18-1	5-1-13-0	1.3-0-11-0	12.3	47	0	1	–	
v. Durham		31-12-68-0	33-12-66-5	4.5-0-14-0		8-3-13-0		33-6-97-3		125.5	314	18	10	–	BCF
(Headingley) 7–10 July		–				–				–	–	–	–	–	
v. Surrey		21.5-3-70-4	20-8-40-5			8-1-19-0		16-5-64-1		81.5	226	13	10	–	ABC
(Oval) 12–15 July		11-3-35-0	18-7-38-1			33-5-119-4		15.5-4-51-2		100.5	345	7	8	–	AC
v. Somerset		18-7-47-3	3.1-1-12-0				12.5-7-44-2	14-5-30-2		61	182	5	10	–	AC
(Scarborough) 19–21 July		21-7-50-5					16-4-42-2	20-9-65-1		70.3	212	13	10	–	ACG
v. West Indians						12-4-25-0	6.5-1-24-0		21-4-44-1	87.1	209	15	10	–	EGH
(Headingley) 24–25 July						2.2-1-7-0	–		3-1-3-0	5.2	12	2	0	–	
v. Lancashire		23-4-70-4			20-4-59-2			22-3-49-1		92	267	8	10	–	ABE
(Headingley) 28–31 July		13-3-32-0			7-1-26-0			12-2-34-1		42	127	7	2	–	BE
v. Somerset		29-7-82-2		22-2-73-3				28-7-62-1	28-8-66-3	128	359	10	10	–	AI
(Taunton) 2–5 August		9-3-38-1		13-1-45-0				9-1-27-1	33-6-91-0	108	368	27	3	–	AJ
v. Leicestershire				24-2-82-2				25.3-4-60-4	26-2-103-2	110.3	351	8	10	–	ACE
(Leicester) 16–19 August				–						–	–	–	–	–	
v. Surrey (Scarborough)		30-1-100-3		20-6-53-2				23.3-6-76-1		110.3	356	30	10	–	ACK
30 August–1 September		15-2-36-0		5-1-11-1				13-2-24-2		37	89	8	3	–	
v. Kent		22.1-8-46-4		22-8-49-1					28-11-71-1	123.1	317	10	10	–	ABK
(Canterbury) 7–10 September		20-4-48-2		15-5-34-4					16.4-4-45-3	68.4	197	15	10	–	ABK
v. Hampshire		13-3-44-2		9-3-27-1		28.5-11-82-6			16-1-58-1	66.5	213	2	10	–	
(Southampton) 13–15 September		5-0-16-0		3-1-20-0		30-4-88-4			21-7-40-3	72	185	5	10	1	

	D Gough	MJ Hoggard	RJ Sidebottom	GM Hamilton	C White	JD Middlebrook	PM Hutchison	CEW Silverwood	ID Fisher
Overs	100.5	488.4	134.2	313.4	76	281.1	129.3	292.3	211.1
Maidens	22	132	46	80	18	68	32	80	48
Runs	245	1274	300	866	194	771	420	762	588
Wickets	16	50	24	40	12	31	16	26	16
Bowler's average	**15.31**	**25.48**	**12.50**	**21.65**	**16.16**	**24.87**	**26.25**	**29.30**	**36.75**

A   GM Fellows 4-0-11-0; 13-4-24-1, 5-0-18-1; 12-2-16-0, 13-2-61-1; 9-2-35-1, 2-1-3-0; 6-1-24-0; 13-4-32-1, 13-1-54-1; 17-5-49-1; 14-5-27-2; 16-5-40-0, 2-0-9-0.

B   MP Vaughan 4-1-10-1; 12.5-5-33-2; 2-1-4-0; 8-2-17-1, 3-1-10-0; 15-1-32-2, 7-1-21-0.

C   DS Lehmann 5-0-19-0; 1-1-0-0; 10-3-17-2, 6-0-30-0; 9-2-15-0; 3-0-10-0; 3-0-5-0; 2-2-0-0, 10-1-34-0.

D   G Ramsden 8-1-32-1, 4-0-36-0.

E   E Elstub 13-3-36-1; 20.1-3-37-3; 13-2-40-2, 7-2-18-1; 17-3-44-1.

F   D Byas 0.1-0-0-0; 4.1-1-8-0.

G   S Widdup 2.3-0-22-1.

H   LC Weekes 23-10-56-6.

I   SM Guy 4-1-8-0.

J   VJ Craven 8-1-15-0.

K   GA Lambert 14-2-36-1, 4-0-10-0; 20-5-62-2, 8-0-25-1.

FIELDING

43 – RJ Blakey (41ct/2st)	
23 – SM Guy (21ct/2st)	
22 – D Byas	
8 – GM Fellows, DS Lehmann, A McGrath	
7 – GM Hamilton	
6 – VJ Craven, S Widdup	
5 – JD Middlebrook, MJ Wood	
3 – PM Hutchison	
2 – MJ Hoggard, RJ Sidebottom, MP Vaughan	
1 – CJ Elstub, ID Fisher, D Gough, SA Lambert, CEW Silverwood	